An Iron Age Settlement outside Battlesbury Hillfort, Warminster, and Sites along the Southern Range Road

by

Chris Ellis and Andrew B. Powell
with John Hawkes

An Iron Age Settlement outside Battlesbury Hillfort, Warminster, and Sites along the Southern Range Road

by
Chris Ellis and Andrew B. Powell
with John Hawkes

with contributions by

Michael J. Allen, Phil Andrews, Alistair Barclay, Wendy Carruthers, Alan J. Clapham, John Crowther, Rachel Every, A.P. Fitzpatrick, Rowena Gale, Jessica M. Grimm, Ellen Hambleton, Phil Harding, Claire Ingrem, Moira Laidlaw, Stephen Legg, Matt Leivers, Richard I. Macphail, Jacqueline I. McKinley, Marco Madella, Mark Maltby, Lorraine Mepham, Pippa Smith, and Chris J. Stevens

and illustrations by S.E. James

Wessex Archaeology Report 22

Wessex Archaeology and Defence Estates 2008

Published 2008 by Wessex Archaeology Ltd
Portway House, Old Sarum Park, Salisbury, SP4 6EB
http://www.wessexarch.co.uk/

British Library Cataloguing in Publication Data
A catalogue record for this book is available from the British Library

Edited by Philippa Bradley
Produced by Julie Gardiner
Cover design by Karen Nichols

ISBN 978-1-874350-47-7

Printed by Henry Ling (Dorset Press) Ltd, Dorchester

Cover photographs

Front: Battlesbury Hill and Battlesbury Bowl excavation site from the south-east
Back: Battlesbury Bowl excavation site from the north-east

Wessex Archaeology Limited is a Registered Charity No. 287786

Contents

List of Figures

List of Plates

List of Tables

Acknowledgements

Wessex Archaeology

The fieldwork was commissioned by Parkman Ltd, Project Manager for the Southern Range Road, and Wessex Archaeology is grateful for the co-operation and assistance of Mr M. Butterfield and Miss P. Cowman. The fieldwork was monitored on behalf of Parkman Ltd by John Hawkes of AC Archaeology, for the Defence Estates Organisation by Jane Hallet and Ian Barnes with assistance from Bob McAlister, for Wiltshire County Council Archaeological Service by Helena Cave-Penny and Duncan Coe, and for English Heritage by Peter Addison. Roy Canham, formerly County Archaeologist Wiltshire County Council, is thanked for his interest and support, particularly in progressing the post-excavation project. The helpful comments and observations of these individuals were gratefully received. J D Hill (British Museum) is thanked for valuable discussions during the excavation and early stages of post-excavation analysis. The interest and enthusiasm for the project, shown by Colonel Morris and Mike Butterfield (Parkman Ltd) is also gratefully acknowledged. Many thanks also to Colonel Skerry and the staff from Explosive Ordnance Disposal who visited the Battlesbury Bowl site and put our minds at rest over some 'suspicious objects'. Thanks also to Ian Barnes for organising the helicopter flight to enable aerial photographs of the site to be taken during the excavation.

The Battlesbury Bowl excavation and Southern Range Road work were managed for Wessex Archaeology by Mick Rawlings and Roland Smith. The fieldwork was directed by Chris Ellis (Battlesbury Bowl) and Vaughan Birbeck (Southern Range Road), with assistance from Dave Murdie, Joe Whelan, Stephen Legg, Julie Lovell, Jo Best, Gemma Smith and Jamie Wright, as well as volunteers from the Wiltshire Archaeological and Natural History Society.

The post-excavation and publication phase of the Battlesbury Bowl excavation and Southern Range Road was commissioned by Defence Estates. The support and encouragement of Ian Barnes and Richard Osgood, Defence Estates, in achieving the post-excavation programme and this publication is gratefully acknowledged. The post-excavation assessment and early stages of analysis was managed by Mick Rawlings and subsequently by Roland Smith, Karen Walker, and Philippa Bradley. Analysis of the finds and environmental remains commenced in 2000 and a substantial draft of the Battlesbury Bowl report, written by Chris Ellis, was completed in 2003. The descriptive text on the SRR sites excavated by Wessex Archaeology was edited by Andrew Powell from original text by Chris Ellis and Vaughan Birbeck. Andrew Powell and Philippa Bradley edited these draft texts for publication. Limited additional specialist analyses, illustrations, and discussions were produced in 2006–7. Other than editing, however, the majority of the specialist work has not been updated since it was finished in 2002. The descriptive text on the SRR sites excavated by AC Archaeology (Chapters 8–12), was edited for publication by Andrew Powell and is based on preliminary post-excavation analysis undertaken by AC Archaeology.

Andrew Lawson, Andrew Fitzpatrick and Richard Osgood are thanked for their helpful comments on earlier drafts of the report. We would like to thank Paul White for providing information about the Eastern Tank Track and for discussing the methodology. The specialists are thanked for their contributions and forbearance during the project. Illustrations were drawn by Elizabeth James and Linda Coleman scanned and cleaned photographs of selected human bones (Plates 5.1–4). The cover was designed by Karen Nichols and Chris Ellis took the cover photographs (also Pl. 2.1). Lorraine Mepham and Michael J. Allen managed the finds and environmental analyses respectively. Michael J. Allen co-ordinated the radiocarbon dating for Battlesbury Bowl, and Dawn Chambers (Rafter Radiocarbon Laboratory, New Zealand) is thanked for assistance during the dating programme. Christine Butterworth undertook the archiving. Alan Clapham would like to thank the George Pitt-Rivers Laboratory, Department of Archaeology, University of Cambridge for use of their facilities. Richard Macphail and John Crowther would like to thank Ian Clewes, Lampeter University, for undertaking the laboratory analysis and to Stirling University for making the thin sections. Our thanks also go to Lindsay Jones of English Heritage for kindly granting permission for the use of the RCHME survey of Battlesbury Hill.

AC Archaeology

The mitigation works during construction were managed for AC Archaeology by John Hawkes. Fieldwork on site was directed by Philip McMahon with much of the supervisory and watching brief work undertaken by Sandra Clark, John Privett and Joseph Whelan with the assistance of a dedicated site team: Emma Allen, Steven Asplin, Charlie Bosworth, Sarah Cottam, Andy Crabb, M. Davies, K. Ely, D. Fox, Brigid Gallagher, F. Gibson, John Hodgson, Aaron Johnston, Jim Keyte, Charlotte Kimber, Steve Leach, Richard McConnell, Emma Markiewiecz, P. Marter,

T. Mellor, Rebecca Montague, Stewart Morris, Dave Murdie, Simon Portet, Keiron Power, Gina Radcliffe, A. Sole, Sean Taylor, Matthew Thompson, T. Walker, Sean Wallis, and Samantha Worrall.

The successful conclusion of the archaeological site works during construction owes much to the efforts of the main contractor, Alfred McAlpine Civil Engineering. Geoff Ind, the contractor's Project Manager, remained unfailingly positive despite the various and repeated difficulties which archaeology presented to his programme, and the efforts which he, sub-agent Lee Emery and the rest of the construction team made to the project are gratefully acknowledged.

Location of the archive

The archive is currently stored at the Wessex Archaeology offices under the following project codes:

Battlesbury Bowl excavations – 44894, 44896, 44898
Southern Range Road (WA) – 44893, 44897
Southern Range Road (AC Archaeology) – AC 444

Abstracts

In 1998–9 a programme of archaeological mitigation works was undertaken in advance of, and during, the construction of a 23 km tank road – the Southern Range Road (SRR) – running across the south-western part of the Defence Training Estate Salisbury Plain (DTE SP) (formerly the Salisbury Plain Training Area, SPTA), Wiltshire, from Warminster in the west to Tilshead in the east.

The DTE SP has been used for military training since the end of the 19th century with the result that much of it enjoys a high level of archaeological preservation, with prehistoric monuments, Romano-British settlements, and multi-period field systems largely unaffected by modern agriculture. The remains, however, have been vulnerable to impacts such as military vehicles crossing the landscape, and the construction of the SRR was part of DE's response to concerns about the fragility of the archaeological and ecological resources. The purpose of the road was to channel non-tactical military traffic onto a purpose-built concrete track and so reduce the impact on the surrounding terrain.

Following an evaluation of the proposed route a two-stage programme of works was undertaken at some 30 sites, including excavation, earthwork survey, strip-and-record, and watching brief, as well as the evaluation of areas previously not accessible. Among the latter was an evaluation north of Battlesbury Camp hillfort which confirmed the presence of an extensive area of Late Bronze Age–Iron Age settlement activity, and on the basis of which a full-scale excavation was undertaken – the Battlesbury Bowl site.

The route of the SRR was designed, successfully, so as to minimise the impact on the known archaeology. Nonetheless, the archaeological works uncovered remains of all periods, from the Mesolithic through to the Plain's modern military use, these findings largely confirming what was previously known of the changing patterns of settlement and land-use.

The limited finds of Mesolithic flintwork reflect the generally low levels or largely invisible character of Mesolithic activity on the chalk downs, and while long barrows are evidence of a more overt and established presence there during the Neolithic, the finds of this period threw little new light on the character of contemporary settlement. From the Early Bronze Age, however, was a partly exposed round barrow ditch on the western slope of the Imber valley, associated with which was a grave containing an inhumation burial in a timber mortuary chamber, followed by multiple inhumation and cremation burials, features with parallels in later Beaker graves.

The Middle Bronze Age was well represented along the SRR with part of a small enclosure revealed on Knook Down and, towards the east (north-west of Tilshead), two ditches possibly forming parts of more extensive field systems, one containing the burial of a young woman, the other containing articulated cattle and sheep carcasses. The Late Bronze Age was represented by settlement activity in a number of locations along the SRR, as well as by the Old Ditch Wessex Linear crossed by the road on Breakheart Hill, and possibly also by a shaft or well, similar to the Wilsford shaft, north-east of Knook.

The most significant evidence for later prehistoric activity, however, was from Battlesbury Bowl where a substantial settlement established in the 8th to 7th centuries BC continued in occupation into the Middle Iron Age when it was replaced by the adjacent Battlesbury Camp hillfort. Only a thin corridor through the settlement was revealed by the excavation, but this showed roundhouses, four-post 'granaries', post-holes, and pits grouped in recognisable clusters across the top of the chalk ridge linking Battlesbury Hill to the downs to the north, with a sequence of ditches close to the hillfort influencing the accessibility of the settlement from the low ground to the east. The often rich deposits of finds and environmental remains in the ditches and pits provided a wealth of information about the character of domestic, economic, agricultural, and social activity on the site, and its place within the wider region.

Although evidence of Romano-British activity, often in the form of field boundary ditches, was found along much of the route, confirming the extensive nature of contemporary agriculture, the main evidence for settlement was that suggesting a possible farmstead on the low ground east of Battlesbury Hill. The earthwork surveys recorded strip lynchets of possible medieval date, and features probably associated with 20th-century military training.

Zusammenfassung

1998–9 wurden archäologische Untersuchung vor und während des Baus einer 23 km langen Panzerstrasse, der Southern Range Road (SRR), duchgeführt, die von Warminster im Westen bis Tilshead im Osten durch den südwestlichen Teil des Truppenübungsplatzes (Defence Training Estate Salisbury Plain, DTE SP, formals Salisbury Plain Training Area, SPTA) in der Ebene von Salisbury, Wiltshire, verläuft.

Der Truppenübungsplatz wird seit Ende des 19. Jahrhunderts für militärische Ausbildung verwendet, was zur Folge hat, dass auf einen Großteil seines

Areals hervorragende Bedingungen für archäologische Hinterlassenschaften herrschen und vorgeschichtliche Denkmäler, romano-britische Siedlungen und mehrperiodige Feldsysteme von Beeinträchtigungen durch moderne Landwirtschaft weitgehend verschont geblieben sind. Beeinträchtigungen des Denkmalbestands ergeben sich jedoch auch durch die derzeitige Nutzung, z.B. wenn militärische Fahrzeuge die Landschaft durchqueren. Der Bau der Panzerstrasse ist Teil der Maßnahmen, die von der Truppenübungsplatz-Verwaltung zum Schutz der Boden- und Naturdenkmäler ergriffen wurden. Zweck der Strasse ist es, nicht-taktischen Militärverkehr auf eine speziell dafür vorgesehene Betontrasse zu lenken, und somit Beeinträchtigungen des umgebenden Geländes zu reduzieren.

Nach Voruntersuchungen entlang der geplanten Trasse wurden an etwa 30 Fundstellen archäologische Maßnahmen durchgeführt, darunter Ausgrabungen, Vermessungen von Bodenmerkmalen und baubegleitende Untersuchungen sowie Voruntersuchungen von zuvor nicht zugänglichen Bereichen. Eine Voruntersuchung nördlich des Ringswalls Battlesbury Camp bestätigte die Existenz eines ausgedehnten Areals mit Besiedlungsspuren der späten Bronze- und vorrömischen Eisenzeit. Aufgrund der Ergebnisse wurde an dieser, Battlesbury Bowl genannten, Fundstelle eine vollständige Ausgrabung durchgeführt.

Die Trasse der Panzerstrasse wurde – erfolgreich – so geplant, dass Beeinträchtigungen bekannter Bodendenkmäler auf ein Minimum beschränkt blieben. Dennoch wurden im Zuge der archäologischen Untersuchungen Hinterlassenschaften aller Perioden von der Mittelsteinzeit bis zur heutigen militärischen Nutzung der Ebene gefunden. Die Ergebnisse bestätigten im Großen und Ganzen das bisher bekannte Bild des sich wandelnden Besiedlungs- und Landnutzungsmusters.

Die wenigen Funde mittelsteinzeitlicher Feuersteinartefakte spiegeln das geringe Ausmaß oder den großenteils unsichtbaren Charakter mesolithischer Aktivität im Bereich der Kreidehügellandschaft wider. Obwohl Langhügeln Hinweise auf eine offensichtlichere, etablierte Besiedlung während der Jungsteinzeit liefern, lassen die Funde aus diesem Zeitraum kaum neue Aussagen zum Charakter der zeitgleichen Besiedlung zu. Aus der frühen Bronzezeit stammt ein teilweise freigelegter Kreisgraben eines Grabhügels am Westhang des Imbertals, zu dem eine Körperbestattung in einer hölzernen Grabkammer gehört, gefolgt von mehrfachen Körper- und Brandbestattungen. All diese Befunde haben Parallelen in becherzeitlichen Gräbern.

Die mittlere Bronzezeit war entlang der Strassentrasse gut vertreten. Ein Teil einer Einfriedung wurde auf Knook Down freigelegt, und im Osten (nordwestlich von Tilshead) wurden zwei Gräben gefunden, die vermutlich zu einem ausgedehnteren Flursystem gehören; einer der Gräben enthielt die Bestattung einer jungen Frau, in dem anderen fanden sich, noch im anatomischen Verband, Skelette von Rindern und Schafen. Siedlungsspuren der späten Bronzezeit stammen von einer Reihe von Fundstellen entlang der Strassentrasse sowie aus der Nähe des „Old Ditch“ genannten „Wessex Linear“-Landgrabens, der von der Trasse am Breakheart Hill gekreuzt wird. Aus dem gleichen Zeitraum stammt vermutlich auch ein Schacht oder Brunnen nordöstlich von Knook, der mit dem Wilsford Schacht verglichen werden kann.

Die bedeutendsten Hinweise vorgeschichtlicher Besiedlung stammen jedoch von Battlesbury Bowl, wo im 8.–7. Jahrhundert v. Chr. eine umfangreiche Siedlung angelegt wurde, deren Besiedlung bis in die mittere vorrömische Eisenzeit reichte und dann in den nahegelegenen Ringwall von Battlesbury Camp verlagert wurde. Die Ausgrabungen legten nur einen schmalen Korridor durch die Siedlung frei; es fanden sich jedoch Rundhäuser, Vier-Posten Speicher, Pfostenlöcher und Gruben in erkennbaren Gruppen entlang des Höhenrückens, der Battlesbury Hill mit den Hügeln weiter nördlich verbindet. Eine Reihe von Gräben in der Nähe des Ringswalls regulierten den Zugang zur Siedlung vom tiefer gelegenen Gelände im Osten. Die an Funden und paläokologischen Resten oft sehr reichen Fundschichten der Gräben und Gruben lieferten eine Vielzahl an Informationen zum Charakter der haus- und landwirtschaftlichen, ökonomischen und sozialen Verhältnisse der Siedlung und ihrer Stellung im regionalen Umfeld.

Obwohl Spuren romano-britischer Besiedlung an vielen Stellen entlang der Trasse gefunden wurden, meist in Form von Flurbegrenzungsgräben als Zeugnis der extensiven Landwirtschaft dieser Periode, stammen die bedeutendsten Siedlungsspuren von einem möglichen Gehöft im tiefer gelegenen Gelände östlich von Battlesbury Hill. Die Vermessung von Bodenmerkmalen erfaßte Hangterrassen vielleicht mittelalterlicher Zeitstellung und Befunde, die wahrscheinlich zu militärischen Trainingszwecken im 20. Jahrhundert angelegt wurden.

Jörn Schuster

Résumé

En 1998–99, on a mis en place une campagne de travaux archéologiques de sauvegarde avant, et pendant, la construction d'une route militaire de 23 km, la Southern Range Road (SRR), qui traverse la partie sud-ouest de la zone de manoeuvres militaires de la plaine de Salisbury, le Defence Training Estate Salisbury Plain (DTE SP) – (anciennement connue sous le nom de Salisbury Plain training Area, SPTA), dans le comté de Wiltshire, elle relie Warminster à l'ouest à Tilshead à l'est.

C'est depuis la fin du 19ème siècle que l'on utilise le DTE SP pour des manoeuvres militaires, ce qui a eu comme résultat que sur une grande partie il bénéficie d'un niveau élevé de préservation archéologique, les monuments préhistoriques, les occupations romano-britanniques et les systèmes de champs couvrant plusieurs périodes n'ayant pratiquement pas été touchés par les pratiques agricoles modernes. Les vestiges ont toutefois pu être atteints par des impacts tels que ceux provoqués par la traversée de la zone par des véhicules militaires, et la construction de la route militaire était, en partie, la réponse du département de la défense aux préoccupations face à la fragilité des richesses archéologiques et écologiques. Le but de la route était de canaliser tout trafic non-stratégique de véhicules militaires sur une piste de béton construite à cet effet et d'en réduire ainsi l'impact sur les terres environnantes.

A la suite d'une évaluation du trajet proposé, on a établi pour quelques 30 sites un programme de travaux en deux tranches qui comprenait fouilles, prospection des levées de terre, décapage et répertoriage et vigilance par la suite, ainsi que l'évaluation de zones jusqu'alors inaccessibles. Parmi celles-ci se trouvait une évaluation au nord de la forteresse de Battlesbury Camp qui a confirmé la présence d'une zone étendue d'activités associée à un campement de l'âge du bronze final-âge du fer, et sur la base de laquelle on a entrepris une excavation à grande échelle– le site de Battlesbury Bowl.

Le trajet de la SRR a été conçu pour, et a réussi à, minimiser l'impact sur l'archéologie dont on avait connaissance. Néanmoins les travaux archéologiques ont mis à jour des vestiges de toutes les époques, du mésolithique jusqu'à l'utilisation militaire moderne de la plaine, ces découvertes ont largement confirmé ce que nous savions déjà sur les changements dans les schémas d'occupation et d'utilisation des sols.

Les rares trouvailles de silex du mésolithique reflètent le niveau généralement bas, voire la nature invisible, des activités mésolithiques sur les collines calcaires, et tandis que les tumulus allongés sont la preuve d'une présence plus manifeste et mieux établie à cet endroit pendant le néolithique, les trouvailles de cette période n'ont apporté que peu de nouvelle lumière sur la nature de l'occupation contemporaine. Datant de l'âge du bronze primitif, il y avait, cependant, un fossé de tumulus arrondi en partie exposé sur le flanc ouest de la vallée de l'Imber auquel était associée une tombe qui contenait une sépulture à inhumation dans une chambre mortuaire en bois, suivie de multiples sépultures à inhumation et incinération, traits qui ont des parallèles dans les tombes de la période finale des peuples à vases.

L'âge du bronze moyen était bien représenté le long de la SRR avec la mise au jour d'une partie d'un petit enclos sur Knook Down et, vers l'est (au nord-ouest de Tilshead), deux fossés qui faisaient peut-être partie d'un système de champs plus étendu, l'un recelait la sépulture d'une jeune femme, l'autre contenait des carcasses articulées de bovins et de moutons. L'âge du bronze final se manifestait par la présence de témoignages d'occupation à divers endroits le long de la SRR, ainsi que par le vieux fossé linéaire de Wessex (Old Ditch Wessex Linear) que la route traverse au niveau de la colline de Breakheart Hill, et peut-être aussi par un puits de mine ou un puits qui ressemble au puits de Wilsford, au nord-est de Knook.

Toutefois, le témoignage le plus révélateur d'activité à la fin de la préhistoire provenait de Battlesbury Bowl où un campement substantiel établi du 8ème au 7ème siècles avant J.-C. avait continué à être occupé jusqu'à l'âge du fer moyen, date à laquelle il avait été remplacé par la forteresse adjacente de Battlesbury Camp. Les fouilles n'ont mis au jour qu'un étroit couloir à travers l'occupation, mais il a révélé des maisons rondes, des 'greniers' à quatre poteaux, des trous de poteaux et des fosses rassemblées en groupes reconnaissables tout au long du sommet de la crête calcaire qui relie Battlesbury Hill aux collines au nord, avec une série de fossés à proximité de la forteresse qui a joué un rôle dans l'accessibilité du site à partir des basses terres à l'est. Souvent d'une grande richesse, les dépôts de trouvailles et les vestiges environnementaux dans les fossés et les fosses ont fourni une importante quantité de renseignements sur la nature des activités domestique, économique, agricole et sociale du site et la place qu'elles occupaient dans la région plus étendue.

Bien qu'on ait retrouvé le long d'une grande partie de la route des témoignages d'activité romano-britannique, souvent sous la forme de fossés limitrophes de champs, ce qui confirme le caractère extensif de l'agriculture contemporaine, le principal indice d'occupation était celui qui indiquait présence éventuelle d'une ferme sur les basses terres à l'est de Buttlesbury Hill. Des prospections des ouvrages de terrassement ont répertorié des terrasses en bandes datant peut-être de l'époque médiévale et des éléments probablement associés aux exercices militaires du 20ème siècle.

Annie Pritchard

Chapter 1
Battlesbury Bowl and the Southern Range Road

This volume describes the results of archaeological fieldwork undertaken before and during the construction, in 1999, of the Southern Range Road (SRR), a 23 km long tank road running across the south-western part of the Defence Training Estate Salisbury Plain (hereafter DTE SP) (formerly the Salisbury Plain Training Area, SPTA) Wiltshire, from Warminster in the west to Tilshead in the east (NGR 390000 146670 to 404610 147630) (Fig. 1.1). Thirty-nine sites were examined, providing evidence for activity spanning the Mesolithic, Neolithic, Bronze Age, Iron Age, and the Romano-British period, as well as more recent activity relating the use of Salisbury Plain for military training. The work, managed by the Defence Estates Organisation (DEO) (now Defence Estates, DE), was undertaken by Wessex Archaeology and AC Archaeology, and this volume integrates the results.

At the west, the SRR passes the Iron Age hillfort of Battlesbury Camp – a Scheduled Ancient Monument (Wiltshire SM 10081). The hillfort is sited on the chalk outcrop of Battlesbury Hill overlooking the Wylye valley and is connected by a narrow ridge to the downland to its north, the resulting natural amphitheatre east of the ridge being referred to as the 'Battlebury Bowl'. An excavation along this ridge revealed a concentration of Late Bronze Age–Iron Age features, including almost 200 pits, many containing apparently 'structured deposits'.

The report on the Battlesbury Bowl excavation, the largest of the fieldwork events, forms Part A of this volume. Part B describes the more dispersed findings from the other sites along of the SRR running east from Battlesbury. The road passes close to the Iron Age hillfort of Knook Castle and the adjacent Romano-British settlement, as well as crossing extensive 'Celtic' field systems, 'Wessex linear' ditches and other features identified from earthworks and cropmarks.

Background to the Project

The DTE SP has been in military ownership since the end of the 19th century with the result that large areas of this rich archaeological landscape have been spared the depredations of modern agriculture. There is a high level of preservation of prehistoric monuments, Romano-British settlements and field systems, as well as remains of later periods, including those relating to the landscape's recent military use. Over the last century, however, that use for military training has had its own significant affects on the archaeology of Salisbury Plain (as reported in the 1973 *Nugent Report* (House of Commons Defence Lands Committee 1973)), and as training intensified after the Army's withdrawal from bases in continental Europe, following the end of the Cold War, there was a heightened awareness of the fragility of the DTE SP's archaeological and ecological resources. The SRR was built, as part of the response to these concerns, in order to channel non-tactical military traffic onto a purpose-built concrete track and so reduce the impact on the surrounding terrain.

In 1996, the route of the SRR was subject to an Environmental Impact Assessment (Frank Green Environmental 1996), during which 95% of the route was evaluated by Gifford and Partners by means of a narrow trench excavated along the centre line of the proposed road (Gifford and Partners 1997a; 1997b). The EIA recommended a two-stage programme of archaeological mitigation, involving work at 30 sites along the route (each assigned an SRR number). These works, commissioned by Parkman Limited, the Project Manager for the SRR, were undertaken in accordance with briefs prepared by DEO (1998a; 1998b).

The pre-construction (Stage 1) mitigation works, undertaken by Wessex Archaeology in March–June 1998, involved small-scale excavations at eight sites and earthwork surveys at a further three (Wessex Archaeology 1999a; Wiltshire Studies 2000), as well as the evaluation of two areas (SRR 11 and SRR 91) that had been previously been unavailable (Wessex Archaeology 1998a; 1998b), and of a third (SRR 85) where the proposed route had been changed and therefore required a second evaluation (Table 8.1). One of these evaluations was at the Battlesbury Bowl, where the lack of Scheduled Monument Consent had prevented earlier evaluation. The Scheduled area includes not only the hillfort, but also the southern end of the chalk ridge, where Iron Age settlement remains were first recorded in 1956 (Chadwick and Thompson 1956), and the northern and south-eastern slopes of Battlesbury Hill. Following the granting of Scheduled Monument Consent by English Heritage, the proposed route of the SRR along the southern end of the ridge and descending into the Bowl was evaluated (SRR 11), confirming the presence of an extensive area of Late Bronze Age–Iron

Age settlement activity (Wessex Archaeology 1998a). Based on the results of the evaluation, a full-scale excavation of the road corridor along the ridge, between the hillfort and Harman Lines (tank works), was undertaken by Wessex Archaeology in June–September 1998.

Further mitigation works along the SRR (Stage 2) were undertaken by AC Archaeology during the road construction phase in 1999 (AC Archaeology 2000). These included 17 locations, selected on the basis of known or anticipated archaeological content, where a 'strip-and-record' exercise was undertaken in advance of the main contract works; a number of these locations were subsequently amalgamated, see Table 8.1. One of these sites (North-West of Middle Barn Farm, SRR 80/5) was the subject of additional investigation for an episode of BBC Television's *Meet the Ancestors* programme (*Hunter of the Plain*). In addition, a watching brief of the whole route during construction identified a further eight sites and a number of isolated features (Wiltshire Studies 2001).

Location, Topography and Geology of the SRR Route

The Defence Training Estate Salisbury Plain (DTE SP) can be divided on topographical grounds into three broad 'ranges' – east, central, and west – as divided by the Avon valley in the east and the Till valley to the west. The SRR starts from near the south-western edge of the western range and traverses the edge of the chalk downland overlooking the Wylye valley, before turning north-east and crossing the Imber valley and the head of the Till valley into the central range (Fig. 1.1).

At the west, it runs south from Harman Lines (at NGR 390000 146670), north-east of Warminster, to the north side Battlesbury Camp (Fig. 2.1). It then descends east into the Battlesbury Bowl at the east of which it joins a spur road running from Battlesbury Barracks south-east of the hillfort. It then turns south over West Hill before ascending north-east onto the downs. A second spur road running north-east from Knook Camp joins it on Knook Down, from where it passes south of the Iron Age hillfort of Knook Castle, then north-east across extensive 'Celtic' fields onto Breakheart Hill, crossing the Old Ditch – a 'Wessex linear' (a major prehistoric boundary). It then drops down into Breakheart Bottom, passing north-west of Middle Barn Farm in the Imber valley, before curving north-east onto Breach Hill at Vedette Point Four, and passing west of the Tilshead Lodge Neolithic long barrow on Tilshead Down. From north-west of Tilshead it arcs round the north of the town before reaching its eastern end at Westdown Camp (at NGR 404610 147630).

For most of its route the SRR was constructed along the lines of existing earth tracks, crossing and forming junctions with a number of other military tracks, including the Imber valley stone track. However, for some of its length it was constructed on undisturbed grassland. The SRR generally crosses a landscape of open, arable-free chalk downland typical of Salisbury Plain, lying almost entirely on deposits of Upper Chalk with superficial deposits of colluvium in dry valleys. Deposits of Lower and Middle Chalk occur in the west of the route in the vicinity of Battlesbury Camp (BGS 1985).

General Archaeological Background

The History of Investigation on the DTE SP

The DTE SP has a long history of archaeological investigation, prompted in part by the unique level of preservation, not only of individual monuments but also of extensive archaeological landscapes, particularly of prehistoric and Romano-British date. Interest in the archaeology of Salisbury Plain began around the same time as 18th century improvements in agriculture were starting to have the greatest impact upon it. Antiquarians such as Richard Colt Hoare and William Cunnington made numerous exploratory investigations of burial monuments, field systems, and other earthworks which were among earliest systematic archaeological investigations in Britain. These early investigations do provide valuable information about their survival and condition at that time (Colt Hoare 1812). Colt Hoare's surveys of the three hillforts close to the SRR – Battlesbury Camp, Scratchbury Hill, and Knook Castle were among the first measured surveys of archaeological sites on Salisbury Plain. In the late 19th century Knook Castle was subject to large-scale survey by Flinders Petrie, as was the Iron Age enclosure at Mancombe Down, north of Battlesbury.

Although access to the DTE SP was restricted following its acquisition by the Government in 1897, the first detailed excavations of its monuments were undertaken in the early decades of the 20th century, such as Maud Cunnington's excavation at Battlesbury Camp (Cunnington 1924). Further interest was kindled by the first aerial photographic surveys by OGS Crawford and Alexander Keiller in the 1920s. There followed intermittent excavations in the DTE SP, but it was not until Collin Bowen and Peter Fowler drew attention to the level of preservation of some of the earthworks, particularly of Romano-British nucleated 'village' settlements, that the scale of the preserved landscape was fully appreciated (Bowen and Fowler 1966). Two research programmes by Reading University have examined the development

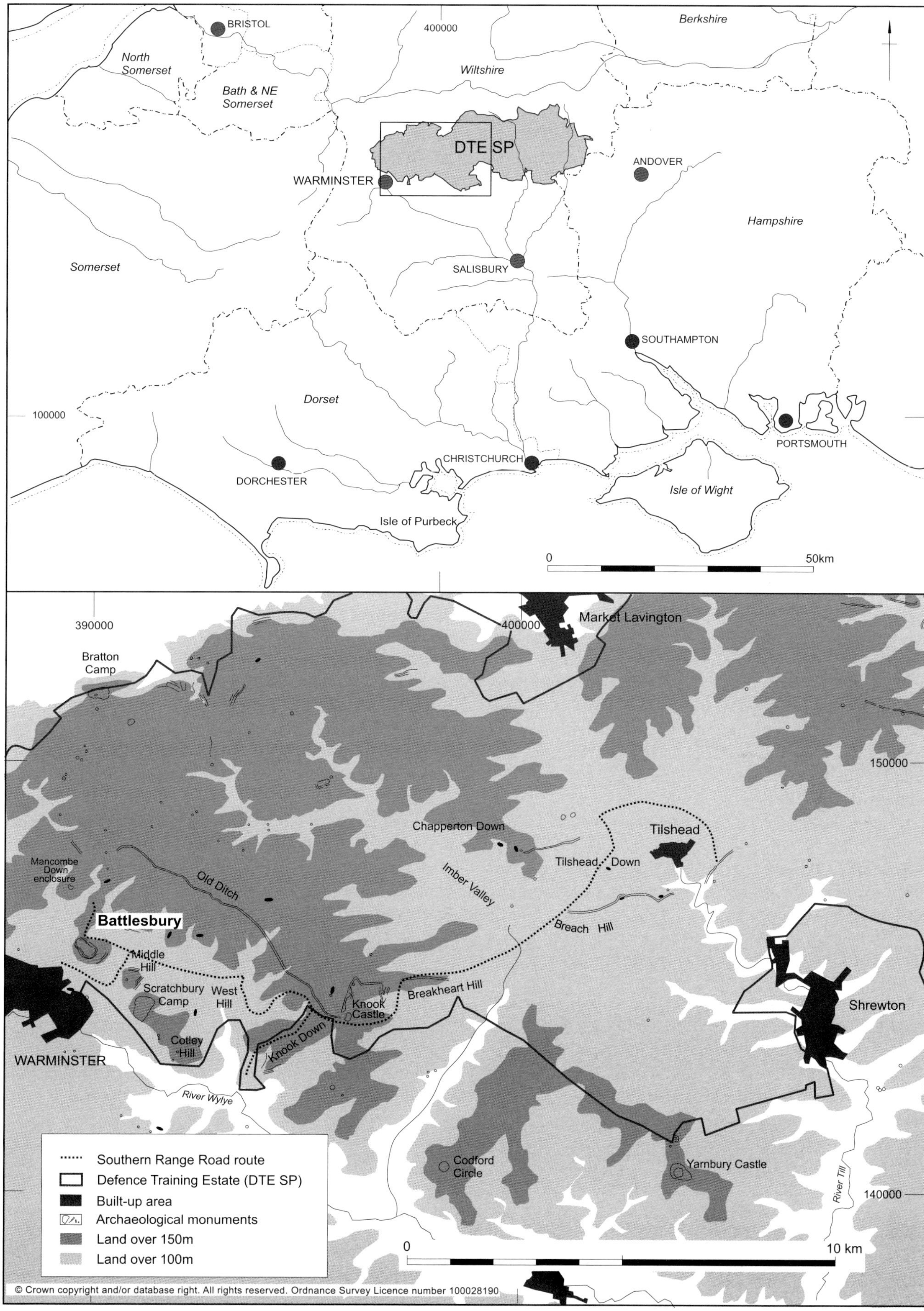

Figure 1.1 Battlesbury and the Southern Range Road

of the later prehistoric and Romano-British landscape on Salisbury Plain (Bradley *et al.* 1994; Fulford *et al.* 2006) and, from the 1980s, the Royal Commission on Historical Monuments (England) (RCHM(E)) began a comprehensive survey of the archaeology of the DTE SP, comprising ground survey of major earthwork complexes and aerial photographic transcription of the remainder, culminating in the publication of *The Field Archaeology of the Salisbury Plain Training Area* (McOmish *et al.* 2002).

The Archaeological Background of the SRR Route

The SRR represents a transect across the south-western DTE SP landscape from the edge of the Wylye valley (along the Battlesbury and Knook spur roads) into the heart of the Plain north of Tilshead. The archaeological fieldwork provided an opportunity to examine activity in a range of landscape zones that have been occupied and exploited through time (Wessex Archaeology 2004).

Although direct evidence for Neolithic settlement is sparse, the SRR passes within 1 km of seven long barrows, with a further four lying within *c.* 2 km – the 'Salisbury Plain West Group' (Ashbee 1984). Some overlook or lie on the edge of the Wylye valley, matching those on the south side of the valley (Allen and Gardiner 2004), others were built further into the downland of the DTE SP, although these too, appear to have been sited to provide views over the valleys that bisect the downs, possibly indicating the significance of these lower lying areas, potentially for settlement. It has been suggested that a small earthwork enclosure within the Scratchbury hillfort may be a Neolithic causewayed enclosure (McOmish *et al.* 2002, 32, fig. 2.6) although Oswald *et al.* dismiss this as being the result of post-medieval ploughing (2001, 157).

Late Neolithic/Early Bronze Age activity is represented largely by the many round barrows on the Plain, and while those in the DTE SP are concentrated in the east, north of Stonehenge and flanking the River Avon and Nine Mile River, there is a significant group also along edge of the Wylye valley on the chalk outcrops of Battlesbury Hill, Middle Hill, Scratchbury Hill, and Cotley Hill. The SRR also passes close to barrows on West Hill, Knook Down, and Breakheart Hill, but to the east around Tilshead barrows are more dispersed.

In later prehistory, from the Middle Bronze Age onwards, the character of activity on the Plain changes, with the first substantial monumental evidence for agriculture and settlement in the form of field systems, land boundaries, settlements and enclosures. The field systems are hard to date, and continued into use through the Romano-British period (some of the strip lynchets on the steep downland edge slopes may be the remains of medieval cultivation). They are also susceptible to damage by ploughing, and although extensive tracts are recorded across the Plain, medieval and post-medieval cultivation may be responsible for some of the gaps in their recorded distribution.

The SRR crosses extensive field systems (presumed to be of predominantly Romano-British date) at Knook Castle, as well as remnants of other systems elsewhere along its route. It also crosses a 'Wessex linear' ditch, Old Ditch, a major later prehistoric land boundary extending, at the west along the top of the downs, roughly parallel to the SRR, before turning north-east at Knook and passing south of Tilshead. Other ditches run off it dividing the landscape into smaller blocks. Occupying this managed landscape are a range of enclosures and settlements, of widely varying form and scale, and in many cases of uncertain date. As well as passing close to the Iron Age hillforts at Battlesbury and Knook (and smaller enclosures both within Battlesbury Camp and on the ridge to its east – McOmish *et al.* 2002) (see Fig. 1.2 and Chapter 2), the SRR crosses the known settlement on the chalk ridge above Battlesbury Bowl and, west of Knook, cuts the southern end of a rectangular enclosure (SMR ST94SW641) and passes a small earthwork enclosure; the SRR also passes two enclosures north-east of Tilshead (SMR SU04NW 613 and 659).

The DTE SP also contains extensive evidence for Romano-British British settlement and agriculture, both on the high downs and in the valley floors. Within the DTE SP, Roman villas are only known from the Avon valley to the east, but there was a villa in the Wylye valley at Pit Mead near Warminster. However, the most striking evidence for settlement comes from the well preserved earthworks of Romano-British nucleated 'villages', such as those at Knook Down West and Knook Down East (Fulford *et al.* 2006). The SRR was diverted to the south of Knook Castle in order to avoid these settlements, although it cut across the associated and extensive system of rectangular fields around them. The SRR passes south of another Romano-British nucleated settlement on Chapperton Down (Malim and Martin 2007).

Aims and Objectives

The archaeological potential of the SRR route, as outlined in the EIA for the 30 sites it identified, led to a number of specific project and research aims concerning the prehistoric and historic land-use of the area:

- to establish the extent, character and date of the prehistoric and Romano-British activities taking place at each site;
- to establish the nature of prehistoric and Romano-British activity, in particular to confirm or refute the interim interpretations suggested during the evaluation phase, and to establish where these activities were taking place within the topography, geomorphology and palaeo-environment of each site;
- to compare and contrast the evidence for prehistoric land-use recovered from the downland with that recovered from the fringes of the Wylye valley and to establish the post-depositional processes that have contributed to the survival or otherwise of evidence for prehistoric activities at each site;
- to compare and contrast the evidence for prehistoric land-use with models previously established for the chalk downlands of Wiltshire.

In addition, further specific research aims were formulated for the Battlesbury Bowl excavation, including:

- to examine the archaeological evidence for the transition from the Late Bronze Age to the Early Iron Age;
- to investigate intra-site variation in the nature of the deposits, both spatially and chronologically, with regard both to formation processes and differentiation in activities/processes;
- to identify and characterise 'structured deposition' and to understand its role within the local and daily activities within the settlement;
- to establish the site's relationship to the adjacent hillfort and enclosure;
- to compare the site to other excavated sites of the period in the region (eg, Longbridge Deverill Cow Down, Mancombe Down, Potterne, East Chisenbury, All Cannings Cross).

PART A: BATTLESBURY BOWL

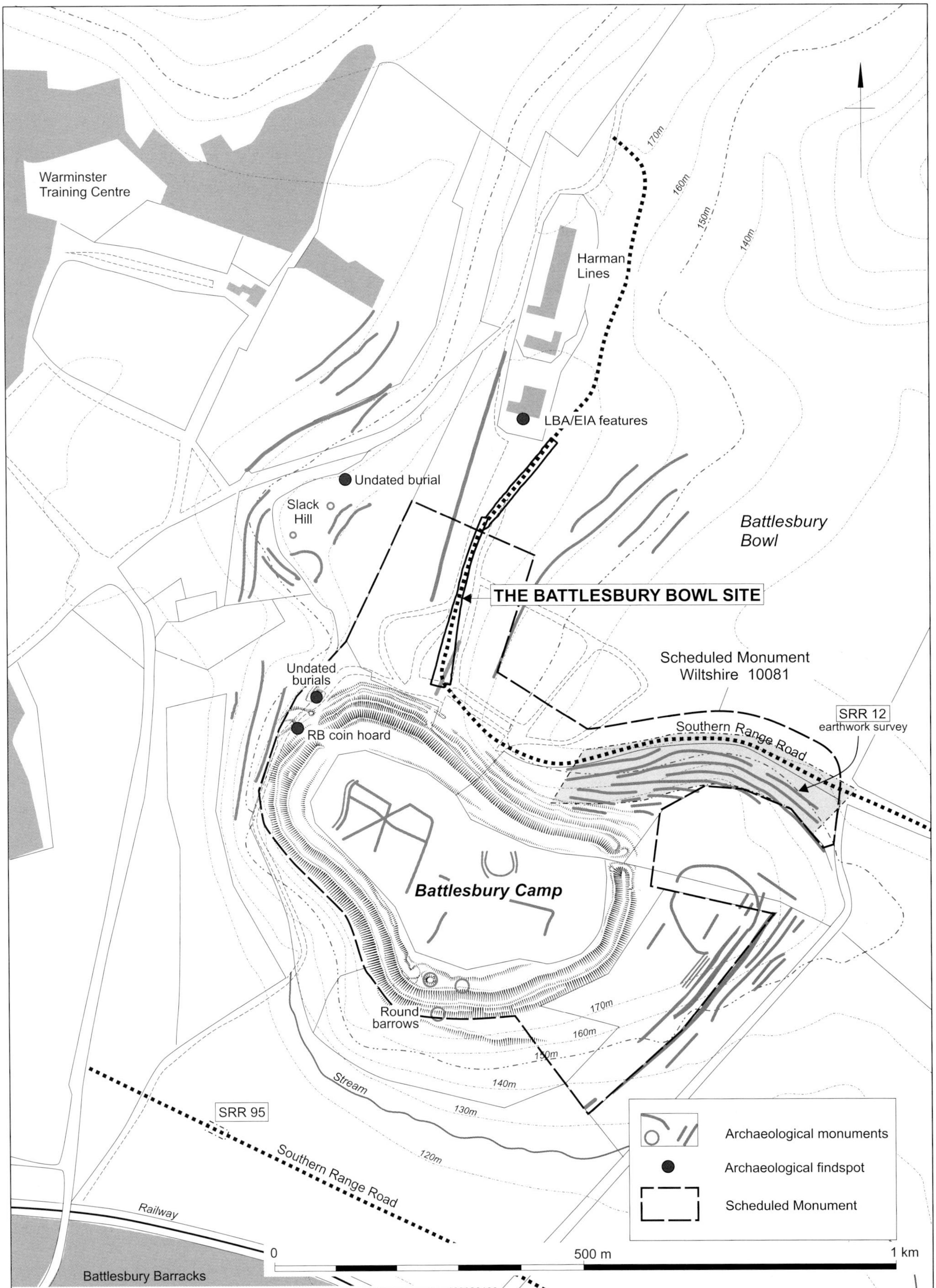

Figure 2.1 Location of the Battlesbury Bowl excavation site. Hachured survey of Battlesbury Camp ©English Heritage. NMR

Chapter 2
Introduction

Site Location, Topography, and Geology

The site lies on the southern margins of Cretaceous deposits of Upper, Middle, and Lower Chalk (Pl. 2.1). The ridge on which it lies is comprised of Middle Chalk, while the hillfort to the south is sited on an outcrop of Upper Chalk (BGS 1985). Battlesbury Hill is one of a number outlying hills separated from the main body of the downs by a *c.* 5 km long strip of low ground running between the Battlesbury ridge and Heytesbury. Battlesbury ridge projects south-south-west into the Wylye valley, the river flowing only *c.* 1 km to the south-west, and the hillfort would have been strategically placed overlooking a point where the valley widens markedly to the west (McOmish *et al.* 2002, 74). Within 6–9 km west of the site there is a major change in the basal geology, with the north-east–south-west aligned Corallian Ridge of Jurassic deposits becoming dominant. Numerous strip lynchets are recorded on the steep slopes of Battlesbury Hill and ridge, and of the adjacent downs.

The excavation area, covering *c.* 0.6 ha, extended for 418 m along the Battlesbury ridge, from below the hillfort's northern ramparts to Harman Lines (NGR 489812 145904–489986 146275) (Fig. 2.1). It was orientated approximately north-north-east to south-south-west, running *c.* 50 m east of the crest of the ridge. It was widest (29 m) at its southern end where the SRR turned eastwards down into Battlesbury Bowl, and narrowed to the north – after *c.* 140 m it was only 9 m in width, the width of the road at this point. After 265 m the road curved to the east and widened to *c.* 12 m, terminating close to the south-east corner of Harman Lines. Its highest part lay near the centre, at *c.* 174 m above Ordnance Datum (aOD), the ground dipping slightly to the north to *c.* 172 m aOD and to the south to *c.* 170 m aOD.

The ridge was relatively flat at the north, the ground sloping no more than 0.4 m from west to east. However, at the south the difference in height was *c.* 3 m as the ground dips down to *c.* 130 m aOD into the Battlesbury Bowl. The chalk ridge drops down steeply to the west, although there is a large relatively flat area, Slack Hill, bowing out to the west at its southern end before the ridge narrows to the north.

The topsoil comprised a greyish–brown compacted silty clay with occasional chalk inclusions, 0.25–0.3 m thick at the north, but thickening downslope (to the east) to a maximum of *c.* 0.7 m at the south. It was already compacted, and the grass rutted, along the existing military road. The topsoil had been totally removed and replaced by scalpings, which formed the bedding layer for the existing military road, along the western side of much of the southern half of the site. Immediately west of the site, south of Harman Lines, a military training area was still in use and extensive machine groundworks associated with the training area had already been carried out prior to the excavation.

The topsoil directly overlay Chalk bedrock. A weathered or degraded chalk horizon was discernible in places within the site and was characterised either by a deposit, up to 0.15 m thick, of greyish–brown clayey silty 'puddled chalk' which molluscan analysis suggested had a periglacial origin, or by a horizon of 'rubble-like' chalk *c.* 0.2–0.3 m thick (Wessex Archaeology 1999b). The relationship between the 'puddled chalk' and the archaeological features was unclear in places due to recent localised disturbance, probably by tanks and lorries. Cleavage planes in the chalk bedrock were clearly discernible in the sides of the deeper/larger features, aligned north-north-west to south-south-east below the weathered chalk. These were used to advantage by the original excavators of the Iron Age pits, resulting in slightly flat, straight, parallel western and eastern sides to pits in their lower sections.

Previous Investigations

As well as the hillforts of Battlesbury Camp, immediately south of the site, and Scratchbury 2 km to the south-east, the hillforts of Bratton Camp, Cley Hill, and Knook lie *c.* 6 km distant, to the north, west, and east, respectively. In addition there are a number of smaller earthwork enclosures of broadly Iron Age date, such as on Mancombe Down (Fowler *et al.* 1965) *c.* 1 km to the north-north-west, Codford Circle *c.* 2 km to the south-east (Allen and Gardiner 2006) and Longbridge Deverill Cow Down (Chadwick-Hawkes 1994) on the south side of the Wylye valley. Other undated enclosures are known from aerial photographs, such as those both within the hillfort (SMR ST84NE702) and on the eastern slope of Battlesbury Hill (SMR ST94NW677), pointing to the complex history of this chalk headland (McOmish *et al.* 2002, 83, fig. 3.30). A possible enclosure on Slack Hill was identified in an aerial photographic survey (SMR ST84NE635), although its interpretation should be treated with some caution (Cox 2002, 8).

Plate 2.1 Battlesbury Hill and Battlesbury Bowl excavation site from the south-east

'Celtic' field systems and lynchets are especially common features near to the site and while most are not positively dated, they could be later prehistoric. Some of these features certainly pre-date the construction of some enclosures, such as Battlesbury Camp, Scratchbury, and Mancombe Down (McOmish *et al.* 2002, 73–8), suggesting that these locations were already extensively utilised, possibly in the Middle–Late Bronze Age. Linear embanked and sometimes ditched features were recorded on Battlesbury ridge aligned generally north–south and following its contours (Cox 2002).

Previous archaeological investigations at Battlesbury have provided ample evidence for Iron Age settlement and burials both on the hill and along the chalk ridge to the north (Fig. 2.1). Colt Hoare, who excavated two of the three Bronze Age barrows on the south side of the hill, recorded a central cist burial in one and a double inhumation within the mound of the other (Colt Hoare 1812, 68). A bead found with one of the skeletons was later confirmed as being of opaque yellow glass with a date range of mid-3rd–late 1st century BC (Guido 1977–8, 177) proving the burials were secondary in nature. Hoare states that the tail of the hillfort rampart overlay the two westerly barrow mounds (Colt Hoare 1812, 68), suggesting a Middle–Late Iron Age date for the construction of the defences. However, the evidence is equivocal as it is not certain that the rampart sealed the secondary burials. Nonetheless, the scale and complexity of the hillfort defences, particularly the entrances, are characteristic of 'developed' hillforts of the Middle–Late Iron Age.

An investigation of the interior of the hillfort was undertaken by Maud Cunnington in 1922, during the construction of a water reservoir on the highest point of the hill and a 285 m long pipe trench running down to the north-west entrance. Nine pits were excavated containing pottery, animal bones, quernstone fragments, clay slingshots, iron objects as well as worked and burnt flint, all pointing to a 'pre-Roman Iron Age' period of occupation (Cunnington 1924, 368).

One question about Battlesbury Camp, as yet unresolved, concerns its relationship, chronological and functional to the adjacent Scratchbury hillfort for which the only date derives from Professor Grimes' fieldwork carried out on the smaller, banked and ditched enclosure within its interior, which recovered mid-3rd century BC pottery (*cf.* Guido 1977–8, 178). It has often been assumed, although not archaeologically proven, that Battlesbury Camp post-dates Scratchbury as it is more defensible, a large part of the interior of the latter being visible from the valley floor (Guido 1977–8, 178; McOmish *et al.* 2002, 75).

Below the north-western entrance of the Battlesbury Camp, Colt Hoare also recorded numerous inhumation burials, many in crouched positions, and a horse burial, during chalk quarry excavations (Cunnington 1924, 373). In some cases as many as four or five skulls were found close together, leading to the interpretation of these burials as being the result of a massacre or a war cemetery (*VCH* 1957, I(1), 118). A number of human skeletons were also found near the western entrance of Scratchbury hillfort (Whimster 1981) and similar remains have been found close to many hillfort entrances, such as at Maiden Castle, Dorset (Wheeler 1943), and South Cadbury, Somerset (Barrett *et al.* 2000), as well as in 'charnel pits' at Danebury, Hampshire (Cunliffe 1984). Colt Hoare's finds, therefore, could well be of Iron Age date. The crouched inhumation burial of a child, aged *c.* 8 years, in a shallow, oval pit on Slack Hill, was excavated during cuttings for a new road (SMR ST84NE153); although there were no grave goods to date the burial, it is possible that it is also Iron Age in date.

In 1956 an access road was constructed north of the hillfort along the eastern side of the ridge, close to its summit, related to the construction of the existing military road (Chadwick and Thompson 1956). The positions of at least 40 pits and *c.* 45 post-holes were recorded in detail along a *c.* 60 m stretch of the road at the south, and further occupation evidence was recorded for at least another *c.* 275 m to the north. The features were recorded as filled with a 'greasy black soil' containing animal bone and pottery. Only one pit and one post-hole were excavated and a number of pottery sherds were collected from the machine-stripping. The datable finds indicated substantial settlement activity along the ridge dated to the Early–Middle Iron Age. Fieldwork at the southern edge of Harman Lines prior to the construction of new buildings (Wessex Archaeology 1995; 1996; 1997) revealed a number of ditches/gullies as well as two post-holes and two pits. The features included two parallel ditches aligned north-west–south-east, one producing material of Late Bronze Age/Early Iron Age date, which were thought to be a continuation of the Iron Age activity recorded in 1956.

A small number of Romano-British period find-spots lie close to the site. In 1773 a hoard of 36 bronze and silver Roman coins was found in a pottery vessel during quarrying outside the north-west entrance of the hillfort, and further Roman coins, as well as three Saxon *seaxes* (single-edged knives), are recorded from the interior (*VCH* 1957, I(1), 118).

Methodology

Evaluation

The Stage 1 Battlesbury Bowl (SRR 11) evaluation comprised the excavation of a 564 m long trench. The trench ran southwards along the eastern edge of the chalk ridge, east of the existing road, before turning east down the northern side of Battlebury Hill into the Bowl, running along the north side of the existing road. A further 90 m length of trench was excavated beyond the north end. Sample excavation of the many exposed features and deposits was designed to be minimally intrusive, sufficient to achieve the aims of the evaluation. The results are not reported here, as the trench was subsequently incorporated within the excavation area.

Excavation and Recording Methods

The site was machine-stripped down to the natural geology or archaeological deposits using a mechanical excavator. A site grid, tied to the Ordnance Survey grid and to Ordnance Datum, was established to enable 1:100 scale pre-excavation plans to be made of the whole site. The site was excavated in two parts, the first extending approximately north for some 270 m from outside the hillfort's defences, the second continuing north-east for a further 170 m to the south-east corner of Harman Lines (Pl. 2.2).

All pits were at least half-sectioned. Those containing inhumation burials and/or finds assemblages suggesting 'structured deposition' (see below) were fully excavated. All relationships between ditches were excavated, along with other sections across the ditches in areas that were not disturbed by other features. In ditch sections containing evidence for possible 'structured deposits', excavation was extended to recover that evidence. When post-built structures were identified, each of the post-holes that made up the structure was half-sectioned. A representative sample of the remaining post-holes on the site was examined by half-section.

Sampling was undertaken where appropriate deposits were recorded, in particular from around human skeletal material in order to obtain possible bone fragments from the associated deposit. Samples were also taken where possible 'structured deposition' was encountered as discrete events within the filling sequence of a pit or ditch.

Assemblage characterisation and recording

It has long been noted that certain features on Iron Age settlements, in particular re-used storage pits, contain apparently deliberate and formalised deposits including assemblages of human and animal bones as well as combinations of other materials (Bersu 1940; Whittle 1984; Cunliffe and Poole 1991, 153–62; Cunliffe 1992; 1995, 80–5), a phenomenon examined in detail in Hill's statistical study of Iron Age pits on a number of settlement sites (predominantly in Hampshire) (Hill 1995). This phenomenon, often referred to as 'structured deposition', suggests that there was a symbolic or ritual dimension to what had often been viewed as predominately mundane Iron Age domestic contexts.

It was one of the initial aims of the Battlesbury Bowl excavation 'to identify and characterise 'structured deposition' and to understand its role within the local and daily activities within the settlement' (see Chapter 1). As a result, a set of criteria was established in an attempt to characterise finds assemblages that may have resulted from 'structured deposition', as follows:

- artefacts occurring in association with an inhumation burial or recognisable human skeletal remains;
- a relatively rich and varied assemblage of artefact types (and materials) occurring in association;
- articulated animal skeletal elements or complete skeletons appearing alone or in association with a relatively rich artefactual assemblage;
- animal skulls appearing alone or in association with a relatively rich artefactual assemblage;
- a relatively rich bone assemblage occurring alone or in association with a relatively rich artefactual assemblage (the latter were ascribed during post-excavation analysis due to the number and/or range of artefact types and materials within the feature assemblage).

Where specific assemblages fulfilling these criteria were recorded in the field they were photographed and planned *in situ* and, where practicable, ascribed individual Object Numbers (ONs) for each element within the deposit. If individual numbering of animal bone elements was impracticable due to their large numbers, they were grouped together in skeletal groups (where discernible) or spatially discernible, discrete groups. Where such bone groups were not discernible, the bones were collected *en masse* and given a single Object Number. Small finds (as isolated examples) were also allocated Object Numbers, but were not planned *in situ*, although they were photographed *in situ* where appropriate.

However, as excavation, assessment, and analysis progressed it became evident that the characterisation of deposits as potentially resulting from 'structured deposition' did not

Table 2.1 Features containing 'structural depositon' by phase and feature group

Feature group	*Cut*	*Feature*	*Human remains*	*Animal bone group*	*Small finds*	*Pot density*	*Bone density*
					Standard deviation (SD)		
Phase 1/2							
1	4012	ditch	yes			>3	1–2
	4023	ditch		yes	1–2	2–3	1–2
	4079	ditch	yes			<1	<1
	4080	ditch	yes		1–2	2–3	2–3
	4090	ditch	yes	yes	1–2	1–2	2–3
	4096	ditch	yes		1–2	1–2	<1
	4105	ditch	yes	yes	>3	1–2	>3
	4113	pit		yes	2–3	1–2	<1
	4162	pit		yes		<1	<1
	4199	p-h	yes			<1	<1
	4221	pit		yes	1–2	<1	>3
	4293	ditch	yes			1–2	1–2
	4305	pit			1–2	<1	1–2
	4455	ditch			>3	1–2	<1
	4751	pit		yes		1–2	>3
2	4470	pit		yes	1–2	<1	>3
	4612	pit		yes		<1	2–3
	4704	pit		yes	>3	>3	1–2
3	4836	pit			2–3	<1	<1
	4865	pit	yes			<1	<1
	4937	pit	yes			<1	<1
	4993	pit	yes	yes	1–2	<1	1–2
	5004	pit	yes			<1	<1
	5216	pit	yes			<1	<1
	5318	pit			1–2	<1	<1
4	5588	p-h			2–3	<1	<1
	5636	p-h	yes			<1	<1
	5760	pit		yes	>3	<1	1–2
	5688	pit		yes	>3	<1	1–2
Phase 3							
1	4195	pit			1–2	>3	>3
	4223	pit	yes			<1	<1
	4332	pit	yes	yes	>3	<1	<1
	4423	pit		yes		<1	2–3
	4436	pit			1–2	<1	<1
	4486	pit		yes	1–2	1–2	1–2
	4553	pit			1–2	<1	1–2
	4796	pit		yes	1–2	1–2	>3
2	4458	pit			1–2	<1	<1
	4572	pit			1–2	1–2	2–3
	4584	pit		yes	1–2	<1	2–3
	4598	pit		yes	1–2	<1	1–2
	4606	pit		yes	1–2	1–2	2–3
	4641	pit		yes	>3	2–3	>3
	4707	pit		yes	>3	<1	<1

Table 2.1 (continued)

Feature group	*Cut*	*Feature*	*Human remains*	*Animal bone group*	*Small finds*	*Pot density*	*Bone density*
					Standard deviation (SD)		
Phase 3							
3	4868	pit		yes		<1	1–2
	5043	pit	yes	yes	1–2	<1	<1
	5073	pit			>3	<1	<1
4	5358	pit	yes	yes	>3	1–2	>3
	5592	pit		yes	1–2	<1	1–2
	5750	pit		yes		>3	<1
	6162	pit		yes		>3	>3
Phase 4							
1	4272	pit	yes			1–2	1–2
	4320	pit	yes			<1	2–3
Unphased							
2	4625	pit		yes		<1	2–3
	4716	pit			1–2	<1	<1
3	5102	pit		yes		1–2	2–3
4	5777	p-h	yes			<1	<1

Small finds mean = 0.70; SD = 3.10
Pot density mean = 194.41 (g/m^3); SD = 771.73 (g/m^3)
Bone density mean = 316.90 (g/m^3); SD = 841.28 (g/m^3)
p-h = post-hole

adequately describe or explain the varied processes by which whole sequences of deposits came to fill individual features. Consequently it was decided to give a greater emphasis to understanding the specific depositional histories of a sample of individual features displaying variant fill sequences. While a consideration of 'structured deposition' has formed part of the site's analysis (the detailed results of which are in the archive), a summary only of it is presented here.

Summary of Analysis of 'Structured Deposition'

Following Hill (1995), features were considered to display 'structured deposition' where they contained human remains, relatively large numbers (>1 standard deviation) of small finds, or articulated animal bone group or skulls (Table 2.1). Structured deposition was recorded in 57 features, including 44 of the pits (22.3%), nine ditch sections (19.6%), and four post-holes (0.9%). Twenty-one of these features (36.8%) contained human remains, 30 (52.6%) contained significant animal remains, and 36 (63.2%) contained significant numbers of small finds. Many had combinations of two (31.6%) or even three (10.5%) criteria, and 38.6% of those features that contained significant animal remains also appeared to have significant numbers of small finds.

The greatest proportion of pits with structured deposition lay within feature groups 2 (35.3%) and 4 (33.3%) (see Chapter 3, Figs 3.2–3.5), followed by feature groups 1 (23.4%) and 3 (13.4%). The percentage of pits with structured deposition increased through time from 21.7% in phase 1/2 (see below) to 54.5% in phase 3; both phase 4 pits contained structured deposition. There is no discernible correlation, however, with pit shape.

The two larger ditches recorded at the south of the site (ditches 4293 and 4043) had relatively high concentrations of structured deposits. The original terminal of the earliest ditch (4293) contained not only articulated cattle vertebrae but also a human humerus, while ditch 4043 also contained a number of structured deposits, especially to the south of a marked change in its direction (Fig. 3.2). Section 4105 of ditch 4043 contained an exceptional deposit of cattle and horse skulls (many of the cattle skulls having been very carefully defleshed), as well as a dog skull and an articulated cow foreleg. The distribution of structured deposition in these ditches may indicate the significance of this location with a long-lived and frequently modified boundary.

The structured deposition in the post-holes were represented in three cases by fragments of human bone in the post-hole fills, and in the fourth by quernstone fragments re-used as packing stones, and although these fulfilled the criteria for structured deposits it is considered that the features are so small, and the human remains so ephemeral, that they probably do not represent practices of a special nature.

Environmental Sampling Strategy

A total of 151 samples (generally of 30 litres, and totalling *c.* 3090 litres) was taken. The main deposits of archaeological interest in pits were sampled. Yellowish–green staining characteristic of cess and mineralisation noticed in pit and ditch fills was also targeted. Because of the large number of pits, care was taken to ensure that sampling was representative in terms of location, phase, type, and nature of the pits and their fills.

Samples were processed by initial flotation in a double, internal-weir flotation system (based in the

Siraf tank), followed by reprocessing of the residues by laboratory wash-over flotation. The flots were retained on a 0.5 mm mesh and residues on 1 mm except, except where field records indicated the possible presence of cess and mineralisation. In these cases the flot size was reduced to 0.25 mm and residues to 0.5 mm. All flots were scanned and recorded to facilitate selection for the analytical programme. The residues to 1 mm of all samples selected for analysis of charred plant and/or charcoal remains, or 0.5 mm for mineralised remains, were fully sorted and added to the material recovered from the flots. A total of 35 samples was analysed for charred plant remains, 77 for mineralised remains, and 16 for charcoals. During the initial stages of analysis the preservation of 'plates' of articulated phytoliths (opal silica bodies of plant origin), were noticed and some of these were subsequently also analysed.

Samples for land snails and soil micromorphology were also taken from specific sequences or contexts. One column of samples through a ditch was analysed for snails and augmented by spot samples from the pits. Four soil thin sections were reported upon together with samples for soil chemistry.

Samples were taken from inhumation burials for the recovery of small human bones. Soil was retained from the areas around the hands and feet for the recovery of small finger and toe bones. The area of the thorax was sampled in order to recover any gall stones, kidney stones, tapeworms, and the possibility of foetal bone. The head area was sampled to ensure full recovery of teeth, and sometimes also the fragments of cranium and other skull parts (eg, hyoid bone). These samples were sieved to a 2 mm mesh.

Chronology and Phasing

There are three strands to the dating: ceramic chronology, radiocarbon dating, and site phasing. These have been combined to understand the chronology of the settlement. These are discussed in detail below.

Ceramic chronology

Vessel forms and other diagnostic ceramic attributes were used to create a date range for the pottery assemblage from Late Bronze Age–Middle Iron Age. Within this range, three ceramic phases (CP) were defined, based largely on the sequence from Potterne, Wiltshire, for the Late Bronze Age and Danebury, Hampshire for the Early–Middle Iron Age (*c.* 8th–3rd centuries BC; for details, see Chapter 4).

Ceramic phase 1) Range of vessel forms typical of the early All Cannings Cross ceramic style, and of the later phases of Potterne (Morris 2000a): date range 8th–7th centuries BC.

Table 2.2 Radiocarbon dating results

Feature	*Context*	*Material*	*Lab. No.*	*Result BP*	*δC¹³‰*	*cal BC (2σ)*
Phase 1/2: 800–350 cal BC						
Ditch 4043	4101 (section 4105)	cattle skull frags (3029)	NZA-17103	2503±40	-20.53	790–420
		cow radius	NZA-13629	2435±70	-21.07	770–400
	4170 (section 4090)	cow femur	NZA-13630	2445±55	-20.86	770–400
Phase 3: 350–200 cal BC						
Pit 5043	5137	pig humerus (3282)	NZA-13634	2247±70	-20.09	420–100
Pit 4707	4811	corvid skeleton (3423)	NZA-17107	2277±40	-19.23	400–200
		horse skull (3219) – cleaned	NZA-17106	2225±50	-21.59	400–160
Pit 4332	4385	horse metapodial, articulated	NZA-17104	2276±45	-21.61	400–200
		human right foot (3016), articulated	NZA-17105	2262±40	-19.62	400–200
	4571	human right femur	NZA-13633	2258±55	-20.11	410–190
Hearth 5711	5959	charcoal: *Prunus spinosa*	NZA-13635	2265±55	-24.24	410–180
Pit 5750	5752	cow 1st phalanges	NZA-17102	2236±50	-21.46	400–180
Pit 5358	5848	cow vertebra, articulated	NZA-13635	2168±55	-21.38	380–100
		cattle vertebrae (3420), articulated	NZA-17108	2241±40	-20.61	390–190
Pit 4868	4884	hornless cattle skull (3238)	NZA-17101	2232±40	-21.28	390–190
Phase 4: 200 cal BC–AD 43						
Pit 4272	4346	human right femur	NZA-13632	2127±85	-20.04	300–AD 20
Pit 4320	4322	human right femur	NZA-13631	2083±70	-19.82	360–AD 60

Plate 2.2 Early stage of cleaning the northern end of the site, with Battlesbury Bowl at top right and the Harman Lines buildings beyond

Ceramic phase 2) Range of vessel forms typical of later All Cannings Cross ceramic style (Cunliffe 1991, fig. A:6) and equivalent to CP (ceramic phase) 1–3 at Danebury (Cunliffe 1984, fig. 6.17): date range 6th–mid-4th centuries BC.

Ceramic phase 3) Range of undecorated vessel forms, equivalent to CP 4–5 at Danebury, but possibly also extending into CP 7 (*ibid.*, figs 6.18–19): date mid-4th–3rd centuries BC.

Radiocarbon dating

Sixteen radiocarbon dates were obtained in two batches, from pits, a ditch, and a hearth. All radiocarbon results have been calibrated using OxCal v2.15 (Bronk Ramsey 1995; 2001; Stuiver and Kra 1986; Stuiver *et al.* 1998) and are expressed at the 95% confidence level with the end points rounded outwards to 10 years following the form recommended by Mook (1986).

The primary aim was to help define the chronology of the site and to confirm and refine the ceramic phasing. A second aim was to help characterise the nature of specific events, and to determine the contemporaneity of materials in specific deposits; in four cases, more than one determination was obtained from the same deposit in order to investigate aspects of taphonomy, including the possibility of the curation of materials.

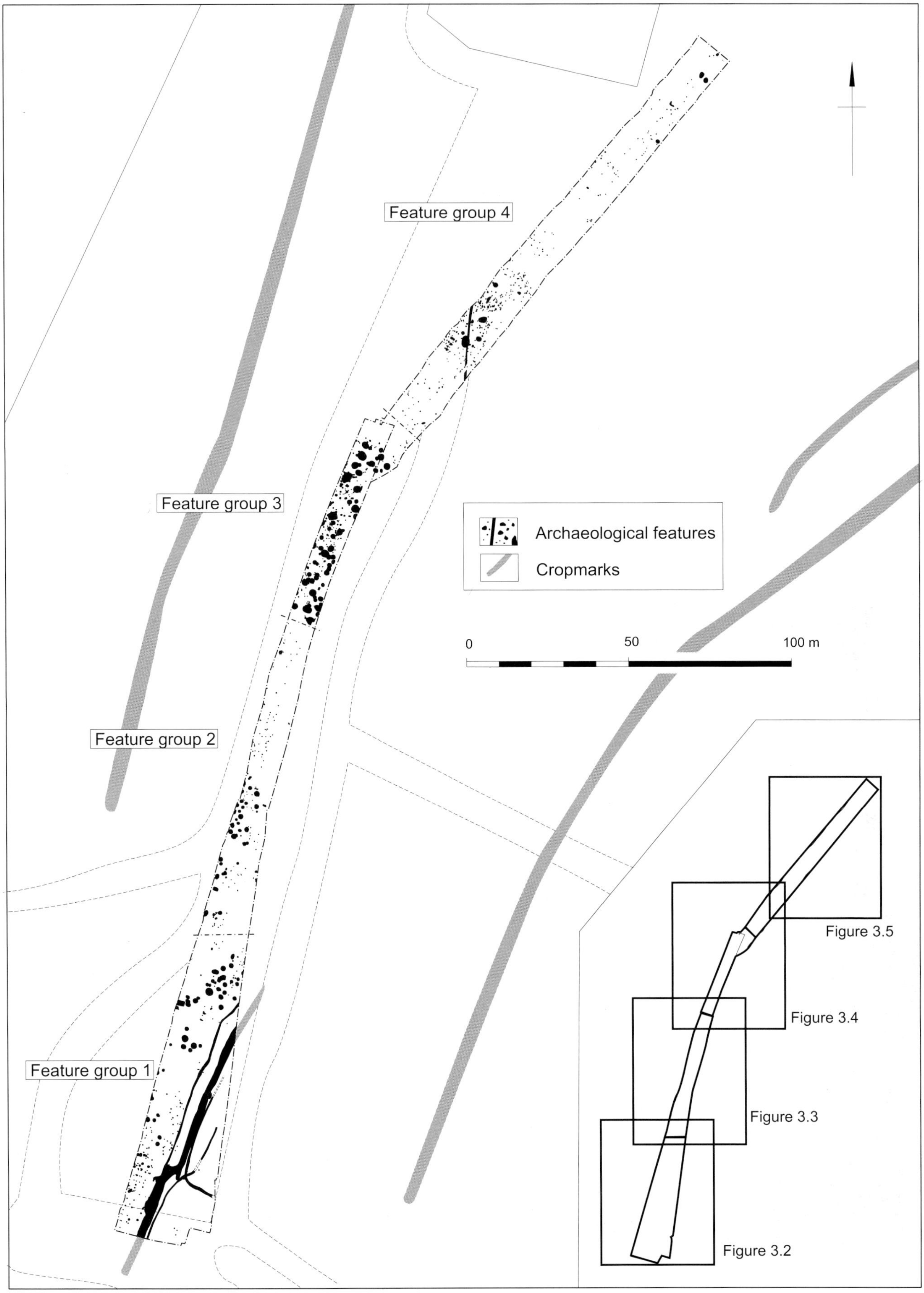

Figure 3.1 The site, showing feature groups

Chapter 3
Results

More than 900 archaeological features were recorded including 725 post-holes, 198 pits, and seven ditches (Fig. 3.1). Although found along the full the length of the site, four major clusters of features were discernible. These clusters or 'feature groups' (FGs) are numbered 1–4 from south to north (Figs 3.2–3.5).

Early Prehistoric Finds

A small number of early prehistoric finds was recovered from the site, but none came from demonstrably contemporary features.

A Neolithic bifacial flint axe (ON 3088, Pl. 3.1) was found associated with human remains in phase 3 pit 4332 (FG 1), while a large fragment of a Neolithic dolerite macehead (ON 3091) with one very smooth, polished, rounded surface, possibly from a source in

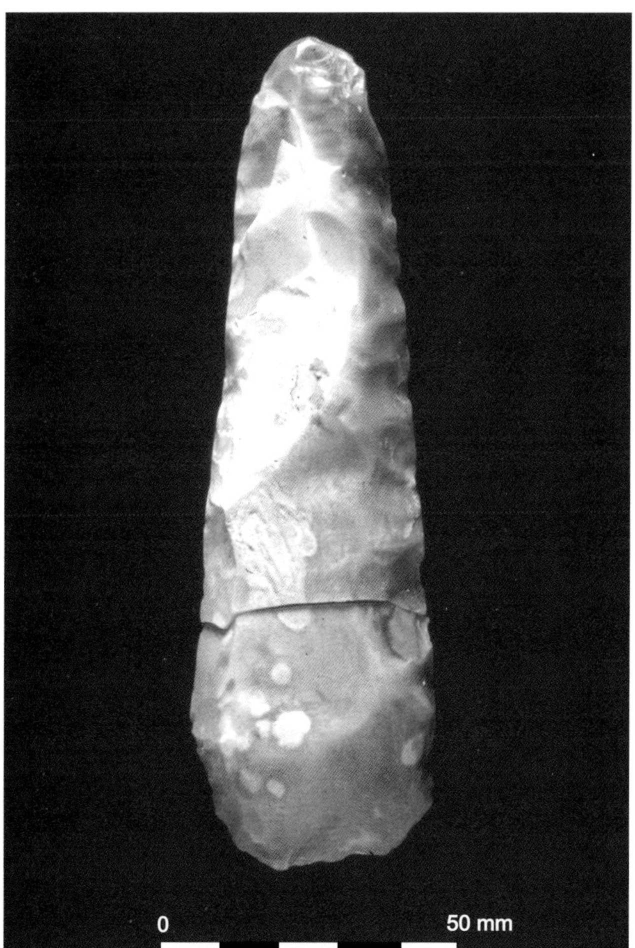

Plate 3.1 Neolithic flint axe from phase 3 pit 4332

south-west England, was found in unphased Iron Age pit 4412 (FG 1). Although some of the patinated flints recovered from the site represent residual material of Neolithic or Early Bronze Age date accidentally incorporated into the later features, the particular nature of these two finds, both of which came from Iron Age features at the southern end of the site (in FG 1) suggests that they may have been curated items, possibly found in the area and retained as curios, of some inherent interest, value, or significance.

An oval pit (5613) at the northern end of the site (in FG 4) (Fig. 3.5) contained 17 small sherds (113 g) of Early Bronze Age pottery. A single small body sherd with traces of comb-impressed decoration was identifiable as Beaker, but there were no other diagnostic sherds, and this small group has been assigned to the Early Bronze on the basis of fabric type. However, all the sherds are in a poor, abraded condition, suggesting they were residual, and all other finds from the pit were consistent with an Iron Age date.

Late Bronze Age/Iron Age Features

Of the 707 potential Late Bronze Age and Iron Age features excavated on the site, a third (230) were attributable to a phase on the basis of ceramic or stratigraphical evidence; a further six were phased using radiocarbon determinations.

Although no formal graves or features dug specifically for burial were found, 21 features (five ditches, three post-holes, and 13 pits) contained human skeletal remains. These varied between almost complete inhumations, articulated elements, single bones, and tiny fragments. Six almost complete inhumation burials were found in four nearby phase 3 or 4 pits in the southern part of the site. Two of these each contained single burials and two contained two almost contemporaneous burials. In addition to these human burials, complete and partial animal skeletons were also recovered from a range of deposits but mainly pit and ditch fills. These included sheep or lambs (contexts 4486, 4612) and a partial dog skeleton (4482). Horse and cattle skulls were recovered from ditch 4083 and other selected elements, such as feet, groups of vertebrae, or limbs were also recovered (see Hambleton and Maltby, Chapter 6)

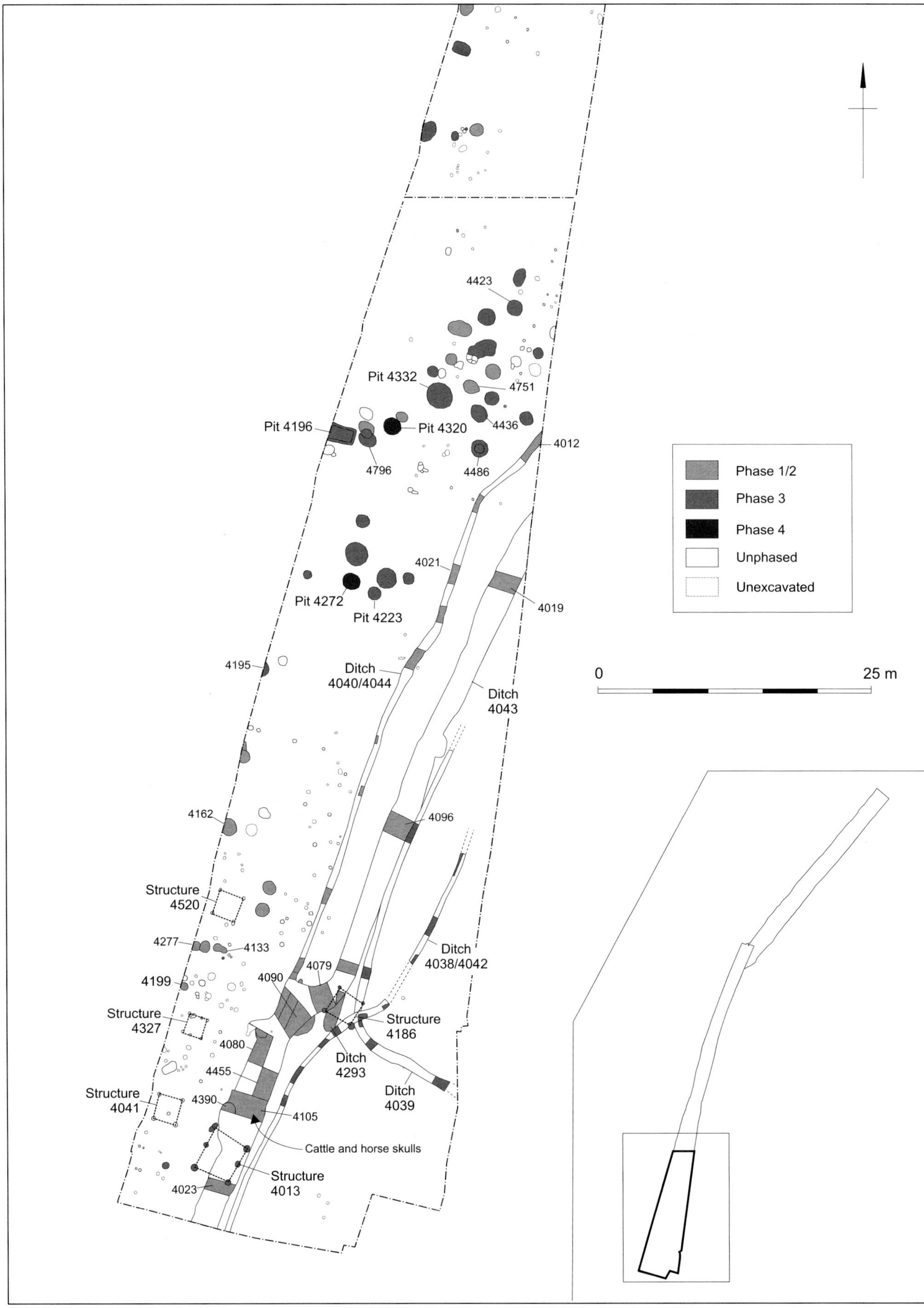

Figure 3.2 Feature group 1

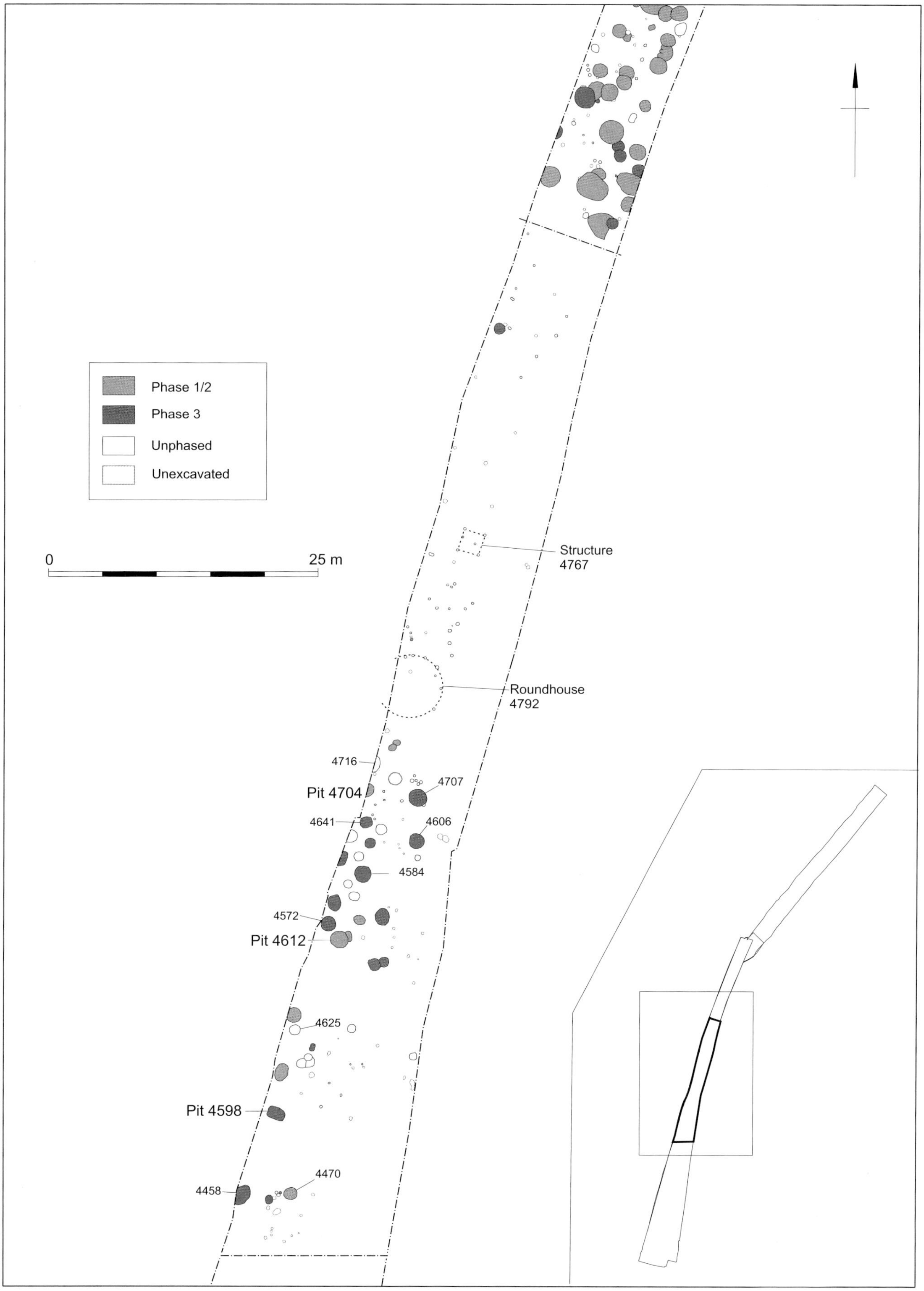

Figure 3.3 Feature group 2

Figure 3.4 Feature group 3

Ditches

Six ditches were recorded, all but one sharing a north-north-east to south-south-west alignment at the southern end of the site, the sixth being recorded at the north end of the site. Most were dated to the Late Bronze Age/early Middle Iron Age (phase 1/2) except for two small ditches dated to the later Middle Iron Age (phase 3) – the single ditch (5795) at the northern end of the site (Fig. 3.5) and one of the southern group (4038/4042). The southern ditches (Fig. 3.2) intercut and it was possible to establish much of their stratigraphic sequence. A number of sections excavated through the ditch fills contained high numbers of small finds and high densities of pottery and animal bone, including articulated animal bones and skulls.

The ditches followed a contour line along a relatively flat area on the east side of the ridge, before the ground fell sharply into Battlesbury Bowl, and they formed the eastern boundary to the area of the pits on the top of the ridge – there were no pits to the east of any of the ditches. However, they did not appear to have been significant boundaries when a number of square and rectangular post-built structures were constructed (see below), as some of these straddled the line of some ditches

Ditch 4293

The earliest of the ditches was recorded for only a short length from the terminal at its southern end to where it was truncated by ditch 4043 to the north. The rounded terminal was 1.8 m wide and 0.8 m deep with steep, slightly concave sides and a flat base. Its fills contained more chalk components than later ditches in this part of the site; a primary fill (4308) of dark brown clayey silt with common chalk represents a mixed deposit of dumped material and weathering products. Fills 4249, 4250, and 4308 contained a small, mixed assemblage with phase 1/2 pottery, an articulated cattle spine (ON 3051), and a gnawed and trampled human humerus (ON 3050). The south-east

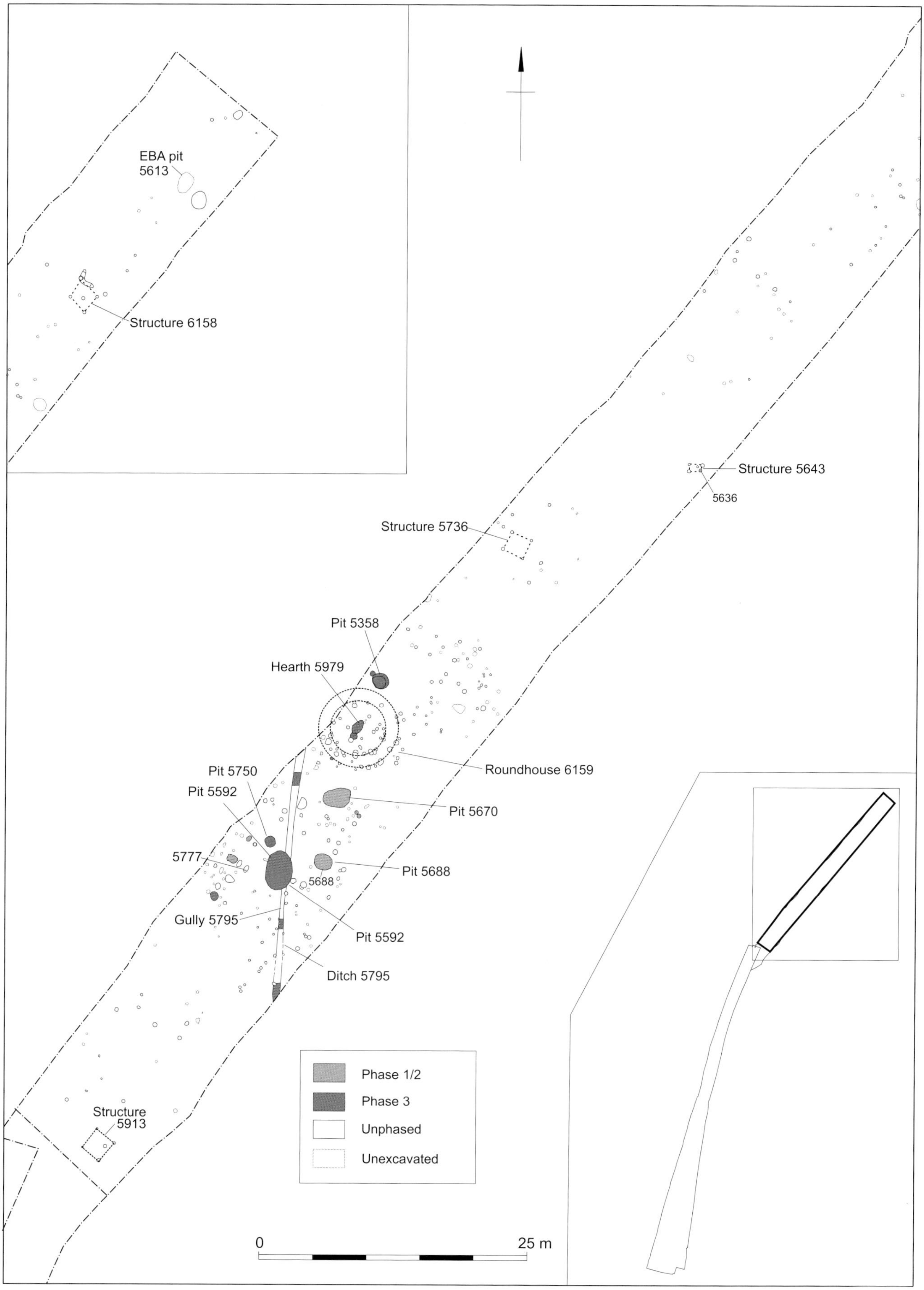

Figure 3.5 Feature group 4

edge of the ditch terminal was cut by phase 3 ditch 4038/4042.

It is unclear what this ditch was demarcating. The northern extent of ditch 4293, where truncated by ditch 4043, could not be determined, and no matching terminal was recorded on the same line to the south (the site continuing for a further 20 m south). However, the position of the terminal was subsequently marked by changes in direction of two later ditches; this may have been a route between the ridge top and Battlesbury Bowl below.

Ditch 4040/4044

This *c.* 55 m long ditch, heavily truncated at its mid-point, was generally aligned north-north-east to south-south-west but turned north-east at the north. Towards the south it was cut by ditch 4043. It remained visible on the western edge of ditch 4043 in some of the excavated sections (Fig. 3.6), but it could not be established whether it had continued to the southern end of the site or had terminated before that point. It was generally 0.6–0.8 m wide and *c.* 0.3 m deep with steep to near-vertical straight sides and a slightly concave or flat base, and one or two fills. It contained a relatively small and mixed finds assemblage which included 360 g of iron slag (from section 4021) representing 8.4% of all the slag from the site. The northernmost section (4012) contained a relatively large quantity of pottery in a dark brown clay loam matrix which also contained charcoal throughout.

This phase 1/2 ditch was the westernmost of the recorded ditches and very few features (pits or post-holes) lay to its east, even between it and ditch 4043, suggesting that even after the construction of the large ditch, the line of ditch 4040 may have remained a significant boundary.

Ditch 4043

The largest ditch was recorded for 73 m within the excavation area, but was visible in aerial photographs continuing to both north and south (Figs 3.1, 3.2). It ran parallel to ditch 4040 some 3–4 m to the east, possibly matching that ditch's slight turn to the north-east at its northern extent within the site. It cut ditches 4293 and 4040 to the east and west, respectively. It was 2–3 m wide, being generally wider to the south, and 1.1–1.4 m deep, with by steep, slightly convex sides, and in places with a 0.4–0.6 m wide steep to vertical slot above the flat base (Fig. 3.6). There was no indication of any internal or external bank constructed from the upcast of the ditch – although with the ground sloping to the east it is material from any bank on the eastern side would not have eroded into the ditch.

Although chalk rubble formed the primary fills, and there were lenses of weathered chalk higher up the ditch, the ditch fills were predominantly of soil deposits which appear to have resulted largely from the dumping of occupation material, rather than from the weathering of soil dumps or soil profiles in the area. Some of the basal deposits had a slightly greenish tinge very similar to midden-like deposits recorded at Potterne (Lawson 2000) and Maiden Castle (Sharples 1991) and, in places, these deposits contained mineralised plant remains (see Chapter 6).

A number of the ditch sections contained large finds assemblages. Human remains were recovered from ditch sections 4079, 4090, and 4096 and animal bone groups from ditch sections 4090 and 4105, and all the excavated sections contained relatively large quantities of pottery and bone. The average sherd weight of the pottery was relatively high (12.8 g). Other finds included a number of quernstone and whetstone fragments as well as worked bone objects and flint hammerstones. A copper alloy penannular brooch of 1st century BC–1st century AD date was recovered from the surface of the ditch.

The animal bone group from the upper fills of ditch section 4105 consisted of substantial parts of at least seven cattle skulls and three horse skulls (ONs 3029–32, 3054–58), and an articulated cattle foreleg (ON 3059) (Pl. 3.2). Some of the skulls displayed knife marks indicating the careful removal of the tissue, as well as removal of bone at their bases, so exposing the brain case. It has also been suggested that this would allow the skulls to be displayed on the tops of poles (see Hambleton and Maltby, Chapter 6).

Plate 3.2 Animal skulls in top of ditch 4043 (section 4105)

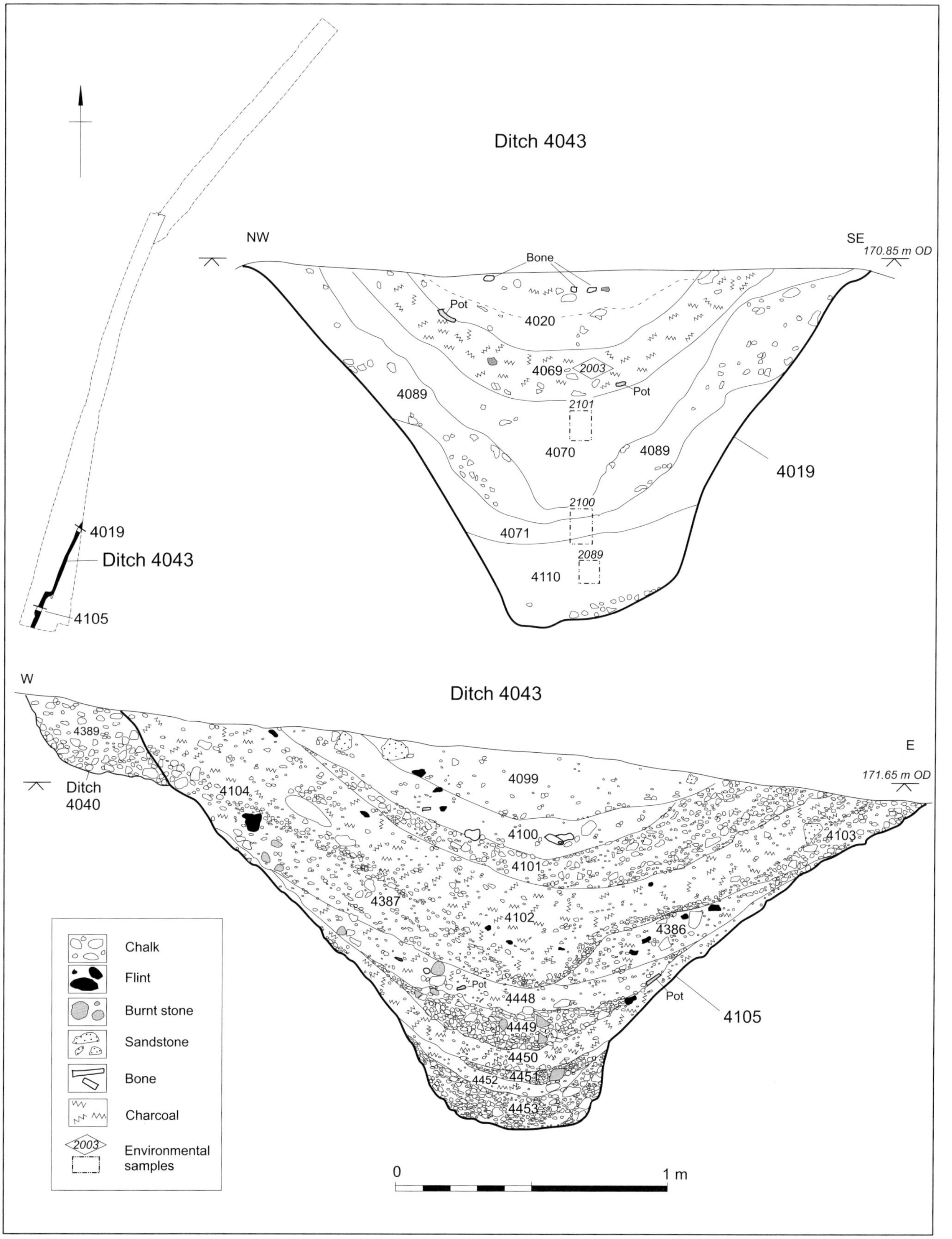

Figure 3.6 Sections 4019 and 4105 of phase 1/2 ditch 4043

The loss of teeth suggests that the skulls had been left exposed for some time before being placed in the largely infilled ditch. One of the cattle skulls and the associated foreleg produced radiocarbon dates of 790–420 cal BC (NZA-17103, 2503±40 BP) and 770–400 cal BC (NZA-13629, 2435±70 BP), respectively, while a cow femur from ditch section 4090 also produced a radiocarbon date of 770–400 cal BC (NZA-13630, 2445±55 BP) (Table 2.2). Although these lie on a radiocarbon 'plateau', they are barely distinguishable at the 95% confidence level and they are consistent with the phase 1/2 date obtained from the ceramic evidence.

The ditch had a noticeable kink towards the southern end of the site, the reason for which is unclear, although it corresponds closely to the earlier terminal of ditch 4293. It is possible that ditch 4043 also originally ended at this point, with an in-turned terminal, and was subsequently extended to the south, although no evidence for such a terminal was identified in the many ditch sections excavated in this area. Moreover, no features were recorded that the ditch might have turned to avoid or pass around. If ditch 4293 had marked a point of access between ridge and low ground, the continuation of ditch 4043 south of that point would appear to have closed off that access.

Ditch 4039

This ditch was 0.6–0.9 m wide and 0.2–0.3 m deep, with moderate to steep concave sides and a shallow concave to flat base, and had a single fill of compacted mid–dark greyish–brown clayey silt/silty clay loam with very common chalk coarse components. It contained a moderate, mixed finds assemblage with a predominance of animal bone, especially towards the south. It also contained 766 g of iron slag (18% of the total recorded on the site).

To the north it was parallel to the other ditches along the line of the ridge, just cutting the eastern edge of ditch 4043 (Fig. 3.2) which, by then, was partly filled. However, at the point adjacent to the terminal of ditch 4293 and the kink in ditch 4043 it turned south-south-east down the slope towards Battlesbury Bowl. This turn supports the suggestion, above, that this point on the ridge may have marked a point of access between the high and low ground. If so, however, this access appears to have been intermittent, being blocked first by ditch 4043 and later by phase 3 ditch 4038/4042 (below), as well as by a number of post-built structures.

Ditch 4038/4042

This phase 3 ditch was the latest within the sequence of ditches at the southern end of the site (Fig. 3.2). It was recorded for *c.* 43 m, again aligned north-north-east to south-south-west, and lay immediately east of ditch 4043 whose alignment it followed closely, suggesting that the latter was still visible at this time. As with ditch 4040/4044, construction of the original tank road in the 1950s had severely truncated the ditch at its mid-point and at its southern end where it was barely discernible in the chalk. No terminal was recognised at its northern end. It was 0.3–0.5 m wide and up to 0.15 m deep with shallow, concave sides and a shallow, concave to flat base. It had a single fill of medium greyish–brown clay loam containing a small finds assemblage. As with ditches 4039 and 4040/4044 it contained some iron slag (220 g), suggesting that some metalworking activity was occurring around in the southern part of the site.

The southern ditches: summary

The sequence of ditches in the south of the site appears to represent the changing configuration of the eastern boundary of ridge-top activity and an intermittent point of access between it and the low ground of Battlesbury Bowl. Although some of the ditches were cut by post-built structures (see below), in general there were few archaeological features, and certainly no pits, to their east. The terminal of the ditch 4293 appears, therefore, to mark a significant break in that boundary possibly defining one side of a route running down the northern slope of Battlesbury Hill. The importance of this point is marked in the layout of the later ditches, first being reflected in the conjectured terminal of ditch 4040/4044 at approximately the same position, then by the marked kink in the line of ditch 4043 which appears to block that access (at least within the area of the site). The later line of ditch 4039 suggests reinstatement of that access and, finally, there is the matching kink in phase 3 ditch 4038/4042 which, again, cuts across the point of access.

Ditch 5795

Towards the north end of the site (Figs 3.4, 3.5), ditch 5795, running north–south for *c.* 23 m (in FG 4), was dated by its stratigraphic relationship to phase 3 pit 5592, which it cut. It was 0.4–0.7 m wide and up to 0.2 m deep with moderate to steep concave sides and a shallow concave base, its recorded depth affected by modern truncation in this area of the site. It had up to three fills (generally two) comprising a sterile, primary fill of weathered chalk and later fills of medium brown silty clay loam, the latter containing a very small finds assemblage of worked and burnt flint, undiagnostic pottery, and animal bone. The line of the ditch passed immediately west of phase 3 roundhouse 6159 (see below), although it could not be established whether or not they were contemporary. Although the line of the ditch is parallel to that of a linear feature to the west visible in aerial photographs (Fig. 2.1), it does not seem to correspond with any of those recorded in earlier fieldwork at the southern edge of Harman Lines (Chapter 2).

Post-holes and Post-built Structures

A total of 725 post-holes was recorded on the site of which 458 (63%) were excavated (Table 3.1), some fully, if they were thought to be components of identifiable structures. The post-holes were generally circular or sub-circular, 0.4 m or less in diameter, and of varying depths. A few were up to 0.6–0.7 m in diameter. The largest numbers of those excavated were recorded towards the north of the site, in FGs 3 (24%) and 4 (46%). Only 48 could be dated either directly or by stratigraphic association, with approximately equal numbers being assigned to phases 1/2 and 3. Of these, as with the pits, the earlier post-holes were predominantly in the north of the site with a higher proportion of the later ones being in the south.

Approximately 120 of the post-holes were assigned to possible post-built structures, comprising two roundhouses and 11 square/sub-rectangular structures. However, the density of post-holes in some areas of the site was such that a number of the structures that have been identified, particularly the small square structures, may in fact consist of post-holes whose apparent arrangement is entirely fortuitous, or post-holes associated in some other way.

The majority of post-holes formed no obvious structures, although some have the appearance of being directly associated with adjacent pits. For example, five shallow post-holes (5029, 5361, 5363, 5365, 5367) appear to be arranged in an arc 0.1–0.4 m out from the north-eastern side of phase 1/2 pit 4993 (or earlier pit 5163 in almost the same location), in FG 3 (Fig. 3.4). The post-holes, averaging *c.* 0.3 m in diameter and 0.1 m deep, had identical single fills of brown silty loam with moderate to abundant chalk inclusions, one (post-hole 5365) containing a single undiagnostic sherd of Iron Age pottery. If associated, these post-holes may have formed some form of partial screen around either of the pits, although the purpose of such a structure is not known, nor whether it related to the pits' original use, presumably for storage, or the later processes of deposition within them. A possibly similar arrangement was recorded around a large sub-rectangular pit (5043) in FG 3 (Fig. 3.4). Although the edges of some of the post-holes appeared to be cut by the edge of the pit, this may simply be due to erosion around its lip.

Even if these post-holes were not directly associated with the pits, their density in such areas still appear to point to an intensity of activity associated either with the pits' original use for storage or their later use as receptacles for varied types of domestic, economic and possibly ritual deposits.

Table 3.1 Post-holes by feature group and phase

FG	*Phase 1/2*	*Phase 3*	*Unphased*	*Total*
1	1	12	71	84
2	1	3	50	54
3	19	6	84	109
4	4	2	205	211
Total	25	23	410	458

Roundhouses

Of the two possible roundhouses, the more complete example (6159) in FG 4 was recognised from a dense, circular concentration of post-holes, including larger (possibly entrance) post-holes to the east-south-east, and a sequence of well made central hearth pits (Figs 3.5, 3.7). The other (4792 in FG 2) comprised an unphased arc of post-holes in an area of the site where tank road construction in the 1950s had truncated the natural chalk (Fig. 3.3). A number of other post-holes, appearing to form short arcs, were also recorded, and these may be the truncated remains of other roundhouses.

Roundhouse 6159

The outline of roundhouse 6159, located towards the northern end of the site (Fig. 3.7), was indicated by a concentration of *c.* 60 post-holes along the western edge of the site within which two possible concentric arcs of post-holes were discernible positioned around of two intercutting hearth pits. The two arcs had projected diameters of *c.* 5.1 m and 7.1 m, placing the structure at the low end of the size range one would expect for Middle Iron Age roundhouses. Comparable double-ring roundhouses of similar scale (or even smaller) have been proposed from Moel y Gaer, Denbighshire, and New Barn Down, West Sussex (Guilbert 1981, 313). Four relatively large post-holes (*c.* 0.5 m in diameter and 0.4 m deep) on the south-east side of the outer arc (5900, 5903, 5951, 5964) may represent a slight shift in the alignment of its entrance, with paired post-holes 5900 with 5951, and 5903 with 5964, giving entrances 2.3 m and 2.6 m wide respectively, dimensions comparable with buildings at Danebury (Cunliffe and Poole 1991, 45–6).

The finds assemblage from the roundhouse was quite small and consisted of pottery, animal bone, worked flint, burnt stone, and fired clay. In addition, two quernstone fragments, a loomweight fragment, and a hammerstone were recovered from the hearth or post-holes in the south of the structure. Although nearly a third (18) of all the post-holes possibly

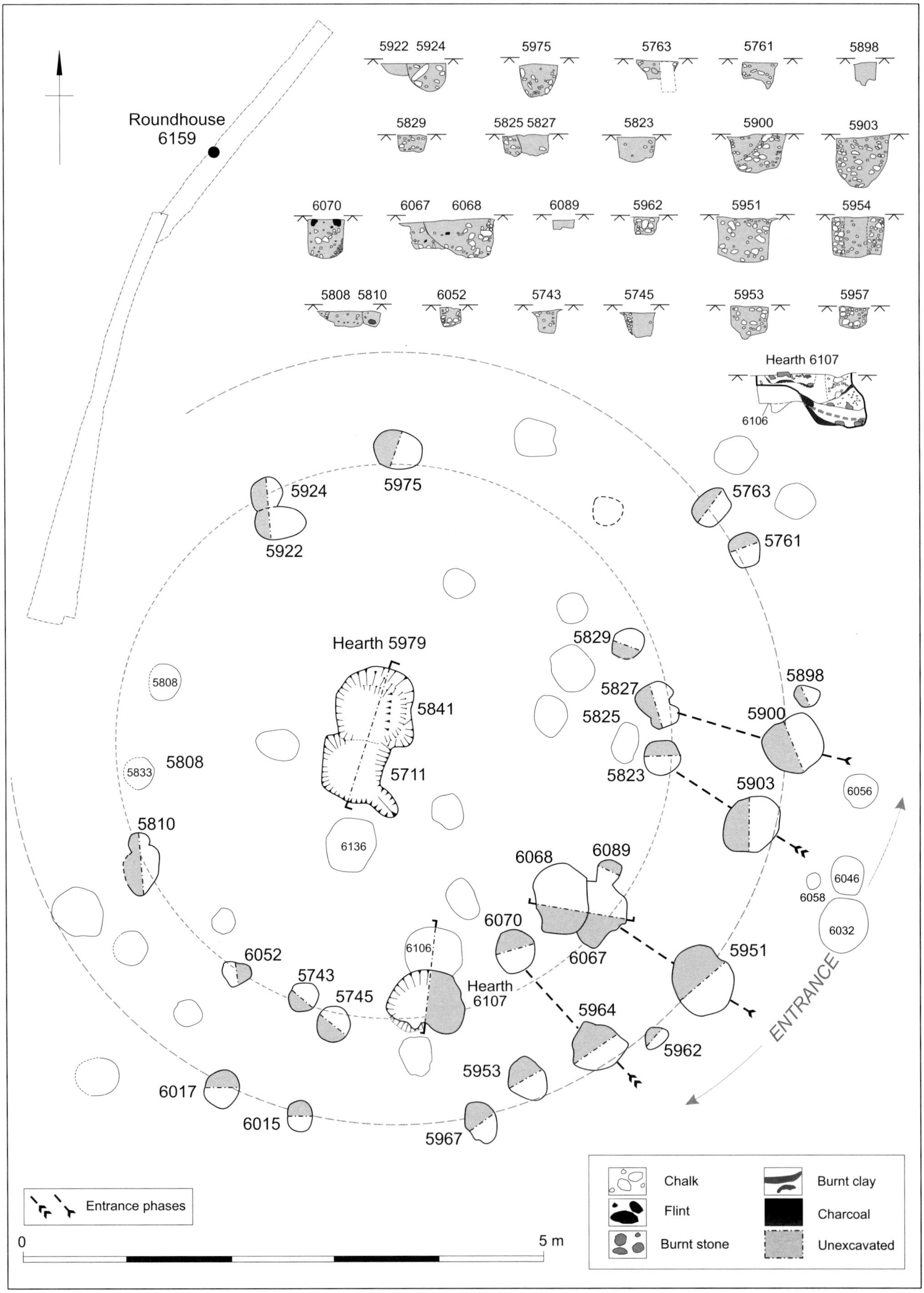

Figure 3.7 Roundhouse 6159

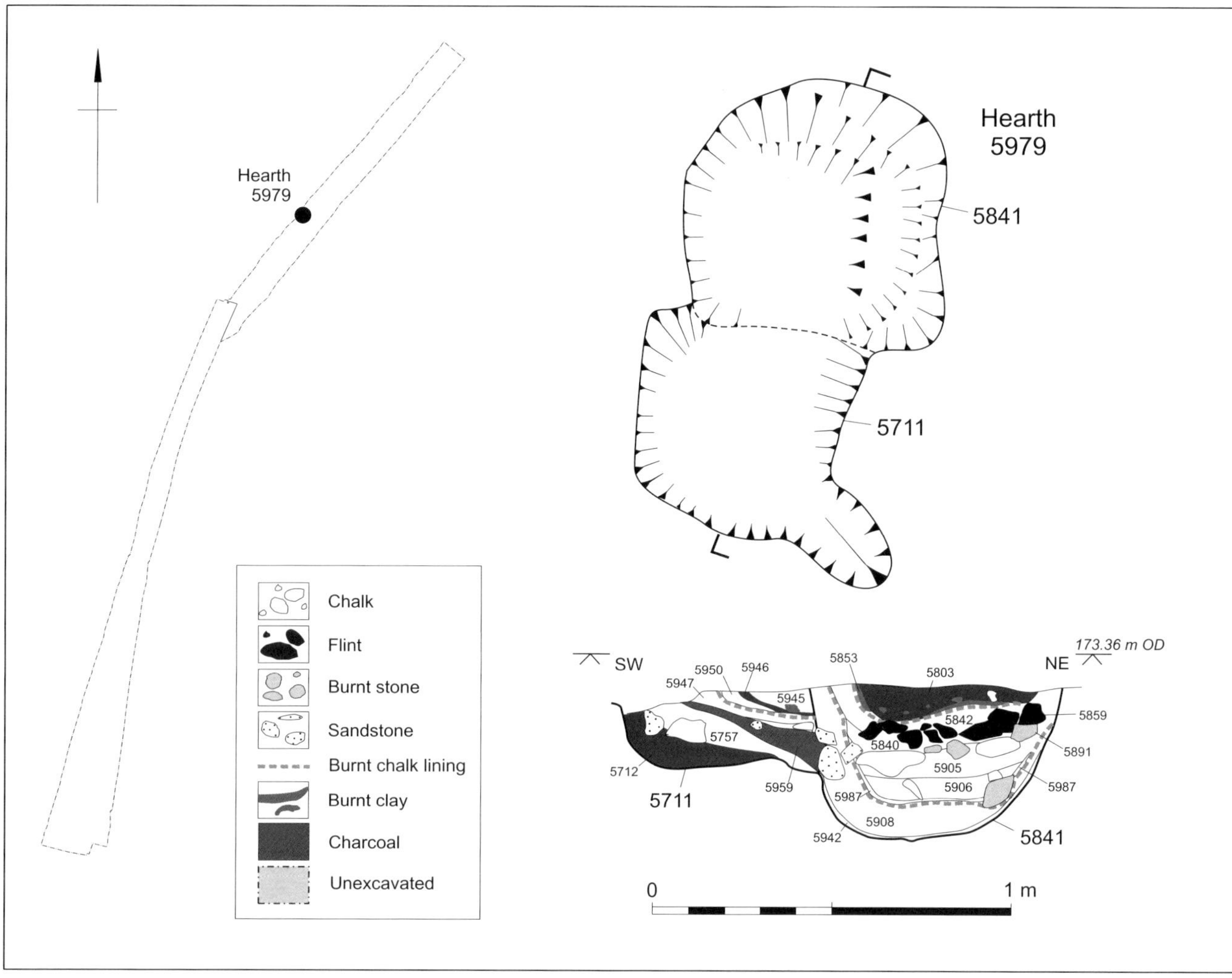

Figure 3.8 Hearth pits in roundhouse 6159

associated with the roundhouse contained pottery, only one (6017, in the south of the structure) contained datable pottery (phase 3).

The central hearth (5979) consisted of two consecutive pits (5711 and 5841) (Fig. 3.8). The initial pit (5711) to the south measured *c.* 0.9 m by 0.6 m and up to 0.15 m deep, with a short extension to the south-east possibly representing a flue facing prevailing draughts from the roundhouse entrance. It contained a dump of charcoal-rich material (5712), overlain by a layer of large (0.08–0.1 m) burnt sandstone blocks and then by a layer of rammed chalk (5757). Later deposits indicated an alternating pattern of charcoal-rich fills (5759, 5946) and rammed chalk deposits (5960, 5957, 5947, 5950, 5945), two of which (5960, 5947) showed evidence for burning. A radiocarbon date of 410–180 cal BC (NZA-13635, 2265±55 BP) (Table 2.2) from charcoal within layer 5959 confirmed the Middle Iron Age date suggested by the phase 3 pottery from posthole 6017.

The second phase of the hearth (5841) was a circular cut *c.* 0.6 m diameter and 0.4 m deep with steep to nearly vertical concave sides and a shallow concave base. A fine layer of silt (5942) at the base of the pit might suggest some collapse from the earlier hearth before the incorporation of the first layer of rammed chalk. A sequence of rammed chalk deposits (5908, 5906, 5905, 5853, 5842), two of which (5906, 5863) showed evidence for burning, were interleaved with silty layers (5942, 5987, 5840). The stratigraphic position in the upper part of the cut of layer 5840 between a layer of chalk and sandstone blocks (0.05–0.1 m) (5891), including some re-used quernstone fragments, and a layer of similarly-sized flint nodules (5859), suggests it was a bedding for the upper flint layer. The sequence of layers also included two baked clay linings. One (5926), towards the base (not seen in section) lay between rammed chalk deposits 5928 and 5906, while the other (5853) was recorded near the top. A charcoal-rich layer (5803) represented the final use of the hearth.

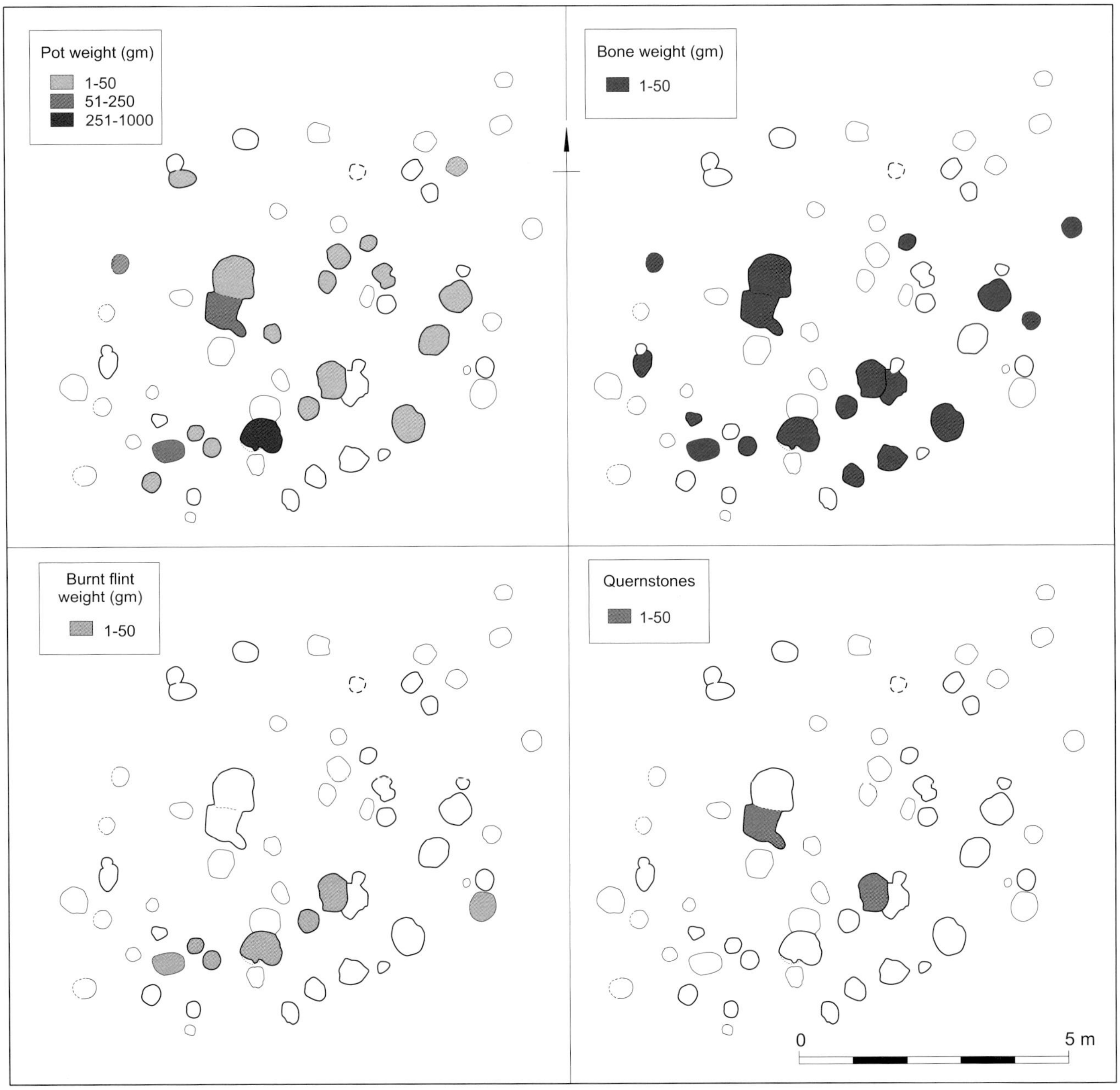

Figure 3.9 Finds distributions in roundhouse 6159

These were the only hearths recorded, and they were comparable in size and shape to hearths recorded at Danebury (Cunliffe and Poole 1991, 145), where just over half the 44 examples were sited within roundhouses (*ibid.*, 141). Three hearth types were recognised at Danebury – daub-lined (27%), rammed chalk (48%), or natural pits with burning in evidence (16%) (*ibid.*, 145). Hearth 5979 incorporated elements of both the daub-lined and rammed chalk types.

Roundhouse 6159 contained relatively few small finds, these including a flint hammerstone, a loomweight fragment, and two quernstone fragments and, like the distributions of pottery, animal bone, and burnt flint, they were found largely around the southern part of the structure (Fig. 3.9). Although pottery was more common in the south, the larger sherds were more prevalent in the eastern part (both north and south). This spatial patterning has been noted previously in Late Bronze Age and Iron Age roundhouses in Wessex, for example, Longbridge Deverill Cow Down, Wiltshire and Dunston Park, Berkshire (eg, Chadwick-Hawkes 1994; Fitzpatrick 1994; 1997; Parker Pearson 1999), and may reflect the organisation of living space, for example for sleeping, food preparation, eating, and craft activities. The predominantly south-east facing entrances to roundhouses of these periods are sometimes marked by special deposits and while no clearly 'placed' deposits were recorded for roundhouse 6159, entrance post-hole 5900 did contain the highest density of animal bone of all the post-holes but as this consisted of only 48 g, no conclusions can be drawn.

Possible roundhouse 4792
The other possible roundhouse was located towards the northern part of FG 2 as represented by an arc of six truncated post-holes (Fig. 3.3). These would have comprised the northern and eastern parts of a structure *c.* 5.6 m in diameter, possibly representing the inner circle of posts of a double-ring roundhouse comparable to roundhouse 6159. The post-holes were all oval in shape *c.* 0.3 m by 0.25 m and up to 0.1 m deep, with fills of dark brown and greyish–brown silty clay containing few chalk components. The only finds were two undiagnostic fragments of pottery (from post-holes 4756 and 4758) and a fragment of animal bone (from post-hole 4758).

Square and sub-rectangular structures
Of the 11 possible square and sub-rectangular structures that were identified, five were at the southern end of the site (in FG 1) (Fig. 3.2). None could be dated by finds although there were stratigraphical indications that two belonged to phase 3 or later. Post-holes of structure 4186 cut the fills of phase 2 ditches 4043 and 4039, while post-holes of six-post structure 4013 also cut the fills of ditch 4043. Although structure 4186 spanned the phase 3 ditch 4038/4042, there was no stratigraphical relationship between them, but it is not unreasonable to suggest that the structure post-dated the ditch and it is consequently dated to at least phase 3, and potentially to phase 4 (Table 3.2). None of the other such structures, which included the other three in FG 1 (4041 (Fig. 3.10), 4327, 4520), one in FG 2 (4767), one in FG 3 (5349) and four in FG 4 (5913, 5643, 5736, 6158) contained datable material but those in FG 1 at least may have been broadly contemporary with 4013 and 4186.

Where the post-holes of 4013 and 4186 cut through relatively soft ditch fills, as opposed to natural chalk, they contained chalk (in structure 4013, Fig. 3.10), or chalk and greensand blocks (in structure 4186), as packing material. Finds from these two structures included undated pottery, animal bone, worked and burnt flint, burnt stone, and a rib knife of worked animal bone (ON 3009, from structure 4013).

Post-built structures of this kind are familiar features on Late Bronze Age and Iron Age sites, and a range of possible functions have been suggested, including houses, animal byres, watch towers, shrines, and excarnation platforms, or even two sets of paired post-holes possibly used for drying racks (eg, Ellison and Drewett 1971). The two pairs of post-holes in structure 5643 (Fig. 3.5) were only 1.25 m apart. These kinds of structures are most frequently interpreted as above-ground stores for grain or other foodstuffs ('granaries'), equipment, and raw materials. At Danebury, 499 examples were recorded (Cunliffe and Poole 1991, 104), and examples from this site falls within the range of 'small' and 'large' Danebury structures (Cunliffe 1984, 89). The post-holes of the structures at this site contained relatively few finds including pottery, worked and burnt flint, burnt stone, and, from structure 5643, a partially worked fragment of human skull (Chapter 5).

The location of the cluster of five structures in FG 1 may be related to the suggested former access point

Table 3.2 Summary of square and sub-rectangular structures (all unphased except * = phase 3+)

Structure	*FG*	*Dimensions (m)*	*Size m^2*	*Ave. p-h diam. (m)*	*Ave. p-h depth (m)*	*Comment*
four-post structure						
4041	1	2.4x2.3	4.8	0.50	0.29	all contained chalk block packing
4186*	1	2.9x2.5	7.3	0.59	0.15	chalk and greensand block packing; cuts ditch 4043
4327	1	2.0x1.6	3.2	0.32	0.17	chalk packing in all but one post-hole
4520	1	2.4x2.2	5.3	0.34	0.20	truncated by tank road
4767	2	2.0x2.0	4.0	0.35	0.10	truncated by tank road
5349	3	2.0x2.0	4.0	0.71	0.24	large post-pits with chalk block packing
5643	4	1.3x0.6	1.0	0.36	0.26	human skull frag. (ON 3371) in post-hole 5584
5736	4	2.0x1.9	3.8	0.33	0.16	
5913	4	2.1x2.0	4.2	0.34	0.27	
6158	4	2.0x2.0	4.0	0.37	0.26	
six-post structure						
4013*	1	4.2x3.4	14.3	0.60	0.16	chalk block packing; cuts ditch 4043; truncated to E by tank road

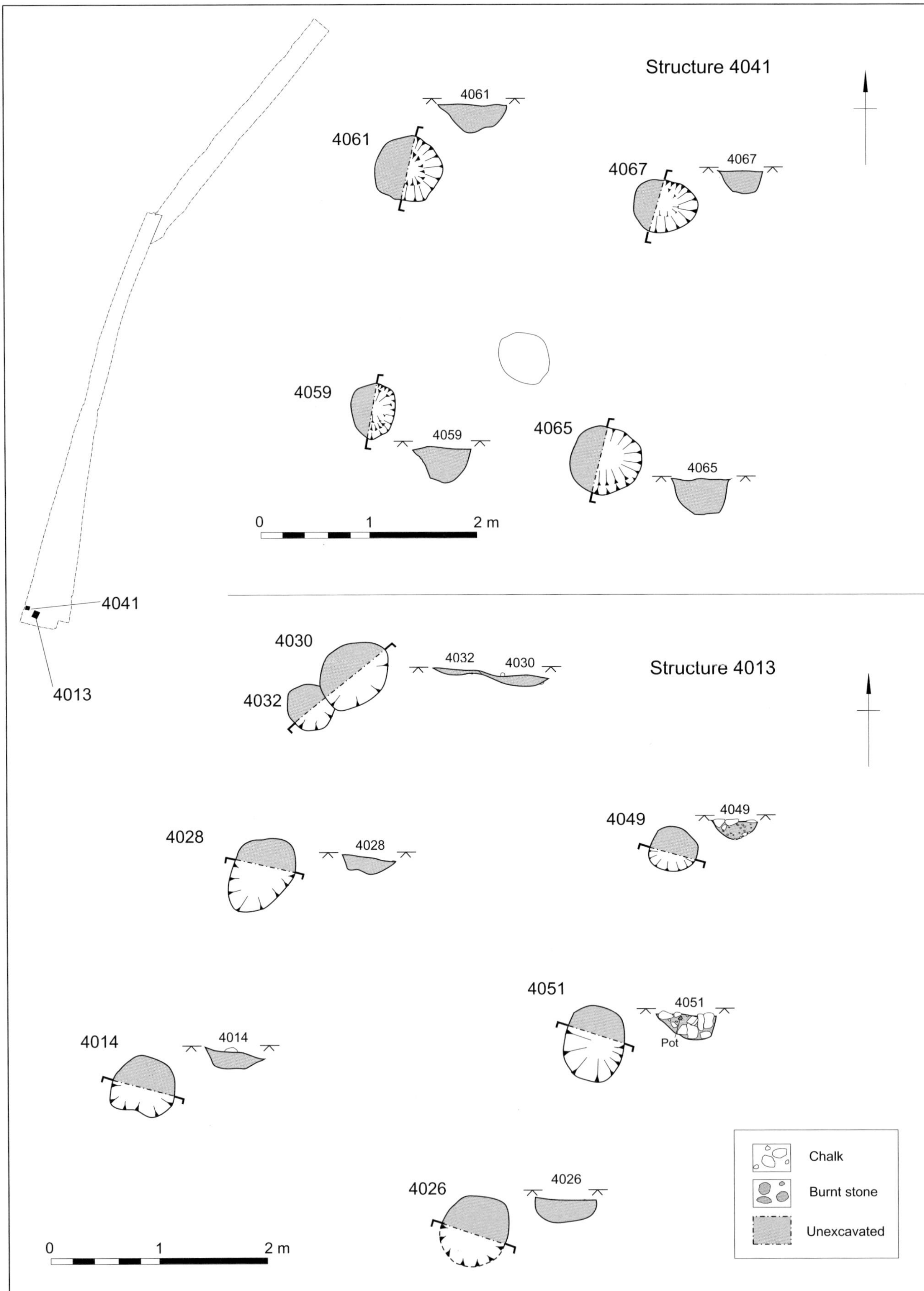

Figure 3.10 Square and sub-rectangular structures 4041 and 4013

between the ridge and Battlesbury Bowl, appearing to emphasise a significant change in activity in this part of the site. Although any interpretation of their location is hampered by the limited area of the excavation, it is noticeable that three of the structures were arranged in a line roughly parallel to the ditches, and that all of them had been built across this access point. The largest structure (4013) almost spanned the largest ditch (4043) raising the possibility of some functional relationship between the two features, while the post-holes of structure 4186 managed to span three of the ditches, again pointing to a change in emphasis.

Pits

Of the 198 Late Bronze Age–Iron Age pits only a few intercut, particularly in FGs 1 and 2 (Figs 3.2 and 3.3). Although more intercutting was evident in FG 3, where there was the greatest concentration of pits *(c.* 41%) (Fig. 3.4; Pl. 3.3), existing features generally appear to have been deliberately avoided. There were relatively few pits at the extreme north of the site (in FG 4, Fig. 3.5). Fifty-seven of the pits were unphased (Table 3.3). The overall chronological pattern suggests that the earlier pits were located in the north of the site, particularly in FG 3, with later pits concentrated towards the south.

The shapes of pits, in both plan and profile, give an indication of their original function, perhaps for grain storage. As nearly all had vertical or near-vertical sides and flat or near-flat bases, they were classified on the basis of their shape in plan alone. The most common were cylindrical (45%), particularly in phase 3 when they accounted for 56% of the pits (compared to 44% in phase 1/2); most of the rest were oval (28%), sub-circular (14%), or sub-rectangular (12%) (Table 3.4).

Circular or sub-circular pits ranged in size from 0.5 m to 2.2 m diameter (mean of *c.* 1.3 m). The elongated (oval and sub-rectangular) pits were 0.35–3.8 m long (mean of *c.* 1.3 m) and 0.2–2.5 m wide (mean *c.* 1.1 m). Most pits were 0.45–0.7 m deep (mean *c.* 0.5 m), except for sub-rectangular pits which had an average depth of 0.7 m (Table 3.5; eg,

Table 3.3 Pit distribution, by feature group and phase

FG	*Phase 1/2*	*Phase 3*	*Phase 4*	*Unphased*	*Total*
1	19	25	2	18	64
2	9	13	–	12	34
3	51	12	–	19	82
4	3	7	–	8	18
Total	82	57	2	57	198

Plate 3.3 Pits of FG 3 with the earthwork defences of Battlesbury Hillfort in the background, looking south

pit 5318 in FG 3, Pl. 3.4). Pit volumes were calculated 'as found', representing therefore, their final rather than original volumes. On average, the largest were the sub-circular and sub-rectangular pits with average volumes of over 3 m³, which is comparable with the general volumes of all pit shapes at Gussage All Saints, Dorset (Jeffries 1979), Danebury (Whittle 1984; Cunliffe and Poole 1991), and Maiden Castle (Rawlings 1991). The other pit shapes fell short of these values, because they were relatively shallow – pits from comparable sites were *c.* 1.3–1.8 m deep on average.

Table 3.4 LBA/IA pit shapes by phase

Shape	*Phase 1/2*	*Phase 3*	*Phase 4*	*Unphased*	*Total*
Conical	–	1	–	–	1
Cylindrical	36	32	–	21	89
Irregular	–	–	–	1	1
Oval	22	9	2	21	55
Sub-circular	14	6	–	8	28
Sub-rectangular	10	9	–	5	24
Total	82	57	2	57	198

Plate 3.4 Sub-rectangular phase 1/2 pit 5318 under excavation (FG 3)

In addition to variations in their size, shape, and form, the pits differed significantly in their fill sequences, the nature of their deposits, and their contents. In order to better characterise and understand the different depositional histories selected pits are examined in detail below. Full details of these and all the other pits can be found in the archive.

Late Bronze Age to early Middle Iron Age (phase 1/2)

Eighty-two pits could be assigned to the earlier part of the site's occupation on ceramic or stratigraphical grounds although none was considered suitable for radiocarbon dating. Seven pits (all in FG 3) were dated to the Late Bronze Age/Early Iron Age, and

Table 3.5 Pit depths (m) and volumes (m³) by pit shape

Shape	*No.*	*Max. depth*	*Mean depth*	*Mean volume*
Conical	1	–	1.10	1.10
Cylindrical	76	1.5	0.55	0.95
Irregular	1	–	0.15	–
Oval	50	1.4	0.50	1.20
Sub-circular	24	1.2	0.45	3.05
Sub-rectangular	17	1.7	0.70	3.20

contained relatively small quantities of pottery and bone and very few 'small finds'. A further 60 pits fell within the broader date range of Late Bronze Age–early Middle Iron Age, again most of them (57%) in FG 3, and to a lesser extent in FG 1 (25%), FG 2 (15%), and FG 4 (3%). They include pits 4612 and 4704 (both in FG 2) and 4993 in FG 3 which contained deposits of animal bone, and in the case of 4993 also human bone. Another 15 pits were dated specifically to the early Middle Iron Age, four in FG 1, one in FG 4, and in FG 3 (Table 3.3).

Pit 4612

Pit 4612 was among the cluster of pits south of possible roundhouse 4792 in FG 2. It cut and therefore post-dated a smaller, shallow pit 4698 on its north-east side (Fig. 3.11). Pit 4612 was *c.* 1.4 m in diameter and 0.9 m deep with near-vertical sides and a flat base. A primary fill of chalk rubble (4821 = 4831) up to 0.2 m thick, containing some animal bone, was overlain by two dumps of occupation debris (4697 and 4613), both containing large animal bone assemblages, along with pottery and small quantities of burnt flint, burnt stone, and fired clay, as well as (from 4697) an iron fragment, possibly from a blade (ON 3211). The lower dump contained a group of seven sheep/goat vertebrae that appear to be from the same animal, displaying knife cuts and representing secondary butchery waste. Several other sheep/goat bones in this context may have been from the same skeleton; other bones included a worked bone offcut (ON 3865). At the interface between the two dump layers was a lamb skeleton (ON 3168), aged 2–3 months, the carcass of which had been skinned, beheaded, and possibly partially dismembered. Many of the bones from this context appear to have belonged to animals that died in the later spring or early summer and were deposited shortly afterwards after processing. The upper dump layer contained small groups of horse foot bones, cattle skull fragments, and four dog bones possibly from the same adult animal.

Pit 4704

Pit 4704 lay 12 m north of pit 4612, on the western edge of the excavation area. It was 1.6 m in diameter and 1.8 m deep with irregular steep to vertical, and in places undercut sides, and an irregular base (Fig. 3.11). Fill 4882 was up to 0.4 m thick, comprising at least two phases of chalk rubble deposition and two silting episodes, was overlain by a substantial dump of occupation debris (4817) rich in charcoal and finds, including quernstone fragments, a whetstone and fragments, as well as most of a cattle mandible (ON 3233) with knife cuts, and an almost complete, albeit slightly gnawed, cattle humerus (ON 3258). This layer, which filled the pit to around half its depth, was

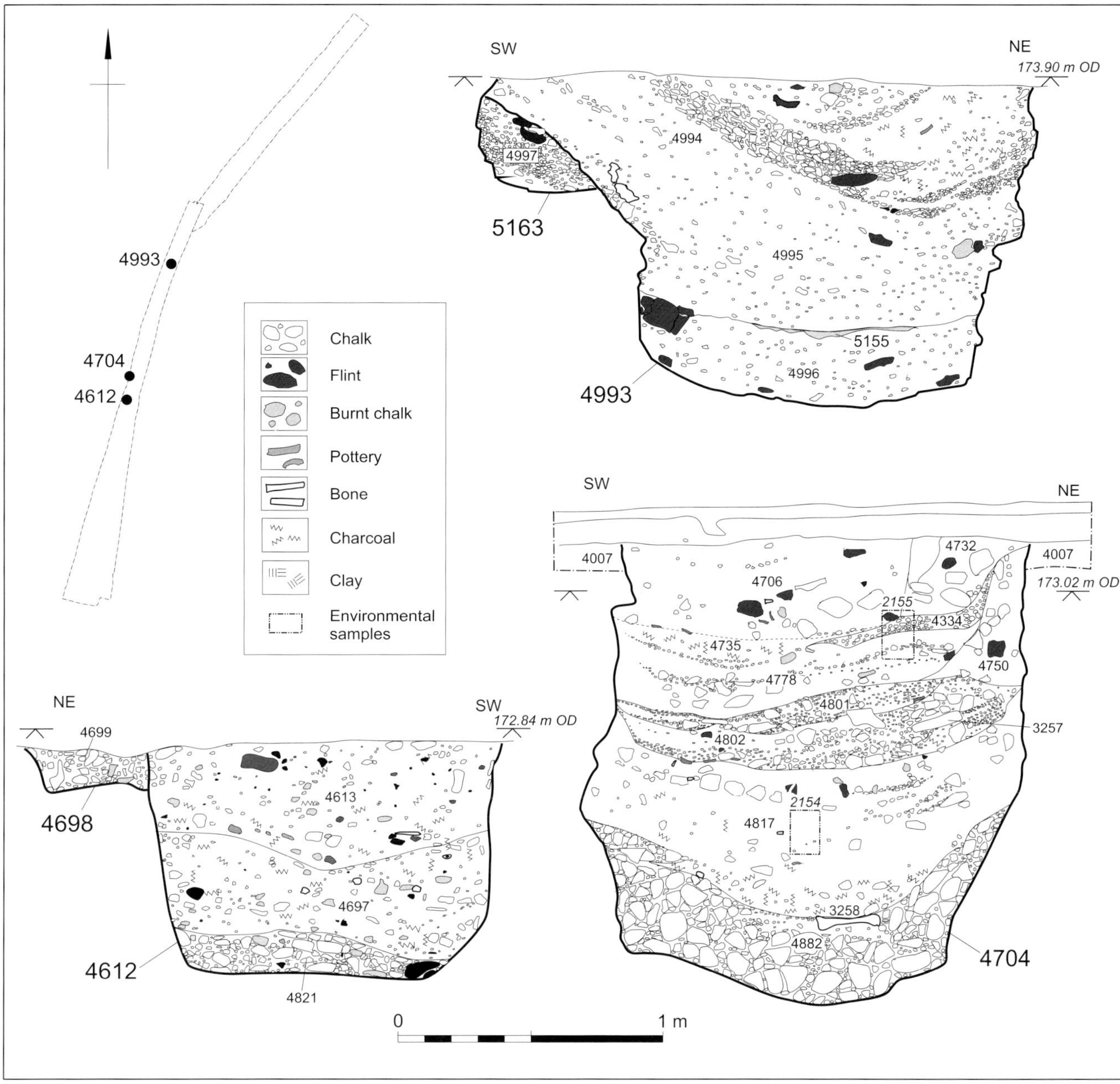

Figure 3.11 Phase 1/2 pits 4612, 4704, and 4993

followed by a longer period of weathering and natural inwash and erosion, interspersed with smaller dumps of waste (4802, 4801, 4750, 4778, and 4706), eventually filling the pit. The upper dump layers contained numerous further fragments of quernstone and whetstone, as well as a cattle ulna shaft sharpened and polished to form a gouge (ON 3232) and, from layer 4750 against the north-eastern edge of the pit, two chalk loomweights and a chalk spindlewhorl. In contrast to pit 4612, there were no large animal bone dumps from the pit, the largest assemblage (from 4817) being dominated by sheep/goat bones, including several complete limb bones and an unusually high number of phalanges and other small bones, representing at least four sheep/goats. There were similar but smaller bone assemblages from other contexts.

Pit 4993

Pit 4993, which was 1.7 m in diameter and 1.3 m deep, cut and almost completely obliterated broader (1.8 m diameter) but shallower (0.5 m) pit 5163 (Fig. 3.11), and the possible arc of post-holes (5164, above) could have been associated with either feature. Pit 4993 had near vertical sides (although shallower where these cut into fills of 5163, and a slightly concave base. There was no primary fill of eroded chalk rubble, but the basal fill (4996) of brown silty

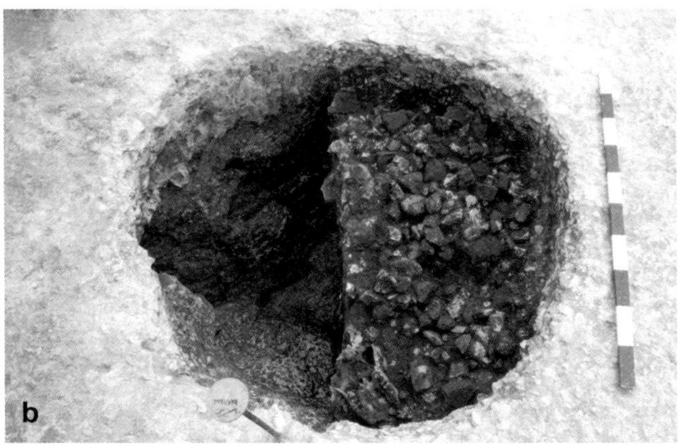

Plate 3.5 a) Section of pit 4436, showing dense layer (4435) containing pottery, charcoal, a whetstone (Fig. 4.3, 10) and burnt animal bone, stone, and chalk; b–c) rubbish deposit 5084 in pit 4641

clay loam, containing pottery, worked and burnt flint, animal bone (including a badger tooth), and a pink coral bead (ON 3286) (Fig. 4.4, 18), may have derived from the eroded fills of the earlier pit. This layer was overlain by a thin organic lens (5155), possible of cess, above which were two layers of dumped domestic waste (4995 and 4994), the lower layer displaying slight tip lines but were still relatively homogeneous, the upper layer comprising discrete dumps interspersed with lenses of chalk rubble. The lower layer contained parts of a cattle skull and a sheep skull (both possibly representing processing waste) and a bone needle point, while the upper layer contained a fragment of human skull.

Later Middle Iron Age (phase 3)

Fifty-seven pits were dated to this phase (Table 3.3), being concentrated in FG 1 at the south (44%) and diminishing towards the north in FG 2 (23%), FG 3 (21%), and FG 4 (12%). Dense concentrations, probably dumps, of cultural material and/or charcoal were found in some pits (eg, pits 4436 and 4641; Pl. 3.5). Two pits (4223 and 4332) both in FG 1, contained inhumation burials, while one rectangular pit (4196) with a distinct stratigraphic sequence comprising layers of puddle and chalk, appears to represent a sequence of cuts used for some form of industrial activity.

Pit 4223

This relatively shallow pit at the southern end of the main concentration of pits in FG 1, was 1.3 m in diameter and 0.6 m deep with near-vertical sides and a flat base (Fig. 3.12). It contained two crouched inhumation burials. The lower skeleton (4345) lay on the *c.* 0.15 m thick basal fill, which contained pottery and animal bone, suggesting that the pit had initially been used (or re-used), for a short period for waste disposal before being used as a grave. The body, of a man aged over 40 years, was laid on its right side with its head to the west. A horse lower mandible (ON 3085) had been placed over the pelvis, and a fragment of bone from another adult (aged over 18 years) was also recovered from this level. Although a layer of soil (4398) was recorded between the two inhumations, it is possible that the two burials were not separated by any great length of time. The upper skeleton (4251; Pl. 3.6a), of an adult female aged 35–55 years, was more tightly crouched, lying on its left side and with the head to the east, and further fragments of horse mandible were recovered from the surrounding soil

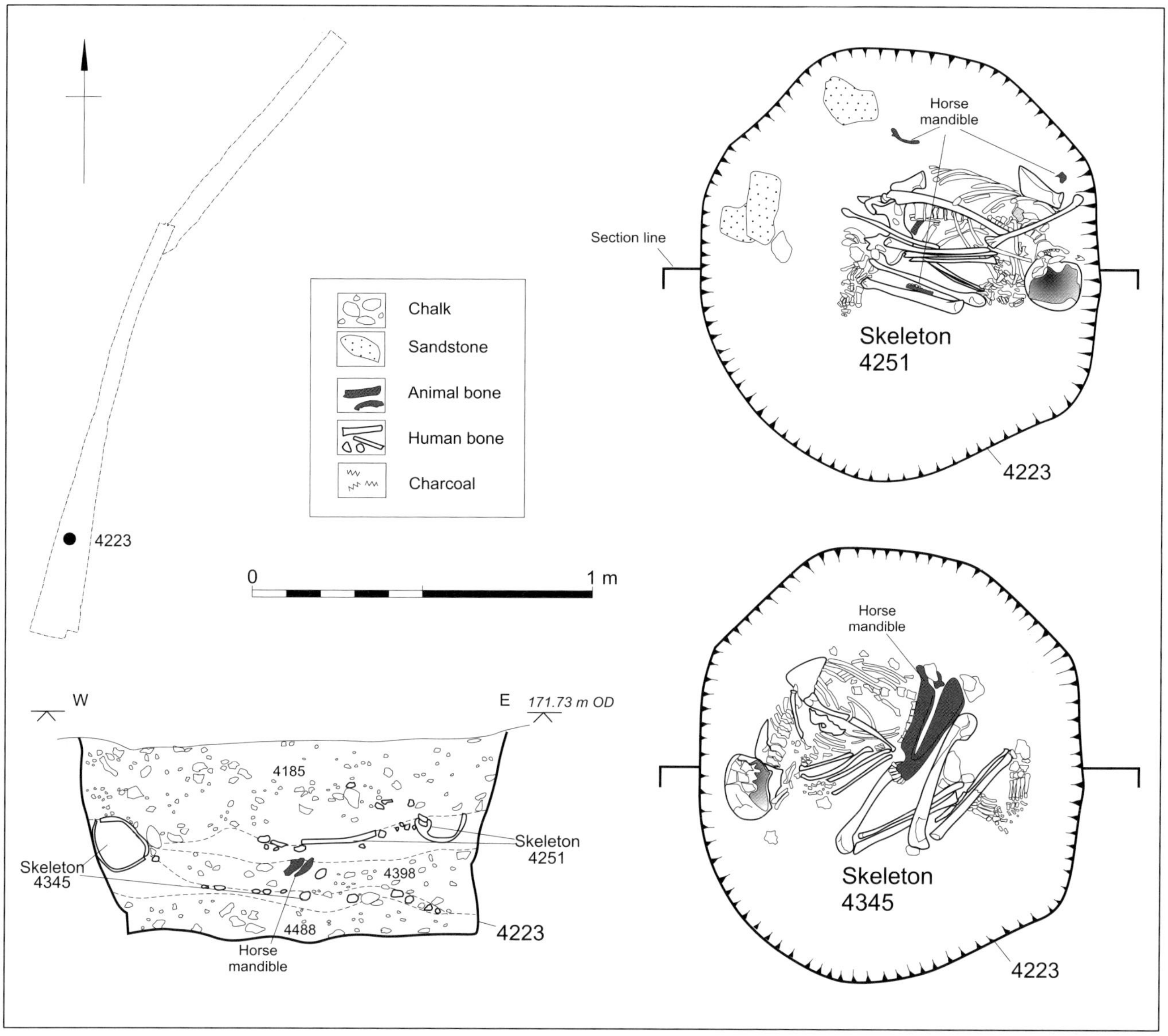

Figure 3.12 Phase 3 pit 4223 with inhumation burials

along with a number of large pieces sandstone to the north-west of the skeleton. Sealing the burial was a 0.3 m thick upper fill (4185). This may have been deposited shortly after the burials as part of the grave fill. Alternatively, the subsequent infilling of the pit may have occurred later, its contents of pottery, worked and burnt flint and stone, and animal bone being typical of the general waste material found in other pits.

Pit 4332

This pit, in the centre of the cluster of pits in FG 1, was *c.* 2 m in diameter and 1.5 m deep, with near vertical sides and a flat base (Fig. 3.13). In contrast to pit 4223, the crouched inhumation in this pit had been placed directly on the base, suggesting either that the burial was made immediately after the pit had been dug, or after it had been emptied of its stored contents, or after it had been cleaned of any redeposited waste material in preparation for the burial. The skeleton (4571; Pl. 3.6b), of a juvenile aged about 10 years, possibly a male, was laid on its left side with the head to the south-east. Probably directly associated with the burial was a Neolithic flint axe (ON 3088, see above; Pl. 3.1), part of a chalk loomweight (ON 3127), and three articulated sheep/goat vertebrae (ON 3128). The latter were recovered from the layer of backfilled soil (4385) surrounding the skeleton, along with other elements of human bone, including an articulated right foot (ON 3016) with the distal ends of the leg bones (Pl. 3.6c). This layer, filling the base of the pit to a depth of *c.* 0.4 m, the upper surface of which appears to have been deliberately levelled, also contained four

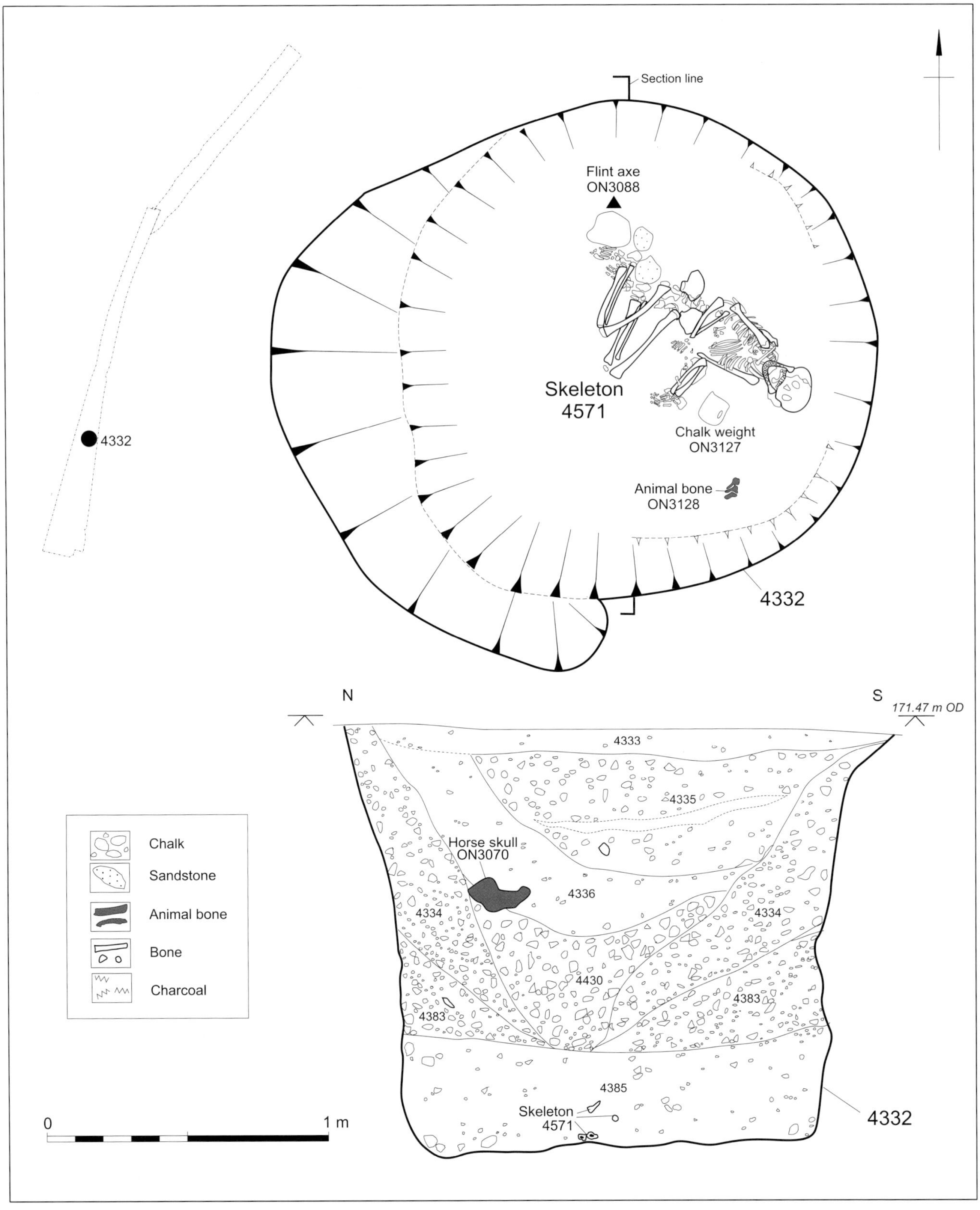

Fig. 3.13 Phase 3 pit 4332 with inhumation burial

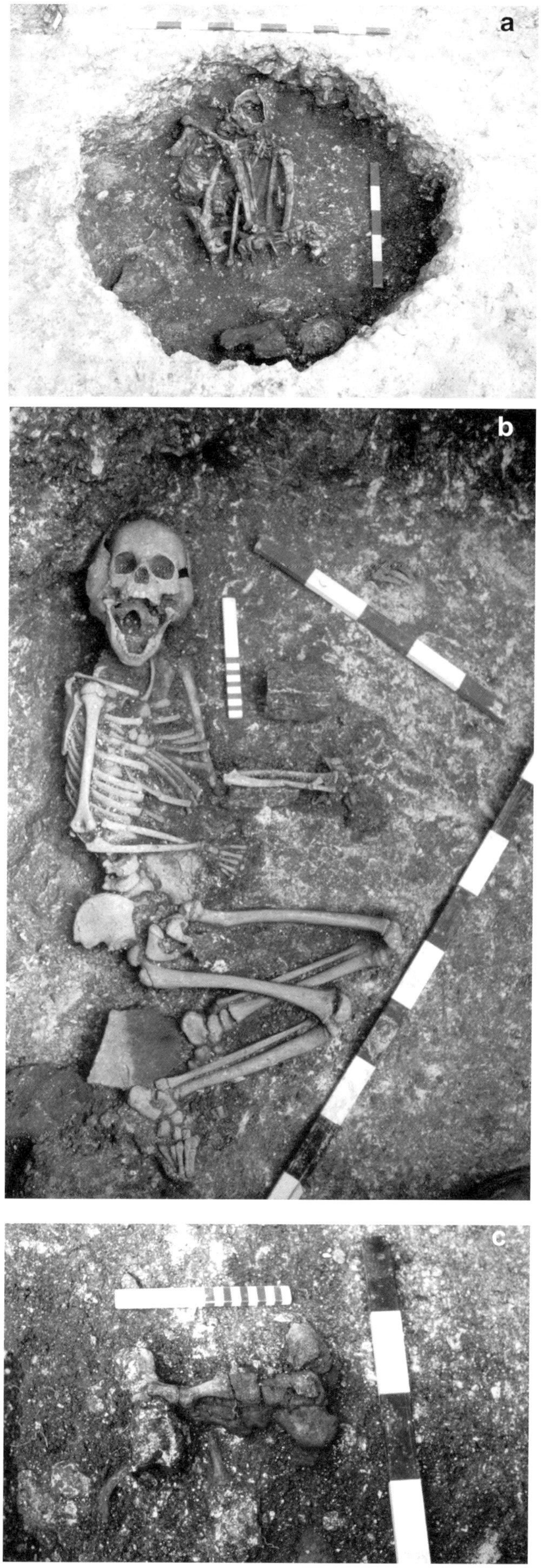

Plate 3.6 a) skeleton 4251 in pit 4223; b) skeleton 4571 in pit 4332; c) articulated foot bones in pit 4332

jaws of lamb and kid and other animal bones, sherds of pottery, worked and burnt flint, and burnt stone. Whether any or all of these latter finds were also deliberately placed in the grave, or were simply incorporated within the backfilled soil, is unclear. The deliberate placing of a finely made axe suggests that this was a collected item that was incorporated into the burial. Both the burial and animal bones from this layer produced radiocarbon dates in the range 410–190 cal BC (NZA-17104, 2276±45 BP; NZA-17105, 2262±40 BP; NZA-13633, 2258±55 BP) (Table 2.2).

The two layers (4383 and 4334) overlying the burial backfill appear to represent medium- to long-term weathering deposits, both having high chalk rubble contents and accumulating around the sides of the pit. Both contained domestic waste as well as horse, cow and sheep/goat butchery waste, layer 4334 also containing an antler handle (ON 3075).

The pit may have been partly recut at this point down to the level of the burial backfill, the base of the recut then immediately filling (or being filled) with sterile chalk rubble (4430) on top of which was placed the skull of a foal (ON 3070); this skull showed no evidence for butchery. Evidence of immature horses are rare on Iron Age sites in southern England (Harcourt 1979; Grant 1984a) and the skull may therefore have some significance because of its rarity. The overlying layers (4336, 4335, and 4333) represent a slower process of natural weathering, incorporating waste material, including a bone needle (ON 3079 from layer 4336).

Pit 4196

This large sub-rectangular pit orientated east–west, with three possible recuts (6163, 6164 and 4553) on the same alignment as the original cut, lay against the western edge of the site (in FG 1) (Fig. 3.14). It contained numerous layers of burnt or baked puddled chalk, charcoal-rich soil, chalk rubble backfill, and 'soily' occupation deposits, and (with the exception of recut 6164) produced a small finds assemblage including animal bone, worked flint, burnt stone, quernstone fragments, pottery (including phase 3 and residual phase 2), and iron slag.

The original cut (4196) was at least 2.6 m long, up to 1.6 m wide and 1.7 m deep, with near-vertical sides and a flat, slightly sloping base, its profile showing little sign erosion of the sides. At the bottom were two layers of chalk rubble in greyish–white silty clay (4569 and 4404) which had the appearance of deliberate backfill, Within layer 4404, which contained small quantities of pottery, animal bone, burnt stone, and

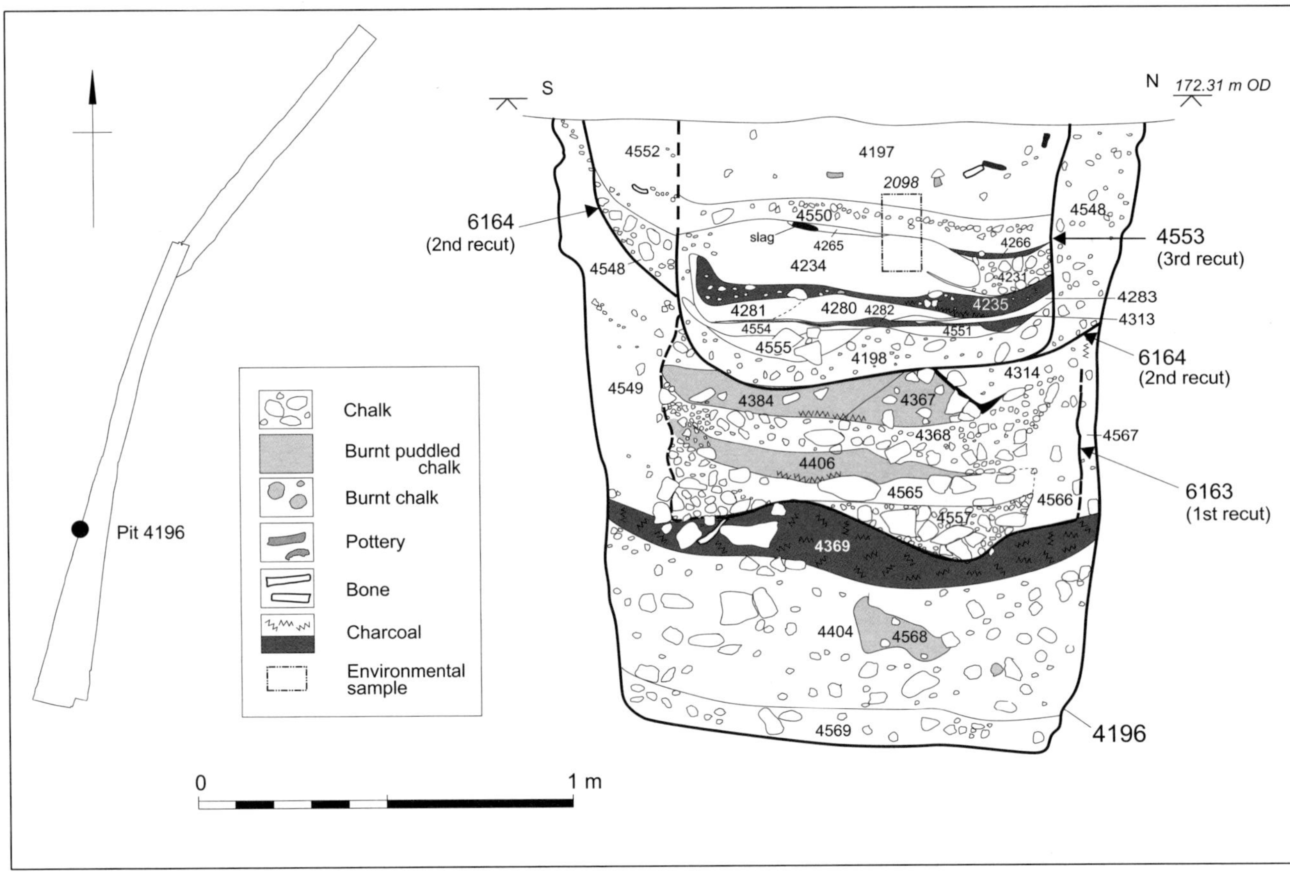

Figure 3.14 Phase 3 rectangular pit 4196

flint, was a deposit of burnt chalk (4568) 0.8 m long, aligned east–west, 0.25 m wide and up to 0.1 m thick. Overlying layer 4404 by was a charcoal-rich occupation deposit (4369) up to 0.15 m thick, which contained most of the pottery, animal bone, and worked flint from this cut. Above this, on the south side of the cut, was a further chalk rubble layer (4549) displaying multiple tip lines of chalk coarse components, extending up to the top of the pit; this was cut into by the later recuts, leaving a width of only 0.2–0.3 m of rubble against the side of the pit. Against the north side of the pit there were two vertical bands of mid-brown silty loam (4567, *c.* 0.05 m wide, on the outside, and 4566, *c.* 0.15 m wide, on the inside), again apparently defined on the inner face (of 4566) by the near vertical side of a recut. The difference in character of these northern layers to the rubble backfill on the south side is hard to explain, as is the vertical interface between them which was defined by a very small trace of possibly organic material, unless the remains of some form of wattle or timber structure/lining within the pit that had rotted *in situ*.

The layers against the south and north sides appear to have been cut into, down to the charcoal layer (4369), by the first recut 6163. This was also sub-rectangular in shape, at least 1.1 m long, *c.* 1 m wide and 1.2 m deep, with vertical sides and an irregular base. It contained successive deposits of chalk rubble, 'puddled' chalk (some burnt/baked *in situ*), and charcoal. Of the 'puddled' chalk deposits (4406, 4367, 4384), the upper two had a reddish colour reflecting localised burning which was not intense enough to affect the underlying contexts.

A possible second recut (6164) was visible cutting the upper levels of the upper rubble fill (4549) of the original pit on its southern side; on the northern side it appears to have cut the earlier deposits back to the chalk bedrock. This cut was also sub-rectangular, centrally located within recut 6163, with a steep concave to near-vertical southern side and a probably concave base (although most of the base was truncated by the third recut – 4553). It was at least 1.5 m long and 0.6 m deep, and appears to have been partly backfilled with sterile chalk rubble (4548), above which was a sterile mid-brown silty loam with chalk lenses (4552). These layers were largely cut away by recut 4553.

Recut 4553 was sub-rectangular and again located centrally within pit 4196. It was at least 2.4 m long, 1 m wide and 0.7 m deep with vertical sides and a slightly uneven, but flat base. It contained a moderate number of finds, including pottery, animal bone, worked and burnt flint, worked bone, worked stone, and quernstone fragments. The significantly greater quantity of finds, compared to the earlier cuts, was due to the predominance of occupation deposits (4198, 4313, 4282, 4235, 4197) and the relative lack of sterile chalk rubble 'backfill' deposits (4555, 4283, 4550). The earliest fill of light grey/brown silty clay (4198) extended across the whole cut (as exposed), but many of the later deposits – of chalk rubble (4555), puddled chalk (4554, 4280, 4281, 4234, 4265) and charcoal-rich soil (4313, 4282, 4235) – only extended *c.* 0.4 m from the feature section, suggesting the possible presences of a small hearth in the centre of the recut. The soil micromorphology of the deposits sampled in upper fills 4234 and 4550 suggest dumps of phosphatic, organic-rich material, some of it burned. The material appears to be derived from ash/soil waste from stabling as well as chalky in-wash lenses (see Macphail and Crowther, Chapter 6).

In the later phases of infilling of recut 4553, four small closely-spaced stakes (stake-holes 4257, 4259, 4261, 4263) were driven into chalky layers 4231 and 4234 in the north-west part of the pit (not seen in section). The stake-holes were up to 0.08 m diameter and 0.06 m deep with steep sides, but their function is unknown and they do not seem to represent structural features within the pit. The end of use of recut 4553 is represented by a small hearth (4215) cutting chalky layer 4231 at its south-east (not seen in section). The hearth pit, which was 0.6 m diameter and up to 0.12 m deep with steep, concave sides and a concave base, contained three fills – two 'puddled' chalk deposits (4213, 4214), the upper of which (4214) was burnt/baked, and an intervening charcoal-rich ashy deposit of very dark brown/black silty loam (4216) containing burnt stone. A second charcoal-rich layer (4212), which was identical to 4216, overlay 4214 and spread slightly to the north of the feature, and probably represents the final use of the hearth. A chalky layer (4550) and an occupation deposit (4197) overlying the hearth represent the final filling of recut 4553.

Large sub-rectangular pits have been recorded on many Iron Age sites but beyond stating that they do not seem practicable for grain storage and are often associated with human remains (Hill 1995) (although not in this case), there is little to indicate their 'primary' function. However, the presence of four successive sub-rectangular pit cuts, two with comparable sequences of layers, points to a continuity of general function at this one location. This clearly involved the laying down of puddled chalk layers, and their *in situ* burning/baking, and episodes of dumping of, variously, charcoal-rich soil, occupation debris, chalk backfill, or organic waste possibly from animal stabling. Even when the feature was almost completely filled, the location was still used for a small hearth, its comparable layers pointing to an apparently related function. The activity of burning, however, is difficult to reconcile with a number of characteristics that may suggest the use, on a number of occasions, of some form of organic linings within the feature. These characteristics include the trace of possibly organic material at the interface between layer 4566 and 4567, the apparent absence of weathering or erosion of the existing pit fills into which vertical-sided recuts 6163 and 4553 had been cut, and the vertical edge of the puddled chalk layer 4281 slightly away from the side of the recut.

Pit 5358

This pit, immediately north of roundhouse 6159 in FG 4, suggests that it may too have been subject to successive recuts. The pit was 1.6 m in diameter and 1.3 m deep with vertical sides and a flat base (Fig. 3.15). It was filled to a depth of at least 0.5 m with an accumulation of probable occupation debris (5848) which included as groups of articulated animal bones, some lying on the base of the pit and with some of the bones bearing knife marks. One group comprised 14 cattle vertebrae and seven ribs, another cattle group comprised both pelves, the sacrum, and two lumbar vertebrae, and a third group comprised 13 bones of a lamb. The layer also contained parts of two cattle skulls and one horse skull. Whether this combined material simply represents butchery waste, or had some other symbolic significance is unclear. The two bone groups containing cow vertebrae produced radiocarbon dates of 380–100 cal BC (NZA-13635, 2618±55 BP) and 390–190 cal BC (NZA-17108, 2241±40 BP).

The profile of the layer's upper surface suggests that it had been cut into, the base of the recut (6160) having moderately steep sides and a flat base 0.15 m above the base of the original pit. A cattle skull lying on the base of the recut was overlain by a dump of occupation debris (5771).

It is possible that a thin humic layer sealing layer 5771 had, in turn, been truncated by a second recut (6161). This was filled to the top of the pit with two layers containing few finds, the lower charcoal-rich layer representing a single dump of material, the upper layer (5769) resulting from a slower process of small-scale deposition and weathering. These layers may then have been largely cut away by a third, 0.5 m deep, recut (6162) on the base of which was a dump of humic and charcoal-rich debris (5735) containing animal bone, pottery (one sherd joining with one from layer 5771), and a bone needle. Two further dumps of material (5734 and 5359) filled the pit, the upper being particular rich in finds including pottery, quern fragments, burnt stone, and animal bone.

Why this pit should have been repeatedly recut in this way is unclear, although it may be related to its proximity to the roundhouse immediately to its south which, as described above, may have been modified

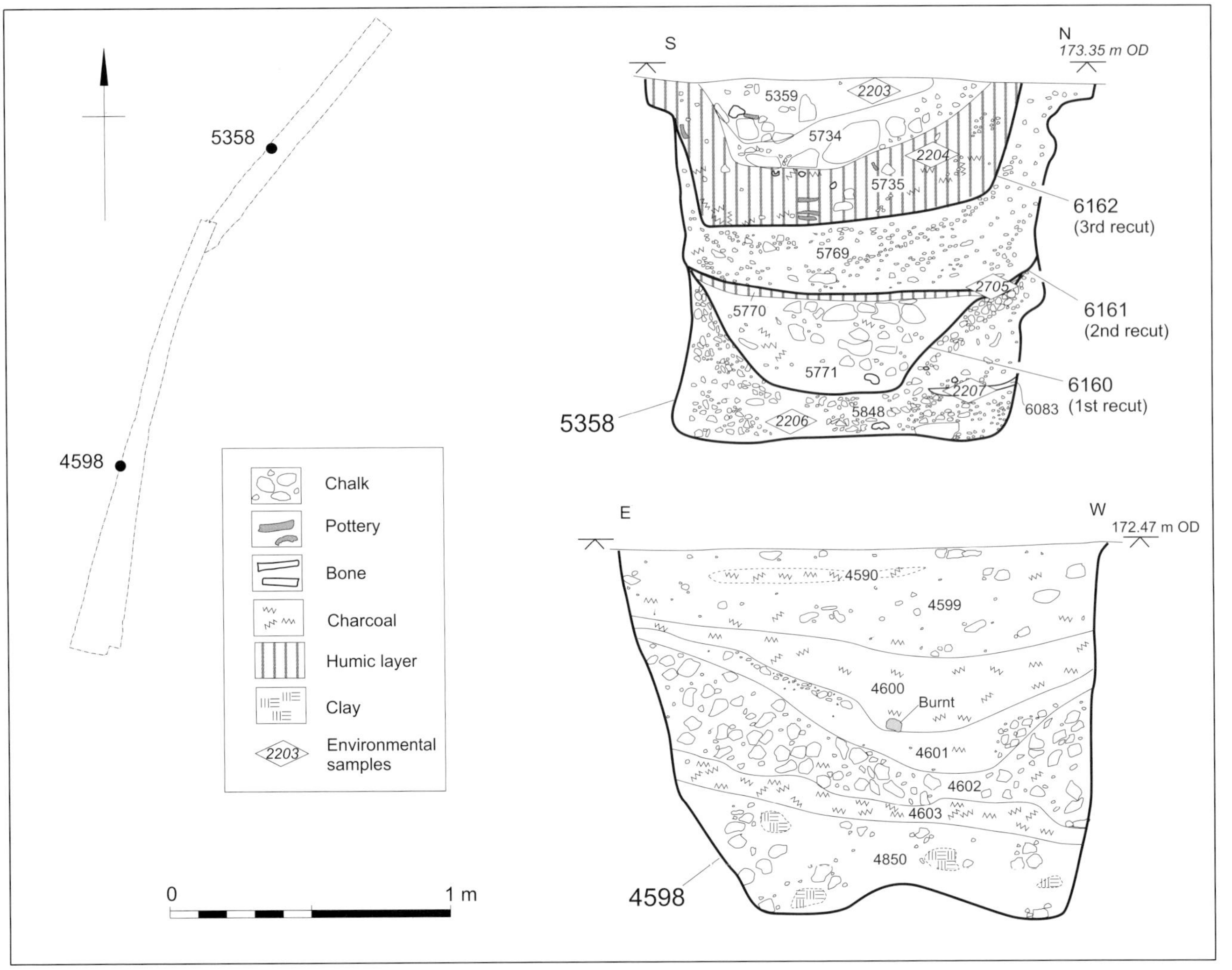

Figure 3.15 Phase 3 pits 5358 and 4598

on at least one occasion, as indicated by the shifting of its entrance. The rather confusing cluster of post-holes in the area of the roundhouse suggests that there may have been a longer sequence of alteration and rebuilding at this location. If the pit was specifically related to the roundhouse, this may help explain its re-use and recutting. Interestingly, an area some 3.5m surrounding the pit to its north and east (the west lay outside the excavation area) was empty of other features; beyond this was a further concentration of post-holes but few pits, suggesting that this area may have been in some way reserved for this pit.

Pit 4598

This sub-rectangular pit, towards the south of the main concentration of pits in FG 2, was 1.7 m long, 1.2 m wide and 1.4 m deep with steep to vertical sides and a slightly irregular base (Fig. 3.15). The basal fill (4850) contained some chalk rubble but may represent a deliberate backfill rather than a naturally accumulated primary fill. Its upper surface may have been smoothed out prior to the deposition of a small dump of possible occupation debris (4603) containing a cattle skull and other bones, a large saddle quern fragment, and a chalk loomweight. This was followed by a period of natural inwash (4602) and then further episodes of dumping (4601, 4600, and 4599).

Late Iron Age (phase 4)

Two pits containing inhumation burials in FG 1 (4272 and 4320) have been dated to the Late Iron Age (phase 4) on the basis of their radiocarbon determinations (although 4320 contained phase 3 pottery).

Pit 4272 was very shallow, grave-like and lay just below the earlier modern road along the ridge. It contained the badly fragmented remains of two closely contemporaneous burials lying on a layer of burnt chalk fragments. It contained no pottery, but a

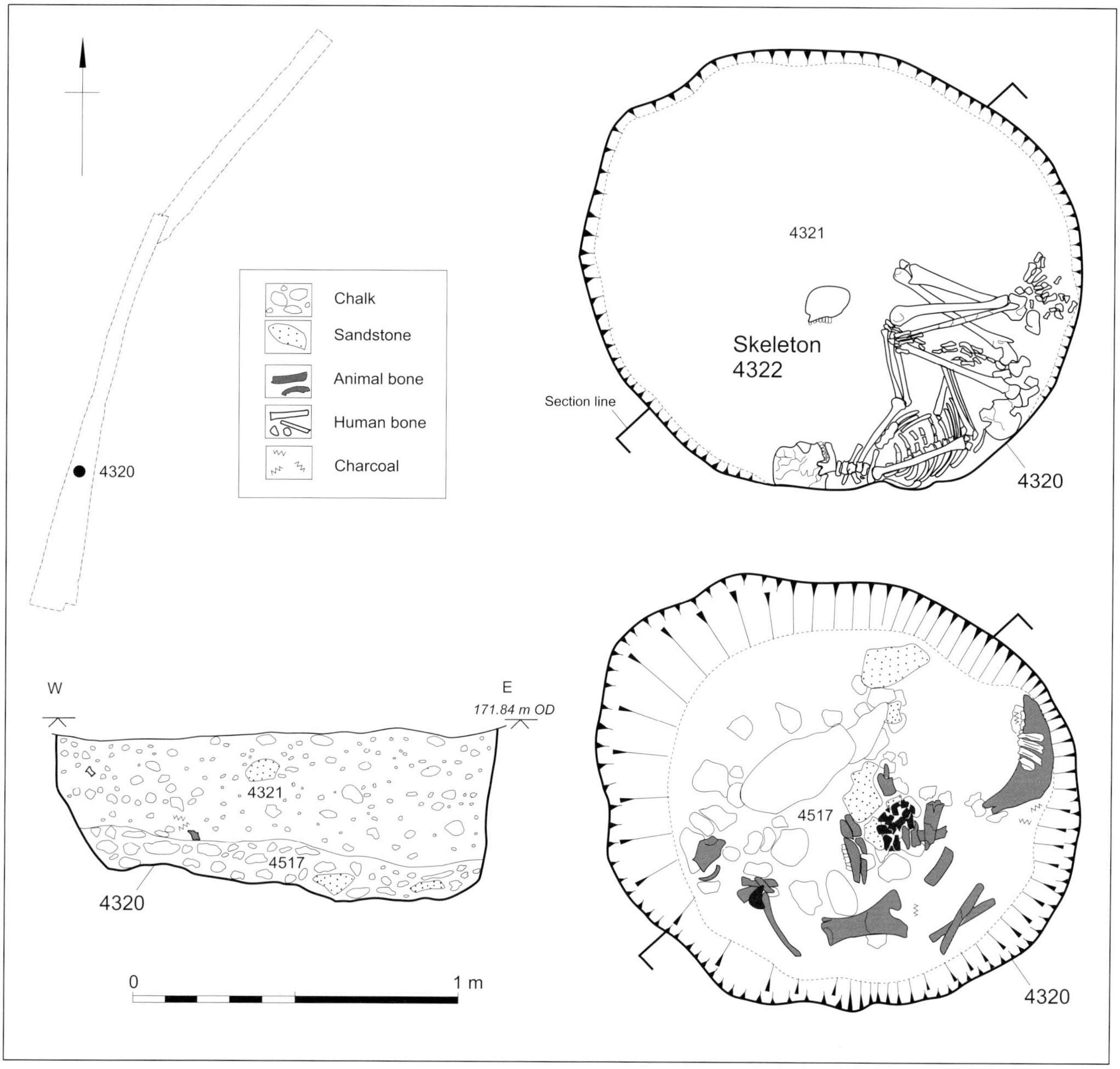

Figure 3.16 Phase 4 pit 4320 with inhumation burial

radiocarbon date of 300 cal BC–cal AD 20 (NZA-13632, 2127±85 BP) was obtained from the lower inhumation (4346), a female aged 30–45 years (Table 2.2). The upper inhumation (4347) was possibly male and aged 20–40 years. Further fragments of adult human bone (4273) were also recovered from the pit.

Pit 4320 contained the single inhumation of an adult male (4322) lying directly on a deposit comprising a broken phase 3 pottery vessel, animal bone, and large blocks of chalk and greensand (Fig. 3.16). However, a radiocarbon date of 360 cal BC–cal AD 60 (NZA-13631, 2083±85 BP) obtained from the inhumation places it in phase 4 (later than *c.* 200 cal BC), at the very end of Iron Age settlement activity at the site (Table 2.2). A single fragment of bone from another individual (an adult aged over 18 years) was recovered from the pit fill.

Re-phased pits

Three pits (5043, 5750 and 4320), initially phased on the basis of ceramic evidence, were re-assigned to later phases in the light of the radiocarbon determinations (Table 2.2). Although the diagnostic pottery in the basal fills of pit 5043 (5136, 5137) was almost exclusively phase 1/2, an articulated pig limb from the basal fill (5137) produced a radiocarbon result in phase 3 of 420–100 cal BC (NZA-13634, 2247±70 BP). Similarly, an articulated cattle foot from the lower fill of pit 5750 (5752) produced a result in phase 3 of 400–180 cal BC (NZA-17102, 2236±50 BP), despite the fact that the diagnostic pottery in both pit fills (5751, 5752) was exclusively phase 1/2, including a deposit of large parts of several pottery vessels in basal fill 5752.

Pit 4320, which contained an inhumation as well as a leg bone fragment of another individual (Table 5.1), contained exclusively phase 3 diagnostic pottery, including a large part of a pottery vessel directly below the inhumation, yet the radiocarbon determination of 360 cal BC–cal AD 60 (NZA-13631, 2083±70 BP) clearly places this feature in phase 4 (later than *c.* 200 cal BC), at the very end of Iron Age settlement activity on the site.

There a number of possible explanations for these inconsistencies. Although the probability distribution for the 4 phase radiocarbon result, for example, suggests that the actual date falls outside the date range of ceramic phase 3, it is statistically possible that it falls nonetheless within the latter part of phase 3; the same applies to the earlier re-phased features. Alternatively, it may be that the date ranges for the ceramic phases need to be revised in the light of these results. A third possibility is that the deposition histories of these (and presumably other) features were in fact more complex than evident from a simple reading of their stratigraphical sequences. It may be, for example, that special deposits of articulated animal or human remains were inserted within features already infilled with soil deposits, and either placed within or covered by layers containing residual, earlier diagnostic pottery and possibly other materials.

Chapter 4
The Finds

Copper Alloy Objects

by Stephen Legg with a contribution
by A.P. Fitzpatrick

Seven copper alloy objects were recovered, of which four are of Iron Age date. Of the other three objects, two are Romano-British and one is post-medieval.

Iron Age Pin

by A.P. Fitzpatrick

A pin fragment, made from circular-sectioned wire that is bent and broken at one end (Fig. 4.1, 1), came from pit 4909 which is dated by pottery to the 8th/7th centuries BC. Although the pin might be from a brooch (Hull and Hawkes 1987, 7–47; Haselgrove 1997, 53) it is more likely to be from a ring-headed or perhaps a small swan-headed pin. Swan-headed pins remain rare (Dunning 1934), but iron examples are known from the Wiltshire sites of All Cannings Cross (Cunnington 1923, 126, pl. 21, 1) and Swallowcliffe Down (Clay 1927, 82, pl. xi, C3).

Other Objects

A British Type B1 penannular brooch (Fig. 4.1, 2) was recovered (Fowler 1960). Fowler suggested that such brooches, commonly termed 'omega' brooches, are normally associated with Roman military contexts and noted that they occur on several hillforts in the south-west captured by Vespasian. She suggested that the type developed from the Type B penannular brooch during the 1st century BC, and that most brooches were deposited before the end of the 1st century AD (*ibid.*, 166–7). However, an earlier date cannot be excluded (Haselgrove 1997, 67, n. 2).

A Roman coin was found unstratified in an evaluation trench. It is an *as* of Domitian (AD 81–96).

Two rings were recovered. The first (Fig. 4.1, 3) is small (ext. diam. 11 mm), and formed from circular-sectioned wire bent round to a penannular shape. The second (Fig. 4.1, 4) is larger (ext. diam. *c.* 43 mm) and is fragmentary, with is no evidence for terminals. Rings of varying sizes are relatively common Iron Age finds, some being interpreted as finger rings and others being of unknown function (eg, Cunliffe 1984, fig. 7.6, 1.31; Montague 1997, 100–2, fig. 49).

A domed sheet object, with a centrally placed suspension loop, probably derives from a bell of Romano-British date (Fig. 4.1, 5). Parallels are known, for example, from Wanborough, Wiltshire (Hooley 2001, 76–8, fig. 29, 6–8), where a military association is suggested, but these objects are also fairly common on civilian sites (*ibid.*). This object came from an Iron Age pit, but could be regarded as intrusive, occurring as it did in the upper fill.

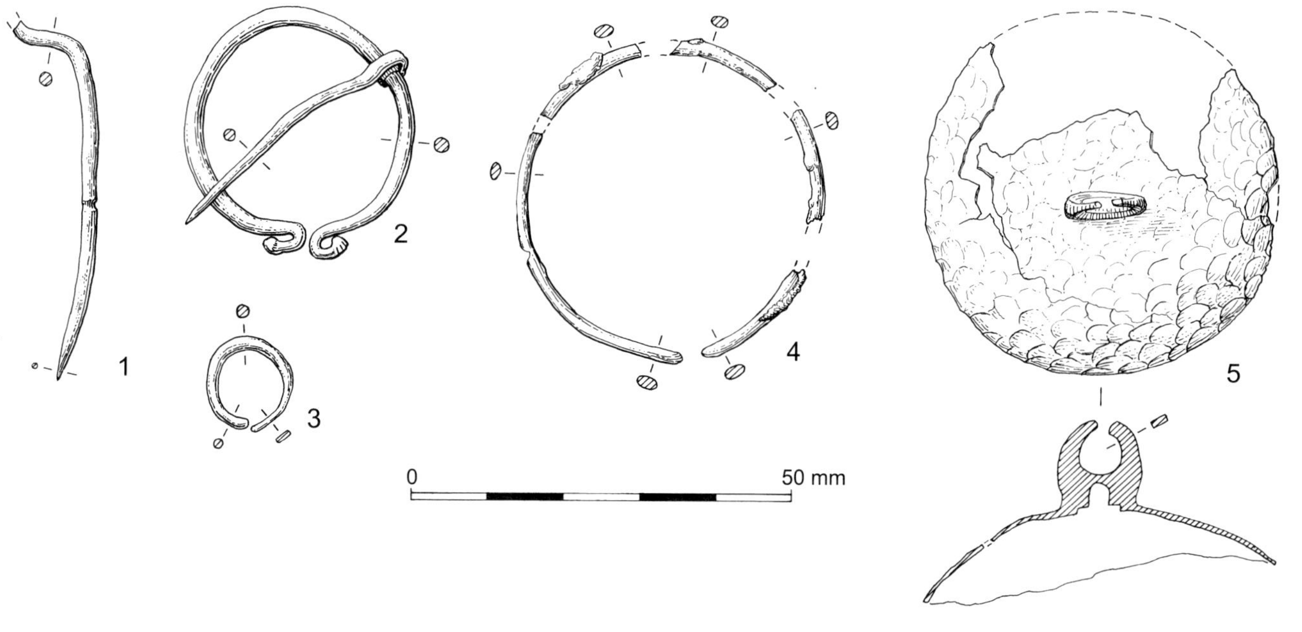

Figure 4.1 Copper alloy objects

The seventh object, recovered during initial cleaning and therefore not securely stratified, is a post-medieval lace-end.

List of illustrated objects (Fig. 4.1)

1. Pin fragment. Object Number (ON) 3244, context 4908, pit 4909 (FG 3, phase 1/2)
2. Penannular brooch. ON 3002, context 4037, cleaning layer over ditch 4043 (FG 1)
3. Small ring. ON 3188, context 4699, pit 4698 (FG 2, phase 1/2)
4. Large ring. ON 3012, context 4024, upper fill of ditch 4043, section 4023 (FG 1, phase 1/2)
5. Bell fragment with suspension loop. ON 3277, context 5044, upper fill of pit 5043 (FG 3, phase 1/2).

Iron Objects

by Stephen Legg with a contribution by A.P. Fitzpatrick

Eight iron objects were recovered from Iron Age pits. These comprise a brooch, a holdfast, two nails, and four miscellaneous objects.

Iron Age Brooch

by A.P. Fitzpatrick

The brooch (Fig. 4.2, 1), from the upper fill of pit 4221, is a La Tène 1Cb fibula. It is badly corroded with the pin bent out beyond the bow of the brooch, and the catchplate is damaged. Hull and Hawkes included related brooches in their Types 1Ca and 2Aa-b, of La Tène I and II type respectively, noting that they appeared to 'coalesce' (1987, 123). It is not clear whether the foot was attached to the bow, but the long flat bow of this brooch suggests that it is of La Tène II type (Stead 1991, 82) and of 3rd century date. Several similar brooches are known from the nearby site of Cold Kitchen Hill, Wiltshire (Hull and Hawkes 1987, 125, 139–42).

Other Objects

A holdfast (Fig. 4.2, 2) is essentially a square-sectioned rivet with a roughly triangular rove at each end. Parallels from Iron Age contexts are known from Westhampnett, West Sussex (Montague 1997, fig. 49, ON 27426) and Danebury (Cunliffe and Poole 1991, fig. 7.25, 2.347–9).

Two nails (one illustrated: Fig. 4.2, 3) both have square-sectioned shafts; one example (from pit 4849) is missing its head. Similar nails were recovered from Danebury (Sellwood 1984, fig. 7.24, 2.176–180).

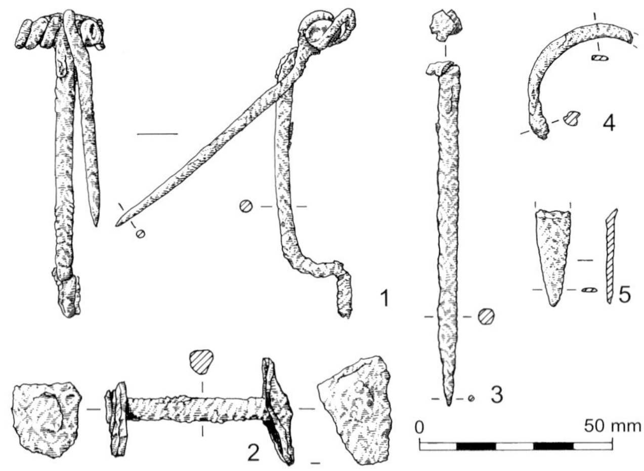

Figure 4.2 Iron objects

The remaining four objects are of uncertain function. The first is a small, fragmentary ring with a rectangular cross-section (Fig. 4.2, 4). The second is a small, triangular fragment tapering to a rounded tip (Fig. 4.2, 5). The third is a thin D-shaped, round-sectioned object (pit 4514, FG 1, phase 3), although it may be a small bent nail with some distorting corrosion. The fourth comprises two small pieces of sheet iron (pit 4612, FG 2, phase 1/2).

List of illustrated objects (Fig. 4.2)

1. Brooch. ON 3042, context 4222, pit 4221 (FG 1, phase 1/2)
2. Holdfast. ON 3131, context 4573, pit 4572 (FG 2, phase 3)
3. Nail. ON 3992, context 5713, pit 5670 (FG 4, phase 1/2)
4. Fragmentary ring. ON 3321, context 4728, pit 4641 (FG 2, phase 3)
5. Triangular fragment. ON 3313, context 4728, pit 4641 (FG 2, phase 3)

Slag

by Lorraine Mepham and Phil Andrews

The excavation produced a small quantity of metalworking slag. This was found in small quantities across the site, within 14 pits and three ditches. Table 4.1 gives the breakdown of slag by phase and by feature group. The main concentrations were in ditches in FG 1 (4039, 4040/4044, 4038/4042) and in pits in FG 2, three of which (4606, 4625, 4641) produced more than 500 g of material.

Most of the slag is likely to be from iron smelting, but there is some which probably indicates iron smithing. The material includes relatively light vesicular slag as well as some much heavier, denser

Table 4.1 Distribution of slag by period and feature group (weight in g)

FG	*Feature*	*Phase 1/2*	*Phase 3*	*Unphased*	*Total*
1	ditch	360	986	–	1346
	pit	578	–	61	639
FG 1 total		*938*	*986*	*61*	*1985*
2	pit	96	1385	666	2147
3	pit	–	10	–	10
4	pit	64	102	–	166
Total		1098	2483	727	4308

fragments. A small amount of the material is very light fuel ash slag which may not necessarily derive from iron working, but this is its most likely source here. No ore, nor any hearth or furnace lining was recovered, and the iron working activity may have been located some distance from the excavated area.

The dense slag includes several rather 'blocky' fragments (eg, from pit 4606) with occasional 'drips' on the surface, but with no obvious 'ropey' flow structure. The nature and appearance of this material is characteristic of furnace slag from pre-Roman non-tapping (shaft) furnaces where the slag and iron bloom had to be removed from the furnace by partly breaking open the wall. However, it is difficult to be certain given the paucity of evidence and nature of the material that this slag was not derived from primary, bloom smithing (the reheating and consolidation of the bloom to remove slag inclusions) or even secondary smithing (the production of artefacts). Indeed, there are two small, hemispherical hearth bottoms which are more indicative of smithing: one example from context 4626 measures *c.* 80 x 45 mm and weighs 570 g, and the other, from context 4163 measures *c.* 115 x 90 mm by 35 mm (485 g).

Flint

by Phil Harding

The flint from the site has been quantified and is shown by feature and artefact type in Table 4.2 (full results in archive). Some 818 pieces of worked flint were found in 272 individual contexts. The mean total from individual features is five pieces which is insufficient for detailed analysis. Most of the flint was found in pits, of which the largest individual group was 23 pieces from pit 5645. The artefacts from sealed contexts are in near-mint condition with only 13% showing a white surface patina. Three flakes from pit 4564 refit indicating that limited flint working was being undertaken on the site in the Early Iron Age.

The most frequent tools are 13 well-worn hammerstones with two others which were made on abandoned cores. This number is too high for them to be considered as flint knapping hammers in view of the small quantity of flint knapping debris from the site. Flint and sarsen hammers, as well as 'mullers', tools for dressing sarsen quernstones, occurred in relatively large numbers at the Late Bronze Age sites (Gingell 1992, 118) on the Marlborough Downs. A small quantity of Greensand fragments may have derived from quernstones which were made locally and may indicate a use for these implements.

The retouched flint implements comprise six scrapers, one piercer, one knife, and a flaked axe. The remainder are unclassifiable miscellaneous retouched flakes. Two side scrapers are patinated as is a well-made end scraper on a flake. A further end scraper shows unpatinated retouch on a patinated flake blank. This suggests that much of the patinated material was residual material of Neolithic or Early Bronze Age date. The well made, bifacial Neolithic flint axe (Pl. 3.1), seems to have been collected during the Iron Age occupation and deposited with a burial in pit 4332 (Fig. 3.13, see Chapter 3). The flakes with miscellaneous retouch, much of which is denticulate, would not be out of place in a Late Bronze Age assemblage.

Burnt Flint

by Lorraine Mepham

Burnt, unworked flint was recovered in some quantity (totalling 42,933 g). The largest quantity from any

Table 4.2 Summary of worked flint

Feature	*No. contexts*	*No. cuts*	*1*	*2*	*3*	*4*	*5*	*6*	*7*	*8*
Ditch	69	27	21	6	142	84	5	7	1	8
Post-hole	21	21	–	–	18	12	–	–	–	1
Hearth	1	1	–	–	–	–	1	–	–	–
Pit	175	97	21	2	239	194	17	11	5	11
Others	6	6	–	–	7	5	–	–	–	–
Total	272	152	42	8	406	295	23	18	6	20

1 = core; 2 = broken core/frag.; 3 = unbroken flakes/blades; 4 = broken flakes/blades; 5 = burned worked flint; 6 = retouched flakes; 7 = scrapers; 8 = other tools

Table 4.3 Distribution of burnt flint by period and feature group (weight in g)

FG	*Feature*	*Phase 1/2*	*Phase 3*	*Phase 4*	*Unphased*	*Total*
1	ditch	10,185	722	–	102	11,009
	pit	2564	3949	47	64	6624
	p-h	–	133	–	373	506
	Total	*12,749*	*4804*	*47*	*539*	*18,139*
2	pit	1880	8052	–	766	10,698
3	pit	1885	780	–	4	2669
	p-h	–	6	–	62	68
	Total	*1885*	*786*	–	*66*	*2737*
4	ditch	–	30	–	70	100
	pit	3609	6704	–	66	10,379
	p-h	54	–	–	822	876
	hearth	–	–	–	4	4
	Total	*3663*	*6734*	–	*962*	*11,359*
Total		20,177	20,376	47	2333	42,933

single feature was 5447 g (pit 4641; phase 3, FG 2), and only nine other features produced more than 1000 g. Table 4.3 gives the breakdown of burnt flint by phase and by feature group. Most of the burnt flint came from features within FGs 1, 2, and 4, with comparatively little from FG 3. Burnt flint occurred in different feature types, but mainly in pits; only in FG 1 were significant quantities recovered from ditches (4043, 4040/4044, and 4038/4032). In terms of chronological distribution, in phase 1/2 burnt flint was concentrated within the ditches of FG 1, while phase 3 saw a wider distribution across the site, with burnt flint deposited in pits rather than ditches.

The origin and/or function of this material type remains unclear; derivation from either domestic or industrial activities is possible. In this instance it shows no clear correlation with any other specific material type. Within FG 1 the concentrations of burnt flint appear to correspond to higher quantities of pottery, while in FGs 2 and 4 there is a slight correspondence with the distribution of metalworking slag – pit 4641, for example, was one of the most productive pits in terms of slag.

Worked Stone

by Stephen Legg

A total of 298 worked stone objects was recovered, 169 of which were identified to type. The assemblage includes quernstones, loomweights, whetstones, and rubbers. Spindlewhorls, a macehead, and a slingshot were also recovered. The remainder of the assemblage are mostly fragmentary examples from this range of objects.

Raw Materials

Objects made from sandstone and greensand dominate the assemblage, with micaceous sandstone outnumbering greensand objects. Both medium- and fine-grained sandstones were utilised, although the fine-grained sandstone has a generally restricted usage. The overall variety of sandstone and greensand types suggests that raw materials were collected from a number of locations, potentially including both local and regional sources. Greensand outcrops below the chalk in the nearby valleys, and the Vale of Wardour lies near to the south. Chalk, which was mainly used to make loomweights and spindlewhorls, is also widely available locally.

The Pennant Sandstone example most likely derives from the South Wales/Bristol area to the west, whereas the sarsen-type stones are more likely to derive from the plains to the east.

As the settlement is on Upper Chalk almost all of the stone will have been imported to the site. Indirect evidence for stoneworking is represented by the 13 well-worn hammerstones and two others made from rejected flint cores (see Harding, above).

Quernstones (Fig. 4.3, 1–4)

This was the most numerous type of stone artefacts encountered, and 126 fragments were recovered. While they all appear to be from saddle querns, a variety of shapes and sizes can be inferred (Fig. 4.3, 4). The assemblage includes the two basic types recognised at Danebury (Brown 1984) – large block-shaped querns and smaller oval-shaped querns. Also recognised are querns with a well-rounded base, as well as much flatter querns which are reminiscent of the later rotary querns in profile, but which still function as saddle querns.

Nearly all of the quernstones appear to have come from lower stones. These are generally pecked but worn, smooth and with a granular texture, or showing varying degrees of polish of the 'stone-on-stone' type. Only two examples of upper stone were recognised (though more may be present in the miscellaneous worked stone). These were distinguished on the basis of a convex grinding surface with wear similar to the lower stones.

Greensand and micaceous sandstone types dominate. These are generally of medium-grained sandstone, although finer-grained sandstone was also used. One example of Pennant Sandstone was identified. Four other examples come from a coarse-grained quartz conglomerate, while seven associated examples come from a sarsen-type stone.

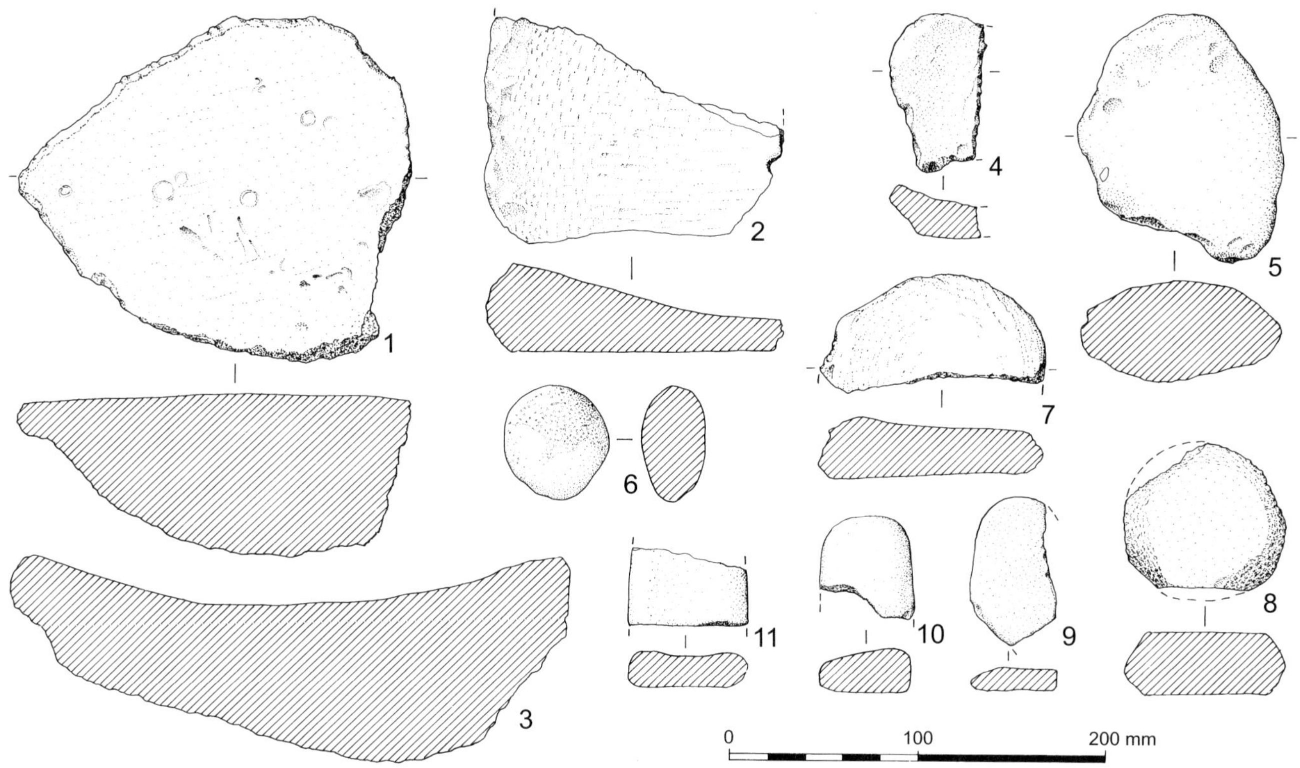

Figure 4.3 Stone object (1–11)

At least one third of all quernstones are burnt or heat-affected. Six show an orange–brown staining on the concave surface. This staining shows clear signs of use-wear, in the form of longitudinal and oblique longitudinal wear polish marks, suggesting that the staining resulted from the 'crushing' of an iron ore, or similar iron-rich material. The working of these iron materials is not consistent with the direction of use of the quernstone were it being used for crop processing only. Such staining was also noted at Danebury (Laws *et al.* 1991, 396).

In terms of distribution quern fragments came from a range of different feature types: eight post-holes (where they are likely to have been used in at least some cases as post-packing material); five ditches and 38 pits. Pit 5670 (FG 4, phase 1/2), produced 16 quernstone fragments. The other features contained seven or less fragments. Features containing quernstones occurred mainly in FGs 1, 2, and 4, with few examples in FG 3, and they displayed no apparent chronological bias.

Rubbers (Fig. 4.3, 5–8)

Two groups of rubbers were identified, forming a total of eight worked stone objects in this category. The paucity of upper quernstones within the assemblage (only two were identified), may show that other objects, such as rubbers, were readily utilised in such a fashion.

The first group, consisting of two objects (Fig. 4.3, 5, 6), is characteristically oval in shape with at least one convex surface, and are very similar in appearance to mullers. However, they are both made from a greensand, which is softer than many of the quernstones. The softness of the stone may also be due to subsequent treatment, as both stones show differing degrees of burning. The surfaces of both stones show use-wear smoothing, and one shows what may be very slight pecking evidence (Fig. 4.3, 6).

The second group, consisting of six objects (Fig. 4.3, 7, 8), is characterised as circular (or near circular) in shape, with a thickness often less than 40% of the surface diameter, and generally closer to 20%. They all have at least one smooth, flat surface, sometimes showing a slight hollowing of the surface. Use-wear polish of this surface is usually high. In many cases the opposing surface also shows signs of smoothing. One or two of the more concave examples could even have been used as lower grinding surfaces themselves. Some of the objects show a deliberate chamfering of the edges (eg, Fig. 4.3, 8), itself an aid to grip.

These rubbers are generally made of medium- and medium/fine-grained micaceous sandstone, ferruginous to varying degrees, and were recovered only from pits.

One circular rubber (Fig. 4.3, 8) shows an orange–brown staining lightly present over one half of its smoothest surface. It does not appear to be post-depositional as the staining itself shows signs of wear polish. Such staining was also present on a few of the quernstones (see above), and it is suggested that the staining on this rubber was a result of its encounter with such a similar surface. This does not mean that this object was used for the direct 'grinding' of an iron ore as that would, in all likelihood, have left a deeper, more extensive staining. The possibility of ore crushers is also suggested at Danebury (Laws *et al.* 1991, 396).

Whetstones (Fig. 4.3, 9–11)

Eight whetstone fragments were recovered. These all seem to be of sandstone, with (generally micaceous) fine-grained sandstone preferred, although some softer sandstone was used. They are characterised by the presence of one or more very smooth surfaces, with varying degrees of polish. The whetstones are often longer than they are wide.

Spindlewhorls (Fig. 4.4, 12)

Only two stone spindlewhorls were recovered, both made from chalk (with a third clay example, see below). One was from a ditch and the other from a pit. They are disc-shaped and have a perforation, near centrally placed, with an hour-glass section.

Weights/Loomweights (Fig. 4.4, 13–16)

A total of 21 chalk weights was recovered (no loomweights in other material types were identified). Some undiagnostic body fragments are also expected to be included in the miscellaneous worked stone. All of the weights were recovered from pits with the exception of one from a posthole.

The shape of the weights shows some variety, but can generally be categorised under the following: sub-rectangular with a slight taper, triangular (Fig. 4.4, 13, 16), cylindrical (Fig. 4.4, 15), oval, near-diamond (Fig. 4.4, 14), and irregular. These classifications broadly conform to the range of types from Danebury (Brown 1984). The most commonly shaped weights are triangular and sub-rectangular. Only two complete examples were recovered, and a further two are substantially complete.

The perforations tend to occur towards the top and were worked from both front and back. Two weights have an off-centre perforation, which runs obliquely through the top, one at a gradient. One triangular loomweight has a side-to-side perforation, although tooling marks suggest a similar process of manufacture. Grooves from wear are rare but where they do occur they tend to rise vertically, or at a slight angle, from the top of the perforation.

Two weights are clearly unfinished and it is suggested that they broke prior to completion, most likely during perforation. Blade/adze marks suggest that the chalk was roughly chopped to shape, and that finer tools were used to prepare the surface for smoothing. Many of the weights have smoothed surfaces in which tool marks are only faintly visible, and show evidence for the rounding of the sides, base, and apical end. Weights were deposited in all phases, and within all four feature groups.

Slingshot (Fig. 4.4, 17)

A single chalk slingshot was recovered from ditch 4105. It is nearly oval in shape with one end rounded to a point and the opposing end flattened. The flattening of one end may be due to use-impact. It is 42 mm long, a maximum width of 29 mm, and weighs 30 g. It is comparable to an example from Danebury (Brown 1984, 424–5, fig. 7.62, 8.70), and is within the size range for the clay slingshot from Danebury (40–50 mm by 27–31 mm, Poole 1984a, 398) and Maiden Castle, Dorset (Poole 1991, 210, 206, fig. 166, nos 2–3), although it is towards the lower end of the weight range from both these sites for stone slingshot (Brown 1984, 425). This slingshot is similar to, but larger and heavier than, the fired clay examples recovered from the site (see fired clay, below), and the difference in size and weight may be a reflection of different uses – hunting game as opposed to offensive weapons (Poole 1984a, 398).

Miscellaneous Worked Stone Fragments

The remaining 130 objects could not be readily ascribed to any category. The majority of these (115 pieces) appear to have at least one worked surface and are probably small fragments from quernstones, rubbers, or whetstones.

A highly polished fragmentary quartzite pebble came from pit 4784 (FG 2, phase 1/2). There does not seem to be any practical purpose for such an object, pebble is not local to Battlesbury and it may be considered to be 'ornamental'. Another piece which may also be considered ornamental was recovered from pit 4641 (FG 2, phase 3).

Thirteen miscellaneous worked chalk objects were identified within the assemblage, all of which came

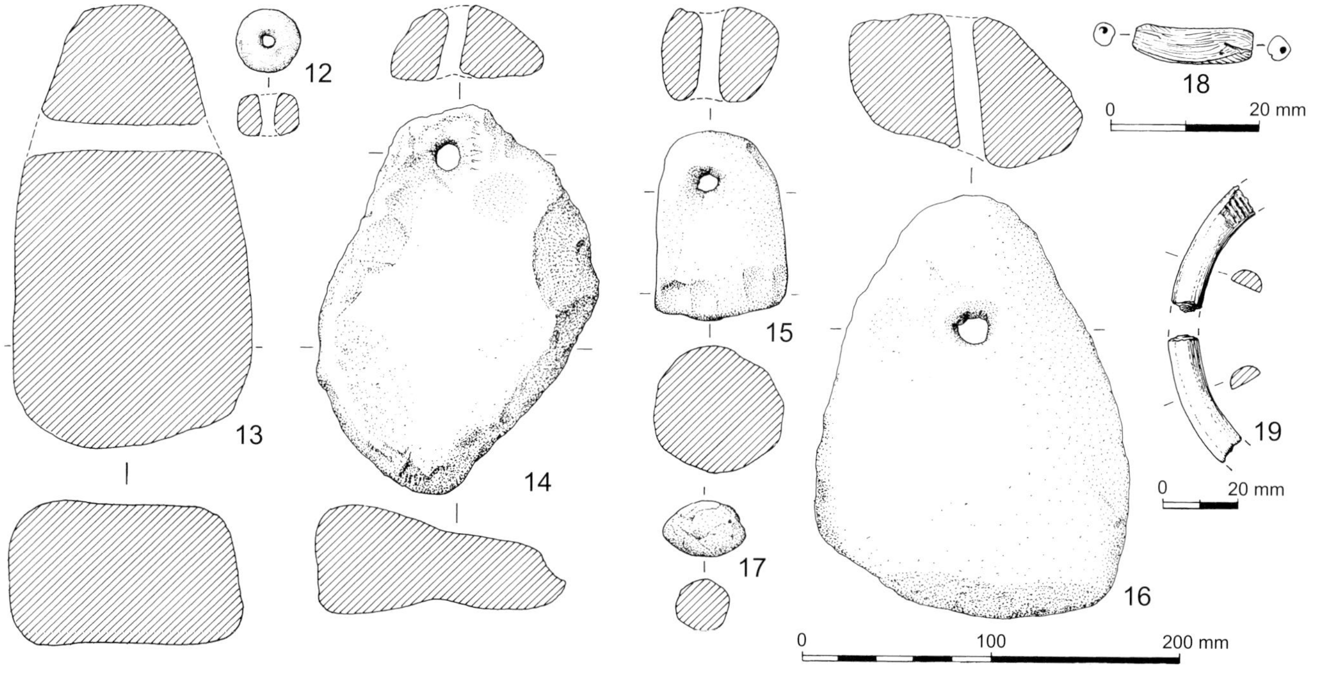

Figure 4.4 Stone objects (12–17), coral bead (18), and shale armlet fragment (19)

from pits. Six of these may be from loomweights but, in the absence of perforations and other identifiable marks, they cannot be identified with any certainty. One object has a large, smooth, flat surface. The chalk on this surface has been scorched/burnt and may indicate its use as a 'fire-plate'. The other objects have at least one, generally smooth, slightly concave surface. Their function is unknown.

Conclusion

The worked stone is typical of the Early–Middle Iron Age. Spatial patterning is apparent within the assemblage depending on its context and category. Chalk objects, for instance, almost exclusively occur within pit deposits, and generally as loomweights. Quernstone fragments were recorded from 55 of the 85 features with worked stone. The lack of rotary querns is interesting given the proposed date range of the settlement.

While the range of material types and object types are consistent with other Early–Middle Iron Age sites (eg, Danebury, All Cannings Cross, Meare Village East), no comparable site shows such a ratio of lower to upper quernstone fragments. There is also a relatively low number of loomweights. This might suggest that the weights were not primarily used as loomweights but had some other function, such as thatch weights.

List of illustrated objects (Figs 4.3–4)

1. Quernstone. ON 3143, context 4616, pit 4614 (FG 2, unphased)
2. Quernstone. ON 3104, context 4448, ditch 4043, section 4105 (FG 1, phase 1/2)
3. Quernstone. ON 3067, context 4312, pit 4553 (FG 1, phase 3)
4. ?Small quern. ON 3887, context 4101, ditch 4043, section 4105 (FG 1, phase 3)
5. Rubber (Gp 1). ON 3352, context 5146, ditch 4043, section 4080 (FG 1, phase 1/2)
6. Rubber (Gp 1). ON 3964, context 5735, pit 5358 (FG 4, phase 3)
7. Rubber (Gp 2). ON 3359, context 5614, pit 5613 (FG 4, unphased)
8. Rubber (Gp 2). ON 3271, context 5211, pit 5201 (FG 3, phase 1/2)
9. Whetstone. ON 3025, context 4100, ditch 4043, section 4105 (FG 1, phase 1/2)
10. Whetstone. ON 3097, context 4435, pit 4436 (FG 1, phase 3)
11. Whetstone. ON 3019, context 4099, ditch 4043, section 4105 (FG 1, phase 1/2)
12. Chalk spindlewhorl. ON 3196, context 4750, pit 4704 (FG 2, phase 1/2)
13. Triangular chalk loomweight. ON 3195, context 4750, pit 4704 (FG 2, phase 1/2)
14. Diamond-shaped chalk weight. ON 3191, context 4750, pit 4704 (FG 2, phase 1/2)
15. Cylindrical chalk weight. ON 3045, context 4254, pit 4221 (FG 1, phase 1/2)

16. Triangular chalk weight. ON 3035, context 4166, pit 4165 (FG 1, phase 1/2)
17. Chalk slingshot. ON 3315, context 4386, ditch 4043, section 4105 (FG 1, phase 1/2)
18. Coral bead. ON 3286, context 4996, pit 4993 (FG 3, phase 1/2)
19. Shale armlet fragments. ON 3155, context 4640, pit 4639 (FG 2, unphased)

Coral Bead

by Stephen Legg

A single piece of worked pink coral measuring 16.5 mm long and 5 mm in diameter at its widest point, was retrieved from pit 4993 (FG 3, phase 1/2). It is pierced longitudinally with a hole 1.5 mm in diameter and probably used as a bead (Fig. 4.4, 18). Coral, which was used to decorate objects such as brooches and pins, was never common in Iron Age Britain, with many of the finds coming from burials in Yorkshire (Stead 1979, 86–8; 1991, 90). In Wessex it seems likely to have been used mainly as small inlays on La Tène brooches (Hull and Hawkes 1987) but a bead similar to the one from Battlesbury Bowl is known from Danebury, Hampshire, where it was suggested that it could be from a necklace (Cunliffe 1984, 396, fig. 7.43, 5.4). At Maiden Castle, Dorset a copper alloy cylinder with a sub-spherical piece of pink coral was recovered from an Iron Age context (Laws 1991a, 156).

Shale

by Lorraine Mepham

Two fragments of a shale armlet were recovered from pit 4639 (FG 2, unphased). The armlet is plain with an oval cross-section (Fig. 4.4, 19). Objects of shale, originating from the Kimmeridge shale beds of Purbeck, Dorset, are relatively common Iron Age finds, and similar armlets have been found, for example, at Maiden Castle, Dorset (Laws 1991b, 233–4, fig. 186) and Danebury, Hampshire (Cunliffe 1984, fig. 7.41).

Pottery

by Rachel Every and Lorraine Mepham

The pottery forms one of the major components of the finds assemblage, amounting to a total of 10,979 sherds (108,650 g). The assemblage is largely of Late Bronze Age to Middle Iron Age date with a small amount of Early Bronze Age material (not discussed).

The condition of the assemblage is variable – most of it (89%) is in a fair condition (slightly rolled edges and abraded surfaces), but 3% is very abraded, the rest (8%) having little abrasion. Surface treatments (burnish and slip coatings) survive but have, in some cases, been removed by post-depositional abrasion. Certain fabrics, particularly the calcareous fabrics, are in a more friable condition and are often heavily leached; sherds have, in some cases, laminated or crumbled badly. The average sherd weight overall is 10 g.

Methods of analysis have followed the standard Wessex Archaeology recording system (Morris 1994a) which accords with nationally recommended guidelines for the recording of prehistoric pottery (PCRG 1997). This focuses on detailed recording of fabric and form. In addition, details of manufacture, surface treatment, decoration, evidence for use (residues and perforations), vessel dimensions, and cross-context joins were recorded. All data have been entered onto the project database (Access), and digital data are held in archive.

The main aims of the analysis were:

- to characterise the range of fabric types present (based on macroscopic inclusions) and to use this information to examine the evidence for local versus non-local production;
- to characterise the range of vessel forms present and to assess any evidence for vessel function;
- to set the assemblage within its local and regional context through an examination of parallels from other published assemblages;
- to examine the chronological implications of the assemblage in terms of the internal ceramic sequence.

Late Bronze Age and Iron Age Pottery

The majority of the assemblage is of Late Bronze Age–Middle Iron Age date and includes a ceramic sequence extending from the decorated wares of the Early All Cannings Cross tradition (8th–7th centuries BC) to 'saucepan pot prototypes' (3rd century BC). This is a substantial and significant assemblage representing a span of several centuries, demonstrating the development of different ceramic styles and also changing patterns of production and distribution through the period. A range of fabric types and vessel forms have been identified which find parallels in other major assemblages from the region, such as Potterne, All Cannings Cross, both in Wiltshire, and Danebury, Hampshire.

Fabrics

The Iron Age assemblage falls into five broad fabric groups based on dominant inclusion type: flint-tempered and flint-gritted (group FL), limestone-

Table 4.4 Iron Age pottery fabric totals

Fabric group	*Fabric type*	*No.*	*Weight (g)*	*% total (by weight)*
Flint-tempered	FL1	149	906	
	FL2	180	1254	
	FL3	328	2381	
	FL4	23	397	
	FL5	147	1460	
	FL6	1	32	
Total		828	6430	5.9
Limestone-tempered	L11	384	5371	
	L12	833	8847	
	L13	1039	8369	
	L14	128	1329	
	L16	23	281	
	L17	5	70	
	L18	163	1302	
Total		2575	25,569	23.6
sandy	QU1	870	9446	
	QU2	3060	26,378	
	QU3	1026	11,491	
	QU4	35	250	
	QU5	400	2544	
	QU6	46	217	
	QU7	251	1696	
	QU8	109	1025	
	QU9	69	523	
	QU10	133	755	
Total		5999	54,325	50.2
Shell-tempered	SH1	812	13,933	
	SH2	455	4217	
	SH3	229	3389	
Total		1496	21,539	19.9
Organic-tempered	VE1	25	173	
	VE2	9	159	
	VE3	3	79	
Total		37	411	0.4
Total		10,935	108,274	

tempered (group LI), sandy (group QU), shell-tempered (group SH), and organic-tempered (group VE). Within these groups, a total of 29 separate fabric types was defined on the basis of the range, size and frequency of inclusions, using a binocular microscope (x20 magnification). Fabrics are described in the Appendix, and fabric totals are presented in Table 4.4.

The range of fabric types reflects a corresponding range in the raw materials exploited, and hence sources or source areas for the pottery. At both Potterne and Danebury, for example, the Late Bronze Age and Iron Age fabric series included wares which were demonstrably locally produced (ie within a radius of 10 km from the site) as well as those which indicated more distant sources, and similar evidence is available for the Battlesbury Bowl assemblage. This information is crucial for understanding the organisation of pottery production and distribution at this period, since it is apparent that both local and regional production and distribution networks were operating (eg, Cunliffe 1984, 251–6; Morris 1994b).

The nearest outcrop of Great Oolite limestone lies just over 14 km to the north-west of Battlesbury at Farleigh Hungerford on the River Frome. The largest outcrop is *c.* 4 km further north-west at Winsley, near Bradford-on-Avon (Sheet 281, BGS). This may be the source for the oolitic-tempered fabrics (LI2, LI4, LI5, and L17), as was suggested for the oolitic fabrics from Potterne (Morris 2000a, 144).

Forest Marble (clay with shelly limestone and limestone) is found to the west of Battlesbury, with the nearest source at Rudge to the west of Westbury and 9.5 km to the north-west of Battlesbury, and this may be the source of the shelly and limestone-tempered fabrics. The Upper Greensand deposits are also to the south-west and west of the site and possibly provide the glauconitic sands identified in many of the fabrics (BGS 1985).

There is one fabric that contains both oolitic limestone and glauconitic sand (L15). One possible source for this combination of inclusions is the Coral Rag series next to Gault clay between 8–10 km from Potterne to the north. This could also be the source of iron oxides in a glauconitic sandy clay matrix (QU5, QU6) (Morris 2000a, 145).

Vessel forms

Given the relatively lengthy time-span of the assemblage, the range of identifiable vessel forms could be considered as limited. Sixteen forms were identified, comprising a range of jars and bowls in both finewares and coarsewares. Vessel forms have been identified on the basis of a combination of rim form, decoration and other diagnostic features such as carinations. Many rim sherds could not be attributed to vessel form. The correlation of vessel form to fabric type is given in Table 4.5.

Bowls

Bowl 1: Short-necked, carinated fineware bowl (Fig. 4.5, 1–4)

Similar to bowl type 3.1 at Potterne (carinated bowl with short upright rim: Gingell and Morris 2000, fig. 48, 20, 21, 24–6), generally occurring there in glauconitic sandy fabrics. Typical of the Early All Cannings Cross style (Cunliffe 1991, fig. A:2; Cunnington 1923, pl. 40, 1). Dated 8th–7th centuries BC at Potterne. The type has been sub-divided on the basis of decorative style.

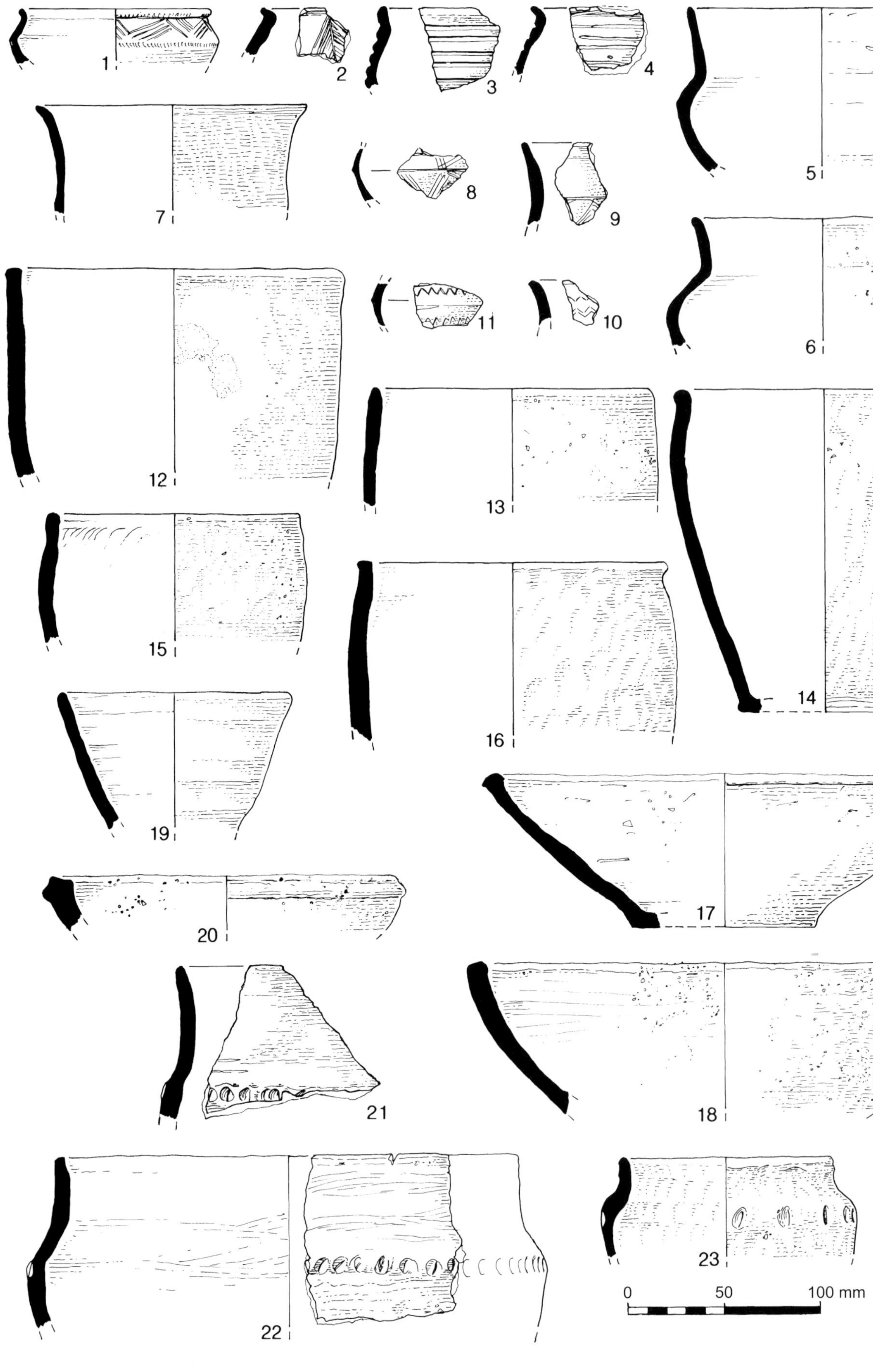

Figure 4.5 Pottery (1–23)

Bowl 1.1: Short-necked, carinated bowl with incised or tooled decoration above carination (Fig. 4.5, 1, 2).

Bowl 1.2: Short-necked, carinated bowl with furrowed decoration above carination (Fig. 4.5, 3, 4) (Gingell and Morris 2000, fig. 48: 18, 19, 22). Most examples are red-finished.

Bowl 2: Long-necked fineware bowls (Fig. 4.5, 5–7)
Similar to bowl type 2 (carinated bowl with long neck) at Potterne (*ibid.*, fig. 47:12, 14), occurring there mainly in glauconitic sandy fabrics (*ibid.*, table 21). Typical of the Later All Cannings Cross style (Cunliffe 1991, fig. A:6; Cunnington 1923, pl. 28, 1). Dated late 8th–early 6th century at Potterne; a significant group of these vessels came from the fire-destroyed roundhouse at Longbridge Deverill Cow Down, dated to the end of the 6th century BC (Chadwick-Hawkes 1994, fig. 5). This type has been subdivided into two on the basis of the extent of the surviving profile.

Bowl 2.1: Long-necked bowls with rounded shoulders, undecorated (Fig. 4.5, 5, 6)

Bowl 2.2: Long-necked bowls, profile uncertain (Fig. 4.5, 7)

Bowl 3: Fineware bowls of uncertain profile
This type encompasses examples of fineware bowls of uncertain profile, many of which may originally have been of types 1 or 2; these have been identified here on the basis of decoration and carination.

Bowl 3.1: Furrowed bowl, carinated but rest of profile uncertain

Bowl 3.2: Carinated or biconical bowl, profile uncertain

Bowl 4: Scratch cordon bowls (Fig. 4.5, 8–11)
Fineware bowls, sharply moulded with faceted shoulder, the facets emphasised by cordons, generally red-finished, and with geometric decoration scratched after firing. Late component of the All Cannings Cross-Meon Hill style (Cunliffe 1991, fig. A:6), found at Danebury in CPs 3–4 (Cunliffe 1984, type BB1, fig. 6.57–8). Cunliffe suggests that they were probably made in the region of Salisbury, and distributed over a well-defined social territory (*ibid.*, 254 and fig. 6.22). No complete profiles survive in the assemblage, and the few examples present have been identified from small decorated and/or carinated sherds. Originally dated mid 6th to mid-5th centuries BC at Danebury, subsequently redated as 5th to mid-4th centuries BC (Cunliffe 1995, 17–18).

Bowl 5: Saucepan pot prototype (Fig. 4.5, 12–16)
Straight-sided or slightly convex vessel with undifferentiated rim, rounded or flattened, sometimes slightly inturned. These vessels are all undecorated, but are generally carefully finished, some burnished. Introduced at Danebury at the end of the Early Iron Age (Cunliffe 1984, type PA, figs 6.67–8). There are no examples here of the later, decorated saucepan pots of the Yarnbury-Highfield or St Catherine's Hill-Worthy Down styles (Danebury type PB); this absence is probably geographical.

Bowl 6: Flared Bowl (Fig. 4.5, 17–20)
Bowl with conical or slightly convex profile and plain or thickened and/or flattened rim. This type may in fact encompass examples of more than one bowl type of various dates, but the single complete profile recovered is closely paralleled by Danebury type DA1.2, dated to the late 4th–1st centuries BC (Cunliffe 1984, fig. 6.65). One squared rim (Fig. 4.5, 19) is also likely to derive from a bowl of this type.

Jars

Jar 1: Shouldered jar (Fig. 4.6, 21–8)
The most common jar form in the assemblage is subdivided here into two variants on the basis of profile, with a third sub-division encompassing examples of uncertain profile. Shoulders are frequently finger-impressed, and rims occasionally similarly impressed. Similar to jar types 31 and 51 at Potterne (carinated jar and shouldered jar: Gingell and Morris 2000, figs 53; 56–8). See also jar type JB2[.2] or JB3[.1] at Danebury. Dated 10th–early 6th centuries BC.

Jar 1.1: Jar with marked shoulder and concave neck (Fig. 4.5, 21–4)

Jar 1.2: Weakly shouldered jar, generally with thickened and/or flattened rim (Fig. 4.6, 25–8)

Jar 1.3: Shouldered jar, identified on shoulder sherds only, profile uncertain.

Jar 2: Biconical jar (Fig. 4.6, 29–31)
Bipartite jar with marked carination, inturned upper profile and plain rim. Comparable to jar type 33 at Potterne (carinated, bipartite jar: *ibid.*, fig. 54, 64–6), dated 10th/9th–early 6th centuries BC.

Jar 3: Jar with rounded shoulder (Fig. 4.6, 32–4)
Jar with flared neck and rounded shoulder and lower profile. Shoulders are occasionally finger-impressed. Comparable to jar type 20 at Potterne (globular/round-bodied jar: *ibid.*, figs 51–2), dated 8th–6th centuries BC.

Jar 4: Fineware jar with rounded shoulder (Fig. 4.6, 35)
Only one example was identified here, lacking its rim, although further examples may be present amongst the undifferentiated fineware shoulder/carinated sherds. This single example is red-finished and burnished. A very similar vessel was found within the substantial group of red-finished finewares recovered from the fire-destroyed roundhouse at Longbridge Deverill Cow Down, dated to the end of the 6th century BC (Chadwick-Hawkes 1994, fig. 5, 17).

Jar 5: Handled jar (Fig. 4.6, 36–8)
No complete profiles of handled jars were recovered, and this type has been identified solely on the basis of the handle attachment. There are six examples of lug/handle attachments, one vertical, two horizontal and three unattached. The attached lugs are on shouldered jars (type

Table 4.5 Vessel form by fabric

Fabric code	*Bowls*									*Jars*												*Total*
	B1.1	*B1.2*	*B2.1*	*B2.2*	*B3.1*	*B3.2*	*B4*	*B5*	*B6*	*J1.1*	*J1.2*	*J1.3*	*J2*	*J3*	*J4*	*J5*	*J6*	*J7*	*J8*	*J9*	*J10*	*no.*
FL1	-	-	-	-	-	-	-	-	-	-	1	-	-	-	-		-	1	-	-	-	2
FL2	-	-	-	-	-	-	-	-	-	-	-	1	-	1	-	-	-	-	-	-	-	2
FL3	-	-	-	-	-	-	-	-	-	-	-	2	-	-	-	-	-	-	-	-	-	2
FL5	-	-	-	-	-	-	-	-	-	-	1	-	-	1	-	-	-	-	-	-	-	2
LI1	-	-	-	-	-	-	-	3	3	-	2	4	-	1	-	-	-	-	-	-	-	13
LI2	1	-	1	2	-	-	-	2	1	2	7	1	1	2	-	1	-	8	2	-	-	31
LI3	-	1	-	-	1	-	-	6	1	4	6	-	-	1	-	-	-	8	2	1	-	31
LI4	-	-	-	-	-	-	-	-	-	-	-	2	-	1	-	-	-	1	-	-	-	4
LI5	-	-	-	1	-	-	-	-	1	-	1	-	-	-	-	-	-	-	-	-	-	3
LI6	-	-	-	-	-	-	-	-	-	1	1	-	-	-	-	-	-	-	-	-	-	2
LI8	1	-	-	-	-	-	-	-	-	-	-	1	-	1	-	-	-	-	1	-	-	4
QU1	1	2	5	4	3	2	1	-	1	4	3	12	1	2	1	1	-	-	-	-	1	44
QU2	-	3	10	21	14	3	1	2	1	6	9	32	2	6	-	3	-	2	-	-	-	115
QU3	-	-	1	2	-	1	-	2	-	1	3	9	1	2	-	-	-	-	-	-	-	22
QU4	-	1	-	-	5	-	-	-	-	-	-	-	-	-	-	-	-	-	-	-	-	6
QU5	4	12	4	8	22	5	-	2	-	-	-	2	1	-	-	1	-	-	-	-	-	61
QU6	-	-	-	-	2	-	-	-	-	-	-	-	-	-	-	-	-	-	-	-	-	2
QU7	-	7	3	14	9	5	1	-	1	-	1	-	-	-	-	-	-	1	-	-	-	42
QU8	-	-	-	1	-	-	-	-	-	1	-	-	-	-	-	-	-	-	-	-	-	2
QU9	-	1	-	1	-	-	-	-	-	-	-	2	-	-	-	-	1	-	-	-	-	5
QU10	-	3	-	3	10	1	-	-	-	-	-	-	-	-	-	-	-	-	-	-	-	17
SH1	-	-	-	-	-	-	-	2	2	4	12	3	2	3	-	-	-	-	-	-	-	28
SH2	-	-	1	1	-	-	-	1	-	1	6	5	-	4	-	-	-	2	-	-	-	21
SH3	-	-	-	-	-	-	-	1	-	1	3	2	-	-	-	-	-	-	3	-	-	10
VE1	-	1	-	1	-	-	-	-	-	-	-	-	-	1	-	-	-	-	-	-	-	3
VE2	-	-	-	-	-	-	-	-	-	-	-	-	1	-	-	-	-	-	-	-	-	1
Total	7	31	25	59	66	17	3	21	11	25	57	78	9	26	1	6	1	23	8	1	1	475

1). There is also one example of an applied, unperforated shoulder lug (Fig. 4.7, 58). Handled jars, all with horizontally or vertically attached lug handles, are known in various Late Bronze Age and Early Iron Age assemblages, although never particularly common. At Potterne, for example, various lug types were identified, most commonly the vertically applied strip forms, used on both rounded and carinated vessels (Gingell and Morris 2000, fig. 52). They are also known from Danebury (Cunliffe 1984, 307). The lugs presumably acted as suspension attachments, since they are too small for manual use.

Jar 6: Jar with cordoned neck (Fig. 4.6, 39)
One sherd has an incised, applied cordon on the neck zone, and is paralleled by a shouldered jar from Potterne, dated 9th–7th centuries BC (Gingell and Morris 2000, jar type 56, fig. 58: 92).

Jar 7: Convex jar with proto-bead rim (Fig. 4.6, 40–3)
A Middle Iron Age form, a common type at Danebury (Cunliffe 1984, type JC2, fig. 6.40), appearing there first alongside the 'proto-saucepan pots' (see Bowl 5, above) and later with decorated saucepan pots of the Yarnbury-Highfield and St Catherine's Hill-Worthy Down style. Examples at Danebury are dated 400–100/50BC.

Jar 8: Large rounded jar with short, thickened rim (Fig. 4.7, 44, 45)
Profiles can be rounded or convex. Comparable to jar type JC1 at Danebury, dated to the later 5th century BC (Cunliffe 1984, fig. 6.35–6).

Jar 9: Rounded jar with bead rim (Fig. 4.7, 46)
Only three examples of this form were recovered, two in limestone-tempered fabrics and one sandy. Comparable to jar form JC2.3 at Danebury, a smaller variant of the basic high-shouldered jar form (JC2), generally well finished and frequently decorated, as one example is here. The style of decoration on this vessel (curvilinear tooling with impressed 'dimples') is more reminiscent of the Maiden Castle-Marnhull style of Dorset (Cunliffe 1991, fig. A:19), although the fabric (LI3) is local. A similarly decorated vessel, with a pedestal base, was found at Suddern Farm, although the dating of associated pottery in that context is ambiguous (Brown 2000a, 104, fig. 3.44). The form is dated 400–100/50 BC at Danebury (Cunliffe 1984, fig. 6.41–2).

Jar 10: Miniature vessel/cup (Fig. 4.7, 47)
A single miniature vessel was recovered. This is essentially a variant of the shouldered jar form (Jar Type 1, above). A miniature vessel from Potterne is similar (Gingell and Morris 2000, type 87: fig. 60, 118).

Briquetage

One piece of briquetage of unknown form, in a very coarse, organic-tempered fabric (VE3), was recovered from pit 5592 (CP 3). Briquetage containers are known from other Iron Age sites in the region, such as Danebury, where a similar organic-tempered fabric was identified (Poole 1984b). A likely source is the Hampshire or Dorset coast, where much of the recorded briquetage is organic-tempered (*ibid.*, 430).

Table 4.6 Range of rim diameters by vessel type

Vessel type	*No. measureable examples*	*Range diam. (mm)*
Bowl 2.1: long-necked	17	100–180
Bowl 2.2: long-necked	15	100–200
Bowl 5: prototype saucepan pot	17	120–280
Jar 1.1: shouldered	18	100–260
Jar 1.2: shouldered	42	80–240
Jar 3: rounded shoulder	19	80–240
Jar 7: proto-bead rim	20	100–260

Rim diameters

External diameters were recorded for all measurable rim sherds. Of the 567 rim sherds recorded, 247 were measurable, and of these 188 could be assigned to vessel form. There is insufficient data here for a valid statistical analysis of the rim diameters, such as has been done, for example, for the Iron Age vessel forms from Cadbury Castle, Somerset (Woodward and Blinkhorn 1997), and hence any consideration of vessel size and standardisation within the Battlesbury Bowl assemblage is very limited. Seven of the vessel forms (all those which included ten or more measurable rims) were selected, and the results are summarised in Table 4.6. All seven forms have a relatively restricted diameter range, particularly the fineware bowls. There is no sign here of the threefold size grouping of coarsewares jars seen at Cadbury and in other Iron Age assemblages (*ibid.*), all the Battlesbury Bowl examples falling within the 'small' or 'medium' size groupings, but the numbers of vessels involved are too small conclusively to demonstrate any bimodal peaks within individual diameter ranges.

Perforations

Two vessels, both in sandy fabrics, have pre-firing perforations in the base, one single and one multiple. A few similar perforated bases were found at Potterne (Gingell and Morris 2000, 153, fig. 60, 122), but the form is not common in Late Bronze Age/Early Iron Age assemblages. The functional implications here are uncertain, but it may be noted that the vessel with a single perforation also has a whitish internal residue, probably limescale.

Decoration

A relatively small proportion of the assemblage is decorated (352 sherds; 3.2% of the total). A fairly restricted range of techniques and motifs is evident here; most are mutually exclusive between finewares and coarsewares. Decoration on coarsewares is almost exclusively limited to finger impressions on rim and/or shoulder, while finewares carry a more varied range of decorative schemes. Table 4.7 correlates decoration and fabric type and Table 4.8 decoration and vessel form – 261 decorated sherds came from 195 vessels of identifiable form; this includes 98 examples of furrowed bowls.

Decoration has been classified both by technique and motif. Four basic techniques were identified: applied, impressed; incised or stabbed (cutting the surface of the vessel) and tooled or furrowed.

Applied

1. Applied neck cordon, finger-impressed (Fig. 4.6, 39).

Impressed

1. Fingertip or fingernail impressions, found on tops of rims and, more commonly, on shoulders of coarseware jars (Figs. 4.5, 21–3 and 4.6, 27, 30–1).
2. Impressed small dots, found on Late Bronze Age/Early Iron Age fineware vessels, generally in zones bounded by incised lines (Fig. 4.7, 49–51). It is possible that these might originally have been infilled with a white paste, such as has been identified at All Cannings Cross and Potterne (Cunnington 1923, pl. 31, 1; Gingell and Morris 2000, 155).
3. Open circles, found on similar vessels, and in similar arrangements to dots. Again, these may originally have been white-infilled. (not illustrated).

Incised

1. Single or multiple lines; some examples may originally have bounded zones of other incised or impressed motifs.
2. Geometric designs (cross-hatched zones or chevrons), used on Late Bronze Age/Early Iron Age fineware vessels, generally above the shoulder or carination. As for the impressed motifs on finewares of this period, designs may originally have been white-infilled (Figs 4.5, 2 and 4.7, 53–7).
3. Stabbed dots, found on fineware vessels (Fig. 4.7, 52).
4. Diagonal incisions, found on necks or shoulders of fineware vessels (Fig. 4.5, 1).
5. Scratched geometric designs on fineware scratch cordon bowls (Bowl Type 4); carried out after firing (Fig. 4.5, 8–11).

Tooled and furrowed

1. Horizontal furrowing on the shoulders of fineware bowls; this ranges from fairly deep 'corrugation' to a few examples where the tooling is shallow and fairly crude (Fig. 4.5, 3–4).
2. Other linear tooling.
3. Tooled lattice design (one example only) (Fig. 4.7, 48).
4. Deeply tooled wave with impressed 'dimples'; one example, from a bead-rimmed jar (Jar Type 9) (Fig. 4.7, 46).

Surface finish

Several different surface treatments were recorded. These range from the fairly crude wiping of coarseware vessels (leaving horizontal or, more commonly, vertical marks on external surfaces), through more careful smoothing, to the well finished vessels (generally finewares) which are burnished and/or red-finished.

Burnishing may be on external surfaces (closed vessels) or internal surfaces (open vessels), or all over; this technique was used on examples of all fabric groups, but particularly on sandy fabrics, and rarely on flint-tempered and limestone-tempered fabrics (Table 4.9). As might be expected, fineware vessels (Bowl Types 1–3) are most frequently burnished, with other vessel forms burnished only sporadically (Table 4.10).

Red-finishing was most frequently used on fineware bowls (Bowl Types 1–4), but was almost certainly also used on jars, as attested by the single identifiable example of a fineware jar (Jar Type 4: Table 4.10). The technique is used almost exclusively on sandy fabrics, with rare examples in flint-tempered, limestone-tempered and shelly fabrics (Table 4.9). Red-finishing is a technique found commonly on Late Bronze Age/Early Iron Age pottery across much of southern England. The term 'red-finished' is used here rather than 'haematite-coated', since analysis on samples of such material has demonstrated the use of several different techniques to achieve a similar effect, of which the application of a haematite coating is only one. Other possible techniques included the application of a ferruginous slip, or the burnishing of iron oxide into the surface of the vessel (Middleton 1987; Gingell and Morris 2000, 155).

Residues

A total of 2196 sherds have residues and these occur on most coarseware vessel forms (jar types 1.1, 1.2, 1.3, 3, 5, 7, and 8, and bowl type 5). These include external sooting, carbonised food residues, and internal residues such as limescale.

Ceramic sequence and dating

Vessel forms and other diagnostic attributes serve to illustrate a date range for the assemblage from Late Bronze Age–Middle Iron Age. Within this range, three ceramic phases (CPs) can be defined, based largely on

Table 4.7 Decoration by fabric

Fabric	*Applied*	*Impressed*			*Incised*							*Furrowed/tooled*				*Total*
code	*1*	*2*	*3*	*4*	*5*	*6*	*7*	*8*	*9*	*10*	*11*	*12*	*13*	*14*	*15*	
FL1	-	1	-	-	-	-	-	-	-	-	-	-	-	-	-	1
FL2	-	2	-	-	-	-	-	-	-	-	-	-	-	-	-	2
FL3	-	6	-	-	1	-	-	-	-	-	-	-	-	-	-	7
FL4	-	1	-	-	-	-	-	-	-	-	-	-	-	-	-	1
FL5	-	1	-	-	1	-	-	-	-	-	-	-	-	-	-	2
FL6	1	1	-	-	-	-	-	-	-	-	-	-	-	-	-	2
LI1	-	3	-	-	-	-	-	-	-	-	-	-	-	-	-	3
LI2	-	3	-	-	-	-	-	-	-	-	-	-	-	-	-	3
LI3	-	1	-	-	-	-	-	-	-	-	-	2	-	-	2	5
LI4	-	1	-	-	-	-	-	-	-	-	-	-	-	-	-	1
LI8	-	1	-	-	-	-	-	-	-	-	-	1	-	-	-	2
QU1	-	18	-	-	1	-	1	1	-	1	1	5	-	-	-	28
QU10	-	1	-	1	-	-	-	-	2	-	-	13	-	-	-	17
QU2	2	41	3	-	8	2	-	2	1	1	1	17	1	-	-	79
QU3	-	15	-	-	-	1	-	-	-	-	-	-	-	-	-	16
QU4	-	-	-	-	-	-	-	-	-	-	-	6	1	-	-	7
QU5	-	3	3	-	5	1	-	-	1	1	-	35	-	-	-	49
QU6	-	-	-	-	-	1	-	-	-	-	-	3	-	-	-	4
QU7	-	1	-	-	2	-	2	1	-	1	-	16	-	1	-	24
QU8	-	1	-	-	-	-	-	-	-	-	-	-	-	-	-	1
QU9	1	4	-	-	1	-	-	-	-	-	-	1	-	-	-	7
SH1	-	4	-	-	-	-	-	-	-	-	-	-	-	-	-	4
SH2	-	6	-	-	-	-	-	-	-	-	-	-	-	-	-	6
SH3	-	2	-	-	-	-	-	-	-	-	-	-	-	-	-	2
VE1	-	1	-	-	-	-	-	-	-	-	-	1	-	-	-	2
Total	4	118	6	1	19	5	3	4	4	4	2	100	2	1	2	275

Key:

1 = applied cordon; 2 = fingertip/fingernail; 3 = dots; 4 = open circles; 5 = lines; 6 = cross-hatching; 7 = herringbone; 8 = scratchings (post-firing); 9 = stabbed dots; 10 = short diagonal slashes; 11 = chevrons; 12 = furrowing; 13 = tooled lines; 14 = tooled lattice; 15 = complex tooling

Table 4.8 Decoration by vessel form

Vessel form	*Applied*	*Impressed*	*Incised*					*Furrowed/tooling*		*Total of ID*
	1	*2*	*5*	*7*	*8*	*10*	*11*	*12*	*15*	
Bowl 1.1	–	–	–	–	–	1	1	–	–	2
Bowl 1.2	–	–	–	–	–	–	–	31	–	31
Bowl 2.1	–	–	–	–	1	–	–	–	–	1
Bowl 3.1	–	–	–	–	–	–	–	66	–	66
Bowl 3.2	–	–	–	1	–	–	–	–	–	1
Bowl 4	–	–	–	–	2	–	–	–	–	2
Jar 1.1	–	5	–	–	–	–	–	–	–	5
Jar 1.2	1	8	–	–	–	1	–	–	–	10
Jar 1.3	1	66	–	–	–	1	–	–	–	68
Jar 3	–	4	–	–	–	–	–	–	–	4
Jar 5	–	1	1	–	–	–	–	–	–	2
Jar 6	1	1	1	–	–	–	–	–	–	3
Jar 7	–	1	–	–	–	–	–	–	–	1
Jar 9	–	–	–	–	–	–	–	–	1	1
Total	3	86	2	1	3	3	1	97	1	197

Key: 1 = applied cordon; 2 = fingertip/fingernail; 5 = lines; 7 = herringbone; 8 = scratchings (post-firing); 10 = short diagonal slashes; 11 = chevrons; 12 = furrowing; 15 = complex tooling

the sequence from Potterne (for the Late Bronze Age: 1100–700 BC) and Danebury (for the Early to Middle Iron Age (700–100 BC). As already discussed (see Chapter 2), the site phasing (phases 1/2, 3, and 4) differs slightly from the ceramic phasing, being a combination of stratigraphic, ceramic and radiocarbon dating evidence.

Table 4.9 Surface treatment by fabric

Fabric code	*Burnished*		*Red-finished*	
	No.	*%*	*No.*	*%*
FL1	5	3.4	–	–
FL2	–	–	1	0.6
FL5	2	1.4	–	–
LI1	13	3.4	–	–
LI2	11	1.3	2	0.2
LI3	32	3.1	2	0.2
LI4	–	–	1	0.8
LI5	–	–	2	1.4
LI6	1	4.3	–	–
QU1	45	5.2	60	6.9
QU2	257	8.4	124	4.1
QU3	41	4.0	2	0.2
QU4	8	22.9	8	22.9
QU5	61	15.3	94	23.5
QU6	5	10.9	8	17.4
QU7	33	13.1	89	35.5
QU8	8	7.3	1	0.9
QU9	4	5.8	2	2.9
QU10	29	21.8	40	30.1
SH1	13	1.6	–	–
SH2	47	10.3	1	0.2
SH3	6	2.6	–	–
VE1	3	12.0	–	–
VE2	1	11.1	–	–
Total	625		437	

- *CP 1*: Range of vessel forms typical of the early All Cannings Cross ceramic style (Cunliffe 1991, fig. A:2), and of the later phases of Potterne (Morris 2000a): short-necked, furrowed bowls (Fig. 4.5, 3, 4) and other fine-wares with geometric impressed and incised decoration (Fig. 4.7, 49–57); shouldered jars,

Table 4.10 Surface treatment by vessel form (no. vessels)

Vessel form	*Burnished*	*Red-finished*
Bowl 1.1	3	–
Bowl 1.2	4	17
Bowl 2.1	9	7
Bowl 2.2	19	20
Bowl 3.1	8	46
Bowl 3.2	7	6
Bowl 4	–	3
Bowl 5	2	–
Bowl 6	2	–
Jar 1.2	3	–
Jar 3	2	–
Jar 4	–	1
Jar 5	1	–
Jar 7	2	–
Jar 9	1	–
Total	63	100

Table 4.11 Fabric types by ceramic phase

Ceramic phase	*1*		*1–2*		*2*		*3*		*Total*
Fabric	*No./g*	*%*	*No./g*	*%*	*No./g*	*%*	*No./g*	*%*	*No./g*
Rg-t	–	–	2/16	<0.1	6/38	0.1	1/3	<0.1	9/57
FL1	2/12	1.0	58/302	1.0	16/109	0.4	2/92	0.4	78/515
FL2	24/127	10.4	78/563	1.9	32/261	1.0	–	–	134/951
FL3	3/5	0.4	115/1002	3.4	30/234	0.9	1/1	<0.1	149/1242
FL4	2/24	2.0	9/168	0.6	1/42	0.2	–	–	12/234
FL5	13/108	8.8	42/408	1.4	49/654	2.4	–	–	104/1170
LI1	9/62	5.1	119/1679	5.6	32/514	1.9	114/1936	8.7	274/4191
LI2	6/70	5.7	190/1741	5.8	100/1057	3.9	325/4307	19.4	621/7175
LI3	9/39	3.2	201/1599	5.3	52/446	1.7	389/3327	15.0	651/5411
LI4	2/7	0.6	31/515	1.7	7/45	0.2	9/167	0.8	49/734
LI5	–	–	5/29	0.1	16/146	0.5	3/40	0.2	24/215
LI6	2/31	2.5	7/100	0.3	–	–	4/31	0.1	13/162
LI7	–	–	4/64	0.2	–	–	–	–	4/64
LI8	1/11	0.9	21/241	0.8	19/201	0.8	70/492	2.2	111/945
QU1	10/71	5.8	220/2944	9.8	262/2737	10.2	53/699	3.1	545/6451
QU2	60/348	28.4	766/7112	23.7	1080/10,953	40.7	348/3018	13.6	2254/21,431
QU3	13/156	12.7	141/796	4.3	386/4577	17.0	44/558	2.5	584/6580
QU4	–	–	13/66	0.2	7/52	0.2	–	–	20/118
QU5	9/27	2.2	143/796	2.7	162/1075	4.0	21/310	1.4	335/2208
QU6	–	–	22/97	0.3	7/12	<0.1	–	–	29/109
QU7	8/45	3.7	70/421	1.4	82/590	2.2	10/86	0.4	170/1142
QU8	–	–	7/103	0.3	97/871	3.2	1/6	<0.1	105/980
QU9	1/6	0.5	21/706	0.6	7/59	0.2	3/16	<0.1	32/257
QU10	1/5	0.4	40/178	0.6	50/375	1.4	13/61	0.3	104/619
SH1	–	–	326/6976	23.2	45/1100	4.1	190/2939	13.2	561/11,015
SH2	9/58	4.7	102/1069	3.6	62/534	2.0	125/1386	6.2	298/3047
SH3	1/8	0.7	40/233	0.8	17/168	0.6	129/2660	12.0	187/3069
VE1	3/6	0.5	5/34	0.1	6/44	0.2	2/31	0.1	16/115
VE2	–	–	2/41	0.1	3/34	0.1	1/74	0.3	6/149
VE3	–	–	3/79	0.3	–	–	–	–	3/79
Total	188/1226		2803/30,041		2633/26,928		1858/22,240		7842/80,435

Rg-t = residual grog-tempered

frequently finger-impressed (Figs 4.5 and 4.6, 20–8); red-finished surface treatment; fabrics flint-tempered, sandy (frequently glauconitic) and oolitic; date range 8th–7th centuries BC.

- CP 2: Range of vessel forms typical of later All Cannings Cross ceramic style (Cunliffe 1991; fig. A:6) and equivalent to CP 1–3 at Danebury (Cunliffe 1984, fig. 6.17): long-necked fineware bowls (Fig. 4.5, 5–7), including scratch cordon vessels (Fig. 4.5, 8–11); continuation of red-finished surface treatment; coarseware shouldered jars; fabrics as CP 1; date range 6th to mid-4th centuries BC.
- CP 3: Range of undecorated vessel forms, equivalent to CP 4–5 at Danebury, but possibly also extending into CP 7 (Cunliffe 1984, figs 6.18–19): rounded and convex jars, some with 'proto-bead' rims (Figs 4.6 and 4.7, 39–46); plain saucepan pots (Fig. 4.5, 12–16); flared bowls (Fig. 4.5, 17–20); fabrics sandy and calcareous; date mid 4th–3rd centuries BC.

Using this ceramic phasing, 121 of the 347 features producing pottery have been dated (on the basis of vessel form and decoration only), with varying degrees of confidence – only 78 produced more than 20 sherds. There are few features which can be definitively dated as CP 1, and many can only be dated broadly as CP 1–2, containing jars of types 1–6, but with no fineware bowls of more closely datable type. Table 4.11 gives the breakdown of fabric types by ceramic phase and Table 4.12 of vessel form by ceramic phase.

Table 4.11 serves to demonstrate that different fabric groups, and hence different source areas, vary in quantity through time. Sandy wares were used

Table 4.12 Vessel form by ceramic phase

Ceramic phase	*1*	*1–2*	*2*	*3*
Bowl 1.1	2	3	2	–
Bowl 1.2	7	8	10	–
Bowl 2.1	–	1	22	–
Bowl 2.2	–	–	46	2
Bowl 3.1	–	39	13	1
Bowl 3.2	–	6	9	–
Bowl 4	–	–	1	1
Bowl 5	–	–	–	17
Bowl 6	–	1	–	9
Jar 1.1	–	12	6	2
Jar 1.2	–	31	8	10
Jar 1.3	–	37	31	2
Jar 2	–	2	3	2
Jar 3	–	17	5	3
Jar 4	–	1	–	–
Jar 5	–	2	3	1
Jar 6	–	–	1	–
Jar 7	–	–	1	20
Jar 8	–	–	–	6
Jar 9	–	–	–	1
Jar 10	–	1	–	–
Total	9	161	161	77

throughout the sequence, although showing a peak in CP 2 when they make up 79.1% of the total assemblage. Limestone-tempered wares are likewise found throughout, peaking in CP 3 (46.3% of total). Flint-tempered wares are most numerous in CP 1 (22.5% of the total), declining sharply thereafter. Shelly wares are scarce in CP 1, but are thereafter present in greater quantities, rising from 27.7% (CP 1–2) to 31.4% (CP 3).

CP 1 is contemporary with the upper zones of the Potterne midden, the earlier activity at All Cannings Cross (Cunnington 1923), and the earliest activity at Houghton Down (Brown 2000b). Although few contexts can be definitively assigned to this phase, more may be included within the broad grouping of CP 1–2. However, the fact that the short-necked fineware bowls characteristic of this ceramic phase occur in smaller quantities than the long-necked bowls of the succeeding phase might indicate a lower level of activity at this period, intensifying thereafter.

The absence of scratch cordon and other round-bodied bowls from Potterne was taken as an indication that deposition on the midden site had ceased prior to the 6th century BC, although long-necked fineware bowls are present in the upper zones of the midden (Morris 2000b, 161–5). At Battlesbury Bowl this ceramic phase (CP 2) is well represented by long-necked fineware bowls, although scratch cordon bowls are scarce.

No radiocarbon dates have been obtained for features dated to CP 1. Three dates were obtained from CP 2 features – two were consistent at 770–400 BC (ditches 4090 and 4105), while the third (pit 5043) seems anomalous at 420–100.

CP 3 is here defined on the basis of a range of plainware forms which at Danebury appeared to post-date the decorated Early Iron Age wares but pre-date the distinctive decorated 'saucepan pot' styles of the Middle Iron Age (Cunliffe 1984, cp4–5). However, it is recognised that CP 4–5 has scant supporting stratigraphic evidence at Danebury, and is represented by a very limited range of vessel forms (Brown 1995, 55). It may well be that these plainware forms continued alongside the decorated 'saucepan pots' of the Yarnbury-Highfield style. Examples of the latter types are, however, completely absent from Battlesbury Bowl. This might argue for an end date prior to CP 6 in the Danebury environs where, it is proposed, decorated wares in glauconitic fabrics appear slightly before those of the local decorated wares, for example at Suddern Farm and Houghton Down (Brown 2000a, 67; 2000b, 78; see also Brown 1995, 63).

Radiocarbon dates from three features (pits 4320, 4332, and 5358) are generally consistent but cover a wide date range from late 5th century BC to mid-1st century AD. Abandonment of the site at the very latest by the end of the 2nd century, however, is indicated by the complete absence of any vessel forms which could be attributed to the Atrebatic ceramic style, but given the lack of decorated Middle Iron Age forms the end date is likely to be earlier, within the 3rd century BC.

Spatial distribution

Pottery was recovered from 629 contexts, which derive from 347 features (36 ditch/gully sections; 155 pits, 144 post-holes, three hearths/ovens; three recuts, two slots, and four unknown features). Of these 629 contexts, 121 (from 72 features) produced more than 25 sherds, and only 47 (from 31 features) produced more than 50 sherds. A crude calculation of the mean sherd weight by feature group shows variation across the site from a low of 7.5 g for FG 3 to a high of 14 g for FG 4 (with 9.4 g and 11.3 g for FGs 1 and 2 respectively) perhaps reflecting different mechanisms of pottery discard in different parts of the site.

There is little in the way of vertical stratigraphy which would allow the examination of a stratified ceramic sequence. In order to explore any chronological or other variation in the assemblage, therefore, the pottery has been examined from the pits in the four feature groups, and from the group of ditches in FG 1.

Table 4.13 gives the quantification of pottery by feature group and ditches, and the presence of

Table 4.13 Pottery distribution by ditch and feature group (% of total FG by weight, presence of vessel forms)

Fabric	FG1 ditches No./g	%	Vessel forms	FG 1 No./g	%	Vessel forms	FG 2 No./g	%	Vessel forms	FG 3 No./g	%	Vessel forms	FG 4 No./g	%	Vessel forms
FL1	2/6	*0.02*		7/134	*0.90*	J7	-	-		115/672	*3.83*		-	-	
FL2	1/3	*0.01*		-	-		-	-		156/1100	*6.27*	J1.3, J3	1/4	*0.02*	
FL3	3/11	*0.04*		2/3	*0.02*		-	-		220/1842	*10.50*	J1.3	1/12	*0.07*	
FL4	1/48	*0.18*		1/28	*0.19*		-	-		19/301	*1.72*		-	-	
FL5	-	-		1/4	*0.03*		-	-		128/1361	*7.76*	J1.2, J3	1/6	*0.04*	
FL6	-	-		-	-		-	-		1/32	*0.18*		-	-	
GR1	5/21	*0.08*		2/4	*0.03*		-	-		1/5	*0.03*		1/11	*0.07*	
GR2	1/17	*0.06*		-	-		-	-		-	-		-	-	
LI1	17/366	*1.37*		120/1107	*7.46*	B5, J1.2, J1.3	109/1964	*9.02*	B5, J1.2, J1.3, J3	51/398	*2.27*		51/1205	*7.47*	B6, J1.3
LI2	92/1086	*4.07*	B2.2, B6, J1.1, J1.2, J1.3, J7	145/1215	*8.19*	J1.2, J5, J7, J8	376/3782	*17.37*	B5, J1.1, J1.2, J2, J7	54/446	*2.54*	B1.1, J1.2, J3	115/1705	*10.57*	B2.1, B5, J1.2, J3, J7
LI3	25/222	*0.83*	B3.1	316/2391	*16.12*	B5, B6, J1.1, J1.2, J3, J7, J8. J9	264/2232	*10.25*	J1.1, J1.2, J7, J8	105/823	*4.69*		96/668	*4.14*	J1.1, J1.2, J7
LI4	5/52	*0.20*	J1.3	7/80	*0.54*	J7	35/252	*1.16*		16/122	*0.70*		46/705	*4.37*	J1.3, J3
LI5	18/177	*0.66*	B2.2, J1.2	-	-		-	-		3/22	*0.13*		6/54	*0.33*	B6
LI6	2/9	*0.03*		2/17	*0.11*	J1.1	1/5	*0.02*		4/46	*0.26*		12/200	*1.24*	J1.2
LI7	-			-	-		-	-		-	-		5/70	*0.43*	
LI8	5/33	*0.12*		70/492	*3.32*	J8	2/9	*0.04*		38/401	*2.29*	B1.1, J1.3, J3	27/315	*1.95*	
QU1	320/4483	*16.82*	B1.1, B1.2, B2.1, B2.2, B3.1, B3.2, J1.1, J1.2, J1.3, J4, J5	100/1152	*7.76*	B3.2, J3	135/1090	*5.00*	B3.1, J1.2, J1.3	127/998	*5.69*	B2.1, B3.1, J1.1, J1.2, J3	49/658	*4.08*	J1.3, J10
QU10	28/128	*0.48*	B1.2, B2.2, B3.2	7/47	*0.32*		-	-		77/497	*2.83*	B1.2,B2.2,B3.1	12/41	*0.25*	B2.2,B3.1
QU2	1077/10557	*39.61*	B1.2, B2.1, B2.2, B3.1, B3.2, J1.1, J1.3, J3, J5, J7	355/2102	*14.17*	B3.1, B4, J1.1, J1.2, J1.3, J7	443/5305	*24.36*	B2.1, B2.2, B3.1, B5, J1.1, J1.2, J1.3, J3, J5	555/3671	*20.93*	B1.2, B2.2, B3.1, J1.2, J1.3, J2, J3	315/2747	*17.03*	B5, B6, J1.1, J1.3, J2, J3

Table 4.13 (continued)

Fabric	FG1 ditches No./g	%	Vessel forms	FG 1 No./g	%	Vessel forms	FG 2 No./g	%	Vessel forms	FG 3 No./g	%	Vessel forms	FG 4 No./g	%	Vessel forms
QU3	424/5479	20.56	B2.2, J1.2, J1.3	82/852	5.74	B5, J3	49/346	1.59	J1.3	136/1256	7.16	B2.2, J1.2, J1.3	49/784	4.86	B2.1, J1.1, J1.2, J3
QU4	4/38	0.14	B3.1	-	-		-	-		23/177	1.01	B3.1	3/159	0.09	
QU5	145/961	3.61	B1.1, B1.2, B2.2, B3.1, B3.2, B5, J2	4/30	0.20	J1.3	-	-		188/980	5.59	B1.1, B1.2, B2.1, B2.2, B3.1, B3.2, J1.3, J5	41/422	2.62)	B2.1, B2.2, B3.1, B3.2, B5
QU6	8/15	0.06	B3.1	2/9	0.06		1/1	0.00		25/130	0.74		5/45	0.28	
QU7	99/743	2.79	B1.2, B2.2, B3.1, B3.2, J1.2	18/176	1.19	B2.1, B2.2, B3.2, B4, B6, J7	2/8	0.04		72/347	1.98	B1.2, B2.1, B2.2, B3.1, B3.2	10/38	0.24	B2.1
QU8	93/840	3.15	B2.2	1/15	0.10		-	-		10/127	0.72	J1.1	2/11	0.07	
QU9	6/98	0.37		-	-		-	-		40/302	1.72	B1.2,B2.2,J1.3, J6	6/51	0.32	
SH1	25/650	2.44	J1.3	121/1374	9.26	J1.2, J3	308/4769	21.90	B5, J1.1, J1.2, J1.3	58/589	3.36	J2, J3	241/5742	35.59	B6, J1.1, J1.2, J1.3, J2
SH2	58/517	1.94	B2.1, J1.3, J3	83/874	5.89	B2.2, J7	158/1647	7.56	B5, J1.2, J3	75/562	3.20	J1.2, J1.3	40/416	2.58	J1.1, J3, J1.2
SH3	9/93	0.35	J1.2, J1.3	128/2649	17.85	B5, J8	49/344	1.58	J1.1	30/214	1.22	J1.2, J1.3	9/74	0.46	J1.2
VE1	1/2		(0.01%)	4/8	0.05		1/25	0.11		12/76	0.43	B2.2, J3	3/13	0.08	B1.2
VE2	-	-		1/74	0.50		-	-		5/42	0.24		3/43	0.27	J2
VE3	-	-		-	-		-	-		-			3/79	0.49	
Total	2474/66552			1579/14837			1933/21779			2344/17539			1153/16134		

diagnostic vessel forms. The data appear to demonstrate clear chronological variations between the five feature groups. FGs 1, 2, and 4 can each be seen to contain a similar range of fabric types (sandy, shelly and limestone-tempered), although FG 4 produced a higher proportion of shelly wares than the other two clusters (38.6%). Vessel forms within all three clusters include those distinctive of CP 2–3 (eg, long-necked fineware bowls and proto-saucepan pots: Fig. 4.5, 12–16), but very little which is likely to derive from CP 1 (one example of bowl type 1.2 from FG 4). FG 3, however, is quite distinct in the range of fabrics and vessel forms represented, with a predominance of flint-tempered (30.3%) and sandy wares (48.4%), with much lower proportions of limestone-tempered and shelly wares. Vessel forms are mainly indicative of CP 1–2 (short-necked and long-necked fineware bowls: Fig. 4.5, 2, 8), with nothing characteristic of CP 3. The ditch/gully group produced a chronologically mixed assemblage of vessel forms from all ceramic phases (eg, Fig. 4.5, 1, 3, 5–7), although sandy wares are predominant (87.6%) at the expense of all other fabric types.

List of illustrated pottery

(Fig. 4.5)

Bowl 1.1: short necked carinated bowl

1. Rim/shoulder sherd; impressed and incised decoration; fabric QU1. PRN (Pottery Record Number) 1258, context 4022, ditch 4040, section 4021 (FG 1)
2. Rim sherd; incised decoration; fabric QU5. PRN 2605, context 5244, pit 5054 (FG 3)

Bowl 1.2: Short-necked furrowed bowl

3. Rim sherd; furrowed shoulder; fabric QU2. PRN 1089, context 4075, ditch 4040, section 4074 (FG1)
4. Rim sherd; furrowed shoulder; fabric LI3. PRN 1102, context 4087, ditch 4043, section 4023 (FG 1)

Bowl 2: long-necked fineware bowl

5. Partial profile; fabric QU2. PRNs 280-1, context 4451, ditch 4043, section 4105 (FG 1)
6. Partial profile; fabric QU2. PRN 1046, context 4071, ditch 4043, section 4019 (FG 1)
7. Rim sherd; fabric QU2. PRN 292, context 4448, ditch 4043, section 4105 (FG 1)

Bowl 4: scratch cordon bowl

8. Body sherd with cordon and scratched decoration; fabric QU2. PRN 755, context 4837, pit 4836 (FG 3)
9. Rim sherd; scratched decoration; fabric QU2. PRN 828, context 4235, pit 4553 (FG 3)
10. Rim sherd; scratched decoration; fabric QU7. PRN 1394, context 4369, pit 4196 (FG 1)
11. Body sherd; cordon and scratched decoration; fabric QU1. PRN 1277, cleaning layer 4037 (over ditch 4043) (FG 1)

Bowl 5: Saucepan pot prototype

12. Partial profile; fabric LI2. PRN 1490, ON 3411, context 5735, pit 5358 (FG 4).
13. Rim sherd; fabric QU5. PRN 1510, ON 3379, context 5359, pit 5358 (FG 4)
14. Profile; fabric LI3. PRN 1362-4, ON 3068, context 4331, pit 4330 (FG 1).
15. Rim sherd; fabric LI2. PRN 599, ON 3208, context 4810, pit 4707 (FG 2)
16. Rim sherd; fabric SH2. PRN 457, context 4728, pit 4641 (FG 2)

Bowl 6: flared bowl

17. Complete profile; fabric LI1. PRNs 1486, ON 3408, context 5735, pit 5358 (FG 4)
18. Rim sherd; fabric LI2. PRN 796, context 4210, ditch 4043, section 4090 (FG 1)
19. Rim sherd; fabric QU2. PRNs 2813-4, context 5731, pit 5592 (FG 4)
20. Rim sherd; profile unknown; fabric QU7. PRN 1320, context 4317, pit 4751 (FG 1)

Jar 1.1: shouldered jar

21. Rim sherd; finger-impressed shoulder; fabric QU2. PRN 1190, context 4100, ditch 4043, section 4105 (FG 1)
22. Rim sherd; finger-impressed shoulder; fabric QU8. PRN 1598, context 5044, pit 5043 (FG 3)
23. Rim sherd; finger-impressed shoulder; fabric QU1. PRN 1210, context 4016, ditch 4040, section 4012 (FG 1)
24. Rim sherd; fabric SH1. PRN 2202, context 5752, pit 5750 (FG 4)

(Fig. 4.6)

Jar 1.2: weak shouldered jar

25. Rim sherd; fabric LI3. PRN 112, context 4617, pit 4564 (FG 2)
26. Rim sherd; fabric LI3. PRN 2822, context 5751, pit 5750 (FG 4)
27. Rim sherd; finger-impressed shoulder; fabric QU3. PRN 1257, context 4022, ditch 4040, section 4021 (FG 1)
28. Rim sherd; finger impressions below rim; fabric LI3. PRN 2792, context 5732, pit 5592 (FG 4)
29. Rim sherd; fabric SH1. PRN 2836, ON 3402, context 5752, pit 5750 (FG 4)

Jar 2: Carinated jar

30. Rim/shoulder sherd; fabric SH1. PRN 1542, context 5136, pit 5043 (FG 3)
31. Rim/shoulder sherd; finger-impressed decoration; fabric QU5. PRN 1623, context 4149, ditch 4043, section 4096 (FG 1)

Jar 3: rounded jar

32. Rim sherd; fabric SH1. PRN 1319, context 4317, pit 4751 (FG 1)
33. Rim sherd; fabric QU3. PRN 1447, context 4385, pit 4332 (FG 1)
34. Rim sherd; fabric QU3. PRNs 2862, context 5594, pit 5592 (FG 4)

Jar 4: fineware shouldered jar

35. Part profile; red finished; QU1. PRN 966, context 4120, ditch 4043, section 4090 (FG 1)

Jar 5: handled jar

36. Shouldered jar with horizontal lug scar; finger-impressed shoulder; fabric QU2. PRN 560, context 4802, pit 4704 (FG 2)
37. Shouldered jar; horizontal lug and incised decoration on shoulder; fabric QU5. PRN 2483, context 5162, pit 5149 (FG 3)
38. Lug; fabric QU1. PRN 171, context 4387, ditch 4043, section 4105 (FG 1)

Jar 6: Cordoned jar

39. Neck sherd with applied, impressed cordon; fabric QU9. PRN 3114, context 4870, pit 4823 (FG 3)

Jar 7: convex jar with proto-bead rim

40. Rim sherd; fabric LI4. PRN 175, context 4417, pit 4416 (FG 1)
41. Rim sherd; fabric LI3. PRN 600, ON 3208, context 4810, pit 4707 (FG 2)
42. Rim sherd; fabric LI2. PRN 320, ON 3153, context 4635, pit 4584 (FG 2)
43. Rim sherd; fabric LI3. PRN 35, ON 3126, context 4515, pit recut 4514 (pit 4486: FG 1)

(Fig. 4.7)

Jar 8: large jar with rounded profile and thickened rim

44. Rim sherd; fabric SH3. PRN 1696, ON 3046, context 4194, pit 4195 (FG 1)

Figure 4.6 Pottery (24–43)

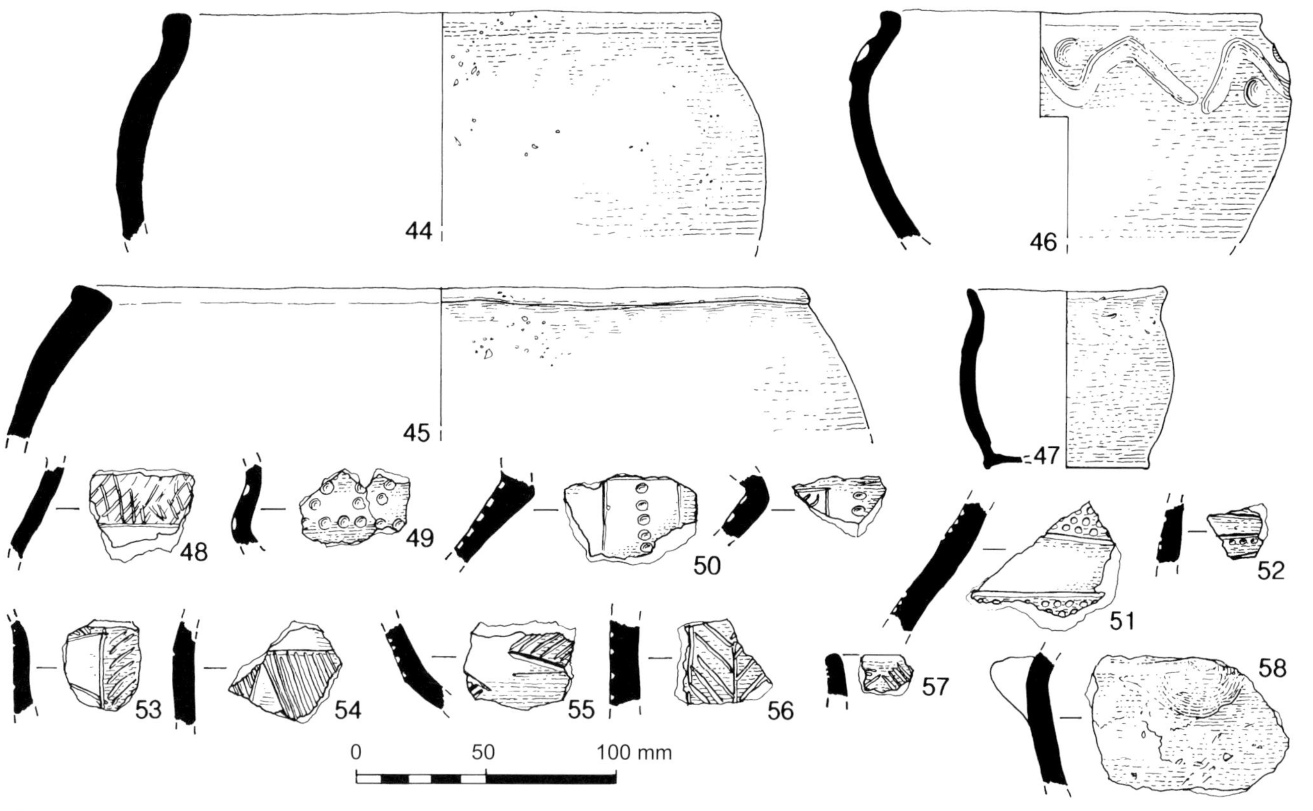

Figure 4.7 Pottery (44–58)

45.Rim sherd; fabric LI3. PRN 608, context 4811, pit 4707 (FG 2)

Jar 9: rounded jar with bead rim

46.Partial profile; tooled and impressed decoration; fabric LI3. PRNs 158-9, ON 3113, context 4507, pit 4486 (FG 1)

Jar 10: miniature vessel

47.Complete profile; fabric QU1. PRN 2784, context 5728, pit 5592 (FG 4)

Decorated sherds

48.Tooled lattice decoration; fabric QU7. PRN 1153, context 4102, ditch 4043, section 4105 (FG 1).

49.Impressed dots; fabric QU2. PRN 425, context 4728, pit 4641 (FG 2)

50.Impressed dots and slashes in banded zones; fabric QU5. PRNs 3102-3, context 4870, pit 4823 (FG 3)

51.Impressed dots in banded zones; fabric QU5. PRN 2403, context 5147, ditch 4043, section 4080 (FG 1)

52.Stabbed dots and incised lines; fabric QU10. PRN 1286, cleaning layer 4037 (over ditch 4043) (FG 1)

53.Incised cross-hatching; fabric QU7. PRN 1287, cleaning layer 4037 (over ditch 4043) (FG 1)

54.Incised cross-hatching in chevrons; fabric QU1. PRN 2603, context 5244, pit 5054 (FG 3)

55.Carinated sherd with incised cross-hatched chevrons; fabric QU7. PRN 1552, context 5135, pit 5043 (FG 3)

56.Incised herringbone; fabric QU5. PRN 2687, context 5323, pit 5318 (FG 3)

57.Rim sherd with incised chevrons; fabric QU2. PRN 291, context 4448, ditch 4105 (Ditch S Section)

58.Shoulder sherd with applied unperforated lug; fabric QU2. PRN 1124, context 4101, ditch 4043, section 4105 (FG 1)

Fired Clay

by Stephen Legg

Four fired clay objects were recovered, comprising one spindlewhorl and three slingshots. The remainder of the fired clay from the site consists largely of featureless fragments, probably of structural origin.

Objects

The spindlewhorl (Fig. 4.8, 1) was recovered from post-hole 5370. The object is of biconical shape, but is incomplete.

Three ceramic slingshots were recovered, respectively from two pits and a ditch (all from the southern end of the site), of which two are substantially complete (Fig. 4.8, 2, 3). All three are ovoid in shape with both ends pointed. One example appears to have been knife-trimmed to shape. Similar clay slingshots occur commonly on Iron Age sites such as Maiden Castle and Danebury (Poole 1984a, fig. 7.44; 1991). Of the two measurable examples, one measures 40 x 26 mm (max.), and weighs 21 g; the second 36 x 22 mm, weight 12 g.

Both these examples are smaller and lighter than the chalk slingshot (see above), and it is suggested that this difference reflects different use, the smaller slingshots being used for hunting game and birds, rather than in warfare. The slingshots fall within the size range of those from All Cannings Cross (30–40 x 18–25 mm, weights not recorded; Poole 1984a, 398) but are smaller than those from Danebury (40–50 x 27–31 mm, weight 30–50 g; *ibid.*).

Other Fired Clay

The majority of the remaining fired clay (280 fragments; 1034 g) is largely undiagnostic, but has been identified variously as hearth lining, pit lining, and wall daub. The fragments derive from 45 individual features. Most of these fragments contain prominent chalk inclusions, sometimes with the addition of small flint inclusions.

A small proportion of the fragments (57) came from two hearths (6107, 5841), and were intensely burnt. A few others showing similar intense burning probably derive from similar features. Some fragments show finger impressions or smearing on surfaces. Many, however, show organic impressions and traces of wattling, indicating they were wall daub. None of the examples was large enough to ensure separation of horizontal 'rods' from vertical 'sails'. Some show a smooth outer surface, which is relatively flat and even, with fine striations evident from the smoothing process. The variety of impressions suggests that some organic tempering of the clay was taking place, generally with grasses or straw. No concentrations of this material were encountered.

List of illustrated objects (Fig. 4.8)

1. Spindlewhorl. ON 3808, context 5372, post-hole 5370 (FG 4)
2. Slingshot. ON 3209, context 4795, pit 4794 (FG 1).
3. Slingshot. ON 3805, context 4127, pit 4113 (FG 1).

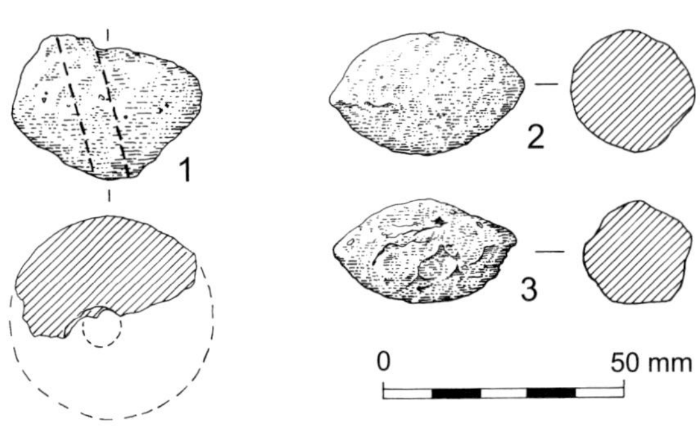

Figure 4.8 Fired clay objects

Worked Bone and Antler

by Stephen Legg

Sixty worked bone and antler objects were identified, and have been categorised according to the classification system set out by Smith (1982), with additions and modifications according to Seager Smith (2000). The finds are comparable to assemblages from Maiden Castle (Laws 1991c, 234–8), Danebury (Sellwood 1984, 371; Cunliffe and Poole 1991, 354–8), Potterne (Seager Smith 2000, 222), and All Cannings Cross (Cunnington 1923).

Pointed Tools

Large pointed tools (Fig. 4.9, 1–3; Pl. 4.1)
Six examples (typically longer than 75 mm and worked to a point at one end) were recovered, of which three are complete. Bone types include horse metapodials, a horse ulna, a cattle ulna, and large ungulate-sized long bone fragments.

Shuttle tips or gouges (Fig. 4.9, 4–5; Pl. 4.1)
Six examples were recovered, all substantially complete. All were formed by an oblique, diagonal cut across the shaft in a longitudinal direction. The tip is usually worked to a point and then worn through use to provide variation of shape. Five are perforated, often at the distal end of the bone. Ovicaprid metapodiae and tibiae seem to have been preferred, with some juvenile bone present. Four of these objects were retrieved from pit deposits.

Awls (Fig. 4.9, 6)
Only one complete example was retrieved, from pit 4836 (FG 3, phase 1/2). It is 40 mm long with a generally rounded section and is pointed at both ends. It was probably produced on a splinter derived from a long bone fragment, of unidentified species.

Needles (Fig. 4.9, 7–11; Pl. 4.1)
Nine examples (six complete) were identified of which four are made from ivory or teeth. They generally have slender pointed shanks with a perforation at the broader part. Both double-pointed and single-pointed examples occur and they were probably worked on a splinter or by shaving a more complete bone. Polish is often evident. Seven examples came from pits, the remaining two from ditch fills.

Miscellaneous bone points
Six points cannot be confidently assigned to the above four sub-types (see Seager Smith 2000). Two may be points from needles, one other appears to be from a large and one from a small pointed tool. Large and medium ungulate-sized long bone fragments and

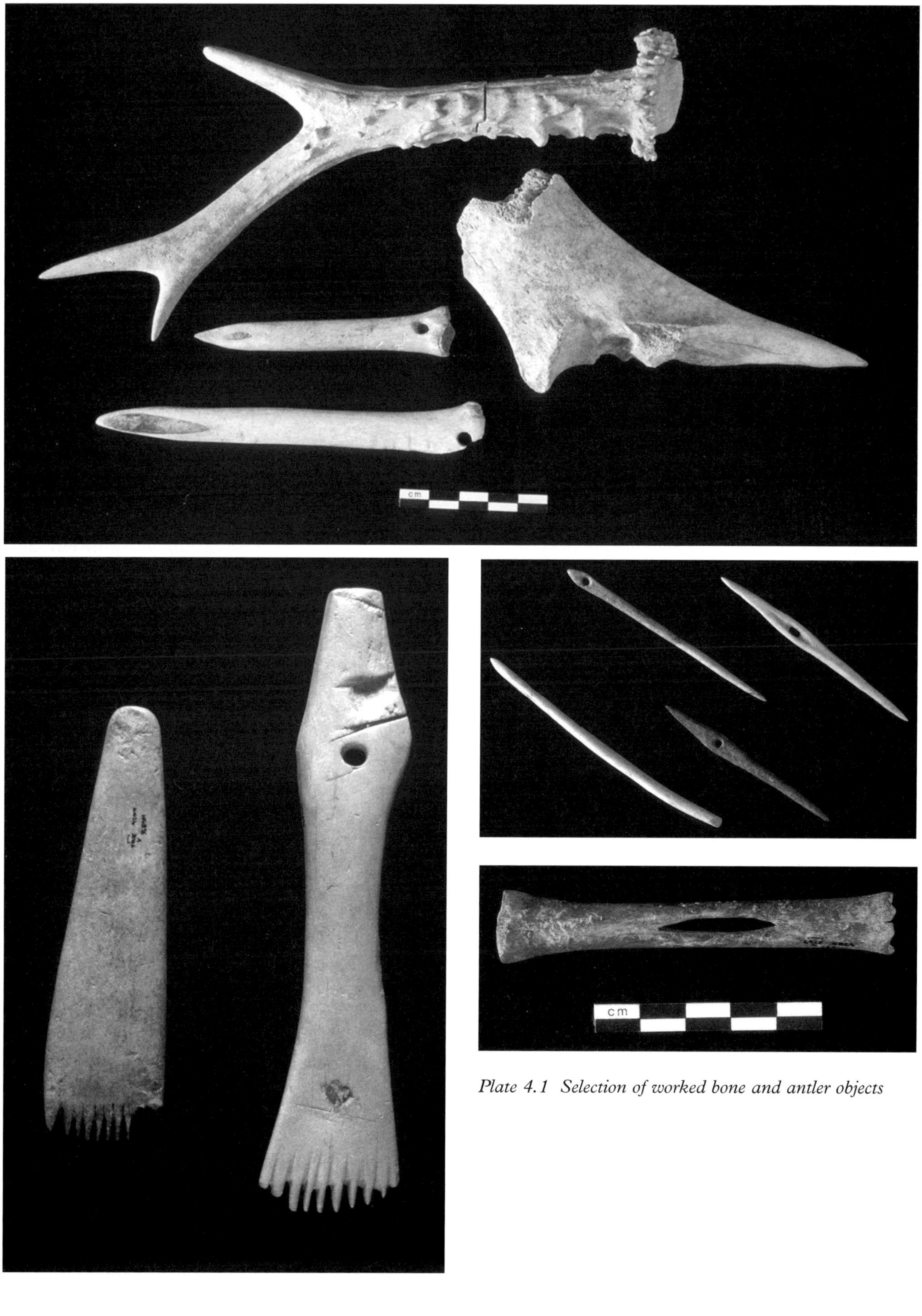

Plate 4.1 Selection of worked bone and antler objects

splinters were probably used. One example appears to be from a jawbone. Five points came from pits and one from section 4096 of ditch 4043.

Miscellaneous shank fragments
The four pieces ascribed to this sub-type (see Seager Smith 2000) comprise a variety of polished and rounded shank fragments probably deriving from pins or needles but they cannot be confidently ascribed to these categories. The species could not be determined for most of them. Three examples were retrieved from pit deposits, the fourth from a ditch.

Bladed Tools

Rib knives (Fig. 4.9, 12)
One complete example from a post-hole was made from a longitudinally split rib forming a blade and handle. It was made from a large ungulate-sized rib fragment and has a smooth finish.

Rib blades (Fig. 4.9, 13)
One substantially complete example from a pit 4704 (FG 2, phase 1/2) is made from a longitudinally split rib from a large ungulate-sized animal, ground to form rounded ends.

Toothed Tools

Weaving combs (Fig. 4.9, 14–15; Pl. 4.1)
Three weaving combs (two complete) were retrieved from ditch 4043, pit 5358 (FG 4, phase 3) and a post-hole. They are made from split beam sections of red deer antler with polished outer tissue for the upper surfaces and the spongey core revealed on the smoothed lower surfaces. The teeth are aligned with the grain. They each have 8–11 teeth surviving, with the narrower end rounded or squared. They have V-shaped notches cut between the teeth which have become more U-shaped with wear. Tooth wear varies but the teeth at the edge of the comb show greater wear; transverse grooves on the undersides of the teeth are also ascribed to use-wear.

The comb from ditch 4043 shows possible bite/chew marks on the narrower butt end. That from pit 5358 is perforated at the butt end and its shape is more complex than the others. These combs can be compared with examples from Maiden Castle (Laws 1991c, 235, fig. 187) and Danebury (Sellwood 1984, figs 373–4).

Dress, Decorative, or Gaming Objects

Sliders (Fig. 4.9, 16)
One almost complete example was recovered from ditch 4455. Two parallel longitudinal perforations extend from the distal end of the bone to a lenticular transverse perforation centrally positioned on the bone. The surface of the bone is highly polished. Its possible use as a simple musical instrument cannot be overlooked. This example was made from the metacarpal of a (?) juvenile ovicaprid.

Decorations pierced for suspension
(Fig. 4.9, 17–18)
One substantially complete object, recovered from a pit, is made from a longitudinally broken beam of red deer antler with a convex upper surface of smoothed outer tissue. A circular transverse perforation occurs near the narrower, more rounded end, with the other end being flatter and wider in cross-section. Only the end of another object survived.

Miscellaneous Bone Objects

Bones with longitudinal holes
One incomplete example was recovered from a pit. It consists of a smoothed and slightly rounded distal shaft end of bone (ovicaprid metatarsal) with a rectangular, longitudinal perforation becoming more rounded as it extends towards the proximal end. The outer surface is polished and smoothed.

Incised or decorated fragments (Fig. 4.9, 19)
One incomplete example (made from a large, ungulate-sized bone) was recovered from pit 5043 (FG 3, phase 1/2). It is decorated with a line of three ring-and-dot motifs and one end is ground smooth.

Other pieces of worked bone
Six other objects are fragments of finished pieces or off-cuts produced during the manufacture of other objects. Some show a high degree of polish and smoothing. Bone types include a horse radius, an ovicaprid tibia, and large and medium ungulate-sized long bone fragments.

Antler

Handle (Fig. 4.9, 20)
Only one example, made from red deer antler, was found. It is a section of beam, which has been sawn and snapped at the wider end. The surface has been deburred and smoothed.

Tines (Fig. 4.9, 21)
Four of the five examples show the characteristic cut and snap technique of removal, while the other appears to have been sawn. They are mostly of red deer antler. Four examples came from pits and one from a post-hole.

Miscellaneous worked pieces (Fig. 4.9, 22–3)
This category consists of four examples, only one of which is complete. Two of the antlers had been

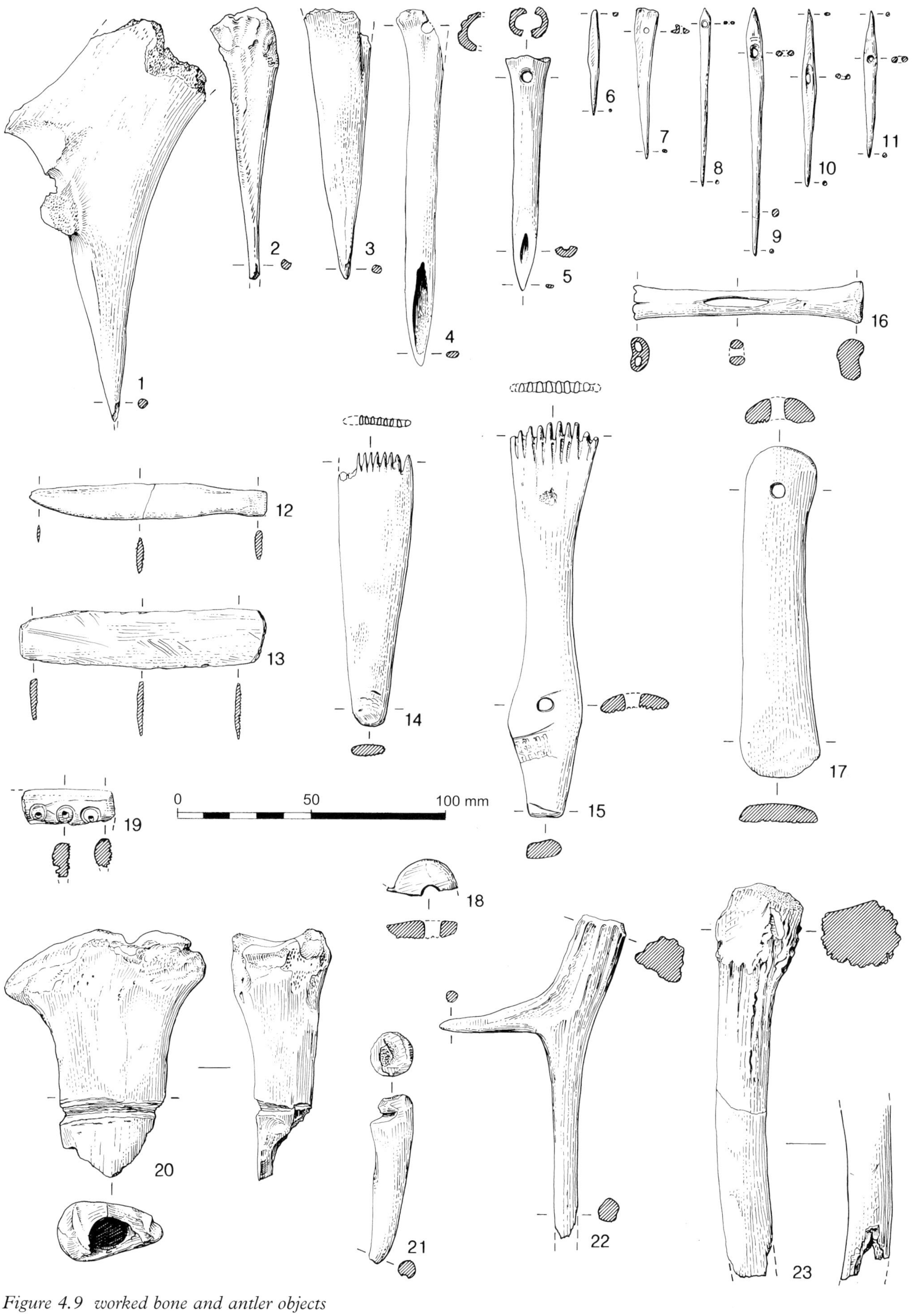

Figure 4.9 worked bone and antler objects

naturally shed, with the burr intact on the complete example. Roe deer and red deer are represented. Tines often show polish. All examples came from pits.

Waste

Three pieces of red deer antler waste were retrieved from pits. They are all beam sections exhibiting saw marks, often on more than one side. Some original surface state remains. They are presumably off-cuts from the manufacture of other objects.

Conclusions

Bones from horse, cattle, ovicaprids, and antler were used as raw materials. Long bones and metapodiae from the principal domesticates appear to have been favoured, especially for the pointed tools, and rib fragments for bladed items, clearly exploiting the natural shape of the bone. Most of the antler shows a characteristic cut and snap technique, seldom retaining the burr end. Where this does exist, on two objects, it can be demonstrated that the antlers were naturally shed and they may well have been picked up locally.

Many objects show clear use-wear polish, indicating that they were well-used. Just over half of the worked bone consists of pointed tools; mostly needles, and fragments of pins and needles. The pointed tools are suggestive of piercing and sewing, generally in association with leatherworking and textiles. This is supported by the presence of worn bone combs. The rest of the assemblage contains items less easily categorised, being 'decorative' and comprising off-cuts which indicate at least some boneworking taking place on or near the site.

The objects came from all phases, with no apparent chronological emphasis, and while there is a slight concentration within FG 1 (28 items), all other feature groups produced objects. The assemblage finds parallels at with other Early Iron Age sites in Wiltshire (Smith 1982), such as Potterne (Seager Smith 2000) and All Cannings Cross (Cunnington 1923). Comparable worked bone assemblages have also been recovered from Maiden Castle (Laws 1991c) and Danebury (Sellwood 1984; Cunliffe and Poole 1991). Some differences occur in the composition of the assemblages, for example, no double-pointed needles were represented at Potterne (Seager Smith 2000, 233) and other weaving combs are relatively poorly represented (*cf.* Seager Smith 2000, 233). Site function, chronology or other factors may account for these differences.

List of illustrated worked bone objects (Fig. 4.9)

1. Large, pointed tool; horse ulna; pointed distal end. ON 3390, context 5728, pit 5592 (FG 4, phase 3)
2. Large, pointed tool; horse metapodial; pointed distal end. ON 3280, context 5074, pit 5073 (FG 3, phase 3)
3. Large, pointed tool; large ungulate-sized long bone; pointed distal end. ON 3076, context 4329, pit 4305 (FG 1, phase 1/2)
4. Shuttle tip or gouge; ovicaprid tibia; worked proximal end; perforated distal end. ON 3350, context 4988, ditch 4043, section 4455 (FG 1, phase 1/2)
5. Shuttle tip or gouge; ovicaprid metatarsal; worked distal end; perforation at proximal end. ON 3309, context 5142, ditch 4043, section 4080 (FG 1, phase 1/2)
6. Awl; species unidentified; bone splinter; pointed both ends. ON 3864, context 4838, pit 4836 (FG 3, phase 1/2)
7. Needle; ivory fragment. ON 3284, context 5084, pit 4641 (FG 2, phase 3)
8. Needle. ON 3010, context 4076, ditch 4040, section 4012 (FG 1, phase 1/2)
9. Needle; ivory fragment. ON 3412, context 5735, pit 5358 (FG 4, phase 3)
10. Needle; ivory fragment. ON 3398, context 5807, pit 5688 (FG 4, phase 1/2)
11. Needle; long bone splinter; wear polished. ON 3007, context 4056, ditch 4011 (phase 1/2)
12. Rib knife; large ungulate-sized rib. ON 3009, context 4069, ditch 4043, section 4019 (FG 1 phase 1/2)
13. Rib blade; large ungulate-sized rib. ON 3207, context 4778, pit 4704 (FG 2, phase 1/2)
14. Weaving comb; rounded butt end; two teeth missing; longitudinally split antler. ON 3006, context 4024, ditch 4043, section 4023 (FG 1, phase 1/2)
15. Weaving comb; squared butt end; teeth very worn; longitudinally split antler. ON 3393, context 5848, pit 5358 (FG 4, phase 3)
16. Slider; lenticular transverse perforation; ovicaprid metacarpal. ON 3349, context 4985, ditch 4043, section 4455 (FG 1, phase 1/2)
17. Object pierced for suspension; red deer antler; polished. ON 3201, context 4806, pit 4809 (FG 3, phase 1/2)
18. Fragment from long bone pierced near end. ON 3033, context 4159, post-hole 4199 (FG 1, unphased)
19. Decorated fragment; long bone fragment; three incised ring-and-dot motifs; one end squared and smoothed. ON 3843, context 5135, pit 5043 (FG 3, phase 1/2)
20. Bone handle; proximal end of horse radius; deep transverse groove around shaft. ON 3813, context 4573, pit 4572 (FG 2, phase 3)
21. Antler tine; red deer; slight transverse groove at tip. ON 3841, context 4634, pit 4584 (FG 2, phase 3)
22. Miscellaneous antler fragment; roe deer beam fragment with protruding tine; sawn at wider end; some polishing. ON 3370, context 5671, pit 5670 (FG 4, phase 1/2)
23. Miscellaneous antler fragment; red deer; proximal end of beam with naturally shed burr; some tooling and transverse cut marks evident; polished surface. ON 3834, context 5192, pit 5191 (FG 3, phase 1/2)

Chapter 5
Human Remains

Jacqueline I. McKinley

Human bone was recovered from 29 contexts within 21 features. The bone from 15 contexts with a date range covering the Late Bronze Age to the early Middle Iron Age (phase 1/2) was all redeposited in either pit (seven; FG 3), ditch (six; FG 1), or post-hole (one; FG4) fills (Table 5.1; Figs 3.2 and 3.4–5). Seven contexts were dated to the later Middle Iron Age (phase 3) including the remains of three inhumation burials made in two pre-existing pits within FG 1, one of which (4332) also contained partially articulated remains. Disarticulated bone was also recovered from both pits and from one other pit in FG 4. The remains of three inhumation burials of Late Iron Age date were recovered from two pits in FG 1, together with redeposited disarticulated bone. Disarticulated bone was also recovered from two undated post-holes within FGs 1 and 4.

Methods

The minimum number count amongst the disarticulated fragmentary bone was based on the most frequently recovered skeletal element in association with the assessed age of the individuals represented (Table 5.1). Age was assessed from the stage of skeletal and tooth development (Beek 1983; McMinn and Hutchings 1985), the length of immature diaphyses (Bass 1987), and the patterns and degree of age-related changes to the bone (Brothwell 1972; Buikstra and Ubelaker 1994; Brooks and Suchey 1990; Iscan *et al.* 1985). Sex was ascertained from the sexually dimorphic traits of the skeleton (Buikstra and Ubelaker 1994). Stature was estimated in accordance with Trotter and Gleser (1952; 1958). Cranial index was calculated according with Brothwell (1972, 88). Platymeric (degree of anterior-posterior flattening of the proximal femur) and platycnemic (meso-lateral flattening of the tibia) indices were calculated according with Bass (1987). The degree of erosion to the bone was recorded using the writer's system of grading (McKinley 2004a, fig. 6). The nature and location of gnaw marks, abrasion from trampling and breaks or fissuring in the bone was also noted.

Results

Taphonomy

Articulated remains

Most of the burials had been made in pits which had not survived to any great depth. The adjacent FG 1 pits 4223 (phase 3) and 4272 (phase 4), each of which contained the remains of two contemporaneous burials, were only 0.2 m and 0.6 m deep respectively. The two other FG 1 burials, 4571 (phase 3, Fig. 3.13) and 4322 (phase 4, Fig. 3.16) were made in individual pits of 1.5 m and 0.5 m depth respectively. The shallow depth of most of the skeletal remains had rendered them vulnerable and there was heavy fragmentation to all except burial 4571, made at the base of the deepest pit. The skull vaults had suffered in particular, especially those in the shallowest pit 4223. The majority of the fragmentation is fresh.

With the exception of the occasionally heavy fragmentation, the bone from the inhumation burials is in good condition, as reflected in the generally high rates of skeletal recovery (Table 5.1). There is evidence for very slight root/fungal marking in some cases. The position of the skeletal remains at the time of excavation indicated that the backfills of the graves were not always packed around the bodies, allowing for some subsequent movement as, for example, with burials 4251, 4345, and 4346 where, in each case, the body had slumped back from a side-on position.

An articulated right foot with the distal ends of the leg bones (pit 4332, layer 4385; Pl. 3.6c) was recovered from the base of the phase 3 pit containing burial 4571. The bone is of fresh appearance, the proximal ends of the broken legs bones (4385) showing uneven angular breaks indicating the blunt fracturing of bone which whilst probably not fully dry – the ligaments had clearly still held the foot bones together – is unlikely to have been totally green at the time of disturbance.

Disarticulated remains

Disarticulated bones, or more commonly fragments of bones, were recovered from 25 – mostly phase 1/2 – contexts, predominantly pit fills (56%) and, less commonly, ditch (28%) and post-hole fills (16%). The only complete skeletal elements recovered were several small bones of the hand (4321) or foot (4345 and 4273) and some teeth (4273), all from phase 3–4

Table 5.1 Summary of human remains by phase and feature group

Phase	*Feature*	*FG*	*Context*	*Deposit type*	*Quantification*	*Age and sex*	*Pathology*	*Condition (roots/abrasion)*
1/2	4012	1	4016	pit fill	3 frags l.	adult >18 yr ??male		<1/<1; canid gnawing
1/2	4079	1	4292	ditch fill	1 frag. 1.	adult >18 yr		-/3; angular breaks
1/2	4080	1	5142	ditch fill	1 frag. l.	older subadult-adult >15 yr		<1/1; angular fractures prox., slightly gnawed distal
1/2	4090	1	4111	ditch fill (above 4112)	1frag. l.	adult >18 yr		-/<1; longitudinal splinter
1/2	4090	1	4112	ditch fill (below 4111)	1 frag. l.	adult >18 yr		<1/1; canid gnawing
1/2	4096	1	4124	ditch fill	1 frag. l.	adult >18 yr		-/1; slightly polished; prox. angular, distal canid gnawing
1/2	4105	1	4100	ditch fill	1 frag. s.	adult >18 yr. ?male		1/<1
1/2	4293	1	4249	ditch fill	1 frag. u.	adult >18 yr ??female		1 / 2-3; trampling; canid gnawing; blackish discoloration
1/2	4865	3	4863	pit fill	1 frag. l.	adult > 18 yr		1/<1
1/2	4937	3	4963	pit fill	1 frag. l.	adult > 18 yr		-/3
1/2	4993	3	4994	pit fill	1 frag. s.	juvenile-adult *c.* 9-25 yr		1/<1; canid gnawing
1/2	5004	3	5003	pit fill	1 frag. u.	subadult-adult > 13 yr		-/1; 'ivoried'; longitudinal fissuring
1/2	5043	3	5044	pit fill	2 frags S.	adult >45 yr.		-/3; trampled?
1/2	5216	3	5218	pit fill	1 frag. u.	subadult-adult > 13 yr		<1/<1; very slightly trampled; old angular breaks
1/2	5636	4	5585	posthole fill	2 frags S.	adult > 18 yr	depressions – endo- & exocranial parietal	-/3
3	4223	1	4251	burial in pit (above burial 4345)	*c.* 96%	adut *c.* 35-55 yr female	pd; calculus; abscesses; amtl; caries; hypoplasia; *cribra orbitalia*; oa – l.1st prox. IP (foot), r.1st MtT-P; pitting – l. temporo-mandibular, r. acromio-clavicular, l. sterno-clavicular, 10-11th costo-vertebral, 2 r. rib facets, 2L; op – r. scaphoid, r. & l. rib facets, r.1st distal IP (foot); ddd – 2L; exo – fibula, patella, calcaneum; eroded – palmar & planter surfaces distal finger & foot phalanges; mv – pegged maxillary I2, squatting facets	1/-; heavily fragmented (recent)
3	4223	1	4345	burial in pit (below burial 4251)	*c.* 98%	adult > 40 yr male	abscess; caries; pd; calculus; hypoplasia; calcified thyroid; *cribra orbitalia*; oa – C2-3, 11-12th costo-vertebral, l. 5th & r. 1st C-MtC joints; ?pyogenic arthritis – l. 5th prox. foot phalanx; op – shoulder, elbow, wrist & knee joints, l. & r. carpals, l. 4-5th C-MtC joint, prox. & distal IP joints (bi-lateral, hand & foot), l. knee, r. talus, C1-3, T1-5, T7, T10-12, 5L, S1; pitting – 1st l. MtC-P, r. talus, r. temporo-mandibular, r. acromio-clavicular; ddd – C5-6, T5, T11, 1L; exo – prox. femurs, r. fibula, patellae, prox. tibiae, calcanea, foot phalanges, foot sesamoids; pnb – proximal tibiae; ?trauma – remodelling ventral surface r. scapula acromion; mv – mandibular molars all 5 cusp, squatting facets	-/-; heavily fragmented (recent)
3	4223	1	4345 <2072>	pit fill (below burial 4345)	9 frags l.	adult > 18 yr		-/-

Table 5.1 (continued)

Phase	*Feature*	*FG*	*Context*	*Deposit type*	*Quantification*	*Age and sex*	*Pathology*	*Condition (roots/abrasion)*
3	4332	1	4571	burial in pit	*c.* 97%	juvenile *c.* 9-10yr ?male	calculus; hypoplasia; *cribra orbitalia*; infection (haematogenous osteomylitis) - r. maxillary c-P1 sockets, C5-6, epiphyseal surfaces humeri, femora, l. tibia and r. distal fibula, metaphyseal surfaces humeri; pitting – T12-L2 ap; destructive lesions – r. 1st metatarsal proximal epiphysis; mv – 3rd centres ossification 1st metacarpal/tarsal & prox. finger phalanges	-/-
3	4332	1	4385	pit fill (above burial 4571)	1 frag. u.	subadult-adult > 13 yr		-/<1
3	4332	1	4385 *obj. 3106*	redep. articulated pit fill (above 4571)	*c.* 5% l.	adult *c.* 18-40 yr ?male	destructive lesions – navicular, 1st prox. phalanx; mv – squatting facets	-/-
3	4332	1	4385 *obj. 3107*	pit fill (above burial 4571)	1 frag. s.	adult >25 yr ?female		<1/1
3	5358	4	5359	pit fill (above 5735)	1 frag. s.	subadult-adult *c.* 13 –25 yr		-/-; very slightly trampled
3	5358	4	5735	pit fill (above 5769, below 5359)	1 frag. u.	adult > 18 yr		<1/<1; slightly trampled; old angular breaks
3	5358	4	5769	pit fill (below 5735)	7 frags S.	adult > 18 yr	pitting – endocranial	-/<1
4	4272	1	4273	pit fill (= 4346, 4347)	4 frags s.l.	adult *c.*20-40 yr	hypoplasia; mv – shovelled I2	-/-
4	4272	1	4346	burial in pit (below 4347)	*c.* 75%	adult *c.* 30-45 yr female	caries; calculus; pd; hypoplasia; pseudo-facet – T1 spine; pitting – l. 1st rib, r. 1st rib, r. sterno-clavicular; Schmorl's – 2T; ddd – 2C, 2T; op – C1-2, 3T, l. rib, r. patella; destructive lesion – r. distal humerus, r. trapezium; exo – calcaneum; mv – maxillary r. I2 malformed, absence r. mandibular M3	-/-; Heavily fragmented (recent).
4	4272	1	4347	burial in pit (above 4346)	*c.* 75%	adult *c.* 30-40 yr ?male	caries; calculus; op – 3r. & 1 l. costo-vertebral, r. medial elbow, r. scaphoid, C1-2; new bone – l. trapezoid; pitting – l. 11th rib, r. acromio-clavicular, 1T ap; exo – proximal femur shaft, calcaneum; mv – retention maxillary deciduous canines & non-eruption permanent, mandibular l. & both maxillary M3 absent, squatting facets	

Table 5.1 (continued)

Phase	*Feature*	*FG*	*Context*	*Deposit type*	*Quantification*	*Age and sex*	*Pathology*	*Condition (roots/abrasion)*
4	4320	1	4322	burial in pit (additional r. scaphoid not from this skeleton)	*c.* 96%	adult >45 yr male	hypoplasia; mal-occlusion; calculus; calcified thyroid; trauma – r. lateral clavicle, r. distal ulna; oa – 11th costo-vertebral; op – r. 1st rib, r. prox. ulna, distal ulnae, r. scaphoid, acetabulae, C1-2, C6, T4-10, L4-S1; Schmorl's – L1; ddd – T9-10; pitting – r. rib, bi-lateral lesser tubercles humerus, l. sterno-clavicular, sacro-iliac; new bone – margins occipital condyles, anterior L5; erosion/rarefaction – hamate hooks; remodelling and erosion – l. middle foot phalanx, r. 2nd proximal & middle foot phalanx; exo – patella, calcaneum; *cribra orbitalia* (r.); mv – squatting facets	-/-; heavily fragmented (recent)
4	4320	1	4321	pit fill (below burial 4322, not linked)	1 frag. l.	adult > 18 yr ??female	pnb – femur shaft	<1/<1; ?trampled; canid gnawing
-	4199	1	4159; obj. 3861	posthole fill	3 frags S.	infant-juvenile *c.* 3-12 yr		<1/-
-	4199	1	4159; obj. 3831	posthole fill	27 frags S.	juvenile-adult c. 9-25 yr	mv - wormians	<1/1
-	5777	4	5886	posthole fill	1 frag. u.	neonate 0-3 months		-/3; dark patch staining

Key: s. = skull; a. = axial skeleton; u. = upper limb; l, = lower limb; mv = morphological variation; pd = periodontal disease; amtl = *ante mortem* tooth loss; os = osteoarthritis; op = osteophytes; exo = exostoses; ddd = degenerative disc disease; pnb = periosteal new bone; C = cervical; T= thoracic; L = lumbar; S = sacral; ap = articular process; C/T-MtC/T = carpal/tarsal-metacarpal/tarsal; IP = interphalangeal

contexts. The majority of the material (84%) represents only fragments of skeletal elements – sometimes further fragmented after final deposition – the broken surfaces all representing old fractures.

The fragments mostly comprise elements of long bone (44.4%) and skull vault (29%). Of the former, femur shaft predominate (25%). Not all fragments could be sided, but 60% of the assemblage comprises bone from the right (including 21% right femur and 12% right humerus) compared with only 21% from the left side. Trabecular bone (eg, vertebrae, pelvic bones, articular surfaces) is almost entirely absent with the exception of the few phase 3–4 hand and foot bones mentioned above. The predominance of skull and long bone fragments amongst disarticulated remains from Early Iron Age settlements and hillforts has been well documented (Whimster 1981, 183; Wilson 1981; Walker 1984; Wait 1985), together with the high percentage of long bones from the right side.

Canid gnawing, evident from the crenulated, worn ends of bone fragments and extant puncture marks (Pls 5.1–2), was observed in 28% of the disarticulated bone assemblage, all except one example deriving from phase 1/2 contexts. The skeletal elements in which gnawing was observed are predominantly the larger long bones (femur, tibia, and humerus), though one fragment of parietal vault also has clear puncture marks in the exocranial surface (4994; Pl. 5.1). Indirect evidence for canid gnawing may be indicated by both the skeletal elements recovered and the age of the individuals from which they derived. It has been observed that the assemblage includes very little trabecular bone and such elements are those most likely to have been removed as a result of total consumption by scavengers (Binford 1981, 171–3). The distinctive patterns in surviving long bone parts following canid gnawing includes the progressive removal of one or both ends of the long bone, the 'cylinder' – a segment of the central part of the long bone shaft – often comprising one of the last surviving parts (*ibid.* and figs 4.56–7). This classic pattern of degradation is illustrated within *c.* 56% of the disarticulated material from the site. The remains of immature individuals would be subject to preferential destruction and loss by exposure to the actions of scavengers, and young immature corpses could have been physically removed from the original site of deposition by the scavenger prior to

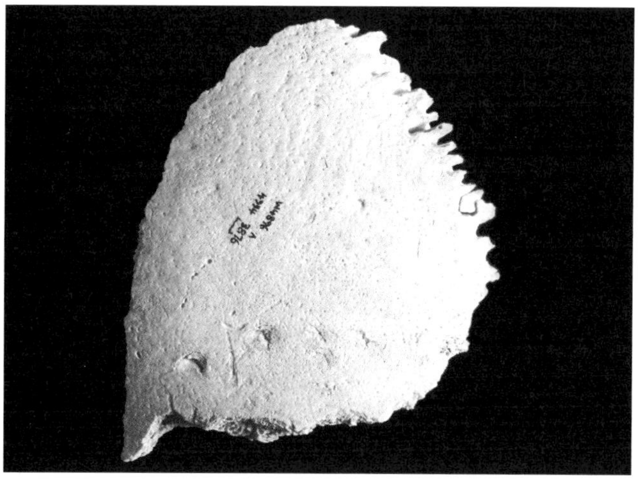

Plate 5.1 Fragment of parietal vault (context 4994) showing puncture marks from canid gnawing in the exo-cranial surface

consumption – wild animals tending to remove their food out of the open to a 'safe place' (Legge, pers. comm.). Whilst caution must be applied with such a small assemblage, the relative dearth of immature remains (see below) may be reflective of such a process. It has also been demonstrated that bone subject to scavenger activity does not always show signs of having been 'cleaned' by animals (Kent 1981). Whatever the precise mechanisms, it is probable that the effects of scavenger activity on the assemblage will have been greater than is evident from the surviving remains.

Similar observations on the affects of scavengers have been made in the disarticulated bone assemblages from various Iron Age sites. At Danebury, for example, canid gnawing was evident in *c.* 6% of the disarticulated bone assemblage (Walker 1984), and a substantial proportion of the long bones recovered were represented by the shafts alone (*ibid.*, fig. 8.5), trabecular bone was also observed to be poorly represented amongst the remains.

There is little evidence for root/fungal marking to the bone, that which was affected (40% of disarticulated bone) being only slightly so. Other abrasion/erosion was also relatively slight, a small proportion (20%) of the material having a fresh appearance, with slight surface 'weathering' to most bone (56%; score up to 1) and moderate weathering ito 24% (score 2–3). All the gnawed bone is at least slightly weathered and that from two contexts have the small, parallel, linear abrasions resulting from trampling. Evidence for trampling was noted in 25% of the bone from the disarticulated assemblage; the effects were generally relatively slight, suggesting limited exposure to this mechanism of abrasion. A single phase 1/2 bone fragment (5003) has a polished

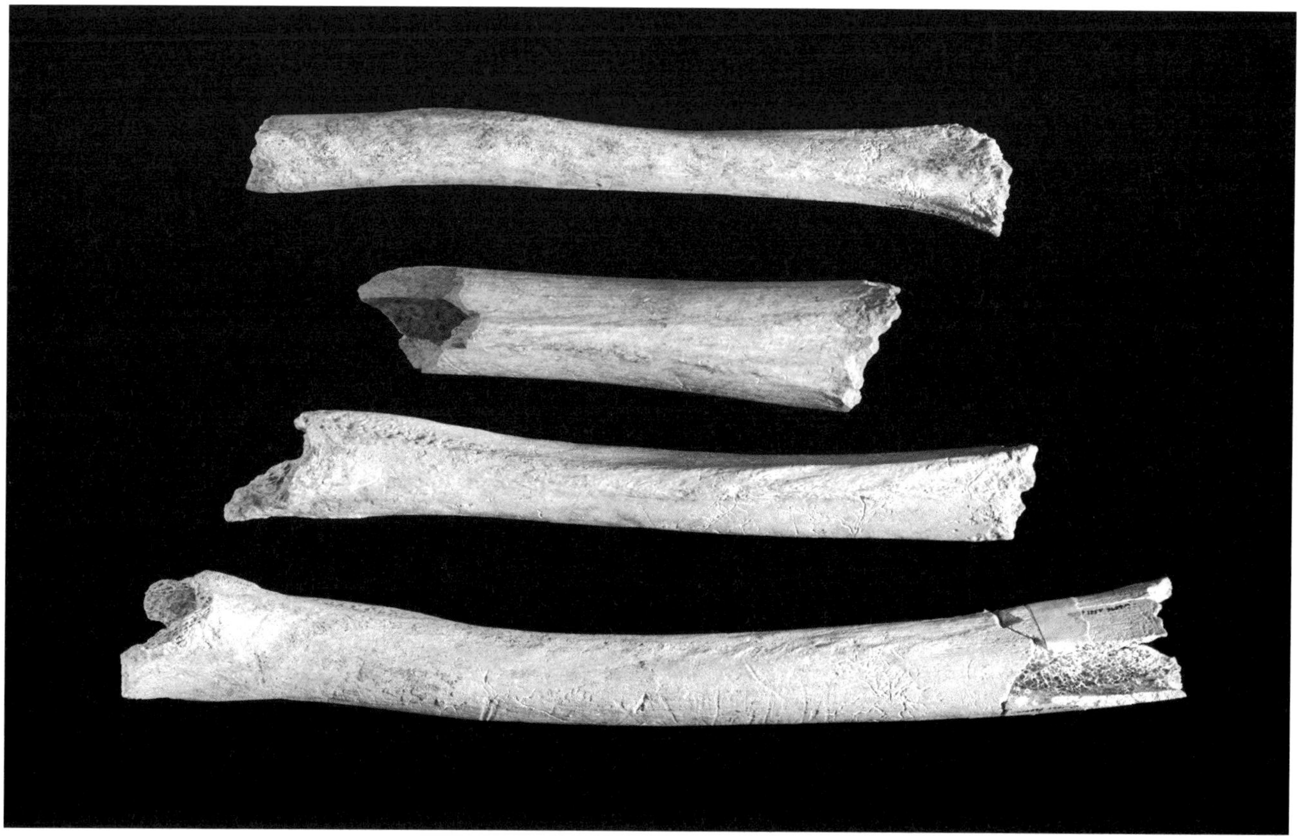

Plate 5.2 Worn, crenulated ends of human long bone shafts (tubes) indicative of canid gnawing

or 'ivoried' appearance, with fine longitudinal fissures; the mechanisms resulting in this appearance are not fully understood but must in some way relate to variations within the burial micro-environment. A patchy dark staining noted on the cortex of bone from two deposits (phase 1/2 and unphased) may represent charcoal or fungal staining.

The bone fragments in which evidence for breakage as opposed to gnawing remain show old, sharp, angular fractures, suggestive of breakage whilst still relatively 'green' rather than totally 'dry'. At least one femur shaft fragment (4111; phase 1/2) had longitudinal splintering of similar appearance to that produced by deliberate impact fracturing for marrow extraction (Binford 1981, 149–63), however, no impact scars (*ibid.*, fig. 4.53) were observed on any of the broken bone fragments. The apparent deliberate fragmentation of relatively green bone has also be observed in material from elsewhere in the Early Iron Age, for example, Salisbury and Figsbury, both in Wiltshire (Whimster 1981) and Danebury (Walker 1984).

A higher percentage of the material from the ditches (57%; all phase 1/2) compared with that from the pits (28%; all phases) show evidence for gnawing, and a slightly higher percentage (28% compared with 14%) was moderately weathered. Conversely, *c.* 43% of the bone from pits show evidence for trampling, compared with only 15% of that from the ditch fills. Approximately 40% of the phase 1/2 material shows signs of gnawing compared with *c.* 8.3% of the disarticulated bone from the other two phases. It is possible, given that the one fragment represented by the latter derived from a pit within FG 1 where much of the early material was recovered, that this fragment of disarticulated bone may have been residual within a later deposit.

The potential significance which may be attributed to these observations carries the caveat of the small size of the assemblage. All the bone conditions observed in the disarticulated human bone are seen to some extent amongst the animal remains, including gnawing to bone from the same contexts. The latter is considerably more extensive within the animal bone assemblage, which as a whole also appears to be more consistently and slightly more heavily weathered, particularly the material from the ditches. This suggests that although there are clearly similarities in some of the biostratinomic processes (those acting between death and final deposition) affecting the two bone assemblages, there are some differences in the factors affecting those processes. In general, the human bone does not have the appearance of material which has been subject to extensive exposure or repeated manipulation prior to its final deposition. The majority of the assemblage has some of the characteristics of material which has been exposed to canid gnawing, but probably not for an extensive period of time and not subsequently subject to repeated manipulation.

Demographic Data

An overall minimum of 13 individuals was identified, six from the inhumation burials and a minimum of seven from amongst the disarticulated material. The three phase 3 burials include the remains of one juvenile and two adults (one male, one female), and the three from phase 4 those of one female and two male adults (Table 5.1). The disarticulated assemblage, viewed as a single entity, includes the remains of a neonate, one infant–juvenile, one juvenile–young adult, and four adults, two of the latter being >45 yr and including at least one male and one female.

The minimum number (MNI) from the disarticulated material was calculated using the methods outlined above, the most frequently occurring element being the right femur shaft. This MNI assumes that disarticulated fragments from any one individual could have been redeposited in features across the entire *c.* 450 m length of the excavated area and views the remains as a single temporal entity. This may have been the case, particularly if the material was subject to deliberate human manipulation or 'curation'. Where, however, the deposits split spatially into their feature groups (FG) – each covering a 75–150 m length of trench – the numbers would show relatively little difference; a minimum of six from FG 1 (one infant–juvenile, one juvenile–young adult, and four adults including one male and one female), a minimum of one adult from FG 3, and a minimum of two individuals from FG 4 (a neonate and an adult). Similarly, if it were assumed – though it could not be proven without radiocarbon dating of the individual deposits, a technique undertaken only on the articulated foot from the phase 3 pit 4332 (ON 3107) – that the redeposited bone from all the phase 3 and 4 features was contemporaneous with those features and not residual, but that the material could have been widely distributed spatially, there is also little significant difference in the MNI overall. On this basis the MNI from phase 1/2 would be three adults, with one adult each from phases 3 and 4, the remaining three immature individuals being from undated features.

These figures, however calculated, are unlikely to be truly representative of the population within the vicinity over such an extensive time span. Through covering an extensive north–south area the excavation was relatively narrow (10–30 m wide) east–west and further features containing articulated or redeposited human remains comprising part of the same assemblage may exist outside the area. Evidence from various sources indicates the presence of several inhumation burials outside the northern entrance to the hillfort, not far from the recent excavations (Fig. 2.1, see Chapter 2). The remains of several burials have been recovered from stone quarries outside the ramparts (Colt Hoare 1812; Cunnington 1924; *VCH* 1957, I, 118), the 'black earth' fill around the burials suggesting similar deposits to those from the recent excavations (ie midden-type material). The remains of a dual burial were also recovered from an earlier barrow partly overlain by the fort rampart (Colt Hoare 1812; Guido 1977–8). Taphonomic processes (see above) and cultural features (see discussion) may have removed some skeletal evidence from the recent assemblage, thereby skewing the appearance of the 'cemetery population', particularly against the recovery of immature individuals.

Evidence from elsewhere (Whimster 1981, 14–15 and 198–225; Cunliffe 1991, table 8.4) show that individuals of both sexes and across the age ranges may be represented within Iron Age pit burials, indicting that neither age nor sex were necessarily qualifying factors for this mode of disposal, though a higher percentage of the adults from Danebury were male (68.5%; Walker 1984). Demographic data pertaining to disarticulated human remains from Iron Age sites is less readily gleaned. Few of the sites listed by Whimster (1981, 198–225) mention the recovery of disarticulated human bone from pits either as isolated deposits (eg, Worlebury, Avon and Stapleford, Cambridge) or in association with articulated remains (eg, Boscombe Down, Wiltshire), and there is little or no detail pertaining to the remains themselves (NB. many of the references are to old excavations where such material may have been overlooked or not recognised). The incomplete skeletons and charnel pits at Danebury (Cunliffe 1991, 421–5) included the remains of both adults and immature individuals, males and females. The deposits comprising skulls and skull fragments were all adult, including both sexes (*ibid.*). The demographic make-up of the isolated human bone fragments is not presented or discussed in any detail though it was noted that both sexes and all age ranges were represented amongst the minimum of 13 individuals identified from the 1969–1978 Danebury excavations (Walker 1984).

Skeletal Indices

Only one skull (4345, phase 3 male) survives sufficiently intact to allow calculation of cranial index, falling into the dolichocrany range at 73.6. It was possible to estimate the stature of four individuals, one female (phase 3) and three males (one phase 3 and two phase 4; Table 5.2). The female is very close to the mean of 1.53 m observed in the Danebury females (Hooper 1991, table 8.7), both being at the lower end of the range of 1.54–1.64 m given for the Iron Age by Roberts and Cox (2003, 103). The males – unsurprisingly with such a small number – have a smaller range but a slightly higher mean than recorded at Danebury (1.66 m), the maximum here falling *c.* 30 mm short of that at Danebury. Both are within the range of 1.64–1.74 m given for the period by Roberts and Cox (*ibid.*). The male mean from the Danebury Environs Project was lower still at 1.64 m (Hooper 2000), the Battlesbury Bowl figure being closest to the average of 1.67 m given for Iron Age males by Manchester (1983) and that of 1.68 m given by Roberts and Cox (2003, 103).

Table 5.2 Range and mean stature estimations

	Range	*Mean*
Female	1.54 (5ft ½ in)	
Male	1.66–1.76 m (5ft 5¼ in–5 ft 9¼ in)	1.70 m (5 ft 7 in)

Platymeric and platycnemic indices were calculated from seven adult femora (one phase 1, two phase 3 and four phase 4) and three tibiae respectively (Table 5.3). All except one set of femora (4251, phase 3 female, eurymeric) fall within the platymeric range, indicating relative homogeneity within the diverse temporal group. The platycnemic index shows greater variability, with one in the eurycnemic (phase 4), and one each in the mesocnemic and platycnemic ranges (both phase 3). There is no link between squatting facets and platycnemia such as has been indicated elsewhere (Brothwell 1972; Molleson 1993); squatting facets were observed in all (10) surviving distal tibiae.

Pathological Lesions

Pathological lesions were observed in all the skeletons recovered from the burials and in redeposited bone from four contexts. Given the small number of

Table 5.3 Platymeric and platycnemic indices, ranges and means

	Range	*Mean*	*Standard deviation*
Platymeric index			
Overall	76.7–91.3	81.8	4.6
Female	76.7–91.3	81.7	6.7
Male	79.8–84.1	81.6	1.8
Platycnemic index			
Overall	59.2–70.5	65.8	4.8
Female	67.6		
Male	59.2–70.5	64.8	5.6

individuals within each temporal group the pathological lesions noted will be presented and discussed for the assemblage as a single entity; a summary of the lesions is presented by context in Table 5.1.

Dental disease

Dental calculus (calcified plaque/tartar) harbours bacteria which predispose to periodontal disease and the development of dental caries. Slight–medium (Brothwell 1972, fig. 58b) calculus deposits were noted in all dentitions, the heaviest deposits being apparent in the juvenile 1571, suggesting a limited age-related link for the condition. Mild–moderate (Brothwell 1972, fig. 58a) periodontal disease (a gum infection which may lead to bone resorption with consequent loosening of teeth and exposure of more of the tooth surface to caries attack) was observed in three adult dentitions; there is no clear link with the severity of calculus deposits or the age of the individual.

The overall rate of *ante mortem* tooth loss (erupted permanent dentitions) is 0.7% (1:138), with a single mandibular incisor having been lost from a female dentition (rate 2.3% for females) in association with a dental abscess, itself probably related to exposure of the pulp cavity in the adjacent tooth. Although the small numbers involved (six dentitions) may not provide a realistic reflection of the populations being served by the 'cemetery', the rate is considerably lower than that of 6.2% recorded from Danebury (Hooper 1991, 1442 surviving teeth), or the 4.2% for the Danebury Environs sites (Hooper 2000), and is slightly lower than the Iron Age average of 3.2% given by Roberts and Cox (2003, table 2.51).

The overall caries rate is 6%, being higher amongst the females (10%) than the males (3.3%) but, as various studies have shown the disease to affect the former to a greater degree than the latter (Hillson 1990, 287), the slightly higher prevalence amongst the females is not unexpected. All the lesions are in the molar teeth (maxillary and mandibular), where they are generally most common (*ibid.*, 294). The lesions are all cervical in origin, ranging in severity from 'pin-hole' lesions with discoloured enamel to complete destruction of the tooth crown and separation of the root branches. A similar overall caries rate (5.6%) was observed at Danebury (Hooper 1991), both being lower than the 8.2% for the Danebury Environs sites (Hooper 2000) or the *c.* 10% recorded for the British Iron Age by Brothwell (1963); though Roberts and Cox give a much lower average rate of 2.9% for the period (2003, table 2.46).

Dental abscesses were observed in two dentitions, with an overall rate of 5%; 6.8% for females and 4.2% for males. Two of the abscesses in one dentition were associated with carious lesions in the tooth crowns (maxillary molars). The rates are slightly higher than those (2.9%) recorded at Danebury (Hooper 1991) and the average of 1.1% given by Roberts and Cox, though there is considerable variation between the individual sites within their sample (2003, table 2.50).

Dental hypoplasia is a developmental defect in the tooth enamel formed in response to growth arrest in the immature individual, the predominant causes of which are believed to include periods of illness or nutritional stress (Hillson 1979). Slight defects, manifest as 1–3 faint lines, mostly in the anterior crowns, were recorded in five of the six dentitions.

The levels of occlusal dental attrition are very light, with only slight polishing or slight–mild exposure of dentine in the individual cusps of molars and only occasional amalgamation in the first molars of individuals where other ageing criteria indicates them to be >35 yr. Wear to the anterior teeth is often relatively heavy, with exposure of the dentine in all dentitions. The anterior teeth in burial 4322 (male >45 yr) are particularly heavily worn, the angle of wear indicating a pronounced over-bite.

The low level of dental attrition amongst the adults is not consistent with a diet of coarse, fibrous foodstuffs or one accidentally adulterated with gritty material during food processing. The presence of calculus deposits suggests the inclusion of some carbohydrates in the diet but the relatively low rate of dental caries implies a diet rich in meat proteins (Hillson 1990). Dental hygiene may also have been a factor in low calculus and caries rates, as may a natural predisposition to be more resistant to caries decay (*ibid.*, 287). The slightly higher rates of caries amongst the females may reflect their natural tendency to suffer more from this condition (see above), or reflect a slight variation in diet between males and females, the former consuming more meat protein and less carbohydrate than the latter.

Metabolic disorders

Cribra orbitalia is generally believed to result from a metabolic disorder connected with childhood iron deficiency anaemia, although Molleson (1993) argues that vitamin C deficiency and intestinal parasites – leading to iron loss – may also have played a contributory role. Porotic lesions (Robledo *et al.* 1995) were noted the orbits of three males (including the juvenile) and slight cribotic lesions in those of a female, with overall rates of 58%, slightly higher at 62.5% in males than in females (50%). The overall rate is higher than that of 49.3% observed from the Danebury Environs assemblages (Hooper 2000) and the 37.5% for the Iron Age presented by Roberts and Cox (2003, table 2.52).

Trauma

Direct evidence for trauma is indicated in the remains of two individuals, both adult males. Burial 4322

(Late Iron Age) shows slight anterior angulation of the distal end of the right ulna with remodelling of the interosseous border (radiographs showed no sign of a fracture) suggesting damage to the pronator quadratus muscle. There is also slight periosteal new bone on the anterior border of the shaft indicative of soft tissue infection. No associated lesions were observed in the radius, but there is considerable new bone growth around the margins of the lateral end of the right clavicle suggestive of damage to the acromio-clavicle capsule, possibly resulting from a sub-luxation of the joint (the scapula acromion is missing so corresponding lesions could not be investigated). This type of trauma may have resulted from a fall on the shoulder and/or hand thereby straining the acromio-clavicular joint and wrist.

The only other evidence for acute trauma is in the right scapula from 4345 (later Middle Iron Age) where there is extensive broadening of the right superior ventral acromion surface with a 28 x 24 mm area of eburnation and pitting in the superior surface and osteophytes on the superior medial and lateral margins of the area (Pl. 5.3). Slight rarefaction of bone at the lateral end of the right clavicle and extensive remodelling of the right humerus greater tubercle suggests traumatic damage to the rotator cuff joint resulting in an abnormal juxtaposition between the acromion and humerus.

Two joining fragments of parietal vault (5585, phase 1/2) from amongst the disarticulated bone assemblage, have a shallow (*c.* 2.3 mm), roughly concave depression *c.* 9 mm diameter in the exocranial surface. A matching depression of similar depth and diameter may be seen in the endocranial surface. There is no exposure of the diploe, the cortical bone being continuous on both surfaces. The lesion is most likely to represent a healed depressed fracture.

Infection

Infection of the periosteal membrane covering bone may lead to the formation of periosteal new bone. Infection may be introduced directly to the bone as a result of trauma, develop in response to some adjacent soft tissue infection, or spread via the blood stream from foci elsewhere in the body. Three individuals have lesions in one or pairs of bones: two males and one female. Only in one case (4322, see above) was it possible to isolate the probable cause of the lesion.

There are numerous lesions indicative of extensive infection from across much of the skeleton of the

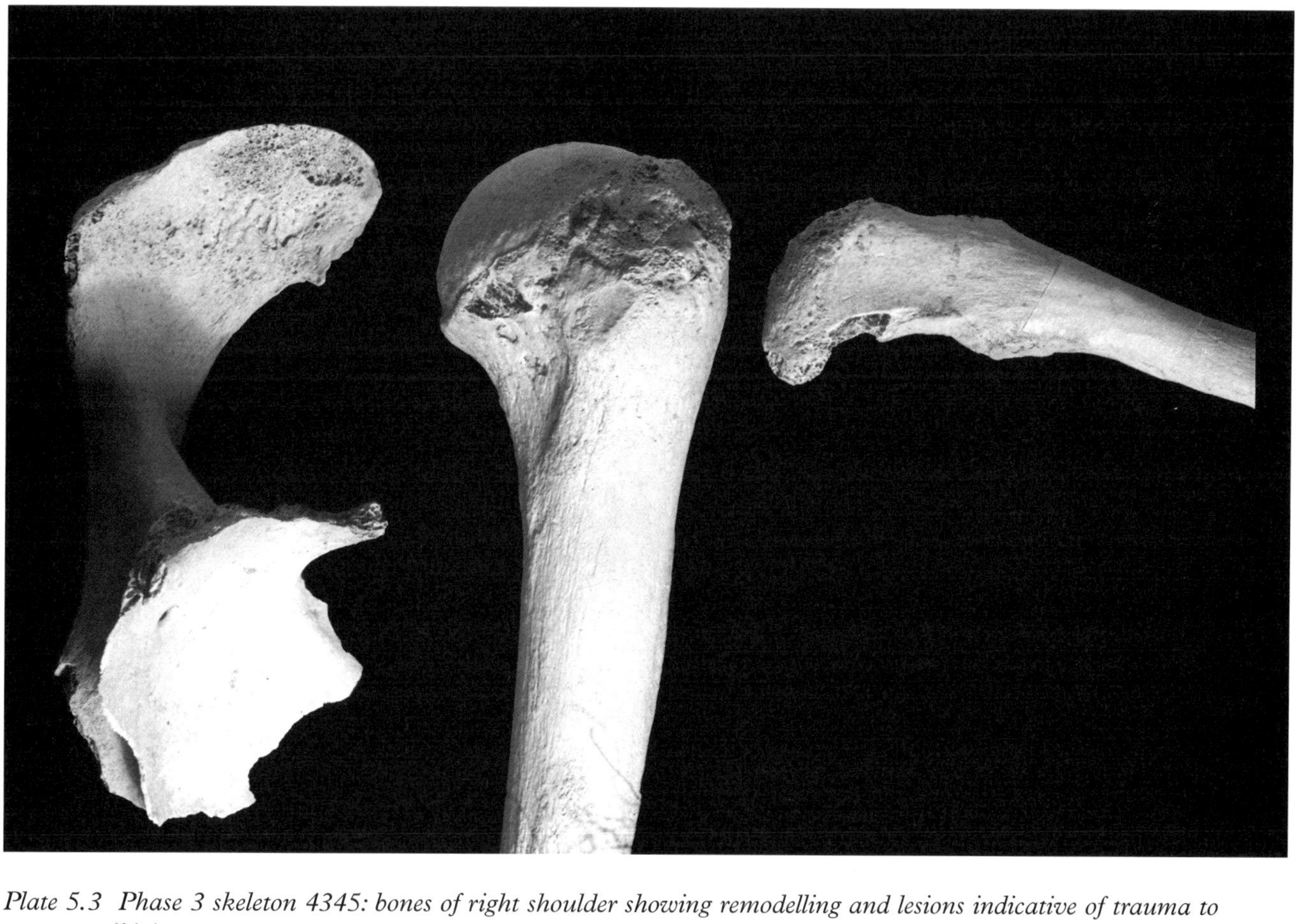

Plate 5.3 Phase 3 skeleton 4345: bones of right shoulder showing remodelling and lesions indicative of trauma to rotator cuff joint

older juvenile 4571. Grainy endosteal new bone was observed along the sagittal and transverse sinus grooves of the occipital vault with patches along the sagittal sinus groove of the right parietal and in the dorsal portion of the right petrous portion at the groove for sigmoid sinus. Erosive lesions were observed in the dorsal margins of the C5 inferior and C6 superior body surfaces. Fine grained surface new bone was seen in both proximal and distal epiphyseal surfaces of the humeri, with pitting and granular new bone in both distal medial metaphyseal surfaces. Similarly, there is fine grained surface new bone over epiphyseal surfaces of both femoral heads and distal epiphyses, the right fibula distal epiphysis and the left tibia epiphyses, with no changes in the metaphyseal surfaces. Although the involvement of the epiphyses is not characteristic of the condition, the lesions in the metaphyses and the vertebrae are indicative of acute haematogenous osteomylitis. This is predominantly a childhood disease, particularly seen in boys (Adams 1986), and was clearly active at the time of death. The affected joints would have been inflamed and painful. The endosteal lesions may have resulted from the spread of infection into the meningeal membranes. The combined conditions are likely to have caused the death of the individual.

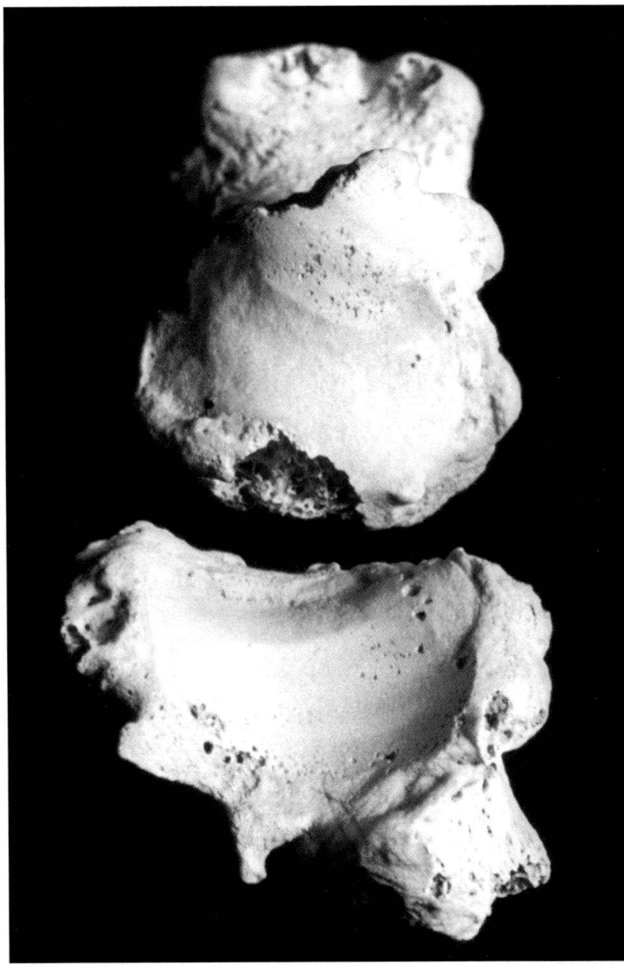

Plate 5.4 Phase 3 skeleton 4345: extensive eburnation (polishing) and remodelling in right 1st carpo-metacarpal joint indicative of osteoarthritis

Joint disease

Osteoarthritis is manifest by eburnation of the joint surface and/or pitting in association with osteophytes on joint surface margins; the aetiology is complicated including the effects of age, mechanical alteration through activity or injury, and genetic predisposition (Rogers *et al.* 1987; Rogers and Waldron 1995). Lesions were recorded in the remains of three adults, one female and two males, and the number of sites involved varied from one to six. Spinal lesions were noted in only one male skeleton (two cervical vertebrae), with an overall prevalence of 1.9%, or 3% for the males. Extra-spinal manifestations of the condition were noted in the remains of all three individuals, two having costo-vertebral lesions (both males; 8% costo-vertebral joints, 21% of male), one carpo-metacarpal lesions (male; 5.3% C-MtC joints, 8% of male), and one with metatarso-phalangeal (female; 2.3% all MtT-P joints, 6.2% of female) and foot proximal inter-phalangeal lesions (female; 2.3% all proximal IP joints, 7.7% of female). The severity of the lesions varied, the most severe lesions being seen in the right 1st carpo-metacarpal joint from 4345 (Pl. 5.4).

Degenerative disc disease – a condition resulting from the breakdown of the intervertebral disc largely related to age and reflecting 'wear-and-tear' (Rogers and Waldron 1995) – was noted in 15% of adult vertebrae (all areas), with a slightly higher rate (16.4%) amongst the males (two individuals) than the females (12.5%, two individuals). Lesions were observed in all areas of the spine but predominantly in the lower thoracic and lumbar. Schmorl's nodes (destructive lesions resulting from a rupture in the intervertebral disc) were observed in two spines, with an overall rate of 2.8%; 1.5% for males and 5% for females. Lesions are confined to the lower thoracic and lumbar regions.

Osteophytes (irregular growths of new bone along joint margins), pitting, and other destructive lesions may develop in response to a number of conditions and it is not always possible to ascertain the specific cause of individual lesions (Rogers and Waldron 1995). The vast majority of these lesions were seen in joint surfaces and are most likely to represent the early stages of some form of joint disease. Lone osteophytes, for example, were observed in 43% of the male spines and 20% of the female, with a similar sexual discrepancy in the extra-spinal joints of 18% for the males and 2.7% for the females, with an overall rate of 12.7%. There is some discrepancy amongst the males in the location of the affected joints, those of the upper limb showing a much higher rate (25%) than for the lower limb (12%). As with the aforementioned lesions it is not always possible to be conclusive with respect to the aetiology of exostoses (bony growths which may develop at tendon and ligament insertions on the bone). Causative factors include advancing age, traumatic stress, or various diseases.

The head of the left 5th proximal foot phalanx from 4345 has been totally remodelled with extensive smooth, but disorganised new bone extending mostly distally but also lateral and medially. A new, poorly defined pseudo-facet has been formed for articulation with the unchanged middle phalanx. Radiography shows partial destruction of the original articular surface. The lesions are indicative of a healed infection, possibly pyogenic arthritis. A similar condition may have affected the distal articular surfaces of several of the middle foot phalanges from 4322, which have been remodelled to give flat surfaces angled planter-wise by *c.* 45°, with erosive lesions within the surface but little remodelling.

The rates of joint disease at Danebury are not given, though it is stated that 75.4% of the adults had some lesions indicative of osteoarthritis (Hooper 1991) and that the populations within the Danebury Environs assemblages (Hooper 2000) were 'not badly affected' by osteophytes. Comparison with some Bronze Age, Romano-British, and post-Roman populations (Table 5.4) show the Battlesbury Bowl assemblage to have consistently relatively low prevalence rates for osteoarthritis and Schmorl's nodes, but occasionally higher rates of degenerative disc disease.

Whilst there are limits to what conclusions may be drawn from the above observations imposed by the small size of the burial group, there are undoubted suggestions that these individuals did not have to endure a marked physically strenuous lifestyle. Whilst clearly not sedentary – the male skeletons are generally large and robust, and both male and females skeletons have relatively strong muscle attachments – they do not have the appearance of individuals who have undertaken a lifetime of grinding physical labour involving much strenuous bending and lifting of heavy loads. The higher rates of joint disease and osteophytes in the upper limbs of the males in particular may be indicative of some specialised activity, many of the muscle attachments in these limb bones were also quite pronounced.

Table 5.4 Comparative indices joint lesions

Site	*Spinal osteoarthritis*	*Degenerative disc disease*	*Schmorl's nodes*
Early–Middle Bronze Age Twyford Down, Hampshire (McKinley 2000b)	10%: 18% f 16% m	5%: 11% f 5% m	8%: 10% f 20% m
Mid–late Romano-British Boscombe Down, Wiltshire (McKinley 1996)	18%: 15% f 26% m	28%: 26% f 39% m	12%: 11% f 17% m
Romano-British Cirencester, Gloucestershire (Wells 1982)	6.8%: 6.9% f 6.8% m		7.1%: 5.6% f 7.7% m
5th–6th century Tolpuddle, Dorset (McKinley 1999)	3%: 2% f 6% m	4%: 8% f 13% m	6%: 6% f 11% m

Morphological Variations

Variations in skeletal morphology may, with other predisposing factors, indicate genetic relationships within a 'population', there are, however, problems with the uncertain heritability of traits (Berry and Berry 1967; Tyrrell pers. comm.). Some traits have been attributed to developmental abnormalities, for instance, extra sutural ossicles or wormian bones (Brothwell 1972, 95–8) and 'squatting' facets' (Brothwell 1972, 92; Molleson 1993, 156; see above).

Wormian bones were not present in any of the three well-represented skulls, the only wormian bone recovered being from amongst the disarticulated remains. Whilst this may simply be fortuitous given the small numbers involved, it does not add support to the variation being very common in Iron Age populations, with 47% from the Danebury Environs assemblages (Hooper 2000) and >70% in general for the period (Brothwell 1972). Tooth crown variations and congenital absence of teeth were the most frequently observed anomalies, one of six dentitions having all 5-cusp mandibular molars and another pegging of the maxillary 2nd incisor. There was a 3.6% congenital absence of the 3rd molars, predominantly from the male dentitions and of the mandibular molar.

Discussion

The majority of the human bone assemblage (all phases) was recovered from pit fills within FG 1, 3, and 4, in association with midden material. There are, however, temporal differences in the form and nature, and, to an extant, in the distribution, of the material.

The Late Bronze Age–early Middle Iron Age (phase 1/2) material all comprises disarticulated bone fragments (representing the remains of a minimum of three individuals) with common evidence for canid gnawing and some weathering. The form and nature of the material is indicative of some level of exposure linked to deliberate human manipulation involving excarnation and possible 'curation'. Much of this material was recovered from midden pits in FG 3 with most of the rest being excavated from ditch segments in FG 1 (Figs 3.2 and 3.4) – the only part of the assemblage to have derived from ditch fills.

The later Middle Iron Age (phase 3) and Late Iron Age (phase 4) material, with the exception of a fragment of bone from a phase 3 pit in FG 4, was all recovered from pit clusters in FG1 (Figs 3.2 and 3.5). The articulated *in situ* remains of burials made in pits were recovered from both phases, each including one pit containing the remains of two individuals (Figs 3.12–3, 3.16). The phase 3 pit containing the single burial (4332) also included an articulated, re-deposited right foot and lower leg (ON 3106; Pl. 3.6) in the fill immediately above the *in situ* remains. All of the pits also contained some disarticulated bone, some of which was similar in form and nature – fragments of certain skeletal elements and at least one with direct evidence of canid gnawing – to the redeposited material from phase 1/2 but, unlike the earlier assemblage, there were also some complete small trabecular bones. None of the disarticulated bone was subject to radiocarbon dating, the attributed phase being that of the feature from which it was recovered. It is probable that some of this bone will be residual from phase 1/2, particularly given the similarity in character between parts of the disarticulated bone assemblage from the various phases.

The practice of making burials in pits, as opposed to specifically cut graves, is a commonly recorded Iron Age rite (Whimster 1981). Formal burial in graves also occurred and, although currently relatively few are recorded, the numbers are likely to increase with more extensive use of radiocarbon dating; there is growing evidence to demonstrate that unaccompanied burials with phasing assigned on the basis of the burial position have been wrongly designated (Haselgrove *et al.* 2001). Although there is some evidence suggestive of 'unceremonious' deposition (Cunliffe 1992), many of the pit burials – including those at this site – were carefully made, formal deposits.

Double burials in the same pit have been recorded from several sites with the inevitable speculation for human sacrifice where females and males are buried together (Whimster 1981, 181–2); the assumption that individuals were buried simultaneously being used in support. Whilst the theory may be a valid one, there are other equally plausible possibilities. The majority of people in the past died of some kind of infection which, if contagious, would be most likely to be caught by those closest to the infected individual who tended them in sickness, laying both open to a similar and closely timed fate. A second consideration is how closely timed such 'dual' burials were. Evidence from the skeletal positions of the burials at Battlesbury suggests that, at least in some cases (including at least three of the four skeletons from the two dual burials), soil was not deposited around the body immediately after burial. The use of some form of organic cover placed over the body/pit would have enabled subsequent deposits to be made. In pit 4272 the burials appear to have been contemporary, the bone from one individual (adult male) immediately overlaying the other (adult female). In pit 4223 (Fig. 3.12) at least one layer lay between the two burial deposits and they were clearly not made at the same time. Similar observations were made in the two graves (not pit burials) containing double burials at Cocky Down, Salisbury, Wiltshire (Lovell 1999). The deposition of two individuals together in one grave/pit implies some form of close connection in life; whilst it is not possible to prove that which may exist between a couple or close comrades, DNA technology could now enable some possible family connections to be analysed, which may help spread further light on the intimacies of social structure in past societies.

Articulated bones, representative of redeposited, partial skeletons (such as the articulated foot from pit 4332) have been reported from several Iron Age sites. A 'burial' from Stanton Harcourt, Oxforshire was recorded as having been 'dismembered'; only the foot bones remaining articulated and placed over other disarticulated elements (Williams 1951, 14; Whimster 1981, 178). Dismemberment would require deliberate human action – chopping bones or cutting the articulations at joints – which would generally leave marks on the bones themselves. The term 'dismemberment' appears to have been used somewhat loosely in some cases: Whimster (1981, 179 and 212–13) refers to several deposits from Danebury comprising partly articulated remains and individual skeletal elements which are referred to as having been 'dismembered', yet there is no mention of cut marks to bone here or in the subsequent Danebury volumes (Hooper 1984; 1991; 2000; Walker 1984; Cunliffe 1991). Walker (1984) refers to an act of 'butchery' inflicted on bone from one context (47) but later states (*ibid.*, 455) that there is no evidence for the human remains having been treated in same way as animal bones subject to butchery in food preparation. The osteologist (Hooper 1984) described the lesions as having been probably inflicted with a 'sword', the 'butchery' perhaps describing a violent attack rather than one undertaken for the purpose of ritual dismemberment. Similarly, the description of remains from Breedon-on-the-Hill, Gloucestershire as 'disarticulated or dismembered' suggests there was no actual evidence for the latter (Whimster 1981, 180 and 251). More secure evidence for deliberate disarticulation is provided by clear knife cuts reported on a distal humerus from Croft Amberly, Herefordshire (*ibid.*, 183), but such evidence appears genuinely rare (Wait (1985).

There is more substantive evidence from both the articulated partial skeletal material and disarticulated fragments for bone having been broken whilst [relatively] 'fresh' (Walker 1984, 455). At Salmonsbury, Gloucestershire (Whimster 1981, 183–4; Walker 1984, 455) the excavator concluded that such breakage had been undertaken to facilitate marrow extraction, leading to the inevitable discussion on cannibalism (*ibid.*). Hill (1995) concluded that other potential explanations were more convincing and certainly the writer would not advocate this as a possibility for the assemblage currently under discussion. Whilst the broken bone from Battlesbury Bowl did have some of the characteristic form of material processed for this purpose it lacked others and the writer believes it more likely to represent a deliberate act associated with assisting in the transformation process after death, accelerating the process of decay.

It has long been recognised that the number of disarticulated and generally fragmentary human bones recovered from Iron Age assemblages must derive from activities other than the disturbance of earlier graves (Whimster 1981, 178). It is widely suggested that at least part of the normal rite of disposal of the dead in the Iron Age was almost certainly by excarnation (Cunliffe 1992), a mortuary disposal mechanism used in several earlier prehistoric periods. The form, condition, and structure (demographic and skeletal) of the disarticulated bone assemblage at Battlesbury Bowl and contemporaneous sites has close similarities with those from Neolithic causewayed enclosures such as Hambledon Hill, Dorset (McKinley in press) and Late Bronze Age middens (Brück 1995; Needham and Spence 1996; Lawson 2001). The midden at Potterne (McKinley 2000a) for example, also shows the predominance of the right side as in Iron Age assemblages and an association with midden material, both characteristics absent from the Neolithic assemblages.

The observed preferential survival of certain skeletal elements amongst remains subject to exposure is not unexpected and may be largely explained by taphonomic factors (see above), but this would not explain the emphasis on bones from the right side. The latter suggests deliberate human manipulation of the material in its disarticulated (or partially so) form. For such deliberate selection to have occurred the bones must have been sufficiently complete at the time to allow the sides to be distinguished. It has been suggested that this material represents lost or discarded curated fragments or accidentally disturbed depositional categories (Cunliffe 1995, 418). It is equally possible, however, that what we are seeing are 'remnants', material selected for ritual use elsewhere having been removed. The fact remains that whilst some bone was clearly lost as a result of animal activity (see taphonomy) some which one may have expected to survive such attention is absent from the assemblage.

The theme of death as a transformation process is commonly accepted (Van Gennep 1977; Brück 1995). Another reoccurring theme is the association of the dead with agricultural fertility and regeneration (Bradley 1981; Walker 1985; Brück 1995; Humphreys 1981; Bloch and Parry 1982). A visible source of both actual and symbolic transformation and fertility are middens (Brück 1995; Parker Pearson 1996); the 'rubbish', via decomposition, attaining the new status of a source of fertility which may be fed back to the land as both a practical organic fertiliser and a symbolic representation of renewal. The link between human dead and midden material, both sharing symbolic characteristics, can hardly be fortuitous. In practical terms – though the distinction between practical and ritual is, as Brück (1999) indicates, likely to represent a modern western concept rather than a prehistoric one – the transformation of the corpse to skeletal remains, ie, from the world of the living to that of the dead, would have been hastened by inclusion of the body in the bacteria-rich midden environment. However, as Hill (1995) observed, 'archaeological deposits of human remains are never simply to do with the treatment of the dead'. By combining the ancestors with that which is used to fertilise the land, a powerful symbolic mixture is obtained, one which actively promotes good crop production whilst symbolically protecting and nurturing it, at the same time reinforcing the community's claim to it.

It is generally considered that the pit burials represent a minority rite (Walker 1985, 561; Hill 1995) with those selected for such deposition representing outsiders, damaged or 'incomplete' individuals, rejects from society. Given the great symbolic and practical significance attached to midden material in later prehistoric societies it is debatable that the important role of the human contribution (or 'mediator'; Sharples 1991; Hill 1995) should fall to outcasts and 'criminals'.

Future analysis of human remains comparing the reflected health and social status (from osteological evidence for diet, physical stress and disease) of individuals from the pit burials with those (currently few) from graves – not possible within this project – may shed further light on the homogeneity or lack of it between the two forms of deposition, and help demonstrate any factors affecting the 'choice' (if any) of individuals destined for different mortuary treatments.

Chapter 6
The Environmental Evidence

Environmental evidence was used to help establish the nature of specific activities and processes on the site, and the function of the features, with particular importance being placed upon the nature of artefact-rich deposits, their depositional environment, taphonomy, and depositional history. This has helped in the interpretation and reconstruction of the site's economy and roles, and allowed comparison with other Iron Age settlements on Salisbury Plain, and possibly comparable sites such as hillforts (such as Danebury, Hampshire and Maiden Castle, Dorset) and occupation accumulations (such as Potterne and East Chisenbury, Wiltshire). Although the nature and landuse of the wider landscape was considered a lower priority, evidence from nearly all strands of palaeo-environmental enquiry touched upon this.

Faunal Remains

by Ellen Hambleton and Mark Maltby

The excavation produced a faunal assemblage of considerable significance which has great potential to further our understanding of the exploitation of animals by Iron Age societies in central southern England, with particular reference to the treatment and disposal of animal remains. In addition to comparison with faunal assemblages from other Iron Age sites in the region, the intrasite variation within the assemblage has also been investigated in some detail. The following is a summary of a comprehensive report (in archive) on the analysis of the faunal remains assemblage which included discussion of metrical and pathological data.

Methods

All bones and teeth recovered were examined and, where possible, identified to species and skeletal element using reference material from the comparative skeletal collection at the School of Conservation Sciences, Bournemouth University. Where appropriate, the following information was recorded for each fragment: context; element; anatomical zone; % completeness; fragmentation; surface condition; gnawing; fusion data; porosity; tooth ageing data; butchery marks; metrical data; other comments such as pathologies or association/articulation with other recorded fragments. The information was recorded onto a relational database (Microsoft Access) and cross-referenced with relevant contextual information such as date and feature type. Groups of four or more bones that belonged to the same skeleton (ie, articulating bones or elements closely matched by size and age) were assigned an 'associated bone group number' (see below). In some instances several separate bone groups were recorded for the same individual, for example where there were several articulating element groups from different body areas but with no clear proof that they came from the same carcass. A summary form was also created for each context. This database, together with supporting charts, tables, and photographs, forms part of the site archive. Methods of quantification employed for the Battlesbury Bowl faunal assemblage include the number of identified specimens (NISP), whole bone equivalents, the minimum number of individuals (MNI), and the minimum number of elements (MNE).

Preservation

Generally the bone surface preservation is good with relatively low numbers of eroded fragments, although the level of fragmentation varies considerably between contexts (and sometimes also within contexts). This variation is primarily a reflection of the depositional history of the bones. Where contexts contained a greater proportion of fairly complete bones, the bone assemblages appeared consistent with having resulted from relatively short term depositional events after which the bones did not remain exposed for long periods. Most commonly these types of context were found near the bases of pits and often contained associated bone groups of four or more bones belonging to a single individual. The more heavily fragmented assemblages may represent more gradual accumulation of material left exposed and incorporated into feature fills over longer periods. Some of the more fragmented material may also represent material that has been redeposited. All of this information contributes to a greater understanding of the site formation processes.

Quantification

A total of 27,813 fragments of animal bone and teeth was recovered from 663 contexts; the majority

Table 6.1 NISP counts by phase for hand-recovered animal bone assemblage

Species	*Phase* 1/2	3	unphased	Total
Sheep/goat	2450	1738	418	4606
Cattle	1591	868	194	2653
Pig	610	246	77	933
Horse	149	214	26	389
Dog	66	138	4	208
Red deer	17	6	16	39
Fox	–	11	–	11
Roe deer	7	1	–	8
Badger	1	1	–	2
Corvid*	2	57	–	59
Raven	1	50	–	51
Mallard	3	2	–	5
Thrush-size (turdidae)	5	–	–	5
Passerine	1	3	–	4
Wader (indet.)	2	1	–	3
Buzzard	–	–	2	2
Duck**	2	–	–	2
Woodcock	–	2	–	2
Crane	–	1	–	1
Rail family	1	–	–	1
Field vole	2	10	8	20
Water vole	–	1	17	18
House mouse	4	1	–	5
Wood mouse	1	4	–	5
Mouse (indet.)	1	1	1	3
Frog/toad (indet.)	8	72	65	145
Frog	8	55	24	87
Toad	3	45	1	49
Total identified	*4935*	*3528*	*853*	*9316*
Unident. medium mammal (sheep/goat-sized)	3338	2212	843	6393
Unident. large mammal (cattle-sized)	1786	1396	444	3626
Unident. mammal	1277	1319	264	2860
Unident. small mammal (rodent-sized)	152	104	15	271
Unident. bird	4	4	–	8
Overall total	11,492	8563	2419	22,474
% ident. to species	43	41	35	41

* = size noted in archive: rook/crow/jackdaw etc)
** = indeterminate species between mallard and teal size
indet. = species indeterminate
Unident. = unidentified

Table 6.2 NISP counts by phased for sieved animal bone assemblage

Species	*Phase* 1/2	3	unphased	Total
Sheep/goat	138	180	44	362
Pig	17	17	26	60
Cattle	16	7	10	33
Dog	–	8	1	9
Fox	–	–	1	1
Red deer	1	–	–	1
Passerine	1	–	–	1
Field vole	2	8	–	10
Mouse (indet.)	4	2	1	7
House mouse	2	1	–	3
Wood mouse	–	2	–	2
Frog/toad (indet.)	–	8	1	9
Frog	–	9	–	9
Toad	–	6	–	6
Total identified	*181*	*248*	*84*	*513*
Unident. mammal	874	1683	455	3012
Unident. medium mammal (sheep/goat-sized)	595	765	305	1665
Unident. large mammal (cattle-sized)	36	35	38	109
Unident. small mammal (rodent-sized)	14	13	7	34
Unident. bird	1	4	1	6
Overall total	1701	2748	890	5339
% ident. to species	11	9	9	10

(22,474 fragments) was recovered by hand (Table 6.1), while a further 5339 fragments were recovered from sieved environmental samples (Table 6.2). From the hand-recovered assemblage, 9316 fragments were identifiable to species (41% of the total assemblage) but substantially fewer were identifiable from the sieved samples (only 10%). In terms of number of fragments identified to species, the assemblage is in a similar order of magnitude to that from Winnall Down, Hampshire (Maltby 1985a) and is one of the largest collections of Early–Middle Iron Age faunal material from Britain.

Phased features of Late Bronze Age–Middle Iron Age date account for 88% of the bone material, with only 3309 fragments coming from unphased Iron Age contexts. Bone was recovered from a variety of feature types but by far the most common were pits, which yielded 80% of the assemblage. A further 16% came from ditches with the remainder coming from post-holes, a hearth, and other features.

The southernmost cluster, FG 1, yielded the largest proportion of the faunal assemblage (40%). Feature group 2 was the next most abundant area of the site and produced 27% of all faunal remains while

Table 6.3 Relative abundance of main domestic species by phase

Phase	*1/2*	*3*	*unphased*	*Total*
		NISP		
Sheep/goat	2450	1738	418	4606
Cattle	1591	868	194	2653
Pig	610	246	77	933
Horse	149	214	26	389
Dog	66	138	4	208
Total	*4866*	*3204*	*709*	*8789*
		%		
Sheep/goat	50.3	54.2	59.0	52.4
Cattle	32.7	27.1	27.4	30.2
Pig	12.5	7.7	10.9	10.6
Horse	3.1	6.7	3.7	4.4
Dog	1.4	4.3	0.6	2.4

20% came from FG 3. The northernmost cluster, FG 4, produced only 13% of the total assemblage.

Species Representation

Domestic species

The hand recovered assemblage is dominated by domestic species. NISP counts show that sheep/goat, cattle, pig, horse, and dog make up 94% of the hand-recovered assemblage, with sheep/goat remains being the most abundant, followed by cattle, pig, horse, and dog in order of abundance. This was true for all three methods of quantification used (NISP, MNE, and MNI counts).

Quantification and comparison of the hand-recovered assemblage concentrates on the five domestic mammal species, as these constitute the bulk of the assemblage. Some variation in the relative abundance of the different domesticates was apparent within the hand-recovered assemblage when compared by phase, feature type, and location (Tables 6.3–5).

Phase

The relative order of abundance of the domestic species remained consistent throughout all phases. Sheep/goat constitute well over half the domestic assemblage and are considerably more abundant than cattle remains, which make up less than a third of the assemblage in phase 1/2 and 3. Pig bone, however, fell from 13% in phase 1/2, to *c.* 8% in phase 3. although it is possible that this reflects intrasite variability rather than chronological change.

The relative abundance of the three most abundant species at Battlesbury Bowl can be compared with a large number of sites from Wessex and elsewhere. Across the whole site percentages of sheep/goat, cattle, and pig were approximately 56%, 32%, and 11% respectively, which fall centrally within the general range encountered on chalkland sites in Wessex. Previous studies have indicated that sheep/goat percentages tend to be slightly higher on hillforts than on non-hillfort sites (Hambleton 1999, 45–6, 55–6). The species ranking was the same at Danebury although the Battlesbury Bowl assemblage had slightly lower percentages of sheep/goat and pig bones (*ibid.*, 109–110; Grant 1984a; 1991), while Early Iron Age samples from Budbury, Wiltshire produced figures of 47% sheep/goat, 43% cattle and 10% pig (Westley 1970), comparable to the assemblage from the Battlesbury Bowl ditches.

There were substantial differences, however, with the assemblage from the extensive Late Bronze Age midden deposit at Potterne, which comprised 40% sheep/goat, 32% pig and 27% cattle (Locker 2000). The high percentage of pigs at Potterne compared with the Early Iron Age percentages at both Budbury and Battlesbury may indicate a gradual decline in pig numbers in the region, and it is possible that there was a further decrease in pig by the Middle Iron Age at Battlesbury. A similar pattern has been observed at Danebury (Grant 1984a; 1991), although rather later in the Iron Age. In contrast, an Early–Middle Iron Age site at Groundwell Farm, Blunsdon St Andrew, Wiltshire (Coy 1981) produced results closely comparable with Potterne including 35% pig, one of the highest percentages encountered on Iron Age sites in Wessex (Hambleton 1999, 45–6). If a decline in pigs is equated with the opening up of the landscape for agriculture and sheep farming, we may be witnessing local variations in the clearance of woodland.

Table 6.4 Relative abundance of main domestic species by feature type

Feature	*Ditches*	*Hearths*	*Post-holes*	*Pits*	*Others*	*Total*
			NISP			
Sheep/goat	563	1	114	3863	65	4606
Cattle	635	1	50	1929	38	2653
Pig	104	1	31	781	16	933
Horse	50	–	15	321	3	389
Dog	24	–	2	181	1	208
Total	1376	3	212	7075	123	8789
			%			
Sheep/goat	40.9	33.3	53.8	54.6	52.8	52.4
Cattle	46.1	33.3	23.6	27.3	30.9	30.2
Pig	7.5	33.3	14.6	11.0	13.0	10.6
Horse	3.6	–	7.1	4.5	2.4	4.4
Dog	1.7	–	0.9	2.6	0.8	2.4

Table 6.5 Relative abundance of main domestic species by feature group

FG	*1*	*2*	*3*	*4*	*Total*
		NISP			
Sheep/goat	1768	1404	784	650	4606
Cattle	1142	536	721	254	2653
Pig	260	145	382	145	932
Horse	187	104	61	37	389
Dog	148	25	7	28	208
Total	3505	2214	1955	1114	8788
		%			
Sheep/goat	50.4	63.4	40.1	58.3	52.4
Cattle	32.6	24.2	36.9	22.8	30.2
Pig	7.4	6.5	19.5	13.0	10.6
Horse	5.3	4.7	3.1	3.3	4.4
Dog	4.2	1.1	0.4	2.5	2.4

Analysis of sheep skulls revealed no evidence for hornless varieties. A total of 83 attached and detached sheep horn cores were found. None of the 73 sheep frontals recovered is from hornless specimens. Horned sheep were also found almost to the exclusion of hornless specimens at Danebury until the latest Iron Age phase (Grant 1984a, 505). No hornless specimens were found at Owslebury in deposits earlier than the late Romano-British period (Maltby 1987). Both male and female horn cores are represented at Battlesbury, although the majority of the older specimens belonged to ewes.

Horse became much more abundant in the phase 3 assemblage (*c.* 7%) than in the earlier phase (*c.* 3%). At Danebury a similar increase was apparent in the material from the second phase of excavations (Grant 1991), although no such pattern was apparent in the material from the earlier excavations (Grant 1984a). On current evidence it seems that horses became more commonly utilised for meat in the Middle Iron Age on some Wessex sites.

Dog remains are also more abundant in the later phase but this is at least partly due to the presence of partial skeletons inflating the fragment count.

Feature type

Different types of feature also displayed some variation in the relative abundance of the different domestic species. Sheep/goat were generally more abundant than cattle in pits and post-holes, while the reverse was true in the ditches. This pattern is not uncommon on Iron Age sites, although the differences between these types of feature at Battlesbury Bowl were somewhat less pronounced than, for example, at Winnall Down (Maltby 1985a). In general, the remains of pigs appear to be slightly more prevalent in pits and post-holes than in ditches. Post-holes appear to contain a higher proportion of horse remains than do pits, ditches, and other linear features, although the assemblage from post-holes is quite small and therefore may be subject to bias. There is also a considerable degree of variation in the relative importance of different species in different pits, with some pits dominated by sheep/goat remains while in others, cattle, pig, or even horse predominate.

Location

In FG 1 and 2, sheep/goat contributed at least half the identified domestic species remains while cattle made up less than a third, and this is reflected in all phases where the samples were large enough to compare them. This suggests that there is no apparent spatial differentiation in faunal assemblage composition between these two areas. Feature group 4 also displays a similar pattern, although pigs appear to be slightly better represented. Feature group 3, however, had a noticeably different assemblage composition. Cattle and sheep/goat were more equally represented and, most strikingly, the relative abundance of pig remains was considerably higher in this area.

Wild species

The wild species, which make up the remaining 6% of the assemblage, include some larger species (red deer, roe deer, fox, and badger) as well as a variety of wild birds, small rodents, and amphibians. There are no fish bones even in the sieved samples. The paucity of finds of wild species is not unusual on Iron Age sites (Grant 1981; Maltby 1996). The incidence of deer remains, however, is particularly low, although it is clear that antlers were utilised for manufacturing purposes. There is no evidence that any of the wild mammals were eaten.

The most likely bird species that could have contributed occasionally to the diet are the ducks and waders, all of which probably would have been captured some distance from the site, most likely in the river valley. Notably absent were bones of domestic fowl or goose. Part of a crane (*Grus grus*) tibiotarsus displayed evidence for butchery but this was probably an imported object or raw material for boneworking. Most of the crows and raven bones were found in associated bone groups and, with buzzards, these species would have been attracted to areas where both rubbish deposits were accumulating in middens and where animals were dying or being slaughtered. This does not explain why they occasionally ended up in pits, although special deposition cannot be ruled out. Corvid bones were also the most common species found at Danebury (Coy 1984; Serjeantson 1991) and Owslebury, Hampshire (Maltby 1987).

The small mammals and amphibians were pitfall victims, indicating that some of the pits were left open for a period before being fully infilled.

Table 6.6 Minimum numbers counts for the main skeletal elements in domestic species

Element	*Sheep/goat*	*Cattle*	*Pig*	*Horse*	*Dog*
Skull	73	57	14	15	3
Atlas	34	18	20	6	–
Axis	12	20	2	2	2
Mandible	252	93	64	11	11
Scapula	97	53	30	9	3
Humerus	126	69	31	15	4
Radius	173	56	21	16	6
Ulna	70	43	21	16	3
Metacarpal	81	42	–	10	1.4
Metacarpal 3	–	–	6	–	–
Metacarpal 4	–	–	3	–	–
Lateral metacarpal	–	–	3	2.5	–
Pelvis	88	60	11	11	3
Femur	100	46	25	5	5
Tibia	227	57	23	12	6
Astragalus	66	33	7	7	2
Calcaneum	56	39	10	3	–
Metatarsal	70	51	–	10	0.6
Metatarsal 3	–	–	2	–	–
Metatarsal 4	–	–	11	–	–
Lateral metatarsal	–	–	–	2	–
Phalanx 1	35.25	13.75	4.5	4.5	0.1
Total MNE	*1560.25*	*750.75*	*308.5*	*157*	*50.1*
MNI	252	93	64	16	11

Body Part Representation

It is possible to recognise the effects of taphonomic biases on the assemblage by comparing the composition of the main domestic species assemblages in terms of skeletal element abundance (ie, the parts of the body represented). A minimum number of elements (MNE) count was calculated for the main skeletal elements of the domestic species (Table 6.6). All the main elements were represented for sheep, cattle, pig, and horse. Certain of the smaller bones were absent from the dog assemblage but this is likely to be a result of the comparatively small sample size. The sheep/goat remains display an abundance of mandibles, radii, and tibiae compared with other elements, which reflects the robustness and, therefore, greater survivability of these elements in a heavily fragmented assemblage. Similar dominance of these bones in sheep/goat samples is common on Iron Age sites, for example Winnall Down, Hampshire (Maltby 1985a). The dog remains, which are of similar size and robustness to sheep/goat, also displayed a similar pattern of element representation. In the smaller species (sheep/goat, pig, and dog) there is also a tendency for the smaller elements to be poorly represented. Low abundance of such small bones may reflect an excavation retrieval bias, but may also be a feature of redeposited material. The larger species (cattle and horse) tend to show a more even representation of skeletal elements.

There is little evidence for any significant variation in the pattern of body part representation between phases for any of the domestic species. When compared by feature type, the pattern for each of the domestic species is broadly similar in pits and ditches. The post-holes tend to be different, however this is most likely a result of small sample bias. Variations in body part representation within and between species at site level reveal broad patterns indicative of the overall state of preservation of the assemblage. Probable cultural selection and deposition of particular body parts, such as the accumulation of cattle and horse skulls from context 4101 (section 4105 of phase 2 ditch 4043), may be more effectively investigated by examining body part representation at feature or context level.

Ageing

Mandibular tooth eruption and wear were recorded following Grant's (1982) system and the age profiles analysed following the methods of Grant (*ibid.*), Hambleton (1999), and Payne (1973). Ageing data from complete mandibular tooth rows was supplemented by additional estimated mandibular wear stage (MWS) values from some incomplete jaws. MWS values were available from 149 sheep/goat, 29 cattle, and 27 pig mandibles (Fig. 6.1). The mortality profiles were typical for Iron Age Wessex (Hambleton 1999) and have parallels with animal husbandry strategies seen at, for instance, Balksbury Camp, Hampshire (Maltby 1985b).

Sheep/goat displayed a high percentage of young individuals, with approximately 50% having died in their first year and almost no individuals surviving beyond 6 years of age. The overall mortality pattern for sheep/goat is almost identical to that seen in all of the Iron Age phases at Danebury (Grant 1984a; 1991) and may reflect exploitation of sheep for both primary and secondary products but with a particular emphasis on yearlings, perhaps representing a cull of animals to pre-empt loss of condition over the first winter (Hambleton 1999). In contrast to Danebury, however, there appears to have been little or no exploitation of this 'prime meat' age group of older juveniles (*c.* 1.5–2 yr), perhaps suggesting a greater emphasis on the importance of secondary products such as milk and wool.

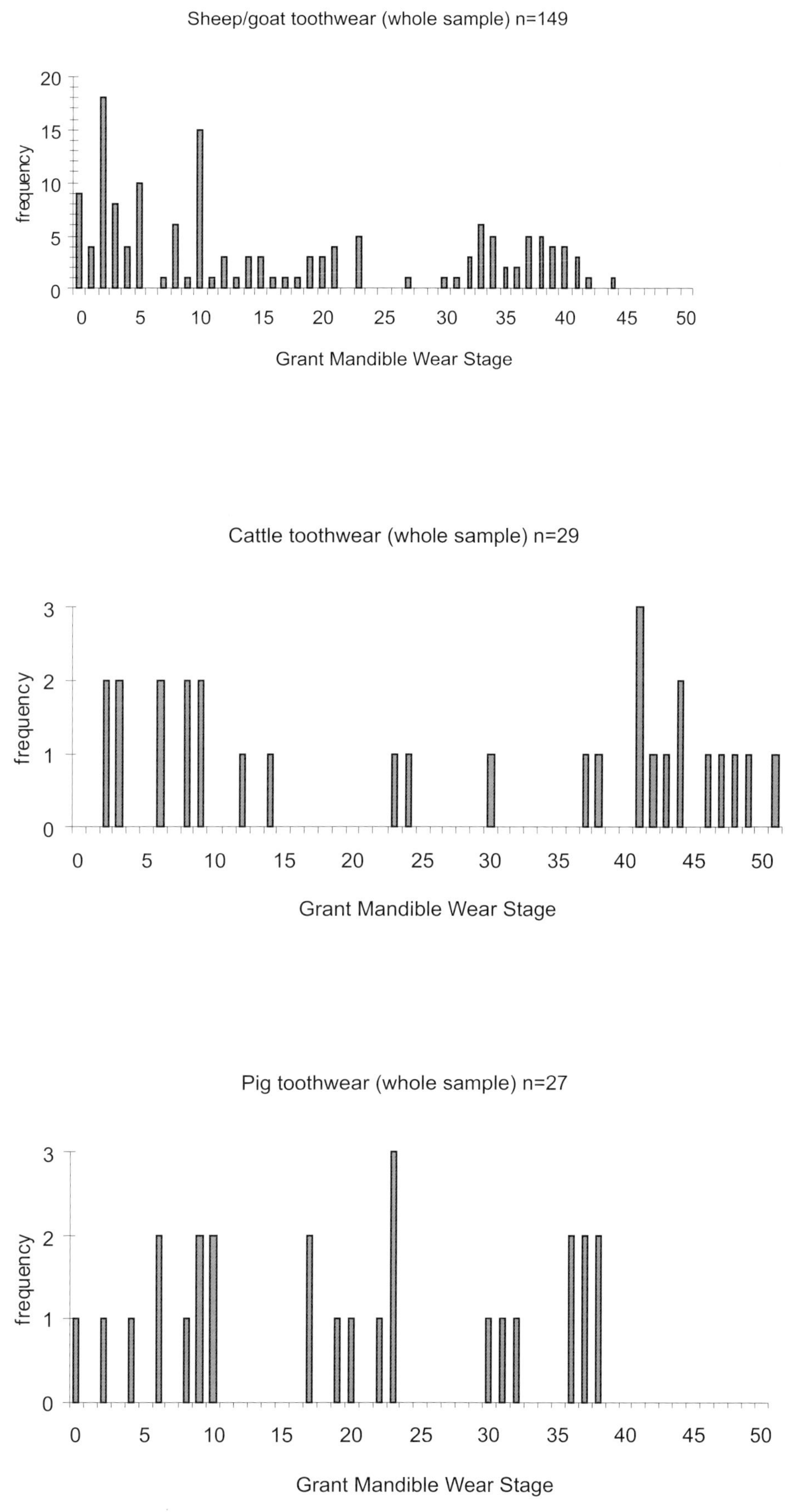

Figure 6.1 Mandible wear stages (including estimates, after Grant 1982) for sheep/goat, cattle, and pig

The cattle assemblage is smaller than the sheep/goat assemblage and, as such, may be less reliable, but none-the-less there is also a marked similarity to the age profile of cattle from the Late Iron Age at Danebury (Grant 1984a; 1991). Almost half the mandibles represent individuals that died before *c.* 18 months, with the remainder comprising mostly adult individuals, some of which were kept into late adulthood. This is again suggestive of a mixed husbandry strategy but with possibly some emphasis on the use of cattle for dairying (Hambleton 1999).

The pig mandibles are all those of young animals killed before the end of their third year, which is entirely consistent of the exploitation of pigs for meat seen at other Iron Age sites from the region (*ibid.*). As with the sheep/goat, peaks and gaps in the mortality profiles may reflect intermittent, possibly seasonal, culling strategy rather than a gradual background accumulation of material resulting from year-round mortality.

The majority of the aged horse assemblage comprised very mature adults, although a small number of juveniles, including one neonatal individual, were also represented in phase 3 contexts.This suggests that, in the later phase, the occupants of the site became more involved in the rounding up and breaking of young horses in addition to their previous exploitation of older animals. A single neonatal horse mandible may just indicate that horses were being bred at the site.

A range of ages is represented in the dog assemblage, suggesting that a breeding population was kept on the site. It has been speculated (Harcourt 1979; Grant 1991) that British Iron Age dogs may have fulfilled a variety of functions as working (herding, guarding, and hunting) animals or as pets. Dogs appear to have been kept in small numbers on most Iron Age sites in the region and puppies and older animals were probably culled as and when necessary to keep the population at a manageable level.

Butchery

In total, 561 specimens were noted as having butchery marks (full details in archive). Including specimens with multiple records, the assemblage provided 596 observations of butchery damage (including five on sieved specimens). Observations of butchery were made on bones of all the domestic species as well as on red deer, roe deer, and crane specimens. In the case of these wild species, all the marks were associated with the manufacture of objects.

Analysis of the types of butchery marks support previous observations from British Iron Age sites that knives rather than cleavers were used for skinning, filletting, and most of the segmentation of the carcass. Cleavers were sometimes used to remove the ribs and loins from the vertebrae of pigs and sheep and occasionally their marks are found on other bones. Saws appear only to have been used for working bones, horn, and antler and seemingly were not routinely employed in butchery.

At least 7.4% of the domesticate bones (excluding loose teeth) bore butchery marks, with evidence in all the species for slight increases in butchery frequencies from phase 1/2 to phase 3. There is some evidence to suggest that bone surface preservation affected butchery observations. Only 13 (3.4%) of the 377 eroded fragments of domestic species also had butchery recorded, whereas 525 (7.6%) uneroded specimens were butchered. Surface erosion tends to mask fine knife cuts. On the other hand, butchery marks were found slightly more frequently on gnawed specimens (8.2%; NISP = 1378) than on ungnawed fragments (7.2%; NISP = 5895).

Context type also appears to have some bearing upon the frequency of butchered bones. The large majority (452) of butchered specimens were found in pits and these unsurprisingly represented a very similar percentage of butchered specimens (7.7%) to that of the overall sample (7.4%). Ditches and other linear features produced 62 butchered specimens (5.5% of the domestic species in that assemblage). As discussed previously, the assemblages in the ditches tended to be less well preserved than in the pits and more butchery marks may have been obliterated. A small sample of 183 bones from post-holes included 17 (9.3%) butchered bones. This is a surprisingly high percentage given the small size of these contexts, although the sample size is limited. Layers and other feature types produced just seven (6.2%) butchered bones.

Of the 538 butchered bones from domestic species, 42.2% belonged to cattle (10.5% of all cattle bones), 40.4% to sheep/goat (5.6%), 11.5% to pig (8.1%), and 6.1% to horse (10.3%). This variation between species may reflect the fact that larger carcasses require more butchery, the pig carcasses being generally larger than sheep/goat but smaller than cattle and horse.

The figures indicate that horse carcasses were commonly butchered for meat, increasingly so in phase 3, and that the carcasses of the large mammals – cattle and horse – were often treated similarly. However, bones from butchered horse carcasses were more likely to be deposited together, possibly indicating that on occasions several horses were butchered at one time, which may be related to special events and communal feasting. The combination of butchery and contextual analysis revealed that some skulls were carefully cleaned prior to possible display and deposition.

Only two dog bones were recorded with butchery marks, both from phase 3 features, providing little evidence to indicate that carcasses were commonly processed for meat or skins.

Although specialist butchers may have been operating, their activities have not been recognised in this analysis of the bones. On the other hand, there are indications that small amounts of waste from bone, horn, and antler working were, on occasions, deposited in the same features, suggesting perhaps that specialists working on a variety of materials were discarding waste.

Associated Bone Groups and Other Deposits of Interest

One aspect of the assemblage which merits particular attention is the nature of deposits of associated bone groups of several skeletal elements belonging to the same individual. A summary is presented here; more detailed descriptions are in the archive. There are numerous examples of such groups. These range from accumulations of several almost complete skeletons, such as context 4507 (pit 4486) which contained the complete and partial skeletons of at least six sheep (as well as the skeleton of a toad); through single complete or partial skeletons (eg, most of a lamb skeleton in context 4613 and the partial skeleton of a dog in context 4482), to smaller sections of domestic species carcasses such as limbs, feet, or groups of vertebrae.

The presence of associated bone groups, particularly when the bones are found in anatomical articulation, has provoked considerable interest when found in pits or ditch terminals on other Iron Age sites, and there is continuing debate as to whether they may be interpreted as 'special' events, perhaps the result of ritual sacrificial or propitiary deposits, or whether they are merely more prosaic deposits of rubbish that are unusual only in the fact of their undisturbed and intact survival (Grant 1984b; Cunliffe 1992; Hill 1995). The discussion of 'special' animal deposits does not confine itself to associated bone groups; single or multiple accumulations of skulls are also often considered in the archaeological literature to be of special significance, particularly if found in significant locations on a site or if having the appearance of having been deliberately 'placed' (Wilson 1999). Several of the Battlesbury pits contained groups of one or more cattle or horse skulls, and there was a much larger group of at least seven cattle and horse skulls in ditch 4043.

The bone assemblages from 37 of the 357 features that produced animal bones were analysed in detail, their selection being based mainly on the size of the assemblage and/or the presence of associated bone groups and substantial portions of skulls. They represent just over 10% of the features but, as they produced 12,074 bones and teeth from hand-collection, over 53% of the total bone assemblage. Most of the assemblages, apart from six from ditch sections, are derived from pits. Although the concentration on larger assemblages imposed a selection bias into the analysis, species representation in the selected features was generally similar to the sample as a whole.

It is clear that within the general pattern of bone deposition some assemblages appear 'unusual', by including one or more groups of associated bones, by containing relatively complete skulls or limb bones, or by simply containing a much denser concentration of bones than generally found. Occasionally all these traits are found in one assemblage.

The most unusual assemblage was undoubtedly that from section 4105 of ditch 4043, where substantial parts of at least seven cattle and three horse skulls were deposited in close proximity in context 4101 (an upper fill), with a similar cattle skull in context 4450 (a lower secondary fill). Several of these skulls display fine knife cuts indicating careful removal of the surrounding tissue and most of the skulls have post-mortem tooth loss from the maxillae, though the loose teeth were not recovered. This combination of taphonomic markers suggests that these skulls (or at least those of the cattle) have been carefully cleaned and left exposed for some time, perhaps as objects of display, before they were finally deposited in the ditch. This would explain why some of the specimens appear to be less decayed than others.

None of the skulls is complete. No occipital condyles survived on the cattle specimens and several lacked the sphenoid bones. Similarly, the horse skulls did not have the sphenoid area. This resulted in the brain case being exposed from underneath, possibly so that it could be removed as part of the act of preparation of the skulls for display, and/or used for food or in some ritual manner. The resulting cavity would also allow the skull to the inserted on top of a pole or hung flat against a wall for display. Therefore, this can be regarded as a possible ritual deposit, the major symbolic significance of the skulls may have related to their use before they were deposited. This could have been on the site itself although their importation from elsewhere cannot be ruled out. Unfortunately, because there was no suitable material with which to date the digging of the ditch, it was not possible to identify whether they were ancient curated items, or broadly contemporary with the time of deposition.

Skulls from other features may have been used in a similar fashion prior to deposition, such as those found in pits 4470 (phase 1/2), and 4606, 4598, and 4868 (phase 3). A portion of cleaned horse skull was also found in pit 4707 (phase 3). This suggests that the practice may have been one that was not restricted to a particular phase or, indeed, a particular area of the site. It would be surprising if such treatment was restricted to this site and re-examination of skulls from other Iron Age assemblages may be revealing. An accumulation of cattle skulls was recorded at an Iron Age enclosure at Harrow Hill, E. Sussex (Holleyman 1937; Manning 1995) and a skinned horse skull and mandible were found in the entrance terminals of the penannular ditch of a Middle Iron Age roundhouse at Farmoor, Oxfordshire (Wilson 1979).

However, not all cattle and horse skulls were treated in this way and most did not produce evidence for careful cleaning. The calf skulls found in pit 5750 (phase 3) have evidence for skinning but not to the excessive extent as the previous specimens; they were probably deposited with their foot bones and are most convincingly interpreted as discarded waste from the skinning process. Two hornless cattle skulls, rarely found on British Iron Age sites, were found in pit 4868 (the only other example being in pit 4796). The presence of two unusual skulls in the same context, with one of them having evidence for careful cleaning, perhaps for display, suggests that their placement could also have had special significance, although there were no unusual bones associated with them.

There were no complete burials of animals. Most associated bone groups consist of relatively small numbers of bones from various parts of the body. The most complete skeletons that show no evidence for butchery belong to dog (eg, phase 3 pit 4423) and corvids (raven in phase 3 pit 4584; crow in phase 3 pit 4707). The fact that the dog skeleton was partially destroyed by gnawing and bones of the raven skeleton were recorded in three different contexts indicates that these may not have been completely articulated when deposited. Indeed, several of the associated bone groups have evidence for slight gnawing damage. It seems likely that most of this damage occurred prior to deposition, particularly in the cases of associated bone groups from the lower pit fills, suggesting that many of the groups may have been secondary depositions. A cattle forelimb in ditch section 4105, on the other hand, may have been disturbed by dogs after disposal.

A substantial proportion of the associated bone groups display evidence for butchery and clearly represent well-preserved carcass processing waste. There are other small groups that, although they do not display butchery marks, were also probably butchered. This is not to say that the evidence for butchery precludes them from being considered as being part of a 'special' deposit, particularly when they are found in association with other associated bone groups or groups of artefacts. A good example of this is from pit 4486 (phase 3), in which a carcass of a sheep has clearly been butchered and segmented but the bones have been collected and deposited together. This could be interpreted merely as the remains of a sheep after it had been fully processed and eaten. However, this does not seem very likely. 'Processed' sheep burials have been identified as foundation deposits in structures from Roman Winchester and on the Iron Age site at Wilby Way, Wellingborough, Northamptonshire (Maltby 2003; in press). The association of the 'processed' sheep in pit 4486 with an almost complete skeleton of a skinned newborn lamb adds to the likelihood that this was a case of structured deposition. Some of the isolated groups of butchered remains, particularly those of small groups of vertebrae are, however, probably best considered as well preserved butchery waste.

Conclusion

The faunal assemblage has provided considerable information concerning the economic exploitation of animals by the occupants of the Iron Age settlement which, in many ways, appears typical when compared to other Iron Age assemblages in terms of overall species proportions and mortality profiles. However, the nature of the preserved archaeological deposits is somewhat atypical in that rather than representing gradual accumulation of background discarded faunal material, it appears likely that much of the faunal the assemblage, in particular from the pits, is largely comprised of multiple examples of well preserved remains from short term depositional events. As such, the assemblage has provided a unique opportunity to investigate the treatment and disposal of animal remains within individual features which should, in turn, provide insights into the cultural significance, as well as the economic importance, of animals in Iron Age societies.

However, it has not been easy to distinguish between what we might regard as mundane butchery waste and deposits that we consider to have a greater significance in their deposition, although the validity of this distinction is in itself problematic. As has been demonstrated, many of these associated bone groups are found with assemblages which do appear to be the waste from basic butchery activities. Some skull depositions would appear to have had special significance; others, it can be argued, would not. It may be that on occasions it was the entirety of the assemblage derived from middens that was considered to be of special significance, in which case one should expect to find bones that were gnawed, burnt, and butchered. On other occasions it is equally possible to envisage that the decision to backfill pits may simply have resulted in the collection and dumping of any convenient soils and associated rubbish that had accumulated nearby.

Indeed, to assign the faunal assemblages (or their components) subjectively along the lines of 'sacred' or 'profane' may be to divide artificially the assemblage in a misleading way. There is every reason to suppose that food consumption and symbolic and ritual behaviour often occurred simultaneously. For example, feasting often accompanies sacrifice. We should not be surprised, therefore, that the residues from these practices are also found in complex associations.

Charred Plant Remains

by Alan J. Clapham with Chris J. Stevens

The 151 processed samples generally produced very rich flots across all features. The majority of flots contained very high numbers of charred grain fragments and small to very large quantities of both charred chaff fragments and charred weed seeds. Mineralised plant remains were also recorded from the majority of the bulk samples (Carruthers below). A total of 35 samples was selected for analysis on the basis of presence and diversity of charred remains, and archaeological context, location, and feature type; 29 of them from pits (Table 6.7).

Methods and Identification

Some samples were very rich in charred plant remains and were sub-sampled using a riffle box. The volume of sample analysed is recorded on the score sheets (archive). Samples were examined using a low-powered stereo-microscope and the charred plant remains were extracted. The critical plant taxa were identified using the modern plant reference collections housed in the George Pitt-Rivers Laboratory, Department of Archaeology, University of Cambridge. The nomenclature follows that of Stace (1997) for the non-cultivated plant taxa and the guidelines provided by Miller (1987) are used for the nomenclature of the wheats.

Table 6.7 Samples analysed for charred plant remains by phase and feature type

Phase	*Pits*	*Ditches*	*Hearth*	*Total*
1/2	7	5	–	12
3	22	–	1	23
Total	29	5	1	35

For some time it has been debated how far it is possible to identify wheat grains to a specific type (Hillman *et al.* 1996, 206). In the majority of cases, given the poor preservation apparent on most sites and the wide variation in cereal caryopsis morphology within one ear, let alone one species, it is accepted that it is usually not possible to identify grains to species level. For this study the grains were divided into those considered to be from hulled wheats and those from free-threshing wheats. The more reliable method of identifying the wheat species is from the chaff remains (spikelet forks, glume bases, and rachis fragments). Wheat grains were, therefore, only given specific status if the majority of the chaff within a context was of one type; then it was deemed that the grains were most likely to be also of that type. Another difficulty is the identification of barley types, especially the six-row variety. The presence of twisted grains is usually used to determine the presence of six-row barley. Although, in most cases, this may be perfectly reasonable, charring itself is bound to cause some distortion and this may manifest itself in the twisting of grains. In this study barley was identified as six-row when the six-row barley internode was present. The use of grain morphology in determining the genetic make-up of a crop (Campbell 2000a, 50) can lead to false conclusions due to the variation of grain even within an ear. The only way to be sure of genetic variations or trends within crops through time is via the genetic record of the crop. This does not mean that some assumptions cannot be made about the genetic make of a crop population, but caution must be exercised.

Results

by Alan J. Clapham

Twelve samples were studied from phase 1/2, five from ditch 4043, the rest from pits (Table 6.8). Twenty-three samples were studied from phase 3 contexts, all but one (from hearth 5979) coming from pits (Table 6.10). The archive records numbers of fragments present (f), but these are calculated to minimum numbers of seeds in the tables. The samples came from both infill deposits and deliberate dumps of material and there was little significant variation between the phases.

In general terms, the samples are very rich in very well-preserved plant remains, especially in the case of the glume bases of spelt wheat (*Triticum spelta*). In the majority of cases it was also possible to determine to species level the non-cultivated taxa. The remains appear to represent the discarding of rubbish which

Table 6.8 Charred remains from phase 1/2 features

	Ditch 4043					Pits						
Feature/section	*4019*	*4096*		*4105*		*4612*	*4751*		*5149*		*5670*	
Context	*4069*	*4124*	*4182*	*4450*	*4102*	*4613*	*4317*	*4318*	*5228*	*5162*	*5715*	*5671*
Sample	*2008*	*2005*	*2012*	*2090*	*2036*	*2139*	*2028*	*2029*	*2164*	*2162*	*2201*	*2177*
Volume (litres)	*13*	*30*	*30*	*30*	*30*	*30*	*30*	*30*	*30*	*30*	*30*	*30*
CEREALS												
Hordeum sp. (grains undiff.)	-	5	-	20	4	-	-	-	-	-	-	-
Hordeum sp. (grains, tail)	-	-	2	-	-	-	2	4	3	2	-	-
Hordeum sp. (grains, hulled)	7	10	16	28	3	-	17	21	21	18	4	6
Hordeum sp. (rachis fragments)	2	-	-	2	-	-	-	-	-	1	3	1
Triticum sp. (grain)	-	-	-	1	-	-	-	21	3	2	-	11
Triticum dicoccum (glume bases)	-	-	-	-	-	-	-	-	1	-	-	-
Triticum dicoccum/spelta (grain)	3	3	10	12	5	-	19	20	8	9	5	56
Triticum dicoccum/spelta (tail-grain)	-	1	-	-	1	-	-	-	-	-	-	-
Triticum dicoccum/spelta (glume bases)	82	106	54	56	42	105	194	400	12	34	162	168
Triticum dicoccum/spelta (spikelet forks)	2	5	4	6	4	4	1	10	-	5	30	9
Triticum spelta (glume bases)	13	4	10	22	8	13	9	10	1	3	32	27
Triticum spelta (spikelet forks)	1	-	2	-	1	-	-	-	-	-	1	6
Triticum spelta (rachis)	9	4	11	1	1	7	-	31	1	2	18	10
Cereals undiff. (grains)	11	47	61	557	51	55	241	576	102	173	80	569
Cereals undiff. (culm internodes)	-	-	-	-	-	3	3	-	-	-	-	-
Cereals undiff. (culm nodes)	3	2	2	-	-	3	1	-	-	-	2	6
Cereals undiff. (basal culm nodes)	-	-	-	-	-	-	-	-	-	-	-	2
Cereals (embryos)	-	-	3	2	-	-	6	10	4	1	2	-
NON-CEREALS												
Ranunculus acris,bulbosus,repens	-	-	4	-	2	-	-	1	-	-	-	2
Papaver sp.	-	1	-	-	-	-	-	1	-	-	-	-
Fumaria officinalis	1	-	-	-	-	-	3	12	-	-	1	2
Corylus avellana	-	4	5	2	3	-	1	6	3	5	2	-
CHENOPODIACEAE (undiff.)	-	-	1	-	-	-	2	-	-	11	1	-
Chenopodium album	12	2	3	1	8	1	-	1	1	-	-	2
Atriplex sp.	-	-	1	-	-	-	1	31	-	-	-	-
Montia fontana ssp. *chondrosperma*	-	-	-	-	-	-	1	-	-	-	-	2
Stellaria media	2	-	1	2	-	-	-	1	-	-	2	4
Fallopia convolvulus	-	2	4	-	2	3	-	15	-	1	2	2
Polygonum aviculare	1	-	1	-	1	-	5	-	-	-	-	1
Rumex sp.	2	2	3	1	2	-	-	16	-	-	4	5
Rumex acetosella group	-	1	1	-	-	-	-	-	-	-	-	-
Anagallis arvensis	1	-	-	-	-	-	-	-	-	-	-	-
ROSACEAE (undiff.)	-	-	-	-	-	-	-	1	-	-	-	-
Rosaceae thorns	-	2	-	-	-	-	-	-	-	-	-	-
Aphanes arvensis	-	1	-	-	-	-	-	-	-	-	1	-
Crataegus monogyna (thorns)	1	2	-	-	-	-	-	-	-	-	-	-
FABACEAE (undiff.)												
Vicia sp.	-	-	-	-	-	-	1	-	-	-	-	-
Vicia/Lathyrus sp.	-	-	3	2	2	1	2	3	-	-	6	-
Pisum sativum	-	-	1	-	-	-	-	-	-	-	-	-
Medicago sp.	-	-	1	-	-	-	-	-	-	-	-	3
Medicago lupulina	-	-	-	2	-	5	-	5	1	-	2	-
Trifolium sp.	-	-	3	6	1	-	9	16	-	-	-	-
Euphorbia sp.	1	-	-	-	-	-	-	-	-	-	-	-
Euphorbia helioscopia	-	-	-	1	-	-	-	-	-	-	-	-
Linum catharticum	-	-	-	-	-	-	-	-	-	-	-	1
APIACEAE (undiff.)	-	-	-	-	1	-	-	1	-	-	2	-
Hyoscyamus niger	-	-	2	-	-	-	-	-	-	-	-	2
Lithospermum arvense	4	9	2	2	1	4	3	7	-	-	11	15
Plantago lanceolata	-	-	-	-	1	-	1	1	-	-	-	-
Veronica hederifolia	-	-	-	-	-	1	-	-	-	-	-	-
Odontites vernus	-	1	1	-	1	3	3	12	-	-	2	3
Galium aparine	11	4	6	2	26	6	2	12	1	1	13	2
Valerianella dentata	1	-	-	-	-	-	-	-	-	1	1	-
Tripleurospermum inodorum	1	1	-	-	-	1	-	2	-	-	2	3
Eleocharis palustris	-	-	-	-	-	-	1	-	-	-	-	-
Carex sp.	1	-	2	-	-	-	-	-	-	-	1	-
POACEAE small (<2mm)(undiff.)	1	15	-	5	9	14	6	14	-	3	18	2
POACEAE large (4-6mm)	-	-	9	-	-	-	-	-	-	-	-	-
POACEAE basal culm nodes	-	-	-	-	-	-	-	73	-	-	1	-
Arrhenatherum elatius var. bulbosum (tuber)	-	2	-	-	1	-	-	-	-	-	1	-
(basal culm node)	-	1	-	-	-	-	-	-	-	-	-	-

Table 6.8 (continued)

	Ditch 4043					Pits						
Feature/section	*4019*	*4096*		*4105*		*4612*	*4751*		*5149*		*5670*	
Context	*4069*	*4124*	*4182*	*4450*	*4102*	*4613*	*4317*	*4318*	*5228*	*5162*	*5715*	*5671*
Sample	*2008*	*2005*	*2012*	*2090*	*2036*	*2139*	*2028*	*2029*	*2164*	*2162*	*2201*	*2177*
Volume (litres)	*13*	*30*	*30*	*30*	*30*	*30*	*30*	*30*	*30*	*30*	*30*	*30*
Avena sp. (grains)	-	3	-	-	-	-	1	-	-	-	-	-
Avena sp. (awns)	3	4	-	1	4	-	2	5	-	1	7	-
Avena sp. (floret indet.)	-	-	-	-	-	-	-	-	-	-	1	-
Avena sp./*Bromus* sp.	2	-	3	1	-	-	-	17	3	1	14	11
Bromus sp.	-	-	-	-	-	3	21	33	-	-	-	-
Anisantha sterilis	-	-	-	-	-	-	-	-	-	-	-	1
Seed indet.	-	-	3	-	4	-	5	78	-	-	1	-
fine chaff/straw fragments	-	-	-	-	-	-	1	-	-	-	-	-

has been burnt accidentally via crop processing or used as a fuel. In some cases, as in the upper fill of pit 5670 (5671), the remains may represent fodder which was burnt as dung and discarded into the pit after being used.

The crops that seem to be present throughout the occupation of this site are spelt wheat (*Triticum spelta*), hulled barley (*Hordeum* sp.) (most likely six-row hulled barley), and possibly oats (*Avena* sp.). In some contexts where the main cereals were present in some quantities (eg, 5735 in recut 6162 of pit 5358) it is possible that wheat and barley were grown together as a maslin, rather than as a monoculture. Emmer wheat (*T. dicoccum*) appears to be sporadically present; this may be as a contaminant of the main spelt wheat crop, or a minor crop in its own right. The differentiation of wild and cultivated species of oats is only possible if the floret bases are present, and, since none was recovered, the status of oat as a crop or arable weed is unresolved. Cereals were sown in both autumn and spring, and harvested by either uprooting and/or by cutting close to the ground. Peas (*Pisum sativum*) were also grown but in small quantities. Table 6.9 shows the number of samples each crop occurs in for each phase.

A list of the non-cultivated taxa identified from the samples analysed and their habitat preferences is given in Table 6.11. Of the 65 taxa which are habitat specific, the majority (44) were from arable/disturbed ground habitats. Most of the arable weeds are found in chalky/base-rich soils and most of the crops,

Table 6.9 distribution of crops within each phase

Crop	*Phase 1/2 (n=12)*	*Phase 3 (n=23)*	*Total (n=35)*
Wheat	12	23	35
Barley	11	22	33
Oats	8	20	28
Peas	1	4	5

therefore, were probably grown on the chalk uplands adjacent to the site. However, some weeds, such as sheep's sorrel (*Rumex acetosella*) and parsley-piert (*Aphanes arvensis*), are found on poorer sandier soils, possibly indicating cultivation in the Wylye valley, or that crops were imported from further afield. A further 16 taxa come from grasslands, five from wood/scrub, and three from wetlands. The percentage occurrence in each phase of those taxa, ie, the most common and recurring species, are shown in Table 6.12.

Because crops were harvested either by being cut low to the ground and/or by uprooting, weeds growing at different heights would be included in the harvest. The presence, for instance in ditch 4043 and pit 4667, of the onion couch-grass (*Arrhenatherum elatius var bulbosum*), twining and scrambling weeds, and the low growing ones, suggests that in the crop was harvested by uprooting. The time of crop sowing can be determined by examining germinating times or flowering times of the associated weeds. Two of the commonest weeds are cleavers (*Galium aparine*) and black bindweed (*Fallopia convolvulus*) and while the former may be present in both autumn and spring sown crops, black bindweed germinates during the spring. Oats and brome (*Bromus* sp.) may also indicate sowing times – as brome flowers between May and August, and oats between June and September, the presence of oats would increase with spring sowing as it is harvested later than autumn sown crops. Because brome seeds mature earlier they are not included in the later harvested, spring sown crops.

On this evidence it appears that crops were sown both during autumn and spring throughout. It is interesting to note the presence of corncockle (*Agrostemma githago*) in pit 4598 (context 4599) as this is usually associated with a Roman introduction (Godwin 1984) but it is quite clear that it was present in the Iron Age.

Many of the grassland taxa are commonly found in grasslands of all types, especially rough grassland,

Table 6.10 Charred plant remains from phase 3 features

Feature	4196			4332				4458		4514	4598			4667	4704			5592			5358		5979
Recut		4553							4486													6162	
Context number	4369	4282	4313	4571		4385	4335	4460	4512	4515	4599	4600	4603	4674	4778	4706	4817	5729	5732	5727	5770	5735	5712
Sample	2051	2023	2026	2115	2117	2118	2055	2062	2095	2094	2119	2120	2144	2125	2141	2135	2143	2191	2193	2183	2205	2204	2198
Volume (litres)	30	30	30	0.5	0.7	30	5	30	5	15	30	30	30	30	30	30	30	30	30	30	30	30	25
CEREALS																							
Hordeum sp. (grains undiff.)	-	-	-	3	-	4	172	1	3	12	-	-	-	18	5	2	-	-	1	1	57	63	-
Hordeum sp. (grains, tail)	-	-	-	-	-	-	3	3	-	2	2	13	-	2	2	-	2	-	-	-	5	1	-
Hordeum sp. (grains, hulled)	9	5	-	-	2	2	58	5	3	5	4	19	3	26	3	-	3	7	-	-	49	50	6
Hordeum vulgare (rachis 6-row)	-	-	-	-	-	-	-	-	-	-	1	2	1	1	-	-	-	-	-	-	12	13	-
Hordeum sp. (rachis fragments)	2	2	-	-	-	2	12	-	1	6	2	36	2	15	-	4	3	2	11	2	59	130	1
Triticum sp. (grain)	7	2	3	3	-	1	32	15	5	6	-	-	7	33	6	-	-	-	13	-	25	76	-
Triticum dicoccum (basal rachis frags)	-	-	-	-	-	-	-	-	-	-	-	-	-	-	-	-	-	-	-	-	-	1	-
Triticum dicoccum (glume bases)	-	10	-	-	-	-	-	-	-	-	-	-	-	-	-	-	-	-	-	-	-	-	-
Triticum dicoccum/spelta (grain)	49	-	3	-	2	9	50	79	3	24	15	36	6	60	18	7	11	66	18	8	81	78	3
Triticum dicoccum/spelta (tail-grain)	-	-	-	-	-	-	-	-	-	-	-	2	1	-	3	-	1	-	-	-	3	9	-
Triticum dicoccum/spelta (glume bases)	340	240	143	-	4	97	127	114	3	81	95	601	415	1029	273	94	187	1135	221	40	1250	1612	139
Triticum diccocum/spelta (spikelet forks)	8	9	5	-	-	5	13	6	-	1	35	105	21	56	23	6	30	73	34	7	97	308	12
Triticum spelta (grain)	-	16	20	-	-	-	-	-	-	-	-	-	-	-	-	-	-	-	-	-	-	-	-
Triticum spelta (glume bases)	77	24	3	1	-	8	12	21	18	18	102	495	50	154	15	17	56	91	51	9	639	733	3
Triticum spelta (spikelet forks)	10	-	-	-	-	2	-	-	2	-	7	24	1	2	-	1	2	7	1	-	16	28	-
Triticum spelta (rachis)	39	11	6	-	-	5	14	18	-	5	62	42	60	67	25	7	18	42	25	1	139	330	3
Triticum spelta (basal rachis)	-	-	-	-	-	-	-	-	-	-	-	-	-	-	-	-	-	-	-	-	4	-	-
Triticum aestivum (rachis)	-	-	-	-	-	-	-	-	-	-	-	-	-	-	-	-	-	-	-	-	-	1	-
Cereals undiff. (grains)	601	118	95	8	5	55	100	150	67	81	100	224	71	529	578	110	149	569	552	39	554	607	29
Cereals undiff. (culm internodes)	-	-	-	-	-	-	-	-	-	-	-	2	-	-	-	-	-	-	-	-	-	-	-
Cereals undiff. (culm nodes)	1	8	12	-	2	2	2	16	5	1	10	22	2	19	-	3	2	14	7	4	12	11	-
Cereals undiff. (basal culm nodes)	-	2	-	1	-	2	1	1	3	4	1	24	4	9	-	-	-	1	4	3	-	-	3
Cereals undiff. (awns)	-	-	-	-	-	-	-	-	-	-	-	-	-	-	-	500	-	1000	1000	-	1000	1000	-
Cereals undiff. (awns)	-	-	-	-	-	-	-	-	-	-	-	-	-	3	-	-	-	-	-	-	1000	1000	-
Cereals (sprouts)	-	-	-	-	-	-	-	-	-	-	1	-	-	-	-	-	-	-	-	-	-	-	-
Cereals (embryos)	3	2	3	-	-	-	18	2	-	3	10	5	2	11	-	-	2	2	1	-	32	62	-
Parenchyma fragments	-	-	-	-	-	-	2	1	-	-	-	-	-	-	3	-	-	-	-	-	-	-	-
NON-CEREALS																							
Pteridium aquilinum (pinnule)	-	-	-	-	-	-	-	-	-	-	-	21	-	3	-	-	-	-	-	-	8	-	-
Ranunculus acris, bulbosus, repens	-	3	-	-	-	-	-	-	-	-	-	1	-	3	-	-	-	1	1	-	1	5	-
Ranunculus parviflorus	-	-	-	-	-	-	-	1	-	-	-	-	-	-	-	-	-	-	-	-	-	-	-
Ranunculus ficaria (tuber)	-	-	-	-	-	-	-	-	-	-	-	-	-	-	-	-	-	-	-	-	-	-	4
Papaver sp.	-	-	-	-	-	-	-	1	-	1	-	-	-	1	-	-	-	-	-	-	-	-	-
Papaver rhoeas	-	-	-	-	-	-	-	-	-	-	-	-	-	-	-	-	-	-	-	-	-	1	-
Fumaria officinalis	-	-	-	-	-	-	4	2	3	1	-	-	2	2	-	1	2	1	2	3	-	1	1
Helianthemum nummularium	-	-	-	-	-	-	-	-	-	1	-	-	-	-	-	-	-	-	-	1	-	-	-
Urtica dioica	-	1	-	-	-	-	-	-	-	-	-	-	-	-	-	-	-	-	-	-	2	-	-
Corylus avellana	-	-	-	-	-	2	-	1	-	3	7	-	-	1	-	-	-	-	-	2	4	-	3
CHENOPODIACEAE (undiff.)	1	-	-	-	-	-	-	-	-	-	5	1	-	-	-	1	-	-	-	-	-	-	-

Table 6.10 (continued)

Feature	4196			4332				4458		4514	4598			4667	4704			5592			5358		5979
Recut		4553							4486													6162	
Context number	4369	4282	4313	4571		4385	4335	4460	4512	4515	4599	4600	4603	4674	4778	4706	4817	5729	5732	5727	5770	5735	5712
Sample	2051	2023	2026	2115	2117	2118	2055	2062	2095	2094	2119	2120	2144	2125	2141	2135	2143	2191	2193	2183	2205	2204	2198
Volume (litres)	30	30	30	0.5	0.7	30	5	30	5	15	30	30	30	30	30	30	30	30	30	30	30	30	25
CEREALS																							
Hordeum sp. (grains undiff.)	-	-	-	3	-	4	172	1	3	12	-	-	-	18	5	2	-	-	1	1	57	63	-
Hordeum sp. (grains, tail)	-	-	-	-	-	-	3	3	-	2	2	13	-	2	2	-	2	-	-	-	5	1	-
Hordeum sp. (grains, hulled)	9	5	-	-	2	2	58	5	3	5	4	19	3	26	3	-	3	7	-	-	49	50	6
Hordeum vulgare (rachis 6-row)	-	-	-	-	-	-	-	-	-	-	1	2	1	1	-	-	-	-	-	-	12	13	-
Hordeum sp. (rachis fragments)	2	2	-	-	-	2	12	-	1	6	2	36	2	15	-	4	3	2	11	2	59	130	1
Triticum sp. (grain)	7	2	3	3	-	1	32	15	5	6	-	-	7	33	6	-	-	-	13	-	25	76	-
Triticum dicoccum (basal rachis frags)	-	-	-	-	-	-	-	-	-	-	-	-	-	-	-	-	-	-	-	-	-	1	-
Triticum dicoccum (glume bases)	-	10	-	-	-	-	-	-	-	-	-	-	-	-	-	-	-	-	-	-	-	-	-
Triticum dicoccum/spelta (grain)	49	-	3	-	2	9	50	79	3	24	15	36	6	60	18	7	11	66	18	8	81	78	3
Triticum dicoccum/spelta (tail-grain)	-	-	-	-	-	-	-	-	-	-	-	2	1	-	3	-	1	-	-	-	3	9	-
Triticum dicoccum/spelta (glume bases)	340	240	143	-	4	97	127	114	3	81	95	601	415	1029	273	94	187	1135	221	40	1250	1612	139
Triticum diccocum/spelta (spikelet forks)	8	9	5	-	-	5	13	6	-	1	35	105	21	56	23	6	30	73	34	7	97	308	12
Triticum spelta (grain)	-	16	20	-	-	-	-	-	-	-	-	-	-	-	-	-	-	-	-	-	-	-	-
Triticum spelta (glume bases)	77	24	3	1	-	8	12	21	18	18	102	495	50	154	15	17	56	91	51	9	639	733	3
Triticum spelta (spikelet forks)	10	-	-	-	-	2	-	-	2	-	7	24	1	2	-	1	2	7	1	-	16	28	-
Triticum spelta (rachis)	39	11	6	-	-	5	14	18	-	5	62	42	60	67	25	7	18	42	25	1	139	330	3
Triticum spelta (basal rachis)	-	-	-	-	-	-	-	-	-	-	-	-	-	-	-	-	-	-	-	-	4	-	-
Triticum aestivum (rachis)	-	-	-	-	-	-	-	-	-	-	-	-	-	-	-	-	-	-	-	-	-	1	-
Cereals undiff. (grains)	601	118	95	8	5	55	100	150	67	81	100	224	71	529	578	110	149	569	552	39	554	607	29
Cereals undiff. (culm internodes)	-	-	-	-	-	-	-	-	-	-	-	2	-	-	-	-	-	-	-	-	-	-	-
Cereals undiff. (culm nodes)	1	8	12	-	2	2	2	16	5	1	10	22	2	19	-	3	2	14	7	4	12	11	-
Cereals undiff. (basal culm nodes)	-	2	-	1	-	2	1	1	3	4	1	24	4	9	-	-	-	1	4	3	-	-	3
Cereals undiff. (awns)	-	-	-	-	-	-	-	-	-	-	-	-	-	-	-	500	-	1000	1000	-	1000	1000	-
Cereals undiff. (awns)	-	-	-	-	-	-	-	-	-	-	-	-	-	3	-	-	-	-	-	-	1000	1000	-
Cereals (sprouts)	-	-	-	-	-	-	-	-	-	-	1	-	-	-	-	-	-	-	-	-	-	-	-
Cereals (embryos)	3	2	3	-	-	-	18	2	-	3	10	5	2	11	-	-	2	2	1	-	32	62	-
Parenchyma fragments	-	-	-	-	-	-	2	1	-	-	-	-	-	-	3	-	-	-	-	-	-	-	-
NON-CEREALS																							
Pteridium aquilinum (pinnule)	-	-	-	-	-	-	-	-	-	-	-	21	-	3	-	-	-	-	-	-	8	-	-
Ranunculus acris, bulbosus, repens	-	3	-	-	-	-	-	-	-	-	-	1	-	3	-	-	-	1	1	-	1	5	-
Ranunculus parviflorus	-	-	-	-	-	-	-	1	-	-	-	-	-	-	-	-	-	-	-	-	-	-	-
Ranunculus ficaria (tuber)	-	-	-	-	-	-	-	-	-	-	-	-	-	-	-	-	-	-	-	-	-	-	4
Papaver sp.	-	-	-	-	-	-	-	1	-	1	-	-	-	1	-	-	-	-	-	-	-	-	-
Papaver rhoeas	-	-	-	-	-	-	-	-	-	-	-	-	-	-	-	-	-	-	-	-	-	1	-
Fumaria officinalis	-	-	-	-	-	-	4	2	3	1	-	-	2	2	-	1	2	1	2	3	-	1	1
Helianthemum nummularium	-	-	-	-	-	-	-	-	-	1	-	-	-	-	-	-	-	-	-	1	-	-	-
Urtica dioica	-	1	-	-	-	-	-	-	-	-	-	-	-	-	-	-	-	-	-	-	2	-	-
Corylus avellana	-	-	-	-	-	2	-	1	-	3	7	-	-	1	-	-	-	-	-	2	4	-	3
CHENOPODIACEAE (undiff.)	1	-	-	-	-	-	-	-	-	-	5	1	-	-	-	1	-	-	-	-	-	-	-

Table 6.10 (continued)

Feature type											pits												hearth
Feature	4196			4332				4458		4514	4598			4667	4704			5592			5358		5979
Recut		4553							4486													6162	
Context number	4369	4282	4313	4571		4385	4335	4460	4512	4515	4599	4600	4603	4674	4778	4706	4817	5729	5732	5727	5770	5735	5712
Sample	2051	2023	2026	2115	2117	2118	2055	2062	2095	2094	2119	2120	2144	2125	2141	2135	2143	2191	2193	2183	2205	2204	2198
Volume (litres)	30	30	30	0.5	0.7	30	5	30	5	15	30	30	30	30	30	30	30	30	30	30	30	30	25
Chenopodium ficifolium	-	-	-	-	-	-	-	3	-	-	-	-	-	-	-	-	-	-	-	-	-	-	-
Chenopodium album	-	2	2	1	-	8	12	6	2	5	-	3	1	13	7	-	1	-	-	6	52	61	2
Atriplex sp.	-	-	-	-	-	-	3	5	-	-	4	-	2	3	4	-	1	-	-	2	3	-	1
Montia fontana ssp. *chondrosperma*	-	-	-	-	-	-	-	3	-	-	-	-	-	-	-	-	-	-	-	-	-	2	-
Stellaria media	6	-	-	-	-	-	2	-	1	1	3	3	2	1	1	-	1	-	5	-	8	4	-
Stellaria graminea	-	-	-	-	-	-	-	-	-	-	-	-	-	-	-	-	-	3	-	-	-	-	-
Sagina sp.	-	-	-	-	-	-	-	-	-	-	1	-	-	-	-	-	-	-	-	-	-	-	-
Agrostemma githago	-	-	-	-	-	-	-	-	-	-	1	-	-	-	-	-	-	-	-	-	-	-	-
Silene sp.	-	-	-	-	-	-	-	-	-	-	1	-	-	-	-	-	-	-	-	-	-	-	-
Persicaria maculosa	-	-	-	-	-	-	-	-	-	-	-	-	-	-	-	-	-	-	-	-	1	3	-
Fallopia convolvulus	-	2	1	-	-	2	3	2	1	2	1	-	2	2	4	1	8	1	2	1	8	14	1
Polygonum aviculare	-	-	-	-	-	-	-	-	-	1	-	-	-	1	1	-	1	-	-	1	1	2	-
Rumex sp.	4	2	11	-	-	4	12	4	2	8	6	2	1	16	10	2	9	1	4	7	12	45	1
Rumex acetosella group	-	2	-	-	-	-	1	-	-	-	-	-	-	-	-	-	-	-	1	-	-	-	-
Hypericum sp.	-	-	-	-	-	-	-	1	-	-	-	-	-	-	-	-	-	-	-	-	-	1	-
Malva sylvestris	-	-	-	-	-	-	-	-	-	-	-	-	-	-	-	-	-	-	-	-	-	1	-
Malva sylvestris	-	-	-	-	-	-	-	-	-	-	-	-	-	-	-	-	-	-	-	-	-	1	-
Viola sp.	-	-	-	-	-	-	-	-	-	-	-	-	-	-	1	-	-	-	-	-	-	-	-
BRASSICACEAE (undiff.)	-	-	-	-	-	-	-	-	-	-	-	-	-	-	-	-	1	-	-	-	-	-	-
Thlaspi arvense	-	-	-	-	-	-	1	-	-	-	-	-	-	-	-	-	-	-	-	1	-	1	-
Brassica sp.	-	-	-	-	-	-	2	-	-	-	-	-	-	-	-	-	-	-	-	-	-	-	-
ROSACEAE																							
Potentilla sp.	-	-	-	-	-	-	-	-	-	-	1	2	-	-	-	-	-	-	-	-	-	-	-
Aphanes arvensis	-	-	-	-	-	-	-	-	1	1	2	-	-	13	-	-	-	-	-	-	1	-	-
Crataegus monogyna (thorns)	-	-	-	-	-	-	-	-	-	-	-	2	-	-	-	-	-	-	-	-	-	-	-
FABACEAE (undiff.)	-	-	-	-	-	-	-	-	-	-	-	1	-	1	-	-	-	-	-	-	-	-	-
Vicia sp.	-	-	-	-	-	-	-	-	-	-	-	-	-	-	-	-	-	4	-	-	-	-	-
Vicia/Lathyrus sp.	2	5	1	-	-	1	6	90	2	2	25	10	18	13	2	-	-	4	4	2	8	18	2
Pisum sativum	4	-	-	-	-	3	-	-	-	-	-	-	-	-	-	-	-	-	-	1	-	1	-
Medicago sp.	-	4	1	-	-	-	-	-	-	-	-	-	-	-	-	-	-	2	-	-	-	-	4
Medicago lupulina	7	-	-	-	1	6	47	3	5	3	3	4	4	51	19	5	3	-	-	-	17	36	-
Trifolium sp.	4	5	-	-	-	-	1	1	-	-	3	1	1	4	4	2	-	1	-	-	-	5	-
Trifolium sp.	-	-	-	-	-	-	-	-	-	-	1	-	-	-	-	-	-	-	-	-	-	-	-
Linum catharticum	-	-	-	-	-	-	-	-	-	-	-	-	-	-	-	-	-	-	-	-	-	1	-
APIACEAE (undiff.)	7	4	1	-	-	1	-	2	1	2	2	2	2	3	-	-	1	-	-	1	6	2	2
Pastiaca sativa	-	-	-	-	-	-	-	-	-	-	-	-	-	-	-	-	-	1	-	-	-	-	-
Hyoscyamus niger	-	2	-	-	-	-	-	-	-	-	-	3	-	-	-	-	2	1	-	-	-	-	-
Lithospermum arvense	15	2	4	2	3	2	14	-	6	9	38	1	3	163	12	3	4	10	13	10	52	12	-
Stachys sp.	-	-	-	-	-	-	-	-	-	-	-	-	-	-	1	-	-	-	-	-	-	-	-

Table 6.11 Common names and habitat preferences of the non-cultivated species

Species	*Common name*	*Habitat (after Stace 1997)*
Pteridium aquilinum (L.) Khun	Bracken	Woods, heaths, moors, usually on acid dry soils, rarely on calcareous ones
Ranunculus acris L./*repens* L./*bulbosus* L.	Buttercups	Grassland, woods, disturbed, & arable land
Ranunculus parviflorus L.	Small-flowered buttercup	Open ground of all sorts
Ranunculus ficaria L.	Lesser celandine	Damp meadows, lawns, woods, hedgebanks, & besides streams
Papaver rhoeas L.	Common poppy	Arable ground, roadsides, & waste places
Papaver L. sp.	Poppy	Waste places & cultivated ground
Papaver dubium L. (+)	Long-headed poppy	Arable, roadsides, & waste
Papaver somniferum L. (+)	Opium poppy	Introduced
Fumaria officinalis L.	Common fumitory	Cultivated & waste ground
Urtica dioica L.	Common nettle	Many habitats, especially woodland, fens, cultivated ground, & where animals defecate
Urtica urens L. (+)	Small nettle	Cultivated & waste ground
Corylus avellana L.	Hazel	Hedgerows, scrub, & woodland
Chenopodium ficifolium Sm.	Fig-leaved Goosefoot	Waste & arable land
Chenopodium album L.	Fat-hen	Waste & cultivated ground
Atriplex L. sp.	Oraches	Waste places & cultivated ground
Chenopodiaceae	Goosefoot family	
Montia fontana ssp. *Chondrosperma* (Fenzl) Walters	Blinks	Many kinds of damp places, from streams to seasonally damp hollows
Stellaria media (L.) Vill.	Common chickweed	Ubiquitous weed of cultivated & open ground
Stellaria graminea L.	Lesser stitchwort	Grassy, often dry places
Sagina L. sp.	Pearlwort	Paths, lawns, ditchsides, short turf (*S.procumbens*)
Agrostemma githago L.	Corncockle	Cultivated and waste ground
Silene L. sp.	Campions	Banks, roadsides, waste, & cultivated land (*Silene latifolia*); woods & hedgerows (*Silene dioica*)
Persicaria maculosa Gray	Redshank	Waste, cultivated, & open ground
Polygonum aviculare L.	Knotgrass	All sorts of open ground
Fallopia convolvulus (L.) Á. Löve	Black-bindweed	Waste & arable ground
Rumex acetosella L.	Sheep's sorrel	Heathy open ground, short grassland, & cultivated land, mostly on acid sandy soils
Rumex L. sp.	Docks	Waste, open, & cultivated ground as well as variety of other habitats
Hypericum L. sp.	St John's-worts	
Malva sylvestris L.	Common mallow	Waste & rough ground
Helianthemum nummularium (L.) Mill.	Common rock-rose	Base-rich grassland
Viola L. sp.	Violets	Woods, scrubs, pasture, grassland, cultivated, & waste ground
Camelina sativa (L.) Crantz (+)	Gold-of-pleasure	Introduced
Thlaspi arvense L.	Field penny-cress	Weed of waste & arable land
Brasssica L. sp.	Cabbages	
Brassicaceae indet.	Cabbage family	
Anagallis arvensis L.	Scarlet pimpernel	Arable & waste land & open ground
Potentilla L. sp.	Cinquefoils	
Aphanes arvensis L.	Parsley-piert	Cultivated & other bare ground on well-drained soils
Crataegus L. sp.	Hawthorn	Wood-borders, scrub, & hedges
Rosaceae indet.	Rose family	
Vicia L. sp.	Vetches	Grassy places, hedge-rows, & rough ground
Vicia L./*Lathyrus* L. *sp.*	Vetches/ Vetchlings	A variety of habitats but most likely here as above
Medicago lupulina L.	Black medick	Grassy places & rough ground
Medicago L. sp.	Medicks	
Trifolium L. sp.	Clovers	Grassy places, waste, & rough ground (*T. repens* & *T. pratense*)
Fabaceae indet.	Pea family	
Euphorbia helioscopa L.	Sun spurge	Cultivated ground & waste places
Euphorbia L. sp.	Spurge	
Linum catharticum L.	Fairy flax	Dry calcareous or sandy soils
Aethusa cynapium L. (+)	Fool's parsley	Cultivated & waste ground
Pastinaca sativa L.	Wild Parsnip	Grassland, rough ground esp. on chalk & limestone
Torilis nodosa (L.) Gaertner (+)	Knotted hedge-parsley	Arable & barish ground
Torilis japonica (Houtt.)DC. (+)	Upright hedge-parsley	Grassy places, hedgerows, wood-borders, & clearings
Daucus carota L. (+)	Wild carrot	Grassy places & rough ground, usually chalky soils
Apiaceae indet.	Carrot family	
Hyoscyamus niger L.	Henbane	Rough & waste ground, esp. manured by rabbits or cattle
Lithospermum arvense L.	Field gromwell	Arable fields, rough ground, & open grassy places
Stachys L. sp.	Woundwort	

Table 6.11 (continued)

Species	*Common name*	*Habitat (after Stace 1997)*
Galeopsis tetrahit L. (+)	Common hemp-nettle	Arable, rough ground, wood clearings, damp places
Prunella vulgaris L.	Self-heal	Grassland, wood-clearings, rough ground
Plantago major L.	Greater plantain	Open & rough ground, either cultivated or grassy
Plantago lanceolata L.	Ribwort plantain	Grassy places
Veronica arvensis L.	Wall speedwell	Walls, banks, open acid or calcareous ground & cultivated land
Veronica hederifolia L.	Ivy-leaved speedwell	Cultivated & waste ground, open woods, hedgerows, walls, banks
Odontites vernus (Bellardi) Dumort.	Red bartsia	Grassy places, arable, & waste ground, waysides
Sherardia arvensis L. (+)	Field madder	Arable, waste, thin grassland
Galium aparine L.	Cleavers	Cultivated & arable land, hedgerows & scrub, other open land
Sambucus nigra L.	Elder	Hedges, woods, waste, & rough ground, especially on manured soils
Valerianella dentata (L.) Pollich.	Narrow-fruited cornsalad	Cornfields & rough ground
Centaurea cyanus L.	Cornflower	Cornfields
Centaurea L. sp.	Knapweeds	Grassland & rough ground
Lapsana communis L.	Nipplewort	Open woods, hedge-rows, waste, rough ground
Tripleurospermum inodorum (L.) Sch. Bip.	Scentless mayweed	Waste, rough, & cultivated land
Asteraceae indet.	Daisy family	
Luzula campestris (L.) DC	Field wood-rush	Short grassland & similar places
Eleocharis palustris (L.) Roem. and Schult.	Common spike-rush	In or by ponds, marshes, ditches, riversides
Carex L. sp.	Sedges	Mainly of wet & damp places
Lolium L. sp.	Rye-grass	Grassy places, waste, & rough ground
Arrhenatherum elatius var *bulbosum*(Willd.) St-Amans	Onion couch	Coarse grassy places, waysides, arable, hedge-rows, rough & waste ground
Avena L./*Bromus* L. sp.	Oats/Brome	Rough & cultivated ground
Bromus secalinus L. type	Rye brome	Weed of cereals, marginal, & waste ground
Bromus l. sp.	Bromes	
Anisantha sterilis (L.) Nevski	Barren brome	Rough & waste ground, waysides, open grass-land, weed of arable
Large Poaceae >1 mm	Larger-fruited grasses	
Small Poaceae <1 mm	Smaller-fruited grasses	

(+) = only identified as mineralised

although common rock-rose (*Helianthemum nummularium*), fairy flax (*Linum catharticum*), wild parsnip

Table 6.12 Percentage abundance of non-cultivated taxa

Species	%	*No. samples (n=35)*
Galium aparine	94.3	33
Lithospermum arvense	88.6	31
Small fruited Poaceae <1 mm	88.6	31
Rumex sp.	82.3	29
Fallopia convolvulus	77.1	27
Chenopodium album	74.3	26
Vicia/Lathyrus sp.	74.3	26
Odonites vernus	68.6	24
Tripleurospermum inodurum	65.7	23
Medicago lupulina	60.0	21
Stellaria media	54.3	19
Apiaceae indet.	54.3	19
Fumaria officinalis	51.4	18
Corylus avellana	48.6	17
Bromus sp.	48.6	17
Valerianella dentata	42.9	15
Atriplex sp.	37.1	13
Polygonum aviculare	34.3	12
Plantago lanceolata	34.3	12
Aphanes arvensis	20.0	7
Anisantha sterilis	14.3	5

(*Pastinaca sativa*), and possibly St John's-wort (*Hypericum* sp.) are indicators of calcareous/base-rich grassland, while the presence of pearlwort (*Sagina* sp.) suggests that, in some places, the grass may have been quite short. The inclusion, for instance in pit 5592 (context 5729), of lesser stitchwort (*Stellaria graminea*), fairy flax, wild parsnip, and self heal (*Prunella vulgaris*), which could have survived for a short time at the edge of fields, may represent the remnants of grassland that had been turned over to cultivation. Alternatively they may have derived from the dung of livestock either grazing on the chalk grassland or fed hay in winter. These species also suggest that the grassland habitat was of some importance, providing grazing for livestock in summer and possibly hay in winter. The presence of henbane (*Hyoscyamus niger*), a species preferring a well-manured environment, suggests that the dung was stored and then used on the fields. Its occurrence in ditch 4043 may indicate that some manure may have been burnt and then dumped in the ditch.

The scrub and woodland species may have derived from the steep scarp slopes that could have been wooded at the time of occupation. Hazel (*Corylus avellana*) nuts would have been gathered as a wild food source in autumn as would have elderberries (*Sambucus nigra*) and, while hawthorn (*Crataegus* sp.) has edible fruits, the fact that thorns were the dominant find suggests that it may have been used as firewood. Tubers of lesser celandine (*Ranunculus ficaria*) may have arrived via the dung of pigs foraging in woodland near the site. Bracken (*Pteridium aquilinum*) pinnules were found in a number of samples (eg, from pits 4598, 4667, and 5358). Bracken is usually found on more acidic soils suggesting that it was brought in either from the valley bottoms or from areas with more acid soils on clay-with-flints over chalk, or from the Greensand and clay vale to the south, where it can be found growing in scrub woodland today. Bracken collected in the late autumn–early winter and dried can be used as bedding for animals.

Wetland habitats were also indicated, as in the assemblage from pit 4751, which included blinks and common spike-rush (*Eleocharis palustris*). The wetland taxa suggest the exploitation of sites in the Wylye valley, or springheads.

The findings from Battlesbury Bowl agree with those from other Iron Age sites on the southern chalk uplands, particularly the sites in the Danebury Environs Project which displayed the exploitation of a similar range of habitats, namely chalk grassland, wetland, and woodland (Campbell 2000a; Cunliffe 2000; Cunliffe and Poole 2000). Both at Battlesbury Bowl and on the Danebury sites, the major crops were spelt wheat and six-row hulled barley, with emmer wheat being rarely encountered. This general pattern seems to be repeated over most of southern Britain such as on sites on Salisbury Plain (Stevens 2006) and several in Hampshire, such as Brighton Hill South (Carruthers 1995, 58), Easton Lane (Carruthers 1989, 131), Lains Farm (Carruthers 1991, 39), Old Down Farm (Green 1981, 118 and 131), and Winnall Down (Monk 1985). Peas were found at Suddern Farm and Nettlebank Copse, Hampshire (Campbell 2000a; 2000b).

The use of rye brome (*Bromus secalinus*) as a fodder crop has been suggested by many authors (Campbell 2000a) and was either tolerated as a weed or grown as a crop in its own right during the Iron Age. Evidence from the Danebury Environs sites suggests that, by the Late Iron Age, rye brome had decreased in importance and cultivated oats taken over, but there is no clear evidence for such a change at Battlesbury Bowl. Campbell (*ibid.*) uses the change in the proportions of brome and oats, along with the introduction of the cultivation of peas, as an indication of a change in agricultural practice, with autumn sown of crops favoured in the Early Iron Age changing to a combination of autumn and winter sowing in the Late Iron Age. She also suggests that this led to a change from growing the crops (spelt wheat and six-row hulled barley) as a mixture to one where each crop is grown as a monoculture. However, the evidence from this excavation does not support this change of agricultural activity. There is also no conclusive evidence for the change in sowing times or in methods of harvesting. The assemblages from Battlesbury are predominately glume-rich and, as such, can be attributed to the burning of waste from the routine processing of crops taken from storage (*cf.* Stevens 2003). In this respect they are consistent with the interpretation of much of the material within the pits as midden waste (Macphail and Crowther, see below).

Analysis of Crop Processing

by Chris J. Stevens

Charred plant assemblages have the potential to reveal ways in which crops were harvested, processed before they were put into storage, and the processing stages that were completed as crops were taken and processed piecemeal when clean grain was required. Assemblages were analysed following Hillman (1981; 1984), van der Veen (1992) and G. Jones (1984; 1987).

It has been suggested that the glumes of hulled wheats would not be removed prior to storage (Hillman 1981; 1984); not only is this highly time-consuming but, in wetter climates, such cereals would store better, using relatively simple storage facilities, in glume or hulled form. It is assumed that glumes were only removed as and when clean grain was required. The generally high proportion of glumes in the samples suggests that the charred remains were the result of the burning of waste from the pounding of spikelets and the removal of the glumes. This suggests that the remains probably derived from the processing of crops taken from storage, as opposed to the processing of crops before storage. Such activities would have been conducted on a regular basis, as and when clean grain was needed for consumption, generating waste within the domestic sphere that may have been burnt on the fire (*cf.* Hillman 1981). Similar patterns have been seen for sites in northern England (van der Veen 1992) and in the Thames valley (Stevens 1996).

The fact that many of the samples were dominated by more than 50% of seeds of larger species suggests that many of the smaller weeds had been removed prior to storage and that, potentially, the crop had been fine-sieved, as well as threshed, winnowed, and coarse-sieved before storage. Processing of crops taken from storage, therefore, would also involve the hand-sorting of large weed seeds, and any remaining small weed seeds, from the crop before it is used. The relatively high proportion of cereal grains to weed seeds suggests that the material is waste from the processing of crops stored as semi-clean spikelets.

Storage practices and scheduling patterns with respect to crop processing appear similar to those recorded at Danebury (M. Jones 1984). However, they differ from Iron Age sites such as Maiden Castle

(Palmer and Jones 1991) and those in the Danebury Environs Project, where the composition of some assemblages suggests that harvested crops had at least not been fine-sieved, and may have been stored in the sheaf or in a partially threshed state.

The reasons for these differences are likely to reflect differences in time and labour constraints and it may be that, at both this site and Danebury, social organisation was such that crops could be both harvested and processed to semi-clean spikelets before they were stored. These differences may reflect differences between small household production, in which crops are stored relatively unprocessed, and community level activities either through the existence of large households or inter-household co-operation. Four scenarios are put forward to explain the differences between the sites:

- Inter-household organisation of agricultural activities existed at both this site and Danebury, but not to the same extent at other sites in England.
- Both sites received crops from elsewhere in the region and processed them to a greater extent than crops kept for household consumption.
- Occupants of other sites participated in the harvesting and processing of crops grown by the inhabitants of the Battlesbury Bowl and Danebury.
- Only communal consumption of communally processed crops occurred at Battlesbury Bowl and Danebury.

At present it is impossible to say which one of these scenarios is most likely to be the reason behind the differences seen. Potentially, Maiden Castle may have had the population needed for such large-scale processing yet the processing and storage of crops at the site appears to have occurred on a smaller, perhaps small household level. It is also curious that while some sites in the north-east of England and the Thames valley show very clear patterns, those from the Wessex region appear to show much more mixed patterns. Given this situation it may be that the patterns represent some collection and redistribution of communally processed grain, or grain that was processed further for exchange purposes.

Mineralised Plant Remains

by Wendy J. Carruthers

Of the 151 samples processed for the recovery of plant remains, 74 were processed specifically for the recovery of both charred and mineralised plant remains. This was because a number of pits and ditches were noted to contain cess-like deposits during excavation.

Methods and Identification

Rapid scanning of some of the flots and residues by the author showed that mineralised plant remains and 'nodules' (Carruthers 1988) were present in many of the samples. Some 82 samples from pits, ditches, and ovens were selected for analysis on the basis of the visual appearance of the residues (the presence of pale brown clinker-like concretions), or mineralised remains observed during scanning, or from contexts from which charred remains were present.

Sorted seeds, unsorted flots, and mineralised seeds recovered from the charred plant remains flots were sent to the author for analysis. After identifying and quantifying the remains, it was decided that only material from the residues would be quantified and included in the analysis. The reasons for this were that there was insufficient time to fully sort all of the flots (as the residues had been much more productive than was expected), and the remains from the flots added very little to the data. Very few mineralised plant remains were present in the flots when compared with the residues (eg, sample 2193: 477 remains in the residue; one in the flot), and remains from the flots added very few new taxa to the list. Where extra taxa were added, these have been marked as + in the species list (Tables 6.13–15).

Mineralised plant remains are often difficult to identify because fruits and seeds have usually been preserved without their seed coats, ie, as naked embryos (Green 1979; Carruthers 2000). This often limits the level of identification to the level of genus (or lower), because distinguishing features are less often found once the seed coat has been removed. For identification purposes, reference material from the Late Bronze Age site at Potterne, Wiltshire (Carruthers 2000) was used, in addition to fresh reference specimens with their seed coats removed. The same species groups and identifying features were used as in the analysis of the assemblage at Potterne.

Results

The results of the analysis are presented in Tables 6.13–15. Nomenclature and much of the habitat information follow Stace (1997). In the following discussion numbers of seeds per 10 litre sample will be used so as to make the data comparable with that from Potterne. The tables give actual seed numbers for each species, and also show total seeds per litre of processed soil at the end of each table.

Site of mineralisation

Preservation by mineralisation occurs under moist to wet conditions when soft plant tissues start to decay anaerobically in the presence of high concentrations of organic waste (Carruthers 2000). The precise

Table 6.13 Mineralised plant remains from phase 1/2 ditch 4043

Feature	*Ditch 4043*																		
Section					*4019*							*4096*					*4105*		
Context	*4010*	*4110*	*4110*	*4171*	*4089*	*4089*	*4070*	*4070*	*4069*	*4069*	*4182*	*4192*	*4124*	*4098*	*4450*	*4387*	*4386*	*4102*	*4101*
Sample	*2103*	*2104*	*2105*	*2106*	*2108*	*2107*	*2109*	*2110*	*2111*	*2008*	*2012*	*2013*	*2005*	*2002*	*2090*	*2044*	*2037*	*2036*	*2007*
Soil vol/l	*2kg*	*2kg*	*2kg*	*2kg*	*2kg*	*2kg*	*2kg*	*2kg*	*2kg*	*13*	*30*	*30*	*30*	*30*	*30*	*30*	*30*	*30*	*30*
Ranunculus repens/acris/bulbosus (buttercup achene) DG	-	-	-	-	-	-	1	-	4	7	14	34	7	-	8	-	-	1	-
Papaver sp. (poppy seed) CD	-	-	2	-	-	-	-	1	-	-	12	344	-	-	14	-	1	-	-
Fumaria sp. (fumitory embryo) CD	-	-	-	-	-	-	-	-	-	1	1	5	-	-	-	-	-	-	-
Urtica dioica L. (stinging nettle achene) CDn	-	-	5	3	6	12	3	1	-	1	16	24	1	-	5	1	2	-	2
Urtica urens L. (small nettle achene) CDn	1	4	1	-	-	-	-	-	-	2	2	62	3	1	3	-	-	1	-
Chenopodiaceae (fat hen etc. embryo) CDn	-	-	4	2	1	-	1	6	1	3	56	60	6	1	14	-	1	4	3
Caryophyllaceae cf. *Stellaria media* (cf. chickweed-type) CD	-	-	-	-	-	-	-	-	-	2	3	3	2	-	1	-	-	-	-
Polygonum aviculare L. (knotgrass achene) CD	-	-	-	-	-	-	-	-	-	-	4	-	1	-	-	-	-	-	-
Fallopia convolvulus (L.)A.Love (black bindweed achene) CD	-	-	-	-	-	-	-	-	-	-	1	2	1	1	-	-	-	-	-
Rumex sp. (dock achene) CDG	-	-	-	-	-	-	-	-	-	-	1	5	-	-	1	-	-	-	-
Viola sp. (violet seed) GHWEMF	-	-	-	-	-	-	-	-	-	-	-	1	-	-	-	-	-	-	-
Thlaspi arvense L. (field penny-cress seed) AD	-	-	-	-	-	-	-	-	-	-	-	-	2	-	1	-	-	-	-
Brassica/Sinapis sp. (mustard, charlock etc. seed) CDG	1	-	1	1	-	-	-	1	-	2	16	37	11	1	19	1	1	4	2
Indeterminate Primulaceae (primrose, loosestrife, pimpernel etc.) CDG	-	-	-	-	-	-	-	-	-	-	-	-	1	-	-	-	-	1	-
Aphanes arvensis L. (parsley-piert achene) Co	-	-	-	-	-	-	-	1	-	-	1	1	-	-	-	-	-	-	-
Malus/Pyrus sp. (apple/pear embryo) U	-	-	-	-	-	-	-	-	-	-	-	-	1	1	-	-	-	-	-
Linum catharticum L. (fairy flax seed) Gdcs U	-	-	-	-	-	-	-	-	-	-	-	3	1	-	-	-	-	-	-
Hyoscyamus niger L. (henbane seed) Dn U	-	-	-	-	-	-	1	-	-	-	24	31	2	1	15	-	1	1	3
Lithospermum arvense L. (corn gromwell embryo) ADoG	-	-	-	-	-	-	-	-	-	-	1	-	3	-	2	1	-	1	-
Lithospermum arvense (whole nutlet) ADoG	-	-	-	-	-	-	-	-	-	1	-	-	-	-	-	-	-	-	-
Myosotis sp. (forget-me-not embryo) GMCW	-	-	-	-	-	-	-	-	-	11	1	-	-	-	-	1	-	-	-
Galeopsis tetrahit L. (common hemp-nettle nutlet) ADWo	2	4	-	-	1	-	1	1	-	-	2	5	-	-	-	-	-	-	-
Prunella vulgaris L. (selfheal embryo) GDWo	-	-	-	-	-	-	-	-	-	1	-	2	-	-	-	-	-	-	-
Lamiaceae *Lamium*-type (dead-nettle-type embryo) CDY	-	1	-	-	-	-	-	-	-	-	-	-	-	-	-	-	-	-	-
Indeterminate Lamiaceae	1	-	-	-	-	-	-	-	-	-	-	-	-	-	-	-	-	-	-
Odontites/Euphrasia sp. (red bartsia/eyebright seed) ADG	-	-	1	4	-	-	-	-	2	-	1	1	-	-	-	-	-	-	-
Sherardia arvensis L. (field madder nutlet) ADG	-	-	-	-	4	1	-	-	-	1	-	2	12	2	-	-	-	-	2
cf. Dipsacaceae (teasel, scabious etc.)	-	-	-	-	-	-	-	-	-	-	3	-	2	1	-	-	-	-	-
Asteraceae *Cirsium/Carduus*-type (thistle-type embryo) DG	-	-	-	-	-	-	-	-	1	-	-	-	2	-	-	-	-	-	-
Asteraceae *Anthemis cotula*-type (mayweed-type embryo) CD	-	-	-	-	-	-	-	-	-	1	-	-	-	-	-	-	-	-	-
Carex sp. (trigonous embryo) MGw	-	-	-	-	-	-	-	-	-	-	-	-	-	-	-	-	-	-	1
Indeterminate Poaceae (indeterminate grass caryopsis) DG	-	-	-	-	-	-	-	-	-	1	-	2	-	1	-	-	-	-	-
Indeterminate mineralised seed	-	-	-	-	1	-	-	-	-	-	-	-	-	-	-	-	-	-	-
mineralised rootlets	-	-	-	2	-	1	-	-	-	-	-	-	-	4	-	-	-	-	-
mineralised worm cocoons	-	-	-	-	-	-	-	-	-	-	-	-	-	1	-	-	-	-	-
mineralised insect pupae	-	-	-	-	-	1	-	-	-	1	-	24	-	-	-	-	-	-	-
mineralised fly eggs	-	-	-	-	-	-	-	-	-	-	-	-	2	-	-	-	-	-	-
indeterminate mineralised invertebrate eggs	-	-	-	-	1	-	-	1	3	1	-	-	1	1	-	-	-	-	-
mineralised mites	-	-	-	-	-	-	1	1	3	4	1	-	-	-	-	-	-	-	-
mineralised nodules	1	-	-	1	-	-	-	-	4	130	13	17	23	14	11	30	40	28	16
Total fruit seeds	*5*	*9*	*14*	*10*	*12*	*13*	*7*	*11*	*8*	*34*	*159*	*624*	*58*	*10*	*83*	*4*	*6*	*13*	*13*
Total seeds per litre	-	-	-	-	-	-	-	-	-	*2.6*	*5.3*	*20.8*	*1.9*	*0.3*	*2.8*	*0.1*	*0.2*	*0.4*	*0.4*
Total mineralised fragments per litre	-	-	-	-	-	-	-	-	-	*13.1*	*5.8*	*22.2*	*2.8*	*1.0*	*3.1*	*1.1*	*1.5*	*1.4*	*1.0*

conditions necessary for this to occur and the time that it takes for tissues to become replaced by minerals are not yet fully understood. It is crucial to the interpretation to establish where the mineralisation occurred, as this will determine whether the taxa represent plants consumed and deposited as faecal waste, or whether they were seeds that had been shed from vegetation growing on a midden-type of deposit, as at Potterne. Of course, a mixture from these two sources could be represented, in addition to domestic waste that may have been dumped in either of the two types of deposit. These sources are particularly difficult to tell apart in prehistoric contexts because exotic imported foods were not being consumed and many of the native species are likely to have been used as foods, flavourings, and medicinal plants.

Mineralised faecal waste has commonly been recovered from Romano-British and later sites, where the construction of cess-pits and garderobes has ensured that the right mineral-rich, moist conditions were provided for preservation to take place. However, such features have not yet been observed on prehistoric sites, which makes the deposits on this site of particular importance. Although the calcareous soils would have been a contributing factor towards the replacement of plant tissues by calcium phosphate, it is unlikely that many of the remains have been preserved *in situ*, as appears to have occurred on the Upper Greensand at Potterne. Distinct spreads of cess-like material were observed in some of the pits and ditches during excavation, and soil micromorphological analysis (Macphail and Crowther, see below) indicated that there was substantial evidence for the input of cess in many of the samples. The archaeobotanical reasons for suggesting that the plant remains were redeposited rather than being preserved *in situ* are discussed below.

Density of mineralised remains

The density of fruits and seeds in the different features was very variable, ranging from 15 items per 10 litre sample (average for pit 5358) to 117 per 10l (pit 4641). There was no clear pattern of distribution or increase in remains in a particular area of the site. Adjacent features often contained very different quantities of mineralised remains and there was no consistent pattern of distribution within features, for example, the mineralisation did not increase towards the top or bottom of all of the features, but varied from feature to feature. This suggests that the remains were more likely to represent redeposited waste rather than material preserved *in situ*. At Potterne, seed numbers varied but there were overall trends which applied to the whole site, such as the increase in mineralisation towards the bottom of the 'midden' and the extensive mineralised 'crust' across the site.

Also notable was the scarcity of rootlet fragments in the samples, compared with their constant presence in the samples from Potterne. Only 17 of the 77 samples produced rootlets and, in most cases, there were only a few rootlets present (average = 1 rootlet per 10 litre sample), whereas all of the Potterne samples contained numerous rootlets, and the average number per 10 litre sample was 188. The frequency of mineralised rootlets was used as an argument for preservation *in situ* at Potterne, and conversely it could suggest that preservation here had not occurred *in situ* on an established vegetation surface.

The frequent presence of 'nodules' in samples is more difficult to interpret, since the origins of these unidentified structures are unknown (Carruthers 1989). They occur in varying sizes, from less that 1mm to over 10 mm diameter, and in very variable quantities. They do not seem to consistently be concentrated in any particular levels in pits and ditches, and can occur in large numbers where there are few seeds, and vice versa. They do, however, appear to be associated with preservation by mineralisation, and can be a useful indicator in flotation samples that mineralised remains might be present in the residues. Their occurrence was not as frequent as at Potterne, averaging 22 nodules per 10 litre sample, as opposed to 78 at Potterne. However, one sample contained a particularly large number of nodules (1431 nodules in 30 litres of sample), many of which were large enough to be mistaken for mineralised peas or beans in the field. These nodules do not appear to be plant in origin, but may be a product of soil chemical processes. They have been examined by soil scientists, mycologists, and a number of other specialists but are still, to the author's knowledge, 'of unknown origin'.

Range of taxa preserved

Sixty-five different taxa were preserved in the samples, many of which were also recovered at Potterne. There were a few notable differences, however, which could provide further evidence for the differences in origins of the material. Although similar quantities of soil were processed at both sites (*c.* 1650 litres here and *c.* 1300 litres at Potterne), 27 grain fragments and several concretions containing cereal bran were recorded, in contrast to just one identifiable fragment of cereal at Potterne. During an evaluation at East Chisenbury, also in Wiltshire (Carruthers, unpublished), a total of only 30 litres of soil from six different contexts produced three cereal fragments and three concretions containing cereal bran (Brown *et al.* 1994; McOmish 1996). Battlesbury Bowl and East Chisenbury also produced evidence for the presence of possible straw, whilst it was absent from Potterne. At East Chisenbury (*ibid.*) matted straw

Table 6.14a Mineralised plant remains from phase 1/2 pits, and phase 3 and unphased post-holes

Feature type	*Pit*														*Post-hole*		
Feature	*4704*				*4751*		*5149*		*4612*	*5670*					*5786*	*4299*	*4324*
Context	*4817*	*4778*	*4726*	*4732*	*4318*	*4317*	*5228*	*5162*	*4613*	*5716*	*5715*	*5714*	*5713*	*5671*	*5787*	*4298*	*4323*
Sample	*2143*	*2141*	*2135*	*2137*	*2029*	*2028*	*2164*	*2162*	*2139*	*2202*	*2201*	*2200*	*2197*	*2177*	*2187*	*2021*	*2031*
Soil vol/l	*30*	*30*	*30*	*2*	*30*	*30*	*30*	*30*	*30*	*15*	*30*	*30*	*30*	*30*	*5*	*15*	*5*
Indeterminate cereal frag.	+	-	-	-	-	-	-	-	2	-	-	-	-	-	-	-	-
cf. cereal bran	-	-	-	-	-	-	-	-	-	-	-	-	-	-	1	-	-
Ranunculus repens/acris/bulbosus (buttercup achene) DG	3	-	-	-	-	-	7	38	-	-	-	-	-	-	-	-	-
Papaver sp. (poppy seed) CD	+	2	-	-	-	-	-	-	+	-	1	-	-	-	-	-	-
Fumaria sp. (fumitory embryo) CD	-	-	-	-	-	-	1	1	-	-	-	-	-	-	-	-	-
Urtica dioica L. (stinging nettle achene) CDn	+	-	3	-	-	-	-	-	-	-	2	-	-	-	-	-	-
Urtica urens L. (small nettle achene) CDn	1	-	5	-	-	-	-	-	-	-	-	-	-	-	-	-	-
Chenopodiaceae (fat hen etc. embryo) CDn	12	1	1	-	-	-	8	23	-	-	4	4	2	5	-	-	-
Caryophyllaceae cf. *Stellaria media* (cf. chickweed-type) CD	-	1	+	-	-	-	-	-	-	1	-	-	-	1	-	-	-
Caryophyllaceae *Cerastium*-type (mouse-ear type) CD	+	-	-	-	-	-	-	-	+	-	-	-	-	-	-	-	-
Polygonum aviculare L. (knotgrass achene) CD	-	-	-	-	-	-	-	1	-	-	-	-	-	-	-	-	-
Fallopia convolvulus (L.)A.Love (black bindweed achene) CD	-	2	-	-	-	-	-	-	-	-	-	-	-	-	-	-	-
Rumex acetosella L. (sheep's sorrel embryo) GEa	-	-	-	-	-	-	-	1	-	-	1	-	-	-	-	-	-
Rumex sp. (dock achene) CDG	4	6	1	-	-	-	2	9	-	-	4	-	-	1	-	-	-
Viola sp. (violet seed) GHWEMF	4	1	-	-	-	-	-	2	-	-	1	-	-	-	-	-	-
Brassicaceae *Capsella*-type (shepherd's purse-type)	-	1	-	-	-	-	-	-	-	-	1	-	1	-	-	-	-
Thlaspi arvense L. (field penny-cress seed) AD	-	1	-	-	-	-	-	3	-	-	-	-	-	-	-	-	-
Brassica/Sinapis sp. (mustard, charlock etc. seed) CDG	524	122	57	3	14		3	4	52	1	34	14	14	10	1	8	
cf. *Camelina sativa* (cf. gold-of-pleasure) C	-	-	-	-	-	-	-	1	-	-	-	-	-	-	-	-	-
Indeterminate Primulaceae (primrose, loosestrife, pimpernel etc.) CDG	1	-	2	-	-	-	-	-	-	-	1	-	-	-	-	-	-
Aphanes arvensis L. (parsley-piert achene) Co	2	1	-	-	-	-	-	-	-	-	-	-	-	-	-	-	-
Linum catharticum L. (fairy flax seed) Gdcs U	1	-	-	-	-	-	-	-	-	-	2	-	-	-	-	-	-
Umbelliferae *Pimpinella* -type (burnet-saxifrage type)	1	-	+	-	-	-	2	9	-	-	3	-	-	-	-	-	-
Aethusa cynapium L. (fool's parsley mericarp) CD	2	-	-	-	-	-	-	-	-	-	-	-	-	-	-	-	-
Torilis sp. (hedge-parsley mericarp)	-	-	-	-	-	-	-	-	+	-	-	-	2	-	-	-	-
Daucus carota L. (wild carrot mericarp) Gc	1	-	-	-	-	-	-	1	-	-	-	-	-	-	-	-	-
cf. *Chaerophyllum* sp. (cf. chervil mericarp) GH	-	-	-	-	-	-	1	-	-	-	-	-	-	-	-	-	-
Indeterminate Umbelliferae	3	1	-	-	-	-	2	5	-	-	-	-	1	-	-	-	-
Hyoscyamus niger L. (henbane seed) Dn U	283	4	9	-	-	-	-	-	-	1	-	-	-	-	-	-	-
Lithospermum arvense L. (corn gromwell embryo) ADoG	5	4	1	-	-	-	-	1	23	-	3	-	1	-	-	6	-
Lithospermum arvense L. (whole nutlet) ADoG	-	-	-	-	-	-	-	-	-	-	-	1	-	1	-	-	-
Myosotis sp. (forget-me-not embryo) GMCW	-	-	2	-	-	-	-	1	+	-	+	3	-	-	-	-	-
Galeopsis tetrahit L. (common hemp-nettle nutlet) ADWod	-	-	-	-	-	-	1	2	-	-	-	-	-	-	-	-	-
Lamiaceae *Lamium*-type (deadnettle-type) CD	-	-	-	-	-	-	-	2	-	-	-	-	-	-	-	-	-
Lamiaceae *Ballota*-type (black horehound-type) DH	-	-	-	-	-	-	-	-	-	-	-	-	-	1	-	-	-
Lamiaceae *Marrubium*-type (white horehound-type) GD	-	+	-	-	-	-	-	-	-	-	-	-	-	-	-	-	-

Table 6.14a (continued)

Feature type							*Pit*								*Post-hole*		
Feature		*4704*			*4751*		*5149*		*4612*			*5670*			*5786*	*4299*	*4324*
Context	*4817*	*4778*	*4726*	*4732*	*4318*	*4317*	*5228*	*5162*	*4613*	*5716*	*5715*	*5714*	*5713*	*5671*	*5787*	*4298*	*4323*
Sample	*2143*	*2141*	*2135*	*2137*	*2029*	*2028*	*2164*	*2162*	*2139*	*2202*	*2201*	*2200*	*2197*	*2177*	*2187*	*2021*	*2031*
Soil vol/l	*30*	*30*	*30*	*2*	*30*	*30*	*30*	*30*	*30*	*15*	*30*	*30*	*30*	*30*	*5*	*15*	*5*
Odontites/Euphrasia sp. (red bartsia/eyebright seed) ADG	-	-	-	-	-	-	-	-	+	-	-	-	-	-	-	-	-
Valerianella sp. (cornsalad embryo) AD	+	+	-	-	-	-	-	-	-	-	1	-	-	-	-	-	-
Asteraceae *Cirsium/Carduus*-type (thistle-type embryo) GD	1	-	-	-	-	-	-	-	1	-	1	-	-	-	-	-	-
Asteraceae *Anthemis cotula*-type (stinking mayweed-type)	1	-	-	-	-	-	-	-	-	-	1	-	1	-	-	-	-
Carex sp. (trigonous sedge embryo) MGw	3	-	1	-	-	-	-	-	-	-	-	-	-	-	-	-	-
Carex sp. (lenticular sedge embryo) MGw	+	-	-	-	-	-	-	-	-	-	-	-	-	-	-	-	-
Indeterminate Poaceae (indeterminate grass seed) GDC	-	-	-	-	-	-	-	-	-	-	1	-	-	-	-	-	-
cf. mineralised straw fragments	+	-	-	-	-	-	-	-	-	-	-	-	-	-	-	-	-
unidentified mineralised seeds	-	1	-	-	-	-	-	-	-	-	-	-	-	-	-	-	-
mineralised rootlets	-	-	-	-	-	-	6	14	1	-	+	2	-	2	-	-	-
mineralised worm cocoons	3	-	-	-	-	-	1	10	-	-	1	1	1	-	-	-	-
mineralised insect pupae	1	-	-	-	-	-	2	10	-	-	-	-	1	-	1	-	-
mineralised invertebrate egg	+	-	3	-	-	-	-	-	-	14	19	15	11	6	-	-	-
mineralised nodules	17	14	19	1	32	194	17	47	152	8	53	30	50	10	1	9	2
Total fruit seeds	*852*	*147*	*82*	*3*	*14*	*0*	*27*	*104*	*78*	*3*	*61*	*22*	*22*	*19*	*2*	*14*	*0*
Total seeds per litre	*28.4*	*4.9*	*2.7*	*1.5*	*0.5*	*0.0*	*0.9*	*3.5*	*2.6*	*0.2*	*2.0*	*0.7*	*0.7*	*0.6*	*0.4*	*0.9*	*0.0*
Total frags per litre	*29.1*	*5.4*	*3.5*	*2.0*	*1.5*	*6.5*	*1.8*	*6.2*	*7.7*	*1.7*	*4.5*	*2.3*	*2.8*	*1.2*	*0.8*	*1.5*	*0.4*

Table 6.14b Mineralised plant remains from phase 3 pits (including hearth 4215 in pit 4196)

Feature type	Pit																		Hearth
Feature	4641				5592									4196					
Recut															4553				4215
Context	4742	4728	5084	4642	5882	5729	5732	5730	5731	5728	5727	5594	5593	4369	4313	4309	4282	4212	4216
Sample	2165	2136	2161	2132	2194	2191	2193	2189	2192	2184	2183	2181	2180	2051	2026	2024	2023	2018	2019
Soil vol/l	30	15	30	30	30	30	30	30	15	30	30	30	30	30	30	1.5	30	2	1.5
Indeterminate cereal fragment	1	4	-	-	-	3	7	2	-	-	-	-	-	-	-	-	-	-	-
cf. cereal bran	-	-	-	-	-	-	-	+	-	-	-	-	-	-	-	-	-	-	-
Ranunculus repens/acris/bulbosus (buttercup achene) DG	2	3	-	-	1	-	15	23	2	-	-	-	-	-	7	-	-	-	-
Papaver sp. (poppy seed) CD	10*	50*	-	4*	1	4	5	4	1	-	-	-	-	-	7	-	-	-	-
Fumaria sp. (fumitory embryo) CD	-	-	-	-	-	1	1	1	-	-	-	-	-	-	-	-	1	-	-
Urtica dioica L. (stinging nettle achene) CDn	10*	-	-	4*	-	-	-	-	1	1	-	-	-	-	-	-	-	-	-
Urtica urens L. (small nettle achene) CDn	10*	20*	-	-	-	-	4	8	1	1	-	-	-	-	6	1	-	-	-
Chenopodiceae (fat hen etc. embryo) CDn	34*	50*	6	31*	-	3	17	7	2	4	2	-	-	7	4	-	-	-	-
Caryophyllaceae cf. *Stellaria media* (cf. chickweed-type) CD	-	10*	-	12*	-	1	8	1	2	1	-	-	-	-	3	-	-	-	-
Caryophyllaceae *Cerastium*-type (mouse-ear type) CD	-	-	-	-	-	-	-	-	-	-	-	-	-	-	1	-	-	-	-
Indeterminate Caryophyllaceae	-	-	-	-	-	1	-	-	-	-	-	-	-	-	-	-	-	-	-
Polygonum aviculare L. (knotgrass achene) CD	-	-	-	-	-	-	-	2	1	3	-	-	-	-	-	-	-	-	-
Fallopia convolvulus (L.)A.Love (black bindweed achene) CD	-	-	-	1	-	-	1	1	-	-	-	-	-	-	-	-	-	-	-
Rumex sp. (dock achene) CDG	17*	10	-	1	-	1	15	7	1	2	-	1	-	1	6	-	1	-	-
Brassicaceae *Capsella*-type	-	-	-	-	-	-	1	1	1	-	-	-	-	-	-	-	-	-	-
Thlaspi arvense L. (field penny-cress seed) AD	-	1	-	-	-	-	4	6	1	-	-	1	-	-	-	-	-	-	-
Brassica/Sinapis sp. (mustard, charlock etc. seed) CDG	140*	264*	16	61*	3	13	357	259	7	110	35	30	8	42	19	3	4	-	-
Indeterminate Brassicaceae	-	10*	-	4*	-	-	-	-	-	-	-	-	-	-	-	-	-	-	-
Indeterminate Primulaceae	-	10*	-	8*	-	-	1	-	1	-	-	-	1	-	-	-	-	-	-
Potentilla sp. (cinquefoil achene)	-	-	-	-	-	-	-	1	-	-	-	-	-	-	-	-	-	-	-
Aphanes arvensis L. (parsley-piert achene) Co	-	-	1	-	-	2	-	-	1	-	-	-	-	-	-	-	-	-	-
Malus/Pyrus sp. (apple/pear embryo) U	-	-	-	-	-	-	-	1	-	-	-	-	-	-	-	-	-	-	-
Linum catharticum L. (fairy flax seed) Gdcs U	-	-	10*	-	-	-	6	3	-	-	-	-	-	-	3	-	-	-	-
Umbelliferae *Pimpinella* -type (burnet-saxifrage type)	1	-	-	-	-	-	-	-	-	-	-	-	-	-	1	-	-	-	-
Torilis nodosa (L.)Gaertn. (knotted hedge-parsley mericarp) Ado	-	1	-	-	-	-	-	-	-	-	-	-	-	-	-	-	-	-	-
Torilis sp. (hedge-parsley mericarp)	-	3	-	-	-	-	-	-	-	-	-	-	-	-	-	-	-	-	-
Indeterminate Umbelliferae	1	-	-	-	-	-	-	-	-	-	1	-	-	-	-	-	-	-	-
Hyoscyamus niger L. (henbane seed) Dn U	-	-	-	-	-	3	6	4	14	2	5	-	-	-	3	-	1	2	-
Lithospermum arvense L. (corn gromwell embryo) ADoG	19	2	-	1	-	3	9	11	2	9	4	1	-	+	-	-	1	-	-
Lithospermum arvense (whole nutlet) ADoG	-	-	-	-	-	1	2	-	-	-	-	-	-	-	-	-	-	-	-

Table 6.14b (continued)

Feature type	Pit																		Hearth
Feature	4641				5592									4196					
Recut															4553				4215
Context	4742	4728	5084	4642	5882	5729	5732	5730	5731	5728	5727	5594	5593	4369	4313	4309	4282	4212	4216
Sample	2165	2136	2161	2132	2194	2191	2193	2189	2192	2184	2183	2181	2180	2051	2026	2024	2023	2018	2019
Soil vol/l	30	15	30	30	30	30	30	30	15	30	30	30	30	30	30	1.5	30	2	1.5
Myosotis sp. (forget-me-not embryo) GMCW	2	30*	-	4*	-	+	2	-	-	1	-	1	-	-	-	-	-	-	-
Galeopsis tetrahit L. (common hemp-nettle nutlet) ADWod	-	-	-	-	-	-	2	1	-	-	-	-	-	-	-	-	-	-	-
Prunella vulgaris L. (self-heal embryo) GD	-	-	-	-	-	-	1	-	-	-	-	-	-	-	-	-	-	-	-
Lamiaceae *Lamium*-type (deadnettle-type)	-	-	-	-	-	-	1	-	-	-	-	-	-	-	-	-	-	-	-
Plantago lanceolata (ribwort plantain seed) G	-	-	-	-	-	-	-	1	-	-	-	-	-	-	-	-	-	-	-
Odontites/Euphrasia sp. (red bartsia/eyebright seed) ADG	-	-	-	-	-	1	2	5	1	-	-	-	-	-	-	-	-	-	-
Rhinanthus sp. (yellow rattle embryo) G	-	-	-	-	-	-	1	-	-	-	-	-	-	-	-	-	-	-	-
Sherardia arvensis L. (field madder nutlet) ADG	1	-	-	-		-	6	2	2	13	2	-	-	-	-	-	-	-	-
Galium aparine L. (cleavers nutlet) CD	-	1	-	-		-	2	-	-	-	-	-	-	-	-	-	-	-	-
Valerianella sp. (cornsalad embryo) AD	-	-	-	-	1	11	-	1	-	-	-	-	-	-	-	-	-	-	-
cf. Dipsacaceae (teasel, scabious etc.) GD	-	-	-	-	-	-	-	-	-	-	-	-	-	-	-	-	1	-	-
Asteraceae *Cirsium/Carduus*-type (thistle-type embryo) GD	-	-	-	-	-	-	-	2	-	-	-	-	-	-	1	-	-	-	-
Asteraceae *Anthemis cotula*-type (stinking mayweed-type) ADh	1	30*	-	-	-	-	-	1	-	-	-	-	-	-	1	-	-	-	-
Carex sp. (trigonous sedge embryo) MGw	1	-	-	-	-	1	1	-	-	-	-	-	-	+	-	-	1	-	-
Indeterminate Poaceae (indeterminate grasses) GC	-	-	-	-	-	-	-	-	-	-	-	-	-	-	1	-	-	-	-
cf. mineralised straw fragment	-	-	-	-	-	1	10	-	-	-	-	-	-	-	-	-	-	-	-
mineralised rootlets	-	-	-	-	-	-	-	-	-	-	-	2	-	-	-	3	-	-	-
mineralised worm cocoons	-	-	-	-	-	-	-	-	-	-	-	-	-	-	-	-	1	-	-
mineralised baby worms	-	-	-	-	-	-	2	-	-	-	-	-	-	-	-	-	-	-	-
mineralised insect pupae	5	-	-	-	-	-	-	3	3	-	-	-	-	-	-	-	-	-	-
mineralised fly eggs	-	-	-	-	1	-	-	-	-	-	-	-	-	-	-	-	-	-	-
Indeterminate mineralised invertebrate eggs	40*	10*	5	24*	-	3	-	8	2	6	3	6	6	-	5	-	-	-	2
mineralised nodules	82*	80*	22	219*	-	8	7	1431	3	47	28	96	20	3	2	-	15	1	-
Total fruit seeds	247	498	23	131	6	49	477	355	41	147	49	34	9	50	63	4	10	2	0
Total seeds per litre	8.2	33.2	0.8	4.4	0.2	1.6	15.9	11.8	2.7	4.9	1.6	1.1	0.3	1.7	2.1	2.7	0.3	1.0	0.0
Total frags per litre	12.5	39.2	1.7	12.5	0.2	2.0	16.5	59.9	3.3	6.7	2.7	4.6	1.2	1.8	2.3	4.7	0.9	1.5	1.3

Habitat keys (Tables 13–15):

A = arable; C = cultivated; D = disturbed, waste; E = heaths, moors; F = fenland; G = grass; H = hedgerows; M = marsh, bog; S = scrub; W = woods

soil preferences: a = acidic; n = nurient-rich; o = open; w = wet, damp

could be observed in mineralised concretions, perhaps indicating stable waste, bedding, or flooring material.

Other remains from obviously edible taxa were scarce from all three sites, although they all produced a few apple/pear (*Malus sylvestris*/*Pyrus communis*) seed embryos. At Potterne, almost all of the edible taxa (which also included bramble (*Rubus* sp.), cf. sloe (*Prunus cf. spinosa*) elder (*Sambucus nigra*) and flax (*Linum usitatissimum*)) were recovered from the pre-midden occupation features. These four economically useful taxa were not present in the mineralised assemblages from Battlesbury Bowl or East Chisenbury, although a charred elder seed was recovered from Battlesbury Bowl. Possible seeds of gold-of-pleasure (*cf. Camelina sativa*) were present in two adjacent pits (4993 and 5149); this is an introduced weed of flax and an oil seed plant (Hjelmqvist 1950), so its presence could be of economic significance.

Table 6.16 summarises the main points of difference between the mineralised assemblages from Battlesbury Bowl and East Chisenbury, and Potterne. It can be seen that the assemblages from Potterne primarily consist of taxa that grow on moist, nutrient-rich soils, such as nettles (*Urtica dioica* and *U. urens*), chenopods (Chenopodiaceae), blinks (*Montia fontana* ssp. *fontana*), and sedges (*Carex* sp.). The other two sites produced greater quantities of cereal remains although in no cases were these numerous. Whether the cereals derived from human faecal waste or from animal bedding and dung is less certain. Relatively few edible taxa were represented in the assemblages, although a number of the remains could have been consumed as flavourings (eg, *Brassica*/*Sinapis* sp.) or medicinal plants. Purging flax (*Linum catharticum*) falls into this latter category, being, as its name suggests, a powerful, if dangerous, purgative. However, it could also have been introduced in animal dung and fodder. It is characteristic of dry, calcareous grasslands, particularly on soils with low levels of available nitrogen. It is, therefore, likely to have been growing around the sites at Battlesbury Bowl and East Chisenbury. It is notable that five out of the ten samples containing purging flax also contained cereal remains, suggesting that these taxa derived from the same source. This does not help in distinguishing between human faeces or stable waste, since cereals and purging flax could have been consumed in both cases. But it is notable that purging flax was not present amongst the wide range of taxa from Potterne and it appears to be more common than might be expected in mineralised assemblages from other sites, such as in the Saxon sunken-featured building at Abbots Worthy, Hampshire (Carruthers 1991). The author suspects, but cannot prove, that purging flax seeds were being collected for medicinal use since it is much less common in medieval mineralised assemblages, when other, safer, purgatives, such as fig became available.

Henbane (*Hyoscyamus niger*) is another potentially poisonous plant that has been used externally, as a poultice, to cure inflammations and relieve pain (Lust 1974). It was relatively frequent on all three sites, and particularly frequent (283 seeds) in the bottom of pit 4704. Henbane is particularly characteristic of nutrient-rich soils such as middens and farmyards, so its frequent occurrence in the samples from Potterne is not surprising. However, the sample from pit 4704 also contained numerous Brassicaceae seeds (524 seeds). Several of the Brassicaceae (*Brassica*/*Sinapis* sp.) and poppy seeds (*Papaver* sp.) can be used to flavour foods. It is possible that these remains were deliberately placed in the base of this pit but this is impossible to prove as the taxa also commonly grow as weeds of disturbed and cultivated soils. Brassicaceae are the most commonly occurring and most frequent taxon, being recorded in 83% of the samples. Since its seeds are the most commonly found mineralised seeds on archaeological sites, it is clear that they are very susceptible to this form of preservation.

Perhaps the most convincing evidence for the presence of human faecal waste was the recovery of apple/pear embryos. These were recovered from two features, pit 5592 and ditch 4043 (section 4096), both of which produced high concentrations of mineralised plant remains, pit 5592 also producing the highest concentration of cereal fragments. The soil micromorphological analysis shows that pit 5592 was phosphate-rich (see below) and, although deposits in ditch section 4096 were not studied, a section of the same ditch to the north apparently contained evidence for cess inputs.

An opium poppy seed (*Papaver somniferum*) was recovered from pit 4598. This introduced taxon was recovered from many of the Danebury Environs sites (Campbell 2000). It may have been grown as a flavouring or as an oil seed plant.

Many of the taxa preserved in the assemblages are common ruderal or segetal weeds, growing in a wide range of disturbed habitats. It is difficult to determine, therefore, whether they were growing locally, shedding their seeds into organic-rich faecal/dung deposits, whether they had been consumed by animals or humans as crop processing waste or crop contaminants, or whether they had been thrown into the faecal/dung deposits as waste during the formation process. Taxa such as nettles, chenopods, docks, and Caryophyllaceae *cf.* chickweed were common in some of the samples (particularly ditch 4043 and pit 4486, close to the ditch), and at Potterne. These taxa are particularly well suited to this type of disturbed, nutrient-rich habitat, and are

Table 6.15 Mineralised plant remains from phase 3 pits

Feature	4332					4458					4598			4667	4993				5358			
Recut						4486																
Context	4385	4385	4385	4336	4335	4460	4507	4512	4515	4540	4603	4600	4599	4674	4996	5155	4995	4994	6083	5770	5735	5359
Sample	2112-7	2085	2118	2048	2055	2062	2069	2095	2094	2091	2144	2120	2119	2125	2159	2160	2158	2157	2207	2205	2204	2203
Soil vol/l	2.9	2	30	30	5	30	15	5	15	30	30	30	30	30	2	15	30	15	2	30	30	30
Indeterminate cereal fragment	-	-	-	-	-	-	2	-	-	-	-	6	-	-	-	-	-	-	-	-	-	-
cf. cereal bran	-	-	+	-	-	-	-	-	-	-	-	-	-	-	-	-	-	-	-	-	-	-
cf. *Triticum dicoccum/spelta* (cf.emmer/spelt rachis) U	-	-	-	-	-	-	1	-	-	-	-	-	-	-	-	-	-	-	-	-	-	-
Ranunculus repens/acris/bulbosus (buttercup achene) DG	-	-	-	-	2	-	2	1	1	-	4	173*	6	-	-	1	4	1	-	-	-	-
Papaver dubium L. (long-headed poppy seed) AD	-	-	-	-	-	-	-	-	-	-	-	+	-	-	-	-	-	-	-	-	-	-
Papaver cf. *rhoeas* (cf. common poppy seed) AD	-	-	-	-	-	-	-	-	+	-	-	-	-	-	-	-	-	-	-	-	-	-
Papaver somniferum L. (opium poppy seed) U	-	-	-	-	-	-	-	-	-	-	+	-	-	-	-	-	-	-	-	-	-	-
Papaver sp. (poppy seed) CD	-	-	1	-	-	-	17	15	-	18	5	-	17	+	-	-	-	-	-	-	-	-
Fumaria sp. (fumitory embryo) CD	-	-	-	-	-	-	-	-	-	-	-	-	-	1	-	-	-	-	-	-	-	-
Urtica dioica L. (stinging nettle achene) CDn	-	-	-	-	-	-	14	-	-	3	1	70*	1	-	-	-	2	-	-	-	-	-
Urtica urens L. (small nettle achene) CDn	-	-	-	-	-	-	3	-	-	-	1	80*	4	-	-	2	-	-	-	-	-	-
Chenopodiceae (fat hen etc. embryo) CDn	-	-	1	-	2	-	21	24	5	24	10	5	3	-	3	2	5	2	-	-	-	-
Caryophyllaceae cf. *Stellaria media* (cf. chickweed-type) CD	-	-	-	-	-	-	6	1	-	1	4	51*	-	-	-	1	2	1	-	-	-	-
Caryophyllaceae *Cerastium*-type (mouse-ear type) CD	-	-	-	-	-	-	1	-	-	-	-	-	-	-	-	-	-	-	-	-	-	-
Indeterminate Caryophyllaceae	-	-	-	-	-	-	-	-	-	-	-	20*	-	-	-	-	-	-	-	-	-	-
Polygonum aviculare L. (knotgrass achene) CD	-	-	-	-	-	-	1	-	-	-	1	16*	3	-	1	-	-	-	-	-	-	-
Fallopia convolvulus (L.)A.Love (black bindweed achene) CD	-	-	-	-	-	-	-	1	1	-	-	2	1	-	-	-	-	-	-	-	-	-
Rumex acetosella L. (sheep's sorrel embryo) GEa	-	-	-	-	-	-	-	-	-	-	-	-	-	-	-	-	-	-	-	-	-	-
Rumex sp. (dock achene) CDG	1	-	-	1	-	-	10	2	8	6	2	11	4	-	-	1	-	1	-	-	-	-
Viola sp. (violet seed) GHWEMF	-	-	-	-	-	-	-	-	-	1	-	-	-	-	-	-	-	-	-	-	-	-
Brassicaceae *Capsella*-type (shepherd's purse-type)	-	-	-	-	-	-	-	-	-	-	-	10*	1	-	-	-	-	-	-	-	-	-
Thlaspi arvense L. (field penny-cress seed) AD	-	-	-	-	-	-	2	-	-	-	-	-	-	-	-	-	-	-	-	-	-	-
Brassica/Sinapis sp. (mustard, charlock etc. seed) CDG	2	1	6	5	14	-	53	7	54	39	8	67*	56	18	-	4	-	1	-	3	1	2
cf. *Camelina sativa* (cf. gold-of-pleasure) C	-	-	-	-	-	-	-	-	-	-	-	-	-	-	-	1	-	-	-	-	-	-
Brassicaceae *Sisymbrium*-type (rocket-type seed) CD U	-	-	-	-	-	-	-	-	-	-	-	-	-	-	-	-	-	1	-	-	-	-
Indeterminate Primulaceae (primrose, loosestrife, pimpernel etc.) CDG	-	-	1	-	-	-	-	-	-	-	-	-	-	-	-	-	-	-	-	-	-	-
Potentilla sp. (cinquefoil seed)	-	-	-	-	-	-	-	-	-	-	-	10*	1	-	-	-	-	-	-	-	-	-
Aphanes arvensis L. (parsley-piert achene) Co	-	-	-	-	-	-	1	-	-	1	4	-	2	+	-	1	-	-	-	-	-	-
Malus/Pyrus sp. (apple/pear embryo) U	-	-	-	-	-	-	-	-	-	-	-	-	-	-	-	-	-	-	-	-	-	-
Linum catharticum L. (fairy flax seed) Gdcs U	-	-	-	-	-	-	5	-	-	-	-	20*	-	-	-	-	-	-	-	-	-	-
Umbelliferae *Pimpinella* -type (burnet-saxifrage type)	-	-	-	-	-	-	-	-	-	-	-	1	2	-	-	-	-	-	-	-	-	-
Aethusa cynapium L. (fool's parsley mericarp) CD	-	-	-	-	-	-	-	-	-	-	-	1	-	-	-	-	-	-	-	-	-	-
Torilis nodosa (L.)Gaertn. (knotted hedge-parsley mericarp) ADo	-	-	-	-	-	-	-	-	-	-	+	-	-	-	-	-	-	-	-	-	-	-

Table 6.15 (continued)

Feature	4332					4458					4598			4667	4993				5358			
Recut						4486																
Context	4385	4385	4385	4336	4335	4460	4507	4512	4515	4540	4603	4600	4599	4674	4996	5155	4995	4994	6083	5770	5735	5359
Sample	2112-7	2085	2118	2048	2055	2062	2069	2095	2094	2091	2144	2120	2119	2125	2159	2160	2158	2157	2207	2205	2204	2203
Soil vol/l	2.9	2	30	30	5	30	15	5	15	30	30	30	30	30	2	15	30	15	2	30	30	30
Torilis japonica (Houtt.)DC (upright hedge-parsley mericarp) GHW	-	-	-	-	-	-	-	-	-	-	+	-	-	-	-	-	-	-	-	-	-	-
Torilis sp. (hedge-parsley mericarp) ADGHW	-	-	-	-	-	-	-	-	-	-	6	-	-	-	-	-	-	-	-	-	-	-
Indeterminate Umbelliferae	-	-	-	-	-	-	-	-	-	-	3	-	-	-	-	-	-	-	-	-	-	-
Hyoscyamus niger L. (henbane seed) Dn U	-	-	-	-	-	-	1	1	-	-	1	130*	2	-	-	-	-	-	-	-	-	-
Lithospermum arvense L. (corn gromwell embryo) ADoG	1	-	-	-	-	-	11	3	5	1	5	4	3	-	-	1	-	1	-	-	-	-
Lithospermum arvense (whole nutlet) ADoG	-	-	-	-	-	-	-	-	-	-	1	-	1	26	-	-	-	-	-	-	-	-
Myosotis sp. (forget-me-not embryo) GMCW	-	-	1	-	-	-	9	3	-	3	4	20*	-	-	-	1	-	1	-	-	-	-
Prunella vulgaris L. (self-heal embryo) GD	-	-	-	-	-	-	-	-	-	-	-	10*	-	-	-	-	-	-	-	-	-	-
Lamiaceae *Lamium*-type (deadnettle-type)	-	-	-	-	-	-	-	-	-	-	-	11*	-	-	-	-	-	-	-	-	-	-
Lamiaceae *Ballota*-type (black horehound-type) DH	-	-	-	-	-	-	-	-	-	-	2	-	-	-	-	-	-	-	-	-	-	-
Plantago major L. (greater plantain seed) G	-	-	-	-	-	-	-	-	-	-	-	-	2	-	-	-	-	-	-	-	-	-
Odontites/*Euphrasia* sp. (red bartsia/eyebright seed) ADG	1	-	-	-	-	-	4	-	-	-	-	-	-	-	-	-	-	-	-	-	-	-
Sherardia arvensis L. (field madder nutlet) ADG	-	-	-	-	-	-	-	-	-	-	-	14	-	-	-	-	-	-	-	-	-	-
Galium aparine L. (cleavers nutlet) CD	-	-	-	-	-	-	-	-	-	-	1	-	-	-	-	-	-	-	-	-	-	-
Valerianella sp. (cornsalad embryo) AD	-	-	-	-	-	-	-	-	-	-	-	-	2	+	-	-	-	-	-	-	-	-
cf. Dipsacaceae (teasel, scabious etc.) GD	-	-	-	-	-	-	-	-	-	-	-	2	1	-	-	-	-	-	-	-	-	-
Asteraceae *Cirsium*/*Carduus*-type (thistle-type embryo) GD	-	-	-	-	-	-	-	-	-	-	-	3	-	-	-	-	-	-	-	-	-	-
Asteraceae *Anthemis cotula*-type (stinking mayweed-type) ADh	-	-	-	-	-	-	-	-	-	1	1	-	-	-	-	-	-	-	-	-	-	-
Asteraceae *Tripleurospermum*-type (mayweed-type) AD	-	-	-	-	-	-	3	-	-	-	-	-	-	-	-	-	-	-	-	-	-	-
Carex sp. (trigonous sedge embryo) MGw	-	-	-	-	-	-	-	-	-	-	+	-	1	-	-	-	-	1	-	-	-	-
Indeterminate Poaceae (indeterminate grasses) GC	-	-	-	-	-	-	2	-	-	2	7	110*	-	-	-	-	-	-	-	-	-	-
cf. mineralised straw fragment	1	-	-	-	-	-	14	-	-	-	11	1	1	-	-	-	-	-	-	-	-	-
Pteridium aquilinum (L.)Kuhn (bracken pinnule fragment) GEW	-	-	-	-	-	-	-	-	-	-	-	1	-	-	-	-	-	-	-	-	-	-
mineralised rootlets	-	-	5	-		-	2	1	-	-	-	-	-	36	-	-	-	1	-	+	-	-
mineralised worm cocoons	2	-	-	-	-	-	-	-	-	-	1	-	-	-	-	-	-	-	-	-	-	3
mineralised baby worms	-	-	-	-	-	-	-	-	-	-	-	-	-	-	-	-	1	-	-	-	-	-
mineralised insect pupae	3	-	1	-	-	-	-	-	-	-	8	3	-	-	-	-	-	-	-	-	-	-
mineralised fly eggs	-	-	-	2	-	-	-	1	-	-	-	-	-	-	-	-	-	-	-	-	-	-
Indeterminate mineralised invertebrate eggs	1	-	1	-	-	-	32	1	-	9	5	-	7	-	1	1	8	7	-	-	-	-
mineralised mites	-	-	-	-	-	-	1	-	-	-	-	-	-	-	-	-	-	-	-	-	-	-
mineralised nodules	4		75	11	5	483	63	63	105	72	63	25	12	15	7	11	15	11	5	7	4	8
Total fruit and seeds	*5*	*1*	*10*	*6*	*18*	*1*	*169*	*58*	*74*	*100*	*71*	*847*	*113*	*45*	*4*	*15*	*13*	*10*	*0*	*3*	*1*	*2*
Total seeds per litre	*1.7*	*0.5*	*0.3*	*0.2*	*3.6*	*0.0*	*11.3*	*11.6*	*4.9*	*3.3*	*2.4*	*28.2*	*3.8*	*1.5*	*2.0*	*1.0*	*0.4*	*0.7*	*0.0*	*0.1*	*0.0*	*0.1*
Total Frag per litre	*5.5*	*0.5*	*3.1*	*0.6*	*4.6*	*16.1*	*18.7*	*24.8*	*11.9*	*6.0*	*5.3*	*29.2*	*4.4*	*3.2*	*6.0*	*1.8*	*1.2*	*1.9*	*2.5*	*0.3*	*0.2*	*0.4*

Table 6.16 Summary of mineralised plant assemblages from Batttlesbury Bowl and East Chisenbury, and Potterne

Battlesbury Bowl & East Chisenbury	*Potterne*
Cereal frags more common & bran present	Only 1 cereal frag. from whole site
cf. straw & matted straw concretions present	No straw recovered
Roots occasional or absent	Roots ubiquitous & often numerous
Purging flax present	Purging flax absent
Blinks absent	Blinks present
Sedges rare	Sedges common & present in most samples
Nettles & Chenopod family in some samples but not dominant.	Nettles &/or Chenopods dominant taxa in all levels of 'midden' & pre-midden .
Brassicas dominant in most samples	Brassicas often present but frequent only in top levels of 'midden'

likely to have been growing locally where organic-rich waste was being deposited, either in the waste's primary or secondary place of deposition.

A few other taxa are more commonly found on cultivated land than on waste ground, but none is totally restricted to arable fields. The more specific weeds of cultivation include corn gromwell (*Lithospermum arvense*), said by Grose (1957) to occur as follows in Wiltshire; 64% arable fields, 28% other cultivated fields, 4% wasteground. Field pennycress (*Thlaspi arvense*) was recorded by Grose as occurring as follows; 58% cultivated, 20% wasteground, also on roadsides, railways etc. These two taxa were also recovered from many of the Potterne samples. It is difficult to determine, therefore, whether they were growing locally on disturbed soils or whether they had been consumed or deposited as crop processing waste. The recovery of these taxa as charred remains (see Clapham, above) demonstrates that they were growing as arable weeds, particularly corn gromwell which was present in 89% of the charred plant assemblages. Field pennycress was only present in small numbers in 9% of the charred assemblages, but it is possible that it does not survive charring as well as the robust, 'stony-coated' corn gromwell seeds.

Comparisons between different types of features, and distribution of the mineralised material

There were no clear differences between phases or between the different types of features or deposits, including deposits containing human skeletal remains. While mineralised remains were found to be more frequent in the central pit group in FG 2, they were also frequent in ditch 4043 and adjacent pit 4486 in FG 1.

It was noted above that there was no consistent pattern of distribution of mineralised material down the soil profile of each feature. However, in many features there were enough similarities in the species composition of adjacent fills to suggest that they had probably come from the same, or a similar, source. Thus, for example, where the seeds of arable/waste ground weed, field madder (*Sherardia arvensis*) occurred in pit 5592, it was present in all of the five central fills, but none above or below. Distributions of several other taxa also occurred in discrete areas of the profile, suggesting that the features had been backfilled over a short period of time from the same, or a similar, source.

The only obvious pattern to be seen from these results is that cereal remains appear to be mainly concentrated (if such an adjective can be used for so few remains) in FG 2 (six out of eight features), although pit 5592 in FG 4 contained the largest number of fragments in total. A second observation is that cereals and bran fragments occurred only in pits and not in ditches. The presence of apple/pear pips in ditch 4043, however, and the soil micromorphology results (see below) suggest that faecal waste was being deposited in the ditches as well as in pits.

Comparisons with the charred assemblages

A large proportion of the weed taxa recovered as mineralised plant remains were also present in the charred assemblages. In the charred assemblage from ditch section 4096, for example (see above), eight of the 11 weed taxa were also recorded as mineralised plant remains. The main differences between the assemblages can be attributed to differences in the methods of preservation. Thus, woody remains such as hazelnut shell do not readily become mineralised, and neither do legumes such as vetches and clovers (Carruthers 2000). As on most archaeological sites, cereal remains are the principal type of waste being burnt that survives charring but these generally have too low a moisture content to become mineralised.

As was found at Potterne, comparisons between the occurrence of the two types of plant assemblages can be instructive (Carruthers and Straker 2000). For example, it was hoped that they could help to differentiate between taxa that were being consumed as medicinal plants and those growing in the vicinity of cess deposits, for example henbane, or being deposited as stable waste, such as purging flax. These two taxa were certainly much more frequent in the mineralised than in the charred assemblages (Table 6.17). This might be expected for henbane, since the typical habitat for this plant is a nutrient-rich waste deposit such as might be provided in the vicinity of

Table 6.17 Comparison of charred and mineralised remains of purging flax and henbane

	Charred	*Mineralised*
purging flax	2 seeds from 6% of samples (2 samples)	54 seeds from 13% of samples (10 samples)
henbane	10 seeds from 14% of samples (5 samples)	551 seeds from 35% of samples (27 samples)

faecal waste or a dung heap. However, purging flax is more typical of dry, calcareous, nutrient-poor grassland. Its presence in the mineralised assemblages is likely to be due to its inclusion in animal dung or bedding, or possibly because it was being consumed for medicinal purposes.

Grassland taxa are fairly frequent in the charred plant assemblages. Clapham notes that the 16 species that are commonly found in grasslands could have been growing in or around the fields, or may have been burnt as dung. Some of the grassland remains, such as buttercup achenes, are equally common in the charred and mineralised assemblages (31% of charred samples, 36% mineralised), suggesting that burnt and unburnt waste bedding or dung contributed to both types of deposit. The increased occurrence of useful taxa such as purging flax in the mineralised assemblages, therefore, could be taken as evidence (though tentative) that these taxa were being deliberately selected for medicinal use. Unless high concentrations of seeds from these potentially useful native plants are recovered, as in a medieval context at Waltham Abbey, Essex (Moffat 1987), it is difficult to demonstrate that they were used medicinally.

One of the most notable differences was the occurrence of brassica seeds in the two types of assemblage. Only one charred sample produced two charred seeds (3%), whereas 83% of the mineralised assemblages contained seeds (64 samples). In many of the mineralised samples these remains were numerous, reaching a maximum of 175 per 10 litre sample (context 4817, pit 4704). Brassica seeds obviously are readily preserved by mineralisation as they are the single most frequently found mineralised taxon. They are also fairly common in charred assemblages although they can easily become fragmented and difficult to recognise. Therefore, although some of the difference could be due to differential preservation, it appears that other explanations are also required.

Unfortunately brassica seeds cannot often be identified to species level, particularly when their seed coats are missing, as with mineralised seeds. The seeds of these two genera, *Brassica* and *Sinapis*, can be used to provide oil or used as a pungent condiment. *Brassica nigra*, black mustard, is the strongest flavoured native species, but its seeds must be collected before the pod shatters. The plants can also be grown to provide leaf fodder and vegetables but since the seed was recovered the two former uses are most likely. Brassicas also grow as weeds in disturbed places but it seems likely that where plants had useful properties, these would have been fully exploited in prehistoric times, when dietary choices were more limited.

Comparisons with other sites

The most relevant sites for comparison, ie, prehistoric sites producing similarly high concentrations of mineralised material, Potterne and East Chisenbury, have already been discussed. Many other Iron Age sites have produced small quantities of mineralised remains, for example Danebury (Campbell 2000a), but concentrated mineralised material was not observed so specific sampling for mineralised plant remains was not undertaken. In the Danebury Environs Project small numbers of mineralised seeds were recovered from Early Iron Age features from Houghton Down, Nettlebank Copse, Suddern Farm, and New Buildings (Campbell 2000a). Only 11 taxa were recorded, and none was well-represented. Opium poppy was the most notable species recorded. A few other Iron Age sites on calcareous soils in southern England, such as Lains Farm (Carruthers 1991) Brighton Hill South (Carruthers 1995), and Maiden Castle (Palmer and Jones 1991) have produced mineralised plant remains, but these have always been in small numbers in pits and ditches, mixed in with other types of waste, and it has not been possible to say whether they were derived from redeposited faecal waste, stable waste, or midden material.

Conclusions

The assemblages appear to represent human faecal waste and possibly also animal dung and bedding, that has become mineralised and then been redeposited in pits and ditches around the site. The features showed no obvious differences according to phasing, although there was an increase in cereal deposition in FG 2, and no cereal remains were recovered from ditches.

The presence of apple/pear seed embryos suggested that at least some of the mineralised material had been of human faecal origin, and it is possible that medicinal plants and flavourings were also represented in the assemblages. This suggestion is difficult to prove, and much of the material could have had very mixed origins, including animal dung, bedding, flooring, crop processing waste, and fruits and seeds shed by the local wasteground vegetation.

There were clear differences between the three sites surrounding Salisbury Plain in Wiltshire: Battlesbury Bowl, East Chisenbury, and Potterne. The former two sites produced very similar assemblages, with more evidence for cereal remains, stable waste, and very few rootlets. Potterne, on Greensand rather than chalk, produced frequent rootlets and more evidence for the local damp, acidic, nutrient-rich 'midden' vegetation, rather than deposited waste.

These analyses have demonstrated the high potential of mineralised deposits in the Salisbury Plain area. Further excavations in the area must take account of the potential for recovering this type of information, and make provision for it in the sampling and processing programmes.

Phytoliths

by Marco Madella

During the analysis of the charred plant remains it was noted that the samples from two contexts (5735 and 5770, samples 2204 and 2205) from the floted material of pit 5358 were extremely rich in phytoliths. Phytoliths are opal silica bodies of plant origin. They can be formed in the cell lumen of many plants and the grass family (Poaceae) is one of the highest producers in the plant kingdom. Phytoliths, being probably the most durable microfossil from terrestrial sediments, may provide an alternative line of research for gathering information on ancient crop husbandry and the intrasite use of plant material, and understanding ancient structures.

Methods

Samples for phytolith are generally collected during excavation in the form of untreated sediments, of 10–50 ml volume, which are then dried and directly processed for phytolith extraction. Those from pit 5358 were recovered as a residue after the flotation of bulk soil samples. The silica skeletons, not-withstanding the high density of opal silica, floated probably because of the presence of microscopic air bubbles trapped between the phytoliths and also between the phytoliths and the residual organic matter on their surface. The air bubbles, combined with the relatively large size of the silica sheets, permitted the recovery of a large amount of silicified material from the flots through the 250 μm and 500 μm meshes.

These samples should not be considered ideal for phytolith analysis and it is impossible to know what components of the original opal silica assemblage was not recovered during the flotation and in what amount; the information related to those components that did not float has been lost. The two samples are indeed extremely poor in single-celled phytoliths which would have had more problems in floating and being trapped in the meshes (small sized compact bodies, no air bubbles trapped). These types of phytoliths, however, normally constitute the bulk of the phytolith assemblages. This missing information needs to be considered when interpreting the assemblage. Nonetheless, the samples are remarkable for the amount of silica skeletons recovered. In consideration of the uniqueness of the finds it was decided to proceed with the analysis of the phytoliths and an alternative approach needed to be devised for their investigation.

Sub-samples of 10 g were selected, after quartering and random sampling, from the total amounts of the 500 μm float residues available from the samples. From each sub-sample originated two micro-samples (A and B) of 0.5 g, each treated in parallel according to the following methodologies:

Micro-sample A (adapted from Madella *et al.* 1998)

- Sample dried in oven at 80°C
- Sample dispersed in a solution of sodium polytungstate with a density of 2.45, centrifuged at low speed and floating portion recovered (final residue)
- Final residue rinsed in distilled water
- Dehydration of the final residue with ethanol
- Final residue mounted on a microscope slide with permanent mounting media (Styrolite)

Table 6.18 Anatomical characteristics of wheat and barley husk silica skeletons (from Rosen (1992) and Ball *et al.* (1996))

	Long cells width (μm)	*Long cell wave hinge height (μm) (thin waves/thick waves)**	*Papillae size (μm)*	*No. pits*
Wheat (*triticum* sp.)				
T. dicoccum (emmer)	18–23	4–8/10–15	22–30	10–12
T. monococcum (einkorn)	18–23	4–8/10–15	25–50	12–14(?)
Barley (*Hordeum* sp.)				
H. distichon (2-row)	15–18	7/10	18–25	10–12
H. vulgare (6-row)	12–15	7/10	18–25	7–9

*These measurements have been here grouped & considered as overall variability of the sample

Micro-sample B

- Sample mounted directly on a microscope slide with permanent mounting media (Styrolite)

All four micro-samples were scanned at 200x, 400x, and 1000x magnifications. Phytolith silica skeletons were identified and counted from micro-samples 2204A and 2205A while micro-sample 2204B and 2205B were used to estimate the ratio of opal silica/other material. A total of 500 silica skeletons was counted in micro-samples 2204A and 2205A.

The anatomical characteristics utilised for the identification of the grass silica skeletons are summarised in Table 6.18. There are no statistical measurements available for samples of *Triticum spelta* (spelt). However, it is considered here that spelt cells should fall in the same range of variability as emmer and einkorn. The silica skeletons from the samples have been grouped according to the following anatomical categories:

- Wheat (*Triticum* sp.): anatomical characteristics falling into the wheat husk variability
- Barley (*Hordeum* sp.): anatomical characteristics falling into the barley husk variability
- Cereal husk: anatomical characteristics that did not permit an attribution to a specific genus
- Grass awns: from the awns of grass inflorescence (mostly cereals).
- Grass culm/leaf: from the culm and/or leaves of grasses
- Dicotyledons: from dicotyledon leaves.

Results

The absolute counts and the frequencies of the phytoliths from pit 5358 are summarised in Table 6.19. Silica skeletons from the husk of wheat (*Triticum* sp.) represent the primary identified cereal in both samples, with frequencies around 20%. Barley (*Hordeum* sp.) husk is more frequent in sample 2204 (7.8%) than in sample 2205 (3.8%). Grass awns is the most represented category in both samples, with a frequency of more than 60%. Both grass culm/leaf and dicotyledon silica skeletons have very low frequencies, never being more than 1% of the total assemblages. The relative proportions of phytoliths versus other materials is outlined in Table 6.20. The absolute counts correspond to a 2-row count on a 22x22 mm cover-slip. In both samples most of the remains are opaline silica skeletons but sample 2205 is richer in phytoliths, which represent about 77% of the total. Most of the 'other materials' are micro-charcoals (respectively 36.4% and 22.4%).

Table 6. 19 Absolute counts and relative frequencies of opaline silica skeletons from pit 5358

Context	*5735*		*5770*	
Sample	*2204*		*2205*	
	Absolute counts	*Frequency (%)*	*Absolute counts*	*Frequency (%)*
Wheat (*Triticum* sp.)	99	19.8	101	20.2
Barley (*Hordeu* sp.)	37	7.4	19	3.8
Cereal husk	44	8.8	37	7.4
Grass awn	311	62.2	338	67.6
Grass culm	5	1	2	0.4
Dicotyledon	4	0.8	3	0.6
	500	100	500	100

Table 6.20 Relative frequencies of opaline silica *versus* other materials in samples from pit 5358

Context (sample)	*Absolute counts*		*Frequencies (%)*	
	Opaline silica	*Other materials*	*Opaline silica*	*Other materials*
5735 (2204)	56	32	63.3	36.4
5770 (2205)	73	21	77.6	22.4

The composition of the two samples is very similar, being both mainly made up by siliceous sheets from grass inflorescence. More than 98% of the silica skeletons represent the husk or awns while grass culm/leaf or dicotyledon phytoliths are 1% or less. This composition, extremely pure in inflorescence remains, clearly highlights that the origin of the articulated phytoliths is from waste from the final stages of crop processing (see Stevens, above; Hillman 1981). The almost complete absence of remains from culm and leaves shows that hay was not present in the pit during the deposition of contexts 5735 and 5770. With all probability, the two contexts are not related to the structure of the pit as storage facility but to its re-use as a rubbish dump.

Context 5770 was a rather thin and dark humic layer. Unfortunately, as the sample for phytoliths was taken from the flot, it was impossible to calculate the opal silica concentration in the sediment. The flot volumes can give an indirect and approximate estimate of the silica concentration in the original sediment samples. The final flot volume of 450 ml, containing about 77% of silica (see Table 6.20), from an original 500 ml, seems to highlight a high presence of silica in the original sediment. The context should represent the disposal of relatively pure and burned crop by-products. The preservation of the organic matter and carbonised material in the sediments produced a dark colour, which masked the abundance of phytoliths during excavation. Carbonised organic material was sometime also preserved on the phytolith surface. Some of the silica skeletons observed during the counting of context 5770, had lost part of their original anatomical characteristics, acquiring a spongy-like structure. This is due to partial melting of the opal silica, which suggests that the remains discharged in the pit came into contact with temperature of or above 800°C. However, only a tiny fraction (0.2%) of the silica skeletons observed show a spongy-like structure. This is possibly due to the burning of the plant material in an uncontrolled fire where temperature varied greatly – a hearth for example. Only a small fraction of the phytoliths came in contact with temperatures higher than 800°C and partially melted.

Context 5735 was also a dark, humic layer. However, from the flot volumes and the content of silica from the flots (see Table 6.20) it seems that, in this context, opal silica – or at least articulated phytoliths – was less concentrated. Once more, these observations are somewhat conjectural, as direct measure of the opal silica concentration was not possible. This context, however, also contained macroscopic charcoals and pottery. It might be argued that this sediment had a more mixed origin, where burned plant remains were mixed with other refuse from the settlement.

Charcoal

by Rowena Gale

Charcoal was recorded in a wide range of contexts across the site, but was significantly more abundant in the pits and ditches than in the hearths and post-holes. Sixteen of the 74 environmental samples taken for plant remains were selected for detailed analysis of charcoals to procure evidence for local woodlands, their management, and the use of woodland resources in the Late Bronze Age and Middle Iron Age.

Methods

Charcoal fragments measuring >2 mm in cross-section were considered for species identification. Samples were prepared for examination using standard methods (Gale and Cutler 2000). The fragments were supported in washed sand and examined using a Nikon Labophot-2 microscope at magnifications up to x400. The anatomical structures were matched to prepared reference slides. When possible, the maturity of the wood was assessed (ie, heartwood/sapwood), and stem diameters and the number of growth rings recorded. It should be noted that measurements from charred material may be up to 40% less than the living wood.

Results

The results are summarised in Table 6.21. The charcoal was generally firm and well- preserved, and intact sections of roundwood were occasionally present.

Group names are given when anatomical differences between related genera are too slight to allow secure identification to genus level. These include members of the Pomoideae (*Crataegus*, *Malus*, *Pyrus*, and *Sorbus*) and Salicaceae (*Salix* and *Populus*). Where a genus is represented by a single species in the British flora this is named as the most likely origin of the wood, given the provenance and period, but it should be noted that it is rarely possible to name individual species from wood features, and exotic species of trees and shrubs were introduced to Britain from an early period (Godwin 1956; Mitchell 1974). Classification follows that of *Flora Europaea* (Tutin *et al.* 1964–80).

The anatomical structure of the charcoal was consistent with the following taxa or groups of taxa:

Aceraceae. *Acer campestre* L., field maple
Aquifoliaceae. *Ilex aquifolium* L., holly
Betulaceae. *Alnus glutinosa* (L.) Gaertner, European alder; *Betula* spp., birch
Corylaceae. *Corylus avellana* L., hazel
Fagaceae. *Quercus* spp., oak
Oleaceae. *Fraxinus excelsior* L., ash
Rosaceae. Subfamilies:
Pomoideae which includes *Crataegus* sp., hawthorn; *Malus* sp., apple; *Pyrus* sp., pear; *Sorbus* spp., rowan, service tree and whitebeam. These taxa are anatomically similar; one or more taxa may be represented in the charcoal
Prunoideae – *Prunus spinosa* L., blackthorn
Salicaceae. *Salix* sp., willow, and *Populus* sp., poplar. In most respects these taxa are anatomically similar. The ray type sometimes allows the taxon to be named, however this feature is not always a reliable indicator, particularly when examining juvenile wood (as in this instance)

Phase 1/2

Charcoal occurred throughout section 4019 of ditch 4043 (Fig. 3.6). The upper secondary fill (context 4069) contained mostly roundwood fragments (diam. *c.* 20 mm or wider) from the hawthorn/*Sorbus* group (Pomoideae), blackthorn (*Prunus spinosa*) and oak (*Quercus* sp.). Its origin is unknown but seems likely to have been domestic fuel debris since the context also included charred cereal grain and chaff, weed seeds, bone and fruit stones.

A small quantity of charcoal was recovered from pit 4993 in FG3. The charcoal, from a mid-level

Table 6.21 Summary of charcoal from selected features (no. frags)

Feature	*FG*	*Context*	*Sample*	*Acer*	*Alnus*	*Betula*	*Corylus*	*Fraxinus*	*Ilex*	*Pom.*	*Prunus*	*Quercus*	*Sal.*
Phase 1/2													
Ditch 4043, s. 4019	1	4069	2008	–	–	–	–	–	–	85 r/s	12	2r, 2h	–
Pit 4993	3	4995	2158	–	–	–	1	1	–	2	–	2s, 5h	–
Pit 5670	4	5715	2201	–	–	–	8	–	–	25	2	4s, 11h	–
Phase 3													
Pit 4196	1	4369	2051	–	–	–	6	–	1	–	–	26r, 8h	–
Pit 4196, recut 4553	1	4313	2026	–	–	–	1	2	–	27	36	5r, 3h	–
Pit 4458	2	4460	2062	1	–	–	–	–	–	1	15	12r, 5h	–
Pit 4598	2	4603	2144	–	–	–	–	–	–	5	8	6r, 10h	1
Pit 4641	2	4742	2165	–	–	–	5	31	–	5	4	10h	3
Pit 4667	2	4674	2125	2	18	–	2	4h	–	10	–	7r, 4h	–
Pit 4704	4	4817	2143	2	–	–	6	–	1	4	1	16r, 4h	–
Pit 5592	4	5727	2183	–	–	1	5	–	–	2	7	58r, 8h	1
		5729	2191	1	–	–	16r	1	–	21	8	13r, 9h	–
Hearth 5979, cut 5711	4	5712	2198	3	–	–	–	8	–	1	–	11s, r, 4h	–
P-h 5786	4	5787	2187	–	–	–	1	–	–	1	–	2h	–
Unphased													
P-h 4299	1	4298	2021	–	–	–	2	–	–	2	5	1h	–
P-h 4324	1	4323	2031	–	–	–	–	–	–	1	–	3s, 1h	–

Pom = Pomoideae; Sal = Salicaceae; h = heartwood; r = roundwood (diam. <20 mm); s = sapwood (diam. >20 mm or unknown)

context, includes oak, the hawthorn/*Sorbus* group, ash (*Fraxinus excelsior*), and hazel (*Corylus avellana*).

Charcoal from the base of pit 5670 (FG 4) (context 5715) includes hazel, blackthorn, the hawthorn/*Sorbus* group, and oak.

Phase 3

Samples were examined from three charcoal-rich pits (4458, 4598, and 4667) from a central cluster in FG 2. Oak and the hawthorn/*Sorbus* group are common to all three pits; less frequent species include maple (*Acer campestre*), alder (*Alnus glutinosa*), hazel, ash, blackthorn, and willow (*Salix* sp.) or poplar (*Populus* sp.). The oak in pit 4458 is mainly twiggy (*c.* 5 mm diam. with two growth rings), whereas in pit 4598 the deposit included roundwood from fast-grown oak and hazel; two hazel stems with 8 mm diameters include two and four growth rings, and possibly derive from coppiced growth felled in winter. Pit 4667 was not only the most species-rich of all the samples examined from the site but also the only sample from which alder was identified. The charcoal almost certainly represents deposited/dumped material but the significance of the alder (which includes fast-grown wood) in this context remains unknown.

Pits 4641 and 4704 were sited close together, also in FG 2. Charcoal was relatively frequent and both pits contained blackthorn, hazel, the hawthorn/ *Sorbus* group and oak, while maple, ash, holly (*Ilex aquifolium*), and willow/poplar were more sporadic.

A large sub-rectangular pit (4196, including recut 4553) on the western side of the site in FG 3 showed evidence for numerous burning episodes and appeared to have been used repeatedly as fire pits. More or less the same type of fuel was associated with these contexts, composed of wood from a similar range of trees and shrubs. The pit appeared to have been relined with chalk after each event. The use of the pit is unknown and although it is not clear whether the scorching has resulted from its use as a fire pit or from hot ashes thrown in, it seems likely that it was associated with some type of industrial use. Dark charcoal stains occurred in the lower half (context 4369) but charcoal fragments were fairly sparse. The sample includes numerous pieces from young oak stems, although hazel and holly were also recorded.

The fill of a recut (4553), dug into the upper layers of pit 4196, contained lenses of *in situ* burning. The recut appeared to have been used for similar purposes to that of the original pit. The charcoal is predominantly from blackthorn and the hawthorn/*Sorbus* group but also includes oak, ash, and hazel. Blackthorn roundwood ranges from 10–20 mm in diameter. The contexts examined were also rich in charred cereal grains and chaff, weed seeds, and bone; peas/beans also occurred in context 4369. It is not clear whether the charcoal residues relate to the subsequent infill of the pit and recut (associated material indicative of domestic waste suggests this as a strong possibility) or whether all this material derives from sequential burning events in the pit. The charcoal remains from both pit cuts suggests the use of fuel composed mainly of narrow stems but also wider oak roundwood (mature enough to include heartwood). Although the narrow stemwood (and possibly chaff and other flammable materials) may represent kindling, thin stems and faggots probably constituted the bulk of the firewood. The use of this type of fuel may have been determined by the local economy or available resources (see below). Alternatively, its selection may reflect the type of heat source required. The advantage of using narrow roundwood lies in its ability to produce rapidly an intense heat source (due to the large ratio of wood surface exposed to atmospheric oxygen); the addition of narrow roundwood or brushwood to an existing fire quickly boosts the temperature (Hodges 1964), although a fire composed entirely of narrow roundwood is short-lived unless constantly tended. While domestic hearths have traditionally depended on narrow roundwood from faggots and hedge-cutting (Edlin 1949) this type of fuel has also been preferred for some industrial activities, for example firing pottery (Lynne and Jefferies 1979), especially in areas where coppicing was practised.

Pit 5592 (FG 4), a large rectangular pit, contained several charcoal-rich layers. A lens overlying the chalk rubble in the base of the pit (context 5729) included fast-grown roundwood, particularly from oak and hazel. Examples included: oak, diam. 20 mm, 4 growth rings; and hazel, diam. 15 mm, 5 growth rings. Other species present included ash, blackthorn, the hawthorn/*Sorbus* group and maple. Context 5727 from the upper-mid level also contained a large quantity of narrow, fast-grown oak roundwood (some with 5 growth rings), possibly from coppice rods – an oblique tool mark was noted on one fragment. Oak heartwood was also present.

Other taxa identified include fast-grown blackthorn with some stems measuring 10 mm in diameter, hazel, birch, the hawthorn/*Sorbus* group, and willow/poplar.

In hearth 5979, within roundhouse 5786, heavy burning was evident and charcoal was abundant. The taxa identified include oak, ash, the hawthorn/*Sorbus* group, and maple. A small amount of charcoal was also recovered from a post-hole (5786) of the roundhouse; this feature also contained stones (possibly used as packing), charred cereal grains and chaff, and weed seeds. Although initially thought to represent the burnt remains of the post, the charcoal, which includes oak, hazel, and the hawthorn/*Sorbus* group, seems more likely to have originated from fuel debris (probably from the adjacent hearth).

Unphased

Samples from post-holes 4299 and 4324 in FG 1 were examined. In both contexts the charcoal was overlain with blocks of chalk which were probably used as packing, and it was anticipated that the charcoal derived from the burnt remains of the posts. The identification of multiple species, including oak, a member of the hawthorn/*Sorbus* group, blackthorn, and hazel, suggests fuel residues as more likely, especially since other domestic waste (charred cereal grains and weed seeds, fruit stones, and bone) is also present.

Discussion

Environmental evidence

In view of the high concentration of features on the site during the Early Iron Age it is likely that this exposed region on the crest of the Battlesbury ridge was ostensibly clear of trees by this time, or perhaps only supported marginal scrub. Scrubby or shrubby species such as hazel, blackthorn, hawthorn, and holly probably colonised the steep flanks of the spur, which would have been difficult to cultivate but may have provided grazing. If, as seems likely, the site was chosen for its defensive attributes, the banks of the hillfort may have been kept free of tree/shrub growth. Larger trees, for example oak, ash, and field maple, were probably restricted to more sheltered aspects on lower slopes. Birch is calcifuge and although it does occur on leached chalk, it is unlikely to have been frequent in this environment (as confirmed by its paucity in the charcoal).

Trees and shrubs on thin chalk soils and exposed scarps tend to be sparse and slower-growing than those in optimum conditions. More densely wooded areas, probably composed of mixed oak, would have occurred on the lower slopes of the Wylye valley to the west and south, where the moist alluvial soils would have promoted fast growth. This region probably provided the fast-grown wood recorded in the charcoal samples. In addition, wetland species such as alder, willow, poplar, and birch would have flourished on these damper soils.

The management and use of woodland resources

Charcoal was identified from a range of features including a (?domestic) oven/kiln, a possible

(?industrial) fire-pit, and pits. The charcoal almost certainly derives from fuel debris and consistently includes a high proportion of narrow roundwood (often <25 mm diam.). The remains of possible coppice rods were recorded from pits 4598 and 5592 but, apart from these, there appears to be no apparent activity-related preferences for fuel type. In terms of species content and the dimensions of the fuel used, there is little differentiation between the contexts throughout the Iron Age period.

Oak and hazel were clearly important and there is some evidence to suggest that these were coppiced. An oblique toolmark present on an oak stem in pit 5592 indicates that the wood had been cut rather than broken. Shrubby species including blackthorn and (probably) hawthorn were also used frequently (although other members of the Pomoideae could be implicated) and occasional use was made of ash, field maple, birch, alder, holly, and willow/poplar. Some fuel had been felled in the winter – as indicated by hazel roundwood from pit 4598.

Fuel would have been obtained from the closest possible source. The prominent use of shrubby species such as blackthorn and hawthorn suggests that some fuel was obtained from thickets growing on the flanks of the ridge. Fast-growing stems and (possibly) coppice rods (eg, oak and hazel) were probably gathered from the valley, perhaps close to local stream courses or the River Wylye itself. The growth patterns observed in the wood structure of oak and hazel tends to suggest an origin from coppiced woodland. If the demand for fuel and timber had outstripped the local supply, the repeated cropping of young trees and shrubs for fuel may have initiated a simple type of woodland management, although possibly not on any organised or regular basis.

Conclusion

Apart from charcoal found *in situ* in the oven, the remaining samples are attributed to redeposited fuel debris. Fuel mainly consisted of narrow roundwood, although some wider stem or cordwood was also used. Fuel woods included mainly oak, the hawthorn/*Sorbus* group, blackthorn, and hazel; taxa apparently used less frequently included ash, maple, holly, willow/poplar, alder, and birch. Fuel may also have included coppiced oak and hazel. These species are mostly characteristic of chalk soils and the abundance of blackthorn and hawthorn type suggest that thickets of scrub grew at, or close to, the site, perhaps on the steep slopes. Other species may also have grown very locally although larger trees are more likely to have grown in more sheltered aspects. Damp, alluvial soils on the lower slopes and in the valley bottom would have supported denser, faster-growing woodland than that on the upland. Fuel and timber may have been in short supply on the poor soils in the immediate vicinity of the site. The location of the site at Battlesbury Bowl gave access to a source of fast-growing wood in the Wylye valley and it was clear from the charcoal that this was heavily exploited.

Land Snails

by Michael J. Allen

The land snail analysis provided the opportunity to examine and define the nature of the landscape in which this site lay. The specific aims of this research were as follows:

- to record the environmental and land-use history of the Battlesbury spur and its surroundings;
- to examine function and activities associated with the pits as derived from the nature of individual pit contexts;
- to explore the exploitation of wider landscape resources;
- to attempt to detail molluscan, and thereby land-use, changes through time.

Examination of spatial variation in local habitats and environment along this ridge was not considered possible in view of the limited number of samples, the nature of the deposits, and the potential chronological diversity of samples with the Iron Age occupation.

Methods

A column of nine contiguous samples (1750–2000 g) for land snails was taken through section 4019 of ditch 4043 to define and examine change in the land-use and local environment through the period of occupation. These samples were processed following standard methods (Evans 1972). In addition, 22 bulk samples (*c.* 30 litres) from four pits, one post-hole, and section 4096 of ditch 4043 were also examined. These were processed by flotation and residues to 0.5 mm were retained (as mineralisation may have been present), in all but one sample. The methods of recovery from these samples are directly comparable to standard methodologies. Nomenclature follows Kerney (1999). The results are presented in Tables 6.22 and 6.23.

Results

Ditch 4043

No primary fill chalk rubble occurred in the base of this ditch along any of its excavated length, and section 4019 had relatively stoneless silty loam fills (Fig. 3.6). This may indicate either that the chalk locally was too resistant to fracture into rubble, or that

Table 6.22 Land mollusc data from ditch 4043

Ditch section	*4019*									*4096*
Context	*4110*			*4071*	*4089*		*4070*		*4069*	*4098*
Sample	*2103*	*2104*	*2105*	*2106*	*2107*	*2108*	*2109**	*2110**	*2111*	*2002*
Depth (cm)	*114–124*	*104–114*	*95–104*	*84–95*	*74–84*	*64–74*	*50–60*	*40–50*	*30–40*	*spot*
Land										
Pomatias elegans (Müller)	+	+	+	–	+	–	+	+	2	3
Cochlicopa lubrica (Müller)	–	1	–	–	–	–	–	–	–	–
Cochlicopa spp.	–	–	–	–	–	–	–	1	1	4
Vertigo pygmaea (Draparnaud)	–	–	–	–	–	–	–	–	–	1
Vertigo spp.	2	–	–	–	–	–	–	–	1	–
Pupilla muscorum (Linnaeus)	2	1	1	2	–	–	–	–	–	3
Vallonia costata (Müller)	7	2	3	1	–	–	1	–	[1]	22
Vallonia excentrica Sterki	5	–	–	–	–	–	–	–	–	22
Vallonia spp.	2	1	–	–	1	–	–	–	–	6
Punctum pygmaeum (Draparnaud)	1	–	–	–	–	–	–	–	–	–
Vitrina pellucida (Müller)	3	–	–	–	–	–	–	–	–	–
Aegopinella nitidula (Draparnaud)	1	–	–	–	–	–	–	–	–	–
Oxychilus cellarius (Müller)	–	–	–	–	–	–	–	–	–	1
Limacidae	16	2	–	2	4	6	7	17	7	103
Cecilioides acicula (Müller)	–	–	–	–	1	–	5	2	8	132
Cochlodina laminata (Montagu)	–	–	–	–	–	–	–	–	–	1
Helicella itala (Linnaeus)	4	–	1	–	–	–	+	1	+	61
Trichia hispida (Linnaeus)	12	[2]	1	1	–	+	+	1	–	19
Arianta arbustorum (Linnaeus)	1	+	–	–	–	–	–	–	–	–
Cepaea/Arianta spp.	+	+	–	+	1	+	+	+	–	+
Fresh/brackish water										
Valvata cristata (Müller)	–	–	–	–	–	–	–	–	–	2
Armiger crista (Linnaeus)	–	–	–	–	–	–	–	–	–	1
Taxa	12	6	6	5	3	3	6	6	5	14
Total	56	7	6	6	6	6	8	20	11	249
Mollusc per kg/litre	31.4	3.5	3.4	4.4	3.4	3.4	4.6	11.4	6.3	8.3
0.5 mm residue extracted	Y	Y	Y	Y	Y	Y	Y	Y	Y	Y

Specimens in [] retain their periostricum and are considered to be recent intrusions; they are not included in the analysis.
* = soil micromorphology

the feature had been consistently kept clean. Of course the nature of the fills, containing a high quantity of refuse, may indicate a relatively rapid infill sequence which would hinder the formation of a typical primary fill (Evans 1972, 321–8; Limbrey 1975, 290–300; Allen 1995a, 4–6). The main fills contained a greenish hue, reminiscent of cess and mineralistation and resembled Iron Age ditch fills at Maiden Castle (Macphail 1991, 117, table 14).

Snail numbers were low throughout the sequence; only the basal sample produced more that 50 shells (only 32 shells per kg). This assemblage represents open country habitats with no woodland. *Trichia hispidia*, Limacidea, and *Vallonia costata* were the most abundant and tend to indicate lightly grazed or ungrazed grassland that has not become rank, possibly with some relict scrub. There is no evidence for very short and trampled grass that might be concomitant with the density of archaeological features. Very few shade-loving species were present and those that did occur (*Vitrina pellucida* and *Aegopinella nitidula*) can exist in a diverse downland grass sward. Little can be said of the assemblages from the remaining fills except that no major change in this environment is obvious.

A spot sample from possible cess-rich deposits within the secondary fills of the same ditch, 175 m to the south (segment 4096), was no richer, but increased sample size (30 litres, ie, *c.* 31 kg) produced 249 shells. The assemblage was similar but the increased proportions of *Helicella itala* with Limacidea indicates a shorter grassland, with micro-habitats of damp shelter created by dense vegetation at its base, typical of unimproved downland swards.

Rapid examination of the flots of the 23 bulk samples taken from four sections of this ditch showed that shell numbers from segment 4096 were typical, but that numbers from segment 4019 were lower than all other sampled sections. This indicates some lateral variation along the ditch, probably related to ditch infill materials and local preservation conditions rather than to differences in the ditch-side environment. Soil analyses (see Macphail and Crowther, below) have indicated that urine and other waste was prevalent in section 4019 and this may have been concentrated here (hence the greener hues in the ditch fills) and account for poorer shell preservation at this location.

One last point that will be addressed in more detail later, was the occurrence in the latter segment (4096) of aquatic species. Here these were *Valvata cristata* and *Armiger crista* (Table 6.22), and both are allochthonous and must have come from bodies of flowing water such the River Wylye or the stream to the foot of Battlesbury Hill itself.

Pits

Although samples from pits were not taken specifically for land snails, the assessment of the flots of the bulk samples (of *c.* 30 litres) demonstrated the presence of allochthonous freshwater species in a few samples. As deposits showed that the pits had filled up through a combination of dumped material and natural infilling, the snail assemblages were considered to be of interest. A limited number of features, therefore, especially those with aquatic species, were examined to provide data about the local environment, activities, and the exploitation of the wider landscape, for example river and water-edge resources.

The composition and derivation of assemblages from pits can be fraught with difficulties. Materials are clearly dumped and disposed of in the pits and consequently may contain shells from a number of unknown environments and locations. Conversely, pits that fill up naturally will 'sample' the local environment, but may be biased towards species that exploit the local shady habitats created by the pit features itself (see Thomas 1977; Evans and Hewitt 1991 for further discussion). Most of the pits here, like those discussed by Evans and Hewitt (1991) at Danebury, although they may have 'special deposits' or contents that are not wholly discarded waste, were left open to the elements and have infilled naturally. More importantly, most molluscs will have been derived from the immediately local environment, so the pit itself will only provide refuge and favourable habitats for species already present within the local, contemporaneous environment.

All assemblages are predominantly open country indicating open grassland with very little relict scrub. Detailed examination aims to define the changing landscape pressure and character of the grassland quality.

Phase 1/2

Pit 4704: This pit contained basal chalk rubble (4882) and soil infill (4817), above which were many dumped and burnt horizons (Fig. 3.11). The main fills, excluding the basal chalk fill, were sampled as four spot samples from contrasting fills. Despite variation in the fills the land snail assemblages are very uniform, reflecting the same local environment as indicated by the other pits and include aquatic species which, in this case, are represented by *Pisidium* sp. in the lowest sampled fill. Significantly, the upper fill also contains a specimen of the rare Vertignid, *V. moulinsiana* which is common in marshes, especially on *Carex* sp. (sedges), indicating the presence and exploitation of these habitats within the Wylye valley.

Pit 5670: A sequence of six spot samples included all the main fills of this broad pit (*c.* 2.1 m across by 1 m deep) with gradual soil infills and dumped deposits. All six assemblages are very similar showing no significant change in the local environment. *Helicella itala* with *Trichia hispda* and *Vallonia costata* are dominant. *T. hispida* declines in the upper pit fills while *V. costata* increases. Short, lightly grazed and trampled grassland are indicated, with no evidence for truly arable contexts or of any woodland stands. All fills contain aquatic species, including *Valvata cristata*, *Lymnaea truncatula*, and *Gyraulus albus*.

Phase 3

Pit 4707: The assemblage from a single sample from the main fill of this pit displays similar characteristics to the others. The aquatic species *Gyraulus albus* was noted.

Pit 5592: This pit, adjacent to 5670, had chalk rubble side-collapse at base, and gentle soil infills above containing charcoal lenses and possible cess layers as well as artefact-rich deposits. A series of nine samples was taken from the main fills including the basal chalk rubble. The assemblages are very similar to pit 5560 and, as with that sequence, little change can be noted. Short, lightly grazed downland is indicated and, once again, aquatic species are present, but sparse. Species present differ from pit 5670 and include *Bithynia tentaculata* and also *Pisidium subtruncatum*.

Table 6.23 Land mollusc data from phase 1/2 and 3 pits and post-hole 4299

Phase	1/2										3										UP
Feature	4704				5670						4707	5592									4299
Soil micromorphology		✧																✸	✸		
Context	4817	4778	4732	4706	4298	5716	5715	5714	5713	5671	4811	4298	5882	5729	5732	5730	5731	5728	5727	5594	5671
Sample	2143	2141	2137	2135	2021	2202	2201	2200	2197	2177	2150	2021	2194	2191	2193	2189	2192	2184	2183	2181	2177
Volume (l)	30	30	2	30	15	15	30	30	30	30	5	15	30	30	30	30	15	30	30	30	30
Land																					
Pomatias elegans (Müller)	3	3	1	6	3	2	3	4	4	6	3	3	2	9	5	2	5	8	4	2	6
Carychium tridentatum (Risso)	3	1	-	-	1	-	5	5	2	1	-	1	-	1	1	-	1	-	-	-	1
Carychium spp.	-	-	1	1	-	-	-	-	-	-	-	-	-	-	-	-	-	-	-	-	-
Succinea putris (Linnaeus)	-	-	-	-	-	-	-	-	-	-	-	-	-	-	-	-	-	2	-	-	-
Cochlicopa lubrica (Müller)	1	2	-	-	-	-	-	3	1	-	-	-	-	-	-	-	-	1	1	-	-
Cochicopa lubricella (Porro)	-	-	-	-	-	-	-	-	-	-	-	-	-	-	-	-	-	1	-	-	-
Cochlicopa spp.	-	-	-	1	-	-	-	2	2	2	-	-	-	1	2	1	1	2	2	1	2
Vertigo pygmaea (Draparnaud)	16	10	3	21	4	4	5	6	11	9	3	4	3 [+1]	27	5	20	3	21	12	13	9
Vertigo moulinsiana (Dupuy)	-	-	-	1	-	-	-	-	-	-	-	-	-	-	-	-	-	-	-	-	-
Vertigo spp.	-	3	-	6	-	-	5	1	-	6	-	-	-	2	-	-	3	1	-	-	6
Pupilla muscorum (Linnaeus)	14	19	4	51	11	4	28	11	13	34	5	11	13	55	24	11	17	28	28	28	34
Vallonia costata (Müller)	31	73	14	95	73	17	43	33	43	69	5	73	4	25	22	10	14	38	14	48	69
Vallonia excentrica Sterki	31	63	14	87	61	18	42	33	47	84	5	61	2	33	22	13	18	34	22	67	84
Vallonia spp.	3	22	4	16	7	-	2	2	-	8	-	7	-	2	1	-	2	2	3	10	8
Acanthinula aculeata (Müller)	-	1	-	-	-	-	-	-	-	-	-	-	-	-	-	-	-	-	-	-	-
Punctum pygmaeum (Draparnaud)	3	2	-	1	-	-	2	-	-	1	-	-	-	-	2	1	-	3	3	1	1
Discus rotundatus (Müller)	+	-	+	1	1	-	1	1	1	1	1	1	+	3	-	1	-	2	1	+	1
Vitrina pellucida (Müller)	-	-	-	-	-	-	2	-	1	1	-	-	-	-	1	-	-	1	-	-	1
Vitrea contracta (Westerlund)	-	1	-	-	-	-	2	2	-	1	-	-	-	1	1	-	-	1	-	-	1
Nesovitrea hammonis (Ström)	-	1	-	1	-	-	-	-	-	1	-	-	-	-	-	-	-	-	-	-	1
Aegopinella nitidula (Draparnaud)	-	-	1	3	3	3	1	2	1	-	1	3	1	2	-	-	-	2	3	-	-
Oxychilus cellarius (Müller)	1	2	-	3	1	-	1	-	1	-	-	1	-	-	-	-	-	-	-	1	-
Limacidae	21	39	30	82	48	14	33	22	36	116	11	48	6	23	20	4	27	36	25	105	116
Euconulus fulvus (Müller)	1	-	-	-	-	-	-	-	-	-	-	-	-	-	-	-	1	-	-	-	-
Cecilioides acicula (Müller)	79	602	173	1775	749	6	105	119	259	1281	9	749	12	5	11	29	91	59	128	651	1281
Cochlodina laminata (Montagu)	-	-	1	4	+	-	2	-	1	-	-	+	-	-	-	-	1	-	-	-	-
Clausilia bidentata (Ström)	+	1	-	1	-	-	+	2	2	2	+	-	-	1	1	3	1	1	-	+	2
Candidula intersecta (Poiret)	-	-	-	-	-	-	-	-	-	3	-	-	-	1	-	-	-	2	-	-	3
Candidula gigaxii (L. Pfeiffer)	-	2	-	-	-	-	-	2	-	-	-	-	-	-	-	-	2	-	-	-	-
Cernuella virgata (Da Costa)	-	-	-	-	-	-	-	-	-	-	-	-	-	-	1	-	-	-	-	-	-
Helicella itala (Linnaeus)	52	127	19	134	73	19	73	56	79	141	14	73	12	38	29	13	14	61	88	108	141
Trichia hispida (Linnaeus)	33	24	2	27	35	19	55	45	29	35	6	35	7	14	12	11	6	22	20	29	35
Arianta arbustorum (Linnaeus)	-	-	-	-	-	-	-	-	-	+	-	-	-	-	-	-	+	-	-	-	+

Table 6.23 (continued)

Phase	1/2										3										UP
Feature		4704			5670						4707	5592									4299
Soil micromorphology		✧																*	*		
Context	4817	4778	4732	4706	4298	5716	5715	5714	5713	5671	4811	4298	5882	5729	5732	5730	5731	5728	5727	5594	5671
Sample	2143	2141	2137	2135	2021	2202	2201	2200	2197	2177	2150	2021	2194	2191	2193	2189	2192	2184	2183	2181	2177
Volume (l)	30	30	2	30	15	15	30	30	30	30	5	15	30	30	30	30	15	30	30	30	30
Helicigona lapicida (Linnaeus)	-	+	-	-	+	-	+	-	-	+	-	+	+	+	1	-	+	-	+	-	+
Cepaea/Arianta spp.	3	5	+	8	4	2	2	2	3	6	1	4	1	4	+	+	1	9	3	5	6
Helix aspersa (Müller)	-	-	-	-	-	-	-	-	-	-	[1]	-	-	-	-	-	-	-	-	-	-
Fresh-water																					
Valvata cristata (Müller)	-	-	-	-	1	1	1	2	2	-	-	1	-	-	-	-	-	-	-	-	-
Bithynia tentaculata (Linnaeus)	-	-	-	-	-	-	-	-	-	-	-	-	-	-	-	-	-	-	-	1	-
Lymnaea truncatula (Müller)	-	-	-	-	2	-	-	-	-	1	-	2	-	-	-	-	-	-	-	-	1
Gyraulus albus (Müller)	-	-	-	-	-	-	-	-	1	-	1	-	-	-	-	-	-	-	-	-	-
Pisidium subtruncatum (Malm)	-	-	-	-	-	-	-	-	-	-	-	-	-	1	-	-	-	-	-	-	-
Pisidium spp.	4	-	-	-	-	-	-	-	-	-	-	-	-	-	-	-	-	-	-	-	-
Taxa	17	19	13	19	17	11	20	17	19	21	12	17	12	18	17	13	17	19	14	15	21
TOTAL	*218*	*401*	*94*	*548*	*328*	*103*	*308*	*236*	*280*	*528*	*56*	*328*	*51*	*243*	*150*	*90*	*117*	*278*	*229*	*419*	*528*
Mollusc per litre	7.3	13.4	47	18.3	21.9	6.9	10.3	7.9	9.3	17.6	11.2	21.9	1.7	8.1	5.0	3.0	7.8	9.3	7.6	14.0	17.6
0.5 mm residue extracted	Y	Y	Y	Y	N	Y	Y	Y	Y	Y	Y	N	Y	Y	Y	Y	Y	Y	Y	Y	Y

Specimens in [] retain their periostricum and are considered to be recent intrusions; they are not included in the analysis.
Soil micromorphology: * = analysis from this context; open symbol = analysis from this feature

Discussion

In recent years a number of Iron Age hillforts and hilltop locations have been excavated on the chalklands, accompanied by land snail analysis – Danebury, (Cunliffe 1984; 2000; Cunliffe and Poole 1991) and Balksbury (Wainwright and Davies 1995; Ellis and Rawlings 2001), Hampshire, and Maiden Castle, Dorset (Sharples 1991). In the Wylye valley, only 2 km from the site, the Iron Age enclosure at Codford Circle has been excavated (Bryant 2002; Allen and Gardiner 2006). The assemblages from Battlesbury Bowl are all open county and show similarities with grassland assemblages from Danebury (Evans and Hewitt 1991) and Balksbury (Allen 1995b; 2001) and no significant change through time can be discerned. However, in contrast with the assemblages at Danebury, *Pomatias elegans* is present throughout at this site, possibly living in bare earth under small shrubs (eg, hawthorn) and indicating a more diverse downland habitat. Unfortunately there were no old land surfaces with which to examine the open grassland of the pre-hillfort environment, and so enable comparison with those examined at Codford Circle, Balksbury, Danebury, and Maiden Castle.

Landscape and land-use

One of the most significant results of analysis from the pits was the consistent nature of the assemblages both through the individual features and in pits of different phases. Unlike at Danebury (Evans 1984; Evans and Hewitt 1991) and Balksbury (Allen 2001), little chronological variation in land-use can be detected. There is no phase of revegetation which might relate to episodes of abandonment, nor any woodland in the vicinity, as at both Danebury and Maiden Castle (Evans and Hewitt 1991; Evans and Rouse 1991).

The local environment was typical downland, not heavily trampled, but probably lightly grazed, with some relict scrub (*Pomatias elegans*) but little evidence for bare earth despite evidence for disturbance and dumping created by the occupation. There is no evidence for local arable contexts or tilled fields. The virtual absence of any woodland species indicates that these habitats were long removed from the top of Battlesbury Hill and were relatively far removed from the chalk ridge

Table 6.24 Iron Age 'hilltop' sites with freshwater/obligatory marsh species

Site		*Altitude above nearest watercourse*	*Distance to nearest watercourse*
Balksbury, Hants	●	20 m	0.2 km to Anton
Maiden Castle, Dorset	⊗	40 m	0.4 km to Winterbourne
Winklebury, Hants	●	30 m	0.8 km to Loddon tributary
Codford Circle, Wilts	●	100 m	1 km to Chitterne Brook, 1.6 km to Wylye
Battlesbury, Wilts	●	*c.* 65 m	1 km to Oxenbourne Bottom, 2 km to Wylye
Danebury, Hants	❍	80 m	3.4 km to Test
The Bowsings, Gloucs	●	15 m	0.1 km to Windrush valley

Key: = ● pits (or features) with freshwater species; ❍ = pits (or features) with no freshwater species; ⊗ = no pits examined

occupied by the site. One might have expected the steeper slopes around Battlesbury Bowl to the east, for instance, to have supported more substantial scrub and the concomitant molluscan fauna to have recorded greater diversity of species than is evident. A very similar open grazed downland, but with some local tillage, is seen further down the Wylye valley at Codford Circle (Bryant 2002). The lack of evidence for woodland or woodland regeneration in both these sites contrasts with that seen at Danebury and Maiden Castle, suggesting either that regeneration did not occur at the site (as at Codford Circle), or that the sampled pits represent too short a period.

Clearance had obviously occurred well before activity on the site, as indeed it had at Codford Circle. Clearance of the hilltops and slopes overlooking the Wylyle valley is known from the Neolithic period onwards, possibly in relation to the construction of some of the long barrows (Allen and Gardiner 2004)

Exploitation of the wider resources

The presence of aquatic and marsh species must be allochthonous and indicate the exploitation of riverine and river-edge environments within the Wylyle valley. Six aquatic and one marsh species were recorded. The aquatic species include mainly soft water species and include catholic aquatic species, tolerating a wide range of conditions (*Armiger crista*, *Gyraulus albus*, and *Pisidium subtruncatum*), ditch aquatic species, mainly occurring in slow-moving plant-rich streams (*Valvata cristata*), moving-water species (*Bithynia tentaculata*), and amphibious species (*Lymnaea truncatula*). The solitary marsh species, *Vertigo moulinsiana*, can be found in areas adjacent to those inhabited by the true aquatic species. Where the palaeofaunas have indicated the presence of grasses rather than sedge, *V. moulinsiana* is stenotopic and usually lives on the stems of *Carex* sp. or *Glyceria maxima* in fen environments (Butot and Neuteboom 1958; Bishop 1974) but its occurrence as a single specimen suggest that this fen was not rife in the Wylye valley or that this was not the resource exploited.

Function and activities

The interpretation of the function of features can rarely be aided by snail analyses, but the record of freshwater species in a number of contexts suggests the exploitation of riverine resources. Their common occurrence on this site (ten contexts from features including pits, ditches, and a post-hole) can only be accounted for if they are introduced on site with a resource commonly collected from the Wylye valley. This may include water, mud or alluvium (for building, lining pits, etc), or rushes, reeds, and sedges which might be used for number of activities. Charred plant remains indicates blinks (*Montia*), common rush (*Juncus*/*Eleocharis palustris*), and sedges (*Carex*). Such riverside vegetation might have been put to a number of uses including bedding (both human and animals), fodder, flooring, covers for pits, thatching, etc, all of which might be expected on sites like this. This has been suggested for Winklebury, Hampshire, where a number of specimens of *Lymnaea peregra* were found in three samples from one pit (Thomas 1977), and Balksbury where both aquatic (*Gyraulus albus*) and marsh (*Vertigo moulinsiana* and *V. angustior*) were recovered from a pit (Allen 1995b).

The occurrence of freshwater or obligatory marsh species seems to be regular if in small number on sites where relevant features have been examined, eg, Codford Circle, Danebury, Balksbury, Winklebury, and The Bowsings, Gloucestershire (Allen 1998), shows that they are common (Table 6.24). All of these hilltop sites have a source of fresh water nearby, suggesting strongly that the use of resources from the riverine contexts was common, although precisely what that resource was remains uncertain. Only at Danebury, the furthest site from a watercourse, does this not occur.

Soil Micromorphology and Chemistry

by Richard I. Macphail and John Crowther

Ten kubiena and accompanying bulk soil samples were taken through selected deposits. Four soil thin sections and six bulk samples were selected for examination to aid in characterising the activities on site and to study mineralised soil materials and depositional environments associated with those activities. Samples selected for study were from phase 1/2 ditch 4043 and a series of pits. In particular it was noted that mineralisation features (colour and appearance) of deposits in both pits and ditches resembled those described from the enclosure ditch of the Iron Age hillfort at Maiden Castle (Macphail 1991, table 14, figs 105d and e) and, more generally, at Potterne and East Chisenbury (Macphail 2000).

The chief aims of the soil study are to contribute to the archaeological objectives of determining economic activity, landscape, shifting patterns within the settlement, and use of this peripheral occupation on the chalk spur outside the hillfort, with particular emphasis on defining the nature of 'special' or 'placed' deposits. It was also hoped that the study would improve the understanding of the archaeological site formation processes responsible for mineralisation.

These aims and objectives were tackled through a combined soil chemical and micromorphological study that had proved successful at the archaeological experimental earthwork constructed on chalk rendzinas at Overton Down, Wiltshire (Crowther *et al.* 1996). This report presents details of the soil micromorphological findings and integrates the chemical results (*cf.* Crowther 2001).

Samples and Methods

Four thin sections were prepared and studied (Table 6.25): one from ditch 4043, section 4019 (context 4070), and others from microlaminated fills from pits (4704, 4196, 5592; Table 6.28). Six bulk chemical samples were investigated from ditch section 4019 and pit 5592 (see Table 6.26, samples listed below).

Table 6.25 Soil micromorphology thin sections

Feature	*Thin section context*	*Soil chemistry*
Phase 1/2		
Pit 4704	4734 (& laminations)	none
Ditch 4043, section 4019	4070	4 context specific samples inc. 4070
Phase 3		
Pit 4553, within 4196	4197/4550/4234	none
Pit 5592	5728/5727	context 5728 & laminations

Chemistry

Analysis was undertaken on the fine earth fraction (ie, <2 mm) of the fills. pH (1:2.5, water) and $CaCO_3$ (by calcimeter) were determined using the methods presented by Avery and Bascomb (1974). Loss-on-ignition (LOI) was determined by ignition at 375°C for 16 hrs (Ball 1964) – previous experimental studies have shown that there is no significant breakdown of $CaCO_3$ at this temperature. Phosphate-P_i and phosphate-P_o were determined using a two-stage adaptation of the procedure developed by Dick and Tabatabai (1977) in which the phosphate concentration of a sample is measured first without oxidation of organic matter, using HCl as the extractant (P_i); and then on the residue following alkaline oxidation with NaOBr (P_o). A Bartington MS1 meter was used for magnetic susceptibility measurements. χ_{max} was achieved by heating samples at 650°C in reducing, followed by oxidising, conditions. The method used broadly follows that of Tite and Mullins (1971), except that household flour was mixed with the soils and lids placed on the crucibles to create the reducing environment (after Graham and Scollar 1976; Crowther and Barker 1995).

Pearson's product moment correlation analysis was used to examine relationships in the data. Where the skewness of the data for individual properties exceeded 1.00, the data were $\log_{10}$ transformed in order to increase parametricity. Statistical significance was assessed at the 95% confidence level.

Soil micromorphology

Undisturbed Kubiena samples were impregnated with a crystic resin mixture and when cured, cut into blocks for thin section manufacture at Stirling University (Murphy 1986). The four thin sections studied were observed at magnifications from 1x to 400x, under plane polarised light (PPL), crossed polarised light (XPL), oblique incident light (OIL), and fluorescence microscopy (blue light). The last was used to study autofluorescent materials, such as poorly decomposed plant material, pollen, and materials composed of calcium phosphate (~apatite) such as bone, mineralised coprolites, and phosphatised soil (Courty *et al.* 1989; Goldberg *et al.* in prep.; Macphail 2000). Thin sections were described and selected features and inclusions counted (Macphail and Cruise 2001). Soil microfabrics were defined (SMF).

Results

The chemical and magnetic properties of the samples analysed are presented in Table 6.26 and the results of the correlation analysis shown in Table 6.27. The

Table 6.26 Chemical and magnetic properties of micromorphology samples analysed

Context	*Sample*	*LOI (%)*	*$CaCO_3$ (%)*	*pH (1:2.5, water)*	*Phosphate* P_i *(mg g^{-1})*	P_o *(mg g^{-1})*	*P (mg g^{-1})*	P_i*:P (%)*	P_o*:P (%)*	χ *(10^{-8}SI)*	χ_{max} *(10^{-8}SI)*	χ_{conv} *(%)*
Ditch 4019*												
4070	2109	4.85	43.4	8.5	10.4	1.22	11.6	89.5	10.5	7.5	36.2	20.7
4089	2107	4.59	44.6	8.5	8.06	1.62	9.68	83.3	16.7	4.8	38.7	12.4
4071	2106	4.94	48.3	8.5	9.61	1.84	11.5	83.9	16.1	5.6	41.5	13.5
4110	2104	4.84	43.1	8.5	9.71	1.21	10.9	88.9	11.1	7.8	38.7	20.2
Pit 5592*												
5727	5727	5.75	48.5	8.4	10.6	1.00	11.6	91.4	8.6	51.7	113	45.8
5728	5728	4.57	34.0	8.4	8.45	1.00	9.45	89.4	10.6	44.8	114	39.3

* Ditch 4019: ditch with cess/mineralised material in main secondary fill contemporary with occupation/settlement;
Pit 5592: pit contaning cess with microlaminations

general character of the fills, including the nature of the relationships between the properties analysed, are discussed before considering the results of both chemistry and soil micromorphology of individual samples/contexts.

General character of the fills (chemistry)

All six samples are alkaline and $CaCO_3$-rich (range, 34.0–48.5%), and have a moderate organic matter content (4.57–5.75%). From an archaeological perspective, the most striking feature of the results is the exceptionally high levels of phosphate recorded (phosphate-P, 9.45–11.6 mg g^{-1}). These clearly indicate very high levels of phosphate enrichment – as might be associated, for example, with midden-type material containing bone or with cess-type deposits. The majority of the phosphate in all the samples is in the inorganic form (phosphate-P_i:P, 83.3–91.4%), which implies that the fills have been subject to quite high degrees of pre- and/or post-depositional organic decomposition/mineralisation. The significant correlations recorded between the phosphate data (Table 6.27), and lack of correlation between LOI and phosphate, reflect the dominance of the phosphate-P_i fraction.

The samples have very low χ_{max} values (36.2–114 x 10^{-8} SI), which presumably reflect the low iron (Fe) content of the fills. As a consequence, the χ values recorded in the samples (maximum, 51.7 x 10^{-8} SI) are relatively low. On the other hand, the percentage χ_{conv} is high (12.4–45.8%). It is quite unusual for samples to have values ≥10.0%. All the samples would therefore appear to show some signs of χ enhancement, and this seems likely to be associated with burning. Correlation analysis reveals a highly significant relationship between χ and χ_{conv} ($r = 0.980$, $p<0.01$), which confirms that χ is strongly influenced by the degree of conversion that has taken place. χ is, however, also affected quite strongly by χ_{max} ($r = 0.991$, $p<0.001$). There is a statistically significant correlation between phosphate-P_o and χ_{conv} ($r = -0.840$, $p<0.05$). Although this relationship is not necessarily causal, the lower concentrations of organic phosphate-P_o could well be a direct result of the burning – with the phosphate released during the burning of organic matter being retained in a mineralised form within the sediments.

Soil micromorphology and chemistry

The soil thin sections revealed variety of soil types, structure, and included natural and anthropogenic materials (Table 6.28). For example, pit 4704 (context 4734) revealed the presence of five layers (microlaminations), with four layers being identified in pit 5592 (contexts 5727 and 5728). Detailed counting was necessary to show up this micro-stratigraphy (Table 6.28, and archive). Twenty-nine different elements were identified. These included: natural inclusions (chalk and flint), structure types (massive, etc), organic matter (amorphous organic matter, plant fragments, *in situ* roots), pedofeatures (excrements, intercalations, clay coatings, secondary Fe/Mn, phosphate-stained soil), and anthropogenic inclusions (burned bone, bone, charcoal, ash, phytoliths, articulated phytoliths, mineralised coprolites, including likely human material, and ashed herbivore dung). These were identified on the basis of their morphology, autofluorescence under blue light, and composition (see below) (eg, Macphail 2000; Macphail and Cruise 2001; Goldberg *et al.* in prep.). Varieties of ash deposits for example were composed of fine calcite crystals, crystals of calcium oxalate (eg, druses), calcitic faecal spherulites, phytoliths, and fine charcoal (Brochier *et al.* 1992; Canti 1998b; 1999; Wattez and Courty 1987; Wattez *et al.* 1990). Both calcite earthworm granules and slug plates were also

Table 6.27 Pearson's produce moment correlation coefficients $ (r) for relationships between the soil properties analysed#

	CaCo₃	P_i	P_o	P	P_i:P	χ	χ_{max}	χ_{conv}
LOI$	ns	ns	ns	ns	ns	ns	ns	ns
$CaCO_3$		ns	ns	ns	ns	ns	ns	ns
P_i			ns	0.936*	ns	ns	ns	ns
P_o				ns	-0.938*	ns	ns	-0.840
P					ns	ns	ns	ns
P_i:P						ns	ns	ns
χ							0.991**	0.980*
χ_{max}								0.950

$ Statistical significance – $p<0.05$ unless indicated as follows:
** = $p<0.0001$, * = $p<0.01$, ns = not significant
# P_i:P necessarily exhibits a perfect inverse correlation with P_o:P. Correlation coefficients involving P_o:P (not presented in table) are therefore identical to those for P_i:P, but with an opposite sign
$ LOI data were $\log_{10}$ transformed to increase parametricity

found, as evidence for biological activity (Canti 1998a). Burned and unburned grey rendzina and more rarely, decalcified humic topsoil and subsoil materials were found (eg, Upton 1 soil association; Findlay *et al.* 1983).

Ditch 4043, section 4019 (fill 4070: ?cessy secondary fills)
The four contexts sampled from the ditch fill display relatively little variation in their chemical and magnetic properties (Table 6.26). The only noteworthy difference is between the two contexts (4089 and 4071) from the middle of the sequence, and the underlying (4110) and overlying (4070) contexts, with the latter two having lower phosphate-P_o concentrations and a higher χ_{conv}. Examination of the thin sections revealed evidence for burning which would support the causal explanation for the inverse relationship between phosphate-P_o and χ_{conv} outlined above.

In thin section, context 4070 is a homogeneous fine deposit that contains many very fine charcoal and rare sand-size fragments of fine organic matter throughout, but phytoliths were rare (SMF1). A likely cess component is composed of rare ubiquitous silt to sand-size bone and human (?) coprolite (Courty *et al.* 1989, pl. iva), and fine-medium sand-size and rare but ubiquitous parenchymatous plant tissues, with articulated phytoliths possibly of bran (*cf.* Monkton, Kent, Norman cess pit, Goldberg *et al.* in prep). Other incorporated materials included patches of sand-size amorphous organic matter and few stone-size clasts of 'burned' chalky soil and a higher fine charcoal content than the surrounding fill. Specific pedofeatures (see Table 6.28) indicate that laminations and blackening of the matrix in thin section is probably due to phosphate impregnation (*cf.* Macphail and Goldberg 1995).

Overall the main characteristics of these ditch fills are that they homogeneous, contain a significant cess content and include burned 'soil'.

Pit 4704 (context 4734: lenses of burnt chalk and soil)
This is composed of coarse chalk lenses with a fine chalky soil (SMF2) and fine laminated fills (SMF3). The chalky soil only contains a few anthropogenic inclusions (fine charcoal, burned snail shell, pottery and burned soil). In contrast the laminated fill (SMF3) contains much more charcoal and phytoliths. Many fragments of burned chalk, chalky soil, and humic chalky soil, occur in thin layers. Also present within these layers are either humic topsoil or mineralogenic subsoil fragments; some coarse wood and 'straw' charcoal including pieces commonly 120–400 µm long. Less common are strongly burned bone, coprolitic (digested and excreted) stained bone, high temperature ashed dung, and organic/phosphatic inclusions of cess. The fine soil also contains burned specks, amorphous organic matter, many probable monocotyledonous charcoal lengths, and very abundant phytoliths which are occasionally associated with patches of fine calcite ash and micritic transformations of ash.

Soil formation is evident in these layers and is recorded by frequent very broad mammilated organo-mineral earthworm excrements and calcite earthworm granules, and other secondary phosphatic inclusions and staining (Table 6.28).

Pit 5592 (contexts 5727 and 5728: microlaminated fills)
Microlaminated fills were sampled as good examples of features which occur in other pits throughout the site. Sampling was restricted to two contexts with clearly typical and well-defined colour and laminations.

The upper sampled context (5727) has a higher organic matter and $CaCO_3$ content, and also shows stronger signs of phosphate-enrichment and χ enhancement. On the whole, however, the chemical properties of these two contexts differ very little from the fills of ditch section 4019. The only notable difference is in the magnetic properties, with this pit exhibiting both higher χ_{max} values, which suggest a higher iron content, and χ_{conv} values, which provide strong evidence for burning.

At the base of context 5727 the uppermost (20 mm) portion is composed of SMF2 (see above), with other soil microfabrics below (Table 6.28). SMF4 occurs from from 20–35(40) mm, and a mixture of SMF2 and SMF3 from 35(40)–65 mm, and the top of context 5728 from 65–90 mm being represented by SMF5.

SMF4 is mainly coarse components that include wood charcoal (including some twig wood, see Gale above), coarse sand- to stone-size (2–10 mm) burned chalk, and humic soil. Coarse fragments of arenaceous limestone are imported material, possibly used for pottery temper, no quernstones, rubbers, or other artefacts were made of limestone (Chapter 4). Most common, however, are the compacted, mixed residues of burned and ashed plant material, composed of small amounts of probable cereal waste (see SMF3) and common herbivore dung and stabling material. The stabling material includes silt-rich fragments of layered plant residues, with rare articulated phytoliths up to 4 mm in size (see above). Burnt (ashed) coprolites are calcitic with evidence for herbs and grasses including stems as ash crystals, calcium oxalate druses. They also include patches of faecal spherulites (<20 μm). Some 'dung' fragments are still 'humic' with little ash, and display concentrated amorphous organic matter. Secondary phosphate concentrations as found in experimental stables (eg, 'Moel-y-gar' old demonstration area, Butser Ancient Farm, Hampshire) were also present. Phytoliths are ubiquitous and very abundant throughout this layer. Sometimes high temperature burning has 'carbonised' previously calcitic mineral residues-material.

Post-depositional pedogenesis including chemical and physical (small meso-fauna) effects make identification of some dung difficult. Nevertheless, both layered fabrics (as in cattle dung) and short plant tissues (as in sheep/goat dung) occur, indicating that both herbivores are likely to be represented (Goldberg *et al.* in prep.; Macphail *et al.* 1997; Macphail and Cruise 2001; Macphail and Goldberg 1995; Matthews *et al.* 1997).

SMF5 contains small amounts of anthropogenic inclusions (as SMF2) and also includes fragments of SMF4 material. It differs mainly by having an open spongy microstructure, snail fragments, and many thin (100–150 μm) dusty calcareous clay void coatings that seal many pores (vughs) that form the spongy porosity. There is evidence for very strong mixing by earthworms, including burrows and excrements, that pre-date some of the soil forming features.

Pit 4553 with pit 4196 (contexts 4197, 4550 and 4234: puddled and burnt/baked chalk)

Contexts 4197 and 4550 are essentially composed of SMF2 with inclusions of SMF3, but which is particularly characterised by many very dusty and cloudy calcareous clay (0.4–0.8 mm) coatings and infills, and related intercalations, sometimes partially closing vughs. Also present are rare iron and manganese fine impregnations with rare likely calcium phosphate impregnation (blue light auto-fluorescence) following vertical channels. Biological activity is responsible for much fabric mixing and burrow infills (spongy microstructure).

Context 4234 is very similar to context 4550, but with more frequent SMF3 material and minor amounts of SMF4. Calcareous clay inwash, iron and manganese impregnation, likely phosphate staining and biological mixing have similarly affected the deposit.

General character

Chemistry records very high amounts of soil phosphate and, in prehistoric soils, such quantities are normally only found in 'middens' such as at Potterne and East Chisenbury. Comparable levels of phosphate were recorded in the 'cemented' soil (1.3% phosphate-P) at Potterne (Macphail 2000, 61). In thin section, phosphate is clearly present as bone, possible human coprolites, and amorphous mineralised cess that probably include bran. Bran is, for example, a component of the high amounts of mono-cotyledonous ash present and ashed *Triticum sativum* has the potential to produce 3.5% phosphate-P (Wattez and Courty 1987). Phosphate is concentrated within fragments of dung, and ashed dung and stabling crust material, and these are further contributors to total phosphate. In addition to phosphate, there is also evidence of secondary calcium carbonate, impregnation of the soil matrix. Much of the organic matter (cereal material and stabling waste – see below) and its organic phosphate component, have been ashed contributing to the dominant amounts of inorganic phosphate (P_i). Little humic topsoil material has been deposited in the fills, although ditch fill 4070 contains fine organic matter inclusions (cess) that were phosphatised and may be protected from full oxidation.

Inputs of burned material, as recorded by unusually high χ_{conv}, are represented in thin sections by burned snail, bone, and blackened soil, along with mineral material interpreted as high temperature burned dung. Significantly, SMF4 (burned dung) is located within context 5727 which recorded the highest χ_{conv}.

Interpretation of the Fills

Ditch 4019

The high phosphate content and enhanced magnetic susceptibility (χ), and the general homogeneous fine charcoal-rich microfabric that includes burned soil, bone, coprolite, and organic and inorganic cess components, along with evidence for inwash of chalky clay, are all indicative of fine silting, major sewage disposal, and important inputs of washed and blown charcoal/burned soil.

The Tower of London moat, which was employed for sewage disposal, had a similar but much more diluted cess and phosphate character because of the influence of the river Thames (Macphail and Crowther 2004). More similar is the fill of the Early Iron Age (phase 2) ditch at Maiden Castle, where inputs of cess probably stained the fill (Macphail 1991, table 14). At Battlesbury Bowl, it is evident that occupation debris was sometimes dumped as wet slurries that had a high phosphate component.

Table 6.28 Microfacies types (soil microfabric types and associated data)

Material	*Sample no. examples*	*Sampling depth, soil micromorphology (SM), bulk data (BD)*	*Phase, interpretation and comments*
Ditch 4019: context 4070:			
SMF1	M2101	SM: *Structure*: v. homogeneous; (fragmented) massive/prismatic, with rare 2 mm thick laminated areas; originally 10–15% voids, open vugh/chambers & v. fine–medium (200–400 μm); *Coarse mineral*: C:F (limit at 10 μm), 10:90, with few silty patches & laminae of 60:40; v. dominant silt-size quartz, with chalk fossils & calcite, & few chalk, v. few medium sand-size chalk, burned chalk, flint; with rare glauconite & biogenic calcite nodules; *Coarse organic/anthropogenic*: few stone-size inclusions of chalky soil clasts with sand-size quartz inclusions etc, & higher fine charcoal content; many v. fine charcoal with rare sand-size frags; rare ubiquitous mainly silt-size bone & likely human? coprolite, some fine–medium sand-size (parenchymatous plant tissue, articulated phytoliths [bran?], & bone; rare, ubiquitous silt–fine sand-size yellowish parenchymatous plant tissue (cess origin); many–abundant patches reddish brown sand-size amorphous organic matter; *Fine fabric*: v. cloudy grey–blackish grey (patches & included clasts) (PPL), moderately high interference colours (open–close porphyric, crystallitic, XPL), grey with abundant black specks & many brown patches (OIL); occasional–many amorphous organic matter & v. abundant fine charred material, rare phytoliths; *Pedofeatures*: rare 100 μm thick chalky clay void coatings, with intercalations associated with fine laminations; occasional blackening (& reduction of interference colours) of matrix is the likely result of phosphate impregnation (autofluorescent under Blue Light; rare included biogenic calcite (mainly slug plate type, as part of the sediment); (many neoformed micritic calcite hypocoatings, but as it affects fragmented material is assumed to be a sample processing artefact). BD: 4070: 4.85% LOI, 43.4% $CaCO_3$, 11.6 P mg g^{-1}, 7.5 x 10^{-8} SI χ and 20.7% $\chi_{conv.}$. BD: 4089: 4.59% LOI, 44.6% $CaCO_3$, 9.68 P mg g^{-1}, 4.8 x 10^{-8} SI χ and 12.4% $\chi_{conv.}$. BD: 4071: 4.94% LOI, 48.3% $CaCO_3$, 11.5 P mg g^{-1}, 5.6 x 10^{-8} SI χ and 13.5% $\chi_{conv.}$. BD: 4110: 4.84% LOI, 43.1% $CaCO_3$, 10.9 P mg g^{-1}, 7.8 x 10^{-8} SI χ and 20.2% $\chi_{conv.}$.	Massive/prismatic (& now fragmented) v. fine silt & chalky clay fill, containing v. much fine charcoal & more rarely coarse charcoal, with amorphous organic matter & some clasts of similar, but more charcoal-rich material; very fine bone, yellow plant tissues & nodules of bone/plant tissues & articulated phytoliths (coprolites) are evidence of cess inputs; blackish staining of the sediment, autofluorescent under blue light, is further evidence of phosphate inputs. Chemistry confirms high inputs of phosphate & additionally suggests deposition of burned soil. *This is a very fine ditch fill, composed of fine charcoal-rich chalky wash, sometimes as silty slurries, & containing background amounts of fine-sorted cess material (sewage-sludge-like). Evidence of fires, burned cereals locally supplying high amounts of fine charcoal.*
Pit 4704: context 4734			
SMF2	M2155	0–3.0(4.0) cm SM: *Structure*: heterogeneous, massive chalk stone layer; 20% voids, dominant chambers & burrows, & few, fine (50–100 μm) curved planar voids; *Coarse mineral*: C:F (limit at 10 μm), 80:20, v. dominant small stone-size (eg, 35 mm) chalk, few chalk gravel, frequent silt-size to fine sand-size quartz, chalk, calcite & fossils; *Coarse organic/anthropogenic*: rare sand-size inclusions of humic non-calcareous soil (with silt-size quartz & glauconite); occasional fine charcoal with rare burned shell (x2), pottery (x1), burned soil (x1), sand-size frags; occasional inclusions of fine charcoal & phytolith-rich soil (see SMF 3, below) & rare fine amorphous organic matter frags; *Fine fabric*: cloudy grey with some black inclusions specks (PPL), moderately high interference colours (open–close porphyric, crystallitic, XPL), whitish grey & mixed grey with black specks (OIL); rare amorphous organic matter & occasional fine charred material, (patches of fine charcoal & phytoliths); *Pedofeatures*: ubiquitous, occasional, v. thin (20–40 μm) micritic coatings; v. abundant total excremental fabric, with mamillated coarse (>2 mm) excrements, with rare very thin (<50 μm) Enchytraeid/Collembola excrements, with rare likely earthworm granules.	Chalk layer: Chalk stone-dominated layer, with earthworm activity mixing-in natural chalk soil, and small amounts of charcoal and sometimes phytolith-rich soil; alongside rare inclusions of non-calcareous (drift) soil. *A dump of chalk to seal lower deposits or seasonal? pit-wall collapse?*

Table 6.28 (continued)

SMF3		(4.0)-6.0 cm SM: *Structure*: v. heterogeneous, massive, with poorly formed thin (1–2 mm) layers; 25–30% voids, dominant chambers & burrows & open vughs, with few, fine horizontal planar voids; *Coarse mineral*: C:F (limit at 10 μm), strongly heterogeneous, with 80:20 to 40:60, few small gravel-size (eg 2–4 mm) chalk, few–dominant silt-size to fine sand-size quartz, chalk, calcite & fossils; *Coarse organic/anthropogenic*: frequent coarse (>2 mm) burned chalk, chalky soil & humic chalky soil – as layers, with few rounded coarse sand size non-calcareous soil clasts, some humic, some subsoil drift; occasional coarse wood & likely 'straw' charcoal; rare strongly burned & rubified, browned bone; rare shell, bone & likely coprolitic bone, rare silt-size strongly rubified mineral matter – possibly ashed dung?; rare inclusions of organic/phosphatic inclusions of cess?; most common component is fine charcoal & phytolith-rich soil (MF3)(frequent mixed MF2); *Fine fabric*: black streaked & grey (PPL), high interference colours (open–close porphyric, crystallitic, XPL), pale grey with black streaks, rare red specks (OIL); rare amorphous organic matter, abundant likely monocotyledonous charcoal lengths & very abundant phytoliths, including commonly 120–400 μm) pieces or articulated lengths (yellow patches of articulated sheets more likely coprolitic), occasional associated patches of fine calcite ash & likely micritic transformations of ash; *Pedofeatures*: rare fine sand-size sparitic calcite infills; rare–occasional phosphatic inclusions & staining of matrix (non-birefringent, autofluorescent under Blue Light); ubiquitous, rare very thin (20–40 μm) micritic coatings; many (mamillated in places) coarse (>2 mm) excrements, with rare very thin (<50–100 μm) Enchytraeid/Collembola excrements loosely infilling chambers, with rare (x4) earthworm calcite granules.	Laminated layer: thinly laminated layer of burned chalk, chalky soil & non-calcareous soil with common patches & laminated areas of monocotyledonous charcoal, long phytolith lengths & associated ash crystals or weakly transformed ash/micritic patches; with strongly rubified fine soil & burned bone etc; small amounts of coprolitic material/cess & secondary phosphate impregnation are evident; the layer is partially worked by earthworms & other mesofauna. *Dumps of hearth & burned cereal processing debris, alongside minor amounts of other food waste & cess, with possible traces of burned herbivore dung.*
		6.5–7.0 cm SM: As SMF2, but with v. dominant chalk gravel (4 mm) & only few patches of SMF3.	Chalk soil & chalk gravel dump/layer, with small amounts of earthworm-worked included cereal processing/hearth & cess debris. *Sealing or seasonal collapse layer.*
		7.0-8.0 cm SM: As SMF 3.	*Dumps of hearth & burned cereal processing debris, alongside minor amounts of other food waste & cess.*
		8.0-9.0 cm SM: As SMF2, without fine chalky soil.	Chalk dump layer.
Pit 5592: Context 5727:			
SMF2	M2212	0–6.5 cm SM: *Structure*: heterogeneous, layered & laminated, spongy microstructure; 30–40% voids, dominant medium (0.5 mm) open vughs & channels (spongy), with coarse (5 mm) size chambers; three major layers:	
SMF4		0–2 mm: Chalk stone & chalky soil (SMF2) dominated	Layer of chalk stones, with calcareous soil & few charcoal frags. *Chalk soil dump?*
SMF3		2–3.5(4) cm: *Coarse organic/anthropogenic*: few wood charcoal (some twig wood?); with very dominant coarse sand to stone-size (2–10 mm) burned chalk, humic soil & most commonly, the compacted, mixed residues of burned & ashed herbivore dung & stabling crust material (sometimes silt-rich, frags of layered plant residues, rare articulated phytoliths of 4 mm in size; some calcitic with ash crystals, calcium oxalate druses (from herbs and grasses – stem frags present) & rare–concentrated patches of faecal spherulites (<20 μm); some frags still 'humic' with little ash, & display concentrated amorphous organic matter; phytoliths are ubiquitous & v. abundant throughout; commonly ash has been transformed to micritic patches; sometimes high temperature burning had carbonised previously calcitic mineral residues, & this is associated with rubified silt-size material; some material is autofluorescent under Blue Light; fine fragmentation & some working by small meso-fauna makes dung identification difficult, but as both layered fabrics (as in cattle dung) & short plant tissues (as in sheep/goat dung) occur in dung frags (both herbivores are likely represented); occasional sand-size humic soil inclusions; rare bone/cess /coprolite; *Fine fabric*: speckled grey & brown (PPL), patches of high interference colours & isotic material (open–close porphyric, crystallitic, XPL), white, grey & with blackish streaks (OIL); patches of v. abundant amorphous organic matter, with very abundant phytoliths (some long articulated lengths), with various ash & faecal spherulites; *Pedofeatures*: occasional patches of thin (50–100 μm) calcareous dusty clay void coatings (post-dating biological porosity formation); rare neoformed sparitic infills; occasional likely phosphate impregnation (autofluorescent under blue light); v.	Phytolith- (including articulated phytoliths) and ash-rich layer, with organic & charred traces of layered & 'short' plant tissue remains; interlayered silt (humic soil clasts) & ashed remains of herbs & grasses, along with patches of faecal spherulites – all indicate the dumping of the mixed remains of burned herbivore dung (likely both sheep/goat & cattle) along with other mixed domestic debris. Much of the ash has partially weathered & been worked by small meso-fauna & larger earthworms. Chemistry shows the high amounts of phosphate present and markedly reflects the highly burned nature of the deposit (45.8% χ_{conv}). *Dump of mixed ashed stabling remains & domestic*

Table 6.28 (continued)

Sample		Description	Interpretation
		abundant faunal mixing with thin (200 μm) small meso-faunal excrements; abundant mamillated, coarse (>2 mm) excrements & burrow fills. BD: 4070: 5.75% LOI, 48.5% $CaCO_3$, 11.6 P mg g^{-1}, 44.8 x 10^{-8} SI χ and 45.8% $\chi_{conv.}$.	*debris, which became partially biologically worked & weathered.*
SMF2-3		3.5(4)–6.5 cm SM: heterogeneous, open chamber & packing void (& spongy) microstructure; 30% voids, coarse packing voids, open vughs & chambers; *Coarse organic/anthropogenic*: frequent SMF2, with frequent SMF3, but fewer included articulated phytoliths but high charcoal content; frequent stone-size burned chalk & few stone-size (max. 11 mm) & sand-size arenaceous (sandy) limestone, & v. few ironstone; frequent coarse (max. 7 mm) twig? wood charcoal; v. few inclusions of SMF4; rare fine burned bone & bone; rare *in situ* root traces; *Pedofeatures*: rare thin (100 μm) dusty calcareous clay void coatings; rare sparitic infills in charcoal; rare calcium phosphate staining of matrix (blue light autofluorescence); strong fabric mixing; v. abundant broad (>2 mm) earthworm burrow fills (occasional earthworm granules), with many very thin excrements. BD: 5.75% LOI, 48.5% $CaCO_3$, 11.6 P mg g^{-1}, 51.7 x 10^{-8} SI χ and 45.8% $\chi_{conv.}$.	Heterogeneous mix of chalk, burned chalk, charcoal-rich chalky soil, small amounts of soil containing articulated phytoliths, v. much likely twig wood charcoal & fine–coarse arenaceous limestone, the last may have been used in pottery production or as a grindstone? *Domestic/cereal-food preparation hearth waste*
Pit 5592: context 5728			
SMF5	M2212	6.5–9.0 cm SM: partially homogenised, spongy microstructure; 25–30% voids, very dominant coarse (3–5 mm) chambers & channels with fine (200 μm) & closed & open vughs; v. dominant homogenised SMF3, with few SMF4; *Coarse organic/anthropogenic*: few gravel-size chalk & coarse charcoal, rare bone/coprolitic (stained) bone; occasional soil inclusions (humic soil, & frags SMF4 with little calcitic material left – partially decalcified); rare *in situ* root traces; occasional land snail frags including burned material; *Pedofeatures*: many thin (100–150 μm) dusty calcareous clay void coatings (in spongy porosity, sealing vughs); rare microsparitic void coating, rare but ubiquitous thin (50 μm) micritic void coatings (subsequent to dusty calcareous clay coatings); v. strong fabric mixing; v. abundant broad (>2 mm) earthworm burrow fills (occasional earthworm granules), with many v. thin excrements that pre-date dusty calcareous clay coatings. BD: 4.57% LOI, 34.0% $CaCO_3$, 9.45 P mg g^{-1}, 44.8 x 10^{-8} SI χ and 39.3% $\chi_{conv.}$.	Strongly mixed & slightly weathered mixture of chalky soil containing abundant fine charcoal & phytoliths, including articulated phytoliths, with included ashed dung remains which are poorly calcitic. The many excrements & biological porosity testify to a period of faunal mixing, which occurred prior to inwash of dusty calcareous clay that occurred through later infilling of the pit. Chemistry indicates phosphate-rich & highly burned nature of the deposit which is less calcitic (34.0% $CaCO_3$) than overlying deposits. *A partially weathered stabling/domestic/cereal processing debris fill.*
Pit 4196: context 4550			
SMF2(3)	M2098	0–4.5 cm SM: mainly homogeneous with dominant SMT2, & few SMT3 & humic soil inclusions (in burrows); 30% voids, channel, chamber & spongy microstructure; v. dominant medium channels (0.5 mm) & chambers (2 mm), with frequent medium (0.5 mm) open vughs; *Coarse organic/anthropogenic*: frequent–common with depth gravel to small stone-size chalk; occasional biogenic calcite (earthworm granules), rare fine–coarse 2.5 mm) bone & mollusc shell (some burned); occasional fine charcoal; *Pedofeatures*: many v. dusty & cloudy calcareous clay (0.4–0.8 mm) coatings & infills, & related intercalations, sometimes partially closing vughs; rare iron & manganese fine impregnations; rare likely calcium phosphate impregnation (blue light autofluorescent) following vertical channel; many fabric mixing/burrow infills.	Mainly chalky fill with some small amounts of earthworm-mixed cereal processing soil. There are strong indications of wet infilling forming intercalations and coating features & weakly phosphatic solutions have washed down-profile. *Wash & chalky soil dumps adjacent to domestic occupation mainly.*
Pit 4196: context 4234			
SMF2-3(4)		4.5–9.0 cm SM: heterogeneous with dominant SMT2, frequent SMT3 & few SMT4; 35% voids, channel, chamber & spongy microstructure; v. dominant medium–coarse channels (0.5–1.0 mm) & chambers (2–4 mm), with frequent medium (0.2–0.5 mm) open vughs; *Coarse organic/anthropogenic*: common with depth gravel to small stone-size chalk; rare burned SMT4, shell, biogenic calcite & charcoal; rare *in situ* roots; occasional very dusty & cloudy calcareous clay (0.4–0.8 mm) coatings & infills, & related intercalations, sometimes partially closing vughs; rare iron & manganese fine impregnations; rare likely calcium phosphate impregnation (blue light autofluorescent) following vertical channel; many fabric mixing/burrow infills;.	As above, but greater quantities of cereal processing soil, along with humic soil, amorphous organic matter inclusions & burned, likely stabling ash/soil waste. *Wash & chalky soil dumps adjacent to domestic occupation mainly.*

Pit 4704

The context studied (4734) is made up of several layers that were sampled for thin section analysis. Layers of chalk-rich soil that contained small amounts of anthropogenic material, were interlayered with fine fills composed of dominantly anthropogenic material. Burned soil that contained charcoal is indicative of hearths/fires on chalk soils (rendzinas), which often include burned snail and bone. These are consistent with soil evidence for likely domestic fires as described, for example, from Neolithic Easton Down, Hampshire and Windmill Hill, Wiltshire (Crowther *et al.* 1996; Macphail 1999).

The other major component to these fills is very phytolith-rich material that contained long articulated phytoliths and monocotyledonous ('straw') charcoal (see above). The same type of material has been found in the Early Iron Age enclosure ditch at Maiden Castle (Macphail 1991, table 14, figs 105, d–e), and at the similarly dated deposits (zone 4) at Potterne, where its origin is interpreted as burned cereal processing waste (see also Matthews *et al.* 1997). Small amounts of ubiquitous coprolitic material/cess were also present alongside very small amounts of probable herbivore dung. The chalk and chalk soil layers that separate laminae resulting from the dumping of hearths and burned cereal processing waste, may derive from the deliberate dumping of local soil material to seal these layers or occur through unstable pit side collapse. If the latter, this would imply possible seasonal/periodic activity allowing time for pit side soils to collapse and silt into this pit (*cf.* Overton Down experimental ditch, Wiltshire, Macphail and Cruise 1996).

Pit 5592

The fills examined in this pit are apparently more complex and record further aspects of the occupation activities. In the sample studied, a chalk soil lamination (within context 5727) sealed a layer of what can be best described as mainly ashed stabling waste (48.5% $CaCO_3$). Burned and partially burned dung and likely stabling material has been partially worked by small meso-fauna. It seems likely that the stabling/stocking waste was mixed and burned before being dumped. This material is similar to fills of Saxon sunken-featured buildings at West Heslerton, North Yorkshire, where fragmented and mixed burned dung occurs – some very strongly burned as here (Macphail *et al.* forthcoming). Strong burning is consistent with the highest values of χ_{conv} being recorded for this context. It is likely that both cattle and sheep (/goat) dung are represented at the site (see above), and that stabling/stocking material along with likely cereal processing waste and other domestic debris, was burned before being dumped into this pit. This provides evidence for dung being burned and not being solely collected for manuring, the latter as practised, for example, at Butser Ancient Farm. The burning of dung from managed herbivores in prehistory is not unusual and has been associated with cleaning and parasite control (Boschian and Montagnari-Kokelji 2000; Macphail *et al.* 1997). The fact that so few faecal spherulites survive is another indication of the ash being weathered. This calcitic material does not survive in exposed conditions for more than a year even under Mediterranean conditions (Brochier *et al.* 1992).

The underlying layer (within context 5727) contained possible twig charcoal (see Gale), rock fragments (possibly imported pottery temper and possible evidence for querns?) and evidence for probable straw/cereal processing waste (long phytoliths and charcoal). This thin layer occured over context 5728, which appears to be a longer weathered and much more thoroughly mixed and bioturbated deposit composed of cereal processing (food) waste and calcareous soil/hearth deposits, calcitic ash being poorly preserved.

A well developed porosity became coated by calcareous clay inwash, which implies that earlier mixed fill 5728 was left exposed for long enough to become partially weathered (only 34.0% $CaCO_3$) and biologically homogenised, before dumping of the chalk soil/hearth/burned dung fills of context 5727.

Pit 4196

Both contexts studied (4550 and 4234) show dominant inputs of chalk soils influenced by domestic occupation, with context 4234 containing greater amounts of burned domestic and stabling debris. They seem to have been deposited as wet dumps, as shown by both chalky textural features and amorphous iron and manganese staining. The lower fill became strongly worked by biological activity prior to being affected by inwash of calcareous and phosphatic solutions originating in context 4234 and above.

Chapter 7
The Battlesbury Bowl Settlement: Location, Organisation, and Development

Other than slight evidence for Neolithic and Early Bronze Age activity, in the form of residual worked flint and a single pit of Early Bronze Age date, the great majority of the excavated evidence is of Iron Age date. The Battlesbury Bowl settlement was founded towards the end of the Late Bronze Age in the 8th century BC and was occupied through the Early and Middle Iron Age, to the 3rd century BC. The evidence is very similar throughout this span of 500 years and, consequently, the results are presented as a single phase.

In order to appreciate the significance of the excavations it is necessary to look beyond the site. Battlesbury Bowl lies in a landscape which has a long history of archaeological investigation (McOmish *et al.* 2002), and extensive work within the Defence Training Estate on Salisbury Plain has shown that there was considerable activity during the Late Bronze Age and Iron Age (eg, Bowen 1978; Bradley *et al.* 1994; McOmish *et al.* 2002; Fulford *et al.* 2006).

Within the immediate locality of Battlesbury Camp there are several other hillforts and numerous enclosures, field systems, and other evidence for settlement (Fig. 2.1). These hillforts, and also those enclosures that have been identified, tend to be located on the higher ground (Fig. 1.1). The relationship between the two hillforts of Battlesbury Camp and the adjacent Scratchbury Camp is of some interest as they lie so close by that it is possible to see from one hillfort into the interior of the other, and both are sited on prominent locations (McOmish *et al.* 2002, 75; Armit 2007, 30). Without further excavation it is unknown whether one hillfort replaced the other, or if their uses overlapped.

Few of these sites have seen excavation and earlier work within Battlesbury Camp hillfort was limited (Cunnington 1924), so the extensive work at Battlesbury Bowl provides the first detailed insight into the character of Iron Age settlement in the area.

The Setting and Layout of the Battlesbury Bowl Settlement

The ridge linking Battlesbury Hill to the main body of the downs to the north might seem an unsuitable location for settlement, being exposed to the elements and with the ground falling steeply to both east and west, but it was the site of a long-lived Late Bronze Age and Iron Age settlement, the full extent of which has yet to be determined. On this basis, there is no reason why the settlement should not have extended over much, if not all, of the ridge top or plateau, as well as extending onto Battlesbury Hill.

The settlement appears, in the main at least, to have been unenclosed. The clustering of features at intervals along the ridge, as indicated by the four feature groups (Fig. 3.1), points to different activity areas while the ditches running along the eastern edge of the ridge seem likely to have been used to define areas of activity and constrain and direct the movement of people and animals.

Among the earliest features on the site were the phase 1/2 ditches, whose general line is maintained into phase 3 and which consistently provided an eastern boundary to the settlement activity throughout the site's occupation, as represented by the distribution of all features with the exception of two square/sub-rectangular structures (4013 and 4186). However, the suggested sequence of ditches appears to indicate that their role at the southern end of the site, as they neared the northern slope of Battlesbury Hill, changed, sometimes allowing access from the low ground to the east through a break in the boundary and, at other times, blocking off that access. These differences may reflect changes in the organisation of the settlement and in the farming of the surrounding landscape. The settlement had access to a variety of habitats – the downs, the sheltered coombes around their margins, and, via the Battlesbury Bowl, the low lying ground and the floor of the Wylye valley.

The small number of buildings that could be identified during the excavation may simply reflect the narrowness of the SRR corridor, which runs close to the eastern edge of what is quite a broad and flat plateau. It is possible that other roundhouses existed but have since been destroyed by ploughing or that roundhouses were gnereally located in areas beyond that excavated. Possible zoning of other activities may be suggested by the distribution of animal bone (Chapter 6). The suggestion, from aerial photographs, of small enclosures on Battlesbury Hill (McOmish *et al.* 2002, 82–3) and Slack Hill (SMR ST84NE635) and of a series of long linear features, raises the possibility that the excavation exposed only a small part of a more extensive settlement.

Possible four-post structures were identified in all four feature groups, with an apparent concentration at the southern end of the excavation. Although most structures were undated, one clearly post-dated a phase 3 ditch and, if the rest of the group were in some way associated, this would place them towards the end of the period of settlement on the ridge top. Not all of these structures needs to have been a granary or food store. Given their location, it is possible that some four-post structures were related to the intermittent access point between the ridge and Battlesbury Bowl, structure 4013, for example, perhaps deliberately spanning ditch 4043 as a causeway or gate. It may be significant that a collection of cattle and horse skulls, which may have been used for display before their deposition in the ditch, was found next to this structure.

Although the distribution of features by phase varies between feature groups, with higher proportions of earlier pits and post-holes being recorded towards the north of the site (in FG 3) and later ones towards the south, it is notable that the clusters of features retain their character through the site's occupation, with foci of activity and intervening 'open' areas largely being retained.

Craft, agricultural processing, and industrial activities are indicated almost wholly by waste materials from pits and ditches. Few features can be identified as having a specific manufacturing or processing function and, where some such function is suggested, for example pit 4196 with its sequence of layers of puddled chalk and burning, its nature is far from clear. Of the 725 post-holes recorded only a small proportion could be assigned to possible structures but many of the remainder are likely to have belonged to a range of structures such as looms, drying racks, and tethering posts, as well as having other, less utilitarian uses such as markers or mounts for display.

The relationship of the Battlesbury Bowl settlement to Battlesbury Camp hillfort is not clear, mainly because the evidence from within the hillfort is very limited. Maud Cunnington's 1922 excavation of nine pits along a pipe trench within the hillfort can only be held to demonstrate settlement within the Iron Age. The siting of the hillfort, whose scale and relative complexity suggests a Middle–Late Iron Age date (Chapter 2), would have been determined primarily by defensive and strategic concerns and the desire to create a powerful impression. Assuming that the hillfort is later, it would have come to dominate the landscape and so must have provided the main economic, social, and functional context for any surrounding settlement in the later part of the Iron Age. This appears to have led to the contraction of ridge-top settlement at Battlesbury Bowl at some point after the 3rd century BC (ie, during phase 4).

Whether that involved the total abandonment of the ridge or changed the character of the activities undertaken there has not been clearly established by the excavation. Evidence from environmental analyses, including snails, suggests that woodland did not regenerate, perhaps indicating more or less continuous occupation until perhaps phase 4, the settlement being set in a typical downland environment with some probable relic scrub (Chapter 6).

Food Procurement, Production, and Processing

The main activity of the occupants of the site was farming and the arable component of the mixed farming economy is indicated by the remains of crops and the many quernstone fragments. The numerous pits are assumed to have been for used for the storage of seed grain, while some of the four-post structures, frequently interpreted as granaries, may have held processed or semi-processed grain for eating.

Cereal crops included spelt wheat and hulled barley, perhaps grown together as a maslin, rather than as a monoculture, and some emmer wheat. Peas and possibly oats were also grown. The cereals were sown in autumn and spring, the weed seeds showing that they were grown mostly on the chalk downs close to the site but also on poorer soils, possibly in the Wylye valley. They would have been harvested in the autumn by either uprooting or by cutting close to the ground. Crops may have been threshed, winnowed, and coarse-sieved before being stored as semi-clean spikelets, with crop waste used as animal fodder or burnt as tinder and fuel.

The animal bone assemblage indicates the importance of animal husbandry to the inhabitants of the Battlesbury Bowl settlement. As on many Iron Age sites in Wessex, the bones of cattle were the most frequent, followed by sheep/goat, then pig. Horse and dog were also present in small numbers. As well as being kept for meat, the mortality patterns suggest that cattle and sheep/goat were also important for secondary products such as milk, wool, leather, bone, and also dung. The carcasses of these animals were butchered within the settlement and most of the animal bone assemblage probably represents waste from butchery, although some deposits may be ritual.

The varied resources offered by the landscape close to the site would have been used, offering downland grassland, low lying pasture along the Wylye valley, and foraging and browsing in stands of woodland on the steeper downland slopes. Environmental evidence suggests that livestock may have been

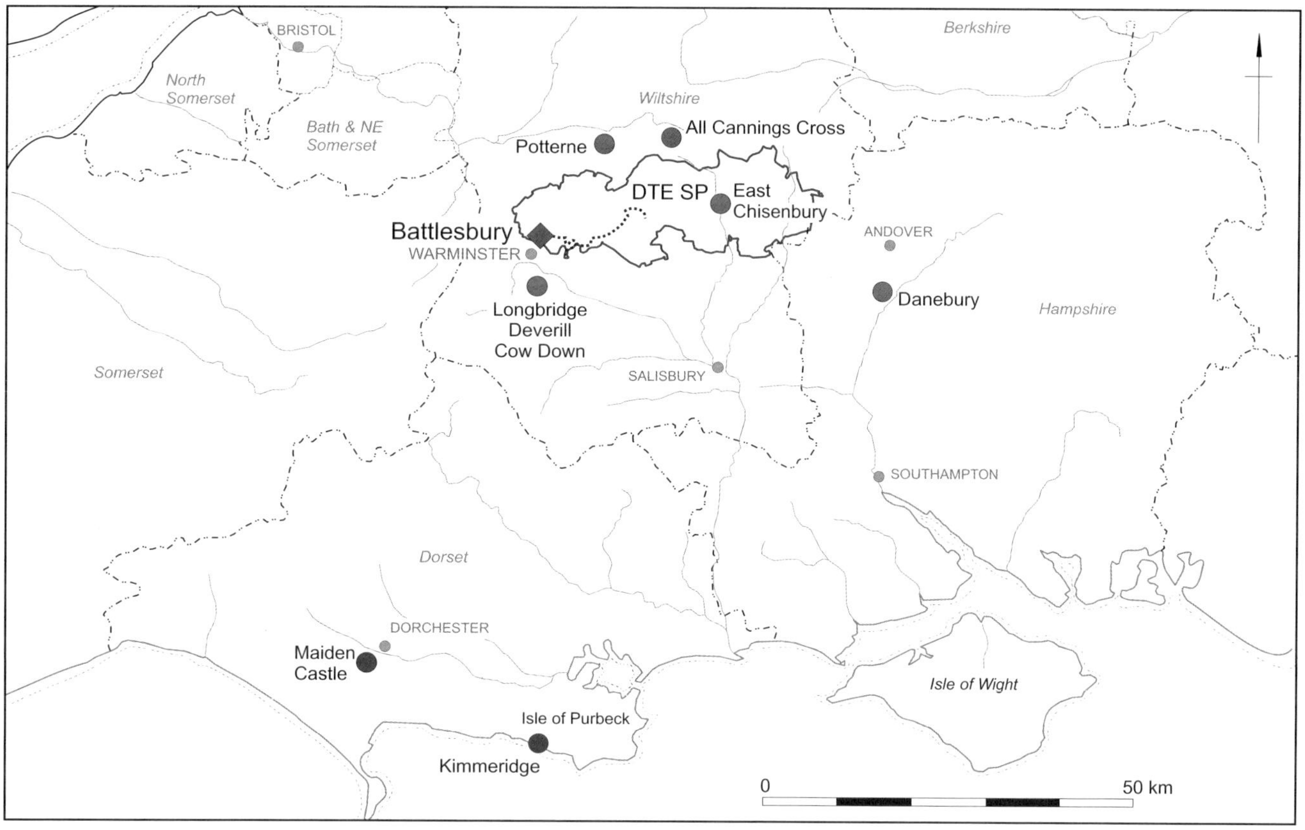

Figure 7.1 Selected later prehistoric sites referred to in text

kept in stockades within the settlement during the winter, with burnt stabling material and burnt dung being found in many of the pits. Some of the ditches at the southern end of the site (see above) may have been used to control the movement of livestock moving on and off the ridge.

Although hunting is suggested by the small number of wild animal bones recovered, and possibly by the small number of slingshots, there is no evidence that it contributed significantly, if at all, to the diet. Edible wild plants, such as hazelnuts and elderberries, however, would have been gathered in autumn probably from woodland edge and scrub on the steeper downland slopes, while other plants, such as bracken, may have been gathered for use as bedding for people and animals, and reeds for thatch.

Status and Society

In many respects the mixed farming regime of the Battlesbury Bowl settlement is typical of the Iron Age in Wessex. A range of craft activities was undertaken and people would have participated in the seasonal cycles of the social and agricultural year. It was through a combination of material deriving from these activities and other, natural, processes that the pits, ditches, and other features were filled with their varied and, in some cases, artefact-rich deposits.

However, careful recording failed to identify any consistency in the pattern of deposition – whether involving rapid dumping events of domestic and other waste, longer-term episodes of accumulating settlement debris, or extended periods of natural infilling. Although much of the material in the features may have been redeposited, no midden deposits were found. However, the soil micromorphology and the presence of henbane (*Hyoscyamus niger*), suggests that dung or byre material was stored in or near to the settlement before being used to manure the fields (Chapter 6). Excavations at the nearby sites of Potterne (Lawson 2000), East Chisenbury (Brown *et al.* 1994; McOmish 1996), and All Cannings Cross (Cunnington 1923) (Fig. 7.1) have revealed large middens, indicating the importance, to Late Bronze Age–Early Iron Age societies, of what is today often viewed as mere refuse.

At Battlesbury Bowl some ditches and pits were rich in animal bones, including articulated remains, and it is possible that some of these represent ritual deposits (Chapter 6). A notable instance is the deposit of seven cattle and three horse skulls in the section of ditch 4043 adjacent to structure 4013 which spans the ditch. At least some of the skulls had been carefully cleaned and possibly displayed before ending up in the ditch and it may be that it was the display, rather than any act of deposition, that was important. A number of animal skulls from other features may also have been used in this way.

The treatment of the human dead was complex. Both sexes and all ages were buried in pits and ditches but disarticulated remains were also found in pits, ditches, and post-holes. The disarticulated remains were dominated by fragments from the skull and long bones, with a notable prevalence of long bones from the right side, as has been noted previously in Iron Age Wessex (Chapter 5). Some of the disarticulated remains may be the result of disturbance of burials but a wide range of mortuary practices, such as exposure and excarnation, is also suggested. However the lack of weathering to some of this material indicates that exposure was not lengthy.

Crafts

There is evidence for a range of craft activities. Metalworking is indicated by iron slag but no metalworking furnaces or hearths were found. Potentially hazardous and noxious activities may have been undertaken away from the settlement, possibly to the south, as suggested by the concentration of slag in FGs 1 and 2.

Textile manufacture is indicated by spindlewhorls of chalk and fired clay, bone weaving combs, and possible chalk loomweights. Some of the bone awls and needles may have been used for leatherworking and are, themselves, evidence, along with bone waste, for bone- and antlerworking, also producing a range of other tools such as 'gouges', knives, and handles.

Stone rubbers and whetstones were also used in craft activities and, while there is evidence for limited flintworking in the Early Iron Age, the relatively high numbers of flint hammerstones were probably mainly used for some other activity.

Some of the finds indicate trade and exchange with communities across the wider, if not very distant, landscape. Some of the pottery fabrics, for example, indicate production some distance from the site but much of it was clearly produced locally. The local Chalk was used for stone and flint, with sarsen probably brought from the plains to the east and Greensand from outcrops below the Chalk in nearby valleys. A quern fragment of Pennant Sandstone may derive from Bristol/South Wales. In the absence of evidence for stoneworking many of these objects are likely to have arrived at the site as finished objects. A fragmentary shale armlet, probably from the Isle of Purbeck in Dorset, indicates links with the south coast and it may be from this area that the coral bead, which probably originated in the Mediterranean, was brought to Battlesbury Bowl.

There is otherwise little that is exotic in the material culture used by the inhabitants of the settlement; a decorated bone object, a few items of personal adornment, such as a small number of metal brooches and fittings, bone sliders, and a small number of possible curios including a polished pebble, an 'ornamental' stone and, most notably perhaps, the Neolithic axe. The few decorated pots bear only a restricted range of motifs.

Regional and Local Context

The work at Battlesbury Bowl provides the first detailed insight into the character of Iron Age settlement in an area that is rich in well-preserved remains thought to be of this date. In the wider context of Late Bronze Age and Iron Age activity in Wiltshire and the surrounding area (Fig. 7.1) it may be compared to a series of important sites: East Chisenbury (Brown *et al.* 1994; McOmish 1996), Potterne (Lawson 2000), All Cannings Cross (Cunnington 1923), Overton Down (Fowler 2000), Longbridge Deverill Cow Down (Chadwick-Hawkes 1994), and Mancombe Down (McOmish *et al.* 2002, 69, fig. 3.18, 73).

There are notable differences between some of these sites and the Battlesbury Bowl settlement, particularly Potterne, East Chisenbury, and All Cannings Cross which were typified by extensive midden deposits and where generally fewer cut features were found, although some elements of their finds assemblages are comparable to that from Battlesbury Bowl. There are also differences between the environmental remains suggesting that different activities took place at the 'midden' sites and what might be thought – but cannot yet be demonstrated – to be more typical settlements such as Longbridge Deverill Cow Down and Battlesbury Bowl.

Many questions remain unanswered about the settlement at Battlesbury Bowl, such as its relationship to the adjacent and neighbouring hillforts of Battlesbury Camp and Scratchbury Camp. The importance of the excavation, however, is in its confirmation of the range of different types of contemporary Late Bronze Age/Early Iron Age settlement, and its provision of the first detailed insight, using modern excavation techniques, into what may be a typical settlement in one part of a region renowned for its evidence for later prehistoric settlement.

PART B: THE SOUTHERN RANGE ROAD

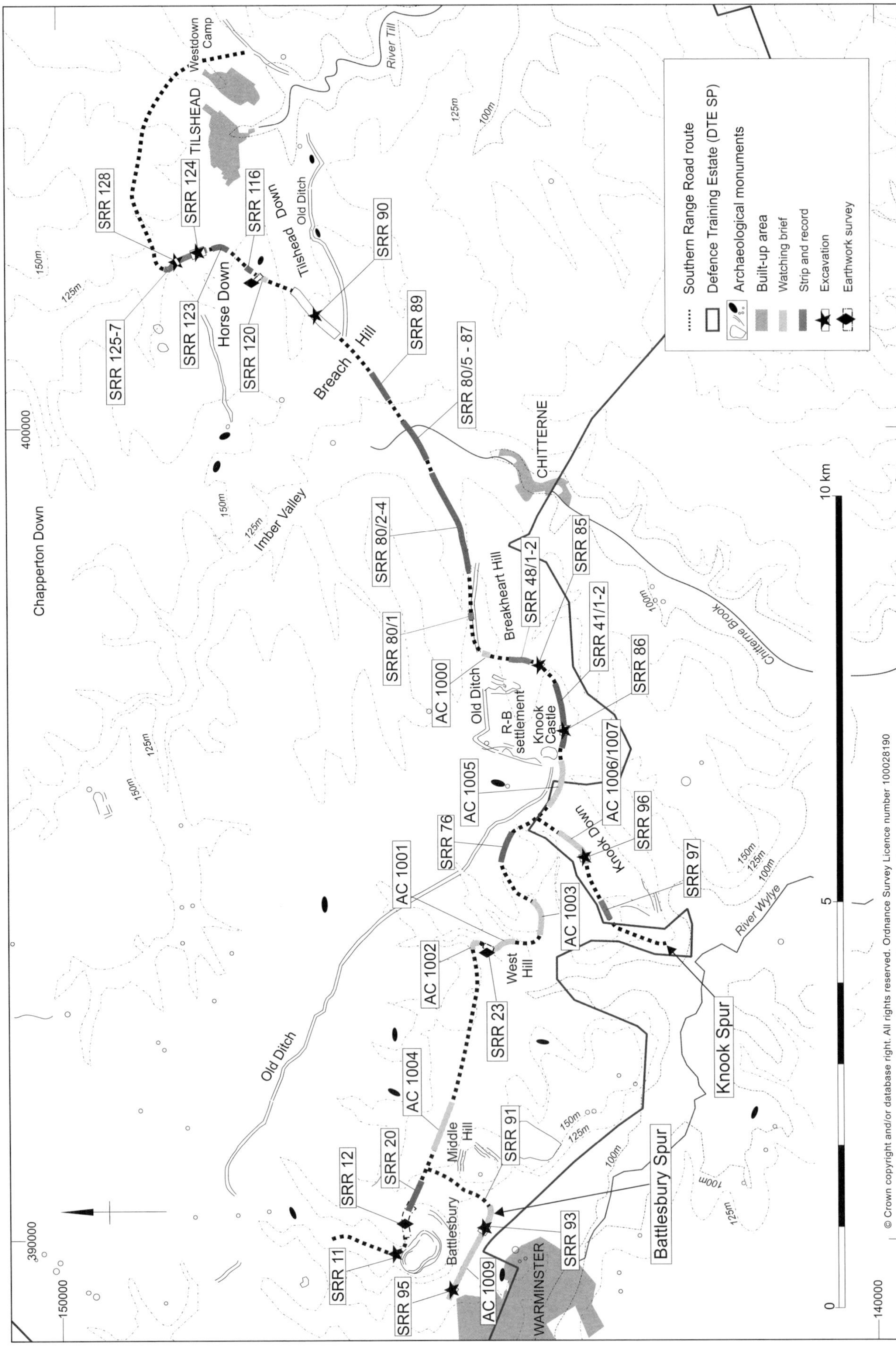

Fig. 8.1 Stages 1 and 2 mitigation sites along the Southern Range Road

Chapter 8
Introduction

This section describes the results of the remainder of the mitigation works along the rest of the SRR (Fig. 8.1). These works were undertaken in two main stages, Stage 1, undertaken by Wessex Archaeology before construction, and Stage 2, undertaken by AC Archaeology during construction (see Chapter 1; Table 8.1).

The Stage 1 works involved small-scale excavations at eight sites, earthwork surveys at a further three, and the evaluation (or re-evaluation) of three areas. As well as Battlesbury Bowl, the evaluations included one at Middleton Farm (SRR 91) where five 1.4 m wide trenches were excavated. No significant archaeological features or deposits were encountered and the site is not reported further. The Stage 2 works involved a 'strip-and-record' exercise undertaken in advance of the main contract works at 17 locations and a watching brief of the whole route (AC 1000) during construction, during which a further eight sites (AC 1001–1007 and 1009) were identified. The watching brief also recorded a number of isolated features along the route.

The results are presented in four chapters: Chapter 9 describes Battlesbury and Battlesbury Bowl; Chapter 10 West Hill to Knook Down; Chapter 11 Knook Castle to Imber Valley; and Chapter 12 Imber Valley to Tilshead.

The methodology for the Stage 1 excavations was largely as described for the Battlesbury Bowl excavation (Chapter 2). Stage 2 strip-and-record sites and watching brief results were recorded by AC Archaeology by their chainage positions along the SRR. These have been subsequently tied to the national grid and locations are referred to by their chainage (for NGRs see Table 8.1). Chainages on the Battlesbury and Knook spur road have B and K prefixes, respectively.

Table 8.1 Stages 1 and 2 mitigation sites along the Southern Range Road (west to east)

Chap.	*Site code*	*Site name*	*Fieldwork*	*Chainages*		*NGR co-ords (end to end)*	
9	AC 1009	Battlesbury Spur	AC watching brief	B0	B1220	389257 145296	390346 144765
9	SRR 95	Boreham Farm Bungalow	WA excavation	B210	B250	389450 145200	389450 145180
9	SRR 93	South-east of Battlesbury Wood	WA excavation	B910	B980	390070 144880	390130 144840
9	SRR 12	East of Battlesbury Bowl	WA earthwork survey	1200	1650	390029 145762	390382 145678
9	SRR 20	East of Battlesbury Hill	AC strip-and-record	1600	2000	390398 145755	390770 145606
9	AC 1004	East of Field Barn	AC watching brief	2500	2900	391077 145490	391196 145274
10	AC 1002	North of West Hill Farm	AC watching brief	4900	5000	393532 145025	393600 144972
	SRR 23	West Hill Farm	WA earthwork survey	5080	5230	393560 144830	393550 144690
	AC 1001	East of West Hill Farm	AC watching brief	5220	5500	393545 144780	393654 144520
10	AC 1003	East of East Hill Cottages	AC watching brief	6000	6400	393848 144130	394180 144274
10	SRR 76	South of Old Ditch	AC strip-and-record	7000	7407	394615 144654	395005 144548
10	SRR 97	North of Bevin's Barn	AC strip-and-record	K800	K1000	393916 143440	394100 143418
	SRR 96	Willis's Field Barn	WA excavation	K1620	K1700	394650 143662	394730 143666
	AC 1006/ 1007	Knook Spur	AC watching brief	K1600	K2100	394618 143662	395044 144022
10	AC 1005	West of Knook Castle	AC watching brief	8000	8500	395325 144130	395774 143974
11	SRR 41/1-2	Knook Castle and East of Knook Castle	AC strip-and-record	8620	9620	395886 143935	396835 143976
	SRR 86	East of Knook Castle	WA excavation	8870	8950	396130 143870	396210 143870
11	SRR 85	East of Quebec Barn	WA (re-evaluation); excavation	9860	9910	397070 144120	397110 144150
	SRR 48/1-2	North-East of Knook Castle	AC strip-and-record	10038	10300	397180 144255	397170 144510
11	AC 1000	Top of Breakheart Hill	AC watching brief	10640	10703	397240 144885	397250 144905
	SRR 80/1	Breakheart Hill	AC strip-and-record	11087	11120	397612 145002	397643 145006
	SRR 80/2-4	Breakheart Bottom	AC strip-and-record	11650	13000	398170 145070	399455 145444
11	SRR 80/5, 087	North-West of Middle Barn Farm	AC strip-and-record	13100	13680	399546 145472	400035 145778
11	SRR 89	Vedette Post Four	AC strip-and-record	14100	14380	400386 146025	146352 146190
12	SRR 90	Tilshead Down	WA excavation	14950	15700	401080 146540	401600 147030
	SRR 120	West of Hotel Crossing	WA earthwork survey; AC strip-and-record	16150	16300	401764 147456	401840 147585
	SRR 116	West of Tilshead, Horse Down	AC strip-and-record	16370	16480	401874 147646	401927 147730
12	SRR 123	West of Golf Crossing	AC strip-and-record	16820	17020	402174 147984	402140 148160
	SRR 124	Horse Down	WA excavation	17110	17266	402119 148255	402066 148388
12	SRR 125, 127	North-West of Golf Crossing	AC strip-and-record	17080	17650	402025 148472	401872 148706
12	SRR 128	South of Foxtrot Crossing	WA excavation	17424	17464	401990 148550	401980 148587

Key:
AC = AC Archaeology; WA = Wessex Archaeology; Chainage: B00 = chainage along Battlesbury spur road; K00 = chainage along Knook spur road (otherwise chainage from Harman Lines to Tilshead)

Chapter 9
Battlesbury and Battlesbury Bowl

Boreham Farm Bungalow Excavation (SRR 95), and Battlesbury Spur Watching Brief (west) (AC 1009)

The site at Boreham Farm Bungalow was immediately south-east of Battlesbury Hill. It lay at 110 m aOD in the base of a broad valley on the north side of a small culverted stream, a tributary of the River Wylye, the natural sub-strata being alluvium and calcareous marl overlying Lower Chalk (BGS 1985). The excavation area, 53 m long (east–west) and 6–8 m wide (310 m^2) (chainage B260–B313), was selected on the basis of a group of small features associated with a ditch/channel filled with a black clay deposit found during the evaluation. During the watching brief (chainage B0–B1220) a number of features were recorded both west and east of the excavation area.

Results

Excavation

Eight features – a large stream channel, two post-holes, two pits, and three natural features – were investigated (Fig. 9.1). These features cut the calcareous marl and were sealed by a 0.2 m of thick greyish–brown alluvial subsoil. A number of modern features were also noted. Topsoil was present only at either end of the site, having been eroded across the rest by a modern trackway.

Few finds were recovered. Mesolithic/Early Neolithic activity in the vicinity is indicated by some of the relatively fresh worked flint found in the stream channel and in a later pit (5008), while a single sherd of residual Romano-British pottery was recovered from a modern feature. Most of the evidence, however, indicated activity of Late Bronze Age to Early Iron Age date.

The channel (5023), probably a former channel of the present culverted stream, was aligned approximately north-west to south-east, parallel with the present stream. It occupied the whole of the western part of the excavation, an 11.5 m length of its north-eastern bank being recorded within the excavation area, and its full profile being determined by a north-east to south-west auger transect that extended 50 m beyond the southern limit of excavation. The auguring showed that the channel was approximately 47 m wide and up to 0.65 m deep, with very irregular, moderately steep sides and a broad undulating base with irregular, presumably natural, hollows. Its earliest fill consisted of patches of a very pale yellow, slightly silty marl (5032), representing eroded and reworked chalk. These were sealed by a dark, organic humic silty clay (5014 and 5031), probably a much degraded peat, which extended across the entire width of the channel and was up to 0.5 m thick towards the banks, but thinned to just a few centimetres in the centre. This deposit produced a few small sherds of very abraded Late Bronze Age pottery, small quantities of worked and burnt flint, and some animal bone fragments. Above it was a pale grey alluvial silty clay (5013 and 5025), the interface between these layers being very diffuse as the peat had stained the alluvium. Two sherds of an Early Iron Age furrowed bowl were recovered from the alluvial deposit, along with some worked and burnt flint. A number of irregular features in the base and sides of the channel, interpreted as stake-holes during the evaluation, proved to be natural root holes, and were not recorded.

The deposits within the channel indicate that it changed from a being one with a high organic content (from decaying water plants) to one of a clean flowing stream, silting up with minerogenic alluvium. The finds suggest that it started to silt up in the Late Bronze Age, although the abraded condition of the pottery may indicate that the archaeological material derived from deposits and features upstream, in which case the channel could have silted up some time after that date.

A group four features, interpreted as two small post-holes (5006 and 5019) and two small pits (but possibly large post-holes) (5000 and 5008), lay close to the northern edge of the channel. The pits were both *c.* 0.65 m in diameter and 0.2 m deep, with moderately sloping, concave sides and concave bases, and both had very dark brown–black silty clay fills similar to that in the channel. Six small abraded sherds of Late Bronze Age pottery and a number of worked flints were recovered from pit 5000, along with 236 charred hazelnut shell fragments and 16 indeterminate cereal grain fragments. Fragments of fired clay (possibly very abraded pottery) and nine pieces of worked flint (some of it Mesolithic/Early Neolithic) were recovered from pit 5008. Of the post-holes, 5006 was 0.3 m in diameter and 0.05 m deep, and 5019 was 0.2 m in diameter and 0.07 m deep. Both had shallow, concave sides and concave bases and, again, similar dark fills; neither produced datable finds.

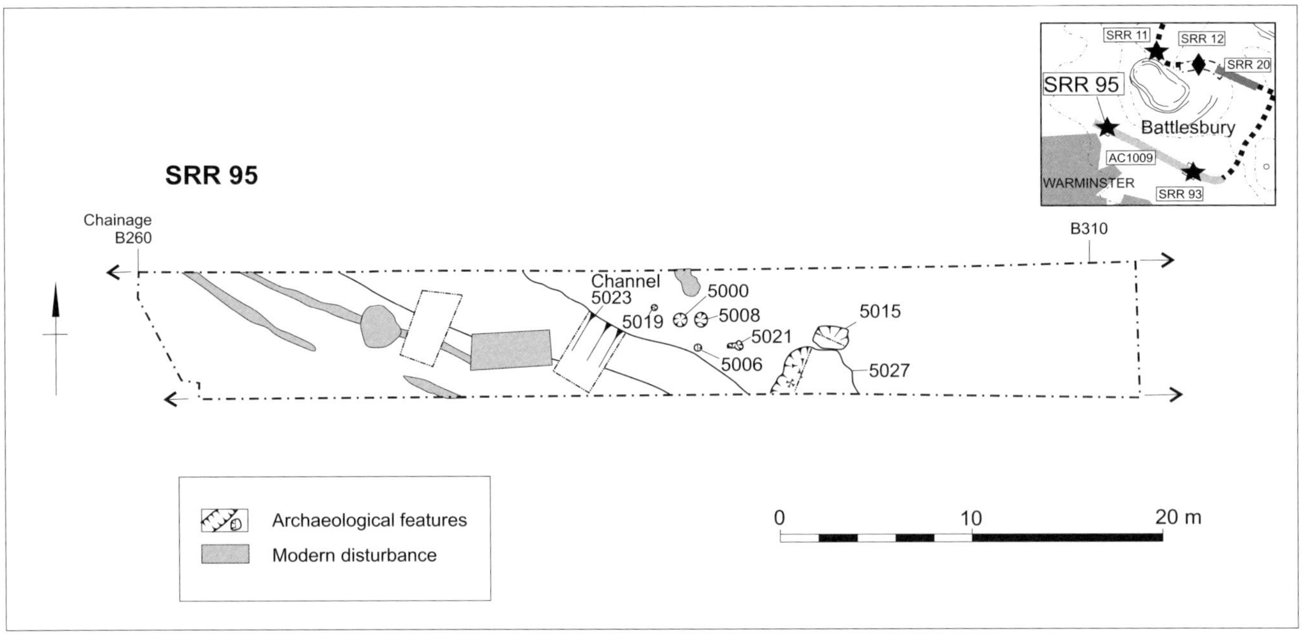

Figure 9.1 Boreham Farm Bungalow (SRR 95)

The similarity in the fills of these features to the natural deposits within the channel, and the presence of very similar pottery, leaves open the possibility that they were natural features, being filled at the same time as the channel. Three irregular natural hollows (5015, 5021, and 5027), varying in depth from 0.06m to 0.13 m, contained similar fills, from which small quantities of degraded animal bone and burnt and worked flint were recovered.

Watching brief

To the west of the excavation site a probable ditch and an undated pit were recorded during the watching brief (chainage B0–B80), while the group of features recorded during the excavation were seen to continue a further 27 m to the east, up to chainage B340, although no recognisable structures were discernible. A small group of dispersed features recorded further east (chainage B420–B660) included an undated post-hole, an undated sheep burial (75), and two pits (81 and 83) containing worked flint, burnt flint, and late prehistoric pottery.

Finds

Excavation

A small quantity of finds was recovered during the excavation (Table 9.1). The worked flint assemblage consists of both patinated and unpatinated flint, some retaining cortex, the unpatinated pieces tending to exhibit a higher degree of edge damage. One piece is burnt. The assemblage includes three blades or blade-like flakes (pit 5008 and channel 5023) suggesting a residual Mesolithic/Early Neolithic component. The burnt, unworked flint is also likely to be of prehistoric date and came mainly from contexts which also produced worked flint, with a concentration in channel 5023.

The only closely datable material is the pottery. Of the 16 sherds, 13 are dated as Late Bronze Age on the basis of their fabric (five are flint-tempered and eight shelly). Two sherds from upper fill 5025 of channel 5023 derive from a furrowed bowl of Early Iron Age type. The remaining sherd, from pit 5011, is a non-distinctive, oxidised sandy ware, possibly Romano-British.

Table 9.1 Boreham Farm Bungalow (SRR 95): all finds (no./wt (g)) by feature

Context/ feature	*Worked flint*	*Burnt flint*	*Stone*	*Prehist. pottery*	*R-B pottery*	*CBM/ fired clay*
Topsoil	1/2	3/16	–	–	–	–
Subsoil	6/14	27/176	–	–	–	1/34
Pit/p-h 5000	3/29	–	1/88	5/9	–	1/1
Ditch 5003	1/4	2/16	–	–	–	–
Hollow 5015	5/7	9/88	–	–	–	–
Hollow 5027	17/194	28/282	–	–	–	–
Pit 5011	–	2/4	–	–	1/2	–
Pit/p-h 5008	9/26	–	–	–	–	4/8
Channel 5023	33/249	92/1434	–	10/20	–	–
Total	75/525	163/2016	1/88	15/29	1/2	6/43

Table 9.2 Boreham Farm Bungalow (SRR 95): molluscs from channel 5023

Context	*5032*		*5031*			*5026*			*5025*		
Sample	*5612*	*5613*	*5602*	*5603*	*5604*	*5605*	*5606*	*5607*	*5608*	*5609*	*5610*
Depth (cm)			*38-43*	*33-38*	*28-33*	*23-28*	*18-23*	*13-18*	*8-13*	*3-8*	*0-3*
Wt (g)	*1000*	*1500*	*1500*	*1500*	*1250*	*1500*	*1500*	*1500*	*1500*	*1500*	*1500*
Land mollusca											
Pomatias elegans (Müller)	–	+	+	+	+	+	+	+	1	+	2
Carychium spp.	–	–	–	–	–	–	–	–	–	–	+
Succinea/Oxyloma spp.	–	1	–	–	–	–	–	–	2	–	–
Cochlicopa spp.	1	4	–	–	+	–	1	+	2	2	1
Abide secale	1	3	1	–	–	–	–	–	–	–	–
Vertigo pygmaea (Draparnaud)	–	–	–	–	2	–	1	1	2	1	–
Vertigo spp.	–	–	–	–	–	1	–	–	–	–	1
Pupilla muscorum (Linnaeus)	2	5	1	1	1	–	–	–	3	–	6
Vallonia costata (Müller)	+	2	–	–	–	1	2	8	9	10	21
Vallonia pulchella (Müller)	–	–	–	–	1	1	–	2	–	–	3
Vallonia excentrica Sterki	5	7	–	–	–	2	4	3	4	2	9
Vallonia spp.	–	–	+	–	–	–	1	–	–	–	2
Punctum pygmaeum (Draparnaud)	2	2	–	–	–	–	–	1	–	–	–
Discus rotundatus (Müller)	–	+	–	+		+	+	+	1	+	+
Vitrina pellucida (Müller)	–	1	–	–	–	–	–	–	–	–	–
Aegopinella nitidula (Draparnaud)	–	1	–	–	–	–	+	–	1	–	–
Limacidae	2	3	–	1	–	5	12	11	13	14	20
Euconulus fulvus (Müller)	1	–	–	–	–	–	–	–	–	–	–
Clausilia bidentata (Ström)	–	–	–	1	–	1	+	1	–	–	+
Helicella itala (Linnaeus)	–	2	–	–	–	1	1	–	–	4	2
Trichia hispida (Linnaeus)	–	–	+	–	1	+	2	3	2	3	2
Helicigona lapicida (Linnaeus)	–	–	–	+	+	1	+	1	+	+	+
Cepaea spp.	+	1	–	–	–	–	–	–	–	–	–
Cepaea/Arianta spp.	–	–	+	+	+	4	+	1	2	+	+
Fresh-/brackish water											
Lymnaea truncatula (Müller)	–	–	–	–	–	–	–	1	–	+	1
Taxa	7	12	2	3	4	9	7	10	12	7	11
Total	14	32	2	3	5	17	24	32	42	36	70

Other finds include a single fragment of probably Romano-British ceramic building material from the subsoil, five small fragments of undiagnostic fired clay, and one fragment of potentially worked stone.

Watching brief

A small worked flint assemblage (19 flints; 128 g) was recovered during the watching brief. The pieces from the features east of the excavation, which included a transverse arrowhead from one of the post-holes (46), appearing to confirm their prehistoric date. Sherds in fine sandy fabric QU2 and shell-tempered fabric SH2/3 were dispersed in small quantities within pits 81 and 83. Although very fragmentary, it is possible to suggest a Late Bronze Age/Early Iron Age date.

Environment

Snails

by Michael J Allen

An open environment, with little or no local woodland, is indicated by the snail assemblages recovered from a series of 11 samples taken through the fill of the channel (Table 9.2). Adjacent to the stream course there was open grassland (*Vallonia costata*, *V. excentrica*), probably with localised bare grass patches (*Abida secale*), but with damper and probably more mesic habitats (Limacidae) indicating longer, damper (*Vallonia pulcella* and *Succinae/Oxyloma* spp.) lush floodplain grassland. Very few obligatory marsh species were present and only one truly aquatic species (*Lymnea truncatula*) was recovered; its occurrence was sparse.

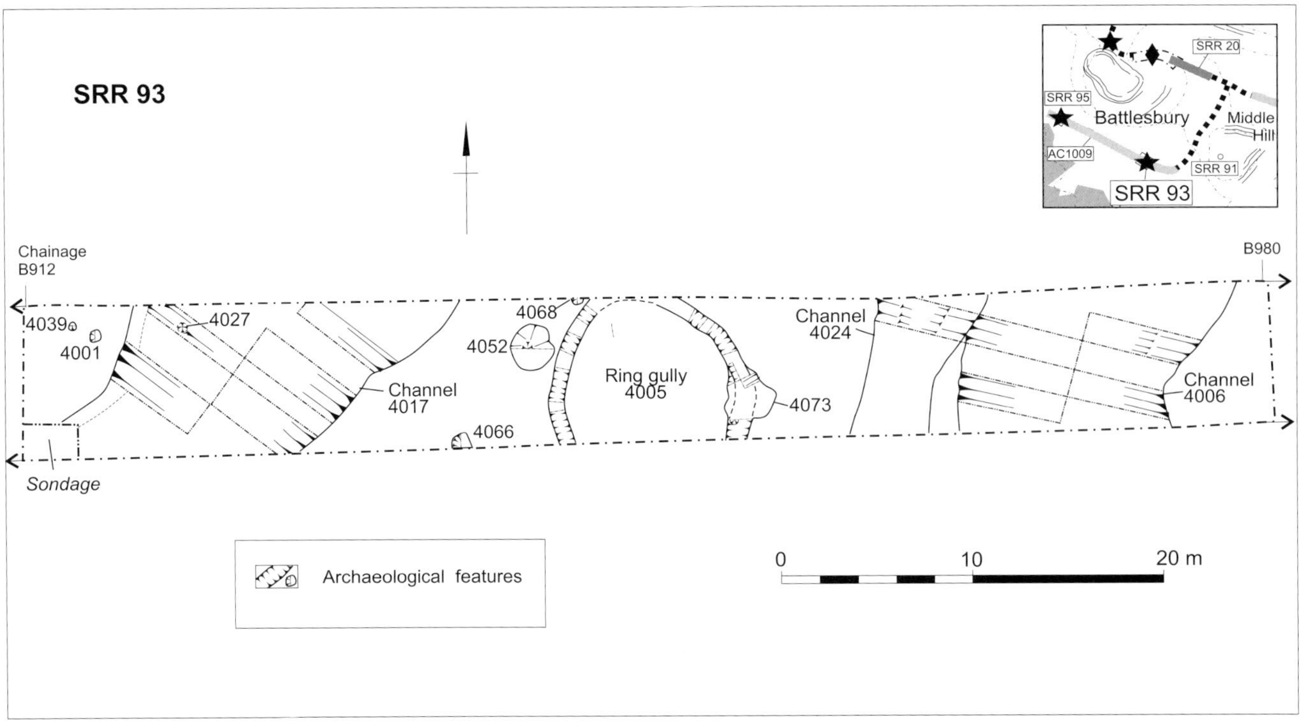

Figure 9.2 South-east of Battlesbury Wood (SRR 93)

Discussion

The nature of the activity on this site is unclear. The regular forms of the pits and post-holes, and their proximity to each other on the edge of the stream channel, suggest that these features were associated, although they form no recognisable structure. While the finds from the site do little to clarify the nature of the activity, the charred hazelnut and cereal fragments from pit/post-hole 5000 suggest the consumption of both wild and cultivated food resources. The open grassland environment indicated by the snail assemblages is one that might be expected from the Late Bronze Age onwards.

The features recorded during the watching brief both west and east of the site appear to indicate comparable, possibly later prehistoric, activity as that found at Battlesbury Bowl, indicating the use of the wider area at this time.

South-East of Battlesbury Wood Excavation (SRR 93) and Battlesbury Spur Watching Brief (east) (AC 1009)

The site, some 500 m south of Battlesbury Hill, lay at *c.* 110 m aOD on a very gentle south-west facing slope at the foot of the low ridge between Battlesbury Wood and Middle Hill. The excavation area, 70 m long (north-west to south-east) and 8 m wide (560 m^2) (chainage B910–B980), was selected on the basis of features, including a series of post-holes or pits and two broad palaeochannels identified during the evaluation (Fig. 9.2). The channels, *c.* 26 m apart, flow south-west from the col between Battlesbury and Middle Hill, across the broad Lower Chalk and Upper Greensand bench towards the Wylye valley floodplain.

Over most of the site the chalk bedrock was overlain by a deposit of very pale grey silty clay alluvium (4059) up to 0.55 m deep which was, in turn, overlain by a 0.2 m thick chalky marl deposit (4058). These appeared to fill a large erosion gully (not shown on Fig. 9.2), possibly periglacial in origin, the eastern edge of which coincided with a later palaeochannel (4006) and the western edge of which lay beyond the western limit of the excavation area. All of the features identified on the site – five post-holes (or small pits) and a ring gully, as well as three palaeochannels and two natural features (4052 and 4073) – cut the marl deposit. They were all sealed by a 0.25 m thick mid-brown silty clay subsoil (4057) containing post-medieval/modern tile and brick fragments.

During the watching brief (chainage B0–B1220) a number of features were recorded to the immediate east of the excavation site.

Results

Excavation

Although few datable finds were recovered from the features it was possible to identify three phases of activity – Mesolithic/Early Neolithic, Late Bronze Age/Early Iron Age, and Romano-British.

Mesolithic/Early Neolithic

The assemblage of worked flints from the site provides evidence for Mesolithic or Early Neolithic activity. Most of the material came from the upper fill of channel 4017, although some also came from near the surface of channel 4006.

Channel 4017, running across the western end of the site, was approximately 12 m wide and up to 0.4 m deep with gently sloping sides and a very irregular base. Its primary fill was a thin (0.02 m) deposit of greyish–brown silty clay from which no finds were recovered although very rare charcoal flecks were noted. Above this was a chalky deposit (4044) of probable post-glacial date as indicated by the snails (see below). This was overlain by a black humic clay deposit (4043), probably degraded peat, from which small amounts of worked and burnt flint, and much degraded animal bone were recovered, approximately 90% of the material coming from the upper 0.05 m. The material may have derived from overlying deposits, although the relative concentration of flints in this channel may indicate that the channel had filled in before the later prehistoric activity on the site.

Channel 4006, which ran roughly parallel to channel 4017 at eastern side of the site, was 11.0–12.0 m wide and up to 0.35 m deep. It had a similar profile to 4017, and a similar sequence of fills, the upper 0.05 m of which, again, produced most of the finds.

Late Bronze Age/Early Iron Age

The upper fill of channel 4006 produced worked flint, burnt flint, and animal bone, and a small number of abraded pottery sherds datable only broadly to the 1st millennium BC. At the other end of the site, however, the primary fill of channel 4017 was cut by a possible post-hole (4027) from which a sherd of Late Bronze Age/Early Iron Age pottery was recovered, again with a number of worked flints. The post-hole was 0.35 m in diameter, and had a visible depth of 0.13 m with steep sides and a concave base but, because its fill (4028) was indistinguishable from the upper fill of the channel, the level from which it had been cut could not be determined. Several other features filled with black humic clay cut the base of the channel, but excavation showed these to be very irregular in form and probably caused by tree roots.

Immediately west of channel 4017 were two further post-holes (or small pits) – 4001 and 4039. These were 0.7 m and 0.4 m in diameter and 0.12 m and 0.07 m deep respectively, with irregular sides and concave bases. Post-hole 4001 also produced a small assemblage of worked flint and Late Bronze Age/Early Iron Age pottery, and although no finds were recovered from 4039 it is assumed to have been of a similar date. Two further post-holes/pits (4066 and 4068) to the east of the channel, both extending beyond the edge of the excavation area, were similar in form. They produced only small quantities of burnt flint but a Late Bronze Age/Early Iron Age date is again likely.

Part of a shallow, sub-circular gully (4005), approximately 9 m in diameter, lay between the two channels, in the centre of the site. The gully was 0.65–1.1 m wide and 0.04–0.23 m deep, with very irregular sides and an irregular concave base. While it may represent the drainage gully around a circular building, no traces of any structure could be located inside it. A small assemblage of fired clay fragments, burnt flint and animal bone fragments was recovered from the gully's light brown silty clay loam fill, and although no datable material was found, the form of the feature suggests a later prehistoric date.

Romano-British

The only evidence for Romano-British activity came from an irregular erosion channel (4024), 3.5–5.0 m wide and up to 0.3 m deep. This ran parallel to channel 4006 and partly cut its upper fill near the northern edge of the excavation area. The two pale grey clay loam fills (4026 and 4035) contained small quantities of worked flint, burnt flint, abraded Romano-British pottery, and a single iron nail (possibly a horseshoe nail). The abraded condition of the finds suggests that they were not *in situ*, but had probably derived from deposits or features upslope.

Watching brief

To the east of the site (chainage B1040–B1220), a shallow pit, three ditches, and two post-holes, all undated, were recorded during the watching brief. A further two pits (96 and 99) produced prehistoric pottery, burnt animal bone, and worked and burnt flint. One recent ditch (41) containing modern material also produced residual 4th century AD pottery.

Finds

Flint

by Phil Harding

Most of the flint was found in the upper levels of channel 4017; it is patinated and includes a relatively large number of blades and bladelets with carefully prepared abraded butts. There is also a single platform flake core and a broken end scraper blade. The smaller assemblage from channel 4006, which includes a core, is similar in condition and technology and is probably contemporary. This material may be of Mesolithic or Early Neolithic date, although the

Table 9.3 South-east of Battlesbury Wood (SR993): finds totals by feature (no./wt (g))

Context/feature	*Worked flint*	*Burnt flint*	*Stone*	*Fired clay*	*Prehist. pottey*	*R-B pottery*	*Iron (no.)*
Pit 4001	1/2	–	–	–	7/18	–	–
Ring gully 4005	–	2/4	–	2+/2	–	–	–
Channel 4006	5/47	20/168	2/50	–	5/2	–	–
Channel 4017	122/605	14/58	–	1/4	–	–	–
Surface over 4024	1/11	2/8	–	–	–	2/14	–
Ditch/channel 4024	6/80	4/2	–	–	–	5/10	1
?P-h 4027	4/26	–	–	–	1/2	–	–
Nat. feature 4052	–	?/18	–	–	–	–	–
Pit 4066	1/7	4/7	–	–	–	–	–
Total	140/878	47/265	2/50	3+/6	13/22	7/24	1

Two fragments of burnt sarsen were recovered from channel 4006, and a nail associated with the Romano-British pottery.

Watching brief finds

The earliest pottery recovered during the watching brief consists of 11 small and abraded, possibly Early Bronze Age, sherds in the fine grog-tempered fabric, GR1, from pit 96 (context 97). Later prehistoric sherds comprise one flint-tempered body sherd (FL2), also from context 97, and a shell-tempered sherd (SH2/3) from pit 99 (context 100).

absence of diagnostic Mesolithic artefacts including microliths, microburins, blade or bladelet cores, and other by-products of blade or bladelet production suggest that it is Neolithic. The material from channel 4024, which was stratigraphically later than channel 4006, is, in contrast, unpatinated with heavy post-depositional edge damage. It is probable that this flint was incorporated into the channel at a much later date. The burnt, unworked flint is likely to have a similar prehistoric date; most of it deriving from channels 4006 and 4017.

Other finds

The prehistoric pottery, all small, plain body sherds, occurs in shelly and sandy fabrics and is not particularly diagnostic, although similarities with the larger assemblage from East of Quebec Barn (Chapter 11) suggest a similar date in the Late Bronze Age. Romano-British sherds, all from the fill of ditch 4024, or from surface cleaning above, are all coarsewares and cannot be dated more precisely.

Table 9.4 South-east of Battlesbury Wood (SRR 93): assessment of molluscs from palaeochannel 4017

Context	*4044*
Sample	*4702*
Depth (cm)	*spot*
Wt (g)	*1500*
Open country species	
Pupilla muscorum (Linnaeus)	C
Vallonia spp.	B
Helicella itala (Linnaeus)	C
Shade-loving species	
Punctum pygmaeum (Draparnaud)	C
Vitrea spp.	C
Aegopinella/Oxychilus spp.	C
Approx. total (in flot)	18

Key: B = 5–9 items, C = <5 items

Environment

Snails

by Michael J. Allen

Samples were taken from both layers of western channel 4017 (context 4043 and 4044) but, because mollusc shells were sparsely preserved, analysis was not pursued. The sample from the upper, humic clays (4043) was void of shells but that from the loose chalky fill (4044) contained an entirely terrestrial, dry land assemblage, deriving from the environment through which the stream flowed; the lack of freshwater species is not unusual as aquatic populations in streams can be very low and highly insular in their locality (Table 9.4). The assemblage is a typical post-glacial one; although *Pupilla muscorum*, *Vallonia* sp. *Helicella itala*, and *Punctum pygmaeum* occur in late glacial contexts (Kerney 1963) species such as *Vitrea* sp, and *Aegopinella nitidula* are not present in biozone Z of the late glacial, Devensian, fauna (Kerney 1977; 1999; Evans 1972). We cannot, however, discount the possibility that these two apices are intrusive down earthworm burrows or root channels. The assemblages indicate that the chalkland stream flowed through open, possibly grazed, calcareous grassland.

Discussion

The evidence for intermittent activity in the vicinity of this site from the Mesolithic/Early Neolithic through to the Romano-British period, probably reflects its attractive location on the lower slopes flanking the Wylye valley, next to a possible seasonal stream, and from where the varied resources of the Chalk and Greensand geology and the river floodplain could be exploited The only two archaeological features on the excavation site to contain any dating evidence (pit/post-hole 4001 and post-hole 4027) both produced small assemblages of Late Bronze Age/Early Iron Age pottery and late prehistoric activity was also identified during the watching brief. The most likely interpretation of the sub-circular gully is as a roundhouse of unknown but probably later prehistoric date, a suggestion possibly supported by the recovery from it of fired clay fragments, burnt flint and animal bone. This activity is similar to that found on SRR95 where a couple of pits and post-holes were identified alongside a channel (see above).

East of Battlesbury Bowl Earthwork Survey (SRR 12)

Six earthwork terraces were surveyed on the steep north-facing slope of Battlesbury Hill, outside the eastern end of Battlesbury Camp hillfort (Fig. 2.1). The survey area (at chainage 1200–1650) was *c.* 430 m long and 70–100 m wide, falling from 162–138 m aOD. North–south sections were taken across the survey area from five base stations located along the north side of a military tank track running around the base of the hill, in order to be able to produce profiles of the terraces and the general terrain. The terraces were clearly discernible as shallow, slightly sloping or nearly flat areas along the steep slope, the three at the east (terraces 2–4) sloping down gradually to the east, and two to the west (terraces 5–6) sloping down gradually to the west.

The surveyed features are part of a large number of similar terraces cut into the north and east sides of the hillfort and around Battlesbury Bowl generally, as well as more widely on many steeper slopes across the Wessex chalklands. Terrace 1, along with others not surveyed, cut into the earthwork defences of the Iron Age hillfort. It has been suggested that they are of medieval date (McOmish *et al.* 2002, 115), perhaps bringing new land into cultivation in response to increasing population and a shortage of suitable arable land.

East of Battlesbury Hill Strip-and-record (SRR 20)

A 400 m length of the route (chainage 1600–2000) immediately east of Battlesbury Hill was subject to strip-and-record on the basis of cropmarks and two ditches recorded during the evaluation. Both ditches were located and excavated further, and a third, truncated ditch was identified to the west, as well as a hollow-way apparently aligned on the eastern entrance to Battlesbury Camp Iron Age hillfort. The largest ditch (F700), whose a upper fill (701) contained two sherds of undiagnostic Romano-British pottery, was cut by the hollow-way.

The hollow-way appeared as a large spread of soil that had been recorded during the evaluation as a natural deposit. It could be traced in adjacent freshly-ploughed fields as a soilmark aligned approximately north-east to south-west, leading up the slope of Battlesbury Hill to the hillfort entrance. It comprised two distinct hollows (706 at the west and 709 at the east), with possible wheel ruts at their bases and with evidence for a major phase of re-use in each. A small group of finds was retrieved. This included two Romano-British coarseware sherds recovered from the uppermost fill (708) of the eastern hollow. A fragment of polished flint axe from a secondary fill (707) of the same hollow was residual.

It is possible that the hollow-way is of late prehistoric origin and directly associated with the Iron Age occupation of the hillfort. However, the fragments of Romano-British pottery, the presence of possible wheel ruts, and the multi-phase nature of the hollow-way suggest longer term use. It may have provided a route between the low ground north-east of Battlesbury and the hilltop accessed through the hillfort entrance, over an extended period, possibly into the medieval period.

East of Field Barn Watching Brief (AC 1004)

Two groups of archaeological features were recorded during easement stripping over 613 m on the low-lying ground to the east of Field Barn, north of Middle Hill (chainage 2330–2943). The western group (chainage 2330–2460), comprised largely undated ditches, gullies, and possible post-holes. An area of Romano-British activity was recorded to the east (chainage 2844–2943). Only the eastern group of features is illustrated (Fig. 9.3)

Results

Western group

At the west, the terminals of two shallow truncated ditches (136 and 140), on the same north-east–south-west alignment, were separated by a 0.6 m wide gap, both terminals cut by a number of shallow post-holes indicating some form of entrance feature. Parallel to them, to their immediate south-east, was a third truncated ditch (146), continuing across the line of the entrance but petering out to the north-east. Some 25 m to the east was an irregular, possibly recut ditch (529) with the orientation, while at the east end of the strip were two ditch terminals 4 m apart. Ditch 119

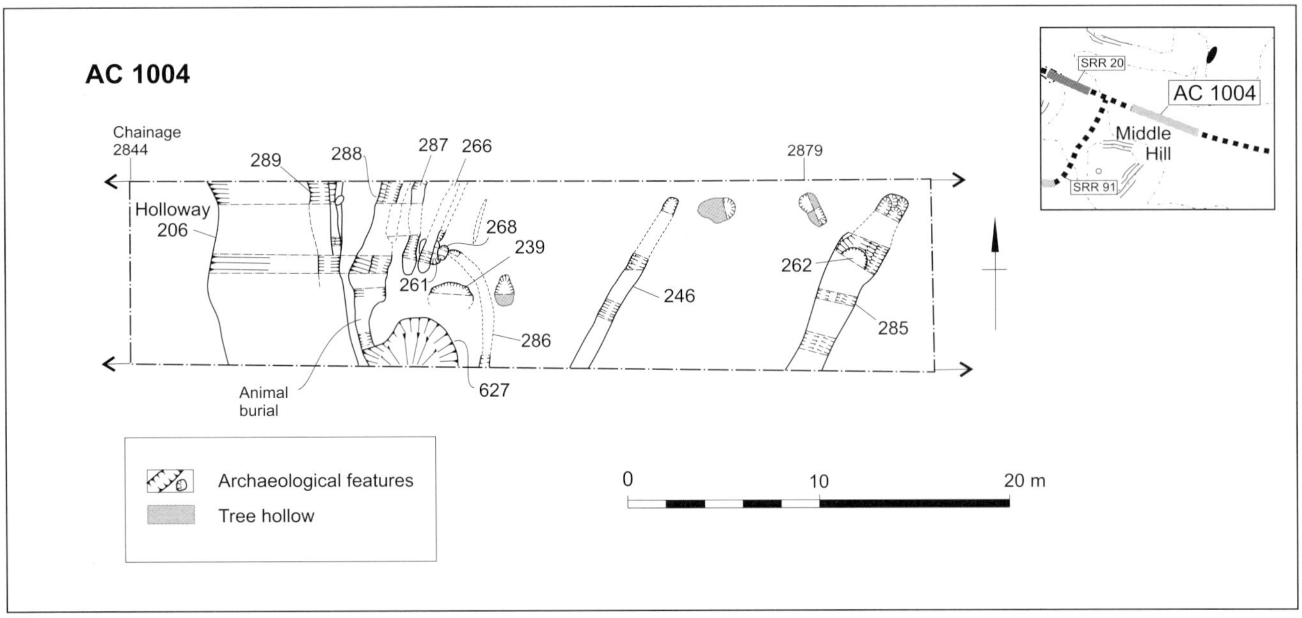

Figure 9.3 East of Field Barn (AC 1004)

was aligned north-east to south-west curving slightly to the south, while ditch 513 was aligned south-south-east to north-north-west.

Two small pits (131 and 504) and 22 possible post-holes were recorded, with a cluster of post-holes between ditches 146 and 529 suggesting a possible structure. Some of these features were badly truncated, and none produced datable finds, although small quantities of worked flint and burnt flint were recovered from some fills. They were sealed by alluvial deposits.

Eastern group

The eastern group of features (Fig. 9.3) was largely bounded at the west by a large north–south aligned hollow-way (206) from the fill of which Romano-British pottery was recovered. There was a fragmentary possible surface along its eastern edge, which was cut by a single post-hole (234). Another post-hole was recorded to the west of the hollow-way.

The eastern side of the hollow-way was flanked by a number of roughly north–south aligned gullies, some intercutting. Gully 289 lay along the eastern side of hollow-way, while, 2 m to the east, irregular gully 288 narrowed before merging with a large scoop/hollow (627). The scoop produced no finds and may have been a drainage sump. The partial skeleton of a horse lay within gully 288 at the point where it narrowed. Two further gullies (287 and 266) lay close together, parallel with and to the east of gully 288, both terminating within the trench, while a further, curvilinear, gully (286) curved round from the south to the north-west terminating just short of gully 266.

There were three pits in the area of the gullies, all containing Romano-British pottery and animal bone. Pit 261 was cut by gully 266 and, on its eastern edge, by pit 268 which also cut the terminal of curvilinear gully 286. Pit 239 lay just to their south.

Approximately 10 m east of the gullies was a north-east–south-west aligned ditch (246) which terminated close to the edge of excavation. Its fill (contexts 3, 5, 7–9) was relatively rich in finds, including a wide selection of Romano-British pottery, iron objects, and a bronze coin of Constantine. A further 10 m to the east, and parallel to 246, was a further ditch (285) that had been the subject of frequent recuts, and which produced a second Roman coin (context 615). It also terminated near to the northern baulk and cut the upper fills of a chalk-sealed cesspit (262) containing Romano-British pottery and animal bone.

Further east there was a north-east–south-west aligned metalled trackway (1030, not illustrated). This was flanked on the west side by narrow gully (1031) and possible hollow-way (1036), and on the east side by two ditches (1027 and 1025) producing Romano-British pottery and a complete horse skull (76 m to the east of the horse skeleton).

Finds

Coins

by Nicholas Cooke

Two small late Roman bronze coins were found (Objects 1 and 1001) (Table 9.5). ON 1 is a 'Constantinopolis' issue of the House of Constantine of AD 330 minted in Lyons. ON 1001 is a *Gloria Exercitus* type issued by Constantius II in AD 340, minted in Trier. Both are common finds.

Table 9.5 East of Field Barn (AC 1004): coins

Object no.	*Context/Feature*	*Description*	*Diam./wt*	*Date*
1	615/Ditch 285	Nummus. Obv: Bust 1, helmeted CONSTAN [TINOPOLIS]; Rev: Victory on prow 1, Lyons, LRBC I, 185.	16 mm/2 g	AD 330
1001	3/Ditch 246	Nummus. Obv: Bust r. laureate, cuirassed/FLIVLC [ONSTA] NTIVSAVG; Rev: 2 soldiers, 1 standard, GLORI AEXER CITVS. Mint mark TRS/palm, Trier. LRBC I, 126.	14 mm/1 g	AD 340

Pottery
by Moira Laidlaw

This site produced an assemblage of largely undiagnostic pottery predominantly of late Romano-British (3rd/4th century) date. The fabrics are mainly local coarsewares, with very few fine wares present (Table 9.6).

Imported finewares are represented by two very small samian sherds recovered from ditch 246 (context 7). British finewares comprise one New Forest colour-coated sherd (Fulford 1975, fabric 1a) found in ditch 246 (context 3), and two abraded colour-coated body sherds from gully 285 and an unlocated soil spread (618), both possibly Fulford's fabric 1b (Tomber and Dore 1998, respectively NFO CC and NFO RS 2), all of which may be broadly dated to the 3rd/4th centuries. A small quantity of mainly plain body sherds (27) were attributed to the catch-all fine oxidised fabric QU100 and represents fabrics from more than one production centre. A number of the sherds may be abraded colour-coated wares either from the Oxfordshire or New Forest industries. Some sherds may also have been produced locally, a possible source being the colour-coated industry of north Wiltshire where a possible production centre near Wanborough has been recorded as producing colour-coated beakers in the second quarter of the 2nd century (Anderson 1979). The only vessel forms present comprise a folded beaker, a small cordoned vessel, and one perforated sherd.

Table 9.6 East of Field Barn (AC 1004): Roman pottery fabrics

Fabric	*No.*	*Wt (g)*
BB	54	457
Colour-coat	3	10
Samian	2	1
G100	1	9
G101	6	54
G102	3	40
Q100	27	136
Q101	29	75
Q102	124	1116
Q103	5	20
Q104	33	191
Mortaria	2	8
Total	289	2117

Coarsewares are the most common fabric types and were sub-divided into eight fabric groups, including one of known source but mainly 'catch-all' types with products from more than one source. The fabric of known source is the Black Burnished ware fabric from the Poole Harbour area of Dorset (Seager Smith and Davies 1993). It should be noted that, in some cases, it was difficult to distinguish between sherds attributed to the moderately coarse fabric QU103 and those of the Black Burnished ware industry.

The bulk of the coarseware sherds are attributed to the sandy fabric QU102 which includes sherds derived from a number of sources such as the Oxfordshire and New Forest industries and more locally the kilns in north Wiltshire, west of Swindon, which are known to have been producing greywares from the 2nd–4th centuries. Each fabric covers a moderate range in the size and abundance of quartz grains and there is, therefore, a degree of overlap between the fabrics. Fabric QU104 is mainly distinguished from QU103 on the basis of being oxidised. Only ten sherds in the grog-tempered fabrics were recovered and probably represent Savernake type wares produced near Mildenhall in the Savernake Forest (Swan 1975).

Only eleven diagnostic rim sherds were recorded plus three rim sherds which were too small to attribute with certainty to a specific vessel form. The three Black Burnished ware forms comprise one everted rimmed jar and two plain rimmed dishes, all forms dated to the 2nd century and later (Seager Smith and Davies 1993, types 2 and 20). The other coarseware forms consist of four jars with curved rims, one jar/beaker with short everted rim, one bead rim jar/bowl, and one storage jar with rounded rim.

Very few sherds are decorated or have traces of surface treatments. The decoration is restricted to one greyware storage jar with a finger-impressed rim, one grog-tempered sherd with an incised band of chevrons, and one Black Burnished ware sherd with incised irregular lines. Some of the Black Burnished ware sherds are burnished or smoothed. Other surface treatments include finger-smearing on grey ware sherds, three sherds with pre-firing perforations, and two greyware sherds with white slip.

With the exception of the grog-tempered fabrics which may represent an earlier element within the assemblage, the bulk of the fabric types and vessel forms, albeit scarce, may be dated broadly to the 2nd–4th centuries. No discrete features contained exclusively early material; the samian and grog-tempered fabrics were all recovered with later fabric types and vessel forms. The larger concentrations of pottery were recovered from ditch 246 (78 sherds from context 3, and 46 from context 7), spread 618 (71 sherds), gully 602 (20 sherds), and ditch 604 (15 sherds).

The bulk of the assemblage is dominated by utilitarian wares and vessel forms such as large storage jars, with only a very small percentage of finewares being present. The assemblage is attributed broadly to the later Roman period and is comparable with pottery recovered at sites in Wiltshire such as Durrington Walls (Swan 1971), Butterfield Down (Millard 1996), Winterbourne (Seager Smith 1995), and Maddington Farm, Shrewton (Seager Smith 1996).

Worked flint

A single retouched flake of noticeably high quality recovered from a gully (context 613) is of black glossy flint with neat shallow retouch on both sides.

Worked stone

Romano-British rotary quern fragments in Old Red Devonian Quartz Conglomerate were recovered; this stone had a relatively limited distribution due to a lack of trade routes eastwards from the Forest of Dean/ Bristol area. Two Pennant Sandstone tile fragments, from the South Wales/Bristol area, were also recovered.

Metalwork

by Lorraine Mepham

Four iron objects were associated with Romano-British pottery, although not in themselves closely datable – these comprise two fragments from ditch 246, and a possible nail shank and a slightly curved iron rod from gully 285.

Animal bone

by Claire Ingrem

A total of 1032 fragments of animal bone (7555 g) was recovered, of which 814 come from Romano-British contexts (Table 9.7). As the assemblage is fragmentary and eroded only a small proportion (15%) is identified to species, and this includes 36 fragments from the skeleton of a horse. Therefore, analysis is limited by sample size but it is clear that the majority of the remaining identifiable fragments belong to sheep/goat (n=35) and that bones belonging to all parts of the body are present although, the only cranial elements are loose teeth and feet are poorly represented. Cattle are represented by a smaller number of fragments (n=19) but again these come from most parts of the body with the cranium represented by loose teeth. Only two fragments of pig are present, one belonging to a femur the other a lateral metapodial. Even discounting the skeleton, horse is more numerous (13 fragments, mostly from the skull and forelimb). Dog is represented by a two fragments, one of which is a skull. The only evidence for wild species is a single lower tooth belonging to roe deer (*Capreolus capreolus*).

Two loose mandibular 3rd molars belonging to sheep/goat indicate that at least one animal was aged 3–4 years at the time of death and another 4–8 years. The mandibular horse 3rd molar from gully 615 suggests that at least one horse was aged 9.25–11.5 years at the time of death. Few bones were able to provide ageing data, a distally-fused humerus and tibia indicate that at least one cow/bull was over 15–20 months at the time of death; a fused sheep distal humerus, proximal radius, and scapula indicate an age >5 months and an unfused pig metapodial an age of <24 months.

The partial horse skeleton from fill 624 of hollow 627 was mature but, in the absence of teeth, it was not possible to estimate age. Osteophytosis, in the form of bony bridging, was observed on seven thoracic vertebrae and provide evidence that the animal suffered from spondylitis deformans. According to Stecher and Goss (1961) this condition is likely to lead to the immobilisation of the spine. The dog skull and axis were both recovered from a soil layer (8), the former is from a very large animal, being intermediate in size when compared to the skull of a German Shepherd and modern wolf hybrid.

Much of the assemblage has been severely affected by root damage to the extent that surface modifications including evidence for gnawing and butchery are likely to be obscured. However, two bones display evidence for gnawing and a cattle humerus showed signs of having been chopped longitudinally through the distal epiphysis.

Discussion

Sample size is too small to provide conclusive evidence regarding animal husbandry practices during the Romano-British period and hence any discussion of such is tentative. It is clear that the major domestic food animals (cattle, sheep/goat, and pig) were all present and it is possible that whole carcasses, at least of cattle and sheep/goat, may originally have been present. There is no evidence for

Table 9.7 East of Field Barn Farm (AC 1004): animal bone from Romano-British contexts

	Cattle	*Sheep/goat*	*Pig*	*Horse*	*Dog*	*Roe deer*	*Large mammal*	*Medium mammal*	*Unid.*	*Total*
Maxilla	1	–	–	–	1	–	–	–	–	2
Upper tooth	1	5	–	1	–	–	–	–	–	7
Mandible	2	–	–	3	–	–	5	2	–	12
Lower tooth	5	12	–	6	–	1	–	–	–	24
Atlas	–	–	–	1	1	–	–	–	–	2
Axis	–	–	–	1	–	–	–	–	–	1
Scapula	–	1	–	4	–	–	–	–	–	6
Humerus	1	2	–	6	–	–	2	1	–	12
Radius	1	3	–	1	–	–	–	–	–	5
Ulna	–	1	–	2	–	–	–	–	–	3
Pelvis	–	2	–	7	–	–	–	–	–	9
Femur	–	–	1	3	–	–	–	–	–	4
Patella	–	–	–	2	–	–	–	–	–	2
Tibia	1	4	–	2	–	–	1	–	–	8
Navicular-cuboid	–	1	–	–	–	–	–	–	–	1
Metacarpal	1	1	–	1	–	–	–	–	–	3
Metatarsal	–	1	–	–	–	–	–	–	–	1
Metapodial	5	2	1	1	–	–	–	–	–	9
Lateral metapodial	–	–	–	2	–	–	–	–	–	2
Phalanx 1	1	–	–	–	–	–	–	–	–	1
Phalanx 3	–	1	–	1	–	–	–	–	–	2
Cervical vertebra	–	–	–	4	–	–	5	–	–	9
Thorcic vertebra	–	–	–	–	–	–	10	–	–	10
Lumbar vertebra	–	–	–	–	–	–	8	–	–	8
Sacrum	–	–	–	1	–	–	–	–	–	1
Rib	–	–	–	–	–	–	10	1	–	11
Tooth fragment	–	–	–	–	–	–	–	–	5	5
Long bone fragment	–	–	–	–	–	–	12	6	–	18
Rib fragment	–	–	–	–	–	–	104	–	–	104
Vertebra fragment	–	–	–	–	–	–	50	–	–	50
Unidentifiable	–	–	–	–	–	–	176	3	292	471
Total	19	36	2	*49	2	1	**383	13	297	802
%	2	4	<1	6	<1	<1	47	2	36	100

* includes 36 frags belonging to skeleton; ** includes 310 frags probably from horse skeleton

immature cattle or sheep/goat but this may be the result of a taphonomic bias. The presence of roe deer suggests that wild species were occasionally hunted. There is much discussion concerning the recovery of complete and partial skeletons from prehistoric and Romano-British sites (see Chapter 6). The presence of a partial horse skeleton from this site could simply represent the disposal of an old or diseased animal which was past its working life (Wilson 1992), as the evidence for *spondylitis deformans* suggests. Alternatively, it is possible that the burial of complete and partial skeletons is the result of structured deposition representing activity of an ideological nature (Hill 1995; 1996; Grant 1991). However, distinguishing these types of activities is not always straightforward (see Chapter 6).

Discussion

The arrangement of ditches and possibly associated post-holes in the western group is hard to interpret, particularly given the size of the area excavated. It seems likely that they were associated, however, with the eastern group of features, which were of predominantly Romano-British date; the latter group flanked on one side by a north–south hollow-way running between the areas of higher ground, and on the other by a ditched and metalled trackway. Although no identifiable structures were recorded, the sealed Romano-British cesspit, the large quantities of Romano-British pottery and animal bone, including a horse skeleton, along with burnt flint, shell, two late Roman coins, and objects of iron, point to settlement activity in the immediate vicinity.

Chapter 10
West Hill to Knook Down

North of West Hill Farm Earthwork Survey (SRR 23) and Watching Brief (AC 1001 and 1002)

Three earthwork features, recorded on aerial photographs north-east of West Hill Farm, were surveyed. The survey area, measuring 150 m by 50 m orientated approximately north-north-east to south-south-west, lay on a north-west facing slope, the ground falling from *c.* 142 m to 119 m aOD (chainage 5080–5230). A modern military road ran across the area along a *c.* 12 m wide terrace. The survey methodology was as described for East of Battlesbury Bowl (see above).

Subsequently, two linear features were recorded during topsoil stripping north of the survey area, where the route crosses the base of a coombe (chainage 4900–5000), while lynchets and a gully were recorded to the south where the route traverses the crest of the hill (chainage 5220–5500).

To the north of the survey area, where the SRR reaches the base of the slope and crosses over the bottom of a coombe running to the north-east, two almost parallel linear features were identified (203 and 206). Both contained post-medieval pottery; feature 205 also containing a single piece of worked flint and a fragment of clay pipe. Some Romano-British pottery was recovered from the subsoil.

Immediately south of the survey area a series of lynchets was recorded cut into the chalk, two on either side of the crest of the hill above West Hill Farm. A little worked flint (two multi-platform cores, 13 flakes, and a scraper), two pieces of non-local stone, and seven pieces of burnt flint were recovered from the surface of one of the lynchets.

Discussion

All of the lynchets, as at East of Battlesbury Bowl, are the result of possibly medieval cultivation of the hillsides. They follow the prevailing topography, both in orientation and in their general altitudes, following certain contour lines along the west-facing slope. These lynchets are part of a larger group seen in aerial photographs. Similar features are also seen on the west- and east-facing slopes of the dry valley to the immediate north-east of West Hill Farm.

The watching brief showed that the lynchets had all been truncated, leaving no trace as upstanding earthworks in the field outside the easement, and none retained any apparent cultivation soil. No feature produced dating evidence, although the collection of fairly unabraded worked flint from lynchet 108 may suggest a prehistoric date for this feature at least. Gully 106 was also undated, but its different alignment to the lynchets suggests that it represents a different phase of activity. The two linear features at the base of the hill to the north probably relate to late medieval or early post-medieval agricultural activity.

East of East Hill Cottages Watching Brief (AC 1003)

Two groups of features were identified during topsoil stripping along the base of the southern flank of East Hill (chainage 6000–6400). The site runs east from the mid-point of the hill to a point where the route leaves the valley floor and ascends a dry coombe to the north-east. Some worked flint, but no datable finds, was recovered from the superficial deposits.

Results

Removal of layer (10) and the underlying subsoil (2) revealed two groups of archaeological features cut into the natural chalk. Two intercutting curvilinear ditches (49 and 52) were exposed at the edge of the excavation (chainage 6000–6100), and three large linear features (25, 28, and 32) at the east (6300–6400).

The earlier curvilinear ditch (52) described a gentle, but regular, arc and was recorded for over 17 m within the easement. It was 1.2 m wide at the east but only 0.6 m at the west, probably as a result of truncation, and up to 0.7 m deep with a roughly V-shaped profile. It was filled with three layers of silt and silty clay loam; burnt and worked flint was recovered from the uppermost fill.

Ditch 52 was intersected at a shallow angle at its west by ditch 49. This also described a gentle arc, although turning more sharply towards the south at the east. It was recorded for over 15 m before petering out to the west, again indicating probable truncation. It was up to 1.1 m wide and 0.6 m deep with steep, fairly straight sides meeting a flattish base. It was filled with clayey silts. Neither fill contained finds.

The eastern group of features comprised two large, parallel linear features (28 and 32) aligned north-east–south-west, both containing Romano-British pottery as well as residual worked flint, and a smaller feature (25) branching off to the west-north-west (and two tree hollows; 21 and 36). The largest of the linear features (32), recorded for over 19 m, was 6.8 m wide with moderately sloping uneven sides and an irregular base, although extensive animal burrowing had disturbed the original profile and its single fill (39) of friable pale brown silty clay loam containing moderate small chalk and flint fragments.

Feature 28, recorded for over 26 m, lay some 2 m to the north-west of feature 32 and, although the two appeared to converge at the south-west, this was due to the presence of remnant subsoil in that area. The feature was 3.1 m wide but less than 0.2 m deep, with shallow uneven sides and an irregular base, again extensively disturbed by burrowing. It was filled with a clayey silt.

Feature 25 appeared to branch of feature 28, but no stratigraphic relationship between the two could be determined due to the similarity of their fills. It was 17.6 m long, 7 m wide and no more than 0.1 m deep. It petered out to the north-west, although its 'shadow' could be discerned continuing beyond the northern baulk.

Finds

The worked flint is almost entirely patinated, and dominated by broad hard hammer struck flakes of probable later prehistoric date. There are very few chronological indicators but a rejuvenation tablet from a blade core and a few pieces with abraded platforms are likely to be earlier than the rest.

A total of 20 sherds (59 g) of Late Bronze Age to Romano-British pottery was recovered from 10 contexts. These are mainly abraded, small, undiagnostic body sherds (there were also two post-medieval sherds) (Table 10.1).

Table 10.1 East of East Hill Cottages (AC 1003): pottery fabrics

Fabric	*No.*	*Wt (g)*
Prehistoric		
F6	2	7
Q1	1	1
Q2	1	2
Roman		
Q100	2	10
Q101	3	4
Q102	4	17
Q104	2	2
Post-med.	2	14
Unident.	3	2
Total	20	59

Four sherds of Late Bronze Age/Early Iron Age pottery were recovered from feature linear feature 28, ditch 49, and a cleaning layer (12). Two were flint-tempered body sherds (FL6), one a body sherd in the sandy fabric QQ1, and one a small upright and flattened rim with finger-impressed decoration in the sandy fabric QU2.

Sixteen sherds of Romano-British pottery were recovered from tree hollow 21 and linear features 28 and 32. With the exception of one plain upright rim sherd and one short everted rim these are small undiagnostic body sherds, mainly attributed to coarseware fabrics. Those from feature 32 included two body sherds in the fine oxidised fabric QU100. On the basis of fabrics and the two vessel forms this small group appears to be early Roman of the late 1st/early 2nd century AD.

Discussion

The curvilinear ditches in the western part of the site are undated, but may, be of prehistoric origin. The presence of a little worked flint within these ditches may support this suggestion. Little of the areas they enclosed was exposed, and their function is unclear. The two wide linear features at the east end of the site, both of which produced Romano-British pottery, were probably part of a poorly-preserved lynchet system.

South of Old Ditch Strip-and-record (SRR 76)

A 407 m length of the route (chainage 7000–7407) along the southern periphery of a known Iron Age settlement site (SMR ST94SW642), south of the later prehistoric Wessex Linear Ditch known as Old Ditch was subject to strip-and-record on the basis of features recorded during the evaluation. Other remains of prehistoric and Romano-British date are known nearby, including two overlapping rectangular enclosures (SMR ST94SW641) visible as cropmarks in aerial photographs, elements of which were crossed by the western end of the road.

Results

The westernmost features, at the top of a dry coombe and sealed by colluvium, were a pit (76006) with a possible post-hole (76005) cutting its south side, and two nearby shallow possible post-holes (76002 and 76004). All were undated, although artefacts recovered from the colluvium included post-medieval pottery, a copper alloy thimble, and an iron calthrop (a four-spiked implement of war which always has one point standing upright).

From *c.* 70–190 m to the east there was a series of five ditches and gullies – ditch 76009, containing late prehistoric pottery (context 76010) and adjacent gully 76011, both aligned north-west–south-east, and ditches 76017, 76020, and 76025, all aligned north-east–south-west. Based on their positions and alignments these appear to be related to the two cropmark enclosures, although the most easterly of the group, U-shaped ditch 76025, may represent a field boundary.

At the east end of the site, two small undated gullies (76027 and 76030) joined at a shallow angle, possibly forming the corner of an enclosure extending to the north. Although no features were recorded within the bounded area, the gullies were cut at the corner by a rectangular pit (76033), the upper fill of which (76034) produced late prehistoric pottery.

Other, curvilinear, features recorded during the evaluation and thought to be associated with either the Iron Age settlement or a 'lost' bowl barrow were shown to be natural features. Two pieces of worked flint were recovered from a tree hollow.

Finds

The site produced a small assemblage of pottery, worked and burnt flint, stone, animal bone, and single pieces of copper alloy and iron – the thimble and calthrop rspectively. The calthrop could be of Romano-British date (Manning 1985, 178, pl. 85, V283) but these are not common finds in this period and it could well be later in date; medieval and later calthrops are of almost identical form.

Six of the pottery sherds are attributed tentatively to the Late Bronze Age/Early Iron Age. They consist of five small body sherds in the fine sandy fabric QU2, from ditch 76009 (context 76008), and one small sandy sherd with a smoothed external surface in the sandy fabric QU1, from pit 76033 (76034). One post-medieval glazed earthenware sherd was also recovered.

Discussion

The site lies within an area of relatively dense archaeology to the south of the Old Ditch Wessex Linear Ditch, with features ranging in date from the Bronze Age to the Romano-British period A number of ditches branch off at angles from the Linear Ditch, including possibly a short earthwork just north of the SRR route, close to a small sub-rectangular enclosure. A round barrow and a pillow mound are also recorded in the area. The two larger and overlapping rectangular enclosures, elements of which were recorded on the site, appear to be associated with a field system extending towards the west, and are probably of late prehistoric date.

Willis's Field Barn Excavation (SRR 96), Knook Spur Watching Brief (AC 1006 and 1007), and North of Bevin's Barn Strip-and-record (SRR 97)

The excavation site at Willis's Field Barn (chainage K1620–K1700) was approximately 2 km to the north-east of the village of Heytesbury, on the Knook spur road. It lay at 175 m aOD on a ridge between the Wylye valley to the south and a large dry valley to the north. The natural geology is Upper Chalk (BGS 1985) which, in this area, is heavily weathered with a very crumbly, granular texture and cut by numerous ploughmarks and solution features. The excavation area, 80 m long (east–west) and 8 m wide (640 m^2) was selected on the basis of a 'ditch and pit complex' identified during the evaluation.

Subsequently, part of the site was re-exposed and extended a few metres to the south (AC 1006) during the Stage 2 topsoil stripping, which also continued to the north-east (up to chainage K2100 – AC 1007). Another section of the route to the south-west of the site (chainage K800–K1000) was subject to strip-and-record (SRR 97).

Results

Although only five definite archaeological features were identified during the excavation – two ditches and three small pits – two main phases of activity, were recognised: Late Neolithic–Early Bronze Age and Middle Bronze Age (Fig. 10.1). Other finds included a sherd of Middle Neolithic Peterborough Ware and an Iron Age brooch, both from the upper fill of a Middle Bronze Age enclosure ditch. Three small undated features towards the west of the site (6023, 6025, and 6049) are probably natural features.

Neolithic and Early Bronze Age

Neolithic and Early Bronze Age activity is represented by a small pit as well as by a number of finds from the two ditches. The earliest material, a single rim sherd of Middle Neolithic Peterborough Ware (possibly Ebbsfleet sub-style) (Fig. 10.2, 1), was recovered from recut 6066 of the Middle Bronze Age enclosure ditch (6004, below). More substantial evidence is provided by a small pit (6047), cut by the enclosure

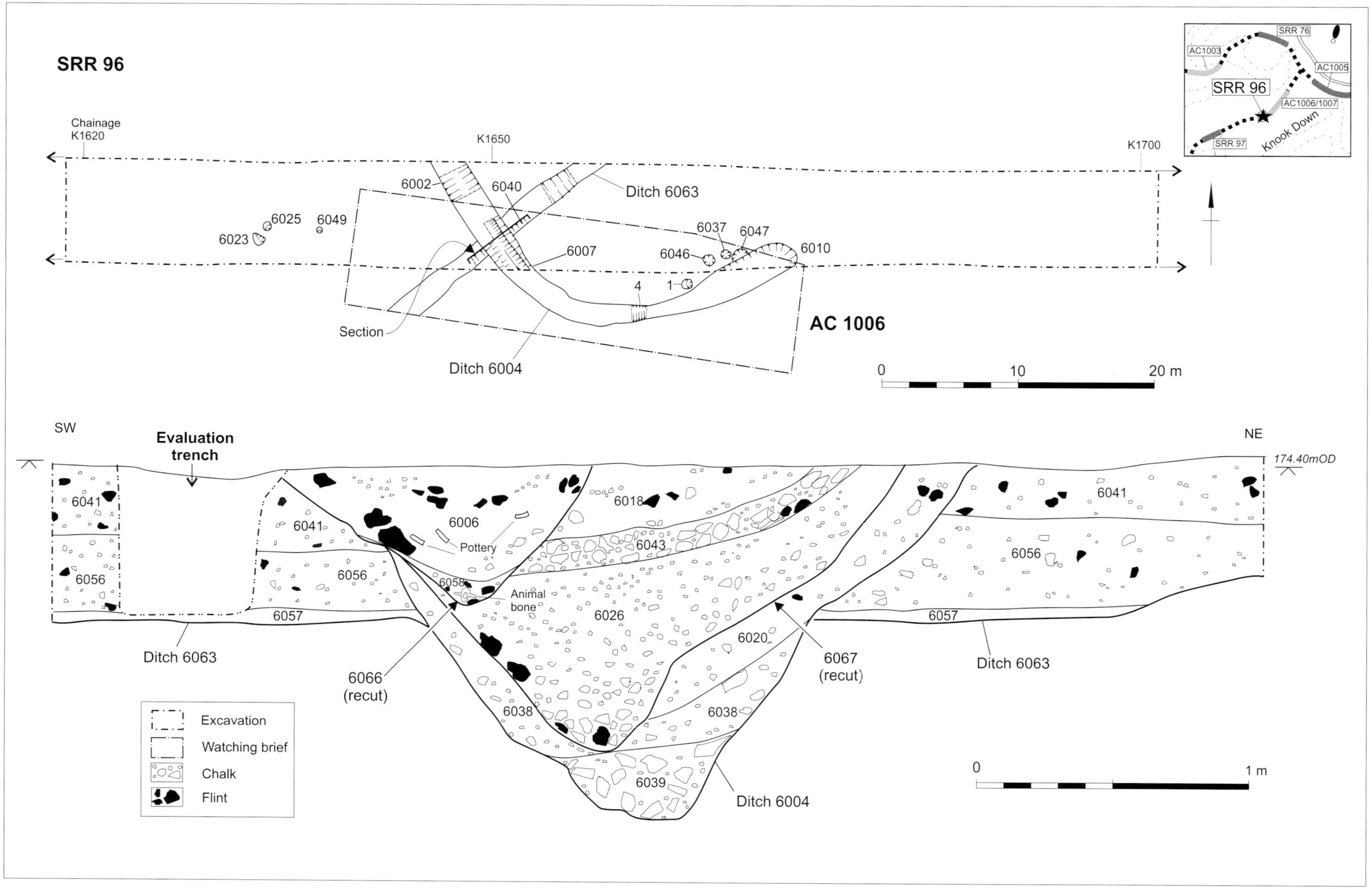

Figure 10.1 Willis's Field Barn (SRR 96/AC 1006)

ditch terminal (6010), which produced a few decorated sherds of Beaker pottery, with further sherds, probably from the same vessel, being also found in the terminal; other Beaker sherds were recovered from other sections of the same ditch (Fig. 10.2, 2–3, 5–7). In addition, two sherds of Early Bronze Age pottery were recovered from ditch 6063 (Fig. 10.2, 4).

Pit 6047 was 0.8 m in diameter and 0.3 m deep with steep sides and a flat base, and was filled with a well-sorted dark brown silty loam with common chalk inclusions containing small quantities of animal bone, Beaker pottery, worked flint (including a small end scraper), a possible greensand quernstone fragment, and burnt flint. A second end scraper and a microdenticulate recovered from the ditch probably derived from the same pit. Flint of probable Late Neolithic–Early Bronze Age date, including a burnt backed knife, was also recovered from other features.

Two other small pits (6037 and 6046), and a pit or post-hole (1) recorded during the watching brief (AC 1006, below), all of them undated, may be associated with pit 6047 on account of their proximity and the similarity of their forms and fills. The features recorded during the excavation produced small amounts of burnt flint and animal bone, including sheep/goat and pig. It is also possible, however, that they were related to the later ditch terminal, as they appear to be positioned along its edge.

Middle Bronze Age

A length of ditch (6063), *c.* 12.5 m long was aligned approximately north-east–south-west across the site. It averaged 1.6 m wide and 0.6 m deep, with an irregular V-shaped profile. Its basal fill (6057, in longitudinal section 6040, Fig. 10.1) was a thin layer of light grey chalky silt, suggesting that the ditch was open for a relatively short period, or that it was maintained. The upper fills (6056 and 6041) consisted of yellowish–brown to greyish–brown silty clays, their unsorted nature suggesting the ditch had been deliberately backfilled, rather than having silted up naturally. The only datable finds recovered from it during excavation was two small probably residual sherds of grog-tempered Early Bronze Age pottery from its secondary fill, although a sherd of later prehistoric pottery was recovered during the subsequent watching brief (AC 1006, below). A small amount of animal bone, from horse, cattle, sheep/goat, and roe deer, and two pieces of worked flint were also recovered.

Ditch 6063 was cut at a right-angle by a *c.* 9 m length of ditch (6004) aligned approximately north-west–south-east. This appeared to curve round to the east outside the excavation area, re-entering it some 18 m to the east and ending at a rounded terminal (6010), a fact that was confirmed during the watching brief (as ditch 4, AC 1006, below). The ditch, which averaged 2.3 m wide at the top and was up to 1.3 m deep, with steep irregular sides and a generally flat though slightly uneven base, appears to form part of an enclosure, with an entrance at the south-east. It is possible that pits 6037 and 6046, and the pit/post-hole (1) recorded during the watching brief, were associated with the ditch terminal, possibly forming part of some entrance structure.

The earliest ditch fills (Fig. 10.1) comprised a thin and patchy layer of chalky silt with rare charcoal inclusions (6061, not visible in section), overlain by a thick layer of loose chalk rubble (6039) containing some animal bone and worked flint. In places, the rubble fills appeared to have derived from the interior of the ditch's curve, suggesting that there may have been internal bank. The overlying deposits of yellowish–brown silty clay (6038 and 6020), from which two fragments (19 g) of unworked shale were recovered, may represent a period of stabilisation. The ditch was recut through these deposits to a depth of over 1 m (6067), the main fills (6026 and 6043) of the recut being substantial deposits of chalk rubble from which small quantities of Middle Bronze Age pottery, animal bone, and worked flint were recovered. These were overlain by a gradual accumulation of yellowish–brown to greyish–brown silty clay loam (6018) almost filling the ditch.

The fills of recut 6067 were cut by a second recut (6066), 1.2 m wide and 0.5 m deep (Fig. 10.1), noted in all three excavated sections. Its primary fill (6058) was a dark brown silty clay loam containing Middle Bronze Age pottery, animal bone, worked flint, and fragments of a greensand saddle quern and a sarsen quernstone. The main fill (6006) contained further sherds of Middle Bronze Age pottery (as well as the residual Peterborough Ware sherds). In the terminal, the primary fill of the recut (6014) was overlain by a deposit of chalk rubble (6015) which contained articulated cattle vertebrae and a tapered bone point. This object, which had signs of wear on its point and may have been a needle or been used in weaving, has a parallel in a bone awl from Bishops Canning Down, Wiltshire (Gingell 1992, fig. 83.9). The overlying layer of silty clay loam (6008) contained a complete cattle skull; the material from these layers appearing to have been deliberately placed. The uppermost layer in the terminal (6003) yielded two iron objects – a small flat fragment and a Late Iron Age brooch.

AC 1006

The subsequent re-opening of the site during the watching brief, extending the excavated area a few metres to the south, confirmed that ditches 6004 and 6010, linked by ditch 4, were the same feature. An undated post-hole or small pit (1) was recorded on the edge of the ditch, on the same line as the

Table 10.2 Willis's Field Barn (SRR 96): all finds by context No./wt (g)

	Burnt flint	*Worked flint*	*Pottery*	*Stone*	*Iron (no.)*	*Worked bone (no.)*
Late Neolithic/Early Bronze Age						
Pit 6037	5/156	–	–	–	–	–
Pit 6046	17/378	–	–	–	–	–
Pit 6047	6/140	7/30	12/61	1/162	–	–
Middle Bronze Age						
Ditch 6063	–	2/18	2/13	–	–	–
Enclosure ditch 6004	103/2895	61/483	24/148	8/498	–	1
Ditch upper recut 6066	103/3713	49/541	132/1136	18/308	5	–
Undated						
Evaluation trench backfill	1/46	–	1/12	–	–	–
?Natural feature 6023	1/18	–	–	–	–	–
Total	236/7346	119/1072	171/1370	27/968	5	1

previously recorded pits 6046, 6037, and 6047 immediately to the east. An additional section cut through ditch 6063 produced a single coarse flint-tempered body sherd of later prehistoric date.

Finds

The excavation produced a relatively large but restricted finds assemblage, mainly flint (worked and burnt) and pottery, with smaller quantities of stone and metalwork (Table 10.2).

Flint

by Phil Harding

Late Neolithic activity is represented by a small quantity of undiagnostic flakes and a well made end scraper on a flake from ditch 6063 and pit 6047 (Table 10.3). The remainder of the flint assemblage was collected from ditch 6004 and recut 6066 which have been dated to the Middle Bronze Age.

Most of the flakes are in mint or sharp condition and appear to be contemporary with the silting of the ditch. However, the most diagnostic pieces, which include a finely made end scraper and a microdenticulate from 6012, are likely to date from the earlier phase of activity. This material was probably derived from pit 6047 which was cut by the terminal of ditch 6004 and contained a small assemblage of Beaker pottery and flint. A burnt backed knife from ditch 6004 (secondary fill) may also represent redeposited material from the earlier activity at the site. (A second end scraper was recovered from AC 1006 – ditch 5 (6063) – during the watching brief). Most of the remaining flint, including a piercer and a naturally backed knife, is undiagnostic and may be contemporary with the silting of the ditches. Material from the upper ditch fills includes flakes with edge damage from reworking in ploughsoil contexts.

Table 10.3 Willis's Field Barn (SRR 96): flint by context

	1	*2*	*3*	*4*	*5*	*Comment*
Late Neolithic/Early Bronze Age						
Pit 6047	–	–	4	2	1	well made scraper on flake
Middle Bronze Age						
Ditch 6063	–	–	2	–	–	
Ditch 6004						
Primary	–	–	3	1	1	utilised flake
Secondary	2	–	28	11	7	3 scrapers (1 pressure flaked end scraper), 1 microdenticulate, 1 backed knife (burnt), 1 retouched (?scraper), utilised flake
Tertiary	–	–	4	–	–	
Terminal	–	–	3	1	–	
Ditch upper recut 6066						
Primary	–	–	11	1	1	piercer
Secondary	1	1	20	6	2	Naturally backed knife; flake with distal notch
Surface	–	–	6	–	–	
Total	3	1	81	22	12	

1 = blades; 2 = broken blades; 3 = flakes; 4 = broken flakes; 5 = tools

Pottery

by Rachel Every

The pottery assemblage comprises 171 sherds (1370 g), including material of Middle Neolithic, Early Bronze Age, and Middle Bronze Age date. Five broad fabric groups were identified on the basis of dominant inclusion types: flint-tempered fabrics (Group FL), grog-tempered fabrics (Group GR), calcareous-tempered fabrics (Groups SH and LI), and sand-tempered fabrics (Group QU). These groups were then sub-divided into eight separate fabric types based on the range and coarseness of the inclusions present. Fabric totals given in Table 10.4 (see Appendix for fabric descriptions).

Middle Neolithic

The earliest material from the site comprises a single sherd in a moderately coarse flint-tempered fabric (FL16), decorated on the top of the rim and on the outside with round-toothed comb impressions (Fig. 10.2, 1). This can be identified as Peterborough Ware, possibly of Ebbsfleet sub-style.

Early Bronze Age

A total of 22 sherds (126 g) has been identified as Early Bronze Age, with varying degrees of confidence. Three fabric types have been defined within this small group, one grog-tempered, one sandy, and one containing fine calcite inclusions. The most diagnostic material comprises three decorated Beaker sherds, in fabric LI 14, recovered respectively from pit 6047, recut 6066 (of ditch 6004), and from the evaluation trench backfill (Fig. 10.2, 3–5). These sherds all bear similar decoration: alternating bands of square-toothed comb impressions and small triangular impressions, probably made with a pointed instrument, and are so similar as to suggest that they all derived from a single vessel, originally dispersed when pit 6047 was cut by the terminal of ditch 6004. The overall form of the vessel(s) is unknown.

Ten further small body sherds from pit 6047 probably represent a second Beaker. These are in sandy fabric QU16 and are decorated with deeply incised diagonal lines. Two more Beaker sherds with incised lines, but in grog-tempered fabric GR5, came from ditch 6004 (Fig. 10.2, 6) and recut 6066 respectively; these may both come from the same vessel, while three grog-tempered sherds with comb-impressed decoration (Fig. 10.2, 2, 7), all from recut 6066, may represent a fourth vessel.

One further plain base sherd in fabric QU16 (ditch 6004), and three small plain body sherds in fabric GR5 (ditch 6004 and recut 6066) are less certainly identified as Beaker.

Middle Bronze Age

The remainder of the assemblage (148 sherds; 1240 g) is dated as Middle Bronze Age. All but one sherd (from pit 6047) came from ditch 6004 and its recut 6066. This group comprises sherds in a range of grog-tempered, flint-tempered, and calcareous (containing either calcite or shell) fabrics. Seven different fabric types have been defined, one grog-tempered, three flint-tempered and three calcareous (Table 10.4; see Appendix for fabric descritions).

Table 10.4 Willis's Field Barn (SRR 96): pottery fabric totals

Date	*Fabric*	*No.*	*Wt (g)*
MNEO	FL16	1	4
MBA	FL17	7	44
MBA	FL18	1	4
MBA	FL19	6	88
EBA	GR5	8	26
MBA	GR6	27	176
MBA	LI 12	20	209
MBA	LI 13	73	696
EBA	LI 14	3	79
EBA	QU16	11	21
MBA	SH8	14	23
Total		171	1370

Fabrics

Most of these fabric types could have been made using raw materials which were locally accessible (ie, within a 10 km radius of the site). The three calcareous fabrics, however, one shelly and two calcite-tempered, may represent regionally traded vessels. These wares have a potential source within the band of Kimmeridge Clay which outcrops at various points across Wiltshire at the foot of the chalk downs – the nearest outcrop is to the north-east of Westbury.

Forms

Diagnostic material within this group comprises several vessels of bucket-shaped or slightly convex profile, both plain and decorated, which appear to derive from vessels of two types within the Deverel-Rimbury tradition – the Barrel Urn and Globular Urn, while the third Deverel-Rimbury form, the Bucket Urn, could also be present.

Rim sherds derive from a maximum of nine vessels. Five of these, all from straight-sided, bucket-shaped vessels in calcite-tempered or shelly fabrics, are from decorated vessels of Barrel Urn type – two with finger-impressions below the rim (one illustrated: Fig. 10.2, 9), one with an expanded, finger-impressed rim (Fig. 10.2, 12), one with applied bosses around the rim (Fig. 10.2, 13), and the most elaborate with an expanded, 'notched' rim, applied, finger-impressed cordon and incised cross-hatching above the cordon (Fig. 10.2, 10). Further decorated vessels are represented by a second finger-impressed cordon and two fingernail-impressed shoulders, all in calcite-tempered fabrics. Three sherds (perhaps from a single vessel, in fabric FL17) with shallow ?comb tooth impressions, are of

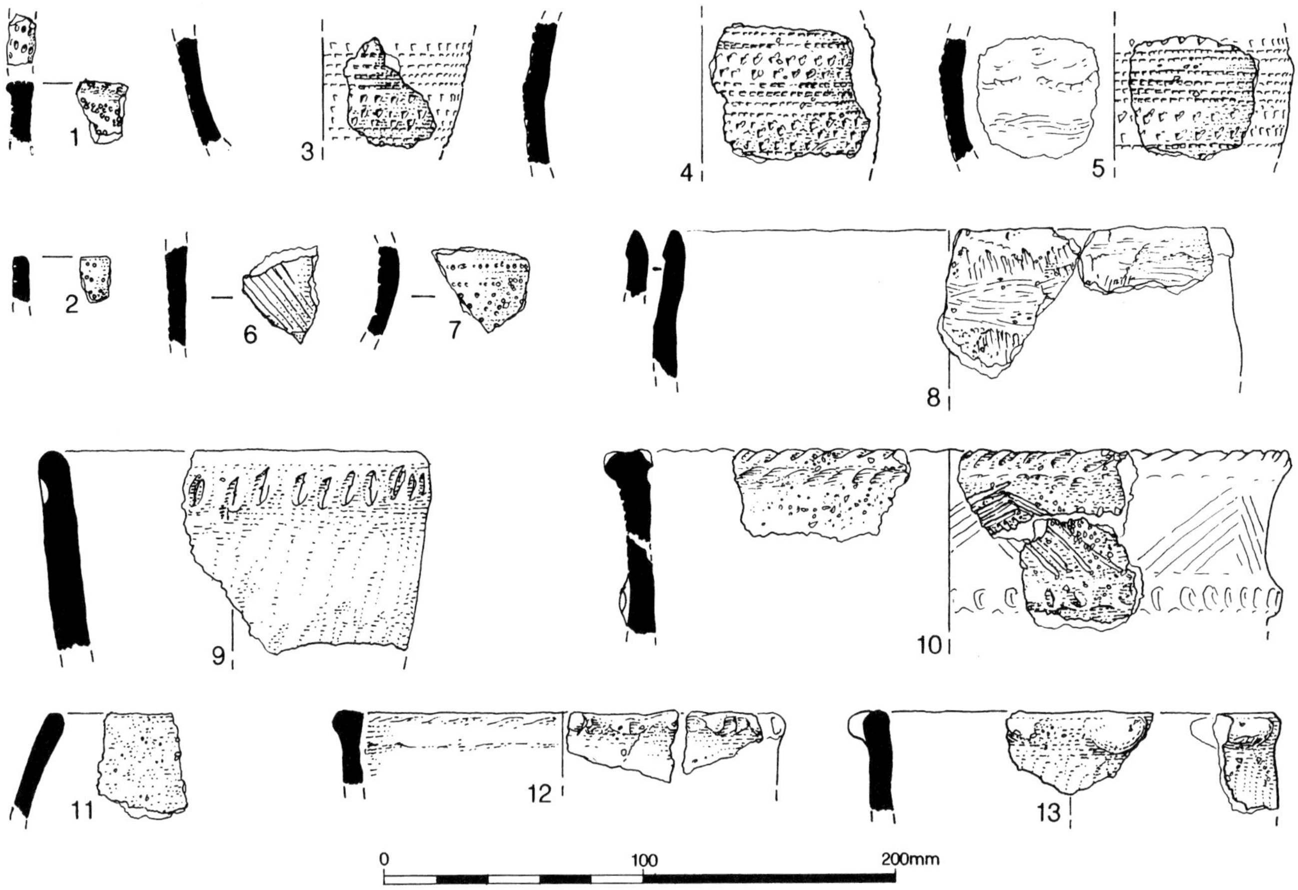

Figure 10.2 Willis's Field Barn (SRR 96): pottery

uncertain vessel form, but could be either from Barrel or Bucket Urn(s). Undecorated rims appear to derive from convex vessels of uncertain ceramic tradition, in grog-tempered fabrics (eg, Fig. 10.2, 8), and from at least one probable Globular Urn, identifiable from the relatively thin vessel walls and the well-sorted flint temper (Fig. 10.2, 11).

Chronology and affinities

This small group finds parallels amongst the Deverel-Rimbury assemblages of Wiltshire, such as those from Bishops Cannings Down and other sites on the Marlborough Downs (Gingell 1992). Traits from the Bishops Cannings Down assemblage which can be recognised in the Willis's Field Barn assemblage include the small quantity of Globular Urn material (represented by sherds in fabric FL19), the medium to large vessels of the Barrel Urn tradition, in calcite-tempered fabrics (LI 12 and LI 13), and a very small quantity of coarse flint-tempered sherds (fabric FL17), which could represent either Barrel or Bucket Urns. As at Bishops Cannings Down there is an emphasis on Barrel Urns (although here in calcite-tempered rather than shelly fabrics) at the expense of Bucket Urns. Globular Urns, comprising the 'fineware' component, are not common within either assemblage. There are, however, interesting variations between the two assemblages in terms of the division between 'heavy-duty' and 'everyday' wares. At Bishops Cannings Down the former comprised the Barrel Urns, made in fabrics deriving from locally outcropping Kimmeridgian Clay, while everyday wares occurred in the flint-tempered Bucket Urn fabrics. At Willis's Field Barn, the Barrel Urn tradition appears to supply both heavy-duty and everyday wares, with the former only marginally supplemented by possible Bucket Urns.

Distribution

The overwhelming majority of the Middle Bronze Age assemblage came from the recut (6066) of ditch 6004. There is insufficient material from the original ditch (and no diagnostic sherds) to examine the possibility of any ceramic sequence between the two features, but the range of fabric types is comparable and it seems that the whole assemblage represents a relative short time-span. Cross-context joins between upper and lower fills of recut 6066 suggests relatively rapid deposition of the pottery within this feature.

AC 1006

In addition, a number of sherds assigned tentatively to the Late Bronze Age/Early Iron Age, were recovered during the watching brief. They included one coarse flint-tempered body sherd from AC 1006 (context 15 in ditch 5 [6063]). These finds are not discussed further.

List of illustrated vessels (Fig. 10.2)

1. Rim of Peterborough Ware vessel; fabric FL1; PRN 3, context 6006, recut 6066
2. Rim of Beaker vessel; fabric GR1; PRN 34, context 6012, ditch 6004
3. Beaker vessel; comb decoration; fabric LI 3; PRN 1, context 6001, backfill of evaluation trench.
4. Beaker vessel; comb decoration; fabric LI 3; PRN 52, context 6048, pit 6047
5. Beaker vessel, comb decoration; fabric LI 3; PRN 39, context 6015, ditch 6004
6. Decorated incised sherd; fabric GR1; PRN 49, context 6033, ditch 6004
7. Beaker vessel; decorated; fabric GR1; PRN 32, context 6012, ditch 6004
8. Plain rim; fabric GR2; PRN 20/26, contexts 6008/6009, recut 6066
9. Barrel Urn rim; finger impressions below rim; fabric LI 2; PRN 15, context 6006, recut 6066
10. Bucket Urn rim; fabric LI 1; PRN 8, context 6006, recut 6066
11. Plain rim; fabric FL4; PRN 6, context 6006, recut 6066
12. Rusticated rim; fabric LI 2; PRN 16, context 6006, recut 6066
13. Rim with applied bosses; fabric LI 2; PRN 11, context 6006, recut 6066

Other finds
by Rachel Every

A total of 27 fragments (968 g) of stone was recovered. Two fragments of greensand were identified, respectively from pit 6047 and ditch 6004. These have worn surfaces and one is possibly part of a saddle quern. A sarsen quern fragment was recovered from recut 6066. A fragment of sandstone from ditch 6004 has possibly been utilised as a rubber. The remaining fragments consist of burnt and unutilised coarse sandstone fragments. None of them shows conclusive signs of working although some have flat surfaces suggestive of a derivation from quernstones.

Two fragments (19 g) of apparently unworked shale came from ditch 6004 and their presence here is of interest. Shale from the Kimmeridge deposits in Dorset was certainly reaching sites in Wiltshire in various forms (unworked pieces, rough-outs, and finished artefacts) in the Late Bronze Age (Wyles 2000, 210), but evidence for the earlier distribution of unworked shale, as here, appears to be lacking.

A worked bone point was recovered from ditch 6004. It has signs of wear on the tapered point but has snapped along the length it may have been used as a needle or point for weaving.

Five fragments of iron from recut 6066 consist of four unidentified fragments and a brooch. The latter object came from the surface of the recut. It is in poor condition, corroded and fragmentary, and comprises the straight bow and catchplate from what is probably a Nauheim derivative brooch of the 1st century AD.

Environment

Charred plant remains
by Alan J Clapham

Four samples were analysed – one from Late Neolithic–Early Bronze Age pit 6047, and three from Middle Bronze Age ditches 6063 and 6004 and recut 6066. The results are shown in Table 10.5.

Late Neolithic/Early Bronze Age

There were few remains from pit 6047 (context 6048). The dominance of the hazelnut shells suggests that this pit was used to store nuts or as a dump for the charred nutshells and indicates that hazelnuts were exploited by the local population. White campion (*Silene alba*) is a plant of both cultivated and waste ground.

Middle Bronze Age

Very few charred plant remains were recovered from samples from ditches 6063 and 6004 with cleavers

Table 10.5 Willis's Field Barn (SRR 96): charred plant remains

Period	*LN/EBA*		*MBA*	
Feature	*Pit 6047*	*Ditch 6063*	*Ditch 6004*	*Recut 6066*
Context	*6048*	*6031*	*6019*	*6014*
Sample	*6709*	*6715*	*6714*	*6711*
Size (l)	*15*	*11*	*10*	*15*
Vol. (ml)	*58*	*15*	*30*	*15*
Crops				
Triticum sp. indet., grain	–	–	–	1+1f
Triticum sp. indet., glume base	–	–	2	3
Hordeum vulgare hulled, grain	4	–	–	4
Avena sp., grain	–	–	–	1
Cerealia indet.	16f	3f	6f	89f
Culm node	1	–	–	–
Weeds				
Corylus avellana	427f	3f	2f	10f
Chenopodium album	–	–	–	4f
Silene alba	1	–	–	–
Vicia sp.	–	–	–	1f
Veronica hederifolia	–	–	–	2f
Galium aparine	–	2	2	–

(*Galium aparine*) probably representing a background flora alongside the cereal remains. The remains from recut 6066 (context 6014) are more varied and include one grain of oats (*Avena* sp.). Non-cultivated plant remains include fat-hen (*Chenopodium album*), vetch (*Vicia* sp.) and ivy-leaved speedwell (*Veronica hederifolia*). These remains may indicate that crop-processing waste had been dumped in the ditch. Hazelnuts were still an important part of the diet.

Charcoal

by Rowena Gale

The charcoal in Late Neolithic–Early Bronze Age pit 6047 (context 6048, sample 6709) was fairly firm in texture but too fragmented to include intact radial segments of roundwood. Taxa identified included oak (*Quercus* sp.) heartwood (3 residue fragments) and sapwood (1 fragment), ash (*Fraxinus excelsior*, 15 fragments), hazel (*Corylus avellana*, 3 fragments), and member/s of the hawthorn/*Sorbus* group (Pomoideae, 7 fragments).

Although the function of the pit is unknown, its fill (6048) included a range of domestic type debris suggesting that the charcoal originated from domestic fuel. The charcoal was too fragmented to assess the type of wood selected, ie, narrow roundwood or larger logs or billets, although the presence of oak heartwood suggests that fairly wide roundwood was probably included. All the species identified would have provided high-calorie fuel (Webster 1919; Porter 1990).

Relatively little is known about the extent and distribution of woodland on the chalklands of Salisbury Plain during the Late Neolithic–Early Bronze Age period. The frequency of earthworks and other features in this region suggests a fairly high density of settlements and, by implication, that the exploitation and/or clearance of woodland began early in the prehistoric period. Supporting environmental evidence, however, is still relatively sparse.

The taxa identified are characteristic of chalk downland. Fuel woods would have been gathered from the most convenient source close to the settlement or point of use. The more sheltered and humid aspects of the lower slopes were probably more wooded and supported taller species such as oak and ash, while the more exposed upper reaches were probably colonised by scrubby or shrubby species, such as hawthorn or hazel. Comparative evidence from elsewhere on Salisbury Plain has identified a similar, although sometimes wider, range of taxa. For example, charcoal from Early Bronze Age sites close to Stonehenge (Coneybury Henge, North Kite, Durrington Down Round Barrow) included oak, hazel, blackthorn (*Prunus spinosa*) and the Pomoideae group (Gale 1990); and in addition to the species named at Willis's Field Barn, a Bronze Age settlement at Dunch Hill, Tidworth, included maple (*Acer* sp.), willow (*Salix* sp.), or poplar (*Populus* sp.) (Gale 2006a). Charcoal from Beaker and Middle–Late Bronze Age features at Breach Hill identified the presence of oak, hazel, Pomoideae, willow/poplar and pine (*Pinus* sp.) (Gale 2006b).

Snails

by Michael J. Allen

Middle Bronze Age ditches 6063 and 6004 with recut 6066

No samples were taken for land snails from ditch 6063, although the flot of a large bulk sample from the basal primary fill (6031) did contain shells. This did not allow detailed analysis, but some indication of a mixed, and not wholly open downland landscape is provided. There is a mixture of typical open country species (*Pupilla muscorum*), catholic species (esp. *Trichia hispida*), and species common in shade, rock rubble, or decaying vegetation (*Discus rotundatus*, *Aegopinella* spp. and *Oxychilus cellarius*).

Ditch 6004 and its upper recut (6066) were sampled for land snails in a continuous column from section 6002, augmented by spot samples. The assemblage from the initial chalky infill is very sparse (10 shells), but open country and catholic species predominate and tend to indicate that the ditch was constructed in a cleared and established open downland environment. What is significant, however, is that chalk rubble primary fill (6035) and, to a lesser extent, the secondary fills (6019 and 6054) are dominated by shade-loving species, in particular *Vitrea contracta*, *Aeopinella nitidula*, and *Oxychilus cellarius*. Of these, *Vitrea* and *Oxychilus* commonly frequent loose rock-rubble habitats (Evans and Jones 1973) but are often found in ditches. The occurrence of these species in the primary fill indicates the close proximity of such habitats (see below). Other shade-loving species such as *Aegopinella*, are rare or absent in rock-rubble and, therefore, indicate the presence of shady habitats (Evans 1972). *Oxychilus cellarius* is found in leaf litter accumulating in ditches (Allen pers. obs.; *cf.* Bell *et al.* in press). Although the larger portion of these assemblages from the primary fills can be attributed to rock-rubble habitats, the lack of open-country species and presence of shade-loving species that are not common in rock-rubble indicate the presence of shady refugia in, or close to, the ditch.

Similar assemblages prevail throughout the secondary fills (contexts 6054 and 6019), where there is no evidence for rock-rubble in either the context or in the coarse particle size data. Here, therefore, the predominantly shade-loving elements and intermediate species that inhabit more mesic environments suggest local shady refuges in the ditch and bank-side and the accumulation of decaying leaf litter. Much of this may reflect the presence of a large unkempt and ungrazed bank as seen, for instance, around the reconstruction of the Pimperne Iron Age house at the Butser Experimental Farm. The wider nature of an unkempt downland is indicated by the very low pro-portions of open country species (*c.* 10–15%).

The upper secondary fill (context 6054) contains a ten-fold increase in shells (571) and a concomitant expansion of open country species. Subtle changes in the assemblage composition include an increase of intermediate species which enjoy ungrazed grassland (*Carychium tridentatum*) and species common in colonising vegetation in ditches, that is Evans' *Punctum* group (Evans 1972, 195: *Punctum pygmaeum* and *Vitrina pellucida*), all increase. Such changes indicate more open conditions locally, but the presence of long grassland in the ditch or its bankside edges.

In contrast, the fills of ditch recut 6066 were almost devoid of shells (<5 examples each of *Carychium* sp., *Pupilla muscorum* and *Vallonia* spp.) but the presence of only open country species and the colluvial and ploughwash nature of its fills tend to suggest a more open, local vegetation with a bare ditch and bank.

Table 10.6 Willis's Field Barn (SRR 96): land molluscs from Middle Bronze Age ditch 6004

Context	*6055*	*6035*		*6019*	*6054*	*6021*
Sample	*6701*	*6702*	*6703*	*6704*	*6705*	*6706*
Depth (cm)	*110–115*	*95–105*	*85–95*	*70–77*	*61–68*	*45–55*
Wt (g)	*1500*	*1500*	*1500*	*1500*	*1500*	*1500*
Pomatias elegans (Müller)	–	–	–	+	–	1
Carychium tridentatum (Risso)	–	2	1	–	10	51
Carychium spp.	–	3	2	1	2	26
Cochlicopa lubrica (Müller)	–	–	–	–	–	3
Cochlicopa spp.	–	2	–	1	1	6
Vertigo cf. *pygmaea* (Draparnaud)	–	–	–	1	–	1
Pupilla muscorum (Linnaeus)	–	–	–	1	–	2
Vallonia costata (Müller)	4	9	6	4	5	118
Vallonia excentrica (Sterki)	1	1	2	1	–	11
Vallonia spp.	–	–	–	–	–	5
Ena spp.	–	+	–	–	–	–
Ena obscura (Müller)	–	–	–	–	–	7
Punctum pygmaeum (Draparnaud)	–	3	2	3	–	4
Vitrina pellucida (Müller)	1	6	2	–	3	31
Vitrea chrystallina (Müller)	–	6	1	–	–	6
Vitrea contracta (Westerlund)	1	19	20	10	22	82
Aegopinella pura (Alder)	–	1	1	–	3	13
Aegopinella nitidula (Draparnaud	–	11	5	6	6	24
Oxychilus cellarius (Müller)	–	7	4	3	3	29
Limacidae	–	11	14	18	3	52
Ceciliodes acicula (Müller)	1	1	–	1	–	–
Clausilia bidentata (Ström)	–	–	–	–	2	3
Helicella itala (Linnaeus)	–	1	–	3	2	23
Trichia hispida (Linnaeus)	3	9	6	4	4	66
Cepaea hortensis (Müller)	–	–	–	1	–	–
Cepaea/Arianta spp.	5	+	1	+	2	7
Taxa		14	12	13	13	20
Total	10	91	67	57	68	571

Discussion

In the primary fills it is clear that the presence of shade-loving fauna is a consequence of the coarse and loose chalk rubble fill. Their rapid arrival in the ditch, probably within a few seasons of weathering, indicates the very close proximity of either other rock-rubble habitats or, more likely, established shady environments. By contrast, in the secondary fills, much of the shade-loving element is a result of longer vegetation and shrubs, but these too may have been heavily influenced by the ditch and bankside environment. Nevertheless, we can assume that environments conducive to the presence of these species existed well beyond the ditch and, as a consequence, we can envisage a generally open but not grazed nor arable landscape, perhaps comprising coarse grassland and shrubs of hawthorn or juniper.

The ditch and its associated snail assemblage is typical of many later Bronze Age ditches and can readily find parallels among a number of sites elsewhere on Salisbury Plain (see for instance the Wessex Linear Ditch project; Bradley *et al.* 1994).

Animal bone

by Pippa Smith

This excavation yielded an assemblage of 385 animal bones, of which 135 were identified to species. Domesticates are strongly represented, with only three bones coming from wild species (red and roe deer). The assemblage is in generally good condition although fragmentary. Two complete cattle skulls were recovered; one from ditch 6004 and one from the recut of ditch terminal 6010, along with two articulated cattle mandibles and four articulated cattle bones from the left hind leg (all from ditch 6004). A group of articulated cattle vertebrae was also found in terminal 6010. The presence of complete cattle skulls and articulated bones hints at more formalised disposal of animal bones but, given the limited nature of the excavation it is difficult to draw firm conclusions.

Discussion

Neolithic to Early Bronze Age activity is represented by a small quantity of residual finds and a single feature, pit 6047, of Beaker date (broadly 2400–1600 cal BC). The recovery of residual material from the later ditches may suggest that more extensive activity of this date was occurring in this area. The finds and environmental evidence provide few clues, however, as to the nature of that activity, other than suggesting a possibly domestic context. Charcoal from the primary fill (6048) of pit 6047 (oak, ash, hazel, and hawthorn) probably represents domestic fuel and a small amount of charred plant remains, including hazelnut shell fragments and cereal grains, reflect the use of both wild and cultivated food resources. Molluscs from the same feature indicated a mixed, not wholly open, downland landscape.

Ditch 6063 is probably dated by a single late prehistoric sherd found during the watching brief, rather than two Early Bronze Age sherds (and some of the worked flint, see Harding above) recovered from it during the excavation. It had fully silted when it was cut by ditch 6004/6010, suggesting that it represents some form of land boundary pre-dating the Middle Bronze Age enclosure.

The Middle Bronze Age ditch appears typical of many later Bronze Age enclosure ditches, there being a number of parallels elsewhere on Salisbury Plain (eg, Bradley *et al.* 1994; McOmish *et al.* 2002). The finds, including pottery, quern fragments, a sandstone rubber (from the ditch), a bone point, animal bone, worked flints, and burnt flint, suggest domestic activity, while the charred plant remains, including wheat, hulled barley, and oats, provide evidence for cereal cultivation. The deposits of animal bone in the ditch are notable, particularly in light of the Middle Bronze Age animal burial in a ditch at South of Foxtrot Crossing (Chapter 12). Molluscan evidence indicates that the enclosure was constructed in cleared and established downland, although with shady areas in the immediate vicinity.

AC 1007

Some 280 m to the north-east, a south-west–north-east aligned ditch (2) was recorded for over 55 m, along with two shallow pits (6 and 15), during the watching brief. Pit 15 produced 11 flint-tempered sherds. They are all small and abraded and, with the exception of one small upright rim, bear slight finger-impressions. A little worked flint and animal bone was also recovered from this pit. Four coarse sandy sherds came from context 3.

SRR 97

A 200 m length of the spur road, 640 m to the south-west of the site, was stripped to investigate possible settlement activity suggested by the presence of two supposed pits recorded during the evaluation. No pits were encountered and the only features recorded were two shallow, undated gullies associated with an extant hedgeline and a single tree hollow.

West of Knook Castle Watching Brief (AC 1005)

A number of approximately north–south aligned gullies and a substantial ditch were recorded during topsoil stripping over a length of some 500 m (chainage 8000–8500) immediately west of Knook Castle Iron Age hillfort and the adjacent Romano-British nucleated settlement (see Chapter 1). The SRR runs here approximately parallel to the Old Ditch Wessex Linear earthwork, and crosses a number of field boundaries recorded from aerial photographs. The site occupies the base of a dry coombe and the east-facing slope to its west.

Results

The most westerly feature, gully 9, was 0.9 m wide and 0.35 m deep at the north with moderately steep, slightly convex sides and a concave base. To the south it narrowed and ended at a rounded terminal. Two silty fills were recorded at the north (11 primary and 10 upper fill). No finds were recovered, but the gully's orientation and position corresponds with a ditch (SMR ST94SE644) recorded from aerial photographs.

Some 90 m to the east, the profile of ditch 17 had been largely truncated by a substantial recut (24) 3.8 m wide and 1.4 m deep, leaving only a single fill (25) producing no finds. Of the three fills in the recut (20, 19, and 18), only the secondary fill (19) produced finds – five fragments of animal bone. These features correspond with a ditch (SMR ST94SE631) recorded from aerial photographs.

A further 40 m to the east, ditch 7 was 2.6 m wide and 0.2 m deep, with moderately steep straight sides and a flattish base. The single fill (8) was a mid-brown compacted silty clay with moderate small chalk fragments and sparse small flint fragments. It contained three sherds of Romano-British pottery, comprising one fine sandy sherd, one moderately coarse oxidised sandy sherd, and one Black Burnished ware sherd.

Two similar parallel gullies (1 and 3), 20 m apart, were recorded a further 90–110 m further east, both with moderately steep sides merging with a concave base. Gully 1 which, like gully 9, ended at a rounded terminal at the south, was *c.* 1 m wide and 0.1 m deep, its fill (2) of pale brown clayey silt producing no finds. Gully 3 was 0.7 m wide and 0.25 m deep with a fill (4) of very pale brown compacted calcareous silt clay, containing two fine sandy sherds of Romano-British pottery.

The most easterly features were a pair of identical, parallel cuts (12 and 14), *c.* 0.5 m wide and 0.2 m deep with steep straight sides and flat bases, which ran south-west–north-east across the route of the SRR near the base of the dry coombe. They had similar fills comprising thin primary fill of degraded chalk and upper fills of friable greyish–brown silty loam, the only find being a fragment of animal bone from cut 14. They were interpreted as probably modern tank tracks, although it may be significant that their alignment corresponds to that of parallel linear features recorded aerial photographs (SMR ST94SE623) some 90 m to the north-east to the north of the Old Ditch earthwork.

Discussion

The site lies immediately west of a north–south boundary, corresponding to the line of the Old Ditch linear earthwork which turns sharply to the north at this point and along which the Romano-British nucleated settlement at Knook Down West (McOmish *et al.* 2002, 95–8, figs 4.11–12), appears to have been laid out. The line is now followed by a modern track and it defines the western boundary of an area of intensive 'Celtic' fields around the Knook Castle hillfort and the Romano-British settlement. It is unclear whether the apparent absence of a similar field system to the west of the boundary reflects a difference in land-use contemporary with these settlements or of more recent times with cultivation essentially flattening earlier features. However, with the exception of cuts 12 and 14, most of the features recorded on this site were shallow gullies and may represent the truncated remnants of once-deeper features, possibly Romano-British field boundaries. The large recut ditch (17) was undated, although its size and profile is comparable to Romano-British ditches elsewhere on Salisbury Plain (Fulford *et al.* 2006).

Chapter 11
Knook Castle to Imber Valley

East of Knook Castle Excavation (SRR 86) and South and East of Knook Castle Strip-and-record (SRR 41)

The excavation area (chainage 8870–8950) was approximately 100 m east-south-east of Knook Castle (Fig. 8.1), lying on an east facing slope at 162–164 m aOD, the natural geology being weathered Upper Chalk (BGS 1985). The area, 80 m long (east–west) and 8 m wide (640 m^2), was selected on the basis of a series of features (interpreted as pits) and a lynchet identified during the evaluation. Subsequently, a 1 km length of the route, running east from near the south-west corner of Knook Castle (chainage 8620–9620) was subject to strip-and-record, focusing on the relict field systems in this area.

Results

Excavation

Upon investigation, only two archaeological features – a small hearth (2004) and a positive lynchet (2005) – were identified, the other features identified during the evaluation proving to be either tree throws or solution hollows.

Feature 2004, continuing beyond the northern edge of the excavation area, was *c.* 0.9 m in diameter and 0.25 m deep, with steep concave sides and base. Its two fills produced two flint flakes and a large quantity of burnt flint, but no datable finds. A few patches of the surrounding chalk bedrock appeared to have been affected by heat, suggesting that it was a small hearth.

The positive lynchet (2005) ran for 46 m across the excavation area, continuing across the slope beyond its eastern edge. It consisted of a deposit of a dark brown silty loam with common flint and chalk inclusions, the coarser material being more abundant towards the base. The deposit was thickest (0.45 m) *c.* 22 m from the eastern end of the site, thinning to 0.3 m at the eastern end. It produced one small flint-tempered body sherd of probable Late Bronze Age date and a small amount of worked and burnt flint.

Strip-and-record

At the western end of the strip-and-record area, a large, approximately north–south, ditch (41006) was recorded aligned on the south-west corner of Knook Castle. It produced a single sherd of probably Late Bronze Age flint-tempered pottery (from context 41009). A smaller, parallel ditch (41003) lay to its west. A north–south ditch at this location is recorded in the SMR forming part of an extensive field system (ST94SE623).

A number of small gullies, one (41020) producing three small sherds of probably residual Neolithic pottery, were recorded in the area of field systems to the east, although they were not all aligned with the locations of the field banks, which were poorly-preserved. Two partially ploughed-out positive lynchets were also recorded with no evidence for associated revetments or retaining structures.

A group of four pits (41022, 41027, 41036, 41041) was excavated at the eastern end of the strip-and-record area, containing prehistoric pottery and quantities of worked flint as well as evidence for burning. Pit 41022 (contexts 41023, 41024, and 41039) contained significant quantities of Neolithic pottery (as well as five Late Bronze Age sherds) together with worked flint and a quantity of carbonised cereal grain. The other pits may be contemporary with the later prehistoric activity at Knook Castle, sherds from pit 41027 being of Late Bronze Age and Iron Age date, while pit 41041 contained a single Romano-British sherd. Several tree hollows were also recorded.

Finds

Flint

by Matt Leivers

The bulk of the assemblage from the strip-and-record (1151/1188 pieces) was recovered from pit 41022, which also contained portions of five Early Neolithic pots (Table 11.1). Given this, it is evident that the lithics represent a closed group of this date, although in the absence of the pottery the flint would have been only very broadly datable. Mostly consisting of flake debitage, the assemblage is characterised by rather broad flakes which fall predominantly into two sorts: those with irregularly arranged dorsal scars and those with dorsal scars indicating blade removal. There are only a very small number of blades, blade-like flakes, and bladelets present in the pit. This is also true of cores (a single blade core), primary flakes (less than 1%), crested or other core preparation pieces (no examples), and retouched tools (four scrapers). The

Table 11.1 Knook Castle and East of Knook Castle (SRR 41): worked flint

Feature	*Context*	*1*	*2*	*3*	*4*	*5*	*6*	*7*
Gully 41020	41021	–	–	–	2	–	–	–
Pit 41022	41023	–	3	–	26	6	–	–
	41024	50	2	2	540	329	–	4
	41039	6	–	–	130	52	1	–
Pit 41027	41028	–	–	–	10	3	–	–
Pit 41036	41037	–	–	–	15	7	–	–
Total		56	5	2	723	397	1	4

Key: 1 = debitage; 2 = blades; 3 = bladelets; 4 = flakes; 5 = broken flakes; 6= cores; 7 = scrapers

assemblage evidently consists of debitage from the reduction of previously prepared cores (secondary and tertiary flakes and trimming flakes) and the absence of chips particularly suggests that the material has been collected and placed deliberately in the pit. The cores themselves, and the products of the knapping (blades and the tools presumably made from them; possibly core tools) are not present. In terms of technology, both soft and hard hammers are attested; core platforms seem to have been prepared in some instances, and there was a general, although not universal, maintenance of edge angle. The assemblage is, on the whole, in a very fresh condition, still sharp and with very limited edge damage, although almost universally patinated to a pale grey.

Pottery

by Moira Laidlaw

The small pottery assemblage from the strip-and-record comprises an interesting group of at least five Neolithic vessels. Smaller quantities of Late Bronze Age and Iron Age pottery were also present. A single small Romano-British sherd from pit 41041 is not discussed further.

Neolithic

At least five Neolithic vessels were recovered from pit 41022, comprising one small cup/bowl and four bowls. Most sherds are small but several are large and in a relatively good condition. The cup has a plain inturned rim and occurs in the fine flint-tempered fabric, FL3 (Fig. 11.1, 1). The bowls include one open straight-sided bowl with a rolled rim, one with an upright, slightly rolled rim, and one with an open plain rounded rim, and all occur in the shell-tempered fabric SH1 (Fig. 11.1, 2–4). The remaining bowl is in the oolitic limestone-tempered fabric LI1 and has a curved profile and inturned plain rounded rim (Fig. 11.1, 5). A further three very small limestone-tempered sherds were recovered from gully 41020.

This group of vessels is comparable to Early Neolithic undecorated bowls of the Hembury or South-Western Style and the flint and shell-tempered fabric types fit within the two major fabric groups of the region, of which shell-tempered fabrics are most commonly represented (Cleal 1995). Flint would have been easily accessible as a tempering agent. Shell-tempered vessels, however, are likely either to have been produced further afield or the shell inclusions were brought to a production site, possibly derived from the Kimmeridge Clay deposits in the area. Tomalin records that shell occurs as exposed areas beneath the Lower Greensand at the foot of the chalk downs and also in faults near the mouths of the Vales of Wardour and Pewsey (Tomalin 1992).

Other comparable Early Neolithic pottery includes bowls with simple inturned rims from Burderop Down, Marlborough Downs and, although the group of vessels from Knook Castle lacks decorated or carinated examples, a similarly broad 4th millennium BC date may be postulated (Cleal 1992, fig. 49). Other assemblages with similar vessel forms and fabric types include pottery recovered from an area outside Windmill Hill (Hamilton 2000), heavy rimmed bowls from King Barrow Ridge, barrow G39, which are noted as being a characteristic feature of the Windmill Hill or decorated style of central southern England (Cleal 1994, fig. 7, 21–3), material from the pre-barrow occupation at Wilsford cum Lake (Smith 1991), and from Horslip long barrow (Ashbee *et al.* 1979, fig. 8, P1–9), all in Wiltshire.

Late Bronze Age

A small quantity of flint-tempered body sherds is attributed to the Late Bronze Age period on the basis of fabric type and comprise two sherds in the coarse flint-tempered fabric FL1 and five in the finer flint-tempered fabric FL2. The coarse sherds were recovered from ditch 41009 with one from pit 41022. Four sherds in Fabric FL2 were also found in pit 41022 and one in pit 41027. A further single sherd was recovered during the excavation from lynchet 2005.

Iron Age

A total of 14 sherds was found in pit 41027 comprising 10 in the shell-tempered fabric SH2, three body sherds in fabric SH1 and one flint-tempered sherd in fabric FL2. It is likely that the SH1 and FL2 sherds are residual. Those in the well-finished fabric SH2 are derived from the same vessel, a slack-shouldered jar with a slight neck constriction and everted rim (Fig. 11.1, 6). The fabric matches that of Peacock's group 4 Glastonbury Wares with a possible Jurassic origin (1968). The vessel is comparable to Middle Iron examples such as those in the Yarnbury-Highfield style (Cunliffe 1991, fig A:16,9) and JC2 type jars from ceramic phases 7 and 8 at South Cadbury (Woodward 2000, fig, 152).

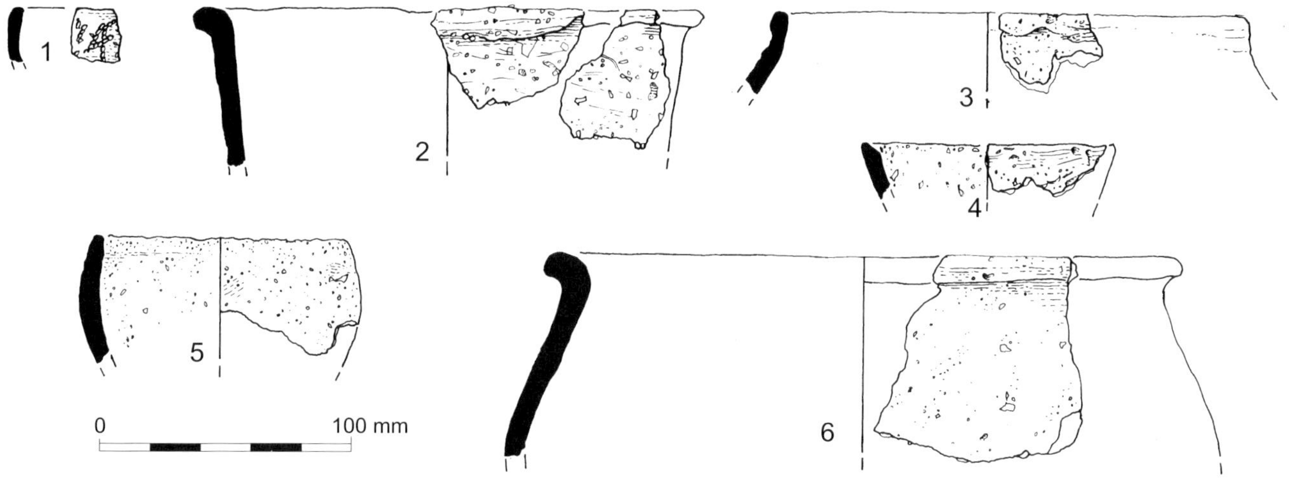

Figure 11.1 South and East of Knook Castle (SRR 41): pottery

List of illustrated vessels (Fig. 11.1)

1. Early Neolithic; plain inturned rim from small cup; fabric FL3; context 41023
2. Early Neolithic; four rolled rim sherds from open straight sided bowl; fabric SH1; context 41024
3. Early Neolithic; two upright slightly rolled rims from a bowl; fabric SH1; context 41023
4. Early Neolithic; two plain rounded rim sherds from an open bowl; fabric SH1; context 41024
5. Early Neolithic; four inturned plain rounded rims from a closed bowl; fabric LI1; context 41024
6. Middle Iron Age; everted rim and three joining body sherds from a slack-shouldered jar; fabric SH2; context 41027

Discussion

The small pit containing Neolithic flints and pottery from five vessels and carbonised grain is of uncertain, but possibly symbolic and ritual, function. Pits are typical contexts for such deposits, although all these materials could be found together within a domestic context and further sherds and flints were found nearby, either residual in later contexts or incorporated within the upper fills of natural features. Neolithic activity is represented in the wider area by the Knook long barrow to the north-west. The group of pits indicates small-scale activity of probable Late Bronze Age and Iron Age date. This may be contemporary with activity at Knook Castle.

This section of the route crosses a landscape of intense archaeological activity, as represented particularly by the extensive field systems around Knook Castle Iron Age hillfort and the Knook Down West and Knook Down East Romano-British nucleated settlements (McOmish *et al.* 2002, 95–8). While the regular layout of these field systems suggests that they were closely associated with the settlements it is possible that they represent the reworking and reorganisation of earlier, possibly Iron Age or even Bronze Age, systems. However, only limited direct evidence for these periods was found.

East of Quebec Barn Excavation (SRR 85) and North-East of Knook Castle Strip-and-record (SRR 48, 48/2)

The site, some 2 km west of the village of Chitterne lay, at 140.5–142 m aOD, on the north-facing slope of a large dry valley, the natural geology being heavily weathered Upper Chalk with frequent solution hollows and periglacial striations (BGS 1985). The initial stage of work at this site involved the machine excavation of a 325 m long evaluation trench, revealing three Late Bronze Age features, one of which, a small heavily truncated pit (1003), was in an isolated position. At the north-east end of the trench, an area 50 m long (south-west–north-east) and 8.5 m wide (425 m^2) (chainage 9860–9910) was selected for excavation on the basis of the other two features (Fig. 11.2).

Subsequently, a *c.* 260 m long section of the route (chainage 10038–10300), starting 130 m to the north of the excavation area and crossing the head of the dry valley, was subject to strip-and-record (SRR 48). This revealed, among a small number of other features, a large, deep circular feature, possibly a prehistoric shaft (*c.* chainage 10090 – Fig. 11.4). As this was considered to be of high potential, the route was re-aligned 20 m to the west, leading to a second stage of strip-and-record (SRR 48/2) at this point of the route.

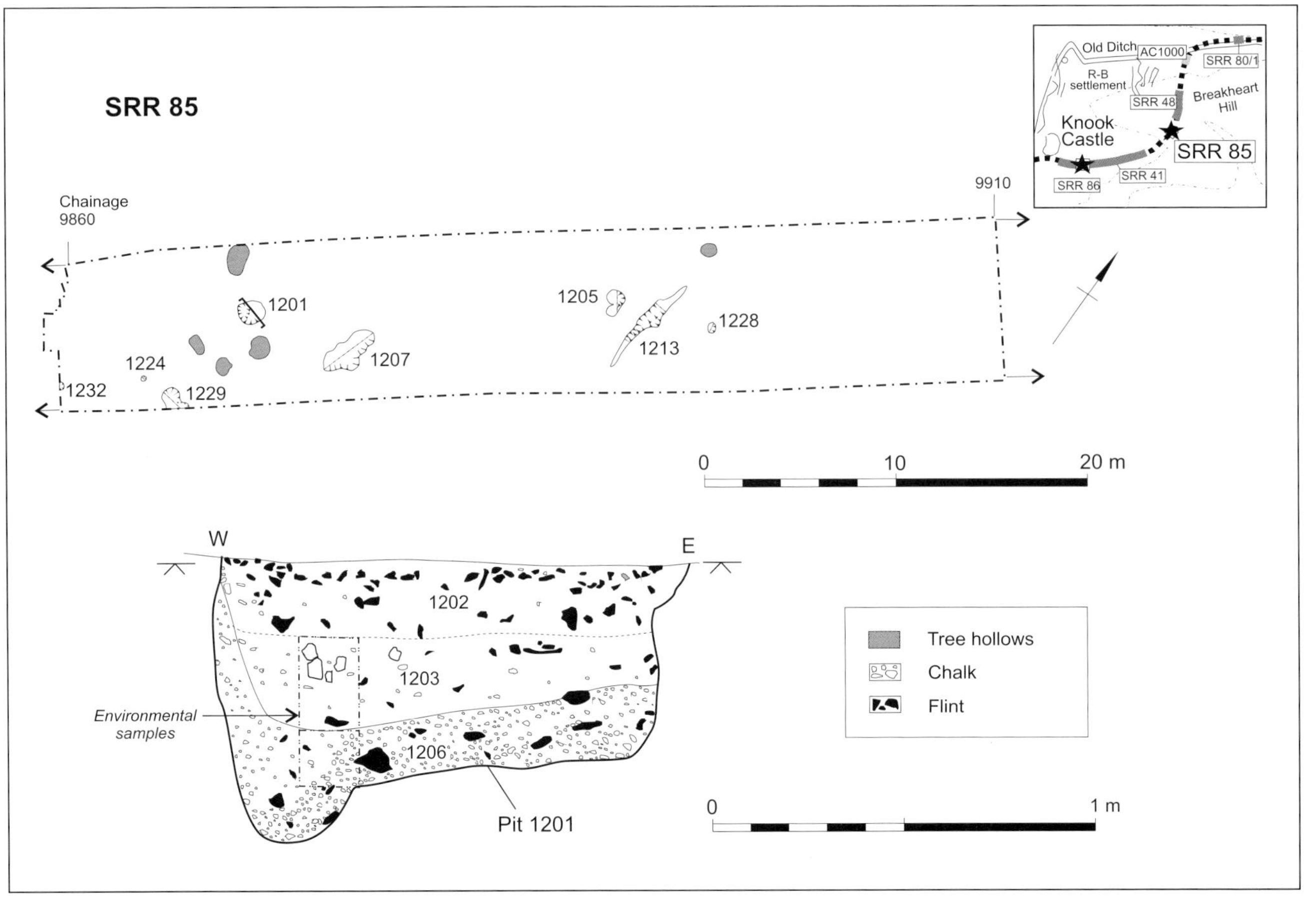

Figure 11.2 East of Quebec Barn (SRR 85) and sections of pit 1201 and ditch 6007

Results

Excavation

Following the mechanical removal of the topsoil, during which small quantities of Late Bronze Age pottery, worked flint, and possible quernstone fragments were recovered, 13 features were investigated. These included two pits (1201, 1205), two post-holes (1224, 1232), a possible hearth (1228), and a short, irregular gully (1213), all of probable Late Bronze Age date (1100–700 cal BC), as well as a number of natural features, some of which, particularly tree hollows 1207 and 1229 (Fig. 11.2), produced material of a similar date.

The largest number of finds came from sub-circular pit 1201. This was 1.4 m long, 1.1 m wide, and up to 0.76 m deep with irregular, vertical sides and a very irregular base. Its three fills produced a quantity of Late Bronze Age pottery including, from its lowest fill (1206), diagnostic sherds from a barrel-shaped jar (Fig. 11.4, 1) and a bucket-shaped vessel with a post-firing perforation below the rim (Fig. 11.4, 2). Worked flints (including flakes, cores, and a piercer), animal bone, burnt flint, and non-local stone were also recovered. The worked flint was characterised by large, unprepared hard-hammer struck flakes with low angles of percussion and the cores were unsystematic pieces typical of the Late Bronze Age.

Similar pottery and worked and burnt flint, but in smaller quantities, were recovered from pit 1205, an irregular feature (possibly two small intercutting pits, although with a single fill) 18 m to the north-east. This was 1.2 m long, 1 m wide, and up to 0.3 m deep with moderately steep, irregular sides and base.

Immediately to its north-west was a length of irregular gully (1213), 5.2 m long, up to 1 m wide and 0.4 m deep, with steep sides and an irregular base. It produced a concentration of Late Bronze Age pottery, possibly from a single vessel, from towards its southern end (1220), with further sherds elsewhere along its length. Diagnostic sherds from 1220 include the rim from a barrel-shaped jar (Fig. 11.4, 3). In addition, three intrusive sherds of Romano-British pottery were recovered from the upper 0.1 m of the fill. The irregular form of the feature and the combination of finds suggest that a Late Bronze Age gully had been subsequently disturbed, possibly by tree roots or animal burrowing, incorporating the Romano-British pottery within the fill.

A small sub-circular feature (1228), 0.5 m long, 0.3 m wide, and 0.07 m deep, with gently sloping

Table 11.2 East of Quebec Barn (SRR 85): finds totals by feature: no./wt (g)

Feature	*Burnt flint*	*Worked flint*	*LBA pottery*	*R-B pottery*	*Stone*
Topsoil	–	3/55	19/154	–	3/429
Pit 1002	–	3/22	6/6	–	–
Pit 1201	64/1159	63/1167	156/1072	–	13/1128
?Pit 1205	3/108	3/11	29/95	–	–
Tree throw 1207	2/20	1/4	19/30	–	–
?Gully 1213	7/411	8/252	159/912	4/28	–
Solution hollow 1217	2/14	–	–	–	–
Post-hole 1224	–	–	1/13	–	–
Natural feature 1225	–	7/60	–	–	–
?Hearth 1228	–	–	–	–	1/262
Pit/tree throw 1229	10/270	8/62	23/93	–	–
?Post-hole 1232	–	–	16/26	–	–
Pit/root-hole 1233	3/38	3/22	3/13	–	–
Total	91/2020	99/1655	431/2414	4/28	17/1819

straight sides and a flat base was excavated 2 m north of gully 1213. It contained a single dark yellowish-brown fill comprising *c.* 40% heat-affected chalk fragments. However, as there was no charcoal in the fill and the surrounding chalk bedrock did not appear to have been affected by heat, there remains doubt as to its interpretation as a hearth. It produced a single quernstone fragment but no datable finds.

The only other relatively undisturbed features were two post-holes (1224 and 1232), both containing small quantities of Late Bronze Age pottery. Both were circular and 0.3 m in diameter, lying 4 m apart at the south-western end of the site.

Strip-and-record

Approximately 300 m to the north, (at chainage 10077), a large, deep, circular pit (48007) was recorded at the base of the valley head, sealed by a colluvial deposit. It was *c.* 7 m in diameter at the top, with very steeply sloping upper sides becoming near vertical and *c.* 3.5 m wide at the limit of excavation, at a depth of 1.8 m (further excavation was precluded on health and safety grounds) (Fig. 11.3). Finds from the upper fills include Late Bronze Age/Early Iron Age and Romano-British pottery and worked flint. Immediately to its east and also sealed by the colluvium, was a small elongated pit (48008) containing burnt flint and carbonised seeds.

A number of tree hollows were also recorded. Two on the original road alignment (48003 and 48005) both yielded worked and burnt flint, but tree hollow 48004 also contained five sherds of Neolithic pottery (context 48003), including three Middle Neolithic Peterborough Ware sherds, as well as one of Late Iron Age/Early Roman and a sherd of samian. Two tree hollows (48812 and 48815) on the realigned road section, again contained worked and burnt flint.

At chainage 10128 there was a tree hollow (48812), which had been cut by a small pit (48810) containing a large portion of a Peterborough Ware jar of Middle Neolithic date and a small assemblage of worked flint including flakes, a retouched flake and a multi-platform core (context 48/2(811)). A little burnt unworked flint (8 pieces weighing 208 g) was also recovered from this feature.

The end of a poorly-preserved, undated contour lynchet (48038), aligned east–west, was recorded close to the large pit, with another 50 m to the north (48001). A third lynchet (48801) was recorded on the realigned section of the road.

Finds

Excavation

The site produced moderate quantities of finds, consisting mainly of flint (burnt and worked), pottery, and a small quantity of potentially worked or utilised stone. Table 11.2 presents finds totals by context.

Flint

by Phil Harding

The flint assemblage has been quantified and the results tabulated by phase in Table 11.3. The assemblage comprises groups of stratified material from Late Bronze Age pits 1002, 1201, and 1205, with material also from Late Bronze Age gully 1213. The remaining material comprises small groups of flint from the upper levels of tree throws, hollows, and irregular pits which were thought to be natural. There is a clear distinction between the condition of the flint from the Late Bronze Age features, which is unpatinated, and material from elsewhere, which is usually patinated.

Most of the Late Bronze Age material was recovered from pit 1201. It is characterised by large, unprepared hard-hammer struck flakes with low angles of percussion. The accompanying cores, including one from gully 1213, are unsystematic pieces and are typical of those found in Late Bronze Age industries.

The two retouched tools from pit 1201 include a piercer which are also more prevalent in flint industries of this date. The patinated flakes demonstrate a higher level of core control including platform abrasion and are likely to represent activity in the area of Neolithic or Early Bronze Age date.

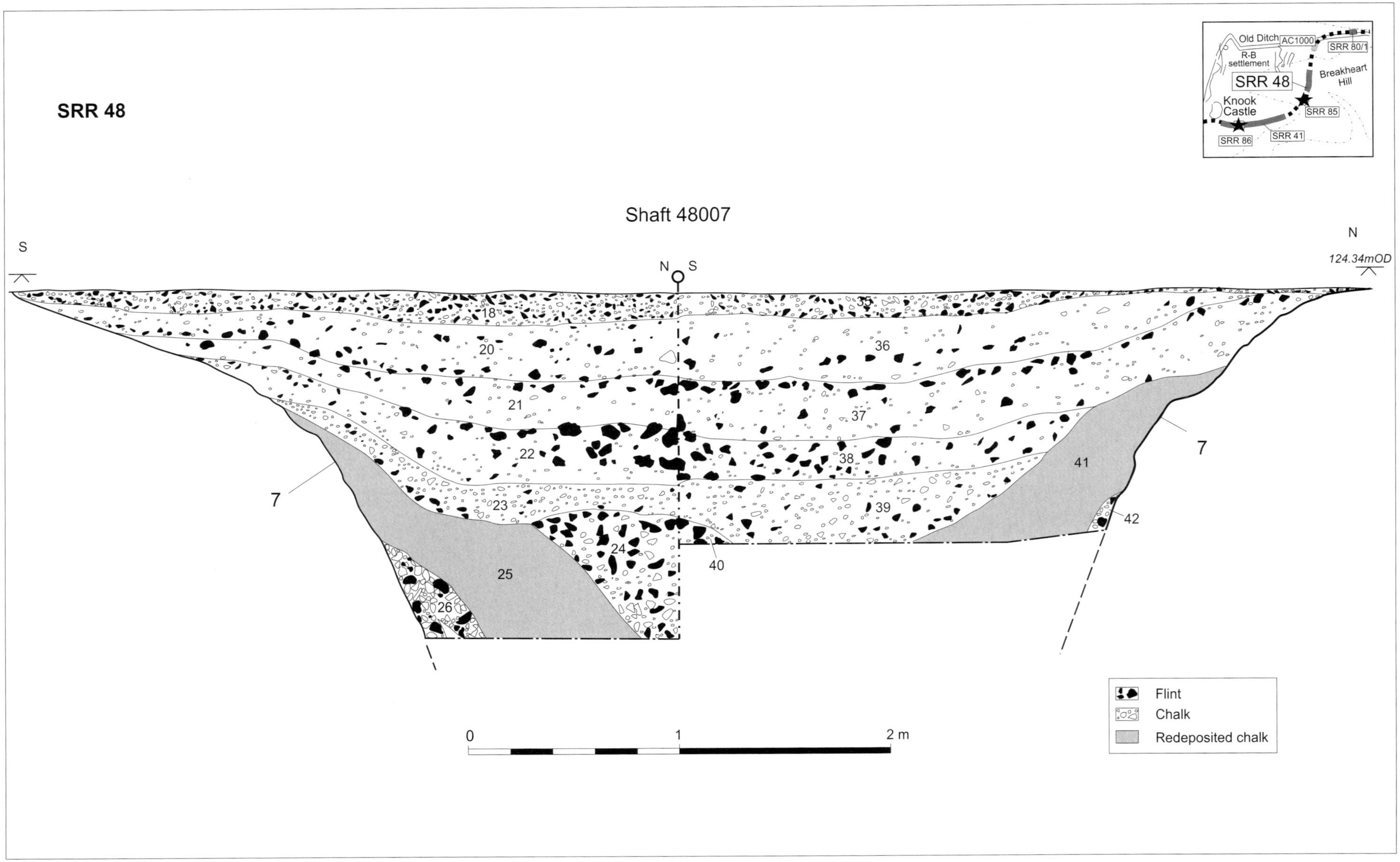

Figure 11.3 North-east of Knook Castle (SRR 48): section of top of pit/shaft 48007

Table 11.3 East of Quebec Barn (SRR 85): flint by context

	1	*2*	*3*	*4*	*5*	*Comment*
Late Bronze Age						
Pit 1002	–	–	2	1	–	
Pit 1201	3	4	32	27	2	1 core on cylinder; 1 single platform core; 1 crested rejuv. flake; 1 flake bifacially ret. on 1 edge; 1 piercer
Pit 1205	–	–	1	2	–	
Gully 1213	1	–	6	1	–	single platform core with prepared platform
Undated						
Topsoil/unstrat.	–	–	4	6	–	
Tree throw 1207	–	–	–	1	–	
Tree throw 1229	–	–	7	–	–	
Pit/hollow 1233	–	–	2	1	–	
Total	4	4	54	39	2	

Key:
1 = cores; 2 = broken cores; 3 = flakes; 4 = broken flakes; 5 = tools

Pottery
by Rachel Every

The pottery assemblage consists of 435 sherds (2442 g), mainly Late Bronze Age in date with just four sherds (28 g) of Romano-British material; only the prehistoric material is discussed here. Four broad fabric groups were identified on the basis of dominant inclusion types – flint-tempered fabrics (Group FL), sandy fabrics (Group QU), calcareous-tempered fabrics (Group CH), and a group with unidentified inclusions (Group D). These groups were then sub-divided into nine separate fabric types based on the range and coarseness of the inclusions present. Fabric totals are presented in Table 11.4 (see Appendix for fabric descriptions).

Sherds were recovered from pits 1201, 1205, 1229, and 1233, post-holes 1232 and 1224, gully 1213, tree throw 1207, and from the topsoil – the two largest groups came from gully 1213 (159 sherds) and pit 1201 (156 sherds). The condition varies; much of the assemblage comprises relatively small sherds with surface and edge abrasion (mean sherd weight overall is 5.6 g), although sherds from pit 1201 are larger and fresher (mean 6.9 g).

Table 11.4 East of Quebec Barn (SR 85): pottery totals by fabric

Fabric	*No.*	*Wt(g.)*
FL14	264	1439
FL15	18	58
QU14	3	11
QU15	123	867
CH1	4	6
D1	19	33
Total	431	2414

Diagnostic material from pit 1201 includes an inturned rim from a barrel-shaped jar (Fig. 11.4, 1) and a bucket-shaped vessel with slightly inturned rim, and a post-firing perforation, probably a repair hole, below the rim (Fig. 11.4, 2). Both vessels are in the sandy fabric QU15. One rim sherd from gully 1213, in flint-tempered fabric FL14, also appears to belong to a barrel-shaped jar (Fig. 11.4, 3). Other rims, from pit 1205, gully 1213, tree throw 1229, and topsoil contexts, in both flint-tempered and sandy fabrics, are less diagnostic but are likely to derive from further jar forms, with plain or everted rims.

No decoration was noted, nor any attempt at surface treatment beyond a crude wiping of external surfaces, leaving vertical fingermarks (eg, Fig. 11.4, 2). The coarse fabric, fairly simple jar forms, and the lack of decoration place this assemblage within the plainware phase of the post-Deverel-Rimbury ceramic tradition, with a date range at the end of the 2nd or beginning of the 1st millennium BC. Parallels for both fabrics and forms can be found within the post-Deverel-Rimbury assemblages from Rockley Down and Burderop Down on the Marlborough Downs (Gingell 1992, figs. 71, 74, and 75) although at these sites flint-tempered fabrics are clearly predominant, with sandy wares forming only a minor component of the assemblages. It was noted that it was difficult to distinguish between post-Deverel-Rimbury ceramic traditions and those of the preceding Deverel-Rimbury phase in the Marlborough Downs assemblages (*ibid.*, 103), but there are no elements within the assemblage from East of Quebec Barn which could be certainly identified as Deverel-Rimbury.

List of illustrated vessels (Fig. 11.4)

1. Rim from barrel-shaped jar; fabric QU15; PRN 33, context 1206, pit 1201
2. Bucket-shaped vessel with a post-firing perforation; fabric QU15; PRN 34, context 1206, pit 1201
3. Rim from barrel-shaped jar; fabric FL14, PRN 47, context 1220, gully 1213

Other finds

A shale object was recovered from pit 1229, possibly part of an armlet. Unworked fragments of shale, probably from the Kimmeridge deposits in Dorset were found at Willis's Field Barn (see Every, Chapter 10).

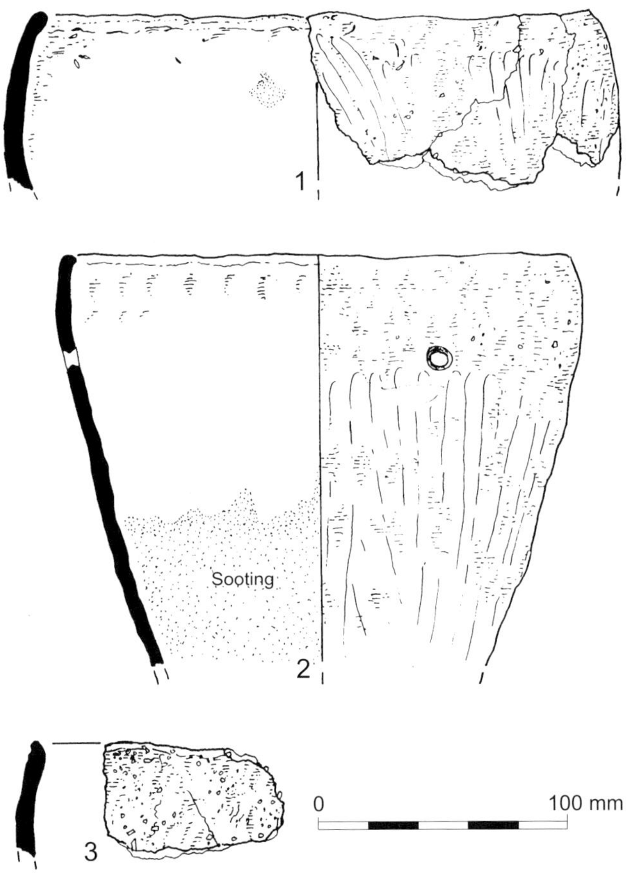

Figure 11.4 East of Quebec Barn (SRR 85): pottery

Table 11.5 North-east of Knook Castle (SRR 48): pottery fabrics

Fabric	*No.*	*Wt (g.)*
Prehistoric		
Flint-tempered		
FL8	1	5
FL10	2	12
FL11	3	1
Calcareous		
L19	1	1
L110	31	46
SH4	32	1693
Sandy		
QU11	6	15
QU12	4	6
QU13	2	6
Roman		
QU101	4	10
Samian	1	1
Total	87	1796

Pottery from the strip-and-record

Neolithic

The earliest pottery to be recovered from the strip-and-record was found in the tree hollow 48004 (context 48003), and comprises three small flint-tempered Middle Neolithic Peterborough Ware sherds with cord impressed decoration (Fabric FL5) and two flint-tempered sherds in fabric FL10, also assigned to the Neolithic period (Table 11.5). Two intrusive sherds comprising one very small abraded South Gaulish samian sherd and one sandy sherd in fabric QU13, possibly Late Iron Age/early Roman, were also recovered from the tree hollow.

Fengate Ware vessel

by Alistair Barclay

Just under half of a shell-tempered (SH4) Fengate Ware style vessel was recovered from the fill of pit 48810 (context 811). Nearly all of the recovered fragments (34 sherds) refit along fresh and old breaks, possibly indicating that deposition had involved either one or more (?four) large fragments. Old breaks run vertically from the rim to the base angle indicating that the vessel was probably slab built (see Fig. 11.5). Only part of the rim (10%) is present while the base is completely absent.

Figure 11.5 shows approximately one-third of the surviving sherds, while the profile is based on further refitting sherds and is considered to be relatively accurate. The form is without doubt a jar with a rim diameter of 240 mm and an estimated height of 290 mm. Two sherds contain enough of the upper part of a base angle to indicate that the vessel had a flat rather than a rounded base. Charred residue on the interior surface of these and other sherds indicates that the vessel had been used for cooking. It can be further noted that sherds belonging to the lower part of the vessel were more worn than those from the upper part and were, in places, pitted which could have been as a result of use (heating, boiling, and cleaning) rather than post-depositional damage.

The collared rim, decorated with short lengths of twisted cord maggot impressions arranged in a nested chevron pattern, has a slight concave profile. Its bevel is decorated with a herringbone pattern made from impressed fingernail. Beneath the collar is a row of evenly spaced neck pits made from the repeat impression of a fingertip. The body of the vessel is decorated all-over with paired fingertip impressions. The outside of the rim and the upper part of the inside have been smoothed. Much of the interior has been ?grass-wiped to form a crude criss-cross pattern.

The vessel displays typical characteristics (collared rim with fingernail decorated internal bevel, neck pits, and paired fingernail body decoration) of the Fengate style of Peterborough Ware (Piggott 1962, 33–4 and fig. 12, P12–3). The jar form with flat base is known from, for instance, Icklingham (Piggott 1954, pl x.2), Sawdon Moor, Yorkshire (Manby 1995, fig. 54. 1;

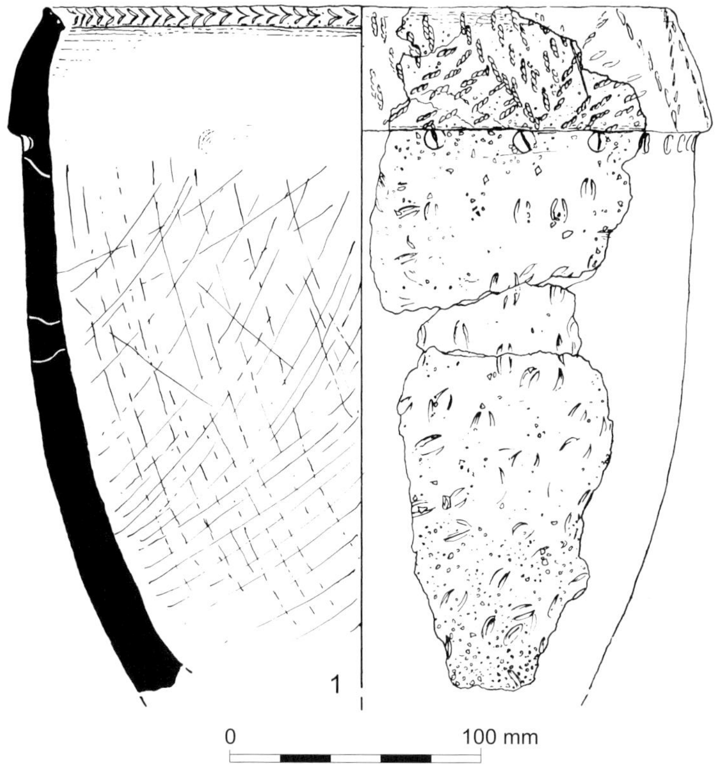

Figure 11.5 North-east of Knook Castle (SRR 48): Fengate Ware jar

1988, 67–9 and fig. 4.14); Yarnton, Oxfordshire (Barclay and Edwards forthcoming) and, within the region, can be closely compared with probable jar-shaped vessels from Downton (ApSimon 1962, 128 and fig. 11, 17–8). It is possible that wider bases represent a simple technological development from the rounded and flattened bases that are generally found on Mortlake and Ebbsfleet vessels. The development of forms within the Peterborough Ware tradition and, indeed, the range of vessel shapes, is in need of definition. Certainly large assemblages from sites like West Kennett (Piggott 1962) and Windmill Hill (Smith 1965) indicate the potential range that can occur.

The vessel is likely to belong to the period 3350–2800 cal BC (Barclay 2007, table 15.1). The Peterborough Ware style (Ebbsfleet) is thought to develop out of bowl pottery in the 36th or 35th century cal BC with the Mortlake and Fengate sub-styles first appearing during the 34th or 33rd century and going out of use perhaps during the 29th.

Late Bronze Age/Early Iron Age

Pottery recovered from the upper deposits of large pit 48007 is predominantly attributed to the Late Bronze Age/Early Iron Age on the basis of fabric type. With the exception of one very small, flat- topped rim sherd and two possible carinated sherds in the fine sandy fabric QU11, the bulk of the sherds are small, often abraded, undiagnostic body sherds. The carinated sherds are from Early Iron Age fineware bowls typically found in the area.

The majority of sherds were attributed to the moderately fine limestone fabric LI 10 and the remainder comprise one flint-tempered body sherd in fabric FL8 and a total of 12 sherds in the sandy fabrics QU11, QU12, and QU13. The sandy fabrics cover a slight range from very fine to moderately coarse and it should be borne in mind that, due to the lack of associated vessel forms, it is possible that the sandy sherds could date anywhere from the Late Bronze Age through to the Late Iron Age.

The bulk of the remaining sherds are small, non-diagnostic body sherds and attributing them to a particular date on the basis of fabric types alone was, in some cases, problematic. Fabric types present comprise flint- and limestone-tempered and sandy. However, the fabrics and forms are comparable with other Late Bronze Age/Early Iron Age assemblages in the area, particular the large assemblage from Potterne (Morris 2000b).

Environment

Charred plant remains

by Alan J. Clapham

The single sample analysed from this site was taken from a secondary fill of the pit 1201 and produced a considerable range of charred plant remains (Table 11.6). Cereals are dominated by indeterminate grain fragments but include spelt wheat (*Triticum spelta*) grains and glume bases (quite well preserved), indeterminate wheat grains (*Triticum* sp.), spikelet forks, glumes bases (of which 32 were recorded), and rachis fragments. Hulled barley (*Hordeum vulgare*) grains and grain fragments were also identified including a single rachis fragment. It is not possible to determine whether the barley was two-row or six-row. Non-cultivated taxa include three fragments of hazelnut shell (*Corylus avellana*) and weed seeds, all of which are indicative of either arable practices or disturbed ground. Four mineralised seeds of a goosefoot (*Chenopodium* sp.) were also recovered.

Discussion

Cereals which could have been grown in the area include spelt wheat and hulled barley. Indeterminate wheat chaff was also present suggesting that crop

Table 11.6 East of Quebec Barn (SRR 85): charred plant remains from Pit 1201

Context	*1203*
Sample	*1600*
Sample size (l)	*11*
Volume (ml)	*25*
Crops etc	
Triticum spelta, grain	1+1f
glume base	11
Triticum sp. indet., grain	1
spikelet fork	2
glume base	32
rachis fragment	2
Hordeum vulgare hulled, grain	6+6f
?rachis fragment	1
Cerealia indet.	94f
Embryo	1
Weeds	
Cenococcum geophilum sclerotia	125
Corylus avellana	3f
Chenopodiaceae	4f
Stellaria media	1
Fallopia convolvulus	1f
Medicago sp.	1
Odontites vernus	1
Galium aparine	10+8f
Asteraceae indet.	1
Arrhenatherum elatius rootlet	1
Small Poaceae	1
Unidentified	1
Mineralised	
Chenopodium sp.	4+1f

processing may have occurred in the area, especially as it is associated with weed seeds. Whether the pit represents a rubbish or storage pit is difficult to determine. Glume wheats such as spelt are commonly stored as spikelets and the assemblage in this pit may represent the dumping of crop processing waste as it is mixed with other cereal remains, the number of grains being small. The presence of the weed seeds may suggest that the crops were stored in a semi-cleaned state, with crop processing only being completed on a piecemeal basis.

The crops usually associated with the Bronze Age include emmer (*Triticum dicoccum*), spelt, and hulled barley. This combination has been found at, for instance, the Early–Middle Bronze Age site at West Row, Mildenhall, Suffolk (Martin and Murphy 1988), at the Late Bronze Age site at Lofts Farm, Maldon, Essex (Murphy 1988), at Runnymede, Berkshire (Greig 1991), and more locally at Potterne (Carruthers 1986). Sclerotia of the soil fungus *Cenococcum geophilum* were present; these can be found in a wide range of soil types

Discussion

Middle Neolithic activity is indicated by the presence of a large part of a Fengate Ware jar in the fill of pit 48810. A little worked flint was also recovered from the pit. A few other small Neolithic sherds came from tree hollow 48004. A small group of features recorded during the excavation indicates Late Bronze Age settlement activity. None of those features forms any recognisable structure although the proximity of the two post-holes may be significant. A series of pits and ditches of Late Bronze Age date lying approximately 100 m south of the site, identified during the evaluation, are likely to form part of the same dispersed settlement.

The large pit recorded during the strip-and-record closely resembles in geographical location, morphology, and excavated profile prehistoric shafts known elsewhere on the southern chalk. Although this feature could only be excavated to a depth of 1.8 m, the steeply shelving fills are virtually identical to the 'weathering cone' of tertiary fills at the top of the Middle Bronze Age well, the Wilsford Shaft, sited 12 km to the south-east (Ashbee *et al.* 1989). Earlier shafts, with possibly ritual functions, are also known, for instance at Fir Tree Field, Cranborne Chase (Green and Allen 1997). The earliest pottery from the upper fills of the weathering cone was of Late Bronze Age/Early Iron Age date, although the presence also of Romano-British pottery in its upper fills means that it would have remained a visible and possibly significant feature throughout later prehistory.

As with the features recorded to the south and east of Knook Castle, the lynchets recorded during the strip-and-record, are probably part of the extensive field system associated with the Romano-British nucleated settlements on Knook Down.

Breakheart Hill Watching Brief (AC 1000), Breakheart Hill (SRR80/1) and Breakheart Bottom Strip-and-record (SRR 80/2–4)

The watching brief recorded the Old Ditch linear earthwork where it was crossed by the SRR route at the top of Breakheart Hill (chainage 10640–10703). A further section of the road just to the east (centred on chainage 11000) was subject to strip-and-record in order to examine part of a field system but revealed no features. However, features were recorded in Breakheart Bottom (chainage 11650–13000).

Results

Old Ditch comprised a large east–west aligned V-shaped ditch (1088) with a narrow vertical-sided slot at the base, measuring *c.* 8.5 m wide and 2.4 m deep, and containing a sequence of six fills. Small quantities of worked flint and animal bone were recovered as well as two iron objects from an upper secondary fill, and Romano-British pottery (2nd–early 3rd century) from the tertiary fill.

Parallel to the ditch, *c.* 5 m to its south, was a smaller ditch (1074) with steep sides and a slightly concave base, also containing Romano-British pottery from its upper fill. The ditch had a truncated gully (1072) on its southern edge. Approximately 23 m to the north of Old Ditch was a small, undated, east–west aligned gully (1070) filled with chalk rubble.

To the east, in Breakheart Bottom, four widely spaced north–south aligned ditches recorded during the evaluation (between chainage 11990 and 12860) were located and further sections excavated (80020, 80025, 80021, and 80023, west to east). The ditches are probably associated with the fragmentary field systems recorded in aerial photographs (SMR ST94NE649 and 654) which lie towards either end of the stripped area.

A discontinuous, north–south aligned spread of abraded flint nodules compacted into a silty clay soil, may represent evidence for a former trackway (80030) (*c.* chainage 12120). This was undated, although it was noted that it respected the line of the field boundaries to the north and south of the easement. A number of tree hollows were investigated, one of which (80031) produced three sherds of Romano-British pottery, tile, and worked flint.

Discussion

The excavation of a section through the Old Ditch linear earthwork revealed little new about this major prehistoric landscape boundary, It can be traced for over 15 km along the top of the down from north-east of Battlesbury to Knook, at which point it turns north-east and passes south of Tilshead. At the site of the watching brief it crosses south to north, at a shallow angle, over the Breakheart Hill ridge that drops to the east from the high point of Knook Down to the Imber valley. Although a bank was apparent in the well-preserved section of the monument to the east of the route, only traces of a possible bank were evident on the south side in the extensively vehicle-rutted easement. Immediately west of the site the ditch appears to define the northern limits of the later, Romano-British settlements at Knook, where it was subsequently used as a parish boundary.

A 450 m long section of the Old Ditch was exposed at Breach Hill, on the west side of the Imber valley south-west of Tilshead and revealed it to consist of two, probably broadly contemporary, parallel ditches, the larger ditch lying on the southern (upslope) side (Birbeck 2006). A single sherd of Late Bronze pottery from Breach Hill is consistent with the suggested date for similar features in the eastern part of Salisbury Plain (Bradley *et al.* 1994).

North-West of Middle Barn Farm Strip-and-record (SRR 80/5, 87)

This section of the route (chainage 13100–13680), which crosses the lower slopes of a ridge between Breakheart Bottom and the Imber valley, and the base of the valley itself, was subject to strip-and-record in order to investigate a dispersed group of features identified during the evaluation. Following the identification of part of a round barrow ring ditch and an adjacent grave (Figs 11.6–7), the excavation became the subject of an episode of BBC television's *Meet the Ancestors* programme (*Hunter of the Plain*).

Results

A group of seven small pits was recorded over *c.* 100 m towards the western end of the area, from some of which sherds of Late Bronze Age/Early Iron Age pottery were recovered, indicating prehistoric occupation in the vicinity. Three pits contained evidence for burning, one (80076) containing 10 flint flakes (two of them burnt). Pit 80134 contained a small Late Bronze Age vessel (Fig. 11.8, see below).

On the lower east-facing slope of the Imber valley (*c.* chainage 13500), a length of curvilinear ditch (80126) was recorded projecting out from the northern edge of the easement and a subsequent geophysical survey of the field to the north confirmed the presence of a probable round barrow ring ditch (or just possibly a small hengiform enclosure). The ditch was 2.3 m wide and 0.8 m deep with sides steep at the top and nearly vertical towards the flat base (Fig. 11.6). Up to four fills were recorded, producing three sherds of prehistoric pottery – two of Early/Middle Bronze Age date (context 80139), and one, associated with a multi-platform flint core, of Late Bronze Age/Early Iron Age date; a Romano-British sherd (context 80093, not shown in section) is presumably intrusive.

An oval grave (80042) just outside the ditch contained two successive inhumation burials and a cremation deposit (Figs 11.6–7). The steep inner faces of the chalk rubble (80043) lying against the sides of the grave indicate that the earlier inhumation (80088), an adult male, was interred within a timber mortuary structure (80038). Although no timber survived, slots cut into the chalk and stake-holes used

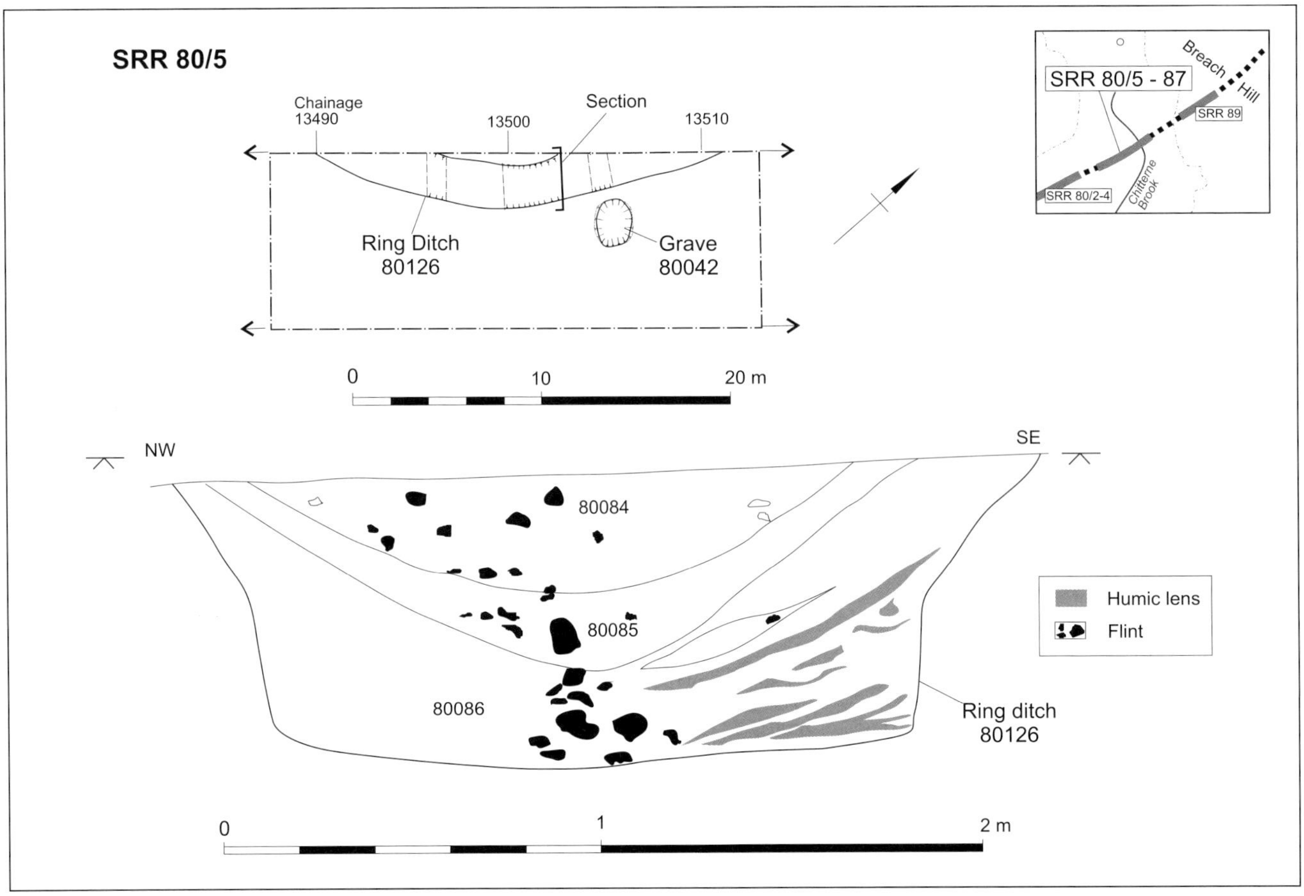

Figure 11.6 North-west of Middle Barn Farm (SRR 80/5) and section of ring ditch 80126

to hold the structure in place were recorded in the base of the grave. The chamber was then packed around with chalk rubble (80043) into which several fragmentary red deer antler picks and a single piece of roe deer antler (not shown in Fig. 11.7, see below) that had probably been used to excavate the grave, were placed. The grave was then backfilled with chalk rubble (80079). Above the skeleton within this chalk rubble was a concentration of flint nodules. There were no artefacts.

At some later date, the chalk rubble and grave fill were cut into, to a fairly shallow depth, by a second grave (80113). This contained a second inhumation burial (80077), again of an adult male, accompanied by an unurned, probably female, cremation burial (80078). Two burnt antler or bone objects, a pin and a gouge or spatula, were recovered from the cremation burial (see below). A retouched flint flake (initially misidentified as a transverse arrowhead, hence the title of the *Meet The Ancestors* programme – *Hunter of the Plain*) was found near the left hand of the skeleton. The upper burials were covered with large flint nodules. A series of small stake-holes was also recorded around the surface of the feature, indicating again that some form of minor structure was erected following the backfilling of the later grave. A bone sample from the skeleton of the later inhumation (80077) produced a radiocarbon date in the Early Bronze Age of 1975–1760 cal BC (Beta-134258, 3550±40 BP). Although no grave-goods were found, the two inhumation burials are classically Beaker in aspect: flexed adult males placed on their left sides with heads to the north-west and the radiocarbon date places the most recent of them late in the period in which Beakers were current.

Two substantial ditches were also recorded (not illustrated). One, undated, was located near the centre of this road section. The other, a large V-shaped ditch (80101) with a flanking parallel gully (80102), both containing Romano-British pottery, was located in the base of the Imber valley at the east end. The ditches seem too large for regular field boundaries and may represent territorial or property boundaries.

Human Bone

by Jacqueline I. McKinley

Human bone from two flexed inhumation burials (80077 and 80088) and one unurned cremation burial (80078) was received for analysis. The cremation burial was made directly above, and

Table 11.7 North-west of Middle Barn Farm (SRR 80/5): summary of human bone

Context	*Burial type*	*Quantification*	*Age & sex*	*Pathology*	*Pyre goods/debris*
80077	inhumation	*c.* 98%	adult *c.* 30–35 yr, male	calculus; pd; hypoplasia; Schmorl's node - T4-L4, S1; ddd - C5-6; op - C1, L4, L5 body surface margins, l. auricular surface; pitting - C3, l. auricular surface, r. 3rd metatarsal, l & r foot sesamoids; exostoses - patellae, calcanea; mv- squatting facets	
80078	unurned cremation	1010.6 g	adult *c.* 30–45 yr, ??female	ddd - T/L	antler/bone pin, gouge/ spatula; burnt flint
80088	inhumation	*c.* 45%	adult >40 yr, male	amtl; caries; abscess; calculus; oa - r. temporo-mandibular, 1C, 1T; op - 2L body surface margins, atlas; exostoses - tibia shaft	

For key see Table 5.1

possibly contemporaneously with, inhumation burial 80077, having been laid in a discrete concentration over the right hand and left arm of the former (Fig. 11.7). Bone from burial 80077 has been radiocarbon dated to the Early Bronze Age: 1975–1760 cal BC (Beta-134258, 3550±40 BP). The grave for the latter (80113) was cut directly through the upper levels of the earlier grave in which inhumation burial 80088 had been made.

Methods

Analysis of the cremated remains followed the writer's standard procedure (McKinley 1994a). Age (cremated and unburnt remains) was assessed from the stage of tooth development and ossification/ epiphyseal bone fusion (Beek 1983; McMinn and Hutchings 1985; Webb and Suchey 1985), and the pattern and extent of degenerative changes in the skeleton (Brothwell 1972; Bass 1987). Sex was ascertained from the sexually dimorphic traits of the skeleton (Bass 1987; Gejvall 1981; Wahl 1982). Levels of reliability reflect the quantity and quality of available traits on which to base the assessment; '??' denotes 'possible', '?' denotes 'probable'. Skeletal indices were calculated (Brothwell 1972; Bass 1987) and stature was estimated (Trotter and Gleser 1952; 1958) for the inhumation burials. This report was written in 1999 and uses a slightly different methodology to that employed for Battlesbury Bowl (Chapter 5).

Results

A summary of the results is presented in Table 11.7.

Disturbance and condition

No direct evidence indicative of disturbance to any of the burial deposits was noted in excavation. However, the recovery of 33.6 g of cremated bone (originating from burial 80078 and representing *c.* 3% of the total weight of bone recovered) from various areas of skeleton 80077, mostly from inside the skull vault (150 mm distant), implies there had been some level of disturbance. The recovery of several fragments of rodent skeleton from the pelvic area of 80077 suggests animal activity was probably the mechanism of disturbance.

The unburnt bone is in poor condition, especially that from the lower burial 80088. The bone from 80077 is all slightly degraded, the left foot bones being in particularly poor condition. The exocranial surface of the skull is moderately weathered and worn with common root marking, the right parietal vault being particularly affected. Experiments have shown that the upper surface of bone generally suffers heavier erosion in the burial environment (Armour-Chelu and Andrews 1996). All the trabecular bone from 80077 has gone and the cortical bone is heavily eroded; the back of the skull, particularly the uppermost right side, is extensively eroded. In contrast, the cremated bone is in good condition and fragments of trabecular bone are common, the latter being the first to suffer in adverse burial conditions. The difference in preservation between the two types of burial deposit is demonstrative of the effects of an alkaline micro-environment.

Demographic data

Three individuals were identified from the skeletal remains, all mature or older adults, the two inhumation burials being of males, the cremation burial probably female. As there is no date for the lower burial, it is unclear how closely contemporary the two deposits were.

As stated above, the burials were laid out in a manner that is typical of males buried with Beakers, although no grave-goods were present. The

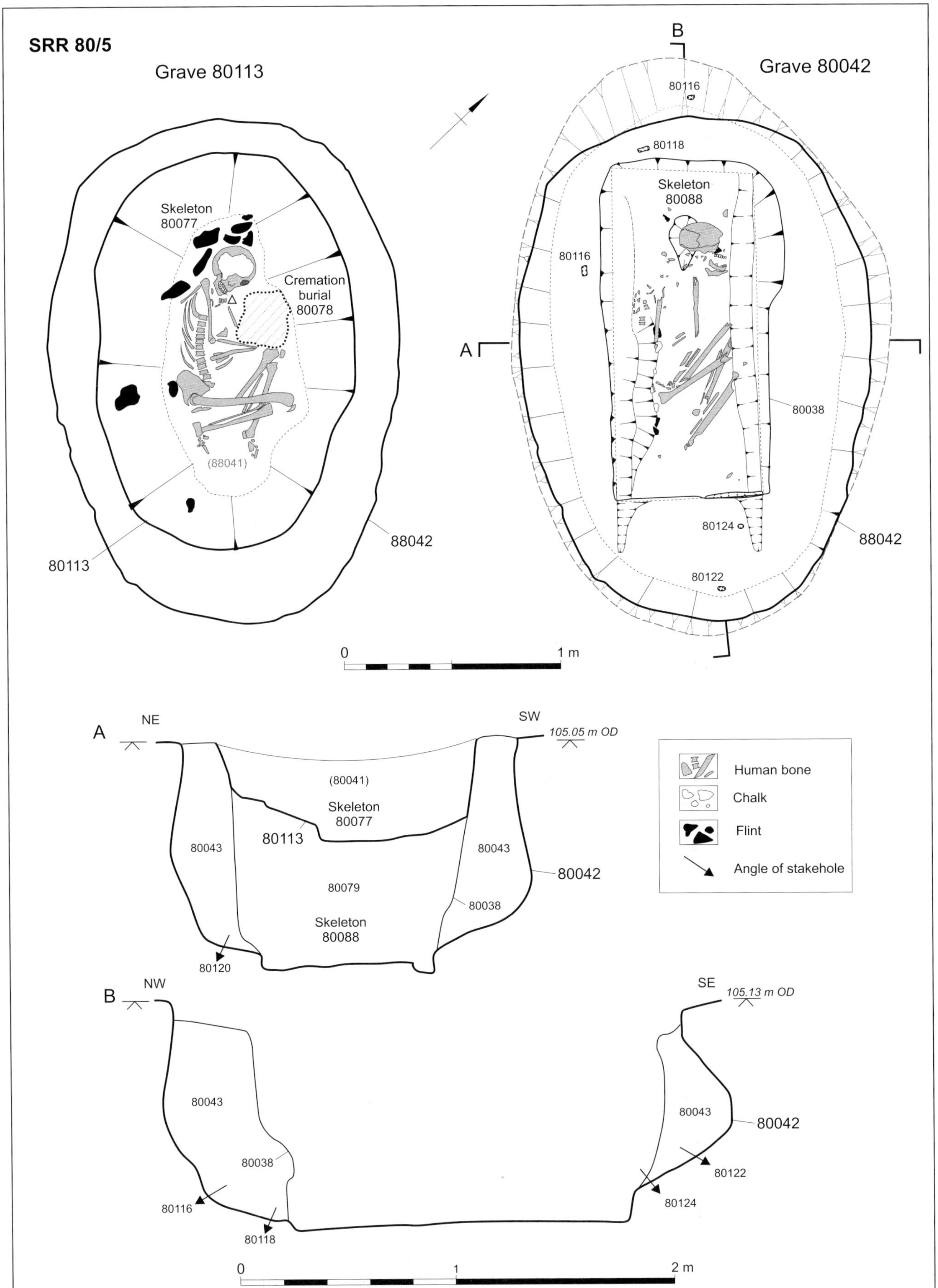

Figure 11.7 Burials in grave 80042/80113

radiocarbon date would put the upper burial at least very late in the Beaker period and there is no clear indication as to the length of time that may have elapsed between interment of the bodies or between that of 80077 and the cremation remains. The overall dating of this small group of burials is, therefore, undetermined. Such small groups of burials are, however, common in the Bronze Age generally. Where the sex of the cremated adults within such groups can be ascertained there is a predominance of females amongst the adults (49% of adults compared with 5% males from a sample of 22 small sites with 1–10 burials each; pers. obs.), and of infants amongst the immature individuals (54% immature individuals, 8% total number). The potential cultural significance of this observation should be set against the fact that 45% of the adults in the sample could not be sexed.

Skeletal indices

Cranial index was calculated for both adult males; 80077 at 86.5 (hyperbrachycrany range); 80088 at 75.9 (dolichocrany range). The platymeric index (degree of anterior-posterior flattening of the proximal femur) was calculated at 80.7 (platymeric) for 80077 and 86.6 (eurymeric) for 80088; the platycnemic index (meso-lateral flattening of the tibia) was 73.2/70.1 (eurycnemic) for 80077 and 60.5 (platycnemic) for 80088. The femoral robusticity index for 80077 is 13.1.

Stature could only be estimated for 80077 at 1.71 m; although the long bones from 80088 were insufficiently well preserved to allow stature to be calculated, comparison with those from 80077 suggest the former was taller than the latter. The estimated heights are similar to those noted for males from other small Bronze Age assemblages, for instance, the average of 1.7 m recorded from Twyford Down, Hampshire (McKinley 2000b).

Pathological lesions and morphological variations

Very slight periodontal disease (gum disease) was noted in the distal alveolus from burial 80077, (80088 was too poorly preserved to ascertain the presence or absence of the condition). Moderate calculus deposits (tartar) were noted in both adult male dentitions, mostly affecting the distal teeth. *Ante mortem* tooth loss at a rate of 1.6% was observed in the older male dentition and was probably directly associated with carious lesions (rate 5.1%, limited to same dentition) and formation of dental abscesses (6.4%, same dentition). The rates are all lower than those noted at the Early to Middle Bronze Age site at Twyford Down, Hampshire (McKinley 2000b), where *ante mortem* tooth loss was at 4% (2% for males), caries at 9% (10% for males) and abscesses at 7% (12%) for males. No lesions were observed in the nine mandibular or five maxillary tooth sockets available for examination from the cremation burial.

The very poor condition of skeleton 80088 means that evidence for joint disease was largely limited to skeleton 80077. This relatively young adult male had extensive Schmorl's nodes (destructive lesions in the vertebral body surface) in 58% of the vertebral bodies from T4 down, and degenerative disc disease (pitting in the vertebral body surface and new bone on the margins) in 8% of his vertebrae. These lesions, together with the obvious strength of the arm and thigh muscles as demonstrated by the robusticity of the attachments, indicate this individual was frequently engaged in heavy lifting, thereby placing stress on the mid-lower spine. Lesions indicative of osteoarthritis (Rogers *et al.* 1987; Rogers and Waldron 1995) were observed in the right temporo-mandibular joint from 80088 (1:4 joints).

Osteophytes (irregular growths of new bone along joint margins) and pitting may develop in response to a number of conditions and it is not always possible to ascertain the specific cause of individual lesions (Rogers and Waldron 1995). The majority of these lesions (Table 11.7) were slight–mild in severity, and are most likely to represent the early stages of some form of joint disease. Similarly, it is not always possible to be conclusive with respect to the aetiology of exostoses, bony growths which may develop at tendon and ligament insertions on the bone. Causative factors include advancing age, traumatic stress, or various diseases.

Pyre technology and the rites and rituals of cremation

The majority of the cremated bone was the buff/white colour indicative of a high degree of oxidation (Holden *et al.* 1995a; 1995b). Minor variations of blue or slightly grey bone fragments were observed amongst elements of skull and the lower vertebrae, but most frequently fragments of lower limb. The distribution suggests some general inefficiency such as shortage of time or temperature necessary to complete oxidation.

The quantity of bone included in the burial is within the upper range of weights noted from cremation burials across the temporal range (McKinley 1997), and represents *c.* 63% of the expected bone weight from an adult cremation (McKinley 1993). The majority (86%) of the bone was recovered from the 10 mm sieve fraction and the maximum recorded fragment size was 87 mm. There is no evidence to suggest deliberate fragmentation of bone prior to burial, the size of fragments seen here being commensurate with those expected in consequence of various of the 'normal' factors which affect bone fragmentation (McKinley 1994b). The relatively large size of the fragments and quantity of bone recovered indicate that the recorded burial position was the primary place of deposition and that relatively little disturbance (see above) has occurred. Skeletal elements from all areas of the body were represented, with no significant prevelance of any specific elements.

Several fragments from two bone/antler pyre goods were recovered from the burial; a polished pin and a spatula or gouge (see below). Most of both items were recovered which, in view of the fact that not all the human bone was recovered for burial (a characteristic of the cremation rite), suggests either the items had not fragmented prior to deposition or that care was exercised to collect most of them. On average, *c.* 16% of Bronze Age cremation burials include some form of pyre good (McKinley 1994c), worked bone artefacts – particularly the type of polished pin seen here – being the most common inclusions, though flint flakes and tools are also recovered.

A relatively substantial quantity (26.8 g) of burnt flint was recovered from amongst the cremated bone within the burial. It may have been a deliberate inclusion; Bronze Age urns filled with nothing other than burnt flint have been found deposited in the vicinity of cremation burials, where they appear to represent some form of mortuary deposit (eg, Portsdown, Nicholls 1987; Twyford Down, McKinley 2000b and Langstone Harbour, Seager Smith *et al.* 2000, all in Hampshire; and Cippenham (CSOWL 96), Berkshire, McKinley 1998). Alternatively, the burnt flint may represent the incidental inclusion of pyre debris in the burial, ie, naturally occurring flint from the base of the pyre.

The excavator believed the cremation burial to have been made at the same time as inhumation burial 80077, over which it was deposited with no intervening fill (see above and Fig. 11.7). If this were so, the inhumation burial would have had to be in position prior to the deposition of the cremation remains. It is also possible that the grave of 80077 was not immediately backfilled with soil/rubble; there may have been another form of cover over the grave, allowing for the later interment of the cremation burial, though this is unlikely to have been at a substantially later date.

Finds

Flint

Twenty-one worked flints were recovered from contexts on this site, 10 of them from a single pit. Most were flakes, three of which were burnt. One long thick flake from the grave fill overlying burial 80088 displayed edge damage. A multi-platform core was recovered from a secondary fill of the ring ditch fill. A single retouched flake came from near the left hand of skeleton 80077 and seemed to have been deliberately placed.

Coin

by Nicholas Cooke

A small late Roman bronze coin, from context 80056, was badly corroded and dated by size alone (17 mm diam., 1.6 g), but is likely to be an antoninianus or nummus of the late 3rd or 4th century.

Pottery

by Moira Laidlaw

A small group of Early Bronze Age and Late Bronze Age/Early Iron Age sherds including one almost complete vessel were recovered from the small cluster of pits and the ring ditch (24 sherds weighing 189 g). Two Romano-British sherds were also recovered.

Early–Middle Bronze Age

Two grog-tempered (GR2) and one undiagnostic sandy sherds (QU1) were recovered from the ring ditch (contexts 80139 and 80093 respectively). On the basis of fabric the grog-tempered sherds may be attributed to the Early/Middle Bronze Age but the sandy sherd is possibly Late Bronze Age/Early Iron Age.

Late Bronze Age/Early Iron Age

Late Bronze Age/Early Iron Age pottery was recovered from a cluster of pits towards the western end of the area. With the exception of one almost complete vessel from pit 80134 the sherds are all very fragmentary and attributing them with certainty to fabric types and date was difficult. The vessel from pit 80134 is a small tub-shaped vessel of probable Middle or Late Bronze Age date, with a plain rounded rim, in the flint-tempered fabric FL2 (Fig. 11.8, PRN 80134). The remaining pottery comprises two fine sandy and five flint-tempered sherds from pit 80076, and one sandy sherd from pit 80092.

Romano-British

Romano-British pottery, comprising one sherd from a necked jar/bowl with a rounded rim and one body sherd, both in the fine oxidised sandy fabric Q100, were recovered from the two linear ditches.

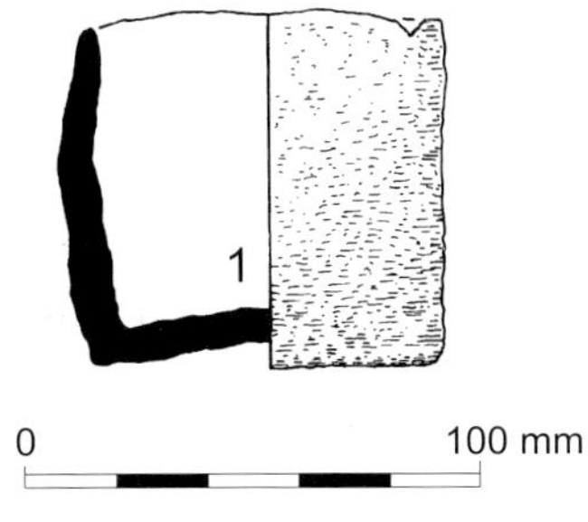

Figure 11.8 North-west of Middle Barn Farm (SRR 80/5): Late Bronze Age pot

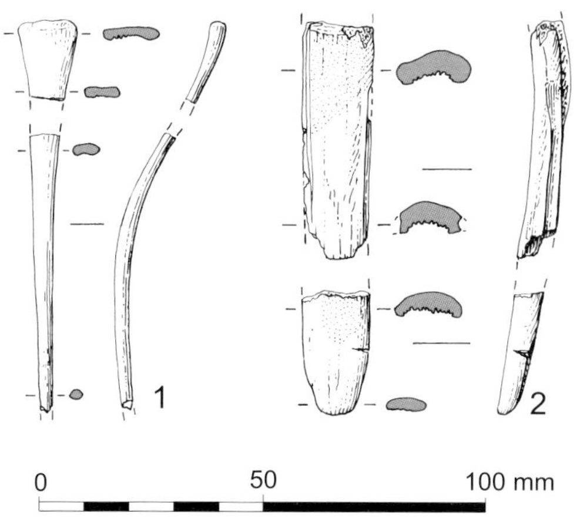

Figure 11.9 North-west of Middle Barn Farm (SRR 80/5): bone and antler objects

Worked bone and antler

by Lorraine Mepham and Jessica Grimm

Fragments of two worked bone/antler objects were recovered from the unurned cremation burial (80078) (Fig 11.9). These comprise four fragments (three joining) from a pin, slightly curved, with a surviving length of *c.* 80 mm, lacking the tip and part of the shaft; and three fragments (two joining) from the shaft and tip of a probable gouge or spatula, also with a surviving length of *c.* 80 mm. Both objects have been burnt on the pyre, which is reflected in their white to bluish-grey colouring, although the curvature of the pin is likely to represent the original form, rather than resulting from deforming through burning. Both objects find parallels in Early Bronze Age contexts elsewhere in Wiltshire, for example from a bowl barrow at nearby Upton Lovell (Annable and Simpson 1964, nos 244–9).

Five fragments of antler were recovered from fill 80043 of grave 80042 (objects 2–6). All but one derive from red deer, the other is roe. The antlers are fragile and some surface erosion is visible. The coarse nature of the chop marks as well as their presumed Early Bronze Age date makes it likely that they were made by flint axes rather than bronze ones. As none of the red deer antlers had their bases preserved it cannot be said if they derive from butchered animals or from collected antler. Object 2 is part of an antler beam with a broken-off tine. Repeated, coarse chop marks at the base-end show that this piece was severed from the rest of the antler. One side (of the 'base' end) shows darkening and possible traces of charcoal, ?burnt. Object 3 is probably part of the beam ending at the top in the terminal tines. Coarse scraping marks are seen towards these terminal tines. Object 4 is a tine tip with no visible working marks. Object 5 is part of the beam with a tine showing similar chopping marks to Object 2. Chop marks are also visible on the tine as this was shaped like a chisel/small axe blade and there are indications of use-wear at the tip. The beam was split in two by repeatedly incising the same opposite lines. Fine cuts are visible on the beam-tine junction. It is unclear why the beam was split and if this was done before or after the tine was shaped into a tool. Object 6 is a piece of roe deer skull with antler (left side?). Fine cut marks at the cranial base indicate that this animal had been skinned. It is possible that objects 2–4 originally formed one large red deer antler and it is likely that the material was worked at or near the site. Object 5 might have been used to dig out the adjacent ditch, or indeed one of the graves.

Other finds

by Lorraine Mepham

An iron cleat from context 80065 is of Romano-British form.

Discussion

The probable round barrow ring ditch was not previously known, but its location on the slopes immediately above the slope on the west side of the Imber valley is typical for such monuments on Salisbury Plain (McOmish *et al.* 2002, 43). The associated grave, however, is of particular interest, containing, unusually, a single inhumation burial interred in a mortuary structure, followed by an inhumation and cremation burials.

Only the middle funerary deposit within grave 80042 has been radiocarbon dated (1975–1760 cal BC) and, therefore, the duration between this burial and the one below remains uncertain. However, it seems probable that the cremation deposit (80078) was made either at the same time or shortly after the inhumation (80113) (see McKinley above). The worked bone grave/pyre goods found with the cremated bone find parallels with similar items from barrows in Wiltshire (see Mepham above). It is likely that all three deposits were made during the Early Bronze Age (2250–1700 cal BC) and potentially within a relatively short period of time (within one or two generations).

The exact relationship between the grave and the barrow remains uncertain. It could have been at the centre of a ditchless turf mound that pre-dated the barrow; it could have been a flat grave with a modest turf mound; or it could represent a secondary/satellite burial. It is even possible that it was contemporary and associated with a small hengiform enclosure rather than a barrow, as in the case of Beaker burials at Thomas Hardye School, Dorchester, Dorset and elsewhere (Gardiner *et al.* 2007). It is not unusual for cremation deposits to be placed within pits that recut such graves (eg, Barrow 5e, Shrewton, Wiltshire; Green and Rollo-Smith 1984, fig. 7).

The burial deposit is best described as a sequential grave, where one or more graves are placed above an earlier grave; such graves are found throughout the Beaker/Early Bronze Age periods. However, it can be noted that, although the two graves were sequential, there is a notable change in character between the structure of the lower and upper graves (see above). On the whole such graves tend to be found at the centre of barrows (eg, Barrows 5k and 24, Shrewton; Green and Rollo-Smith 1984, figs 11–12 and 16) and, from this aspect, the Middle Barn Farm grave is slightly unusual. The structure of the lower grave with a timber-lined mortuary structure is also reminiscent of some Beaker-associated graves at, for example, Chilbolton, Hampshire (Russel 1990), where a sequence of two graves was identified. The form of the mortuary structure at Middle Barn Farm remains unclear as no timber survived. It may have been a timber-lined grave with timbers supported in the chalk-cut slots and stake-holes or a roofed mortuary structure; there was no evidence for more complex timber coffins or biers as seen as some other sites eg, Sutton Veny, Wiltshire (Johnston 1980), Site XII, Dorchester-on-Thames, Oxfordshire (Whittle *et al.* 1992).

The layout of the inhumation burials is typical of adult male Beaker burials though no grave-goods were present. On the other hand, the absence or near absence of grave-goods is not unusual in Early Bronze Age contexts and such an absence would indeed be more typical of secondary and/or satellite graves. The use of flint nodules to cover the burials is a common practice in Wiltshire (eg, Barrows 5a and 5j, Shrewton; Green and Rollo-Smith 1984, 313) and could be interpreted either as a sealing or closing deposit, as an attempt to prevent wandering spirits, and/or to simply mark the grave.

Vedette Post Four Strip-and-record (SRR 89), and Tilshead Down Excavation (SRR 90), Earthwork Survey (SRR 120) and Strip-and-record (SRR 116 and 120)

Five small investigations were undertaken over a distance of 2.4 km on Tilshead Down, from the upper slopes on the east side of the Imber valley, to a coombe between Tilshead Down and Horse Down that runs east into the Till valley. They included an attempt to relocate a grave noted during the evaluation, the survey of a small linear earthwork, and three sections of strip-and-record. They are described below from south-west to north-east.

Results

Strip and record

This strip-and-record site at Vedette Post Four (chainage 14100–14380), on the east side of the Imber valley, was centred on a large ditch, aligned approximately west-north-west–east-south-east, that had been partially excavated during the evaluation and was further investigated (89069). Parallel to it, 5 m to its south, was a smaller, poorly-defined ditch, that had not been identified during the evaluation. The ditches followed a slightly sinuous line running down the slope of the hill. Both produced Roman pottery – one small abraded sherd of South Gaulish samian ware, five fine sandy and six grey coarseware sherds which, on the basis of fabric types, may tentatively be attributed to the early Romano-British period.

A short length of curvilinear gully (89057) was recorded immediately south of the smaller ditch, and a large sub-circular scoop (89089) on the southern edge of the larger ditch. A group of tree hollows was recorded beside the ditches, two of which yielded quantities of worked flint, burnt flint, and non-local stone. A well-preserved earthen bank to the east of the site proved to be of modern military origin.

Excavation

A section of the route between the 'India' and 'Juliet' tank crossings (chainage 14950–15700) was stripped in order relocate an inhumation burial of possible Romano-British date noted, but not investigated, during the evaluation (Gifford and Partners 1997a, gazetteer 22, 56), and the location of which had not been recorded precisely. A series of cross trenches were machine-excavated in order to relocate and then re-excavate the evaluation trench, but its line was not discernible at the south-west due to subsequent damage by vehicles, and the grave could not be found. No other archaeological features were recorded in any of the trenches.

Earthwork survey and strip-and record

A small linear earthwork, aligned north-west–south-east, was surveyed, where it crossed the SRR at chainage 16220, west of Hotel Crossing. A tank track had created a *c.* 4 m wide and 0.7 m deep rut cutting through the southern end and three other tank tracks were recorded across and along the west side. Two areas of the earthwork contained abundant buried metal, with rabbit holes in the voids between the metalwork. The regular form of the earthwork suggested that it was a modern military feature. The subsequent strip-and-record confirmed its recent date, with modern finds being noted in the machine-sectioned bank material.

A further section of strip-and-record (chainage 16370–16480), which focused on two probable pits recorded during the evaluation, identified one undated possible pit, and two small features, either post-holes or natural solution hollows, containing burnt flint and slag. Three other features proved to be of recent military origin.

Chapter 12
Imber Valley to Tilshead

Horse Down Excavation (SRR 124), and West and North-West of Golf Crossing Strip-and-record (SRR 123 and 125/127)

The excavation area (chainage 17110–17266) to the west of Tilshead lay across the top and upper northern slope of an east–west chalk spur between two coombes, sloping from *c.* 119 m aOD at the south down to an east–west lynchet at the north at *c.* 115 m aOD. The excavation was targeted on two ditches and three possible pits recorded during the evaluation.

Subsequently, the coombe to the south of the excavation was subject to strip-and-record (SRR 123), as was the area covering the excavation site and continuing to the north (SRR 125/127), the latter revealing further, and in some cases associated, features. Unfortunately, there is some uncertainty as to the precise locations of some features recorded during the strip-and-record, with the result that some of the relationships between features recorded during the two phases of work remain unclear.

Moreover, for ease of recording, the northern strip-and-record area amalgamated two adjacent sites (SRR 125 and 127, chainage 17080–17650) which also encompassed the excavation at SRR 128 to the north (see below). For the purposes of this report, therefore, the strip-and-record features recorded up to the coombe north of the excavation site are described whilst those further north are dealt with separately. However, both areas were treated as a single site in the analysis of the finds; in some cases it has not been possible to distinguish between finds from the two sites.

Results

Excavation

A subsoil (7420) was recorded in the northernmost 18 m of the site. Six features were excavated, of which only two ditches were of archaeological origin; the others were a periglacial solifluction hollow (7424) and three tree hollows (7417, 7422, and 7435), one of which (7417) contained worked and burnt flint in its upper fill.

A *c.* 6 m length of ditch (7433), aligned east–west, was recorded at the southern end of the site. It was up to 1.8 m wide at the east but only 0.9 m wide at the squared terminal at the west (within the evaluation trench), and it was 0.6–0.9 m deep. Sherds of Late Neolithic/Early Bronze Age pottery were recovered from the lower ditch fills (7403 and 7431) as well as rare animal bone, burnt flint, and worked flint.

A parallel ditch (7416) was recorded *c.* 90 m to the north; it was traced for 7.5 m and had a terminal at its western end. It was 0.8 m wide and 0.7 m deep with a similar profile to ditch 7433 but produced no finds.

Strip-and-record

The section of strip-and-record south of the excavation area (chainage 16820–17020) was targeted on a ditch and two other possible features recorded during the evaluation. It confirmed the presence of the ditch, which was aligned approximately north-east–south-west with a V-shaped profile and which yielded a small quantity of Romano-British pottery and worked flint. The other possible features noted during the evaluation were not found and no other evidence for archaeological remains was encountered.

The strip-and-record area widened the western part of the excavation site, revealing further features at the southern end of the site (Fig. 12.1). These included a matching ditch terminal (12659) to the west of ditch 7433, forming a 4 m wide entrance, with a third ditch (12567) lying at an angle across the entrance to its south. Within the gap between the terminals of ditches 7433 and 12567 there was a small crescentic pit (12611) containing a partial inhumation burial, comprising the skull and long bones only and accompanied by a Late Iron Age/early Romano-British jar (Table 12.1, Fig. 12.3, no. 2). A single undated post-hole and a stake-hole (12683 and 12685) were recorded some 20 m to the south. A possible pit (12604) was identified to the east of ditch 12567, although its relationship with this feature was not clearly defined.

Some 70 m to the north of the ditches, on the western side of the route easement (outside the earlier excavation area), a 30 m long ditch (12621) was recorded, aligned north–south but curving slightly to the east, with terminals at either end (Figs 12.1–2). In the southern terminal, which was *c.* 2.2 m wide and up to 1.3 m deep, the skeleton (12578) of a female aged *c.* 16–18 years (Fig. 12.2; Table 12.1) lay face down on the primary fill (12579) with its head to the north, its posture suggesting that the body had been thrown into the ditch rather than being carefully placed. Probable trauma to the face had resulted in the loss of anterior maxillary teeth when the individual was 10–14 years old. A bone sample

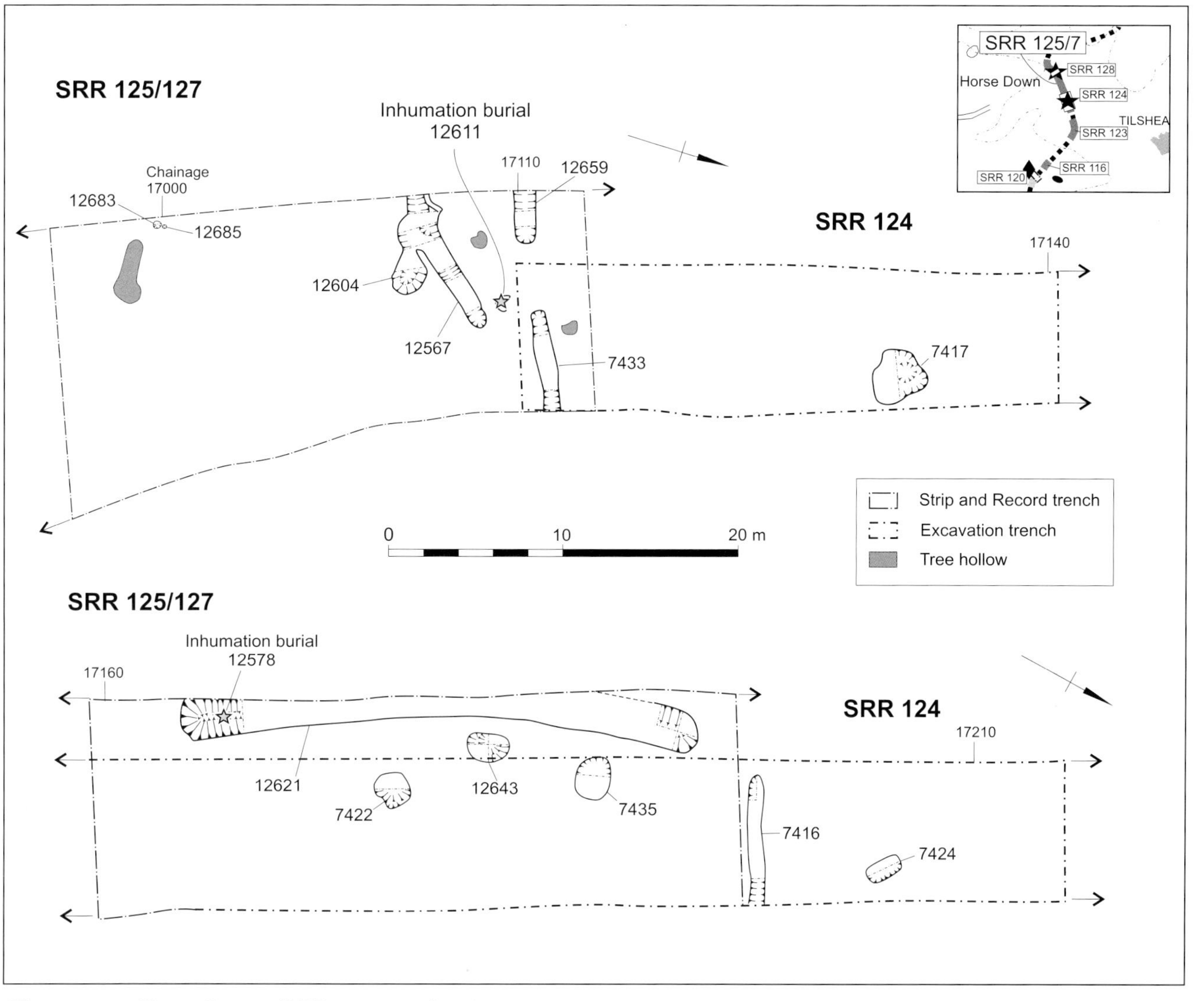

Figure 12.1 Horse Down (SRR 124, 125/127)

from the skeleton produced a radiocarbon date in the Middle Bronze Age of 1520–1400 cal BC (Beta-167360, 3190±40 BP) and other evidence of activity in this period is provided by a decorated rim sherd from a Middle Bronze Age vessel recovered from a secondary fill (12658) from the opposing ditch terminal. The remainder of the pottery from the ditch, much of it abraded, was of Late Bronze Age/Early Iron Age date. A possible pit (12643) lay just inside the curve of the ditch.

The initial interpretation of ditch 12621 was as possibly the western flanking ditch of a long barrow (AC Archaeology 2000, C25). The opposing ditch, it was suggested, lay outside the road easement to the east, with the barrow mound and any internal features having been levelled by ploughing. However, the subsequent radiocarbon dating of the burial to the Middle Bronze Age discounts this interpretation. It is probable, therefore, that this ditch represents part of a field enclosure system or drainage ditch; burials within such ditches being relatively common.

A poorly-preserved negative lynchet (12541) was recorded close to the base of the coombe to the north, and in the base of the coombe were two large tree hollows (12600 and 12627). These yielded very large quantities of burnt flint and evidence for *in situ* burning, along with, from 12600, 10 pieces of worked flint of probable later prehistoric date. No more precisely datable artefacts were recovered from these tree hollows, which were sealed by 0.6 m of colluvium (12522). A large east–west ditch (12585) on the flank of the coombe yielded pottery of probable Late Bronze Age date (contexts 12585 and 12586).

Finds

Excavation

by Lorraine Mepham

The human bone is summarised in Table 12.1. The small assemblage of finds from the excavation is all likely to be of prehistoric date (Table 12.2), although

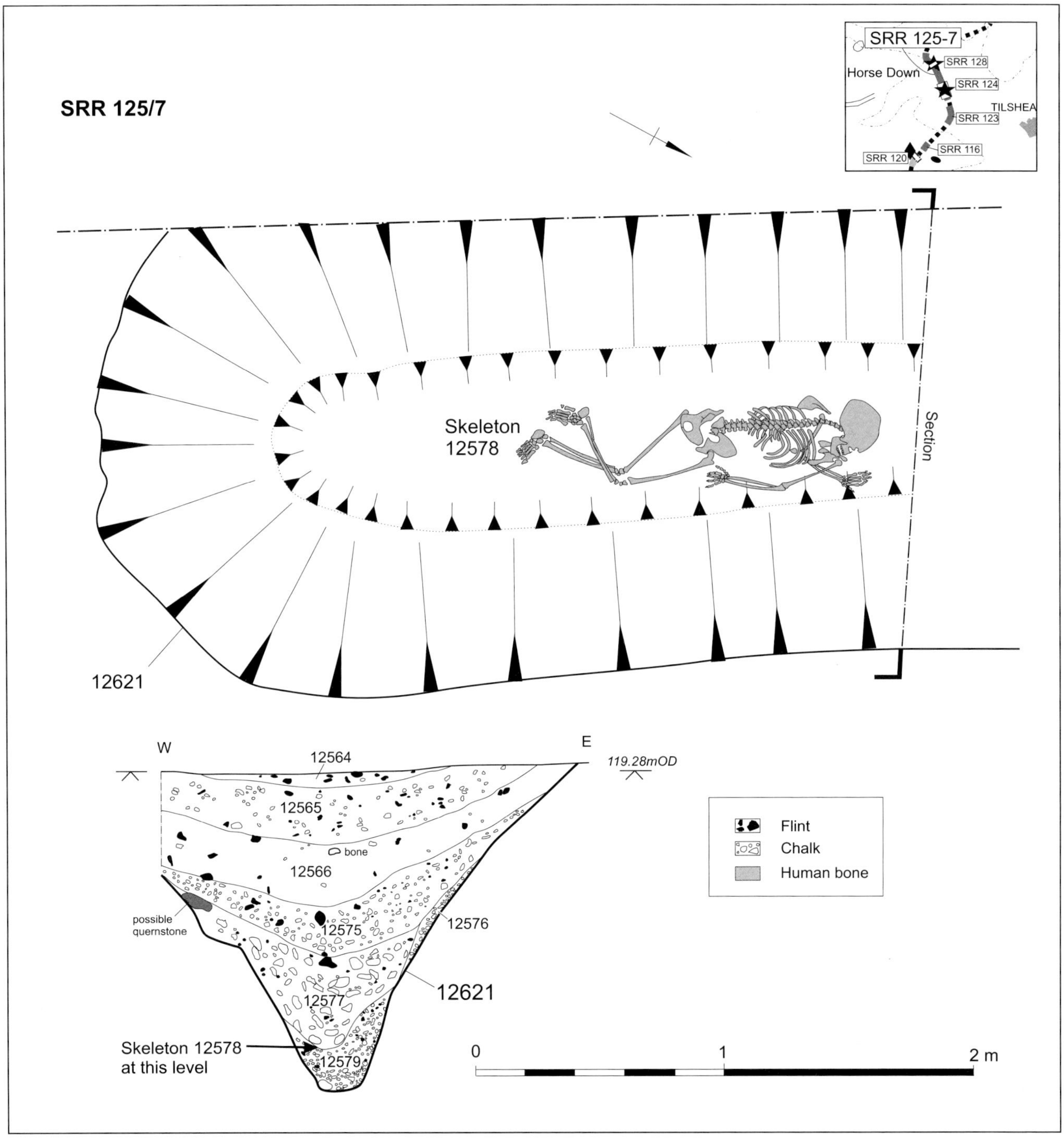

Figure 12.2 North-West of Golf Crossing (SRR 125/127) plan of terminal of ditch 12621 with detail of skeleton 12578, and section through the ditch

Table 12.1 North-West of Golf Crossing (SRR125/127): summary of human bone

Context	*Cut*	*Burial type*	*Quantification*	*Age/sex*	*Pathology*
12578	12621	inhumation	*c.* 99%	subadult *c.* 16–18 yr female	*am*tl (?trauma); caries; pd; calculus; ?dental abscess; pnb - mandible; exostoses - humerus shafts; strong adduction & medial rotation both arms
12611	12610	crouched inhumation	*c.* 15%	adult *c.* 25–40 yr ?female	*am*tl; caries; ?dental abscess

See Table 5.1 for key

Table 12.2 Horse Down (SRR 124): finds totals by feature: no./wt (g)

Feature	*Burnt Flint*	*Fired clay*	*Worked flint*	*Pottery*	*Animal bone (no.)*
Ditch 7433	3/54	–	4/28	9/21	17
Tree hollow 7417	1/4	–	2/12	–	–
Tree hollow 7422	137/998	1/2	–	–	–
Hollow 7424	5/50	–	–	–	–
Total	146/1106	1/2	6/40	9/21	17

the only clearly datable material comprises nine sherds of pottery from the lower fills of ditch 7433. These are dated, on the basis of their grog-tempered fabric, to the Late Neolithic/Early Bronze Age. None of the worked flint is chronologically distinctive and it can only be given a broad Neolithic/Bronze Age date range. The fired clay comprises a small undiagnostic fragment. None of the 17 fragments of animal bone recovered was identifiable.

Strip-and-record

Pottery

by Moira Laidlaw

The only vessel rim sherds recovered were from an expanded flat-topped rim with incised decoration on the external neck in fabric FL7 (Fig. 12.3, 1; PRN 12658). This rim is comparable to a Middle Bronze Age Biconical Urn recorded at Easton Lane, Hampshire (Ellison 1989, fig. 88, 55) and is perhaps slightly earlier than the later Bronze Age fabric types.

There was also a small assemblage of Late Bronze Age/Early Iron Age body sherds, mostly from ditch 12621. The sherds are very small and featureless and were attributed to this period mainly on the basis of fabric type, the majority occurring in the coarse flint-tempered fabrics FL2 and FL6. The later Bronze Age/Early Iron Age fabric types and decoration, albeit scarce, are comparable with the large pottery assemblage from Potterne (Morris 2000a, fig. 105, motif 8.3). Other late prehistoric pottery fabrics recorded from SRR125/127 are described below.

There was a complete, deliberately placed Late Iron Age/Early Romano-British vessel in a moderately coarse sandy fabric (QU103) recovered from burial 12611 (Fig. 12.3, 2; PRN 12610). The jar has an upright slightly everted rim, is decorated with an incised band of chevrons, and is burnished. This form and decoration is typical of the continuation of Durotrigian forms and decoration in the area.

Other finds

by Lorraine Mepham

Two Pennant Sandstone tile fragments were recovered from context 12575, while ditch 12585

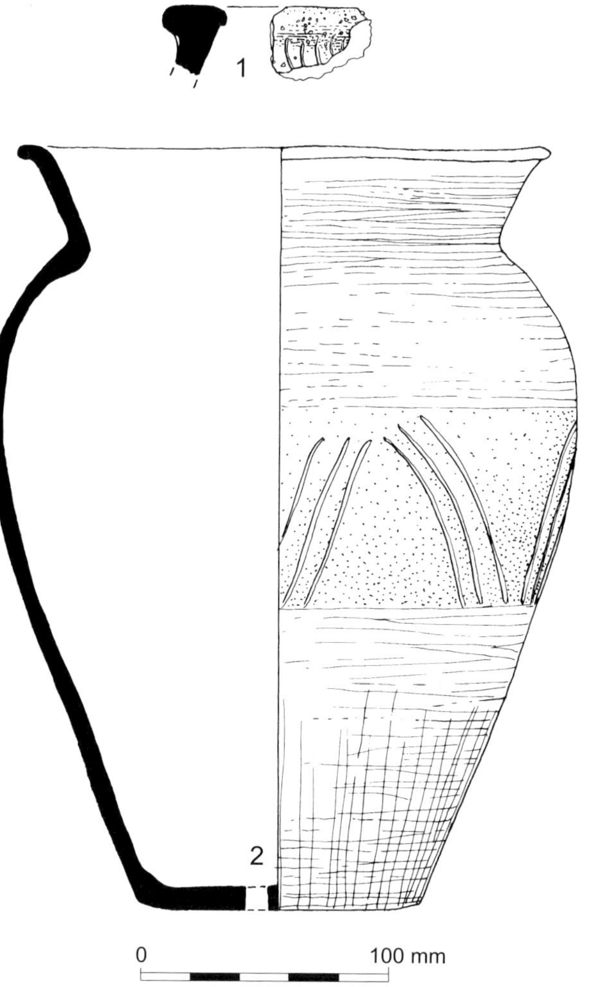

Figure 12.3 Horse Down (SRR 125/127): pottery

(contexts 12585 and 12586) produced a curved, perforated iron strip of unknown function, and a small undiagnostic fragment of ceramic building material, possibly Romano-British.

Discussion

A few sherds of residual Late Neolithic/Early Bronze Age pottery were recovered from ditch 7433 during the excavation. Activity of this period may be represented by a circular feature, possibly a ring ditch *c.* 12 m in diameter, recorded in the SMR (SU04 NW667) just west of the SRR route but close to the suggested location of the northern terminal of ditch 12621.

Ditch 12621, dated to the Middle Bronze Age, seems to be a fragment of a wider field enclosure or ditch system. It may be significant that the other main evidence for Middle Bronze Age activity along this section of the SRR is in the northern part of the same strip-and-record site (SRR 125/127), 350 m to the north (see below), where one of a series of animal burials in a ditch produced an almost identical date of 1510–1380 cal BC (Beta-167361, 3160±40 BP).

The later inhumation burial, accompanied by the Late Iron Age/Early Romano-British jar, was located within the apparent entranceway between the three small ditches 70 m to the south, and although there is nothing else to directly associate it with the ditches, a Late Iron Age/Early Romano-British date would be reasonable for an enclosure formed by them. The ditch recorded in the coombe to the south was of Romano-British date and it is possible that the majority of ditches recorded on this site were components of the same organised landscape, with ditch terminals marking points of access between adjacent fields or paddocks. Remnants of such field systems have been recorded from aerial photographs in the vicinity of the site, with more extensive areas surviving on the higher downland, such as on Chapperton and Lavington Downs to the west and north.

South of Foxtrot Crossing Excavation (SRR 128) and Strip-and-record (SRR 125/127)

The excavation site (chainage 17425–17465), to the north-west of Tilshead, was located on a low ridge with the ground falling gently, from 118 m aOD, to the north, east, and south. The site was targeted on three possible linear features of Romano-British date recorded during the evaluation. Subsequently, the site was encompassed by an area of strip-and-record.

Results

Excavation

Two features were excavated in the northern part of the site – an area of intercutting quarry pits and a curvilinear ditch which crossed them.

The large, sub-circular area of quarrying (8440) comprised at least 10 discrete pits of different sizes. It was up to 10 m across and *c.* 2 m deep, with a ridge of intact chalk across its centre indicating at least two zones of quarrying. The pits produced occasional pieces of worked flint, burnt flint, and animal bone, as well as two sherds of samian from pit fill 8436.

A slightly curvilinear ditch (8441), 3.4 m wide and 1.2 m deep, cut through the upper fills of the quarry, running north-east–south-west. It produced a single sherd of Romano-British coarseware, along with pieces of burnt flint and worked flint. Slumping of the quarry and ditch fills had created a wide, shallow depression which had filled with colluvial deposits (8418 and 8422). These sealed a buried soil or turfline (8419) containing a further eight sherds of Romano-British pottery.

Strip-and-record

Towards the base of the dry coombe south of the excavation site there was evidence for a poorly-preserved negative lynchets (12502).

Some 70 m north of the excavation site there was a shallow, possibly truncated north-west–south-east aligned ditch (12525) that petered out to the south and extended beyond the trench to the north-west. It contained along its base the complete skeletons of a pregnant cow and two sheep, the ditch having been locally widened to accommodate the cow carcass, along with the partially articulated and disarticulated remains of other animals (Pl. 12.1).

A bone sample from one of the sheep skeletons produced a radiocarbon date in the Middle Bronze Age of 1510–1380 cal BC (Beta-167361, 3160±40 BP), while Late Bronze Age/Early Iron Age pottery and quantities of worked and burnt flint were also recovered from the ditch.

Just beyond the south-eastern end of 12525 was a large V-shaped ditch (12528). It ran north-east from the edge of the easement then turn north where it was truncated by the edge of a large unexcavated feature (12647). A human skull, possibly from a female, and aged 30–50 years, was recovered from ditch 12525 (context 12668).

Finds

Excavation

by Lorraine Mepham

A small quantity of prehistoric and Romano-British finds was recovered from the site (Table 12.3). The small worked flint assemblage, which includes flakes/flake fragments and cores/core fragments but no tools or other retouched pieces, consists of locally accessible chalk flint, mostly patinated and in relatively fresh condition. In the absence of diagnostic pieces it can only be dated broadly to the Neolithic or Bronze Age.

All the pottery from the site was Romano-British. The three sherds of samian, from quarry pit 8433, are

Table 12.3 South of Foxtrot Crossing (SRR 128): finds totals by feature: no./wt (g)

Feature	*Burnt flint*	*Worked flint*	*Pottery*	*Iron (no.)*	*Animal bone (no.)*
Buried soil 8419	1/2	5/178	8/2	–	1
Colluvium 8422	–	–	–	1	–
Quarry pit 8433	–	6/51	3/5	–	2
Ditch 8441	2/82	21/358	1/18	–	2
Quarry pit 8447	1/190	9/190	–	–	1
Quarry pit 8452	–	3/40	–	–	3
Total	4/274	44/817	12/25	1	9

of later 1st or early 2nd century AD date. A possible sherd of Black Burnished ware was found in ditch 8441. The remaining sherds, from the buried soil, are coarseware and are not more closely datable within the Romano-British period.

An iron nail was recovered from the colluvium (8422). In addition, nine animal bone fragments were recovered – three are horse, two cattle, and the remainder could not be identified.

Strip-and-record

Flint

by Matt Leivers

The assemblage of 110 pieces from the two ditches is almost entirely patinated and dominated by broad, hard hammer struck flakes of probable later prehistoric date. There are very few chronological indicators but a few pieces have abraded platforms and may be earlier. Most are likely to be redeposited (Table 12.4), the exception being the group from context 12665 in ditch 12528: the 27 flakes all look as though they derive from the same nodule, and are very fresh – possibly they represent limited knapping in the Early Iron Age. All of the scrapers are rather crude, and would not be out of place in the Middle Bronze Age or later.

Table 12.4 South of Foxtrot Crossing (SRR 125/127): worked flint

Context	*1*	*2*	*3*	*4*	*5*
Ditch 12525					
12525	1	3	–	–	–
12527	–	8	1	–	–
12533	–	1	1	–	–
12540	–	5	2	1	–
12552	–	1	–	–	–
12636	–	1	–	–	–
12638	–	3	–	–	–
12617	–	5	1	–	–
12640	–	5	–	–	–
12644	–	1	–	–	–
12646	–	9	1	–	–
Ditch 12528					
12529	–	1	–	–	1
12530	–	2	–	–	1
12531	–	2	–	–	–
12560	–	1	–	–	–
12663	–	3	–	–	–
12665	–	27	–	2	1
12666	–	7	–	–	–
12667	–	2	–	–	–
12668	–	7	–	1	–
12670	–	2	–	–	–
Total	1	96	6	4	3

Key:
1 = debitage; 2 = flake; 3 = broken flake; 4 = core;
5 = scraper

Pottery

by Moira Laidlaw

The bulk of the pottery recovered from ditch 12525 comprises very small and featureless sherds, which are attributed to the Late Bronze Age/Early Iron Age mainly on the basis of fabric type, the majority occurring in the coarse, flint-tempered fabrics FL2 and FL6. Other fabrics recovered from SRR 125/127 comprise four shell-tempered sherds including one decorated with two slightly curving furrowed bands and six very small sherds in the sandy fabric QU2. The later Bronze Age/Early Iron Age fabric types and decoration, albeit scarce, are comparable with examples in the large pottery assemblage from Potterne (Morris 2000a, fig. 105, motif 8.3).

Other pottery of this period comprises one coarseware sherd (QU102) and one abraded fine grog-tempered sherd which may possibly be Early Bronze Age or Late Iron Age/Early Romano-British.

Animal bone

by Claire Ingrem

A total of 1933 fragments of animal bone was recovered (Table 12.5), the great majority of it from the northern section discussed above. Although cattle are the most numerous taxon according to NISP, most of the fragments belong to the partial skeletons of a pregnant cow (with foetal calf) and two sheep skeletons. Additional fragments not associated with the skeletons represent a minimum of one other sheep/goat and cattle.

Cattle are represented by elements from all parts of the body including skull bones and vertebrae, as are sheep, from which loose teeth, humeri, tibiae, carpals, and proximal phalanges are most numerous. Fragile skull bones are poorly represented as are vertebrae and ribs especially when considering the presence of partial skeletons and taking account of the fragments assigned to the medium mammal category. Pig is represented solely by loose teeth and horse by a tibia.

Dental ageing data are scarce, an isolated mandibular third molar belonging to cattle indicates that one cow was aged over 6 years at the time of slaughter. Apart from the partial skeletons, few bones were able to provide epiphyseal fusion data although an unfused proximal epiphysis of a femur indicates that one sheep/goat was less than 42 months at the time of slaughter.

All of the partial skeletons were recovered from ditch 12525 (Pl. 12.1), which was widened to accommodate that of the cow. The sheep came from contexts 12599 and 12620, the cow from context 12597. The sheep skeleton from context 12620 belongs to an animal aged 3–4 years according to

Table 12.5 South of Foxtrot Crossing (SRR125/127): animal bone

	Cattle	*Sheep/ goat*	*Pig*	*Horse*	*Large mammal*	*Medium mammal*	*Unid.*	*Total*
Horn core	–	1						1
Zygomatic	1	–						1
Occipital condyle	2	2						4
Upper tooth	14	11						25
Mandible	17	5				1		23
Lower tooth	17	20	1					38
Hyoid	1	–						1
Atlas	1	–						1
Axis	1	1						2
Scapula	6	3						9
Humerus	4	16				2		22
Radius	1	8						9
Ulna	3	3						6
Pelvis	10	5						15
Femur	4	6			1			11
Patella	2	1						3
Tibia	4	15		1		1		21
Carpal	–	10						10
Astralagus	5	2						7
Calcaneus	1	2						3
Navicular-cuboid	–	3						3
Lateral malleolus	1	–						1
Sesamoid	3	–						3
Metacarpal	2	5						7
Metatarsal	–	5						5
Metapodial	16	1						17
1st phalanx	5	10						15
2nd phalanx	6	7						13
3rd phalanx	2	1						3
Cervical vertebra	5	–				2		7
Thoracic vertebra	11	3				3		17
Lumbar vertebra	6	1			1			8
Sacrum	1	–			–			1
Caudal vertebra	1	–			–			1
Rib	10	2			14	1		27
Skull fragment	40	–			120	7	1	168
Tooth fragment	2	2	5		1	–	1	11
Long bone frag.	8	–			14	14		36
Rib fragment	14	28			162	30		234
Vertebral frag.	81	19			39	15		154
Unidentifiable	9	77			188	–	716	990
Total	317[a]	275[b]	6	1	540[c]	76[d]	718[e]	1933
%	16	14	<1	<1	28	4	37	

Includes [a]308 and [b]236 frags belonging to skeletons
Includes [c]399; [d]42 and [e]441 frags probably belonging to skeletons

tooth-wear data, and epiphyseal fusion data indicate that it was adult. This animal displays evidence for butchery on its left humerus in the form of multiple cut marks on the medial side of the distal epiphysis. A few bones were probably gnawed but severe root damage masks evidence for other surface modifications. The sheep skeleton from context 12599 belongs to an immature individual with epiphyseal fusion data indicating that it was about 3 years of age at the time of death. The cow skeleton belongs to an immature animal aged somewhere between 36–48 months according to epiphyseal fusion. There is no evidence for butchery on either the immature sheep or cow skeletons although this may have been obscured by root damage.

The sample size is too small to provide conclusive evidence regarding animal husbandry practices. It is clear that cattle, sheep/goat, and pig were all present but the interpretation of other aspects must remain speculative. The presence of partial skeletons belonging to immature sheep and a pregnant cow raises the question of whether these represent the disposal of diseased animals or the result of ritual activity. However, the presence of immature and foetal animals indicates that some livestock were reared at the site. The under-representation of fragile and less dense elements such as ribs and vertebrae belonging to sheep/goat, suggests that the assemblage is biased by density-related preservation bias, given the presence of partial skeletons. Butchery marks on the adult sheep skeleton indicate that one of the skeletons had been utilised and, from their location, that the forelimb was disarticulated at the elbow joint.

Discussion

Ditch 12525 provided inconsistent dating evidence. The Middle Bronze Age date from one of the sheep burials in its base and, by association probably the other animal burials, contrasts with the predominantly Late Bronze Age/Early Iron Age date provided by the pottery

Plate 12.1 Animal bone in ditch 12525

assemblage. This appears to lack a Middle Bronze Age component, although the dating of the small featureless flint-tempered sherds is not precise. As discussed above, the reason for the animal burials could not be determined, but whether it was purely functional or had some primarily symbolic significance, it suggests the likely presence of contemporary settlement in this area. The burial of a human skull from the same ditch also suggests some symbolic activity. The burial of a young girl within a short length of ditch at SRR125/127 (see above), is also of interest here and seems to be part of the same tradition of burial within ditches during the Middle Bronze Age.

Ditch 12525 corresponds closely in its location and orientation with a ditch forming part of a field system recorded in the SMR (SU04NW611), which lies on the south-eastern margins of the more extensive field systems on Lavington and Chapperton Downs. The possible Middle Bronze Age date for this ditch is therefore of some interest in understanding the early development of these systems, elements of which are known to date from the Middle Bronze Age (McOmish *et al.* 2002, 53), and to have continued in use or been modified into the Iron Age and Romano-British period. Romano-British quarry pits and a ditch were recorded *c.* 100 m to the south, and it is possible that the large unexcavated feature (12647) recorded during the strip-and-record may have been a further area of quarrying.

Chapter 13
Discussion

Early Prehistory

The earliest evidence for activity along the SRR is represented by a few pieces of flintwork, including blades and blade-like flakes, of possible Mesolithic or Early Neolithic date, that were recovered from a stream channel and a later pit at Boreham Farm Bungalow (Chapter 9); there may have also been a Mesolithic component to the small worked flint assemblage at South-east of Battlesbury Wood (Chapter 9). Both sites, located south of Battlesbury Hill, were on relatively low lying ground on the edge of the Wylye valley, a potentially favourable location for the exploitation of the varied wild resources available across a range of ecological zones. The low level of Mesolithic finds from the SRR is consistent with the limited evidence from across the rest of the DTE SP, as well as more widely on the chalk throughout southern England. This does not mean, however, that exploitation of the downs was not an integral part of the subsistence activities of hunter-gatherer communities with settlement patterns weighted towards the valleys that flank and bisect Salisbury Plain, where finds are predominantly of large core tools (Wymer 1977). An assemblage of 261 Mesolithic or Early Neolithic flints, for example, was recorded in a possible tree hollow on Breach Hill, Tilshead (Harding 2006), indicating activity higher on the downs.

Much of evidence for Neolithic activity along the SRR comprised isolated features or residual material. An Early Neolithic presence would not be unexpected given the proximity of both Battlesbury Bowl itself and of several sites along the SRR to known long barrows. There are four on the ridge top to the north of Battlesbury Bowl and three lie close to the SRR route at Heytesbury, Knook and the King's Barow at Bishopstrow (Allen and Gardiner 2004, fig. 5, E, F, and G respectively). The latter lies almost on the floor of the Wylye valley, positioned on the edge of the Greensand bench, less than 1 km from Boreham Farm Bungalow (see Allen and Gardiner 2004 for a discussion of the Wylye long barrows). A pit at East of Knook Castle (Chapter 11), contained sherds from five different Early Neolithic pots along with worked flint and cereal grain (the few Late Bronze Age sherds from the same feature are probably intrusive). A substantial portion of a Middle Neolithic Peterborough Ware vessel was found with worked and burnt flint in a small pit cutting a tree hollow at East of Knook Castle (Chapter 11, Fig. 11.5), and the residual Neolithic pottery and flints recovered from Willis's Field Barn (Chapter 10). In the absence of a clear settlement context, however, the deposition of such material in pits during the Neolithic is frequently (perhaps inevitably) interpreted as having a ritual dimension. Further indications of non-domestic later Neolithic activity in the area include a possible henge in the Wylye valley at Sutton Veny (Gardiner in prep.) and a barrow containing an antler macehead on Cop Heap in Warminster (Simpson 1996). It was also suggested, as early as 1930, that a discontinuous inner bank and ditch circuit within Scratchbury might be a causewayed enclosure (McOmish *et al.* 2002, 32 and figs 2.16–17), though this has been disputed (Owald *et al.* 2001, 157). Residual Neolithic and Early Bronze Age flintwork was recovered from Battlesbury Bowl although the flint axe from an Iron Age pit may have been an item found and retained as a curio (Chapter 3).

The dearth of clear evidence for settlement activity continues into the Early Bronze Age, the main feature of this period being the previously unknown round barrow and adjacent multiple inhumation/cremation burials recorded at North-West of Middle Barn Farm. Round barrows in this part of the Plain are quite widely dispersed, at least relative to the concentrations of such monuments along the edge of the chalk around Battlesbury and more notably to the east around Stonehenge, the Avon valley, and Nine Mile River. However, the ring ditch's highly visible location on a ridge overlooking the Imber valley is typical of many such monuments. The positioning of the body, the timber chamber in which the earlier inhumation had been interred, the re-use of the grave for subsequent burials and the presence in the upper grave of a multiple burial (inhumation and cremation) are all features which have parallels in late Beaker graves. The radiocarbon date from the upper inhumation burial of 1980–1760 cal BC is consistent with a date towards the end of the Early Bronze Age, the earlier burial preceding it by an unknown period. If the grave was marked in some way, there could have been a long interval between the two burial events.

Isolated pits of Late Neolithic/Early Bronze Age date on the SRR include small pit at Willis's Field Barn containing Beaker sherds, flints, hazelnut shells and cereal grains, with further residual Late Neolithic/Early Bronze Age sherds and flintwork being recovered from adjacent ditches (Chapter 10). Residual material of this general period was also identified in the assemblages from a number of sites including, to the west, flints and pottery from Battlesbury Bowl (Chapters 3–4) and pottery from the Battlesbury Spur watching brief (Chapter 9), and to the east flints from South of Foxtrot Crossing (Chapter 12). The evidence for Neolithic and Early Bronze Age activity is somewhat limited, partly due to the nature and extent of the excavations. However the general pattern of activity fits into the known evidence.

Later Prehistory

Middle Bronze Age settlement on the chalk is more widely known from the Marlborough Downs to the north (Gingell 1992), and on Cranborne Chase to the south (Barrett *et al.* 1991), than on Salisbury Plain itself, although the excavation of a Middle–Late Bronze Age settlement on Dunch Hill, Tidworth (Andrews 2006), in the eastern part of the Plain suggests, that this may simply reflect the restricted access to the military training area, and the relative lack of investigation sites of Bronze Age date.

Nonetheless, as recorded more widely across Salisbury Plain, and beyond, it is only from the Middle Bronze Age that the weight of the evidence changes from the ritual and monumental to the domestic and agricultural, with the first clear although limited evidence for settlement, land division and enclosure. This was demonstrated in the various phases of activity at Willis's Field Barn (Chapter 10) where a ditch, possibly a field boundary, was subsequently crossed by the ditch of a possible enclosure. Undated post-holes on the inner edge of the enclosure ditch close to its entrance may have been associated with it, but no domestic structures were identified within the enclosure, although only a small area was exposed. Nonetheless, the materials recovered from the enclosure ditch, which was recut on at least one occasion, are all characteristic of domestic and agricultural assemblage. It included Deverel-Rimbury pottery probably of relatively local manufacture, worked flint, quern fragments, fragments of unworked shale, and a worked bone point possibly used for weaving, along with animal bone, cereal grains and hazelnut shells. Articulated animal bones including cattle mandibles, vertebrae and hind leg bones were recovered, some of which was deposited in ditch terminals along with two complete cattle skulls. The enclosure would have been sited on the relatively flat top of a promontory ridge on the edge of the Wylye valley, the environmental evidence pointing to cleared and established downland, although with shady areas close by.

This would have been the only significant evidence for activity in this period were it not for the two radiocarbon dates from SRR 125/127 (North-west of Golf Crossing and South of Foxtrot Crossing), which indicated that both the possible unceremonious burial of a young female in the bottom of a ditch terminal (Fig. 12.2), and, some 350 m to the north, the burials of animal carcasses in another ditch (Pl. 12.1, 1520–1400 cal BC and 1510–1380 cal BC, respectively) were also of Middle Bronze Age date. The majority of the pottery from the ditches appeared to indicate a Late Bronze Age/Early Iron Age date, although it may be that some to the undiagnostic flint-tempered pottery encountered at that site and more widely along the SRR, belongs to the Middle Bronze Age.

The proximity of these human and animal burials is intriguing and raises the question of whether there may have been some symbolic/ritual association between them, cremation rather than inhumation being the more common mortuary rite for humans in the Middle Bronze Age. A close association between Middle Bronze Age human and animal burials is found at other Middle Bronze Age sites, such as at the settlement on the Old Sarum Spur, Salisbury where a human burial and a cow burial (buried with a foetal sheep/goat) were dated to 3179±40 BP, 1520–1320 cal BC (NZA-18419) and 3211±40 BP, 1600–1400 cal BC (NZA-18418) respectively (Powell *et al.* 2005). Middle Bronze Age animal burials in ditches are quite widely known, as for instance at Kingsmead Quarry, Horton, Berkshire (Wessex Archaeology 2006a), where the ditches formed parts of a more extensive system of land division. At Corporation Farm, Oxfordshire human and animal burials together with fragmentary human remains were made in ditches and other features in significant positions such as the terminals (Shand *et al.* 2003, 38–9, fig. 3.8). Yates has noted in his study of Bronze Age field systems that special deposits including human remains were placed in ditches with entrances being particularly favoured locations (2007, 136–7). As only short lengths of Middle Bronze Age ditch were revealed along the SRR it is not possible to determine whether they were associated with more extensive field systems, although the alignment of the ditch containing the animal burials on one axis of a rectilinear field system identified in aerial photographs may not be coincidental.

Activity in the Late Bronze Age/Early Iron Age, however, is even more widely represented, not least by the beginnings of settlement activity in a landscape location not dissimilar to that of Willis's Field Barn – the chalk ridge at Battlesbury Bowl, where the pottery sequence starts with the decorated wares of the Early All Cannings Cross tradition dated to the 8th–7th centuries BC (Chapter 7).

Beyond Battlesbury, however, although there is evidence for activity of this period at a number of other sites along the SRR and at varying locations within the landscape, this evidence consists in many cases of either relatively isolated features, such as individual pits at South of Old Ditch (Chapter 10), Willis's Field Barn (Chapter 10), East of Knook Castle (Chapter 11), and North-west of Middle Barn Farm (Chapter 11), or residual material in later features. A few sites, however, have hints of possible settlement activity, including those on the Battlesbury spur road. At Boreham Farm Bungalow (Chapter 9), a group of possibly contemporary post-holes and pits in an open grassland environment produced Late Bronze Age pottery, worked flints, and fired clay, along with cereal grain and hazelnut shells, while to the east, at South-east of Battlesbury Wood (Chapter 9), a circular gully, possibly representing a round-house, was closely associated with a group of postholes containing Late Bronze Age/Early Iron Age pottery and flints. While these sites, both located on the edges of former stream channels, may indicate foci of settlement separate from that at Battlesbury Bowl, it is also possible that they represent small-scale activity by parts of the same community exploiting an adjacent ecological zone, perhaps on a seasonal or other short-term basis.

A similar small cluster of pits, post-holes, a hearth, and a gully were also recorded at East of Quebec Barn (Chapter 9). The likely domestic nature of these features is indicated by the finds comprising post-Deverel-Rimbury pottery dating from around the end of the 2nd or beginning of the 1st millennium BC, worked flints (including flakes, cores, and a piercer), animal bone, burnt flint, part of shale armlet, and a quern fragment. Also recovered were grains of spelt wheat and hulled barley, these crops being typical of this date and possibly processed in the immediate area, and hazelnut shells.

The impression gained from such evidence is small-scale settlement activity largely dispersed across a landscape increasingly subject to changing patterns of division and organisation. No dating evidence was recovered from the Old Ditch, where the SRR crossed this major spinal Wessex Linear on Breakheart Hill (Chapter 9), but excavations at Breach Hill (Birbeck 2006), on Copehill Down (Wessex Archaeology 1988), and in the eastern range of the Plain have shown that these linear ditches, which appear to divide the landscape into large, possibly territorial or landuse blocks, had their origins in the Late Bronze Age (Bradley *et al.* 1994). In some cases these ditches cut across earlier field systems, and many, including Old Ditch, had smaller subsidiary ditches running perpendicular from them (McOmish *et al.* 2002). Although there is a noticeably greater concentration of field systems to the south of the Old Ditch on Breakheart Hill, possibly reflecting differences in contemporary land-use, it cannot be established that these are actually associated with the ditch's construction, rather with its use in later periods.

Whether it was the particular location of the initial Battlesbury Bowl settlement which accounts for the continued nucleation and expansion of settlement on the site into and through the Iron Age (until its ultimate replacement by the hillfort of Battlesbury Camp), or whether the wider pattern of smaller-scale dispersed settlement remained the norm is unclear. However, the extensive middens discovered at Potterne (Lawson 2000) and East Chisenbury (Brown *et al.* 1994; McOmish 1996) indicate that certain locations in the landscape developed as important foci in the economic and social lives of communities on and around the Plain. While no middens approaching this scale were found at Battlesbury Bowl, there appears nonetheless to have been a substantial accumulation of midden material resulting in part, as at Potterne and East Chisenbury, from the burning of stabling waste. In the same way, therefore, the site's potentially strategic location, both agriculturally and economically, may contributed to the development of this ridge as a focus for more widely dispersed settlements.

Battlesbury Bowl was the only site along the SRR producing substantial evidence for Iron Age settlement. This is despite the fact that the route passes close to other known Iron Age sites, including an enclosure adjacent to the SRR at South of Old Ditch (Chapter 10), and Knook Castle hillfort. It is probable, that other, as yet unrecognised, open settlements on a similar scale are to be found in the landscape crossed by the SRR, but were not directly impacted by it. Although a number of burials had been found outside the north-west entrance to Battlesbury Camp in the early 19th century (Cunnington 1924, 373, it was not until an access road was constructed in 1956 that the presence of settlement features on the chalk ridge north of the hillfort were first identified (Chadwick and Thompson 1956). While some of the ditches are recognisable in aerial photographs, the extensive settlement is not.

Romano-British and Later

The partial inhumation burial between ditch terminals at Horse Down (Chapter 12) was accompanied by a decorated jar of Late Iron Age/ Early Romano-British date. Elsewhere along the SRR, however, with the exception of East of Field Barn (Chapter 9), evidence for Late Iron Age and Romano-British activity consisted largely of few ditches dated by Roman pottery, and small quantities of residual finds from other features.

The evidence from East of Field Barn, located on the low ground east of Battlesbury Bowl, however, suggests the possibly intensity of Romano-British exploitation of the landscape, comprising field boundaries and track-ways. Other features included a cesspit and a horse burial in a gully located probably on the edge of a settlement. The substantial finds assemblage included pottery dominated by utilitarian wares and vessel forms such as large storage jars, and there is nothing to indicate a particularly high status for such a settlement. Although the scale and extent of the settlement associated with these features was not established, it appears to fall between the villa settlements that are known from the river valleys, such as at Pit Mead (Colt Hoare 1821, 108), in the Wylye valley near Warminster and others in the Avon valley (Grinsell 1957, 91), and the downland 'village' settlements such as those at Knook and on Chapperton Down (McOmish *et al.* 2002, 95).

Although no medieval features were recorded, the earthworks surveyed at East of Battlesbury Bowl (Chapter 9) and West Hill Farm (Chapter 10), comprising strip lynchets formed through cultivation on the steep chalk slopes, may well be of medieval date, although the subsequent excavation of the West Hill lynchets produced no datable finds. Those to the east of Battlesbury Bowl are probably associated with the shrunken medieval village that lies at the foot of Middle Hill, recorded in *Domesday Book* as Mideltone (see Smith 1997, fig. 34), where house platforms and enclosure earthworks can still be seen (Gardiner, pers. obs.).

Two short earthwork banks, recorded at Vedette Post Four (Chapter 11) and West of Hotel Crossing (Chapter 12), were shown to be modern features, most probably associated with military training.

Conclusion

The route of the Southern Range Road, between Harman Lines in the west and Tilshead in the east, represents a transect across part of a well-preserved archaeological landscape, about which much is known from aerial photographic and earthwork surveys, but relatively little excavation has taken place. The different stages of fieldwork undertaken before and during the road's construction, therefore, offered a valuable opportunity to enhance the understanding of that landscape's development and of the changing influences which have created and preserved the diverse range of archaeological monuments known to exist there.

However, the line chosen for the SRR, which sought to minimise its archaeological impact by avoiding where possible the known archaeological resource, is not the line that would have been selected by archaeologists seeking to answer the many questions about the archaeology of Salisbury Plain. Moreover, where elements of more extensive activity were recorded along the route, their interpretation was necessarily constrained to the route of the road. As a consequence, the results of the fieldwork, with the major exception of the excavation at Battlesbury Bowl, raise as many questions as they answer. Although even at the latter site interpretation was hampered by the excavation area and an important question of the relationship of the settlement to the hillfort remains unanswered (see Chapter 7).

Nevertheless, not only have important individual finds been made, but together the results reveal patterns of social, economic, and ritual activity which suggest how the use of the landscape changed over time. Along its 23 km, the SRR passes within sight of a number of known Neolithic long barrows and Early Bronze Age round barrows; it cuts across extensive 'Celtic' field systems, whose construction and use may date from the Middle Bronze Age through to the Romano-British period, as well as across the line of a major late prehistoric linear ditch; and it passes close to the defences of two Iron Age hillforts, and to two Romano-British nucleated settlements. In addition, as it passes from valley floor, across downland edge and dry coombe onto chalk ridge, it crosses medieval strip lynchets and post-medieval field boundaries, as well as features relating to the use of Defence Training Estate Salisbury Plain (DTE SP) for military training. Features from all these periods of activity were investigated along the route, adding (to varying degrees) to a fuller understanding of how this upland landscape was exploited in different ways and at different times in the past. A range of finds and environmental remains has been recovered which has assisted the interpretation of activities being carried out and also the appearance of the landscape from early prehistory through the post-Roman period. Despite limitations dictated by the road specification valuable information has been gained from these analyses.

Importantly the results of these archaeological investigations have helped inform the probable impact of the proposed Eastern Tank Track. As with the Southern Range Road it is hoped that this road will help manage the flow of heavy traffic across the Plain. Archaeological desk-based assessment and field evaluation among other techniques (Wessex Archaeology 2006b; 2007), have revealed a similar landscape to the Southern Range Road, with remains dating from the Neolithic up to the modern use of Salisbury Plain for military training. Known areas of relatively high archaeological potential also exist along this route but the impact of the Tank Track is being mitigated as far as possible by utilising existing tracks and building up selected areas in order to protect any archaeological remains. Excavation is being undertaken only where absolutely necessary in order for the construction of the road to take place.

Bibliography

AC Archaeology, 2000. *Salisbury Plain Training Area Southern Range Road: Stage 2 archaeology contract assessment report*, Hindon, unpubl. rep.

Adams, J.C., 1986. *Outline of Orthopaedics*, London, Churchill Livingstone

Allen, M.J., 1995a. Ditch and feature fills, in R.M.J. Cleal, K.E. Walker and R. Montague, *Stonehenge in its Landscape: Twentieth-century Excavations*, 4–6, London, English Heritage Archaeol. Rep. 10

Allen, M.J., 1995b. Land molluscs, in Wainwright and Davies 1995, 92–100

Allen, M.J., 1998. *The Development of Prehistoric Landuse in the Guiting Power Landscape; the land snail evidence*, unpubl. rep. for Guiting Power Ltd

Allen, M.J., 2001. Land snails; evidence for landscape and landuse change, 54–67 in C.J. Ellis and M. Rawlings, Excavations at Balksbury Camp, Andover 1995–97, *Proc. Hampshire Fld Club Archaeol. Soc.* 56, 21–94

Allen, M.J. and Gardiner, J., 2004. Neolithic of the Wylye valley 1: Millennium re-investigation of the Corton Long Barrow, ST 9308 4034, *Wiltshire Archaeol. Natur. Hist. Mag.* 97, 63–77

Allen, M.J. and Gardiner, J., 2006. Codford Circle: Iron Age pits and feasting, *Past* 53, 1–3

Anderson, A.S., 1979. *The Roman Pottery Industry in North Wiltshire*, Swindon, Swindon Archaeol. Soc. Rep. 2

Andrews, P., 2006. A Middle to Late Bronze Age settlement at Dunch Hill, Tidworth, *Wiltshire Archaeol. Natur. Hist. Mag.* 99, 51–78

Annable, F.K. and Simpson, D.D.A., 1964. *Guide Catalogue of the Neolithic and Bronze Age Collections in Devizes Museum*, Devizes, Wiltshire Archaeol. Natur. Hist. Soc.

ApSimon, A.M., 1962. The prehistoric pottery, 128–38 in P.A. Rahtz, Neolithic and Beaker Sites at Downton, near Salisbury, Wiltshire, *Wiltshire Archaeol. Natur. Hist. Mag.* 58, 116–41

Armit, I., 2007. Hillforts at war: from Maiden Castle to Taniwaha Pa, *Proc. Prehist. Soc.* 73, 25–38

Armour-Chelu, M. and Andrews, P., 1996. Surface modification of bone, in M. Bell, P.J. Fowler and S.W. Hillson, *The Experimental Earthwork Project 1960–1992*, 178–85, York, Counc. Brit. Archaeol. Res. Rep. 100

Ashbee, P., 1984. *The Earthen Long Barrow in Britain*, 2nd edn, Norwich, Geo Books

Ashbee, P., Bell, M. and Proudfoot, E. (eds), 1989. *Wilsford Shaft: Excavations 1960–2*, London, English Heritage Archaeol. Rep. 11

Avery, B.W. and Bascomb, C.L. (eds), 1974. *Soil Survey Laboratory Methods*, Harpenden, Soil Survey Technical Monogr. 6

Ball, D.F., 1964. Loss-on-ignition as an estimate of organic matter and organic carbon in non-calcareous soils, *J. Soil Sci.* 15, 84–92

Barclay, A., 2007. Connections and networks: a wider world and other places, in D. Benson and A. Whittle (eds), *Building Memories. The Neolithic Cotswold Long Barrow at Ascott-Under-Wychwood, Oxfordshire*, 331–44, Oxford, Cardiff Stud. in Archaeol.

Barclay, A. and Edwards, E., forthcoming. The prehistoric pottery, in G. Hey (ed.), *Yarnton Neolithic and Bronze Age*, Oxford, Thames Valley Landscapes Monogr.

Barrett, J.C., Bradley, R., and Green, M., 1991. *Landscape, Monuments and Society. The Prehistory of Cranborne Chase*. Cambridge, Univ. Press

Barrett, J., Freeman, P.W.M. and Woodward, A., 2000. *Cadbury Castle Somerset: the later prehistoric and early historic archaeology*, Swindon, English Heritage Archaeol. Rep. 20

Bass, W.M., 1987. *Human Osteology*, Columbia, Missouri Archaeol. Soc.

Beek, G.C., van, 1983. *Dental Morphology: an illustrated guide*, Bristol, J. Wright

Bell, M.G., Allen, M.J., Smith, R.W. and Johnson, S., in press. Mollusc and sedimentary evidence for the palaeoenvironmental history of Hambledon Hill and its surroundings, in R. Mercer and F. Healy (eds) in press, *Hambledon Hill, Dorset, England. Excavation and survey of a Neolithic complex and its surrounding landscape*, Swindon, English Heritage Archaeol. Rep.

Berry, A.C. and Berry, R.J., 1967. Epigenetic variation in the human cranium, *J. Anatomy* 101, 361–79

Bersu, G., 1940. Excavations at Little Woodbury, Wiltshire, part 1: the settlement as revealed by excavation, *Proc. Prehist. Soc.* 6, 30–111

BGS, 1985. *British Geological Survey of Great Britain, 1:50,000 Solid and Drift Series*, Sheet 281, Frome

Binford, L.R., 1981. *Bones: ancient men and modern myths*, New York, Academic

Birbeck, V., 2006. Excavations of the Old Ditch linear earthwork, Breach Hill, Tilshead, *Wiltshire Archaeol. Natur. Hist. Mag.* 99, 79–103

Bishop, M.J., 1974. The molluscs of Wicken Fen with some additional records, *Cambridgeshire & Isle of Ely Natur. Trust Ann. Rep.* 1–4

Bloch, M. and Parry, J., 1982. Introduction: death and the regeneration of life, in M. Bloch and J. Parry (eds), *Death and the Regeneration of Life*, 1–13, Cambridge, Univ. Press

Boschian, G. and Montagnari-Kokelji, E., 2000. Prehistoric shepherds and caves in the Trieste Karst (northeastern Italy), *Geoarchaeology* 15(4), 331–71

Bowen, C., 1978. 'Celtic' fields and 'ranch' boundaries in Wessex, in S. Limbrey and J.G. Evans (eds), *The Effect of Man on the Landscape: the Lowland Zone*, London, Counc. Brit. Archaeol. Res. Rep. 21, 115–22

Bowen, C. and Fowler, P.J., 1966. Romano-British settlements in Dorset and Wiltshire, in C. Thomas (ed.), *Rural Settlement in Roman Britain*, 43–67, London, Counc. Brit. Archaeol. Res. Rep. 7

Bradley, R., 1981. Various styles of urn: cemeteries and settlement in southern England c. 14000–1000bc, in R. Chapman, I. Kinnes, and K. Randsborg (eds), *The Archaeology of Death*, 91–104. Cambridge, Univ. Press

Bradley, R., Entwistle, R. and Raymond, F., 1994. *Prehistoric Land Division on Salisbury Plain: the work of the Wessex Linear Ditches Project*, London, English Heritage Archaeol. Rep. 2

Brochier, J.E., Villa, P. and Giacomarra, M., 1992. Shepherds and sediments: geo-ethno-archaeology of pastoral sites, *J. Anthrop. Archaeol.* 11, 47–102

Brooks, S.T. and Suchey, J.M., 1990. Skeletal age determination based on the os pubis: a comparison of the Acsádi-Nemeskéri and Suchey-Brooks methods, *Human Evol.* 5, 227–38

Bronk Ramsey C., 1995. Radiocarbon calibration and analysis of stratigraphy: the OxCal program, *Radiocarbon* 37(2), 425–30

Bronk Ramsey C., 2001. Development of the radiocarbon program OxCal, *Radiocarbon* 43(2A), 355–63

Brothwell, D. (ed.), 1963. *Dental Anthropology*, London, Pergamon

Brothwell, D.R., 1972. *Digging up Bones: the excavation, treatment and study of human skeletal remains*, London, Brit. Mus. (Natur. Hist.)

Brown, L., 1984. Objects of stone, in Cunliffe 1984, 407–26

Brown, L., 1995. Pottery production, in Cunliffe 1995, 53–65

Brown, L., 2000a. The pottery, in Cunliffe and Poole 2000, 65–113

Brown, L., 2000b. The pottery, in Cunliffe and Poole 2000, 75–102

Brown, G., Field, D., and McOmish, D., 1994. East Chisenbury midden complex, Wiltshire, in A.P. Fitzpatrick and E. L. Morris (eds), *The Iron Age in Wessex: recent work*, 46–9, Salisbury, AFEAF/Trust for Wessex Archaeology

Brück, J., 1995. A place for the dead: the role of human remains in Late Bronze Age Britain, *Proc. Prehist. Soc.* 61, 245–77

Brück, J., 1999. Ritual and rationality: some problems of interpretation in European archaeology, *European J. Archaeol.* 2(3), 313–44

Bryant, A., 2002. *The Landscape and Landuse of Codford Circle: the Molluscan evidence*, unpubl. dissert., Univ. Bristol

Buikstra, J.E. and Ubelaker, D.H., 1994. *Standards for Data Collection from Human Skeletal Remains*, Arkansas Archaeol. Survey Res. Ser. 44

Butot, L.J.M. and Neuteboom, W.M., 1958. Over *Vertigo moulinsiana* (Dupuy) en haar voorkomen in Nederland, *Basteria* 22, 52–63

Campbell, G., 2000a. Plant utilization: the evidence from charred plant remains, in Cunliffe 2000, 45–59

Campbell, G., 2000b. Charred plant remains, in Cunliffe and Poole 2000, 72–4

Canti, M., 1998a. Origin of calcium carbonate granules found in buried soils and Quaternary deposits, *Boreas* 27, 275–88

Canti, M.G., 1998b. The micromorphological identification of faecal spherulites from archaeological and modern materials, *J. Archaeol. Sci.* 25, 435–44

Canti, M., 1999. The production and preservation of faecal spherulites: animals, environment and taphonomy, *J. Archaeol. Sci.* 26, 251–8

Carruthers, W.J., 1988. Mystery object no. 2 – animal, mineral or vegetable? *Circaea* 6, 20

Carruthers, W J., 1989. The carbonised plant remains, in, P.J. Fasham, D.E. Farwell and R.J.B Whinney (eds), *The Archaeological Site at Easton Lane, Winchester*, 131–4, Winchester, Hampshire Fld Club Monogr. 6

Carruthers, W.J., 1991. The carbonised and mineralised plant remains, 36–41 in P.S. Bellamy, The investigation of the prehistoric landscape along the route of the A303 road improvement between Andover, Hampshire and Amesbury, Wiltshire, 1984–1987, Hampshire Fld Club Archaeol. Soc. 47, 5–81

Carruthers, W.J., 1995. Plant remains, and medieval plant remains, 56–60 and 139–42 in P.J. Fasham and G. Keevill with D. Coe, *Brighton Hill South: an Iron Age farmstead and deserted medieval village in Hampshire*, Salisbury, Wessex Archaeol. Rep. 7

Carruthers, W.J., 2000. Mineralised plant remains, in Lawson 2000, 72–84

Carruthers, W.J., unpublished, Mineralised plant remains, in G. Brown, D. Field and D.

McOmish, *The Late Bronze Age–Early Iron Age Site at East Chisenbury, Wiltshire*, English Heritage unpubl.

Carruthers, W.J. and Straker, V., 2000. Comparison between charred and mineralised plant assemblages, in Lawson 2000, 91–5

Chadwick, S.E. and Thompson, M.W., 1956. Notes on an Iron Age habitation site near Battlesbury Camp, Warminster, *Wiltshire Archaeol. Natur. Hist. Mag.* 56, 262–4

Chadwick-Hawkes, S., 1994. Longbridge Deverill Cow Down, Wiltshire, house 3: a major roundhouse of the Early Iron Age, *Oxford J. Archaeol.* 13, 49–69

Clay, R.C.C., 1927. An inhabited site of La Tène I date, on Swallowcliffe Down, *Wiltshire Archaeol. Natur. Hist. Mag.* 43, 59–93

Cleal, R., 1992. The Neolithic and Beaker pottery, in Gingell 1992, 61–70

Cleal, R., 1994. The pottery, 54–84 in R. Cleal and M.J. Allen, Investigation of tree-damaged barrows on King Barrow Ridge and Luxenborough Plantation, Amesbury, Wiltshire Archaeol. Natur. Hist. Mag. 87, 54–84

Cleal, R., 1995. Pottery fabrics in Wessex in the fourth to second millennia B.C., in I. Kinnes and G. Varndell (eds), *'Unbaked Urns of Rudely Shape'; essays on British and Irish pottery for Ian Longworth*, 185–94, Oxford, Oxbow Monogr. 55

Colt Hoare, R.C., 1812. *The Ancient History of Wiltshire, Volume 1*, London, Miller

Colt Hoare, R.C., 1821. *The Ancient History of Wiltshire, Volume 2*, London, Miller

Coy, J.P., 1981. The animal bones, 68–72 in C. Gingell, Excavation of an Iron Age enclosure at Groundwell Farm, Blunsdon St Andrew, 1976–7, *Wiltshire Archaeol. Natur. Hist. Mag.* 76, 33–75

Coy, J.P., 1984. The bird bones, in Cunliffe 1984, 527–31

Courty, M.A., Goldberg, P. and Macphail, R.I., 1989. *Soils and Micromorphology in Archaeology*, Cambridge, Univ. Press

Cox, C., 2002. *Aerial Photographic Assessment: Battlesbury Bowl, Warminster*, unpubl. CgMs Consulting rep.

Crowther, J., 2001. *Report on chemical and magnetic properties of ditch and pit fills from the Iron Age hillfort at Battlesbury*, unpubl. rep.

Crowther, J. and Barker, P., 1995. Magnetic susceptibility: distinguishing anthropogenic effects from the natural. *Archaeol. Prospection* 2, 207–15

Crowther, J., Macphail, R.I. and Cruise, G.M., 1996. Short-term burial change in a humic rendzina, Overton Down experimental earthwork, Wiltshire, England, *Geoarchaeol.* 11(2), 95–117

Cunliffe, B., 1984. *Danebury: An Iron Age Hillfort in Hampshire. Volume 1, The Excavations, 1969–1978: the site; Volume 2, The Excavations, 1969–1978: the finds*, London, Counc. Brit. Archaeol. Res. Rep. 52

Cunliffe, B., 1991. *Iron Age Communities in Britain*, 3rd edn, London, Routledge

Cunliffe, B., 1992. Pits, preconceptions and propitiation in the British Iron Age, *Oxford J. Archaeol.* 11(1), 69–83

Cunliffe, B., 1995. *Danebury: An Iron Age Hillfort in Hampshire, Volume 6*, York, Counc. Brit. Archaeol. Res. Rep. 102

Cunliffe, B., 2000. *The Danebury Environs Programme; The Prehistory of a Wessex Landscape; Volume 1 Introduction*, Oxford, Oxford Univ. Comm. Archaeol. Monogr. 48

Cunliffe, B. and Poole, C., 1991. *Danebury: An Iron Age Hillfort in Hampshire. Volume 5, The Excavations, 1979–88: the finds*, London, Counc. Brit. Archaeol. Res. Rep. 73

Cunliffe, B. and Poole, C., 2000. *The Danebury Environs Programme. The Prehistory of a Wessex Landscape. Volume 2.* Oxford, Oxford Univ. Comm. Archaeol. Monogr. 49

Cunnington, M.E., 1923. *The Early Iron Age Inhabited Site at All Cannings Cross Farm, Wiltshire*, Devizes, George Simpson

Cunnington, M.E., 1924. Pits in Battlesbury Camp, *Wiltshire Archaeol. Natur. Hist. Mag.* 42, 368–73

DEO, 1998a. *Salisbury Plain Training Area, Southern Range Road: Brief for Stage 1 (Pre-Construction) Archaeological Works*, unpubl. project brief

DEO, 1998b. *Salisbury Plain Training Area, Southern Range Road: Brief for Stage 2 (Construction) Archaeological Works*, unpubl. project brief

Dick, W.A. and Tabatabai, M.A., 1977. An alkaline oxidation method for the determination of total phosphorus in soils, *J. Soil Sci. Soc. America* 41, 511–14

Dunning, G.C., 1934. The swan's-neck and ring-headed pins of the Early Iron Age in Britain, *Antiq. J.* 91, 269–95

Edlin, H.L., 1949. *Woodland Crafts in Britain*, London, Batsford

Ellis, C.J. and Rawlings, M., 2001. Excavations at Balksbury Camp, Andover 1995–97, *Proc. Hampshire Fld Club Archaeol. Soc.* 56, 21–94

Ellison, A., 1989. The Neolithic and Bronze Age pottery, in P.J. Fasham, D.E. Farwell and R.J.B. Whinney, *The Archaeological Site at Easton Lane, Winchester*, 83–91, Winchester, Hampshire Fld Club Monogr. 6

Ellison, A. and Drewett, P., 1971. Pits and post-holes in the British early Iron Age: some alternative explanations, *Proc. Prehist. Soc.* 37, 183–94

Entwhistle, R., 1994. The environmental setting of the linear ditches system, in Bradley *et al.* 1994, 101–21

Evans, J.G., 1972. *Land Snails in Archaeology*, London, Seminar

Evans, J.G., 1984. Land snail analysis, in Cunliffe 1984, 476–83

Evans, J.G. and Hewitt, T., 1991. Land snail analysis, in Cunliffe and Poole 1991, 432–9

Evans, J.G. and Jones, H., 1973. Subfossil and modern land-snail faunas from rock-rubble habitats, *J. Conchol.* 28, 103–29

Evans, J.G. and Rouse, A., 1991. The land mollusca, in Sharples 1991, 118–25

Findlay, D.C., Colbourne, G.J.N., Cope, D.W., Harrod, T.R., Hogan, D.V. and Staines, S.J., 1983. *Soils of England and Wales. Sheet 5, South West England*, Southampton, Ordnance Survey

Fitzpatrick, A.P., 1994. Outside in: the structure of an Early Iron Age house at Dunston Park, Thatcham, Berkshire, in A.P. Fitzpatrick and E. L. Morris (eds), *The Iron Age in Wessex: recent work*, 68–72, Salisbury, AFEAF/Trust for Wessex Archaeology

Fitzpatrick, A.P., 1997. Everyday life in Iron Age Wessex, in A. Gwilt and C. Haselgrove (eds), *Reconstructing Iron Age Societies: new approaches to the British Iron Age*, 73–86, Oxford, Oxbow Monogr. 71

Fowler, E., 1960. The origins and development of the penannular brooch in Europe, *Proc. Prehist. Soc.* 26, 149–77

Fowler, P.J., 2000. *Landscape Plotted and Pieced. Landscape History and Local Archaeology in Fyfield and Overton, Wiltshire*, London, Rep. Res. Comm. Soc. Antiq. London 64

Fowler, P.J., Musty, J.W.G and Taylor, C.C., 1965. Some earthwork enclosures in Wiltshire, *Wiltshire Archaeol. Natur. Hist. Mag.* 60, 52–74

Frank Green Environmental, 1996. *Environmental Statement Proposed Southern Range Road*, unpubl. rep.

Fulford, M.J., 1975. *New Forest Roman Pottery*, Oxford, Brit. Archaeol. Rep. 17

Fulford, M.J., Powell, A.B., Entwistle, R. and Raymond, F., 2006. *Iron Age and Romano-British Landscapes of Salisbury Plain*, Salisbury, Wessex Archaeol. Rep. 20

Gale, R. 1990. Charcoals, in J. Richards, *The Stonehenge Environs Project*, 252, London, English Heritage Archaeol. Rep. 16

Gale, R., 2006a. Charcoal, in P. Andrews, A Middle to Late Bronze Age settlement at Dunch Hill, Tidworth, *Wiltshire Archaeol. Natur. Hist. Mag.* 99, 66–8

Gale, R., 2006b. Charcoal, 95–7 in V. Birbeck, Excavations on the Old Ditch Linear Earthwork, Breach Hill, Tilshead, *Wiltshire Archaeol. Natur. Hist. Mag.* 99, 79–103

Gale, R. and Cutler, D., 2000. *Plants in Archaeology*, Otley, Westbury and Royal Botanic Gardens, Kew

Gejvall, N.G., 1981. Determination of burnt bones from prehistoric graves, *Ossa Letters* 2, 1–13

Gennep, A. van, 1977. *The Rites of Passage* (Transl. M.B. Vizedom and G.L. Caffee), London, Routledge and Kegan Paul

Gifford and Partners, 1997a. *Report on an Archaeological Evaluation of the Salisbury Plain Training Area Southern Range Road*, unpubl. rep. 7428.4R

Gifford and Partners, 1997b. *Report on an Archaeological Evaluation at Southern Range Road Alternative Route A*, unpubl. rep. B0765.2R

Gingell, C.J., 1992. *The Marlborough Downs: a later Bronze Age landscape and its origins*, Devizes, Wiltshire Archaeol. Natur. Hist. Monogr. 1

Gingell, C.J., and Morris, E.L., 2000. Form series, in Lawson 2000, 149–53

Godwin, H., 1956. *The History of the British Flora*, Cambridge, Univ. Press

Godwin, H. 1984. *History of the British Flora* (2nd edn), Cambridge, Univ. Press

Graham, I.D.G. and Scollar, I., 1976. Limitations on magnetic prospection in archaeology imposed by soil properties, *Archaeo-Physika* 6, 1–124

Grant, A., 1981. The significance of deer remains at occupation sites of the Iron Age of the Anglo-Saxon period, in M. Jones and G. Dimbleby (eds.), *The Environment of Man: the Iron Age to the Anglo-Saxon Period*, 205–12, Oxford, Brit. Archaeol. Rep. 87

Grant, A, 1982. The use of toothwear as a guide to the age of domestic ungulates, in B. Wilson, C. Grigson and S. Payne (eds), *Ageing and Sexing Animal Bones from Archaeological Sites*, 91–108, Oxford, Brit. Archaeol. Rep. 109

Grant, A., 1984a. Animal husbandry, in Cunliffe 1984, 496–547

Grant A. 1984b. Survival or sacrifice? A critical appraisal of animal burials in Britain in the Iron Age, in C. Grigson and J. Clutton-Brock (eds), *Animals and Archaeology 4: husbandry in Europe*, 221–7, Oxford, Brit. Archaeol. Rep. S227

Grant, A, 1991. Animal husbandry, in Cunliffe and Poole 1991, 447–87

Green C., and Rollo-Smith S., 1984. The excavation of eighteen round barrows near Shrewton Wiltshire, *Proc. Prehist. Soc.* 50, 255–318

Green, F.J., 1979. Phosphate mineralisation of seeds from archaeological sites, *J. Archaeol. Sci.* 6, 279–84

Green, F.J., 1981. The plant remains, 96 in Davies, S.M., Excavations at Old Down Farm, Andover Part II, *Proc. Hampshire Fld Club Archaeol. Soc.* 37, 81–163

Green, M. and Allen, M.J., 1997. An early prehistoric shaft on Cranborne Chase, *Oxford J. Archaeol.* 16, 121–32

Greig, J.R.A., 1991. The British Isles, in W. van Zeist, K. Wasylikowa and K.-E. Behre (eds), *Progress in Old World Palaeoethnobotany*, 229–334, Rotterdam, Balkema

Grinsell, L.V., 1957. Archaeological gazetteer, in *VCH* 1957, 21–272

Grose, D., 1957. *Flora of Wiltshire*, Devizes, Wiltshire Archaeol. Natur. Hist. Soc.

Guilbert, G., 1981. Double-ring roundhouses, probable and possible, in prehistoric Britain. *Proc. Prehist. Soc.* 47, 299–317

Guido, M., 1977–8, An Iron Age burial from Battlesbury, *Wiltshire Archaeol. Natur. Hist. Mag.* 72/73, 177–8

Hambleton, E., 1999. *Animal Husbandry Regimes in Iron Age Britain: a comparative study of faunal assemblages from British Iron Age sites*, Oxford, Brit. Archaeol. Rep. 282

Hamilton. M. A., 2000. Pottery, 144–8 in A. Whittle, J.J. Davies, I. Dennis, A. Fairbairn. and M. A. Hamilton, Neolithic activity and occupation outside Windmill Hill causewayed enclosure, Wiltshire: survey and excavation 1992–93, *Wiltshire Archaeol. Natur. Hist. Magazine* 93, 131–80

Harcourt, R.A. 1979. The animal bones, in G.J. Wainwright (ed.), *Gussage All Saints: an Iron Age settlement in Dorset*, London, Dept Environ. Archaeol. Rep. 10, 150–60

Harding, P., 2006. Flint, in Birbeck 2006, 87–9

Haselgrove, C., 1997. Iron Age brooch deposition and chronology, 51–72 in A. Gwilt and C. Haselgrove (eds), *Reconstructing Iron Age Societies: new approaches to the British Iron Age*, Oxford, Oxbow Monogr. 71

Haselgrove, C., Armit, I., Champion, T., Creighton, J., Gwilt, A., Hill, J.D., Hunter, F. and Woodward, A., 2001. *Understanding the British Iron Age: an agenda for action*, Salisbury, Iron Age Research Seminar and Prehistoric Society

Hawkes, S.C., 1994. Longbridge Deverill Cow Down, Wiltshire, house 3: a major roundhouse of the Early Iron Age, *Oxford J. Archaeol.* 13(1), 49–69

Hjelmqvist, H., 1950. The flax weeds and the origin of cultivated flax, *Bot. Not.* 103, 257–98

Hill, J.D., 1995. Ritual and Rubbish in the Iron Age of Wessex, *Oxford, Brit. Archaeol. Rep.* 242

Hill, J.D., 1996. The identification of ritual deposits of animal bones: a general perspective from a specific study of 'special animal deposits' from the southern English Iron Age, in S. Anderson and K. Boyle, *Ritual Treatment of Human and Animal Remains*, 17–32, Oxford, Oxbow

Hillman, G., 1981. Reconstructing crop husbandry practices from charred remains of crops, in R. Mercer, *Farming Practice in British Prehistory*, 123–62, Edinburgh, Univ. Press

Hillman, G., 1984. Interpretation of archaeological plant remains, the application of ethnographic models from Turkey, in W. van Zeist and W.A. Casparie (eds), *Plants and Ancient Man: studies in palaeoethnobotany*, Rotterdam, Balkema, 1–42

Hillman, G.C., Mason, D., de Moulins, D., and Nesbitt, M., 1996. Identification of the archaeological remains of wheat: the 1992 London workshop, *Circaea* 12, 195–209

Hillson, S.W., 1979. Diet and dental disease, *World Archaeol.* 2, 147–62

Hillson, S.W., 1990. *Teeth*, Cambridge, Univ. Press

Hodges, H., 1964. *Artifacts*, London, John Baker

Holden, J.L., Phakley, P.P. and Clement, J.G., 1995a. Scanning electron microscope observations of incinerated human femoral bone: a case study, *Forensic Sci. Int.* 74, 17–28

Holden, J.L., Phakley, P.P. and Clement, J.G., 1995b. Scanning electron microscope observations of heat-treated human bone, *Forensic Sci. Int.* 74, 29–45

Holleyman, G.A., 1937. Harrow Hill excavations, 1936, *Surrey Archaeol. Collect.* 78, 230–52

Hooley, D., 2001. Copper alloy and silver objects, in A.S. Anderson, Wacher, J.S. and Fitzpatrick, A.P., *The Romano-British 'Small Town' at Wanborough, Wiltshire*, London, Britannia Monogr. 19, 75–116

Hooper, B., 1984. Anatomical considerations, in Cunliffe 1984, 463–74

Hooper, B., 1991. Anatomical considerations, in Cunliffe and Poole 1991, 425–31

Hooper, B., 2000. The human population, in Cunliffe 2000, 127–8

House of Commons Defence Lands Committee, 1973. *Report of the Defence Lands Committee (The Nugent Report)*, London, HMSO

Hull, M.R. and Hawkes, C.F.C., 1987. *Corpus of Ancient Brooches in Britain: pre-Roman bow brooches*, Oxford, Brit. Archaeol. Rep. 168

Humphreys, S., 1981. Death and time, in S. Humphreys and H. King (eds), *Mortality and Immortality*, 261–71, London, Academic

Iscan, M.Y., Loth, S.R. and Wright, R.K., 1985. Age estimation from the ribs by phase analysis: white females, *J. Forensic Sci.* 30, 853–63

Jeffries, J.S., 1979. The pits, in G.J. Wainwright, *Gussage All Saints: An Iron Age Settlement in Dorset*, 9–15, London, Dept Environ. Archaeol. Rep. 10

Jones, G.E.M., 1984. Interpretation of plant remains: ethnographic models from Greece, in W. van Zeist, W. and W.A. Casparie (eds), *Plants and Ancient Man: studies in palaeoethnobotany*, 43–61, Rotterdam, Balkema

Jones, G.E.M., 1987. A statistical approach to the archaeological identification of crop processing, *J. Archaeol. Sci.*, 14, 311–23

Jones, M.K., 1984. The plant remains, in Cunliffe 1984, 483–95

Johnston, D.E., 1980, The excavation of a bell-barrow at Sutton Veny, Wilts, *Wiltshire Archaeol. Natur. Hist. Mag.* 72/3, 29–50

Kent, S., 1981. The dog: an archaeologist's best friend or worst enemy – the spatial distribution of faunal remains, *J. Field Archaeol.* 8, 367–72

Kerney, M.P., 1963. Late glacial deposits on the chalk of south-east England, *Phil. Trans. Roy. Soc. London* B246, 203–54

Kerney, M.P., 1977. A proposed zonation scheme for late-glacial and postglacial deposits using land mollusca, *J. Archaeol. Sci.* 3, 387–90

Kerney, M.P., 1999. *Atlas of the Land and Freshwater Molluscs of Britain and Ireland*, Colchester, Conch. Soc. Great Britain and Ireland

Laws, K., 1991a. The copper alloy objects, in Sharples 1991, 153–6

Laws, K., 1991b. The shale, in Sharples 1991, 233–4

Laws, K., 1991c. The worked bone and antler, in Sharples 1991, 234–8

Laws, K., Brown, L. and Roe, F., 1991. Objects of stone, in Cunliffe and Poole 1991, 382–404

Lawson, A.J., 2000. *Potterne 1982–5: Animal Husbandry in Later Prehistoric Wiltshire*, Salisbury, Wessex Archaeol. Rep. 16

Limbrey, S., 1975. *Soils and Archaeology*, London, Academic

Locker, A., 2000. Animal bone, in Lawson 2000, 101–19

Lovell, J., 1999. Further investigations of an Iron Age and Romano-British farmstead on Cockey Down, near Salisbury, *Wiltshire Archaeol. Natur. Hist. Mag.* 92, 33–8

Lynne, M.A.B. and Jefferies, R.S., 1979. *The Alice Holt/Farnham Roman Pottery Industry*, London, Counc. Brit. Archaeol. Res. Rep. 30

Lust, J.B., 1974. *The Herb Book*, London, Bantam

Macphail, R.I., 1991. The archaeological soils and sediments, in Sharples 1991, 106–18

Macphail, R.I., 1999. Soils, in A. Whittle, J. Pollard and C. Grigson (eds), *The Harmony of Symbols: the Windmill Hill Causewayed Enclosure, Wiltshire*, 119–24, Oxford, Oxbow

Macphail, R.I., 2000. Soils and microstratigraphy: a soil micromorphological and micro-chemical approach, in Lawson 2000, 47–70

Macphail, R.I., Courty, M.A., Hather, J. and Wattez, J., 1997. The soil micromorphological evidence for domestic occupation and stabling activities, in R. Maggi (ed.), *Arene Candide: a functional and environmental assessment of the Holocene sequence (Excavations Bernabò Brea-Cardini 1940–50)*, 53–88, Romae, Memorie dell' Istituto Italiano di Paleontologia Umana

Macphail, R.I. and Crowther, J., 2004. Sediment micromorphology, particle size, chemistry and magnetic properties, in G. Keevil, *Tower of London Moat Archaeological Excavations 1995–9*, 41–3, 82–3, 155, 183, 186, 202–4, Oxford, Historic Roy. Palaces Monogr. 1

Macphail, R.I. and Cruise, G.M., 1996. Soil micromorphology, in M. Bell, P.J. Fowler and S.W. Hillson (eds), *The Experimental Earthwork Project 1960–1992*, 95–107, London, Counc. Brit. Archaeol. Res. Rep. 100

Macphail, R.I. and Cruise, G.M., 2001. The soil micromorphologist as team player: a multianalytical approach to the study of European microstratigraphy, in P. Goldberg, V. Holliday and R. Ferring, R. (eds), *Earth Science and Archaeology*, 241–67, New York, Kluwer Academic/Plenum

Macphail, R.I. and Goldberg, P., 1995. Recent advances in micromorphological interpretations of soils and sediments from archaeological sites, in A.J. Barham and R.I. Macphail (eds), *Archaeological Sediments and Soils: analysis, interpretation and management*, 1–24, London, Institute of Archaeology

Macphail, R.I., Cruise, G.M., Gebhardt, A. and Linderholm, J., forthcoming. West Heslerton: soil micromorphology and chemistry of the Roman and Saxon deposit, in J. Tipper (ed.), *West Heslerton Anglo-Saxon Settlement*, Yedingham, Landscape Research Centre

Madella, M, Powers-Jones, A.H. and Jones M.K., 1998. A simple method of extraction of opal phytoliths from sediments using a non-toxic heavy liquid, *J. Archaeol. Sci.* 25, 801–3

Malim, C. and Martin, A., 2007. A Romano-British roadside settlement on Chapperton Down, Salisbury Plain training area, *Wiltshire Archaeol. Natur. Hist. Mag.* 100, 104–30

Maltby, M., 1985a. The animal bones, in P. Fasham, *Prehistoric Settlement at Winnall Down, Winchester*, 97–112, Winchester, Hampshire Fld. Club Monogr. 2

Maltby, M., 1985b. *The Animal Bones from the 1973 Excavations at Balksbury, Hampshire*, London, Anc. Monum. La. Rep. 4542

Maltby, M., 1987. *The Animal Bones from the Excavations at Owslebury, Hants: an Iron Age and Romano-British settlement*, London, Anc. Monum. Lab. Rep. 6/87

Maltby, M., 1996. The exploitation of animals in the Iron Age: the archaeozoological evidence, in T.C. Champion and J.C. Collis (eds), *The Iron Age in Britain: recent trends*, 17–28, Sheffield, J.R. Collis

Maltby, M., 2003. Animal bone, in A. Thomas and D. Enright, The excavation of an Iron Age settlement at Wilby Way, Great Doddington, *Northamptonshire Archaeol.* 31, 48–56

Maltby, M., in press, *Feeding a Roman Town: Environmental Evidence from Excavations in Winchester, 1972–1985*, Winchester, Winchester Archaeol. Rep. 4

Manchester, K. 1983. *The Archaeology of Disease*, Bradford, Univ. Press

Manby T.G., 1995. Neolithic and Bronze Age pottery – implications, in T.C.M. Brewster and A.E. Finney, The Excavation of Seven Bronze Age Barrows on the Moorlands of North-East Yorkshire, 42–51, *Yorkshire Archaeol. Rep.* 1

Manby T.G., 1988, The Neolithic in Eastern Yorkshire, in T.G. Manby (ed.), Archaeology in Eastern Yorkshire. Essays in honour of T.C.M. Brewster, 35–88, Sheffield, Univ. Sheffield

Manning, W.H., 1985. *Catalogue of the Roman-British Iron Tools, Fittings and Weapons in the British Museum*, London: British Mus.

Manning, W.H., 1995. Ritual or refuse: the Harrow Hill enclosure reconsidered, in B. Rafferty, V. Megaw and V. Rigby (eds), *Sites and Sights of the Iron Age: essays on fieldwork and museum research presented to Ian Mathieson Stead*, 133–8, Oxford, Oxbow Monogr. 56

Martin, E. and Murphy, P., 1988. West Row Fen, Suffolk: a Bronze Age fen-edge settlement, *Antiquity* 62, 353–8

Matthews, W., French, C.A.I., Lawrence, T., Cutler, D.F. and Jones, M.K., 1997. Micro-stratigraphic traces of site formation processes and human activity, *World Archaeol.* 29, 281–308

McKinley, J.I., 1993. Bone fragment size and weights of bone from modern British cremations and its implications for the interpretation of archaeological cremations, *Int. J. Osteoarchaeol.* 3, 283–7

McKinley, J.I., 1994a. *The Anglo-Saxon cemetery at Spong Hill, North Elmham Part VIII: The Cremations*, Gressenhall, East Anglian Archaeol. 69

McKinley, J.I., 1994b. Bone fragment size in British cremation burials and its implications for pyre technology and ritual, *J. Archaeol. Sci.* 21, 339–42

McKinley, J.I., 1994c. Pyre and grave goods in British cremation burials; have we missed something? *Antiquity* 68, 132–4

McKinley, J.I., 1997. Bronze Age 'barrows' and the funerary rites and rituals of cremation, *Proc. Prehist. Soc.* 63, 129–45

McKinley, J.I., 1998. *Cremated human bone from Cippenham Sector (CSOWL 97)*, unpubl. rep. for TVAS

McKinley, J.I., 2000a. Human bone, in Lawson 2000, 95–102

McKinley, J.I., 2000b. Human bone and funerary deposits, in K.E. Walker and D.E. Farwell, *Twyford Down, Hampshire, Archaeological Investigations on the M3 Motorway from Bar End to Compton, 1990–93*, 85–119, Hampshire Fld Club Archaeol. Soc. Monogr. 9

McKinley, J.I. 2004. Compiling a skeletal inventory: disarticulated and co-mingled remains, in M. Brickley and J.I. McKinley (eds), *Guidelines to the Standards for Recording Human Remains*, 13–16, Reading, Brit. Assoc. Biol. Anthrop. Osteoarchaeol. and Inst. Fld Archaeol

McKinley, J.I., in press, Human remains, in R. Mercer and F. Healy, *Hambledon Hill, Dorset, England. Excavation and survey of a Neolithic complex and its surrounding landscape*, Swindon, English Heritage Archaeol. Rep.

McMinn, R.M.H. and Hutchings, R.T., 1985. *A Colour Atlas of Human Anatomy*, London, Wolfe Medical

McOmish, D., 1996. East Chisenbury: ritual and rubbish at the British Bronze Age – Iron Age transition, *Antiquity* 70, 68–76

McOmish, D., Field, D. and Brown, G., 2002. *The Field Archaeology of the Salisbury Plain Training Area*, Swindon, English Heritage

Middleton, A.P., 1987. Technological investigations of the coatings on some 'haematite-coated' pottery from southern England, *Archaeometry* 29, 250–61

Millard, J.I., 1996. The pottery, 27–34 in M. Rawlings and A.P. Fitzpatrick, Prehistoric sites and a Romano-British settlement at Butterfield Down, Amesbury, *Wiltshire Archaeol. Natur. Hist. Mag.* 89, 1–43

Miller, T.E., 1987. Systematics and evolution, in F.G. Lupton (ed.), *Wheat Breeding*, 1–30, London, Chapman & Hall

Mitchell, A., 1974. *A Field Guide to the Trees of Britain and Northern Europe*, London, Collins

Moffat, B., 1987. A curious assemblage of seeds from a pit at Waltham Abbey, Essex: a study of medieval medication, *Essex Archaeol. Hist.* 18, 121–3

Molleson, T.I., 1993. The human remains, in D.E. Farwell and T.I. Molleson, *Poundbury Volume 2: the cemeteries*, 142–214, Dorchester, Dorset Natur. Hist. Archaeol. Soc. Monogr. 11

Monk, M.A., 1985. The plant economy, in P. Fasham

(ed.), *The Prehistoric Settlement at Winnall Down, Winchester*, 112–17, Winchester, Hampshire Fld. Club Archaeol. Soc. Monogr. 2

Montague, R., 1997. Copper alloy objects, in S.J. Lobb and J.C. Richards, Excavations at Cheap Street, 1981, in A.G. Vince, S.J. Lobb, J.C. Richards and L. Mepham, *Excavations in Newbury 1979–1990*, Salisbury, Wessex Archaeol. Monogr. 13, 100–105

Mook, W.G. 1986. Business meeting: recommendations/resolutions adopted by the twelfth International Radiocarbon Conference, *Radiocarbon* 28, 799

Morris, E.L., 1994a. *The Analysis of Pottery*, Salisbury, Wessex Archaeology Guideline 4

Morris, E.L., 1994b. The organisation of pottery production and distribution in Iron Age Wessex, in A.P. Fitzpatrick and E.L Morris (eds), *The Iron Age in Wessex: recent work*, 46–9, Salisbury, AFEAF, Trust for Wessex Archaeology

Morris, E.L., 2000a. Dating, in Lawson 2000, 157–66

Morris, E.L., 2000b. Fabrics, in Lawson 2000, 140–9

Murphy, C.P., 1986. *Thin Section Preparation of Soils and Sediments*, Berkhamsted, AB Academic

Murphy, P., 1988. Plant macrofossils, 281–93 in N. Brown, A Late Bronze Age enclosure at Lofts Farm, Essex, *Proc. Prehist. Soc.* 54, 249–302

Needham, S. and Spence, T., 1996. *Refuse and Disposal at Area 16 East, Runneymede*, London, Brit. Mus. Press

Nicholls, J., 1987. Two Bronze Age urns from Portsdown, *Proc. Hampshire Fld Club Archaeol. Soc.* 43, 15–20

Oswald, A., Dyer, C. and Barber, M., 2001. *The Creation of Monuments. Neolithic Causewayed Enclosures in the British Isles*, Swindon, English Heritage

Palmer, C. and Jones, M., 1991. Plant resources, in Sharples 1991, 129–38

Parker Pearson, M., 1996. Food, fertility and front doors in the first millennium BC, in T.C. Champion and J.C. Collis (eds), *The Iron Age in Britain: recent trends*, 117–32, Sheffield, J.R. Collis

Parker Pearson, M., 1999. Food, sex and death: cosmologies in the British Iron Age with particular reference to East Yorkshire, *Cambridge Archaeol. J.* 9(1), 43–69

Payne, S, 1973. Kill-off patterns in sheep and goats: the mandibles from Asvan Kale, *Anatolian Stud.* 23, 281–305

PCRG, 1997. *The Study of Later Prehistoric Pottery: General Policies and Guidelines for Analysis and Publication*, Oxford, Prehistoric Ceramics Research Group Occas. Pap 1/2 (revised edn)

Peacock, D.P.S., 1968. A petrological study of certain Iron Age pottery from Western England, *Proc. Prehist. Soc.* 34, 414–27

Piggott, S., 1954. *Neolithic Cultures of the British Isles*, Cambridge, Univ. Press

Piggott, S., 1962. *The West Kennet Long Barrow. Excavations 1955–56*, London, HMSO Rep. 4

Poole, C., 1984a. Objects of baked clay, in Cunliffe 1984, 398–407

Poole, C., 1984b. Briquetage containers, in Cunliffe 1984, 426–30

Poole, C., 1991. The small objects of daub and clay, in Sharples 1991, 209–10

Porter, V., 1990. *Small Woods and Hedgerows*, London, Pelham Books

Powell, A.B., Allen, M.J., Chapman, J., Every, R., Gale, R., Harding, P., Knight, S., McKinley, J.I. and Stevens, C., 2005. Excavations along the Old Sarum water pipeline, north of Salisbury, *Wiltshire Archaeol. Natur. Hist. Mag.* 98, 250–80

Rawlings, M., 1991. The pits, in Sharples 1991, 89–94

Roberts, C. and Cox, M., 2003. *Health and Disease in Britain from Prehistory to the Present Day*, Stroud, Sutton

Robledo, B., Trancho, G.J. and Brothwell, D., 1995. *Cribra Orbitalia*: health indicator in the late Roman population of Cannington (Sommerset [*sic.*], Great Britain), *J. Palaeopath.* 7(3), 185–93

Rogers, J., Waldron, T., Dieppe, P. and Watt, I., 1987. Arthropathies in palaeopathology: the basis of classification according to most probable cause, *J. Archaeol. Sci.* 14, 179–93

Rogers, J. and Waldron, T., 1995. *A Field Guide to Joint Disease in Archaeology*, Chichester, Wiley

Russel, A.D., 1990. Two Beaker burials from Chilbolton, Hampshire, *Proc. Prehist. Soc.* 56, 153–72

Seager Smith, R.H., 1995. Romano-British finds, in A.B. Powell, M.J. Allen and I. Barnes, *Archaeology in the Avebury Area, Wiltshire: recent discoveries along the line of the Kennet Valley foul sewer pipeline*, 1993, 39–48, Salisbury, Wessex Archaeol. Rep. 8

Seager Smith, R.H., 1996. Pottery, 53–8 in J.I. McKinley and M. Heaton, A Romano-British farmstead and associated burials at Maddington Farm, Shrewton, *Wiltshire Archaeol. Natur. Hist. Mag.* 89, 44–72

Seager Smith, R., 2000. Worked bone and antler, in Lawson 2000, 222–40

Seager Smith, R. and Davies, S.M., 1993. The Roman pottery from excavations at Greyhound Yard, Dorchester, Dorset, in Woodward *et al.* 1993, 229–89

Seager Smith, R., ApSimon, A.M., Mepham, L. and Gardiner, J., 2000. Pottery, in M.J. Allen and

J.P. Gardiner, *Our Changing Coast: A Survey of the Intertidal Archaeology of Langstone Harbour*, 144–58, York, Counc. Brit. Archaeol. Res. Rep. 124

Sellwood, L., 1984. Objects of bone and antler, in Cunliffe 1984, 371–95

Serjeantson, D., 1991. The bird bones, in B. Cunliffe and C. Poole 1991, 479–81

Shand, P., Henderson, E., and R., and Barclay, A., 2003. Corporation Farm, Wilsham Road, Abingdon: A summary of the Neolithic and Bronze Age excavations, 1971–4, in A. Barclay, G. Lambrick, J. Moore and M. Robins, *Lines in the Landscape, Cursus Monuments in the Upper Thames Valley*, 31–40, Oxford, Thames Valley Landscapes Monogr. 15

Sharples, N.M., 1991. *Maiden Castle: Excavations and Field Survey 1985–6*, London, English Heritage Archaeol. Rep. 19

Simpson, D.D.A., 1996. 'Crown' antler maceheads and the later Neolithic in Britain. *Proc. Prehist. Soc.* 62, 293–310

Smith, I.F., 1965. *Windmill Hill and Avebury*. Oxford, Clarendon

Smith, I.F., 1991.Round barrows Wilsford cum Lake G51–G54: excavations by Ernest Greenfield in 1958, *Wiltshire Archaeol. Natur. Hist. Mag.* 84, 11–39

Smith, M.J.C., 1982. *The Worked Bone from Iron Age Sites in Wiltshire*, unpubl. dissert., Univ. Southampton

Smith, R.W., 1997. *Excavations at Emwell Street, Warminster: the early economy and environment of a Wiltshire market town*, Salisbury, Wessex Archaeology

Stace, C., 1997. *New British Flora*, 2nd edn, Cambridge, Univ. Press

Stead, I.M., 1979. *The Arras Culture*, York, Yorkshire Philos. Soc.

Stead, I.M., 1991. *Iron Age Cemeteries in East Yorkshire: excavations at Burton Fleming, Rudston, Garton-on-the-Wolds, and Kirkburn*, London, English Heritage Archaeol. Rep. 22

Stecher, R.M. and Goss, L.J., 1961. Ankylosing lesions of the spine (horse), *J. Amer. Vet. Med. Assoc.* 138, 248–55

Stevens, C.J., 1996. *Iron Age and Roman Agriculture in the Upper Thames Valley Archaeobotanical and Social Perspectives*, unpubl. thesis, Cambridge Univ.

Stevens, C.J., 2003. An investigation of agricultural consumption and production models for prehistoric and Roman Britain, *Environ. Archaeol.* 8, 61–76

Stevens, C.J. 2006. Charred plant remains, in Fulford *et al.* 2006, 152–8

Stuiver, M. and Kra, R.S. (eds), 1986. Calibration issue, Proceedings of the 12th International ^{14}C conference, *Radiocarbon* 28(2B), 805–1030

Stuiver M., Long, A. and Kra, R.S. (eds), 1993. Calibration issue, *Radiocarbon* 35(1)

Stuiver, M., Reimer, P.J., Bard, E., Beck, W.J., Burr, G.S., Hughen, K.A., Kromer, B., McCormac, G., Plicht, J. van der and Spurk, M., 1998. Intcal98 radiocarbon age calibration, 24,000–0 cal BP, *Radiocarbon* 40, 1041–83

Swan, V.G., 1971. The coarse pottery, 100–16 in G.J. Wainwright, The excavation of prehistoric and Romano-British settlements near Durrington Walls, Wiltshire, 1970, *Wiltshire Archaeol. Natur. Hist. Mag.* 66, 76–128

Swan, V.G., 1975. Oare reconsidered and the origins of Savernake ware in Wiltshire, *Britannia* 6, 36–61

Thomas, K.D., 1977. The mollusca from an Iron Age pit at Winklebury, 70–4 in K. Smith, The excavation of Winklebury Camp, Basingstoke, Hampshire, *Proc. Prehist. Soc.* 43, 31–129

Tite, M.S. and Mullins, C., 1971. Enhancement of magnetic susceptibility of soils on archaeological sites, *Archaeometry* 13, 209–19

Tomalin, D., 1992. The Deverel-Rimbury and late Biconical Urn domestic ceramic assemblage from Bishops Canning Down, in Gingell 1992, 71–86

Tomber, R. and Dore, J, 1998. *The National Roman Fabric Reference Collection: a handbook*, London, Mus. London Archaeol. Service Monogr. 2

Trotter, M. and Gleser, G.C., 1952. Estimation of stature from long bones of American whites and negroes, *Amer. J. Physical Anthrop.* 10(4), 463–514

Trotter, M. and Gleser, G.C., 1958. A re-evaluation of estimation of stature bases on measurements of stature taken during life and of long bones after death, *Amer. J. Physical Anthrop.* 16(1), 79–123

Tutin, T.G., Heywood, V.H., Burges, N.A., Valentine, D.H., Walters, S.M. and Webb, D.A., (eds), 1964–80. *Flora Europaea* 1–5, Cambridge, Univ. Press

Veen, M. van der, 1992. *Crop Husbandry Regimes: an archaeobotanical study of farming in northern England 1000 B.C.–A.D. 500*, Sheffield, Sheffield Archaeol. Monogr. 3

VCH (Victoria County History), 1957. *A History of Wiltshire (Part 1)*. Oxford: Inst. Hist. Res./Univ. Press (ed. E. Crittall)

Wahl, J., 1982.Leichenbranduntersuchungen. Ein Überblick über die Bearbeitungs-und Aussagemöglichkeitenvon Brandgräbern, *Prähistorische Zeitschrift* 57(i) 2–125

Walker, L. 1984. The deposition of the human remains, in Cunliffe 1984, 442–63

Wainwright, G.J. and Davies S.M., 1995. *Balksbury Camp Hampshire Excavations 1973 and 1981*,

London, English Heritage Archaeol. Rep. 4

Wait, G., 1985. *Ritual and Religion in Iron Age Britain*, Oxford, Brit. Archaeol. Rep. 149

Wattez, J. and Courty, M.A., 1987. Morphology of ash of some plant materials, in N. Fedoroff, L.M. Bresson and M.A. Courty (eds), *Soil Micromorphology*, 677–83, AFES, Plaisir

Wattez, J., Courty, M.A. and Macphail, R.I., 1990. Burnt organo-mineral deposits related to animal and human activities in prehistoric caves, in L.A. Douglas (ed.), *Soil Micromorphology: a basic and applied science*, Amsterdam, Elsevier, 431–9

Webb, P.A.O. and Suchey, J.M., 1985. Epiphyseal union of the anterior iliac crest and medial clavicle in a modern multiracial sample of American males and females, *Amer. J. Physical Anthrop.* 68, 457–66

Webster, A.D., 1919. *Firewoods: their production and fuel values*, London, Fisher Unwin

Wessex Archaeology, 1988. *Excavations at the SPTA FIBUA Site, Copehill Down 1987–8*, Salisbury, unpubl. rep. 31762

Wessex Archaeology, 1995. *Warminster CATC LAD, Battlesbury Barracks and Harman Lines: Archaeological Desk-based Assessment and Watching Brief*, Salisbury, unpubl. rep. 39922/1

Wessex Archaeology, 1996. *Warminster CATC LAD, Battlesbury Barracks and Harman Lines: Archaeological Evaluation Report*, Salisbury, unpubl. rep. 39922/2

Wessex Archaeology, 1997. *Harman Lines, Warminster, Wiltshire: Assessment Report on the Results of the Archaeological Excavation*, Salisbury, unpubl. rep. 39921

Wessex Archaeology, 1998a. *Battlesbury Bowl (SRR 11) Archaeological Evaluation*, Salisbury, unpubl. rep. 44895.1

Wessex Archaeology, 1998b. *Middleton Farm (SRR 91) Archaeological Evaluation*, Salisbury, unpubl. rep. 44895.2

Wessex Archaeology, 1999a. *Salisbury Plain Training Area, Southern Range Road, Stage 1 Archaeology Contract; Assessment Report*, Salisbury, unpubl. rep. 44897.1

Wessex Archaeology, 1999b. *Salisbury Plain Training Area, Southern Range Road, Stage 1 Archaeology Contract: Site SRR 11 – Battlesbury Bowl Assessment Report*, Salisbury, unpubl. rep. 44898.1

Wessex Archaeology, 2004. *Salisbury Plain Training Area: Historic Landscape Assessment*, Salisbury, unpubl. rep. 51700.01

Wessex Archaeology, 2006a. *Kingsmead Quarry, Horton, Berkshire, Parts of Extraction Phases 4–7: Post-Excavation Assessment Report*, Salisbury, unpubl. rep. 54635

Wessex Archaeology, 2006b. *Salisbury Plain Training Area. Proposed Eastern Tank Track. Archaeological Desk-based Assessment*, Salisbury, unpubl. rep. 63210.01

Wessex Archaeology, 2007. *Eastern Infratructure, Salisbury Plain Training Area, Wiltshire. Archaeological Field Evaluation*, Salisbury, unpubl. rep. 63213.02

Westley, B., 1970. The animal bones from Budbury, 152–3 in G.J. Wainwright, An Iron Age promontory fort at Budbury, Bradford-on-Avon, Wiltshire, *Wiltshire Archaeol. Natur. Hist. Mag.* 65, 108–66

Wheeler, R.E.M., 1943. *Maiden Castle, Dorset*, London, Res. Rep. Comm. Soc. Antiq. London 12

Whimster, R., 1981. *Burial Practices in Iron Age Britain*, Oxford, Brit. Archaeol. Rep. 90

Whittle, A., 1984. The pits, in Cunliffe 1984, 128–45

Whittle, A., Atkinson, R.J.C., Chambers, R., and Thomas, N., 1992. Excavations in the Neolithic and Bronze Age complex at Dorchester-on-Thames, Oxfordshire, 1947–1952 and 1981, *Proc. Prehist. Soc.* 58, 143–201

Williams, A., 1951. Excavations at Beard Mill, Stanton Harcourt, Oxfordshire, 1944, *Oxoniensia* 16, 5–22

Wilson, B., 1979. The vertebrates, in G. Lambrick and M. Robinson, *Iron Age and Roman Riverside Settlements at Farmoor, Oxfordshire*, 128–33, London, Counc. Brit. Archaeol. Res. Rep. 32

Wilson, B., 1992. Considerations for the identification of ritual deposits of animal bones in Iron Age pits, *Int. J. Osteoarchaeol.* 2, 341–9

Wilson, B., 1999. Displayed or concealed? Cross cultural evidence for symbolic and ritual activity depositing Iron Age animal bones, *Oxford J. Archaeol.* 18(3), 297–305

Wilson, C.E, 1981. Burials within settlements in southern Britain during the pre-Roman Iron Age, *Bull. Inst. Archaeol. Univ. London* 18, 127–69

Wiltshire Studies, 2000. Salisbury Plain Training Area sites, in Excavation and fieldwork in Wiltshire 1998, *Wiltshire Archaeol. Natur. Hist. Mag.* 93, 261 and 262–3

Wiltshire Studies, 2001. Southern Range Road, Salisbury Plain Training Area sites, in Excavation and fieldwork in Wiltshire 1999, *Wiltshire Archaeol. Natur. Hist. Mag.* 94, 254–5

Woodward, A., 2000. The late Bronze Age and Iron Age ceramic type series, in J.C. Barrett, P.W.M. Freeman and A. Woodward, *Cadbury Castle, Somerset: the later prehistoric and early historic archaeology*, 325–46, London, English Heritage Archaeol. Rep. 20

Woodward, A. and Blinkhorn, P., 1997. Size is important: Iron Age vessel capacities in central and southern England, in C.G. Cumberpatch and P.W. Blinkhorn (eds), *Not So Much a Pot, More a Way of Life*, 153–62, Oxford, Oxbow Monogr. 83

Wyles, S.F., 2000. Shale and jet, in Lawson 2000, 208–13

Wymer, J.J., 1977. *Gazetteer of Mesolithic Sites in England and Wales*, London, Counc. Brit. Archaeol. Res. Rep. 20

Yalden, D., 1999. *The History of British Mammals*, London, Poyser Natur. Hist.

Yates, D.T., 2007. Land, Power and Prestige. Bronze Age Field Systems in Southern England, Oxford, Oxbow

Appendix
Pottery Fabric Codes

Four separate pottery fabric type series were originally created during analysis of the various pottery assemblages within the Battlesbury Bowl/Southern Range Road project:

1. Battlesbury Bowl (Wessex Archaeology)
2. Other Southern Range Road sites (AC Archaeology)
3. East of Quebec Barn (Wessex Archaeology)
4. Willis Field Barn (Wessex Archaeology)

All fabrics have been defined and coded following the nationally recommended guidelines (PCRG 1997) but, as site-specific series, the four have not been cross-correlated. The original type series, created individually, contained duplicate fabric codes; these have been amended for the purposes of publication to produce a unique sequence. A concordance of original and publication codes is included in each project archive. The pottery type series is presented here within the four original site-specific blocks, arranged chronologically within each block.

BATTLESBURY BOWL

EARLY BRONZE AGE FABRICS

GR1 Moderate sub-rounded grog (<1 mm), rare sub-rounded limestone (0.5 mm), in a coarse matrix; soapy feel; sparse carbonaceous inclusions.

GR2 Frequent to moderate sub-rounded grog (<0.5 mm), in a relatively coarse matrix, slightly micaceous; sparse sub-rounded quartz (<0.25 mm) and sub-rounded limestone (0.3 mm).

EARLY/MIDDLE IRON AGE FABRICS

Sandy fabrics

QU1 Fine, silty, micaceous matrix containing few macroscopic inclusions; rare to sparse linear voids (organic); rare (not universal) patinated flint (<1 mm). Occasionally burnished and/or red-finished.

QU2 Relatively fine sandy matrix, slightly micaceous; frequent, well sorted, sub-rounded quartz (<0.5 mm); moderate iron oxides, sparse carbonaceous inclusions; rare (not universal), sub-angular, patinated flint (<1 mm). Well finished; frequently burnished and/or red-finished.

QU3 Relatively fine, sandy matrix, slightly micaceous; moderate, well sorted, sub-rounded quartz (<0.5 mm); rare to sparse, sub-angular patinated flint (<6 mm); rare (not universal) sub-rounded limestone (<0.5 mm); sparse iron oxides.

QU4 Relatively coarse sandy matrix, slightly micaceous; frequent, well sorted, sub-angular quartz (<1 mm); rare, sub-angular limestone (<0.5 mm); rare, sub-angular, patinated flint (<1 mm). Occasionally burnished and/or red-finished.

QU5 Relatively fine glauconitic sandy matrix, slightly micaceous; frequent, sub-rounded quartz (<0.5 mm), moderate iron oxides. Well-finished; frequently burnished and/or red-finished.

QU6 Fine, glauconitic sandy matrix, slightly micaceous; frequent, well sorted quartz (<0.25 mm). Well-finished; often burnished and/or red-finished.

QU7 Fine, silty matrix, slightly micaceous; moderate fine quartz; sparse iron oxides; rare carbonaceous inclusions. Well finished, frequently burnished and/or red-finished.

QU8 Coarse matrix, slightly micaceous; common, poorly sorted, sub-rounded quartz (<0.5 mm); sparse, prominent iron oxides (<2 mm); moderate carbonaceous inclusions.

QU9 Moderately coarse, sandy matrix, slightly micaceous; frequent, well sorted, sub-rounded quartz (<0.25 mm); moderate, poorly sorted, sub-angular, patinated flint (<1 mm); rare sub-angular limestone (<0.25 mm).

QU10 Fine glauconitic matrix, slightly micaceous; moderate fine quartz; rare (not universal) patinated flint (<0.5 mm). Well finished, frequently burnished and/or red-finished.

Flint-tempered fabrics

FL1 Common, poorly sorted, sub-angular calcined flint (<2 mm), in coarse matrix, slightly micaceous; sparse, sub-rounded quartz (<0.5 mm); sparse iron oxides.

FL2 Moderate, fairly well sorted, sub-angular calcined flint (<1 mm), in fairly coarse matrix, slightly micaceous, sparse iron oxides. Generally well finished.

FL3 Sparse to moderate, poorly sorted, sub-angular calcined flint (<2 mm), in relatively coarse, sandy matrix, slightly micaceous; common, well sorted, sub-rounded quartz (<0.5 mm), rare iron oxides.

FL4 Sparse, very poorly sorted, sub-angular patinated flint (<10 mm) in silty, slightly laminar matrix, slightly micaceous, rare sub-rounded quartz (<1 mm); rare iron oxides.

FL5 Sparse to moderate, fairly poorly sorted, sub-angular calcined flint (<1.5 mm) in relatively fine, glauconitic sandy matrix, slightly micaceous; common, well sorted, sub-rounded quartz (<0.5 mm).

FL6 Sparse to moderate, poorly sorted, sub-angular patinated flint (<2 mm), in coarse sandy matrix; moderate, fairly well sorted, sub-rounded quartz (<0.5 mm); sparse iron oxides.

Calcareous fabrics

LI1 Common, poorly sorted, sub-angular/sub-rounded limestone (<5 mm) in coarse matrix with soapy feel, slightly micaceous; rare (not universal) patinated flint (<0.5 mm); sparse iron oxides.

LI2 Common, fairly well sorted oolitic limestone (<1 mm) and sparse sub-rounded quartz (<5 mm) in relatively fine matrix, slightly micaceous; rare iron oxides; soapy feel.

LI3 Common, well sorted limestone (<0.5 mm, rarely <1 mm); in relatively fine matrix, slightly micaceous; rare carbonaceous inclusions. Generally well finished, although rarely burnished.

LI4 Common, relatively well sorted oolitic limestone (<2 mm) in relatively coarse matrix, slightly micaceous.

LI5 Sparse to moderate, well sorted oolitic limestone (<1 mm), in relatively fine, glauconitic sandy matrix; sparse, sub-rounded quartz (<0.5 mm); rare iron oxides (0.5 mm); rare carbonaceous inclusions.

LI6 Moderate, very poorly sorted, sub-rounded/sub-angular limestone (<6 mm), and sparse, sub-rounded quartz (0.5 mm), in relatively fine matrix, slightly micaceous; sparse iron oxides.

LI7 Abundant, well sorted oolitic limestone (<0.5 mm), in fine moderately coarse matrix, slightly micaceous. Generally well finished, although not burnished.

LI8 Common, poorly sorted, shelly limestone, including both sub-angular and plate-like fragments; in a relatively coarse matrix, slightly micaceous; sparse iron oxides.

Organic-tempered fabrics

VE1 Frequent linear voids (<3 mm) in fine, silty, slightly micaceous matrix.

VE2 Moderate to common linear voids (<10 mm) and sparse , sub-rounded quartz (<0.5 mm); rare (not universal) sub-rounded/sub-angular limestone (<0.5 mm), in relatively coarse matrix, slightly micaceous; rare iron oxides.

VE3 Frequent large linear voids (<8 mm) and frequent sub-rounded quartz (<0.25 mm), in coarse, slightly micaceous matrix; sparse iron oxides. Briquetage.

Shelly fabrics

SH1 Frequent, poorly sorted fossil shell in plate-like fragments (<5 mm); sparse sub-rounded quartz (0.5 mm); in coarse matrix, slightly micaceous; sparse iron oxides.

SH2 Moderate, fairly well sorted fossil shell in plate-like fragments (<1 mm); in relatively coarse sandy matrix, slightly glauconitic; frequent, sub-rounded quartz (<0.5 mm); sparse iron oxides. Well finished; occasionally burnished.

SH3 Sparse to moderate, poorly sorted fossil shell in plate-like fragments (<4 mm); in relatively fine, sandy matrix, slightly micaceous; moderate, sub-rounded quartz (<0.25 mm); sparse iron oxides.

OTHER SOUTHERN RANGE ROAD SITES (AC ARCHAEOLOGY)

NEOLITHIC FABRICS

Flint-tempered fabrics

FL9 Moderately soft, fine matrix, containing rare, angular flint <2 mm; rare rounded quartz 0.25 mm. Unoxidised.

FL10 Moderately soft, fine matrix, containing rare, poorly sorted, angular flint <5 mm, mainly 0.5 mm; sparse rounded quartz 0.25 mm. Unoxidised.

FL11 Moderately soft, fine matrix, containing sparse, well-sorted angular flint 1 mm; rare angular chert/quartz <0.5 mm. Unoxidised.

Shelly fabric

SH4 Soft, irregular matrix, containing common, poorly-sorted shell <5 mm moderate to common large shell, soft fabric. Unoxidised with oxidised external surface.

Limestone-tempered fabric

LI9 Moderately hard, fine textured matrix, containing moderately well-sorted oolitic limestone <1 mm, sparse shell <2 mm. Generally unoxidised.

EARLY BRONZE AGE FABRICS

GR3 Moderately hard, fine matrix with sparse rounded grog <5 mm, rare rounded quartz 0.5 mm. Thick walled, oxidised external surface, coe and internal surface unoxidised.

SH5 Moderately hard, irregular matrix containing common, well-sorted shell <4 mm, mainly 1 mm.

LATE BRONZE AGE/EARLY IRON AGE FABRICS

Flint-tempered fabrics

FL7 Hard, fine textured matrix, containing moderate, poorly-sorted, calcined angular flint <3 mm; sparse, rounded quartz 0.25 mm. Variable firing.

FL8 Hard, moderately fine matrix, containing sparse to moderate angular flint <2 mm, mainly 0.5mm; rare rounded quartz 0.25 mm; rare mica flecks. Generally unoxidised.

FL12 Hard, moderately fine matrix, containing to moderate/common, well-sorted angular flint 1 mm; rare rounded quartz 0.25 mm. Generally unoxidised.

FL13 Hard, irregular matrix, containing common, well-sorted angular flint <2 mm. Unoxidised. (coarse version of F6).

Limestone-tempered fabrics

LI10 Moderately hard, fine textured matrix, containing moderate well-sorted oolitic limestone 0.5 mm, rare shell <2 mm. Generally unoxidised.

LI11 Soft, irregular matrix, containing common, well-sorted angular calcite <2 mm, Sparse shelly limestone, rare quartz. Oxidised external surface, unoxidised core and internal surface.

Shelly fabrics

SH6IA Moderately soft, fine matrix, containing common, well-sorted shell <2 mm. Unoxidised, oxidised external surface.

SH7IA Moderately soft, irregular matrix, containing common, well-sorted shell 1 mm; sparse sub-rounded quartz/chert 1 mm. Unoxidised.

Sandy fabrics

QU11 Moderately hard, moderately fine matrix containing common, rounded quartz 0.25 mm. Unoxidised.

QU12 Moderately soft, fine irregular matrix containing sparse, rounded quartz 0.25 mm. Unoxidised.

QU13 Hard, moderately coarse matrix containing common, rounded quartz 0.5 mm. Unoxidised.

Grog-tempered fabrics

GR4 Soft, fine fabric, containing sparse, poorly-sorted grog <3 mm; rare flint 1 mm. Oxidised.

ROMANO-BRITISH FABRICS

Sandy fabrics

QU100 Moderately soft, fine matrix containing sparse rounded quartz <0.5 mm. 'Catch-all' group for fine oxidised wares.

QU101 Moderately soft, fine matrix containing rare rounded quartz <0.25 mm; sparse mica flacks. 'Catch-all' group micaceous fine wares, includes oxidised and unoxidised wares.

QU102 Hard, moderately irregular matrix containing moderate rounded quartz <0.5 mm. 'Catch-all' group for sandy greywares

QU103 Hard, irregular matrix containing common rounded quartz <1 mm. 'Catch-all' group for coarse grewares.

QU104 Hard, irregular matrix containing common rounded quartz <1 mm. 'Catch-all' group for coarse oxidised wares.

Grog-tempered fabrics

GR100 Soft, moderately fine matrix, containing moderate, moderately-sorted grog <2 mm. Generally orange

GR101 Hard, moderately irregular matrix, containing well-sorted grog <2 mm, rare rounded quartz 0.25 mm. Generally pale grey.

GR102 Hard, moderately irregular matrix, containing common grog <1.5 mm; rare iron oxide. Generally buff/pale pink.

EAST OF QUEBEC BARN (SRR85) (WESSEX ARCHAEOLOGY)

LATE BRONZE AGE FABRICS

FL14 Moderately hard fabric, sparse to moderate, poorly sorted flint <1.5 mm; sparse sub-rounded quartz; sparse voids representing burnt out organic material; variable firing.

F15 Moderately hard fabric, rare, poorly sorted flint <1 mm; sparse, well sorted, sub-rounded quartz <1 mm; variable firing, well finished.

QU14 Moderately soft fabric containing sparse, flint <0.5 mm; sparse sub-rounded quartz; sparse voids representing burnt out organic material <0.5 mm; variable firing, well finished.

QU15 Moderately hard fabric containing moderate, sub-rounded quartz <0.5 mm; sparse flint <1 mm; variable firing and finish.

CH1 Moderately soft fabric containing moderate, sub-rounded quartz <0.5 mm, moderate sub-rounded/sub-angular chalk <0.5 mm; variable firing.

D1 Moderately soft fabric; moderate voids, sub-rounded, possibly calcareous <1.5 mm; poorly finished, variable firing.

WILLIS FIELD BARN (SRR96) (WESSEX ARCHAEOLOGY)

NEOLITHIC FABRIC

FL16 Moderate, poorly sorted, calcined flint <1.5 mm. Moderately hard fabric with variable firing. Hackly fracture. Peterborough Ware.

EARLY BRONZE AGE FABRICS

GR5 Fine grog tempered fabric; common, poorly sorted grog <2 mm. Soft fabric, slightly micaceous, with soapy texture. Oxidised exterior and interior surface; margins and cores black. Beaker.

GR6 Coarse, irregular fabric, slightly micaceous, with 'lumpy' texture; sparse, poorly sorted grog <5 mm; rare calcite <4 mm. Soft; variable firing.

LI14 Sparse, fairly well sorted calcite <1.5 mm; rare grog <2 mm; in a fine silty/sandy matrix, moderately hard fabric. Soft, variable firing, well finished. Beaker.

QU16 Fine sandy fabric; moderate, fairly well sorted, sub-rounded quartz <0.25 mm; sparse grog <0.5 mm; sparse iron oxides. Soft, mainly oxidised. Beaker.

MIDDLE BRONZE AGE FABRICS

FL17 Common, poorly sorted, sub-angular calcined flint <3 mm; rare sub-rounded quartz <0.5 mm. Moderately hard fabric with variable firing, well finished.

FL18 Rare sub-angular flint <1mm; sparse iron oxides. Moderately hard fabric.

FL19 Common, fairly well sorted, sub-angular flint <2 mm; rare sub-rounded quartz <0.5 mm. Moderately hard fabric; variable firing.

LI12 Common, poorly sorted calcite <5 mm, in a soft, coarse matrix; variable firing.

LI13 Sparse, poorly sorted, calcite <3 mm; rare sub-rounded fine quartz; in a fairly fine matrix; variable firing.

SH8 Common, fairly well sorted fossil shell <2 mm; rare sub-angular flint <2 mm; in a coarse matrix. Soft; variable firing; slightly soapy feel.

Index